I0127349

# The Flora of Mount Adams, Washington

by

**David Biek and Susan McDougall**

Sound Books

Seattle, Washington

*This book is our gift to each other, to remember the best of times in the mountains.*

Biek, David.
The flora of Mount Adams, Washington / by David Biek and Susan McDougall.
1st ed.
Seattle, Wash.: Sound Books, c2007.
1. Plants--Washington (State)--Adams, Mount. 2. Botany--Washington (State)--Adams, Mount. 3. Adams, Mount (Wash.). I. McDougall, Susan.

ISBN 978-0-9776285-1-3



First edition 2007

**Sound Books**

13008 37th Ave. NE
Seattle, WA 98125

http://mtadamsflora.clearwire.net

## Contents

## Acknowledgments

We received help and gracious assistance from many people over the course of this project.

David Giblin, herbarium manager at the University of Washington, stands out: he accompanied us in the field and helped in innumerable ways in the herbarium. Ben Legler and Katie Glew also at the UW herbarium deserve mention. At the Marion Ownbey Herbarium at Washington State University, we were assisted by Larry Hufford, John Clark, and Josh Brokaw. Access to collections at Oregon State University was provided by Richard Halse. Andrea Ruchty and John Scott, botanists working for the U.S. Forest Service, shared their knowledge as well as access to herbarium collections held at the Trout Lake ranger station.

Gina King, wildlife biologist for the Yakama Nation, made helpful comments on the manuscript and shared a Native American perspective on Mount Adams. Paul Slichter, who has traveled widely across the slopes of Mount Adams, spent time with us in the field, shared collections and location information, and did much scouting on our behalf. Plant lists compiled by Jim Riley were very useful in early stages of our research.

We were helped with particular groups of plants by Mark Egger, Joy Mastrogiuseppe, and Peter Zika, who generously shared their knowledge.

Paul Dixon and Mike Daly supported us on a particularly long hike and made collections on our behalf during their summit climb. Back in Trout Lake, innkeepers Marilyn and Kelly Enochs were excellent, and tolerant, hosts to a couple of dusty botanists, who spent evenings spreading their plant specimens across the dining room.

Finally, we are grateful to the Washington Native Plant Society for a grant that helped to support our fieldwork.

# Introduction

## Project Methods

The idea for this book originated with an observation made by one of the authors, Susan, as we approached the end of a short hike on the Round-the-Mountain Trail at Mount Adams. It was in the fall of 2003 and most flowers had vanished from the small, dry meadows along the southwest segment of that trail, but the landscape, scenery, trees, and environment were of such compelling interest, that she suggested that we undertake a project to document the flora of Mount Adams.

We soon discovered how little comprehensive work had been done on the floristics of the mountain and that we would thus have to work "from the ground up," beginning in the herbarium.

Susan completed the first stage of the project in the fall of 2003 by producing a finding list of plants. This list was based upon the *Flora of the State of Washington*, written by Charles V. Piper and published in 1906. The entries in this book included brief data for each of the herbarium vouchers that Piper studied -- the place, the collector, and the collector's number.

For example, the entry for the sedge, *Carex rossii*, included these specimens:

Mount Adams, Henderson 2094 and Suksdorf 24
Klickitat River, Suksdorf 48
West Klickitat County Suksdorf 77

An entry such as this, therefore, provided four separate herbarium collections for which to search.

Thus, Piper's information on "specimens examined" for each species gave us a list of plants likely to be at Mount Adams. The full review of his book resulted in an Excel database list of more than 1,400 entries. These entries were derived from the geographical information, which included place names such as "Mount Adams," "Klickitat River," "Bird Creek Meadows," and so on. Collector names were also searched. Additions to the list were also acquired from field trip lists prepared by Jim Riley. Some candidate species known from Mount Rainier or Mount Hood were also included.

Using this finding list, we visited the two major herbaria in the state of Washington -- the University of Washington and Washington State University -- during the winter and spring of 2004. Examination of specimens at these two herbaria resulted in an initial list of 638 verified taxa for our study area at Mount Adams. Later that year, we also visited the Oregon State University herbarium in Corvallis and the small herbarium at the Trout Lake Ranger Station. In addition, we reviewed the archives of Wilhelm Suksdorf's papers at the library of Washington State University. Suksdorf was one of the earliest collectors at Mount Adams, performing his field work in the latter 19th and early 20th centuries. His contributions to knowledge of the Mount Adams flora were very extensive.

The next stage in the project was to undertake field work for the purpose of documenting taxa previously uncollected for the herbaria. The majority of this fieldwork was completed in 2004 and 2005. This work, along with additional herbarium visits, added 198 taxa to the Mount Adams list, for a total of 836 species, subspecies, and varieties by the end of 2005. With a collector's permit from the U.S. Forest Service, we made more than 600 collections in the field; these were placed in the herbarium at the University of Washington. Our database, from which the flora was built, was expanded to include details about the collections and the observations that we made. As we will explain in greater detail in a following section ("Biogeography"), the flora of Mount Adams is as diverse a flora as one can find in any area of comparable size in Washington. The current list, which includes a few additions made in 2006, stands at 841 taxa.

While work on the complete flora has been underway, Susan published a photographic field guide entitled *The Wildflowers of Mount Adams, Washington* (Sound Books, 2006) and has built and maintained a website devoted to news and results of our research, at:

mtadamsflora.clearwire.net/mtadamsflora

That Mount Adams is so little known, compared to Mounts Hood, Rainier, and St. Helens, and therefore that its fascinating plant life is likewise little known, is a clear omission in the knowledge of Northwest flora. Foremost in our minds throughout the project has been the correction of that situation. From its beautiful flowers to its many birds to the grandeur of its glacial and volcanic landscapes, here is a mountain that awaits discovery! It is our most fervent hope that this book will promote such an awakening.

## The Study Area

Mount Adams is located in southern Washington State, astride the boundary of Skamania and Yakima Counties, 31 miles north of the Columbia River at White Salmon. Mount Rainier is about 47 miles north-northwest and Mount St. Helens lies 31 miles to the west of the mountain. To the south, 56 miles away in Oregon, lies Mount Hood. The summit of Mount Adams is 12,276 feet in elevation and is centered upon 46° 12.16'N, 121° 29.44'W.

## Introduction

The area surveyed in this study includes the Mount Adams Wilderness Area and adjacent land above an elevation of 4,000 feet. This contour was chosen for several reasons, the most important of which is the fact that it very closely comports with the geologic "footprint" of the mountain. As noted by geologists Wes Hildreth and Judy Fierstein (Hildreth and Fierstein, 1995): "... the Mount Adams volcanic field, as here depicted appears to have a certain coherence and integrity [with respect to Quaternary era volcanic activity]. Our eastern boundary is the canyon of the Klickitat River, a long-lived barrier never crossed by Adams-derived lavas...." Further, "North of the map area, a cluster of Quaternary basaltic centers in the Walupt Lake area separates Mount Adams from the Goat Rocks stratovolcano."

The 4,000-foot line, therefore, neatly follows the Klickitat River Canyon on the east, the ridgeline at Walupt Lake on the north, includes Council Lake on the northwest, and hews closely to Forest Service Road 23 on the west. Further west, geologically older rivers and ridges lie between Mount Adams and Mount St. Helens. The line on the south is harder to fix. Much of this terrain consists of a debris flow that lacks many distinguishing features, and below 4,000 feet, most land is both in private ownership and has been extensively logged.

Basically, from any point within the study area, one might walk straight uphill to the summit of Mount Adams. From a consideration of geology, topography, and land use, therefore, we infer an ecological integrity to this footprint. Thus defined, the study area encompasses approximately 208,000 acres, less than the 235,612 acres within Mount Rainier National Park.

Administration of the land within the study area is divided between the U.S. Forest Service and the Yakama Nation. On the west side is the Gifford Pinchot National Forest, which includes the Mount Adams Wilderness Area, established in 1964 and comprising 47,280 acres. On the east, the Yakama Nation provides public access to the approximately 17,000 acres of the Mount Adams Recreational Area, including land once known as "Tract D." Here, roads, trails and campgrounds are available to visitors, providing access to the famous Bird Creek Meadows, as well as Hellroaring Meadows, the Ridge of Wonders, Bench Lake, and Bird Lake, plus the southeastern pertain of Mount Adams itself. The remainder of the study area within the Yakama Nation is open only to enrolled tribal members and those with permission of the Yakama Tribal Council.

A very small portion of the study area, on the southeast and within two air miles of Bench Lake, is administered by the Washington Department of Natural Resources. This includes a remarkable collecting location, the "DNR quarry" close to the source of Dairy Creek.

## The Flora of Mount Adams, Washington

Mount Adams and the study area lie east of the Cascade Crest, which roughly parallels Road 23 on the west side of the mountain and Road 2329 on the north. Its slopes drain to the Columbia River. On the north, Muddy Fork, Killen Creek, and Adams Creek drain to the Cispus River, which meets the Cowlitz River and then the Columbia at Longview. On the west, the Lewis River, with tributaries that include Riley Creek, Falls Creek and waters from Swampy Meadows, meets the Columbia near Woodland. On the south, Trout Lake Creek picks up flow from Grand Meadow before meeting the White Salmon River. The White Salmon also gathers water from Cascade Creek, Morrison Creek, and Gotchen Creek, ultimately joining the Columbia at the town of White Salmon. Finally, on the eastside, Bird Creek, Hellroaring Creek, Big Muddy Creek and Clearwater Creek all join the Klickitat River, which meets the Columbia at Lyle.

## Geology and Topography

Mount Adams, at 12,276 feet in height, is one of the largest volcanoes of the western coast, third in height to Mount Rainier and Mount Shasta. In volume of eruptive material, it is second only to Mount Shasta. The rounded summit of Mount Adams tops a great apron of volcanic debris spread down slope.

Most of the eruptions in the vicinity of Mount Adams, except for the main cone, which is composed of andesite, consisted of basaltic or olivine-andesite material. This basalt is undoubtedly derived from the mantle of the earth itself, intruding in this case to the base of the crustal material. Eruptions issued from a north-trending belt more than 20 miles long. The volume constituted the largest flow in Washington for the past half-million years with the greatest flow beneath the mountain's present cone.

The main cone is barely older than a half-million years, with a few older eruptive centers south and east of the mountain. The earliest eruptive process began about five kilometers southeast of the modern summit. As time passed, the eruptive center shifted towards the present cone where a volcanic dome of andesitic and dacitic lavas was built. In geological time terms, the eruption was more or less continuous. More than a single eruptive vent was involved in the construction of Mount Adams and much of the current apron of eruptive material issued from summit as well as flank vents, many of which are located above approximately 6,500 feet of elevation along the south and west sides of the volcano. During the Pleistocene, while andesite erupted in this central region, basalt continued to erupt on the periphery, placing other edifices within close proximity to the mountain. King Mountain, a shield volcano on the southeast side of Mount Adams, is an example of these basaltic outpourings. Red Butte, a basaltic cinder cone located on the northeast flank of Mount Adams, erupted during post-glacial times.

No historical eruptions are known and it appears that most activity ceased 3,500 years ago, with a couple of possible exceptions. Nevertheless, southeast of the volcano, ash layers, aged by comparison to known Mount St. Helens ash falls, are less than 2,500 years old and probably are sourced in vents close to the summit. The summit cap itself is probably more than 8,000 years old.

In general, Mount Adams has not been as explosive as Mount St. Helens; pumice eruptions and pyroclastic-flows were rare. Certainly, Mount Adams has suffered no St. Helens-style eruption in at least 100,000 years. Most flows have been effusive, at most moderately explosive, with few observable ash falls in the geological story. Rather the basalt and andesite have flowed thin and fluid over layers below, with long tongues of thick lava flows present as well. Many of these flows are confined, their viscosity restricting their movement over topographic hindrances, but some large ones moved considerable distances. In particular, basalt flows extended 20 miles from the mountain, exuding very little ash. Evidence of ash layers is thus very rare at the mountain, with Pleistocene layers absent thanks to erosion, and post ice age falls at most a couple of inches thick.

Since much of the cone was built during the latter part of the Pleistocene ice age, eruptions occurred beneath and through an ice cap, which was more extensive than the current cover. The eruption of a small cone on the summit probably occurred near the glacial maximum, while post ice age events took place below the summit but high on the cone itself. The mountain thus was steep and ice-capped during the summit building activity. Rising magma through water melted from such an ice cap would produce steam, perhaps resulting in explosions not unlike those witnessed at Mt. St. Helens, although probably of smaller duration and certainly not as destructive to the mountain itself. Rather, the effusive nature of the mountain created thin and steep layers, some resulting into avalanches of mixed composition.

Pumice as a product of explosive activity is therefore quite rare at Mount Adams. The great apron of the mountain is primarily broken lava, as much of the ash and pumice found its way into river valleys, where it was quickly carried away. Glaciers, too, have moved volcanic products downward, leaving evidence of any small explosive ash flows and debris scant indeed.

Mount Adams is not considered to be a candidate for eruption in the foreseeable future. Earthquakes are entirely absent and the relative age of the summit cone indicates inactivity for the past several thousand years. Small eruptions along the mountains flanks are at least a thousand years old. Eruptions therefore have been small and effusive.

Most basalt flows, too, are old, although recent ones did occur during the latter part of the ice ages. Such flows are possible again and would resemble the type witnessed at Hawaiian volcanoes; that is, rivers of basalt rather than pyrotechnics. Ashfall of any significance is unlikely. This is an interesting phenomenon, since the hyperactive Mount St. Helens stands so close by.

In fact, rather than the worry of ash or fluid rock, the risk from Mount Adams is more likely to be in the nature of a debris avalanche. Any event that causes melting of the icecap could send such floods down the steep sides. Glaciers, too, may be prompted to flood in response to volcanic activity or, more commonly, heavy rain or excessive warmth. These types of events are definitely historical, with such floods moving down rivers from glaciers such as the Avalanche (an appropriate name!), the Adams, and the Rusk.

Debris flows are the most potentially destructive risk at the mountain, more so than glacial events. Lava flows are separated by zones of breccia, composed of broken volcanic parent rock and clay formed from water present in and after the eruption. These layers are slippery and unstable, thus providing an excellent surface for flow. Small flows are common while large ones have also occurred since the glacial maximum. In particular, approximately 5,000 years ago a huge avalanche moved down slope as far as the region of Trout Lake. Most flows, however, are of much smaller extent. Major catastrophes, given the present activity at the mountain, seem unlikely.

## Plant Communities

### Forests

The second highest mountain in Washington State, Mount Adams is a tall stratovolcano located midway between Mount Rainier and Mount Hood. As such, its plant communities share many of the characteristics of those two mountains. However, the location of Mount Adams east of the Cascade crest, and the presence of connections by means of eastward-trending ridges to sagebrush lowlands, adds a significant dimension to its flora that is not seen elsewhere in the Cascades.

Much of the landscape surrounding the volcano is forested, and, with the exception of riparian zones at the lower limit of the study area, these are primarily coniferous forests. Mount Adams is home to eighteen conifer species, some of which are quite rare at the mountain, including *Picea sitchensis* (Sitka spruce) and *Taxus brevifolia* (western yew); other species, such as *Abies amabilis* (Pacific silver fir) form the dominant overstory in many areas. The best available scheme for the description of the forest communities of Mount Adams is that set out in *Natural Vegetation of Oregon and Washington,* by Franklin and Dyrness (1988).

The forests have been extensively logged at the lower elevations, with only the higher regime preserved intact within the boundaries of the Mount Adams Wilderness Area. Forest fire has undoubtedly influenced forest composition, as it has elsewhere in the Northwest; the effects at Mount Adams are most easily observed in the presence of large expanses of *Pinus contorta* var. *murrayana* (lodgepole pine) which exceed those of the other major Northwest volcanoes. Lodgepole pine forests are particularly common on the borders of lava flows that extend tongue-like to lower elevations on the north and south sides of the mountain. Anthropogenic use of fire included that of the Yakama and Klickitat peoples who maintained huckleberry fields in the region.

White pine blister rust (*Cronartium ribicola*), introduced from Asia to the Pacific Northwest at Vancouver, B.C. around 1910, was known at Mount Adams by 1921 and is a serious pathogen of *Pinus albicaulis* (whitebark pine). Evidence of the disease is most observable on the south and southeast slopes. Shoal et al. (2005) found an infection rate of nearly 53% in trees surveyed at Mount Adams. The prickly gooseberry, *Ribes lacustre,* is known to be a host for the alternate generation of this rust. Irregular outbreaks of Western spruce budworm (*Choristoneura occidentalis*) are known to damage Douglas-fir, Engelmann spruce, lodgepole pine, and western larch.

Forests in the Pacific Northwest have been classified Jerry E. Franklin and C.T. Dyrness in their *Natural Vegetation of Oregon and Washington* (1973). In their framework, forests are subdivided into a series of zones, "areas in which a single tree species is the major climax dominant." The boundaries of a zone are set chiefly by elevation. Actual forest composition within a zone at Mount Adams is greatly influenced by the history of disturbance, chiefly through fire and logging. Thus, at particular sites, *Pinus contorta* (lodgepole pine) and *Pseudotsuga menziesii* (Douglas-fir) may be the dominant trees but do not represent climax species.

The discussions that follow look at forest zones separately with respect to the east and west sides of Mount Adams. While the situation on the west is straightforward, with two primary forest zones present, that on the east side of is more complicated, as deep canyons and prominent ridges allow an "interfingering" of zones that, to an extent, overrides elevation as a sorting factor. It is significant, however, that this interfingering is less marked than at Mount Rainier: with a few notable exceptions, large rivers are absent at Mount Adams. The finger-like projections of deeply-cut valleys so common at its northern neighbor are not part of the landscape.

## The Flora of Mount Adams, Washington

### Forest zones on the west side of Mount Adams

#### *Abies amabilis* (Pacific silver fir) Zone

The *Tsuga heterophylla* (western hemlock) Zone, which lies below the *Abies amabilis* Zone and is found at Mount Rainier and on Mount Hood, is absent from Mount Adams above the 4,000-foot line. Rather, the middle elevations of the study area are included in the *Abies amabilis* (or Pacific silver fir) Zone. Pacific silver fir is the dominant tree on the south side of Mount Adams to an elevation of approximately 5,500 feet. Where soils are well-drained, stands may be nearly pure and are often crowded, especially where fire and logging have cleared away older trees. Below about 5,000 feet, especially on west-facing slopes, *Pseudotsuga menziesii* (Douglas-fir) is likely to be the most abundant species, sometimes to the exclusion of Pacific silver fir.

The *Abies amabilis* Zone is not as strongly marked at Mount Adams as it is at Mount Rainier, and thus other conifers are often part of the forest composition. On disturbed sites, *Larix occidentalis* (western larch) is very common around 4,000 feet on the southeast side of the mountain but is only a minor component with increased elevation. *Tsuga heterophylla* is chiefly limited to north slopes and the valleys of streams at elevations not much greater than 4,200 feet. *Picea engelmannii* (Engelmann spruce) is found in small numbers on the north and west sides, where it is most often encountered along meadow edges up to 5,200 feet. *Pinus ponderosa* (ponderosa pine) occurs as scattered individuals to an elevation of approximately 5,000 feet on the south side of the mountain along the road to Cold Springs (the South Climb route); this species is also found in small numbers on the north side. *Abies procera* (noble fir) and *Pinus monticola* (western white pine) are also locally established in this zone.

In general, plant associations within the *Abies amabilis* Zone vary along a moisture gradient. Thus, the common occurrence of the "*Abies amabilis/Xerophyllum tenax*/Lithosol" association may be attributed to the overall dry conditions and southerly location of Mount Adams.

The next association along the gradient, characterized by the dominance of *Gaultheria shallon* (salal) in the understory is not found at Mount Adams, as salal is entirely absent from the study area. However, if one were to take *Berberis nervosa* (dwarf Oregon grape) as a "stand-in" for salal, then one might claim that a variant of the "*Abies amabilis/Gaultheria shallon*" association is present on slopes with a west aspect and beneath a fairly closed canopy.

Remaining associations, ranging from the dry to the moist, are "*Abies amabilis/Vaccinium alaskaense-V. membranaceum,*" "*Abies amabilis/Streptopus lanceolatus*" and "*Abies amabilis/Oplopanax horridus.*" These are, progressively, less frequently seen, typically restricted to forests bordering lakes, streams and meadows on the west side of Mount Adams.

Understory vegetation varies greatly with factors such as canopy cover (which influences light and moisture availability) and aspect. In general, as Franklin and Dyrness note, understories in the *Abies amabilis* Zone around Mount Adams are depauperate, dominated by dry regime specialists such as *Vaccinium membranaceum* (thin-leaf huckleberry) and *Xerophyllum tenax* (beargrass). This is in distinct contrast with the *Abies amabilis* Zone on the Olympic Peninsula, where the understory is rich in herbaceous plants; this, too, is the case in the *Abies amabilis* Zone at Mount Rainier.

In addition to those mentioned above, shrubby species in the *Abies amabilis* Zone at Mount Adams include *Acer glabrum* var. *douglasii* (Douglas maple), *Menziesia ferruginea* (fool's huckleberry), *Nothochelone nemorosa* (woodland beardtongue), and *Rhododendron albiflorum* (Cascade azalea). Common creeping sub-shrubs include *Linnaea borealis* ssp. *longiflora* (twinflower), and two species of *Rubus*, *R. lasiococcus* (dwarf bramble) and *R. pedatus* (five-leaved bramble).

Herbaceous plants frequently seen are *Achlys triphylla* (vanillaleaf), *Cornus unalaschkensis* (bunchberry), *Fragaria virginiana* var. *platypetala* (greenleaf strawberry), and *Maianthmum stellatum* (star-flowered false Solomon's-seal).

### *Tsuga mertensiana* (mountain hemlock) Zone

Franklin and Dyrness propose a division of the *Tsuga mertensiana* Zone into a lower subzone in which the forest canopy is closed, and an upper parkland zone. This is well-illustrated in the vicinity of Cold Springs on the southern slope of Mount Adams, where at approximately 5,500 feet of elevation the forest cover becomes discontinuous and patchy. No one species is truly dominant here: depending upon slope and aspect, one is about equally likely to see, in addition to mountain hemlock, *Abies lasiocarpa* (subalpine fir), and *Pinus albicaulis* (whitebark pine) at higher elevations; *Abies amabilis* may also be found on gentle slopes of southern aspect.

The abundance of mountain hemlock on the south side of the mountain is perhaps somewhat surprising, given the relative dry conditions there. Persisting to high elevations, perhaps seasonal water from snow melt provides the necessary moisture for this species.

At higher elevations, the tree cover becomes progressively thinner, until at a point above 6,000 feet, trees are mostly limited to ridgelines, reflecting the influence of unstable soils and depth of snow cover off of the ridges. At the highest elevation of tree growth, one finds extremely dwarfed trees, called "krummholz" (from the German, meaning "crooked wood"). Subalpine fir and whitebark pine are the major krummholz species on Mount Adams.

A number of associations have been described for the *Tsuga mertensiana* Zone in southern Washington and in Oregon by Franklin and Dyrness, again arranged along a dry to moist gradient: these include "*Abies amabilis-Tsuga mertensiana/Xerophyllum tenax,*" "*Abies amabilis-Tsuga mertensiana/Vaccinium membranaceum,*" "*Abies amabilis/Veratrum viride,*" "*Abies amabilis/Menziesia ferruginea*" and "*Chamaecyparis nootkatensis/Rhododendron albiflorum.*" Perhaps because of summer dryness and rapidly-draining soils on the slopes of Mount Adams, none of the shrub or herb components of these associations is of frequent enough occurrence to make it possible to trace them. For example, *Chamaecyparis nootkatensis* is rare at the mountain and *Vaccinium membranaceum* uncommon above 5,000 feet.

Away from the high elevation meadows, soils on Mount Adams at these elevations are very poorly developed and in many places there is little or no understory vegetation. Shrubs are found locally here, including *Phyllodoce empetriformis* (pink heather), *Ribes montigenum* (mountain gooseberry), *Salix barclayi* (Barclay's willow) in wetter places, and *Sambucus racemosa* (red elderberry).

Herbaceous species in the *Tsuga mertensiana* Zone include *Lupinus* (lupine) species, *Luzula glabrata* var. *hitchcockii* (smooth woodrush), and *Penstemon* species.

## Forest zones on the east side of Mount Adams

An intricate mosaic of forest types is found on the east side of Mount Adams, reflecting topography, soils, and moisture. Species that are uncommon to rare in the study area on the west side are encountered more frequently here, including *Larix occidentalis* (western larch) and *Pinus ponderosa* (ponderosa pine). *Abies grandis* (grand fir) and *Picea engelmannii* (Engelmann spruce) are frequent at middle elevations, while near timberline *Pinus albicaulis* (whitebark pine) and *Tsuga mertensiana* (mountain hemlock) forests are locally well-developed. On the north and northeast sides of the mountain, *Pinus contorta* var. *murrayana* (lodgepole pine) covers extensive tracts on the flats and along the shallow slopes that run out to the Klickitat River. Potato Hill and Devil's Garden are good vantage points from which to view the landscape of the eastern slopes. At the lower limit of the study area, *Quercus garryana* var. *garryana* (Oregon white oak or Garry oak) forms open groves in select locations on thin soils.

## Introduction

### *Pinus ponderosa* (ponderosa pine) Zone

The presence of *Pinus ponderosa* in the forest along the south and southeast aspect sides at the mountain reflects the drier conditions of this area owing to the mountain's position east of the crest. Common herbaceous species in these forests include *Hieracium albiflorum* (white hawkweed), *Lupinus sericeus* ssp. *sericeus* var. *sericeus* (silky lupine), *Phlox diffusa* (spreading phlox), and the lovely *Calochortus subalpinus* (subalpine mariposa lily). Native grasses are also abundant in the ponderosa pine forest understory, including *Bromus* species, *Calamagrostis rubescens* (pinegrass), *Deschampsia danthonioides* (annual hairgrass) and *Poa secunda* (one-sided bluegrass).

The ponderosa pine forests have been heavily logged at Mount Adams and thus climax forests are absent on the east side of the study area. Periodic fire, under natural conditions, serves to maintain an open canopy in the ponderosa pine forest and prevent the establishment of other species. In historic times, it is likely that logging has helped maintain open ponderosa forests; at the same time, fire suppression has made it possible for other tree species to become established. Douglas-fir is frequently more numerous than ponderosa pine; other species include grand fir, western larch, and, at higher elevations, Engelmann spruce.

Individual large ponderosa pine trees are present, however, and one of these, the Trout Lake Big Tree at 213 feet tall is the largest ponderosa pine in Washington State. (Now dead, the Yakama Nation Tree at 179 feet had a thicker trunk and contained a slightly larger volume of wood.)

At the lower edge of the *Pinus ponderosa* Zone on the southeast side of the mountain, ponderosa pine forms an open forest with Oregon white oak on south-facing slopes. The underlying rock is basalt (which is mined at a small quarry operated by the Washington Department of Natural Resources near Dairy Creek), and soil depth varies. Where soils are deeper, the appearance resembles a savannah, with native grasses and perennial herbs in abundance. On shallow soils a landscape reminiscent of the sage-steppe formation typical of lower elevations on the eastern flank of the Cascades is observed. Here, *Purshia tridentata* (antelope bitterbrush) grows, as well as a number of *Lomatium* species and such evanescent spring flowers as *Mimulus breweri* (Brewer's monkeyflower) and *Olsynium douglasii* (grass widows). Annual herbs are also common here, the reverse of the situation in the west side forests. Other frequently encountered species include *Collinsia parviflora*, *Cryptantha affinis*, several *Gayophytum* species, and two *Madia* species -- *M. glomerata* and *M. gracilis*.

## The Flora of Mount Adams, Washington

### *Pinus contorta* (lodgepole pine) Zone

At an elevation above about 4,500 feet on the north and northeast sides of Mount Adams, large tracts of *Pinus contorta* var. *murrayana* (lodgepole pine) are found, to a degree not seen at the other northern Cascade volcanoes. The topography is generally flat and soils well-drained, with little or no surface water after late spring. As the result of seedling establishment following fires, stands may be nearly pure and even-aged. Such stands, therefore, are seral; mature, climax forests of *Pinus contorta* apparently do not have a chance to become established. *Ribes cereum* (wax currant) is common in openings while grasses and sedges are frequent throughout, including *Agrostis scabra* and *Carex halliana*. Along watercourses, *Populus balsamifera* ssp. *trichocarpa* (black cottonwood) and *P. tremuloides* (quaking aspen) are locally common.

### *Pseudotsuga menziesii* (Douglas-fir) Zone

On soil and topography not favorable to lodgepole pine on the east side of Mount Adams, Douglas-fir is the dominant forest tree up to almost 5,000 feet. Western larch and ponderosa pine are also found in these forests up to about 4,500 feet, and both can reach impressive sizes here. Grand fir is also fairly abundant west of the Klickitat River, including sites below the point where Engelmann spruce enters the mix, closer to 5,000 feet. Shrub species found in this open forest include *Rosa pisocarpa* (cluster rose), *Sambucus racemosa* (red elderberry), *Spiraea betulifolia* var. *lucida* (birch-leaf Spiraea) and *Symphoricarpos albus* (snowberry). As in the other eastside zones, grasses are common and include species of *Calamagrostis* (reed-grass), *Festuca* (fescue), and *Hordeum* (squirreltail grass).

### Higher elevations on the east side

Above the reach of Douglas-fir and grand fir, at approximately 5,500 feet, the tree cover is at best discontinuous; in some places small groves are found but even these are scattered. The forest has very much the appearance of the *Tsuga mertensiana* Zone described above with west side forests, although individual trees, especially whitebark pine, may be much larger. Subalpine fir is more common here as well.

### Meadows

Justice William O. Douglas, writing in *My Wilderness, the Pacific West*, described one of his favorite places thusly: "Bird Creek Meadows lies at about a mile high on the southeast shoulder of Mount Adams. It's not a single meadow but a series of alcoves that stretch a mile along the southern rim of the peak. Above each alcove is a series of benches, one higher than the other." Perhaps the most well-known floral feature of the Mount Adams country, Bird Creek Meadows rivals the floral display of Paradise at Mount Rainier.

In midsummer, the lush green of these meadows dims beneath a kaleidoscope of flower color. The species are many. There is the blue of *Lupinus arcticus* ssp. *subalpinus* (subalpine lupine), the mauve of *Castilleja parviflora* var. *oreopola* (magenta paintbrush), and the yellow of *Senecio triangularis* (arrowleaf senecio). *Penstemons* and monkeyflowers, heathers and sedges—all are here, set against the backdrop of moraine and mountain. At the edges of the moraines, subalpine species, such as *Phyllodoce glandulifera* (yellow heather) and *Penstemon procerus* var. *tolmiei* (Tolmie's penstemon) become more common. Near Bird Creek, Hellroaring Meadows supports extensive patches of white *Ligusticum grayi* (Gray's lovage) and subalpine lupine. At the trailhead, colonies of the purple *Penstemon euglaucus* (glaucous penstemon) are established in disturbed areas.

But if the meadows along Bird Creek have gained the most attention, the diversity of meadow types at Mount Adams far exceeds that of its northern neighbor. In fact, the number and large size of many of the middle elevation meadows is one of the most distinctive aspects of the Mount Adams landscape. Wet meadows ranging from a hundred feet on a side to many acres are found on the north and west sides of the mountain. Many of these are sphagnum meadows. Some of these meadows remain partially inundated throughout the summer and often support flowing water, including streams and smaller watercourses.

Such meadows may owe their origins to the type of volcanic eruptions that have occurred at the mountain. Although explosive eruptions, at least in recent times, are rare, the volume of material extruded is second only to that of Mount Shasta in northern California. Most of the upper cone was constructed between 20 and 10 thousand years ago, and the volcanic "thumbprint" of the mountain owes much of its form to debris avalanches that result from its eruptive activity and landform instability. As recently as 1921 a huge landslide originating at the upper levels of Avalanche Glacier traveled more than four miles down slope. Less than 6,000 years ago an immense lahar flowed south and southwest, covering the Trout Lake valley. Debris flows are thus a major factor in the topography.

From a floral community point of view, these eruptive dynamics, coupled with recent glacial history, augment the flora. The number of wetland specialists is thus greater than might be expected. An example of such diversity is found at Grand Meadow and Swampy Meadows, two large meadows located on the mountain's southwest side at an elevation of 4,000 feet. Except for some extensive, slightly elevated shrubby areas, in early summer the water in much of the meadow landscape is ankle deep. Portions of these meadows remain wet throughout the summer and both are characterized by flowing water, including streams and small watercourses, and the presence of ponds. Water plants inhabit the small ponds, and wetland specialists abound in the seasonally drier places. Slightly elevated and extensive areas support shrubby species, such as *Betula glandulosa* (dwarf birch), and *Vaccinium uliginosum* (bog blueberry), both wetland specialists not found at Mount Rainier. *Viburnum edule* (highbush cranberry) is another species with a preference for wetlands. Herbaceous wetland species include *Drosera anglica* (sundew), an insectivore that is most common in Swampy Meadows, and *Comarum palustris* (purple cinquefoil, a wetland *Potentilla* relative). Species requiring inundation include *Utricularia intermedia* (flatleaf bladderwort). Sedges and rushes, too, thrive in these meadows.

On the north side of Mount Adams, Muddy Meadows, as the name implies, constitutes another wet, and seasonally inundated habitat. The large shrubby patches are absent from this meadow; thus, neither dwarf birch nor bog blueberry are found, but the primarily herbaceous community is home to many orchids, including *Platanthera stricta* (slender bog orchid), and large expanses of *Camassia quamash ssp. breviflora* (blue camas), a lily apparently restricted to this side of the mountain.

Even the smallest meadows, such as Babyshoe Meadow, on the northwest side near Takhlakh Lake, support a rich wetland flora, including *Kalmia microphylla* (alpine laurel) and *Dodecatheon jeffreyi* (Jeffrey's shooting star) and *Drosera anglica* (English sundew).

By contrast to these middle elevation wet meadows, the subalpine meadows on the north and west side of the mountain are much less extensive, limited, largely, by restricted water and suitable level topography. At these elevations, the forest extends up ridges and valleys to the edges of steep moraines and barren glacial till. Interspersed are meadows and the occasional small lake, where species of wetland and drier upland environments are encountered. Familiar species in these steep meadows include *Luetkea pectinata* (partridgefoot), *Arabis furcata* var. *furcata* (Cascade rockcress), *Ranunculus suksdorfii* (subalpine buttercup), and *Valeriana sitchensis* (Sitka valerian).

The transition to the alpine region above continuous timberline is subtle in some areas and very abrupt in others. Well-developed meadows are only infrequently encountered. Where steep and barren moraines dominate the landscape, plant life may, for all practical purposes, terminate quite abruptly; this dynamic is visible at places such as High Camp at 6,800 feet on the north side. In other places, such as along the South Climb route, forest patches persist to high elevations, but the herbaceous community changes from a subalpine-type flora to a more alpine community. Thus, tucked amongst the rocks, *Smelowskia ovalis* var. *ovalis* (small-fruit smelowskia), *Polemonium elegans* (elegant Jacob's ladder) and several species of wild buckwheat, including *Eriogonum pyrolifolium* var. *coryphaeum* (dirty socks) and *E. umbellatum* var. *hausknechtii* (Hausknecht's buckwheat) thrive. The sulphur-yellow flowers of the latter are often seen with the blue *Lupinus sericeus* (silky lupine).

A persistent impression of dryness is characteristic of the alpine, perhaps due to the presence of so much rock and the reduced density and diversity of the floral community. By mid-summer, the snowline recedes to the point that it is reached only at high elevation, typically well above 7,000 feet. But dry landscapes are more than an impression. With its summit situated east of the Cascade crest, Mount Adams does include environments with a more southerly, drier flavor.

***

With 769 native species found at and above the 4,000 foot level, on just 325 square miles, the diversity of the flora of Mount Adams is arguably the result of many diverse habitats created by the interplay of a complex topography and a unique geographic location. For example, on the southeast, one can travel from a sage/steppe and oak woodland to alpine tundra in just four miles. The number of forest and meadow communities reflects the same diversity.

Although much of the study area, particularly at higher elevations, was in a pristine environment, the affects of past and present human impact, including logging, grazing, especially by sheep, and road building, was present in many locations. This combination of multiple use and relative insulation from such impacts interplays with the unique geographical factors influencing the mountain's flora. In this respect, it is quite different from Mount Rainier to the north, even though the percentage of introduced species at Mount Adams is much less. And, as is evident from the discussion above, the plant communities at Mount Adams do not always fit into categories previously defined for the Cascade Mountains as a whole. The uniqueness of the flora as contrasted with other Pacific Northwest volcanoes makes Mount Adams a fascinating place and one deserving further study.

## Ethnobotany of Mount Adams

*We have used the past tense in the following overview of native peoples' usage of native plants. However, plants play an important role today; thus, the discussion does not mean to imply that utilization has ceased. Huckleberry fields near Mount Adams, in particular, are protected for Native American use.*

Sacred mountain to the Native Americans, Mount Adams, or "Pahto," meaning, "standing tall," historically provided both spiritual and physical sustenance. A visit to Trout Lake on the mountain's south side in late summer provides a first hand experience of the most important food sources for the first, and subsequent peoples who came to the Mount Adams country. Filled with the small, round sweet blue fruits, flat boxes on the porches of local stores await purchase and shipment. Huckleberries augment the menus of local restaurants and constitute an important business in Trout Lake, and a source of income for the many people who pick and process them.

Mushrooms, too, are important to the local community. Locally common in lower elevations, mushroom collecting is a seasonal means of livelihood for many people living near the mountain.

Rights to and maintenance of huckleberry fields predates the current Trout Lake business endeavors by many generations. For the tribes here, including the Yakama and Klickitat peoples, the tasty huckleberries of summer constituted a mainstay of winter's diet.

That huckleberry species, of which two were most important for gathering, find the Mount Adams terrain much to their liking is evidenced by the abundance of these chest-high shrubs in middle elevations. Open areas with minimal competition suit them best and disturbed areas are rapidly colonized. It is known that huckleberry "fields" were maintained with occasional burning by Native Americans. In fact, early forest managers forbade the practice.

In the Indian Heaven uplands, a high recently active volcanic plateau sprinkled with lakes west of Mount Adams, abundant huckleberry fields provided a valuable food source for the Klickitat Tribe, one of 14 bands of the Yakama Nation. In late summer, the fields became home to many people. Women were responsible for the preparation of the berries. The fields varied in extent and even location, depending on the yearly weather and the competition from brush. Here, too, fire kept the brush under control.

Just north of Indian Heaven, the Surprise Lakes camp served as a site for processing the huckleberries so prolific in the region. Today, signs separate traditional Native American huckleberry fields from publicly accessed sites, a reflection of treaty rights that acknowledge both the important role of berry gathering and the historical reality of people who depended on the harvest.

Later, huckleberries were also canned, thus extending their utility. Huckleberry fields and campsites, including structures left for reuse, were considered personal territory, claims that were verbally honored. This system, too, reflected the importance of the sites, both for personal use, and trading.

Berries awaited consumption until traditional ceremonies could be held, rituals that honored the importance of the fruit and served to unite the people. Yearly harvests provided opportunity, too, for trade and socialization, as separation during other seasons might preclude.

While huckleberry gathering constituted an autumn activity, springtime and summer plants played important roles in the diet. Early season plants, such as several species of lomatium, provided fresh food beginning as soon as February in the lower elevations. The large, succulent stocks of *Heracleum maximum* (cow-parsnip), a wet meadow plant, were a much sought after herb, partly due to their size. Bulbous plants, too, provided valuable food sources from spring through autumn. Camas bulbs could be found at Muddy Meadows, on the north side of Mount Adams. The beautiful little *Fritillaria pudica* (yellowbell) was perhaps less regularly a part of the diet, but was nonetheless sought, along with many other root plants. Other fruits, such as those of *Prunus virginiana* (chokecherry), a lower elevation species, and, to the west, *Vaccinium parvifolium* (red huckleberry) and *Amelanchier alnifolia* (serviceberry), were gathered in season.

*Quercus garryana* (Oregon white oak) is found in a few places on the southeast side of the study area; trees are more extensive on the lower slopes, and their acorns, nutritious and abundant in good years, also served the peoples east of Mount Adams. These acorns had to be leached to remove harmful tannins. The high elevation *Pinus albicaulis* (whitebark pine) provided nuts, too, late in the season, and the inner bark of *Pinus ponderosa* (ponderosa pine) was known to be edible.

The quantity of plant material gathered by women could be considerable. Estimates of as much as 60 pounds daily of root material have been observed. However, plant gathering was always restricted by seasonality, and the time available for digging probably never exceeded a couple of months. Nevertheless, scientists estimate that in some regions plant resources provided up to half of the required daily caloric intake. The amount of protein available from plants, however, was considerably less.

Plants, fresh or dry, provided a necessary food source, but their usefulness was not limited to providing nutrition. Art flourished amongst the native peoples; in particular, basketry achieved a high state of beauty and complexity. Both waterproof and beautiful cedar root baskets decorated with woven designs served utilitarian purposes and artistic sensibilities. The long fibrous leaves of *Xerophyllum tenax* (beargrass) provided excellent weaving material for mats and baskets.

Plants were extensively utilized for medicine as well. One of the most important medicinal plants at the mountain is *Lomatium dissectum* (fern-leaved lomatium), which serves as a vegetable, a fish poison, and, as it turns out, an important medicine. The root pulp could be applied to infected wounds, while a dilute drink treated respiratory infections. Horses, too, benefited from use of this plant.

Mount Adams is located just south of the Klickitat Divide trail, which connected native people on the east and west sides of the Cascades and which has been in use for thousands of years. Plant resources from the Mount Adams country were prominent among the items traded along this trail and to this day the mountain remains important for its ethnobotanical resources to many people.

## The History of the Study of the Flora of Mount Adams

The first botanist to venture up to Mount Adams began his collecting work relatively late, at least in terms of the botanical exploration of the Pacific Northwest. Wilhelm Nicholas Suksdorf arrived in Bingen, Washington, on the Columbia River, in 1876. In September, 1877, Suksdorf undertook his first collecting trip, visiting Bird Creek Meadows. His last trip was made in September, 1925. In between, he made thousands of collections in the Mount Adams country. Indeed, Suksdorf made his living supplying plant specimens to scientists at universities throughout the United States. Most of his work was done on the east and southeast sides of the mountain, with the occasional trip up the Lewis River on the west. *Suksdorfia,* a genus in the Saxifrage family, was named for him by Asa Gray, his friend and mentor at Harvard. *Suksdorfia ranunculifolia* is a small, attractive herbaceous perennial with white flowers that grows on the eastern slopes of the mountain. A number of other species also commemorate Suksdorf: two grasses, *Bromus suksdorfii* and *Poa suksdorfii,* a spikerush *Eleocharis suksdorfii,* a buttercup, *Ranunculus suksdorfii,* a hawthorn, Crataegus suksdorfii, a monkeyflower, *Mimulus suksdorfii,* a pink, *Silene suksdorfii,* and a paintbrush, *Castilleja suksdorfii.*

Thomas Jefferson Howell, the first botanist to work in Oregon, visited Mount Adams in 1882, and made a small number of collections of subalpine species, including *Ivesia gordonii.* A pussytoes, *Antennaria howellii,* is named for him.

Prolific Oregon collector Louis F. Henderson came to Mount Adams in 1882 but made his most important visit in 1892, when he collected plants from Washington for a display he took to the 1893 World's Fair in Chicago. Now in the herbarium at the University of Washington this display consisted of 114 plants from Mount Adams, including *Phlox hendersonii,* a beautiful cushion plant from the summit of Little Mount Adams.

John B. Flett, who worked across most of western Washington and who is especially known for his service as a park ranger and botanist at Mount Rainier National Park between 1913 and 1921, spent June and July of 1899 on the east and southeast sides of Mount Adams. His journals have not been found and his label notes often carry little precise location information. Nevertheless, by collating known dates of his collections with what label data does exist, we were able to reconstruct most of the path of his travels at Mount Adams in 1899.

John S. Cotton worked in the valley of Hellroaring River in 1903, as well as at lower elevations eastwards.

John W. Thompson, associated with the University of Washington and a prodigious collector across the Pacific Northwest, visited Mount Adams in 1934.

Eugene Hunn collected on the east side, from the mountain down to Toppenish, in 1977 and made a number of important collections at Howard Lake, in the northeast corner of the study area.

Beth Skaggs Ryan, working for the U.S. Forest Service between 1980 and 1983, collected at Mirror Lake as well as along the west side in alpine and subalpine habitats. Her specimens are in the herbarium at the Mount Adams Ranger District Office in Trout Lake.

In 1992, Sarah Gage and Sharon Rodman, on behalf of the herbarium at the University of Washington, recreated the 1892 collecting trip of Louis Henderson. Hundreds of their collections are housed at the University of Washington.

Elroy Burnett, Mark Egger, Robert Goff, Don Knoke, Joy Mastrogiuseppe, and Peter Zika have all collected at Mount Adams in recent years.

In mid-June, 2001, Richard Olmstead, Director of the herbarium at the University of Washington, led the herbarium's annual foray to the Gifford Pinchot National Forest, collecting in the Trout Lake area.

Paul Slichter, a science teacher from Gresham, Oregon, is very familiar with the Mount Adams country and made several dozen collections and observations for us in 2005 and 2006, including notable information from Devil's Garden, located on the north slope of the mountain.

Jim Riley, of the U.S. Forest Service, has hiked innumerable miles around Mount Adams; his plant lists are posted on the website of the Washington Native Plant Society.

## The Flora of Mount Adams, Washington

Paul Dixon and Mike Daly, strong climbers both, supported us on a long-distance hike along the Round-the-Mountain trail early in the summer of 2005. They combined this with a summit climb and along the way made the highest collections of plants ever taken at Mount Adams, at more than 9,200 feet, above the Lunchcounter.

Our own travels and collecting have taken us to many fine and wild places on Mount Adams, as well as to clearcuts and heavily-grazed meadows. All have been worthwhile, and our own collections number more than 600.

## Rare Plants and Weeds

### Rare Plants

Many factors can combine to make a plant rare: it may occur only in a very limited place, it may be more widespread but in small numbers where it does occur, or its habitat may be dwindling. Rarity also has a geographic component. Thus, *Calypso bulbosa,* the calypso orchid, easily found at lower elevations at Mount Rainier, is extremely rare in our higher and drier study area at Mount Adams. However, objective measures of rarity have been developed and are used by agencies responsible for environmental laws at both the federal and state level.

No plants federally listed as "endangered" or "threatened" by the U.S. Fish and Wildlife Service were found within the study area.

Washington state law includes different provisions with respect to the classification of plant rarity and endangerment, and, based upon those provisions the list of species from Mount Adams given here is longer than that under federal law. The rare plants inventory for the state is administered by the Natural Heritage Program of the Department of Natural Resources.

**Listed Plants with NHP**

| Scientific Name | Global Rank | State Rank | State Status |
|---|---|---|---|
| *Anthoxanthum odoratum* | G5 | SNR | R1 |
| *Luzula arcuata* | G5 | S1 | S |
| *Microseris borealis* | G4? | S2 | S |
| *Mimulus suksdorfii* | G4 | S2 | S |
| *Potentilla drummondii* ssp. *breweri* | G5 | S1 | T |
| *Salix sessilifolia* | G4 | S2 | S |
| *Spiranthes porrifolia* | G4 | S2 | S |
| *Utricularia intermedia* | G5 | S2 | S |
| *Utricularia minor* | G5 | S2? | R1 |

A "Global Rank" of G4 or G5 means that the species is apparently or demonstrably secure in its worldwide range. "State Rank" indicates relative rarity or endangerment within the state of Washington. A rank of S1 or S2 offers a darker perspective: S1 means "Critically imperiled (5 or fewer occurrences)" and S2 implies "Imperiled (6 to 20 occurrences), very vulnerable to extirpation." "State Status" is the overall assessment of the species made by the Natural Heritage Program. No plants at Mount Adams are considered "Endangered, or in danger of becoming extinct or extirpated from Washington." One species is "Threatened, or likely to become endangered in Washington" ("T" above) while six are "Sensitive, or vulnerable or declining and could become endangered or threatened in the state" ("S" above). State Statuses R1 and R2 refer to plants of concern but in need of review and additional data.

In addition to plants with official designations as "rare," endemic plants should be mentioned here. These are of special interest because of their very limited geographic distributions.

Indeed, one, *Carex constanceana,* may be extinct. It is known from just one collection made by Wilhelm Suksdorf in 1909. It has not been seen since, despite searches by a number of botanists over the years. This species grew at the upper end of Hellroaring Valley and may have been eliminated when the valley was grazed heavily by sheep in the 1920s and 1930s. The species is obviously closely related to a widespread sedge *C. petasata* which is found across the West east of the Cascade Mountains. The likelihood is that *C. constanceana* is a "neoendemic," having evolved in place at Mount Adams from the parent species *C. petasata.*

A second possible neoendemic is *Eucephalus glaucescens,* called the Klickitat Aster that only grows in those parts of Klickitat, Skamania, and

Yakima Counties surrounding Mount Adams. It does not cross the Columbia River into Oregon, nor does it reach the Goat Rocks north of the mountain. Its closest relative is *E. engelmannii*, a species that is widespread in the Rocky Mountains and the interior Pacific Northwest. Unlike the possibly extinct *Carex constanceana*, it is quite common within its limited range.

## Weeds

Of the 843 taxa in the flora of Mount Adams, 770 are native. The 73 introduced species - from well-established invasive plants to casual introductions - amount to 8.6% of the total flora. At Mount Rainier, the figure is 17%.

Several factors account for the difference between these two mountain floras. The first, and most important, is the more limited elevational range at Mount Adams: we collected data only for plants occurring above 4,000 feet. At Mount Rainier, the lowest elevation in the national park is 1,760 feet, along both the Carbon and Ohanapecosh Rivers, which allows many plants that are less tolerant of cold to gain a foothold. Second, human traffic at Mount Adams has been much less and this would seem to more than balance the fact that much of our study area has been logged, unlike the national park. Traffic, whether people on horseback or in automobiles, brings in weed seeds as well as creating disturbed patches in the environment for the establishment of those seeds. Finally, while park staff at Mount Rainier does work to control the worst of the weedy species, annual mowing of the road edges in much of the park helps to maintain favorable conditions for their establishment and spread. This is not the case at Mount Adams.

Only a handful of species are able to move away from roadsides, campsites, and trails to become established in undisturbed habitats. *Mycelis muralis* (wall-lettuce) is able to grow in undisturbed forests to almost 5,000 feet. *Poa annua* (annual bluegrass) is sometimes seen in intact meadow habitats, but never in great numbers. *Plantago major* (common plantain) may do the same. On the other hand, some weeds we found, such as *Viola arvensis* (field pansy) and *Secale cereale* (rye), probably don't reproduce at Mount Adams. Other species fall in between these extremes, reliably seen in, but restricted to, a small set of disturbed habitats.

As with rare plants, federal and state agencies take an interest in weedy plants. No "Federal Noxious Weed" occurs at Mount Adams. In Washington State, the Noxious Weed Control Board rates plants of concern according to their presence and degree of threat into three classes.

## Introduction

Class A weeds are plants which are of limited occurrence in the state at the present time and for which an effort is to be made to eradicate those present and prevent their introduction. No state Class A weeds are found at Mount Adams.

Class B weeds are present but deemed to be not irretrievably widespread. Where a species is already present, control measures are to be decided at the county level. The prevention of introduction in other areas is also a priority. At Mount Adams, several Class B weeds occur: these include *Centaurea stoebe* (spotted knapweed), *Centaurea diffusa* (spreading knapweed), *Daucus carota* (Queen Anne's lace), *Hieracium caespitosum* (yellow hawkweed), *Hypochaeris radicata* (hairy cat's ear), and *Leucanthemum vulgare* (oxeye or Shasta daisy).

Class C weeds are widespread, abundant, and beyond hope of control, although where crops are threatened, counties have the authority to implement control measures. At Mount Adams Class C weeds include *Artemisia absinthium* (wormwood, absinthe), *Cirsium arvense* (field thistle), *Cirsium vulgare* (bull thistle), *Hypericum perforatum* (Klamath weed), *Linaria vulgaris* (yellow toadflax), *Phalaris arundinacea* (reed canary-grass, known from one location along Road 23 on the northwest and at Horseshoe Lake), *Secale cereale* (rye), *Senecio vulgaris* (common groundsel), and *Tanacetum vulgare* (common tansy).

## Biogeography

The degree of species richness that we found at Mount Adams was the major surprise in the course of this project. Certainly, this discovery went against the first impression we had, that the mountain was a dusty and dry place, logged around its lower flanks. Including introduced species, there are 843 known taxa at Mount Adams; this compares with 909 at Mount Rainier. However, excluding weeds, the count at Mount Adams is 769 taxa while that at Mount Rainier is 735. Thus, in terms of numbers, the native flora of Mount Adams is greater than that of Mount Rainier. (For the purpose of the analysis that follows, we will exclude the introduced species.) The area above the 4,000 foot elevation at Mount Adams is 325 square miles, while the area within the park boundary at Mount Rainier is 368 square miles. The number of native taxa at Mount Rainier drops to 552 if only those plants occurring at 4,000 feet and above are counted, making Mount Adams much richer in terms of taxa above this elevation.

In addition to numerical differences, while sharing much in common, there are many taxa distinctive to the two mountains. These differences may be attributed to three major factors, an examination of which will help to introduce Mount Adams to people unfamiliar with the area.

The first factor is the elevation of the study area. The *Flora of Mount Rainier* book (Biek, 2000) included all lands within the national park boundaries. Thus, the lowest elevation for the study area was 1,760 feet at the Carbon River entrance. As mentioned above, the study area at Mount Adams was selected to be the 4,000-foot line "footprint" of the mountain with the addition of one lower area (Cascade Creek basin) that lies within the Mount Adams Wilderness Area. It was expected, therefore, that many lower elevation species at Mount Rainier would be absent from the Mount Adams flora. This is indeed the case; examples are provided by plants such as *Allium validum, Gaultheria shallon, Malus fusca, Oenanthe sarmentosa,* and *Vaccinium ovatum.* All of these are absent from Mount Adams.

A second factor for species differences is the presence of specific habitats in degrees that vary between the two mountains. For example, large wetlands are present on the west and southwestern sides of Mount Adams. These include the acres of flat, seasonally inundated, often sphagnum-based land at Grand Meadow, Swampy Meadows, and Bathtub Meadow. Such large wetlands are absent from Mount Rainier. Thus, wetland plants unique to such areas at Mount Adams include *Callitriche palustris, Carex aquatilis* (both varieties *aquatilis* and *dives*), *Elodea nuttallii, Isoetes lacustris, Potamogeton alpinus, P. epihydrus, P. gramineus, Utricularia intermedia* and *U. minor*. The study area at Mount Adams has also been heavily logged outside the Wilderness Area and one might expect that such extensive human activity might influence floral communities. Conversely, Mount Rainier has extensive high elevation meadows, including those at Sunrise, Paradise, as well as other, subalpine "parks." While Mount Adams supports subalpine meadow communities, they are not as extensive as at Mount Rainier. Lakes, from large bodies of water to small, permanent pools in meadows are a prominent feature of the landscape at Mount Adams, unlike Mount Rainier. Additionally, the deep glacial river valleys that define much of the topography at Mount Rainier are much reduced in number at Mount Adams. Finally, at Mount Adams one finds basaltic slopes and exposures with east and southeast aspects, a situation absent at Mount Rainier; this is discussed in more detail below.

The third factor concerns the location of Mount Adams south and east of the Cascade crest, a geographical reality that suggests a possible impact on the flora. Precipitation is considerably lower than at the nearby Cascade volcanoes, including Mounts Hood, Rainier, and St. Helens, as well as the Goat Rocks. And, from the few records available, Mount Adams is both colder in the winter and warmer in the summer than its neighbors. Thus, on balance, the plants enjoy a longer growing season. (Although Mount Adams is located about one-half a degree of latitude south of Mount Rainier and it is a general phenomenon that the diversity of life increases as one moves southwards along a line of longitude, we feel that this is a minor factor.) As we will show, it is this geographic reality that accounts for the many differences between the two mountains and yields a more diverse flora at Mount Adams.

Taking into account these three factors - elevation, habitat extent, and geographical location -- one way to analyze the distinctiveness of the Mount Adams flora is to consider those species that are at the limits of their ranges at or near the mountain. A large number reach their northern limits here. Typically, these are plants of the Sierra / Cascade axis in Oregon and California. On the other hand, only a handful of species reach their southern limits in our study area. Of these, two are circumboreal species, coming as far south as Mount Adams, and two have distributions north in the Washington Cascades and over to the northern Rockies. The following list thus gives some indication of geographical importance. (Primary sources for this list are distribution data in Hitchcock and herbarium records.)

***Species Distribution Limits at Mount Adams***

| **Northern** | **Southern** |
| --- | --- |
| *Agoseris monticola* | *Agoseris glauca* var. *dasycephala* |
| *Calochortus subalpinus* | *Carex engelmannii* |
| *Carex angustata* | *Carex lasiocarpa* |
| *Carex breweri* | *Carex nardina* var. *hepburnii* |
| *Carex halliana* | |
| *Carex microptera* | |
| *Carex straminiformis* | |
| *Carex subfusca* | |
| *Carex vernacula* | |
| *Eriogonum douglasii* | |
| *Lonicera conjugialis* | |
| *Melica aristata* | |
| *Navarretia divaricata* | |
| *Potentilla drummondii* var. *breweri* | |
| *Spiranthes porrifolia* | |

Part of the Cascade Range but east of the divide, Mount Adams is also home to species that are both at the western end of their range and absent from Mount Rainier, where one might otherwise expect them. Among these are *Betula glandulosa, Camassia quamash* ssp. *breviflora* (also at a northern limit), *Lewisia nevadensis, Zigadenus paniculatus,* and *Zigadenus venenosus* var. *gramineus.*

## A Comparison of the Flora of Mount Rainier and Mount Adams – the Geography

To further study the possible importance of the geographical factor, five genera were selected, based on two criteria. The first was a measure of the numerical divergence between the mountains. Of course, this divergence is influenced by numbers of species in a particular genus; thus, it is perhaps not surprising that *Carex* is well represented at both mountains and that the numbers of unique species is high. However, this genus was also selected for the diversity of habitats occupied by *Carex* species. And, of the 51 *Carex* taxa at Mount Adams, 18 are unique to that mountain; of the 41 taxa at Mount Rainier, 9 are unique.

*Agoseris, Lupinus, Penstemon, Poa,* and *Saxifraga* are the other genera selected for this analysis. The following table summarizes the native species numbers and uniqueness (at one mountain as opposed to the other) status.

| | **Mount Adams** | | **Mount Rainier** | |
|---|---|---|---|---|
| **Genus** | # taxa | #unique taxa | # taxa | #unique taxa |
| *Agoseris* | 7 | 3 | 4 | 0 |
| *Carex* | 51 | 18 | 41 | 9 |
| *Lupinus* | 9 | 5 | 5 | 1 |
| *Penstemon* | 14 | 7 | 8 | 1 |
| *Poa* | 10 | 5 | 8 | 3 |

**Table 1: Selected Genera**

To evaluate the importance of the geographic and habitat factors suggested above, the individual species of the five genera were analyzed for distribution patterns, both in the literature (Hitchcock, 1973, and Jepson 1993) and in the database for the current study as well as the WTU (University of Washington herbarium) online database. The WTU database includes county distribution maps for *Carex;* for the other genera the distribution was ascertained by examination of the individual specimen data specifications provided by the website and from our own Mount Adams database.

From these sources the following table for *Carex* summarizes the distribution for those taxa unique to each mountain. The table shows if the species is primarily found east or west of the Cascades and whether Hitchcock considered it to be either limited to western or eastern Cascades' locations, at the northern end of its range in the Mount

Adams region, or the southern limit at Mount Rainier. The purpose of the summary presented in the table, therefore, is to give an overview of the importance of the southeastern location of Mount Adams in contrast to the northerly one of Mount Rainier.

The "elevation factor" ("E.F.") in this table refers to the lowest elevation of the Mount Adams study area at 4,000 feet.

| Mountain /Taxa | W. Cas-cades | E. Cas-cades | Cosmo-politan | E. F. | Hitchcock locations |
|---|---|---|---|---|---|
| **MOUNT ADAMS** | | | | | |
| *Carex angustata* | | y | | | Mount Adams at northern end of range |
| *Carex aquatilis* var. *aquatilis* | y | | | | East Cascades to California |
| *Carex aquatilis* var. *dives* | y | | | | Western Cascades, to CA |
| *Carex athrostachya* | | | y | | Cosmopolitan, Alaska to California |
| *Carex breweri* | | | y | | Mount Adams south |
| *Carex californica* | y | | | | West Cascades to northern CA |
| *Carex constanceana* | | y | | | East Cascades |
| *Carex disperma* | | | y | | East Cascades, ID, OR |
| *Carex epapillosa* | | y | | | Cosmopolitan, circumboreal |
| *Carex fracta* | | y | | | East Cascades, to southern coastal ranges & CA |
| *Carex halliana* | | y | | | Mount Adams at northern end of range |
| *Carex inops* ssp. *inops* | | | y | | West Cascades, to northern CA |
| *Carex jonesii* | | | y | | Mount Adams at northern end of range, to southern CA |

| | | | | | |
|---|---|---|---|---|---|
| *Carex lasiocarpa* | | y | | | Circumboreal, southern Cascades |
| *Carex multicostata* | | | y | | Central Cascades, to southern CA |
| *Carex straminiformis* | | | y | | Mount Adams at northern end of range, to Sierra Nevada |
| *Carex subfusca* | | y | | | Mount Adams at northern end of range |
| *Carex vernacula* | | y | | | Mount Adams at northern end of range, to Sierra Nevada |
| | | | | | |
| MOUNT RAINIER | | | | | |
| *Carex albonigra* | y | | | | Northern species, Olympics, rare in CA |
| *Carex cusickii* | | | | y | Sea level to moderate elevations, western Cascades |
| *Carex hendersonii* | | | | y | To 3000 ft/western Cascades, nw. CA |
| *Carex leptalea* ssp. *leptalea* | | | | y | To n. CA Coast, lowlands to moderate elevations |
| *Carex nudata* | | y | | | Western Cascades, Columbia River gorge, to central CA |
| *Carex paysonis* | y | | | | Northern, to Wallowas |
| *Carex pellita* | | | | y | Cosmopolitan, low elevation |
| *Carex praticola* | y | | | | Northern, to nw. CA, lowland |
| *Carex stipata* var. *stipata* | | | | y | Cosmopolitan, to CA, lowland to moderate elevations |

**Table 2: Characteristics of *Carex* distribution**

Table 2 clearly demonstrates the importance of the southeastern location of Mount Adams relative to Mount Rainier. The last column shows that Hitchcock gave Mount Adams as the northern limit for the range of seven species. However, five of those have more northerly specimens at the University of Washington herbarium. Thus, only *Carex angustata* and *Carex halliana* remain as northern limit species. *Carex breweri* is problematic as having been previously split into varieties with distinct distributions north and south of Mount Adams. The *Carex* maps provided on the WTU herbarium website reflect the more expanded distribution data and the collections at WTU reflect this fact. Three species show a more western distribution, and thus might be considered "candidate" species for Mount Rainier. However, of these, *Carex californica* is primarily a coastal species; *C. aquatilis* var. *aquatilis* is a Cascades species that misses Pierce County (in which most of Mount Rainier National Park is located) for some reason although it is also found east of the Cascades, and *C. aquatilis* var. *dives* is widely distributed west of the Cascades. We recorded specimens of both varieties of *C. aquatilis* west and north of the mountain. For the other species unique to Mount Adams, our observations tend to support the data acquired from the WTU specimens and from Hitchcock's notes.

In conclusion, the *Carex* species unique to Mount Adams reflect very accurately the distributions noted in both the literature and in modern collections. The south and eastern location of the volcano thus accounts for the absence of these species from Mount Rainier. Conversely, most species found at Mount Rainier but not at Mount Adams are either too low in elevation or are western and/or northern species. Hitchcock reflects this, as do the WTU distribution maps and specimens.

*Lupinus* was selected partly because of the large number of taxa present at Mount Adams as well as for the differences from Mount Rainier. Lupines occupy a wide variety of habitats and are particularly common on the southeastern side of the mountain. Of the five unique taxa at Mount Adams all but one are species found elsewhere in Washington, primarily east of the Cascades. *Lupinus polyphyllus* ssp. *polyphyllus* is the only exception, although it, too, is also primarily an eastern species. *L. polycarpus,* an annual at Mount Rainier but absent from Mount Adams, is typically a lowland species. Our database reflects also the eastern distribution of *Lupinus.*

*Agoseris* species unique to Mount Adams also reflect that southern and eastern distribution. The *Penstemon* species found at Mount Adams are nearly exclusively eastern Cascades species as well.

Thus, a close look at the genera summarized in Table 1 confirms that geography is probably the most important factor in determining the occurrence of those species unique to either of the two mountains. This is not entirely expected, or is at least a stronger indication than might be thought, given that the two are large volcanoes surrounded by forests and support many similar habitats. To examine the possibility that the presence of particular habitats, such as large meadows, is an important factor along with geography, the meadows on the north and west sides of Mount Adams were compared with Mount Rainier in terms of unique species. Excluding *Carex aquatilis aquatilis, C. aquatilis dives, C. jonesii,* and *C. lasiocarpa,* (discussed above) the analysis shows that *Betula glandulosa, Juncus ensifolius* var. *ensifolius, Juncus supiniformis, Potamogeton epihydrus,* and *Scheuchzeria palustris* would be possible "candidate" species for Mount Rainier based on known locations in the WTU and our Mount Adams database. Therefore, habitat (wet, large meadows) may explain their absence. Of the *Carex, C. lasiocarpa,* and *C. aquatilis* var. *dives* are species that might be expected at Mount Rainier, given available habitat. Thus, in spite of the difference in meadow size and type at the two mountains, meadow habitats alone provide a rather short candidate list of species unique to the two mountains.

The other major habitat difference between Mount Adams and Mount Rainier is found on the dry eastern and southern slopes of the former. One of the driest sites in the study area is the quarry operated by the Washington Department of Natural Resources on the southeast. At an elevation of 4,123 feet, the quarry is located on a bald hillside with a south/southeast aspect, surrounded by forest, although historically heavily logged. This bald is home to 67 species, including a small grove of *Quercus garryana.* Here, the number of species in common with Mount Rainier is 32, or nearly half.

To examine the overall differences between the floras of the two mountains, three comparisons were made. The first looks at all native taxa and then the smaller set of those taxa at Mount Rainier found only below 4,000 feet of elevation and also not found at Mount Adams. This seems a reasonable approach to handling the difference in study area elevations. Thus filtered, the comparison is between the 769 taxa of Mount Adams and 648 taxa at Mount Rainier. Of these, 196 are unique to Mount Adams – 25 percent of the flora, and 139 are unique to Mount Rainier, or 21 percent of the flora. (Chart 1)

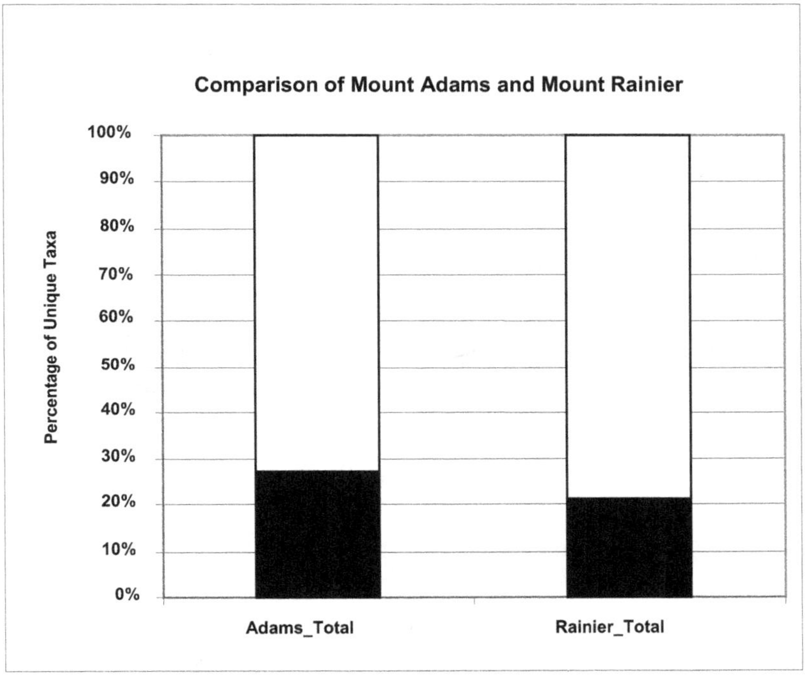


**Chart 1 – Unique Native Taxa Above 4,000 Feet**

The Mount Adams database is composed of approximately 3,300 entries, each of which includes quadrant information, where the quadrants number eight - that is, northwest, north, northeast, east, etc. In considering the east side, we can examine the flora in the northeast, east, and southeast quadrants, comparing them with the remaining five quadrants that will define the "west" for this inquiry. These three were chosen because they are exclusively "eastern", and thus include drier habitat species, such as the DNR quarry. The Rainier list includes 603 taxa for this comparison (using the same elevation criteria as for the entire flora comparison mentioned above), and the Mount Adams list numbers 602. Of these, 139, or 23 percent are unique to Mount Adams, and 208 or 34 percent are unique to Mount Rainier. (Chart 2) On the west, north, and south sides, which includes 523 taxa at Mount Adams, 20 percent are unique; of the 613 Mount Rainier taxa, 36 percent are unique. The higher numbers for Mount Rainier are because of the smaller number compared from Mount Adams (Chart 3).

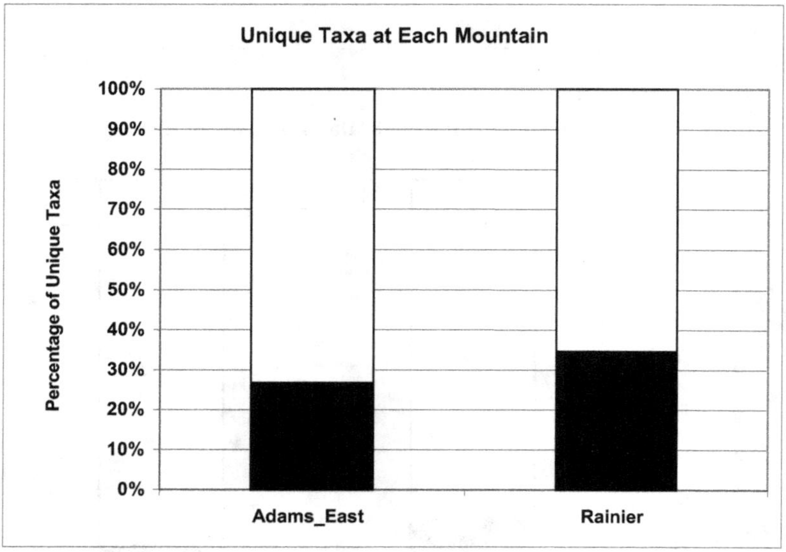


Chart 2 – Eastern Aspects of Mount Adams / Mount Rainier

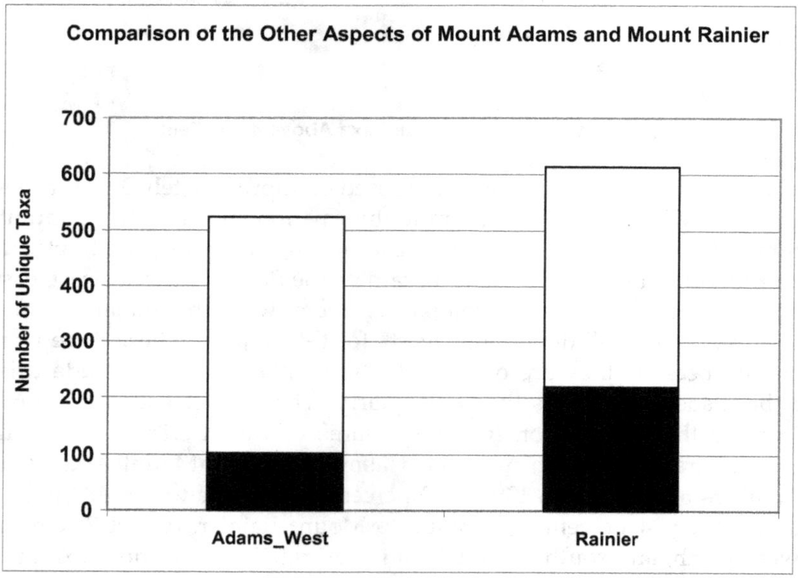


Chart 3 – Mount Adams – West, North, South Sides Mount Rainier

Finally, if we limit the inquiry to Mount Adams and compare the three eastern quadrants with the five western, 21 percent are unique to the western aspects, while 39 percent are unique to the eastern. This comparison alone would indicate the importance of aspect at the mountain.

Summarizing, the number of species unique to each mountains' flora seems large, given their proximity and the variety of habitats afforded by the two volcanoes. The eastern and southern location of Mount Adams accounts for many of the unique species at the mountain. It is most noteworthy that the eastern and southeastern aspects of the mountain are home to 240 species absent from the western, northern, and southern slopes.

## Place Names

As one of the first European explorers and collectors to the Mount Adams region, Wilhelm Suksdorf called many of his favorite collecting locations by German names. His journal also was written in German. In the 1940s, William A. Weber, a graduate student at Washington State University, translated Suksdorf's notes and produced a glossary as well. This paper was very important in ascertaining where his herbarium collections were made. For example, Suksdorf collected many specimens in "Wodan's Vale." This is the modern-day Hellroaring Creek valley. "Donner's Vale" refers to the valley of Big Muddy Creek. In our database, we have recorded both the German names and English translations, but for the purposes of this book, only the English terms have been used.

Many people may be unfamiliar with the various locations at Mount Adams. Bird Creek Meadows is probably the most well known site at the mountain, and certainly Cold Springs is familiar to the thousands who climb the mountain each year. Takhlakh Lake is also a popular camping location, particularly to people who live to the south.

To facilitate understanding of the text, the following table gives many of the place names, the quadrant in which they are located, elevation and modern GPS latitude/longitude readings, if known; these are given to a tenth of a degree accuracy only and are readings taken by the authors or by Paul Slichter. Old collections are often lacking in details, and, so, for example, Flett's many specimens from the Klickitat River and Klickitat Meadows typically do not include elevation.

The authors named a few places as well. These include "Bathtub Meadow," a large, seasonally inundated meadow downhill from and close to the well known Babyshoe Meadow at the intersection of Roads 23 and 2329, and "Three Meadows," a pond and meadow area near the Yakama Nation boundary on the north side of the mountain.

| PLACE | QUADRANT | ELEVATION (FT) | LATITUDE/LONGITUDE |
|---|---|---|---|
| Avalanche Valley | east | | |
| Babyshoe Meadow | northwest | | N 46° 16.1', W 122° 36.3' |
| Bathtub Meadow | northwest | 4,285 | N 46° 16.5', W 121° 36.3' |
| Bench Lake | southeast | 4,850 | N 46° 9.6' , W 121°23.9' W |
| Big Muddy River | east | | |
| Bird Creek Meadows | southeast | 6,500 | |
| Cascade Creek | southwest | | |
| Cold Springs | south | 5,580 | N 46° 08.2', W 121°30.9' |
| Council Lake | northwest | 4,278 | N 46° 58.958', W 121° 34.498' |
| Crofton Butte | south | 5,043 | N 46° 07.9', W 121°32.0' |
| Devil's Garden | northeast | 7,860 | N 46° 13.4', W 121° 27.9' |
| DNR quarry | southeast | 4,123 | N 46° 07.8', W 121° 20.2' |
| Foggy Flat | north | 6,050 | N 46° 15.7', W121° 29.1' |
| Grand Meadow | southwest | 4,080 | N 46° 09.1', W 121° 39.2' |
| Klickitat Glacier | east | | |
| Klickitat River | east | | |
| Hellroaring Creek | southeast | | |
| Hellroaring Meadow | southeast | 5,350 | N 46° 9.4', W 121° 25.7' |
| Hellroaring Overlook | southeast | 6,528 | N 46° 9.5', W 121° 26.6' |
| High Camp | north | 7,050 | N 46° 10.1', W 121°29.4' |
| Horseshoe Lake | northwest | 4,140 | N 46° 18.6', W 121°34.1' |
| Horseshoe Meadow | northwest | 5,916 | N 46° 10.8', W 121° 34.1' |

| | | | |
|---|---|---|---|
| Howard Lake | east | 4,905 | |
| Island Springs | southeast | | N 46° 10.0', W 121° 20.7' |
| Keene's Horse Camp | north | 4,370 | N 46° 18.6', W 121° 32.9' |
| Killen Creek Meadow | north | 4,200 | |
| King Mountain | southeast | | |
| Klickitat River | east | | |
| Lewis River | northwest | | |
| Little Mount Adams | southeast | 6,823 | N 46° 10.3', W121° 25.1' |
| Midway Meadows | north | 4,200 | N 46° 21.3', W 121°32.0' |
| Mirror Lake | southeast | 5,500 | N 46° 08.3', W 121°25.5' |
| Morrison Creek | south | 4,560 | N 46° 07.5', W 121° 31.3' |
| Muddy Meadows | north | 4,360 | N 46° 18.4', W 121° 32.1' |
| Muddy River Canyon | east | | |
| Ollalie Lake | northwest | 4,247 | N 46° 17.3', W 121° 37.1' |
| Pineway trailhead | southeast | 4,300 | N 46° 06.0', W 121°25.8' |
| Potato Hill | north | 5,090 | N 46° 19.9', W 121° 30.5' |
| Ridge of Wonders | southeast | 5,550 | N 46° 10.1', W 121° 25.9' |
| Riley Creek trailhead | west | 3,832 | N 46° 13.0', W 121° 38.1' |
| Road 115 | north | | |
| Road 170 | southeast | | |
| Road 5603 | northwest | 4,066 | N 46° 20.2', W 121°33.3' |
| Road K6900 | southeast | 4,100 | |
| Road 8040 | south | | |
| Road 82 | southeast | | |
| Rusk Creek | east | | |
| Snipes Mountain | southeast | | N 46° 07.2', W 121° 28.4 |
| Spring Creek Meadow | northwest | 4,450 | N 46° 18.3', W 121° 32.7' |
| Stagman Tr. | southwest | 4,185 | N 46° 09.9', W 121° 27.5' |

| | | | |
|---|---|---|---|
| Swampy Meadows | southwest | 3,900 | N 46° 09.9', W 121° 37.8' |
| Takh Takh Meadow | northwest | 4,640 | N 46° 16.1', W 121° 35.2' |
| Takhlakh Lake | northwest | 4,395 | |
| Three Meadows | north | 4,829 | N 46° 19.3', W 121° 29.9' |
| White Salmon River | southwest | | |

## Introduction

## Visiting Mount Adams

The south side of the mountain is approached by car from the Trout Lake valley along Forest Service Road 8040. Seasonally open, depending on snow conditions, this road terminates at the South Climb trailhead (Trail 15) at an elevation of approximately 5,600 feet. This trail leads to a junction with the Round-the-Mountain Trail (Trail 9), an excellent trail that provides access to the subalpine region.

Reaching the south side of the mountain is more difficult when approaching from northern locations, such as the Puget Sound basin, during the off-season. The easiest method is from the Columbia River to Trout Lake. This is the best available route until Road 23 opens along the west side, usually by early June. Much of Road 23 is drivable prior to this time, however, from the south or the north. All but 10 miles of it is paved. On the north, the road terminates at Randle, at State Highway 12; on the south it ends at Trout Lake.

Along the south side of the mountain Road 8290 provides access to the southeast region, including the Bird Creek Meadows area, and also to several good trails. The Aiken Lava Flow, reached by a side road, is a particularly interesting geological feature in this area. Many flowering species are encountered along the trail bordering the flow in late spring.

Good roads traverse the north side of the mountain, too. Muddy Meadows, a truly spectacular meadow and one of the largest wetlands, is directly accessible from Road 2329, close to Keene's Horse Camp. In June, the camas fields await the visitor to this location. Trails from Muddy Meadows intersect with the Pacific Crest Trail and provide access to the subalpine region, including some small lakes. Other meadows, too, as well as lava flows and lakes, including Takhlakh Lake and Olallie Lake, are easily reached from Road 2329. Both Takhlakh and Olallie support rich flora communities; Takhlakh in particular has some nice meadows along the south shore of the lake. Interesting lodgepole pine forests border Road 2329 to the east.

The advantage of the many excellent Forest Service roads is that much of the 4,000-foot line at Mount Adams is accessible by car. These roads also give direct access to several good trails that, in general, climb towards the subalpine and alpine habitats. The Pacific Crest Trail crosses Road 23 on the southwest side of the mountain. Grand Meadows is reached on a spur road from there and Swampy Meadows is a short walk through the nearby forest and a small meadow.

The lower reaches of Bird Creek Meadows are accessible by car with a short hike leading to the open areas. Hellroaring Meadows, with trail access from the road between Bird Lake and Bench Lake, is another spectacular meadow. Trails from this area lead to another climbing route and Sunrise Camp, passing through wet meadows and alpine habitats on the approach to a large moraine near Mazama Glacier.

Most of the higher elevation subalpine as well as the alpine habitat are accessed by foot. The South Climb trail approaches a glacial field at approximately 7,800 feet, providing up to that point an opportunity to encounter species of the harshest environments. On the northwest side, an excellent trail leads to High Camp at an elevation of more than 6,800 feet. By contrast with the south, the plant community at High Camp is richer, up to the highest reaches at the base of a steep and barren moraine. Here, too, on the northwest side, is one of the few places where kinnikinnick (*Arctostaphylos uva-ursi*) is encountered; at lower elevations the common manzanita is pinemat manzanita (*Arctostaphylos nevadensis* ssp. *nevadensis*). The views from High Camp, as with many other high elevation sites, are stunning.

Compared to its neighbors, Hood, Rainier, and St. Helens, Mount Adams is "off the beaten path." It is better known to people around Portland and Vancouver than those in the Puget Sound area, but with a little effort, it is an easily reached destination and deserves to have more visitors!

# Introduction

## How to Use This Book

With 843 separate taxa comprising the flora of Mount Adams - counting species, subspecies, and varieties - an efficient means of identifying plants in the field is essential. We use "keys" in this book to enable the user to work stepwise through this large number to reach a correct identification in as few steps as possible.

Specifically, we use dichotomous keys, in which pairs of contrasting statements are presented. The task of the user is to decide which of the two statements best describes the plant in question.

At the most universal level, in the book's first key, the question is whether the plant reproduces by spores or by seeds. At the other extreme, a key to separate two varieties of a species of wild pea, may ask for as small a detail as the size of the flower.

Consider this example of a short key, for the two species of the genus *Trientalis* (starflowers) in the primrose family. One characteristic, the arrangement of leaves on the stem, is sufficient to separate the species.

1 Leaves whorled at the top of the stems only ............................... *T. borealis* ssp. *latifolia*
1 Leaves whorled as well as scattered on the lower stem ................ *T. europea* ssp. *arctica*

An example of a longer key is that for the entire primrose family.

1 Leaves basal; petals turned back ........................... *Dodecatheon*
1 Stems leafy; petals spreading ............................................. 2

2(1) Leaves alternate, clustered at the top of the stems; flowers pink ..... *Trientalis*
2 Leaves opposite, not clustered at stem tips; flowers yellow ........... *Lysimachia*

The first "couplet," as each pair of contrasting statements is called, focuses upon leaf arrangement and flower form. The first statement leads to the name of a genus, *Dodecatheon*, but the second statement only presents a number. This number, "2," means that it is necessary to consider the second couplet if the plant being identified does not fit the first statement. The second couplet distinguishes the two other genera of the primrose family at Mount Adams, completing the family key.

The number "1" in parenthesis shows that the user arrived at couplet 2 from couplet 1 - a means of racing one's steps through a key. This is perhaps of little use in a short key, but in a longer key - to the 50 species of *Carex* (the sedges) for example – knowing that one arrived at couplet 22 from couplet 13 can be helpful in "backtracking" should a plant fail to "key out" successfully.

Having keyed out the plant, it is necessary to complete the identification of the plant by studying the description in the book. Keys are a sort of shorthand, faster than reading through *all* the descriptions in the book to identify a plant but insufficient for certainty.

The discussion of each plant is standardized. The scientific name is given, including the author of the name, followed by one or occasionally two common names. Descriptions of the plant's features are written with the necessary minimum of technical terms; a glossary provides definitions for terms that may be unfamiliar.

To avoid repetition, details common to all species in a genus or genera in a family are given once. That is, statements of features of a genus should be understood to apply to each of the constituent species.

For each plant, habitat and ecological information is given, derived from our own fieldwork, herbarium specimens, and the technical literature. We also list places where the plant has been found at Mount Adams.

For current, accepted scientific names, we have relied upon two major authorities. The primary source is the *Flora of North America*. This massive work is not yet complete and for groups of plants not covered in the *Flora* we have consulted the PLANTS Database, produced by the National Plant Data Center of the U.S. Department of Agriculture. Where other sources have been relied upon, including *The Jepson Manual: Higher Plants of California* and the *Oregon Vascular Plant Checklist – Asteraceae,* we explain our reasoning in the text.

## Key to the Major Groups of Plants at Mount Adams, Washington

1 Plants reproducing by spores; flowers, seeds and fruits absent....... ................................................ Ferns and Fern Allies (below)

1 Plants producing seeds borne in woody cones or various fruits..... 2

2(1) Seeds on the scales of woody cones or in fleshy, berry-like structures (as with junipers and yew); flowers absent (gymnosperms)................................................... Conifers (p. 62)

2 Seeds produced within a fruit that develops from an ovary; flowers present (angiosperms)....................................................... 3

3(2) Flower parts in 3s (although some parts may be very reduced or even absent); leaves typically parallel-veined; seeds with 1 cotyledon; annual or perennial herbs (also a monocot is *Lemna*: the plant is a tiny floating thallus with a single small root in the water; flowers are almost never seen)...................... Monocots (p. 341)

3 Flower parts in 4s or 5s (rarely in 3s or absent); leaves typically net-veined; seeds with 2 cotyledons; annual or perennial herbs, shrubs, and trees...................................................... Dicots (p. 74)

## Ferns and Fern Allies

This group is of the greatest evolutionary age of the major groups of plants at Mount Adams. All reproduce by means of spores, which may be borne on leaf surfaces, at the tops of leafless stems, in the axils of scale-like leaves, or in sacks underwater. The spores are produced in specialized structures, called sporangia, that are, in general, best observed under the microscope. The account presented here will avoid these microscopic details but will, at points, call for the use of a handlens. Flowers are absent and, indeed, these plants show no structures that even *look* like flowers. And since flowers are absent, seeds are absent as well. As used here, "cones" refers to the cone-like appearance of the sporangia-bearing structures in horsetails and some clubmosses; they are in no way comparable to the cones of a conifer. In the true ferns, the sporangia are grouped into sori (described in the key), the nature of which is critical in separating the genera. The sori may be covered with a protective tissue called an indusium.

All are vascular plants, meaning that their roots, stems, and leaves incorporate specialized tubes for the transportation of water. True mosses and the liverworts, on the other hand, lack this vascular tissue and are not included in this book. Not all of these plants look like ferns: the group includes clubmosses, horsetails, and the quillworts. Most, the so-called true ferns, however, do look like ferns: they are plants lacking an above-ground stem, with leaves rising from a perennial rootstock and with the leaf composed of a slender stem and divided blade (the "frond").

1 Above-ground stems hollow and jointed, more than 2 mm in diameter, with whorls of scalelike leaves at the joints; sporangia borne in a short cone at the top of the stem (horsetails) ............... Equisetaceae

1 Above-ground stems solid, not jointed, less than 2 mm in diameter; leaves green (if scalelike, then arranged along the stem); sporangia in structures other than cones or in cones that are not at the top of a jointed stem ............ 2

2(1) Leaves scalelike to grasslike, undivided, attached directly to the stem (the stem in *Isoetes* obscure); sporangia in cones or small, basal or sacks ............ 3

2 Leaves with a stalk and a blade, the blade often divided or lobes; sporangia borne on the leaf surface or modified leaf surface (grapeferns and true ferns) ............ 4

3(2) Leaves grasslike, basal and slender, base of the stem upright, short, fleshy ............ Isoetaceae

3 Leaves scalelike to needlelike, arranged along prostrate, branched stems ............ Lycopodiaceae

4(2) Plants with mostly 1 frond, 1 branch of which is modified and bears sporangia; sporangia large, in "grapelike" clusters on branched or unbranched spikes (grapeferns) ............ Ophioglossaceae

4 Plants with 2 or more fronds; sporangia very small, grouped into sori (plural of sorus, small dotlike or linelike arrangements) borne on the underside of a blade or at its lower margin (true ferns) ............ 5

5(4) Plant producing fronds of 2 types, fertile and sterile, of greatly different appearance............ 6

5 Plant producing 1 type of frond, the fertile blades not of a different appearance ............ 7

6(5) Fronds once-pinnate ............ Blechnaceae

6 Fronds 2 or more times pinnate ............ Pteridiaceae

7(5) Sori borne at the edge of the underside of the leaflet, more or less covered by the turned back margin (thus, an indusium absent) .... 8

7 Sori borne away from the edge of the underside of the leaflet, an indusium sometimes present ............ 9

8(7) Fronds longer than 100 cm, arising single from the rootstock .................................................................. Dennstaedtiaceae
8 Fronds seldom longer than 80 cm, clustered in tufts ........................................................................................ Pteridaceae

9(7) Indusium present, often persistent at maturity but sometimes fragile and disappearing.............................................. Dryopteridaceae
9 Indusium absent at all stages of the development of the sorus ... 10

10(9) Fronds deeply pinnately lobed or once pinnate ....... Polypodiaceae
10 Fronds 2 or more times pinnate ......................... Dryopteridaceae

## Blechnaceae (C. Presl) Copel.—CHAIN FERN FAMILY

### *Blechnum* L.—DEER FERN

#### *Blechnum spicant* (L.) Sm.—DEER FERN

Two bright green frond types distinguish this fern. The once-pinnate sterile fronds form a rosette; they are 20-75 cm long and often lie flat on the ground with oblong leaflets that are about 15 mm long and 5 mm wide. The fertile fronds are longer, stiffly erect, and rise from the center of the plant. The 10-20 mm long leaflets are widely spaced, 2-3 mm wide and inrolled along the margins. The sori form continuous bands on each side of the midvein. An indusium is present.

A middle elevation species of moist, well-drained forest soils and wetland borders, this is a common fern at the mountain, found up to about 4,500 feet. It grows alongside Road 23, at Takhlakh Lake near the inlet stream, and was collected by Suksdorf in "springs" as well as near Thorn Creek, a tributary of the White Salmon River.

## Dennstaedtiaceae Ching—BRACKEN FAMILY

### *Pteridium* Gled. *ex* Scop.—BRACKEN

#### *Pteridium aquilinum* (L.) Kuhn var. *pubescens* (L.) Underw. NORTHERN BRACKEN

This is the largest of the ferns at Mount Adams, with fronds 1-2 m in height. They arise singly from a vigorous and widely spreading rootstock. The blades are roughly triangular and 3 times pinnate. The leaflets are hairy on the underside, hence "pubescens." There is no indusium; instead, the sori, arranged in lines at the leaflet margins, are partially covered by the inrolled margin.

This fern grows in drier habitats than most other ferns and may be found in large colonies on disturbed ground. This characteristic makes it appear nearly weedy, although this species is a native. It is found in middle elevation open woods and dry areas, up to about 4,500 feet. It grows along the east shore of Takhlakh Lake and occurs on south-facing slopes on Crofton Ridge. Suksdorf collected it in Hellroaring Canyon, close to Bench Lake.

## Dryopteridaceae Herter—WOOD FERN FAMILY

The most diverse family of ferns at the mountain, the wood ferns may be locally abundant but are never common, although they range from low elevation forests to open alpine slopes. The most frequently encountered species is a middle elevation forest dweller, lady fern (*Athyrium filix-femina* var. *cyclosorum*), and the family overall is well-represented by 5 genera and 12 species. Sterile and fertile fronds are alike. The sori are distinct and borne away from the margins of the leaflets. An indusium may be present; its characteristics are important for separating the genera. This family was formerly included in an expanded Polypodiaceae.

The relative dryness of Mount Adams as well as the tendency for snow cover to disappear early, particularly on the south aspects of the mountain, may explain some of the relative scarcity of wood ferns, especially compared to its northern neighbor, Mount Rainier.

1 Indusium cuplike, holding the sorus and splitting into radiating fragments, often obscure .......................................... *Woodsia*
1 Indusium covering the sorus from above or from the side, or indusium absent .......................................................... 2

2(1) Indusium present .......................................................... 3
2 Indusium absent .......................................................... 5

3(2) Indusium round, like a shield over the sorus............... *Polystichum*
3 Indusium curved, attached at the side of the sorus .................... 4

4(3) Fronds 1 m or longer ............................................... *Athyrium*
4 Fronds less than 40 cm long ...................................*Cystopteris*

5(2) Fronds (excluding the stalk) much longer than wide; base of the plant with persistent leaf stalk bases ........................... *Athyrium*
5 Fronds (excluding the stalk) wider than long; base of the plant lacking persistent leaf bases ............................... *Gymnocarpium*

## Dryopteridaceae

### *Athyrium* Roth—LADY FERN

These ferns vary in size from small to large. They bear tufted, deciduous fronds that are 2- or 3-times pinnately compound. The longest leaflets are at the midsection, giving the frond a tapered appearance at each end. Chaffy scales clothe the bases of the leaf stalks while the bases of the dead fronds tend to persist from year to year.

1 Sorus curved, located near the midline of the leaflet; indusium present ..................................... *A. filix-femina* ssp. *cyclosorum*

1 Sorus round, located near the margin of the leaflet; indusium absent ......................................... *A. alpestre* var. *americanum*

#### *Athyrium alpestre* (Hoppe) Clairville var. *americanum* Butters. ALPINE LADY FERN

The fronds of this lady fern can reach over 50 cm in length, although typically they are much smaller. The leaflets are ovate-lanceolate and borne on short stalks. The sorus is round; there is no indusium.

This is the most common fern of open rocky slopes and moraines at subalpine and alpine elevations. It was collected by Suksdorf at the upper end of Hellroaring Meadows.

#### *Athyrium filix-femina* (L.) Roth ssp. *cyclosorum* (Rupr.) C. Christens. WESTERN LADY FERN

Growing in large clumps, this stately fern reaches 1-2 m in height. The leaflets are lanceolate to oblong and not stalked. The slender sorus is curved like a crescent moon (or the letter "J"), and the indusium is also curved.

A middle elevation fern of wet forest sites and stream banks, especially likely to be found on the west side of Mount Adams, it grows in the dense forest near the Pacific Crest Trail parking area near Road 23. Suksdorf also collected it at Hellroaring Canyon.

### *Cystopteris* Bernh.—BLADDER FERN

#### *Cystopteris fragilis* (L.) Bernh.—BRITTLE FERN

The 5-40 cm long once- or twice-pinnately compound fronds of this small fern are deciduous. The name "fragilis" is appropriate, as the leaf stalks are brittle and easily broken. The leaflets are thin and light green. The round sori are partially covered by a fragile, somewhat cuplike indusium that is soon torn apart as the sporangia mature. The remnants remain visible and may be seen with the aid of a handlens.

Fairly common, this species grows alongside Roads 060 and 23. Suksdorf collected it on cliffs above 6,500 feet on the southeast side, at a favorite campsite he called "Wiesehalde," at or near the present Hellroaring Overlook. It is also found on Crofton Butte.

### *Gymnocarpium* Newman—OAK FERN

The fronds of these ferns are triangular in outline and may reach 40 cm in length. They rise singly from a slender, creeping rootstock. The stalk is longer than the blade, while the blade has 3 primary divisions of approximately equal size. The leaflets are 2-4 times pinnate. The sori are round and lack an indusium.

1 Blades 8-24 cm long; leaflets at the base unequal in length; leaflets with small, sharply-tipped teeth ............................ *G. disjunctum*
1 Blades 3-14 cm long; basal leaflets equal in length; leaflets without teeth, rounded ................................................... *G. dryopteris*

#### *Gymnocarpium disjunctum* (Rupr.) Ching—PACIFIC OAK FERN

This medium-sized fern is characterized by broadly triangular fronds up to 40 cm tall, rising singly from a slender, creeping rootstock. The blade of the fronds has 3 primary divisions of nearly equal size. The leaflets are oblong and toothed. The sori are round and there is no indusium.

A species of lower elevation streambanks and moist forests, it is scarce at Mount Adams. Suksdorf collected it near the White Salmon River and in the valley of Big Muddy Creek.

#### *Gymnocarpium dryopteris* (L.) Newman—WESTERN OAK FERN

Similar to *G. disjunctum* but generally much smaller, this oak fern ranges from 3-14 cm in height. The basal leaflets of the lateral lobes of the blade are unequal in size, giving the lobes an asymmetrical appearance. The tip of the terminal lobe is rounded and entire.

More common than *G. disjunctum*, this species grows alongside Road 23 at milepost 34. It is also found at Bathtub Meadow at 4,250 feet. Suksdorf collected it on a moraine near Muddy River Canyon, probably close to 6,000 feet.

### *Polystichum* Roth—SWORD FERN

Most commonly lowland plants, sword ferns are fairly rare within the study area, partly because of the base elevation of 4,000 feet. Additionally, the relative dryness of Mount Adams may preclude their establishment. These ferns grow as small to large tufts of once- or twice-pinnate, evergreen fronds. The fronds are composed of tough, stiff, dark-green, toothed leaflets; the lower leaflets often have an earlike lobe at the base. The leaf stalks are scaly. The round sorus is covered by a round indusium which is held above the sorus rather like a shield.

## Dryopteridaceae

1 Fronds once-pinnate, the leaflets not further divided .................. 2
1 Fronds twice-pinnate, the leaflets pinnately divided again or at least pinnately lobed .......................................................................... 4

2(1) Frond with leaflets nearly to the base; spiny teeth of the leaflets spreading widely ................................................. *P. lonchitis*
2 Frond with leaflets half to ¾ its length; spiny teeth curved towards the tip of the leaflet ............................................................. 3

3(2) Fronds less than 50 cm long, the leaflets overlapping .................. .................................................... *P. imbricans* ssp. *imbricans*
3 Fronds well over 50 cm long, the leaflets not overlapping ............... ........................................................................... *P. munitum*

4(1) Lowest leaflets lanceolate, 1.5 – 3 cm long ............. *P. scopulinum*
4 Lowest leaflets deltoid, 1 – 1.5 cm long .................. *P. kruckebergii*

### ***Polystichum imbricans*** **(D.C. Eat.) D.H. Wagner ssp.** ***imbricans*** **IMBRICATE SWORD FERN**

Similar to western sword fern, and once considered a smaller variety of that species, this fern has narrower, shorter fronds that are typically less than 50 cm long and sometimes no longer than 30 cm. The leaflets overlap one another and each is somewhat folded over its midvein. The indusium may be toothed or toothless, and lacks the marginal hairs of the *P. munitum* indusium.

A middle elevation to subalpine species, often found in exposed areas such as roadcuts and trail borders, this fern grows on the Salt Creek debris flow at the end of Trail 75. It is also found at the junction of Road 23 and Road 90, growing on a road cut. Suksdorf collected this fern at Hellroaring Canyon, at an unspecified elevation.

### ***Polystichum kruckebergii*** **W.H. Wagner KRUCKEBERG'S HOLLY FERN**

This fern resembles *P. lonchitis*, but has much shorter leaflets, up to 2 cm long and more deeply divided. The upper lobe at the base of the leaf midvein is much larger than the other lobes. The leaflets are spine-tipped.

This species is known only from a collection made by David Wagner in Hellroaring Valley, where it grows in rock crevices between 6,000 and 7,000 feet.

### ***Polystichum lonchitis*** **(L.) Roth—MOUNTAIN HOLLY FERN**

Distinguished by the tough and leathery fronds that range from 15-60 cm in length, the fronds are slender, only about 7 cm wide near the middle and are borne on short stalks. The lower leaflets are nearly triangular in outline while those at the middle are longer and curved. The teeth of the leaflets are uneven in size and sharp-tipped. The sori are very close together.

Found on rocky slopes in open forests from middle elevation to the upper subalpine regions, this species grows near Trail 7B on Forest Service Road 2329. It was collected by Suksdorf at "Wiesehalde," a place at or near Hellroaring Overlook, at approximately 6,500 feet.

### ***Polystichum munitum*** **(Kaulfuss) C. Presl**
### **WESTERN SWORD FERN**

This large sword fern has evergreen fronds that may reach 150 cm or more in length and 25 cm across near the middle. The flat leaflets do not overlap, distinguishing this species from *P. imbricans*. The leaf stalk and midvein are chaffy with persistent scales, and on very wide leaflets; the sori may occur in more than one row. The indusium is fringed with short hairs.

More common in lower elevation forests in western Washington, western sword fern is uncommon above the 4,000-foot line at Mount Adams. It is found in middle elevation forests in small numbers, as alongside Road 071 at Bunnell Butte on the southeast side of the mountain, along Road 070 below the Stagman Ridge trailhead, on Crofton Ridge, and near the trail from Muddy Meadow to the Pacific Crest Trail.

### ***Polystichum scopulinum*** **(D.C. Eat.) Maxon—ROCK SWORD FERN**

Chaffy at the base, the fronds of this relatively small fern range from 10-40 cm on stalks 3-20 cm long. There are 20-40 pairs of leaflets of mostly equal length, varying from 1.5-3.2 cm long. The lower leaflets are divided into small but distinct lobes; the other leaflets are toothed with incurved teeth. The sori are present primarily on the middle and upper leaflets and the indusium is irregularly toothed.

Found in cliff crevices and open rocky slopes at middle to subalpine elevations but below timberline, this species is known at Hellroaring Canyon and alongside Hellroaring Creek as well.

## ***Woodsia*** **R. Br.—CLIFF FERN**

### ***Woodsia scopulina*** **D.C. Eat. ssp.** ***scopulina***
### **ROCKY MOUNTAIN CLIFF FERN**

Small, tufted, and delicate, this fern bears deciduous leaves, although the stalks tend to persist on the short rootstalk. The once-pinnate fronds reach 30-40 cm in length and the plant is finely hairy, with whitish hairs. The indusium is cuplike and attached by its base; it splits into narrowly triangular segments as the spores mature.

Named "cliff fern" for its preference for growing in rocky places, woodsias grow on cliffs, ledges, and talus. A tough plant, it has a misleadingly fragile appearance. Found in rock crevices, ledges, and talus slopes, this species is rare at Mount Adams, known only from a Suksdorf collection made at Hellroaring Canyon.

## Equisetaceae DC.—HORSETAIL FAMILY

### *Equisetum* L.—HORSETAIL

The common name refers to the resemblance of the plants to the tail of a horse - or at least the branched members of the genus. The horsetails are borne on extensive horizontal rootstocks. The hollow stems are jointed and are grooved lengthwise, roughened to the touch by microscopic silica crystals on the surface. The stems of the species at Mount Adams are deciduous, lasting just one year. There are two types of stems—sterile and fertile; in some species, the two are dimorphic and differ greatly. When dimorphic, the fertile stems usually appear first, followed, as they wither, by the sterile stems. Some species have branched stems, the branches arising in whorls from the joints of the stems. The actual leaves of the horsetails are reduced in size to small, often dark teeth that surround the stem at each joint. Spores are produced in conelike structures at the tops of the fertile stems.

1 Sterile and fertile stems alike, not branched ........... *E. laevigatum*
1 Stems alike or not, branched, not persisting but deciduous ......... 2

2(1) Stems alike, green............................................... *E. palustris*
2 Sterile and fertile stems different, the latter brownish................. 3

3(2) Sterile stems 10-60 cm tall; teeth of the sheaths 6-14.................. ....................................................................... *E. arvense*
3 Sterile stems 30-100 cm tall; teeth of the sheaths 14-28.............. ....................................................... *E. telmateia* var. *braunii*

### *Equisetum arvense* L.—FIELD HORSETAIL

The sterile stems of this most common horsetail are bright green, much-branched, and may reach nearly 60 cm in height. The stems have 10-14 grooves and the sheaths are 4-5 mm long. The unbranched fertile stems are shorter, thicker, and light brown. They are topped with a cone 2-4 cm long and appear early in spring.

With a preference for the moist and shaded ground of stream banks, thickets, and occasionally road borders, this is a middle elevation species. It grows at Swampy Meadows and alongside Road 23 and was collected at Hellroaring Canyon and Cowslip Springs by Suksdorf.

### *Equisetum laevigatum A. Braun*—SMOOTH HORSETAIL

The single stems of this horsetail are usually unbranched and range from 30-100 cm in height. Occasionally, stems with 1 or a few irregularly placed branches are seen. The stems have 16-30 ridges. The green sheaths are 7-15 mm long and have black bands at the tip only. The 1-2.5 cm long cones are blunt and typically borne on a short stalk.

As with the other horsetails at the mountain, this is a species of stream banks and other wet places. It is less common than *E. arvense,* growing along a small stream in Swampy Meadows and alongside Trail 75 at the edge of a pond in the Cascade Creek drainage.

### *Equisetum palustre* L.—MARSH HORSETAIL

Slender and only about 50 cm tall, the sterile and fertile stems of this horsetail are alike. Regularly branched, the stems show 5-10 lengthwise grooves and 5–10 teeth in the sheath. The teeth are 3-7 mm long, black to dark brown, with transparent margins. The cone is stalked, 1-2.5 cm long, and blunt at the tip.

Uncommon, this species is known from Grand Meadow, where it grows in shallow water in a pond near the east end.

### *Equisetum telmateia* ssp. *braunii* (J. Milde) Hauke—GIANT HORSETAIL

Showy for its size alone, the robust sterile stems of this horsetail may reach 100 cm, although are occasionally much smaller. There are 20-40 grooves on the stems and numerous branches. The stout fertile stems are up to 60 cm tall, and bear 15-30 teeth in the sheath. The fertile stems are yellow-brown and appear early in the spring. The cones are 4-8 cm long.

A lower elevation species elsewhere in the northwest, this large horsetail is found at Mount Adams only along Cascade Creek, on the southwest side, where it grows at the edges of ponds under red alder along Trail 75.

## Isoetaceae Rchb.—QUILLWORT FAMILY

### *Isoetes* L.—QUILLWORT

Quillworts are somewhat grass-like aquatic plants that are common in the shallow lakes and ponds of the Mount Adams region. The leaves arise in tufts from short, thickened stems buried in the mud. Spore-producing vascular plants, the quillworts do not have flowers or seeds. Instead, sporangia of two types are borne in separate small sacks at the bases of specialized leaves, covered by a thin membrane: male spores, or microspores, are extremely small and number in the thousands while female spores, or megaspores, number in the dozens and are larger than the microspores. The megaspores may be ornamented with tiny bumps ridges, or spikes.

Positive identification of the species requires the examination of the female spores with a microscope.

1 Plants often in deep water; leaves flexible; female spores with spines, crests, or high ridges, 0.5-0.8 mm wide ............ *I. lacustris*
1 Plants often in shallow water; leaves stiff; female spores with scattered bumps, or sometimes ridges or wrinkles, seldom over 0.5 mm wide ........................................................ *I. bolanderi*

### *Isoetes bolanderi* Engelm.—BOLANDER'S QUILLWORT

This quillwort prefers water less than about 30 cm deep and often reaches above standing water late in the season. The 6-25 cm long leaves are relatively rigid and unbending. The 0.3-0.5 mm wide megaspores are whitish to almost bluish and have scattered bumps and ridges.

This species grows amongst grasses and sedges at lake margins and in bogs from middle elevations to timberline. Suksdorf collected it at Bird Creek, Bird Lake, and Hellroaring Canyon, as well as in "shallow ponds" at 6,000 feet of elevation. The authors found it at Mirror Lake on the southeast side of the mountain at 5,500 feet. It is also known from Bench Lake.

### *Isoetes lacustris* L.—LAKE QUILLWORT

This species differs from *Isoetes bolanderi* in the megaspores, which are 0.5-0.8 mm wide; these have jagged crests or high ridges. The plants have flexible leaves that are fully submerged, sometimes in water as deep as 1 m.

This uncommon species was collected by the authors at Olallie Lake, and is also known from a herbarium specimen taken at Walupt Lake, somewhat north of the study area.

## Lycopodiaceae Mirb.—CLUBMOSS FAMILY

Two genera of clubmosses are represented at Mount Adams and, of these, only *Lycopodium clavatum* is commonly seen. While sharing the name "mosses," these plants are vascular plants and therefore very different from true mosses. In both species at Mount Adams, the small, evergreen leaves are arranged in loose to dense spirals on the stems; the effect is that the leaves appear to be in "ranks" when viewed from above, although his can be difficult to see. Instead of seeds, the plants reproduce through the production of spores in structures called sporangia. These are emplaced at the bases of specialized leaves called sporophylls, smaller and lighter in color than ordinary leaves. In both species, the sporophylls are grouped into what may be called, for convenience, "cones."

1 Vegetative leaves up to about 3.5 mm long; appearing to be 5-ranked ............................................................ *Diphasiastrum*
1 Vegetative leaves often more than 4 mm long, appearing to be 6- to 10-ranked ............................................................ *Lycopodium*

### *Diphasiastrum* Holub—CLUBMOSS

#### *Diphasiastrum sitchense* (Rupr.) Holub—SITKA CLUBMOSS

The horizontal stems of this clubmoss are about 40 cm long, while the upright, cone-bearing stems are sparsely arranged in tufts and 8-12 cm tall. The scalelike leaves are slender but firm, generally 4-ranked, but often 5-ranked as well; they are up to 3.5 cm long while the horizontal stems are only sparsely leafy. The 1.5-2.5 cm long cones are in 2s or 3s on the fertile branches.

Widespread at Mount Adams in open subalpine meadows but infrequently seen, this species grows at Bird Creek Meadows at 6,600 feet. It was located along the trail to Lookingglass Lake at 5,800 feet on the southwest side, and was also collected by Suksdorf at 7,000 feet, probably above Bird Creek Meadows.

### *Lycopodium* L.—CLUBMOSS, GROUND-PINE

#### *Lycopodium clavatum* L.—RUNNING GROUND-PINE

The common name refers to the great length that the prostrate vegetative stems can reach: 3 m is common at Mount Adams, especially where the plant can trail down a steep hillside. The "running" portion of the stem and shorter branches bear leaves often in 10 ranks, appearing whorled; each leaf is 6-8 mm long and very slender, tipped with a hairlike bristle. The cones are 5-15 cm long, usually 2 or 4 per "fruiting" stem; the portion of the stem bearing the cones is only sparsely leafy.

Frequently seen in forest openings in rather dry places, either in long strands or as more compact mats of stems, this species may be found up to 5,000 feet on the north and west sides of the mountain.

## Ophioglossaceae (R. Br.) C. Argardh—ADDER'S TONGUE FAMILY

### *Botrychium* Sw.—GRAPEFERN, MOONWORT

Similar in appearance to true ferns, each *Botrychium* plant consists of a single stem that rises from a deeply-buried root crown. The stem is divided into 2 portions at about ground level or sometimes well above the ground. One portion is a sterile leaf blade, more or less divided, and fern-like. The other portion, called the sporophore, is fertile and lacks leaflets; it bears a panicle of brown sporangia that are crowded on the branches. (The name "grapefern" is derived from the appearance of these sporangia clusters.)

Except for *B. multifidum*, these species are rarely seen and some are known for Mount Adams only from a single herbarium collection.

1 Sterile leaf blade triangular, 10-20 cm wide, leathery and evergreen ..................... *B. multifidum*

1 Sterile leaf blade oblong in outline, to 5 cm wide, thin and deciduous ..................... 2

2(1) Point of separation of sterile and fertile portions of stem close to ground level ..................... *B. simplex*

2 Point of separation at least half-way up the stem ..................... 3

3(2) Sterile leaf once-pinnate, the leaflets rounded in outline ..................... *B. lunaria*

3 Sterile leaf twice-pinnate, the leaflets blunt to pointed ..................... 4

4(3) Fertile portion multiply-branched, spreading ..................... *B. lanceolatum* var. *lanceolatum*

4 Fertile portion once-branched, the branches ascending ..................... *B. pinnatum*

### *Botrychium lanceolatum* (Gmel.) Angstr. var. *lanceolatum* LANCE-LEAF MOONWORT

Typically less than 15 cm in height, this small species bears a stalkless sterile blade that is attached at the top of the shared stem; it is more or less triangular, up to 6 cm long and about as wide. The blade is 1-2 pinnate, with deeply toothed leaflets that are pointed at the tips. The fertile portion of the leaf has loosely-spreading multiple branches, with loosely clustered sporangia.

Listed as "Watch" by the Washington Natural Heritage rare plants program, this species is known at the mountain from a single Suksdorf collection at Hellroaring Canyon, without additional label information. Elsewhere in Washington, it grows in both mature forests and well-drained meadows.

### *Botrychium lunaria* (L.) Sw.—COMMON MOONWORT

From 6-18 cm tall and hairless throughout, the sterile blade of this species is short-stalked (to about 5 mm in length) and about 1.5-7 cm long. It is pinnate with 3-6 pairs of leaflets; each leaflet lacks a midrib and is rounded in outline (or "lunate," hence both the common and scientific names). The fertile stalk and fruiting spike range from 0.5-7 cm in length with narrowly-spreading branches.

Listed in the "Watch" category by the Washington Natural Heritage rare plants program, this species is known only from a Suksdorf collection made at Muddy Canyon. The plant prefers open, moist, streamside habitats elsewhere in Washington.

#### ***Botrychium multifidum* (Gmel.) Trev.—LEATHERY GRAPEFERN**

The plants of this large grapefern may reach 35 cm in height. Borne on a short, heavy stalk, the sterile blade is broadly triangular, as much as 20 cm in width and length, and is 2- or 3- times pinnately divided. It persists through the winter into the following growing season. The toothed leaflets are ovate to diamond-shaped. The fertile portion of the blade is multiply-branched, the branches ascending-spreading.

The only common grapefern at Mount Adams, this species grows in wet meadows and along lake borders, as well as in middle elevation forest openings where it may be seen at trailsides. It is found at Midway, Swampy, and Bird Creek Meadows. Plants have also been located at Bench Lake, and there is a Suksdorf collection from Hellroaring Canyon.

#### ***Botrychium pinnatum* St. John—NORTHWESTERN GRAPEFERN**

A small grapefern, this species ranges from 8-10 cm in height. The base of the shared stem is a reddish color. The oblong sterile blade is stalkless or very short-stalked, about 4 cm long, and 1- to 2-pinnate; the leaflets are primarily ovate in shape and may be lobed or unlobed. The fertile blade may have a short or long stalk and is twice-divided, with narrow, ascending branches.

Listed as a "Watch" species by the Washington Natural Heritage rare plants program, the type collection for this species was made in 1885 by Suksdorf on a day when he was on the northeast side of Mount Adams, probably on the upper Lewis River. A collection was made earlier by Howell in 1882, but there is no other information on the collection label. In Washington, this grapefern shows a wide range of habitat preferences, from wet forest openings to subalpine meadows.

#### ***Botrychium simplex* E. Hitchc.—LITTLE GRAPEFERN**

Only 3-13 cm high, this small grapefern is best distinguished by the fact that the sterile leaf is borne on the shared stem at the ground level while the fertile portion is elevated well above the ground. The sterile blade has a stalk up to 2.5 cm in length and the blade can reach 4 cm in length. The leaves are 1- to 3- times pinnate. The fertile stalk ranges from 2-8 cm in length, with the fruiting spike is usually compound and 1-4 cm long.

## Pteridiaceae

According to the Washington Natural Heritage rare plants program, this is another "Watch" species in Washington. It is found at Mount Adams in moist to dry meadows at middle elevations. It was collected by Henderson on the south face of a cliff and by Suksdorf at Muddy River Canyon.

## Polypodiaceae Bercht. & J. Presl—POLYPODY FAMILY

### *Polypodium* L.—POLYPODY

The two polypody species at Mount Adams are both small ferns, with once-pinnate fronds and leaflets that are rounded at the tip. The fronds arise singly from slender, creeping, scaly rootstocks that are often found growing on tree trunks and rock faces. The sori are more or less round, relatively large, and lack indusia.

1 Immature sori circular, set close to the leaflet margin; blade of the frond less than 3.5 cm wide ........................ *P. amorphum*

1 Immature sori oval, midway between the midrib and the margin; blade of the frond 5-7 cm wide .......................... *P. hesperium*

#### *Polypodium amorphum* Suksdorf—IRREGULAR POLYPODY

The blade of the frond is typically less than 10 cm long, although occasionally as much as 20 cm, and about 3.5 cm at the widest point. The sori are circular and placed close to the leaflet margins. This species differs from *Polypodium hesperium* in some features of the scales that cover the creeping stem, and in the presence of sterile structures called sporangiasters in the sori. These differences can best be seen with a microscope.

Rare at the mountain, this species was collected by Suksdorf west of Stagman Ridge.

#### *Polypodium hesperium* Maxon—WESTERN POLYPODY

The fronds of this fern reach 20 cm in length and are crowded on the rootstocks; the blade reaches 5-7 cm wide. The species resembles *Polypodium amorphum* except in microscopic details.

Found on cliffs and in rock crevices, up to the subalpine region, Suksdorf collected this species at Hellroaring Canyon. It was also collected on the northwest side of the mountain by Beth Skaggs Ryan.

## Pteridaceae E.D.M. Kirchn.—MAIDENHAIR FAMILY

A family of 3 genera and 3 species at the mountain, only one is at all common—Lace lipfern (*Cheilanthes gracillima*). The study area being above 4,000 feet may preclude the more frequent occurrence of maidenhair fern (*Adiantum aleuticum*), the only wetland species of the three. The other two ferns thrive in rocky, dry places where they are often "tucked" in crevices. All lack an indusium, although the sori are covered by the inrolled leaflets of the fertile fronds.

1 Fronds of 2 types; leaflets of the fertile fronds long and narrow ...... .............................................................. *Cryptogramma*
1 Fertile and sterile fronds alike ............................................ 2

2(1) Fronds twice-pinnate, the blade lanceolate .............. *Cheilanthes*
2 Fronds as wide as long, palmate-pinnate (fan-like in outline .......... .............................................................. *Adiantum*

## *Adiantum* L.—MAIDENHAIR

### *Adiantum aleuticum* (Rupr.) Paris
### NORTHERN MAIDENHAIR, FIVE-FINGER FERN

The glossy black stalk and the graceful, bright green leaflets set this beautiful fern apart. The stalk branches into 2 divisions at the top; each of these is subsequently separated into 3-7 divisions of approximately equal length. This imparts a rounded configuration to the 25-100 cm tall fronds, which arise singly from creeping rootstocks. The leaflets overlap on the midrib, and are rectangular-oblong to occasionally triangular in shape. The sori are oblong and placed at the margin of the leaflets where they are partially covered.

This attractive species is found locally in moist forested sites below 5,000 feet; Suksdorf collected it at Hellroaring Canyon.

## *Cheilanthes* Sw.—LIP FERN

### *Cheilanthes gracillima* D.C. Eat.—LACE LIP FERN

The tufted 5-25 cm tall fronds of this tough but graceful fern are twice-pinnate, firm, oblong-lanceolate in shape and a dull yellowish-green in color. The leaflets are hairy to wooly on the underside. The sori are rounded and covered by a recurved, modified leaflet margin.

Common in rock crevices from middle to subalpine elevations, this species has been found along the cliff north of the junction between the Stagman Ridge trail and the Round-the-Mountain trail. It is also known at Crofton Butte, alongside Trail 20, and was collected by Suksdorf at various sites in Hellroaring Canyon.

## Pteridaceae

### *Cryptogramma* R. Br.—ROCKBRAKE

#### *Cryptogramma cascadensis* E.R. Alverson—CASCADE ROCKBRAKE

The thin fronds of this tufted fern are of two types. The sterile leaf blades range from 3-20 cm in height and the finely-toothed leaflet blades are light to medium green, and so thin as to be translucent when pressed. The fertile fronds bear leaflets that are oblong and podlike in appearance; the sori form a continuous line beneath the turned-under margins. The bases of the leaf stalks drop from the plant in the fall as the leaves wither.

The thinness of the leaflets and the deciduous leaf stalks help separate this species from the similar *C. acrostichoides*, which has not been found in the study area at Mount Adams (the reason for its absence is not evident).

Found in middle elevation to subalpine sites, this fern is relatively common at the mountain. It grows alongside the Snipes Mountain Trail (north of the Pineway Trail), at the eastern edge of the Aiken lava flow on the Round-the-mountain trail, at 6,950 feet on the south side of the mountain, and at Hellroaring Canyon.

## The Flora of Mount Adams, Washington

### Gymnosperms—Conifers

Mount Adams is set amidst coniferous forests, now heavily logged outside the Wilderness Area. Forest cover ranges from dense on the west to more sparse on the east; forest composition varies greatly along this gradient. To a large extent, habitats at Mount Adams are defined by the presence and nature of the tree cover.

All but one of the eighteen conifer species at Mount Adams are evergreens (larch loses its leaves in the fall) and all but two (common juniper and western yew) are trees. Two species -- Sitka spruce and western yew -- are rare. By comparison, seventeen species of conifers are found at Mount Rainier; there, larch is absent and ponderosa pine is rare.

The leaves of the conifers resemble scales or needles that may be attached singly to the twigs or arranged in bundles. Flowers are not present. In most conifers, pollen and ovules are produced in separate cones on the same plant; for convenience, these are here called pollen (male) cones and seed (female) cones, respectively. Pollen is typically shed in great quantities, for the conifers are wind pollinated. The fertilized ovule develops into a seed covered by a papery bract and attached to a woody cone scale. Juniper and yew are the exception: pollen and ovules are produced on separate plants and the typical woody cone is replaced, in juniper, by a blue-black fleshy cone or, in yew, by a juicy red aril. In many species, the bark, twigs, needles, or cones are sticky with an odorous resin.

1 Leaves often scalelike, attached singly, opposite or whorled .................................................................... Cupressaceae

1 Leaves not scalelike, attached in bundles; if attached singly, then alternate ........................................................................ 2

2(1) Plants either male or female; seeds borne singly in a fleshy, red aril .....................................................................Taxaceae

2 Plants with both male and female cones; seeds borne in woody cones ................................................................ Pinaceae

### Cupressaceae Rich. *ex* Bartl.—CYPRESS FAMILY

The conifers of this family are most easily distinguished by their scalelike leaves, borne opposite in pairs or in groups of three on the branches. One shrub and two trees comprise this family at the mountain, each in its own genus. The male and female reproductive structures are borne in separate "flowers," most often on the same plants. The male "flowers" are very small pollen-producing cones borne in the axils of the leaves, while the female cones are small, woody, and rounded to oblong in the case of *Thuja* and *Chamaecyparis*, and a round, bluish "berry" in *Juniperus*.

| | | |
|---|---|---|
| 1 | Prostrate, spreading shrub | *Juniperus* |
| 1 | Upright trees | 2 |
| 2(1) | Cones more or less spherical; leaves green to bluish green; the branchlets drooping | *Chamaecyparis* |
| 2 | Cones egg-shaped or elongated; leaves yellowish green; the branchlets spreading | *Thuja* |

## ***Chamaecyparis*** **Spach—CEDAR**

### ***Chamaecyparis nootkatensis*** **(D. Don) Spach—ALASKA CEDAR, YELLOW CEDAR**

Recognizable by the thin, grayish, scaly bark and the flattened foliage sprays, this tree may reach 50 m in height, although it is typically much smaller. The top leader droops to one side and all the branchlets tend to hang. They are clothed in green to yellowish-green 4-ranked, scalelike leaves with sharp tips that spread. The rounded pollen cones are tiny, and the seed cones are round also, 1 cm in diameter, and consist of 4-6 thick, woody scales, green and glaucous when fresh, turning reddish brown at maturity. Trees in protected or lower elevation sites develop buttresses at the base of a single trunk. Subalpine inhabitants or those on exposed sites often take on a shrubby, multiple-branched configuration; these may spread clonally to form a thicket.

Some authorities now advocate the use of the name *Callitropsis nootkatensis* for this species.

Long-lived, often in excess of 1,000 years, this middle elevation to timberline species shows a preference for wet sites and is relatively rare at the mountain. It grows near Grand Meadow on the southwest side and is found in open, wet habitat along Road 034 on the north, regrowing in a clearcut.

## ***Juniperus*** **L.—JUNIPER**

### ***Juniperus communis*** **L. var.** ***montana*** **Ait.—COMMON JUNIPER**

A shrubby conifer that may spread to more than 2.5 m across, but reach only 50 cm or so in height, the configuration and needle-like foliage set it apart from all other species. The reddish-brown bark is thin and scaly. The 4-8 mm long leaves are densely packed, narrowly lanceolate, sharply tipped, and whitish on the underside. The pollen and seed cones are borne in leaf axils on separate plants. The 4-6 mm diameter male cone is round, and the 5-8 mm seed cone scales mature to form a roundish, fleshy berry that is blue-black and coated with a white bloom.

Found in dry and typically rocky habitats from middle elevations to timberline, this species is relatively common at Mount Adams. It grows at Muddy Meadows at lower elevations, near the Aiken Lava Flow, alongside the Snipes Mountain Trail, South Climb Trail, and the Round-the-Mountain trail. It is also found on the summit of Little Mount Adams and at 7,800 feet of elevation on the southeast side of the mountain.

### ***Thuja*** **L.—ARBORVITAE**

#### ***Thuja plicata*** **Donn** ***ex*** **D. Don—WESTERN RED-CEDAR**

Although this species may reach 60 m in height with a potential diameter of 2-3 m and heavily buttressed bases, the trees at Mount Adams are much smaller. The branches are widely spread and the thin reddish to grayish-brown bark is fibrous, peeling easily in long strips. The young branchlets are flattened, and the leaves are paired; they are not 4-ranked. The leaves are flattened, more or less oval, and pointed at the tip. The tiny pollen cones are borne singly near the ends of the branches, and the seed cones are narrowly egg-shaped; they have about 10 woody scales, are 1-1.5 cm long and borne in small clusters.

Most typically a lowland species with a preference for wet sites, western red-cedar is uncommon at the mountain. Small trees are found near Road 5603 and Road 070 on the west and north.

## Pinaceae Lindl.—PINE FAMILY

There are 18 coniferous species at Mount Adams. With the exception of the rare western yew (*Taxus brevifolia*), and the three Cupressaceae species, all are members of the Pine family. Tree-sized, the pines occupy habitats that range from middle elevation wetlands to high subalpine open, rocky slopes. Common lowland species found elsewhere in the Cascades play a less dominant role above the 4,000-foot line, but all northwestern species are present, including Sitka spruce (*Picea sitchensis*). Four "true firs" (*Abies*) are found here, as well as trees with eastern affinities, such as ponderosa pine (*Pinus ponderosa*) and western larch (*Larix occidentalis*). At timberline, pine family "trees" may be reduced to stunted shrubs. In terms of size, the largest trees are ponderosa pines, but this may in part be due to logging practices outside of the Wilderness Area that would have removed larger middle elevation trees of other species.

Leaves of the pine family members are needlelike, longer than wide, and borne as single, alternate needles, or in bundles of 2-5. The seed cones are long and slender, with woody scales. Two winged seeds develop on each scale and each scale has a papery bract that may protrude. The male (pollen) cones are much reduced in size and vary from yellowish to reddish in color. Male and female cones are borne on the same trees.

The pine family is represented by 6 genera (14 species) at the mountain.

1 Leaves in clusters of 2-5, or more numerous in whorls on spurs ... 2
1 Leaves attached singly, spirally arranged on the branch ........... 3

2(1) Leaves numerous, in whorls on short spurs, deciduous ......... *Larix*
2 Leaves in bundles of 2-5, spirally arranged along branches, not deciduous .................................................................. *Pinus*

3(1) Leaves with woody bases that persist as peglike structures or raised rims on the twigs when the leaves have fallen ................ 4
3 Leaves lacking such woody bases; twigs smooth or nearly so after the leaves have fallen ....................................................... 5

4(3) Leaves sharp-tipped, squarish in cross section .................... *Picea*
4 Leaves rounded at the tip, flattened to angled in cross section ....... ............................................................................ *Tsuga*

5(3) Seed cones pendulous, falling intact ...................... *Pseudotsuga*
5 Seed cones erect on the branches, the scales deciduous and falling separately (cones rarely found intact) .............................. *Abies*

## ***Abies*** **Mill.—FIR**

*Abies* are sometimes called the "true firs" to distinguish them from conifers such as Douglas-fir, which belongs to a separate genus, *Pseudotsuga*. The species are most easily distinguished by the erect seed cones, borne on branches near the tops of the trees; the maturing cones appear quite early in the season. The scales fall away from the cone, thus dispersing the winged seeds, and leaving a spike in their place. Thus, finding whole cones on the ground is rare, although the large seeds may sometimes be seen. Each scale of the seed cone is covered by a papery brown bract that varies in length. The bark is grayish (or somewhat maroon plated in *A. procera*) and typically shallowly furrowed, although much thickened on old *A. grandis* and *A. amabilis*. The young twigs are hairy. The leaves are flattened with 2 stomatal bands (of whitish stomata) on the undersides. Two species also have such bands on the top. The leaves may curve upward or be carried flat in a single plane, as is the case with *A. grandis*. When they fall, they leave a flush, circular scar on the branch.

1 Upper surface of the leaves whitish, two bands of stomata ........... 2
1 Upper surface of the leaves green, lacking white stomata ........... 3

2(1) Leaves flattened; bracts of the cones concealed; subalpine trees or shrubs ........................................ *A. lasiocarpa* var. *lasiocarpa*
2 Leaves angled in cross section; bracts exserted; forest tree of lower elevations ........................................................... *A. procera*

3(1) Leaves in 2 horizontal ranks, alternating longer and shorter on each side of the twig (the top of the twig not covered with leaves) ........................................................ *A. grandis* var. *grandis*
3 Leaves clustered on the top half of the twig, not 2-ranked, of more or less equal length (the top of the twig covered with leaves) ................................................................ *A. amabilis*

**_Abies amabilis_ (Dougl. _ex_ Loud.) Dougl. _ex_ Forbes**
**PACIFIC SILVER FIR**

The denizen of the snow zone, this species reaches about 60 m in height with a diameter of up to 1.5 m. The dark gray bark becomes shallowly furrowed with age. Blunt at the tip, the dark green, glossy leaves bear 2 white bands of stomata on the lower surface and are 2-3 cm long. They curve outward and upward, while beneath they appear flattened. The 8-15 cm long seed cones are purplish-brown and sticky with resin when young; the bracts are shorter than and hidden by the scales.

Common, this species is the dominant conifer in many forests around the mountain at elevations from 4,000-5,000 feet, occasionally higher. It prefers wetter and lower habitats than the similar, and smaller, *A. lasiocarpa.*

**_Abies grandis_ (Dougl. _ex_ D. Don) Lindl. var. _grandis_—GRAND FIR**

Ranging from 25-60 m in height, with a rounded crown, this middle elevation species is most easily identified by the 2-ranked leaves giving the branches a flattened appearance. The leaves range from 1.5-5 cm long and tend to alternate between short and long on the branches. They have stomata on the lower surface, while the upper surfaces are glossy and dark green, with a slight groove along the midvein. The 8-12 cm long seed cones are greenish-brown and resinous, with bracts shorter than the scales.

Typically a lower elevation species in western Washington, grand fir grows as high as 5,000 feet of elevation at Mount Adams. While it prefers moist sites and is most often seen in stream valleys, it is often found in dry forests southeast of the mountain. It can be seen on Crofton Ridge, along the Pineway Trail, on the road to King Mountain at the Tract D boundary, along the Snipes Mountain trail, and alongside Road 782.

## Pinaceae

### *Abies lasiocarpa* (Hook.) Nutt. var. *lasiocarpa*—SUBALPINE FIR

As the common name implies, this is the highest elevation true fir species at the mountain, and the smallest. It may vary from 5-20 m tall, depending on elevation, and is found in open, "broken" forest to elevations above 6,500 feet. Recognizable by the narrow, spirelike crown, the branches are borne to the ground, perhaps because of the open nature of the forests. The bark is gray and thin, roughening some and furrowing with age. The 1-3 cm long leaves curve strongly upward on the branch. The upper surface of the leaves has two bands of stomata and the lower bears a single, more diffuse stomatal line. The 5-10 cm long seed cones are purplish, with bracts that are shorter than the scales.

Common in the subalpine zone, this species is cosmopolitan at the mountain, where it fringes, and invades, moist meadows. It also inhabits windswept ridgelines and talus slopes.

### *Abies procera* Rehd.—NOBLE FIR

The largest and longest lived of the true firs, noble fir may reach a height of 60 m, with a commensurate trunk diameter of more than 2 m. With a tendency to drop the lowest branches, a rounded crown of the topmost branches characterizes mature nobles. Also distinctive, the thickened bark of the older trees alternates between deep furrows and rather smooth reddish-to-maroon, flat patches. The strongly upward-curved needles measure 2.5-3.5 cm long and have two white stomatal bands on both upper and lower surfaces. The 10-20 cm long greenish brown seed cones bear bracts much longer than the scales; the bracts, therefore, protrude beyond the scales and give the immature cone a bristly appearance.

A middle elevation tree with a preference for open, dry sites, noble fir is most commonly encountered on the west and, to a lesser extent, south sides of the mountain. Here, the species seems to be able to exploit the disturbed habitat left in the wake of logging. Several large trees grow alongside Road 23; this species also grows near Grand Meadow and along Road 5603 on the north flank of the mountain.

### *Larix* Adans.—LARCH

#### *Larix occidentalis* Nutt.—WESTERN LARCH

Confined almost exclusively to regions east of the Cascades, this larch also occurs as isolated individuals just west of the Cascade crest at Mount Adams. Fairly common at lower elevations on the south and east sides, individual trees may reach 70-80 m in height, with the lower part of the trunk free of branches on older trees. The bark is thick and furrowed into large plates on mature trees, with cinnamon-colored scales strongly resembling ponderosa pine. The leaves are of two kinds:

bracts on short, spur-like side branches or at the base of the cones, and deciduous green needles arranged in whorls at the tip of spur shoots. The seed cones are 2.5-3 cm long with young scales reddish-brown in color and greenish to yellowish bracts.

Found alongside Trail 75 at Salt Creek, near Grand Meadow alongside Road 8810, and just east of the crest alongside Road 23, this is a middle elevation species at the mountain. Groups of large individuals grow on the south side north of Trout Lake.

### *Picea* A. Dietr.—SPRUCE

Spruce leaves are borne on woody, peglike bases that persist after the leaf has fallen. The twigs, therefore, are "stubbly." The needles are also very sharp at the tips and encircle the twigs. The bark is thin and scaly, with a maroon tinge on flaked pieces. The seed cones hang from the branches only at the top of the tree (a useful point of distinction from Douglas-fir) and are egg-shaped to oblong and pale brown when mature. The bracts are shorter than the scales

1 Young branchlets short-hairy; leaves squarish in cross section, with stomatal bands on both surfaces ............................. *P. engelmannii*

1 Young branchlets smooth; leaves flattened, with stomatal bands on the upper surfaces ...................................................... *P. sitchensis*

#### *Picea engelmannii* Parry *ex* Engelm.—ENGELMANN SPRUCE

Potentially reaching 50 m in height, with a 1 m diameter, most specimens of this spruce are much smaller. It is most easily distinguished from *P. sitchensis* by the hairy twigs and strongly 4-angled needles. These are about 2.5 mm long, and brushed strongly upwards, with white stomatal lines. The 5-10 cm long seed cones are yellowish-brown with thin, papery scales that have irregular margins at their tips.

Preferring wet and cold sites, this species is locally common in middle elevation to subalpine forests and at meadow edges. It is found at Grand, Killen Creek, and Midway Meadows. It also grows near the Lewis River where it crosses Road 23, alongside the Snipes Mountain Trail, on Crofton Butte, and at Hellroaring Canyon. The species reaches about 6,000 feet elevation at Mount Adams, well below its maximum elevation at Mount Rainier, where it can be found in stunted, shrublike form at nearly 8,000 feet.

#### *Picea sitchensis* (Bong.) Carr.—SITKA SPRUCE

Massive trunks characterize the lower elevation individuals of this species. Reaching upwards of 50 m tall, it is the denizen of the coastal forest, making its way inland along river courses. The twigs are hairless and less densely packed than *P. engelmannii*. The 1-1.5 cm long leaves are yellowish-green, and the 6-10 cm long seed cones are reddish brown, with the scales toothed at the tip.

Very rare at Mount Adams, Sitka spruce is found only near the ponds along Cascade Creek, at 3,200 feet, within the Mount Adams Wilderness Area on the southwest side. Here, along Trail 75, fine large trees as well as numerous seedlings occur on wet ground at the foot of a north-facing slope.

It would be interesting to speculate about how this species became established at this isolated location east of the Cascade crest. It does grow near the Columbia River close to Portland, but perhaps the Mount Adams trees have survived here since early post-glacial times.

### *Pinus* L.—PINE

In this genus, each bundle of 2-5 leaves (or needles) is borne in the axil of a short, thin bract; the bundled leaves of the pines tend to remain together even after they have fallen. Although the branches are generally whorled on young trees, older trees tend to drop the lower branches and show a straight, tall trunk with a crown that becomes increasingly irregular in age. Trees such as *P. albicaulis* growing on exposed, high-elevation sites may be reduced to a shrublike "krummholz" form. *P. contorta* tends to be the smallest of the species and *P. ponderosa* the largest.

Pollen cones are numerous and clustered at the bases of the new growth while the seed cones are fewer, woody, and heavy, and sometimes borne in whorls. They take two years to mature. In *P. contorta* they may persist on the branches for many years. *P. monticola* bears long cones, an easy fieldmark to distinguish this pine from the other 5-needled species, *P. albicaulis*. The bracts are smaller than the scales in all species.

| | | |
|---|---|---|
| 1 | Leaves 5 per bundle ........................................................ | 2 |
| 1 | Leaves 2 or 3 per bundle ................................................. | 3 |
| 2(1) | Cones cylindrical, more than 10 cm long, short-stalked; leaves 5-10 cm long, flexible ................................................ | *P. monticola* |
| 2 | Cones ovate, to 8 cm long, stalkless; leaves 4-7 cm long, stiff ........ ........................................................................ | *P. albicaulis* |
| 3(1) | Leaves in bundles of 2 ....................... | *P. contorta* var. *murrayana* |
| 3 | Leaves in bundles of 3 .................. | *P. ponderosa* var. *ponderosa* |

### *Pinus albicaulis* Engelm.—WHITEBARK PINE

Often with multiple trunks, this species varies from an upright 15 m tall tree on protected sites, typically near the lower elevations of its range, to twisted, shrubby krummholz forms in the harsh, windy subalpine habitats. The 4-6 cm long leaves, borne 5 to a bundle, are yellow-green and stiff, distinguishing them from the other 5-needled pine, *P. monticola*. The purplish-brown, egg-shaped cone is only 4-8 cm long, with thick scales pointed at the tip; the cones usually fall before opening. Large seeds attract animals and birds, particularly Clark's nutcracker, often seen in whitebark pine forests. Trees on the south and southeast sides of Mount Adams seem especially vulnerable to white pine blister rust: in some places, dead and dying trees outnumber the living.

Most common on the south side of the mountain where individuals have been located at over 7,800 feet of elevation on the South Climb trail, this species also grows at lower elevations on the north, as on Potato Hill at 5,100 feet. The largest tree found during the study grows at 5,800 feet alongside the Island Springs trail; it has a diameter at breast-height of 1.5 meters (just over 5 feet).

### *Pinus contorta* Dougl. *ex* Loud. var. *murrayana* (Grev. & Balf.) Engelm.—LODGEPOLE PINE

The smallest pine at the mountain, varying from 5-15 m tall, this tree is most easily distinguished from the other *Pinus* species by the 2-leaved bundles and the dark gray, thin, scaly bark. The name "contorta" refers to the 3-5 cm long, dark yellow-green twisted needles. Dark brownish-green seed cones are curved and slender; they persist on the branches, typically opening only when subjected to fire. The knoblike scale tip ends in a stout prickle.

Forests of this species grow alongside roads on the north side of the mountain. Here, there is a history of frequent fires and loose, dry soils, which encourage establishment. Locally common elsewhere, this pine is found at the Lewis River on the west and at Hellroaring Canyon on the southeast.

### *Pinus monticola* Dougl. *ex* D. Don—WESTERN WHITE PINE

Upwards of 50 m tall, this fast-growing species matures to a spirelike form with long spreading branches well-separated by yearly growth increments. Young trees have thin, dark gray bark that becomes pale in color with age and typically breaks into squarish scales or small plates. The 4-10 cm long leaves are pale blue-green in color, due to the prominent bands of white stomata, and flexible; they are borne in bundles of 5. The 10-25 cm long seed cone is cylindrical, slender, and somewhat curved. The thin cone scales lack a prickle.

Easily distinguished from *P. albicaulis* by the flexible, lighter needles, and the long, distinctive cones, this is a middle elevation species of open places where it may compete on the poorest of soils. It can be subjected to the fungal disease white pine blister rust, spread by bark beetles, but most trees at the mountain appear to be healthy. It grows alongside Road 5603 on the northwest, Road 034, and near the Tract D boundary on the road to King Mountain. Trees are also found along the Lewis River on the west and along the borders of Swampy Meadows.

***Pinus ponderosa* P. & C. Lawson var. *ponderosa*—PONDEROSA PINE**

The position of Mount Adams east of the Cascade crest undoubtedly accounts for the presence of this species on the south and east aspects. The largest of the genus at the mountain, this species is easily recognized by the deeply plated, cinnamon-reddish bark, resembling puzzle pieces, and the 12-20 cm long, thick needles, borne 3 to a bundle. Mature trees vary from 30-60 m in height. The cones take two years to mature and vary from deep reddish-purple when young to brown when mature; they are 8-14 cm long and have scales with prickly tips.

Large trees grow near Road 8040 (the South Climb road) in the lower to middle elevations. Rare on the west side of Mount Adams, there are scattered individuals near Midway Meadows alongside Road 2329 on the north side. The species is more common near the Snipes Mountain trail and at the Tract D boundary along the road to King Mountain on the southeast.

### *Pseudotsuga* Carrière—DOUGLAS-FIR

***Pseudotsuga menziesii* (Mirbel) Franco var. *menziesii*—DOUGLAS-FIR**

The dominant tree of the lower elevation western Cascades, this is a disturbance species that may reach 75 m in height in favored locations. At Mount Adams, the trees are much smaller and only a few large individuals are found. Wide furrows of very thick bark, grayish-brown to reddish-brown in color, distinguish maturing trees. Young trees bear dark bark, often shallowly fissured. The 2-3 cm long leaves are 4-sided in cross section and tend to curve upward and, to a lesser extent, around the twigs. There are bands of stomata on the upper side. The 10-20 cm long seed cones are greenish brown, maturing to tan. The forked bracts are longer than the scales, protruding from the cone and bending over the tips of the scales.

Locally common, the higher elevation (4,000 feet) of the study area undoubtedly precludes dominance of this species in most forests at Mount Adams. It grows to elevations of about 5,000 feet.

## *Tsuga* Carrière—HEMLOCK

The leaves of the hemlocks at Mount Adams are thick and short, blunt or rounded at the tip, and leave flat scars when they fall. The shoot at the top of the tree (the leader) droops markedly in *T. heterophylla* and, to a lesser extent, in *T. mertensiana*. The bracts of the seed cones are hidden by the scales. The presence of *T. heterophylla* is often indicated by large numbers of the small, rounded cones on the forest floor; *T. mertensiana* cones are longer. Locally common, *T. mertensiana* is a subalpine tree; *T. heterophylla* is unusual within the study area, being more of a lowland species of wetter habitats.

1 Leaves flattened, with white stomatal bands only on lower side; forest tree of middle elevations .......................... *T. heterophylla*

1 Leaves angled in cross section, with white stomatal bands on both sides; subalpine trees ...................................... *T. mertensiana*

### *Tsuga heterophylla* (Raf.) Sarg.—WESTERN HEMLOCK

A so-called "climax" species, this hemlock is a lower to middle elevation tree, with mature individuals reaching 50-60 m in height. The hanging branches form a pyramidal crown with a typically characteristic drooping top. Mature trees bear reddish brown bark, with broad ridges separated by narrow fissures, a bit like a thin-barked *Pseudotsuga menziesii* (Douglas-fir) but grayer in tone. Young trees also have thinly-fissured bark. The flattened, straight leaves are of multiple lengths (hence, "heterophylla") between 5 and 20 mm; this variation imparts a rather lacey appearance to the foliage. They are green above and whitish below. The 1.5-2.5 cm long seed cones are egg-shaped, with thin scales. Thousands may litter the ground, an indicator of trees in the area.

A species of wetter forests, mature trees are scarce at Mount Adams. Perhaps because western hemlock is slow to become established in logged areas, the fact that most of the younger specimens are found on the logged north and west sides suggests some sort of "invasion" by the species from its more usual lowland habitats. However, where suitable habitat in older forests is available, trees may grow at elevations in excess of 4,500 feet. Many forests in the logged areas are not of sufficient age to support large trees but good specimens may be seen surrounding Swampy Meadow.

### *Tsuga mertensiana* (Bong.) Carrière—MOUNTAIN HEMLOCK

The subalpine counterpart of *T. heterophylla*, this smaller species (10-30 m) is typically more densely foliated in appearance with shorter branches of varying length. The purplish to dark reddish-brown bark can be deeply furrowed on mature trees although it is characteristically thin on younger individuals. The thickened leaves are 1-2 cm long and circle the twigs, giving a star-like appearance. They are bluish green and banded on both sides with white stomatal lines. The 3-7 cm long seed cones are slender and elliptical in shape, with thickened scales.

A subalpine tree of moist environments, mountain hemlock is locally common, including the drier south and eastern aspects of the mountain where presumably it is able to find sufficient subsurface moisture. Near "monoculture" stands are found on the Round-the-Mountain Trail west of the South Climb trail. It grows as low as 4,000 feet near the Lewis River and also is found near the Pineway Trail at 4,500 feet on the southeast side of the mountain.

## Taxaceae Gray—YEW FAMILY

### *Taxus brevifolia* Nutt.—WESTERN YEW

Often a large, spreading shrub, but occasionally a small tree, western yew branches tend to droop and the trunk is often curved. The bark is distinctive—reddish brown, thin, and easily shredding to reveal a purplish to yellowish trunk. The flat leaves are 1-2 cm long, sharply-pointed, and arranged in 2 ranks in a flat configuration. They are typically dark green on the upper surface, and lighter on the lower, but they do not have stomatal bands. The trees are either male or female. The pollen cones consist of a few small bracts surrounding the stamens. The tiny female ovule develops into a bright red, fleshy, berrylike structure, known as an "aril" that encloses a woody seed.

More typically a lower elevation deep forest species, this conifer is very rare at Mount Adams, known only as individuals at two locations on the west side at elevations between 4,000 and 4,500 feet.

## The Flora of Mount Adams, Washington

## Angiosperms – Flowering Plants
## Dicotyledonous Plants (Dicots)

Angiosperms are vascular plants that bear flowers and seeds. The seeds develop from ovules held within an ovary, one or more of which comprise the pistil of the flower. Pollen is borne separately in anthers, which together with filaments comprise the stamens of the flower.

Almost all the dicots, the larger of the two divisions of angiosperms, bear leaves with netlike veination and flowers typically with parts in fours or fives – that is, five sepals, five stamens, and so on. "Dicot" refers to the fact that the seed leaves, or cotyledons, are two in number.

1 Trees or shrubs, with perennial woody stems .................. Group 1
1 Herbaceous plants, annual or perennial (at most, slightly woody in the lowest stems of some perennials or with woody rootstocks at the soil surface ........................................................ 2

2(1) Petals absent, although the sepals may be colored and petal-like ... ..............................................................................Group 2
2 Petals present ........................................................ 3

3(2) Petals distinct, at most united a very short distance at the base ...... ........................................................................ Group 3
3 Petals united part or all of their length .......................... Group 4

**Group 1 – Trees or Shrubs**

1 Petals absent; sepals, if present, never brightly-colored ............. 2
1 Petals present, although sometimes quite small; sepals present, sometimes much reduced in size, colored or green .................. 4

2(1) Leaves pinnately lobed; the female flowers single, the male flowers numerous and in catkins; fruit an acorn (a nut held in a scaly cap) ........................................................................ Fagaceae
2 Leaves smooth-edged or toothed, but not lobed; female as well as male flowers in catkins; fruit a capsule or nutlet (if a nutlet, not in a scaly cap) ........................................................ 3

3(2) Leaves ovate, toothed; seeds in a woody cone or papery husk ...... ........................................................................ Betulaceae
3 Leaves linear, lanceolate or oblanceolate; seeds in a capsule ........ ........................................................................ Salicaceae

4(1) Leaves alternate (whorled in some *Eriogonum*) ........................ 5
4 Leaves opposite ........................................................ 12

5(4) Petals distinct or united only at the bases ............................... 6
5 Petals united most of their length ..........................................11

6(5) Stamens 7-20 or more ..................................................... 7
6 Stamens 5, or sometimes only 4 .......................................... 9

7(6) Leaves evergreen, spiny or prickly; petals more than 5 ................ Berberidaceae
7 Leaves mostly deciduous, if evergreen then not prickly or spiny; petals 5 or 6 .................................................................. 8

8(7) Flowers borne in involucres; corolla 6-parted, with segments in 2 whorls of 3 ................................................ Polygonaceae
8 Flower attachment various, but not in involucres; corolla with 5 petals ........................................................... Rosaceae

9(6) Leaves pinnately-veined; flowers in small umbels in the axils of the leaves ....................................................... Rhamnaceae
9 Leaves palmately-veined; flowers in racemes, or a tall, raceme-like cluster of tiny umbels ......................................................10

10(9) Flowers in simple racemes from the axils of the leaves; leaves less than 10 cm broad ......................................... Grossulariaceae
10 Flowers at the top of the stem in a raceme-like cluster of tiny umbels; leaves 10 cm or more broad ........................ Araliaceae

11(5) Flowers aggregated into a head on a common receptacle, the head subtended by bractlike phyllaries; individual flowers tubular, greenish, inconspicuous ....................................... Asteraceae
11 Flowers solitary, in racemes, or in small clusters, never headlike; flowers saucer-shaped to bell-like, brightly colored ........ Ericaceae

12(4) Ovary inferior, with the remains of the style and other flower parts usually remaining at the top of the fruit ................. Caprifoliaceae
12 Ovary superior, with any remaining flower parts placed below the fruit .......................................................................13

13(12) Petals distinct; flowers regular ........................................... 14
13 Petals united much or most of their length; flowers irregular to strongly 2-lipped ........................................................... 17

14(13) Leaves palmately veined, 5-13 lobed, the margins toothed; fruit a winged samara ................................................. Aceraceae
14 Leaves pinnately veined, not lobed; the margins toothed or not; fruit not winged ........................................................ 15

15(14) Stamens 8-50; flowers large, white .................... Hydrangeaceae
15 Stamens 4-7; flowers small or inconspicuous, greenish or reddish .......................................................................... 16

16(15) Flowers in tiny clusters in the axils of leaves; leaves toothed ................................................................................. Celastraceae

16 Flowers in flat-topped clusters at the ends of the stems; leaves not toothed ................................................................. Cornaceae

17(13) Stems square in cross-section; fruit breaking into 4 nutlets; plant with a mint-like odor ................................................ Lamiaceae

17 Stems round in cross-section; fruit a many-seeded capsule; odor indistinct ......................................................... Scrophulariaceae

**Group 2 – Herbaceous Annuals or Perennials, Petals Absent**

1 Plant aquatic, roots submerged throughout the growing season or becoming stranded late in the summer .................Callitrichaceae

1 Plant terrestrial; if in wet places, then the roots not submerged ........................................................................................... 2

2(1) Plant parasitic on conifers, rooted upon the branches of the host tree ........................................................................ Viscaceae

2 Plant not parasitic, rooted in the soil ....................................... 3

3(2) Stems square in cross-section; leaves opposite; all parts of the plant clothed with stinging hairs ............................... Urticaceae

3 Stems round in cross-section; leaves various; stinging hairs absent ........................................................................................... 4

4(3) Sepals absent .................................................. Berberidaceae

4 Sepals present (although falling soon after the flower opens in some Ranunculaceae) ....................................................... 5

5(4) Sepals 3, the tips long and tapered .....................Aristolochiaceae

5 Sepals more than 3, not long and tapered .............................. 6

6(5) Pistils 2 to many; stamens many ........................ Ranunculaceae

6 Pistil 1; stamens 3-10 ........................................................... 7

7(6) Leaves opposite, not toothed; fruit a capsule with 2 to many seeds.. ............................................................... Caryophyllaceae

7 Leaves alternate or whorled, sometimes toothed; fruit 1-seeded, usually an achene ............................................................. 8

8(7) Leaves broadly toothed, clothed with mealy particles on the undersides; stamens 5 ................................ Chenopodicaceae

8 Leaves usually not toothed, hairy or smooth on the undersides, never mealy; stamens 3, 6, or 9 .......................... Polygonaceae

## Angiosperms - Dicots

### Group 3 – Herbaceous Annuals or Perennials, Petals Present, Distinct

1 Plant aquatic, the roots submerged throughout the growing season and the leaves floating; flowers always yellow ....... Nymphaeaceae

1 Plant terrestrial; if in wet places, then the roots not submerged; flower color various ........................................................ 2

2(1) Plant insectivorous, the leaves covered with sticky gland-tipped hairs . ........................................................ Droseraceae

2 Plant not insectivorous, the leaves not adapted to trap insects ....... ........................................................................ 3

3(2) Plants lacking chlorophyll, the leaves reduced to reddish or brownish scales . ........................................................ 4

3 Plants with normal green leaves ........................................... 5

4(3) Style elongated, often curved, conspicuous; stem slender (leafless forms of some pyrolas) ........................................ Pyrolaceae

4 Style short, straight, usually hidden by petals; stem fleshy ............ ........................................................... Monotropaceae

5(3) Ovary partly or wholly inferior ............................................... 6

5 Ovary superior ........................................................... 10

6(5) Ovary partly inferior, at most the calyx attached to the ovary no more than 2/3 its length .................................... Saxifragaceae

6 Ovary fully inferior ........................................................... 7

7(6) Stamens numerous ............................................. Loasaceae

7 Stamens 2-8 ........................................................................ 8

8(7) Flowers in umbels; leaves lobed or divided .................. Apiaceae

8 Flowers in heads, racemes, or spikes; leaves not lobed or divided... .......................................................................... 9

9(8) Stamens 5; leaves whorled at the top of a short stem, flower heads with conspicuous white bracts ................................ Cornaceae

9 Stamens 2 or 8; leaves arranged along the stem; flowers in racemes or spikes, without conspicuous bracts (if the leaves all basal, then flowers borne directly on the root crown) ... Onagraceae

10(5) Flowers conspicuously irregular and bilaterally symmetrical ...... 11

10 Flowers regular and radially symmetrical ...............................14

11(10) Flowers pea-like: the upper petal rising bannerlike above the others, with 2 petals forming a keel enclosing the style and stamens, and 2 petals forming wings that partly surround the keel ........................................................................ Fabaceae

11 Flowers not pea-like: the petals and/or sepals modified in other ways than above ........................................................ 12

| | | |
|---|---|---|
| 12(11) | Leaves glaucous, deeply divided (fernlike) .............. | Fumariaceae |
| 12 | Leaves not glaucous, if divided then not fern-like .................... | 13 |
| 13(12) | Sepals regular; spur, if evident, from the lowermost petal ............. ...................................................................... | Violaceae |
| 13 | Uppermost sepal modified into a spur or hood ...... | Ranunculaceae |
| 14(10) | Sepals 2 ...................................................... | Portulacaceae |
| 14 | Sepals 3 or more .......................................................... | 15 |
| 15(14) | Sepals 4, petals 4, stamens 6 .............................. | Brassicaceae |
| 15 | Flower parts of different numbers ........................................ | 16 |
| 16(15) | Leaves thick and succulent; flowers numerous, in dense, flat-topped clusters ............................................... | Crassulaceae |
| 16 | Leaves thin, or if thick, then not succulent; flowers arranged otherwise .................................................................... | 17 |
| 17(16) | Leaves opposite or whorled ............................................... | 18 |
| 17 | Leaves alternate or basal ................................................. | 19 |
| 18(17) | Flowers yellow; stamens more than 15 ...................... | Clusiaceae |
| 18 | Flowers not yellow; stamens 5 or 10 ................. | Caryophyllaceae |
| 19(17) | Stamens more than 10 ..................................................... | 20 |
| 19 | Stamens 5-10 ................................................................ | 22 |
| 20(19) | Filaments of stamens united, forming a tube around the pistil ................................................................... | Malvaceae |
| 20 | Filaments of stamens separate, not forming a tube ................. | 21 |
| 21(20) | Sepal partly fused, forming a cuplike receptacle (the hypanthium); stamens attached to the upper part of the inside of the receptacle ... ..................................................................... | Rosaceae |
| 21 | Sepals distinct; stamens attached directly beneath the pistils ....... ......................................................... | Ranunculaceae |
| 22(19) | Sepals and petals 3 or 6 .................................................. | 23 |
| 22 | Sepals and petals 5 (4 in some of the Saxifragaceae) ............. | 24 |
| 23 (22) | Sepals and petals 3 ........................................ | Limnanthaceae |
| 23 | Sepals and petals 6 ......................................... | Berberidaceae |
| 24(22) | Leaves compound, with 3 heart-shaped leaflets ......... | Oxalidaceae |
| 24 | Leaves divided or not, but never with heart-shaped leaflets ........ | 25 |
| 25(24) | Sepals distinct; styles 5, united nearly their full length; style persistent in fruit as a coiled beak ......................... | Geraniaceae |
| 25 | Sepals partly fused at the bases; styles typically 1 or 2 (rarely 3 or 4), not united and not persistent .......................................... | 26 |

26(25) Leaves alternate, although stems sometimes tufted; styles 2 (rarely 3 or 4) .......................................................... Saxifragaceae

26 Leaves basal, opposite, or whorled; style 1 ........................... 27

27(26) Leaves thickish, evergreen; petals distinct ................ Pyrolaceae

27 Leaves thin, deciduous; petals united only at their bases or up to half their length .................................................Primulaceae

**Group 4 – Herbaceous Annuals or Perennials, Petals Present and Fused**

1 Plant aquatic, the roots submerged throughout the growing season and the leaves floating or held above the surface ..................... 2

1 Plant terrestrial; if in wet places, then the roots not submerged .... 3

2(1) Leaves divided into threadlike segments, floating in and on the water ........................................................ Lentibulariaceae

2 Leaves divided into 3 lobes, held above the surface .................... ........................................................... Menyanthaceae

3(~~2~~ 1) Plants lacking green leaves, the leaves reduced to reddish or brownish bracts ............................................................... 4

3 Plants with green leaves (the leaves sometimes scale-like) ......... 5

4(3) Flowers bell-like, in a tall raceme ....................... Monotropaceae

4 Flowers 2-lipped with a long tube, solitary or in a short, few-flowered spike ..............................................Orobanchaceae

5(3) Ovary inferior ................................................................... 6

5 Ovary superior ................................................................ 10

6(5) Flowers aggregated into a head on a common receptacle, the head subtended by bractlike phyllaries; individual flowers tubular and narrow, usually small ........................................... Asteraceae

6 Flowers not aggregated on a common receptacle subtended by phyllaries; individual flowers more or less conspicuous .............. 7

7(6) Trailing plant with evergreen, opposite leaves and slightly woody older stems; flowers in pairs on forked stems ......... Caprifoliaceae

7 Annual or perennial herbs, stems not at all woody; flowers various .. ............................................................................... 8

8(7) Leaves whorled; fruit a pair of nutlets ....................... Rubiaceae

8 Leaves alternate or opposite; fruit a capsule or an achene .......... 9

9(8) Leaves opposite; flowers white or pink; fruit an achene ................ .............................................................. Valerianaceae

9 Leaves alternate; flowers blue; fruit a capsule ...... Campanulaceae

10(5) Flowers irregular, with a tube and 2-lipped corolla (weakly so in *Mentha* in the Lamiaceae and *Veronica* in the Scrophulariaceae) . ........................................................................................11
10 Flowers regular ........................................................................ 12

11(10) Stems square in cross-section; leaves all opposite; plant with a mintlike or distinctive odor ........................................ Lamiaceae
11 Stems round in cross-section; leaves opposite or alternate; distinctive or mintlike odor absent ..................... Scrophulariaceae

12(10) Leaves thick, succulent; flowers in flat-topped clusters ................. ................................................................ Crassulaceae
12 Leaves thin or thickish but never succulent; flowers in other kinds of inflorescence ............................................................. 13

13(12) Stamens placed opposite the lobes of the corolla ........Primulaceae
13 Stamens placed alternate with the lobes of the corolla ...............14

14(13) Stamens 4; lobes of the corolla brownish, of papery texture; leaves basal .......................................................... Plantaginaceae
14 Stamens 5; lobes of the corolla colored, of normal texture; stem leaves present, although basal tufts often present ....................15

15(14) Pistils 2, developing into a pair of follicles ............... Apocynaceae
15 Pistil 1; fruit a capsule or nutlet ........................................... 16

16(15) Ovary 4-lobed, becoming 4 nutlets (1 or more nutlets occasionally failing to develop) ............................................. Boraginaceae
16 Ovary not 4-lobed, becoming a capsule ................................ 17

17(16) Stem leaves opposite ........................................ Gentianaceae
17 Stem leaves alternate ..................................................... 18

18(17) Plant a twining or trailing vine ........................... Convolvulaceae
18 Plant not a twining or trailing vine ........................................ 19

19(18) Style 3-branched at the top .............................. Polemoniaceae
19 Style not branched ..........................................Hydrophyllaceae

# Aceraceae

## Aceraceae Juss.—MAPLE FAMILY

### *Acer* L.—MAPLE

Varying from shrubs to large trees, the maples bear opposite, palmately lobed, deciduous leaves. There are many small flowers borne in racemes or rounded clusters; they are followed by paired, winged seeds called samaras.

None of the maple species is particularly common at Mount Adams, where both are middle elevation species, usually seen at forest edges and openings. *A. douglasii* is more likely to be encountered on the south and east sides, on drier, open sites. *A. circinatum* is often seen along roadsides. A third species, big-leaf maple (*A. macrophyllum*) reaches to just 4,000 feet on the steep bank above Road 23 west of the mountain.

| | | |
|---|---|---|
| 1 | Large trees; flowers in pendant racemes; leaves 20 cm or more broad | *A. macrophyllum* |
| 1 | Shrubs or small trees; flowers in rounded clusters; leaves 15 cm or less broad | 2 |
| 2(1) | Leaves 3-5 lobed; flowers greenish | *A. glabrum* var. *douglasii* |
| 2 | Leaves 7-9 lobed; flowers reddish | *A. circinatum* |

#### *Acer circinatum* Pursh—VINE MAPLE

A shrub with many trunks, this 5-10 m tall maple may occasionally reach tree status. Rounded in outline, the 6-12 cm leaves are divided into 7-9 shallowly toothed lobes. While the species is most noted for its spectacular autumn display of red to gold leaves, the tiny flowers with white petals and purplish-red sepals are also attractive. The wings of the samaras are configured in a straight line and are red at maturity.

A middle elevation species, this species is most common on the west and north sides where it shows a preference for disturbed areas that retain moisture through the summer.

#### *Acer glabrum* Torr. var. *douglasii* (Hook.) Dippel ROCKY MOUNTAIN MAPLE

A tall shrub or sometimes a small tree, at Mount Adams this maple is as common as *A. circinatum*, particularly on the southern aspects. The leaves are pentagonal and typically divided into 5 lobes, although sometimes 3, and are 3-8 cm broad. The sepals and petals are greenish yellow, and the joined samaras form a V-shape. The leaves turn bright yellow in autumn.

Found along the road to King Mountain, northeast of Bench Lake, and in Hellroaring Canyon, this is a species of relatively dry, open places at middle elevations, particularly on rocky slopes.

### *Acer macrophyllum* Pursh—BIGLEAF MAPLE

Reaching perhaps 10 m in height at Mount Adams, at lower elevations this is a massive tree with a rounded crown. The leaves are divided into 3 or 5 major lobes and are typically 20-30 cm broad. Numerous flowers are borne in a long raceme; each blossom is about 5 mm broad, greenish-yellow, and fragrant. The samaras are V-shaped, with wings about 4 cm long.

This species was located just once in the study area, on a cliff above the overlook on Road 23 west of the mountain.

## Apiaceae Lindl.—CARROT FAMILY, PARSLEY FAMILY

The "carrots" vary from short to tall, and may be perennials or biennials. The stems are typically hollow and the leaves are pinnately divided. The bases of the stem leaves are typically expanded and sheathe the stalk. The flowers are small and configured in flat-topped umbels. The umbel itself may be compound, made up of smaller umbelets, each borne on a special stem called a "ray." The yellow or white flowers consist of 5 sepals and 5 petals. The inferior ovary develops into a dry fruit, called a schizocarp, which, when mature, splits into a pair of seeds held by a short, stem-like structure. The fruits may be variously ribbed or winged. Many species have distinctive odors.

Formerly named the Umbelliferae, this family is represented by 9 genera and 16 species at the mountain; only one is a weed.

1 Flowers in a single umbel; fruit with hooked bristles ......... *Sanicula*
1 Flowers in a compound umbel; fruit smooth or variously hairy or barbed .......... 2

2(1) Fruit elongated and linear, at least 1 cm long .............. *Osmorhiza*
2 Fruit rounded to oblong or blocky; if more than 1 cm long, then not linear .......... 3

3(2) Mature fruit flattened, winged on at least two of the ribs ............. 4
3 Mature fruit more or less rounded, not winged on the ribs ............7

4(3) Lateral ribs of fruit as well as midribs winged ................. *Pteryxia*
4 Only the lateral ribs winged .......... 5

5(4) Leaves basal, or with a much reduced stem leaf; plants less than 50 cm tall .......... *Lomatium*
5 Stem leaves present; plants more than 50 cm tall ..................... 6

| | | |
|---|---|---|
| 6(5) | Tall, stout plants, 1.5 to 3 m tall; leaves divided once into broad, lobed leaflets ........ | *Heracleum* |
| 6 | More slender plants, less than 1.5 m tall; leaves divided twice into more narrow, toothed leaflets ........ | *Angelica* |
| 7(3) | Roughly hairy, biennial introduced plant, not found away from roadsides ........ | *Daucus* |
| 7 | Native perennials of meadows, open slopes, or wet places; smooth or softly hairy ........ | 8 |
| 8(7) | Leaflets linear, even-edged ........ | *Perideridia* |
| 8 | Leaflets at least 5mm wide, toothed ........ | 9 |
| 9(8) | Leaflets toothed and lobed, less than 3 cm long; stem not chambered at the base ........ | *Ligusticum* |
| 9 | Leaflets merely toothed, more than 3 cm long; base of stem with hollow chambers ........ | *Cicuta* |

## *Angelica* L.—ANGELICA

### *Angelica arguta* Nutt.—SHARP-TOOTH ANGELICA

Stout and tall (120 cm or more), this perennial has leafy stems. The leaves are divided into 3 major lobes, each divided again into broad, coarsely toothed, lanceolate to ovate leaflets. Numerous, white flowers are configured in large, compound umbels. The fruits are winged on the lateral margins as well as ribbed.

A middle elevation to subalpine, moisture-loving species, this carrot-family member grows near the stream that runs through Swampy Meadows, and along the Cascade Creek trail on the southwest side. It is also found at Hellroaring Creek, and a Suksdorf specimen was collected at an island in Bird Creek on the southeast side of the mountain.

## *Cicuta* L.—WATER-HEMLOCK

### *Cicuta douglasii* (DC.) Coult. & Rose—WESTERN WATER-HEMLOCK

Tall and poisonous, this plant varies between 50 and 150 cm in height. Thickened at the base, the clustered stems have a stack of small air chambers in the base. The leaves are 2 or 3 times divided into narrow lanceolate leaflets, each having the veins that branch off the midvein reaching to the bases of the teeth of the leaflet, rather than to their tips. Numerous whitish flowers are borne in compound umbels that are 6 cm across. The fruits are nearly round and wingless, with thickened ribs.

This is a low to middle elevation species, known for the Mount Adams area from a single collection made along Road 23 near Swampy Meadows, where it grew next to a stream under Engelmann spruce and western hemlock.

## *Daucus* L.—CARROT

### *Daucus carota* L. ssp. *carota*—WILD CARROT

This biennial plant is distinguished by a single stem 20-120 cm in height that rises from a well-developed taproot. The 2-12 cm long, stalked leaves are linear to lanceolate, with the upper leaves more elongate, much-divided and appearing fern-like. The inflorescence is a compound umbel 4-12 cm wide, each umbelet consisting of typically 20 whitish or yellowish flowers. The oval fruit is widest at the middle and about 2 mm broad.

This weed is known from modern collections taken at the summit overlook on Road 23 and at the DNR quarry.

## *Heracleum* L.—COW-PARSNIP

### *Heracleum maximum* W. Bartram—COW-PARSNIP

This 1-2 m tall plant is hard to miss in its wetland habitat. The stems are coarse, thick, and hairy, and the leaves are palmately lobed into 3 divisions, each coarsely toothed. Small white flowers compose the broad umbels that may exceed 15 cm in width. The rounded, flattened fruits are 8-12 mm long; they are ribbed and have broad wings on the lateral margins.

This is a middle elevation species of wet sites, growing in sun or light shade, at streamsides and meadow edges. It has been collected at Spring Creek Meadow, Midway Meadows, and in Hellroaring Canyon.

## *Ligusticum* L.—LOVAGE

### *Ligusticum grayi* Coult. & Rose—GRAY'S LOVAGE

A common species of lower subalpine meadows, this taprooted perennial is characterized by 20-60 cm tall stems that often lack leaves entirely, or sometimes have a single leaflet. The basal leaves are divided into small leaflets. The compound umbels consist of 7-15 rays, each terminating in an umbelet of small, white flowers. The inflorescence thus has an open appearance.

Cosmopolitan at the mountain, this lovage has been collected at Bathtub Meadow and Hellroaring Creek, and was also recorded along the trail above Hellroaring Overlook, an unusually high elevation for the species. It is also found along Road 2329 near Midway Meadows and at the gate to the Bird Creek area.

## *Lomatium* Raf.—BISCUIT-ROOT

Most often species of drier habitats east of the Cascades, the genus is better represented at Mount Adams than at Mount Rainier, where there are only two species. The common name refers to the tuberlike taproot of the plants, which was an important food source for Native Americans. The leaves are dissected into small leaflets in a classic "carrot" form and the flowers are in compound umbels. The individual umbelets may or may not have an "involucel" of bractlets; if present, the bractlets may be separate or united. Flower color typically ranges from white to yellow. Most species have been located on the south and east sides of Mount Adams.

In the key, "ultimate" leaf segments are the final segments of the much-divided leaves.

1 Ultimate leaf segments relatively long, more than 1 cm in length ..... ............................................... *L. triternatum* var. *triternatum*

1 Ultimate leaf segments small, less than 1 cm long .................... 2

2(1) Ultimate leaf segments forming more or less definite leaflets, undivided to deeply cleft ..................................................... 3

2 Ultimate leaf segments narrow and scarcely leaflike .................. 4

3(2) Leaflets strongly toothed or cleft; flowers white or sometimes yellow ............................................................... *L. martindalei*

3 Leaflets mostly untoothed or shallowly toothed; flowers yellow .................................................................. *L. nudicaule*

4(2) Bractlets present and united into a shallow, bowl-like involucel ....... ..................................................................... *L. watsonii*

4 Bractlets, if present, separate ........... *L. dissectum* var. *dissectum*

### *Lomatium dissectum* (Nutt.) Mathias & Constance var. *dissectum*
### FERNLEAF BISCUITROOT

A somewhat open arrangement of hairless, 50-150 cm tall stems rising from a large, woody taproot characterize this robust perennial. The roughened stem and basal leaves are large and thrice-pinnately dissected into segments up to 10 mm long and 2-4 mm wide. The flowers are yellow (rarely purple), the rays number 10-30, the longest reaching 10 cm, and the bractlets are narrow and separate. The elliptic fruit is 8-17 mm long, with narrow lateral wings, and is borne on an obsolete or very short stalk.

Growing from middle elevations to the subalpine regime in open, rocky places, this species has been located on Trail 183 on the south side, and is also known from a Suksdorf collection at Hellroaring Canyon

### *Lomatium martindalei* (Coult. & Rose) Coult. & Rose
### MOUNTAIN PARSLEY

The stems are 15-40 cm tall on this tufted plant. The dark, bluish-green, mostly basal leaves are twice-divided, with the ultimate leaf segments 1-1.5 cm long and toothed. The 3-6 small umbelets of whitish flowers are borne on 1.5-6 cm long rays. The oval fruits are 8-15 mm long.

Found on the southern aspect of the mountain, this species is relatively common on the South Climb route and at Hellroaring Creek. It is also known from a Suksdorf collection at the White Salmon Glacier, on the southwest.

### *Lomatium nudicaule* (Pursh) Coult. & Rose
### BARESTEM BISCUITROOT

Solitary stems or a slightly branched crown form a plant from 20-90 cm tall. The stems and leaves are hairless and bluish in color. The leaves are 3-times divided or pinnately 1-3 times compound. There are 3-30 roundish to lanceolate leaflets, 2-9 cm long, that often have small teeth towards the tips. The stems may be hairy below the umbel. The flowers are yellow, with separated umbelets that range between 6 and 20 cm in length. The fruit is 7-15 mm long and is sometimes narrowed to a beaklike tip.

A middle elevation species of dry, open places, modern collections from the southeast side at 4,000 feet, at and near the DNR quarry, are the only known occurrences of this *Lomatium* at Mount Adams.

### *Lomatium triternatum* (Pursh) Coult. & Rose var. *triternatum*
### NINE-LEAF MOUNTAIN-PARSLEY

This species resembles *L. martindalei*, but has leaflets that are 3 times divided into very slender, untoothed leaflets 2-8 cm long. "Triternate" means "thrice divided into three." The umbel rays number 5-15 and the umbelets are small and composed of yellow flowers. The fruits are 8-10 mm long.

A species of relatively dry middle elevation habitats, this lomatium has been found at the DNR quarry on the southeast side, at the gate to Bird Creek on Road 82, and near the Klickitat Glacier in the Big Muddy Creek valley.

### *Lomatium watsonii* (Coult. & Rose) Coult. & Rose
### WATSON'S DESERT-PARSLEY

The stalked basal leaves rise from the thickened taproot of this nearly leafless plant. The narrow leaf segments measure 1-5 mm long; the end segments are small. The flowers are yellow and the involucre divided into two parts unequal in size with cone-shaped bracts united below the middle or nearly to the tip. The wings of the 6-7 m long fruit are thin.

This is a species typically found in open hillsides or sagebrush habitat. At Mount Adams it has been found at Devil's Garden at 8,000 feet, a dry site on the north side.

### *Osmorhiza* Raf.—SWEET-CICELY

The common name is in reference to the aromatic roots of some species, although this is not the case for the three species at Mount Adams. These are medium-sized perennial herbs ranging from 30-60 cm tall, with leaves that are 3 times divided into toothed leaflets. The umbelets are widely spreading and consist of relatively few flowers. The species are most readily separated by the fruits, and the shape of the stylopodium (a small structure at the tip of the fruit, the remnants of the base of the style) is important.

1 Fruit smooth; flowers yellow .................................. *O. occidentalis*
1 Fruit bristly, at least near the base; flowers greenish-white to white or purplish .................................................................... 2

2(1) Flowers greenish-white to white; fruit beaked .................. *O. berteroi*
2 Flowers purplish; fruit flat at the tip ............................. *O. purpurea*

#### *Osmorhiza berteroi* DC.—COMMON SWEET-CICELY

The bristly fruits distinguish this sweet-cicely. The white to greenish-white flowers develop into fruits that are 12-22 mm long, topped with a conical stylopodium and tapered at the base and somewhat widened toward the upper end.

This species has also been called *O. chilensis*.

Uncommon at the mountain, this species is known only from a Flett collection on the Klickitat River. It's likely that the study area is too high for it to occur elsewhere at Mount Adams.

#### *Osmorhiza occidentalis* (Nutt. *ex*. Torr. & A. Gray) Torr. WESTERN SWEET-CICELY

As with *O. berteroi,* this species is uncommon at the mountain. It has the largest umbels of all three species with umbelets on widely spread rays 3-6 cm long. The plant is distinguished from other genus members by the more clustered and upright stems. Occasionally having a yellowish cast, the greenish-white flowers consist of 5-12 rays that are 1-4 cm long and sometimes longer. The cylindrical-shaped fruits lack hairs or bristles and are 12-18 mm long, blunted at the base, with a conical stylopodium.

This species is known from a Suksdorf collection at Hellroaring Canyon.

### *Osmorhiza purpurea* (Coult. & Rose) Suksdorf
### PURPLE SWEET-CICELY

A crown-like stylopodium at the top of the fruit distinguishes this species. The flowers are purplish or occasionally greenish and the short-hairy fruits are 8-13 mm long, wide above, and tapered to the ray.

Although it is the most frequently seen *Osmorhiza* at Mount Adams, this species is nowhere common. Observed on Road 5603 on the north side, and on the Road 82 on the south – the South Climb route – this species is also known from a Suksdorf collection made at an unspecified location.

## *Perideridia* Reichenb.—YAMPAH

### *Perideridia gairdneri* (Hook. & Arn.) Matthias ssp. *borealis* Chuang & Constance—COMMON YAMPAH

Yampah is a slender plant, from 40 to 100 cm tall, rising from a deeply buried, spindle-shaped root. Leaves up to 10 cm long are arranged along the stem; each is divided pinnately into a few long, slender segments. One or 2 umbels are typical, with 5-9 umbelets of white flowers; the bracts are very small. The fruit is 2-3 mm long, nearly rounded in side view, and ribbed but not winged.

Collections of this species were made by Henderson in 1892 at Bird Creek Meadows and at another, undescribed location at the mountain. Sarah Gage and Sharon Rodman did not find the plant when they re-collected along Henderson's route in 1992. If it persists at the mountain, it would be expected on dry, south-facing slopes below about 4,500 feet on the east and southeast.

## *Pteryxia* (Nutt. *ex* Torr. & A. Gray) Nutt. *ex* Coult. & Rose
## WAVEWING

### *Pteryxia terebinthina* (Hook.) Coult. & Rose var. *terebinthina*
### TURPENTINE WEED

This aromatic perennial rises from a stout taproot and branched rootstock that is clothed with the leaf bases of previous years. The basal leaves are stalked, 3-18 cm long, ovate, and 3-times pinnately divided, with many small segments. The stems vary from 10-60 cm in height, with a few leaves below the middle. The yellow flowers are configured in an umbel, with a few involucels of narrow green bractlets from 2-6 mm long. The 5-11 mm long fruit is ovoid to ovoid-oblong, with broad lateral wings.

Formerly included in the genus *Cymopteris*, this species resembles *Lomatium martindalei*, but is quite rare at the mountain. It is found at

5,050 feet on the steep, rocky, east-facing slope of Crofton Butte, and was also collected by Howell at an unspecified location.

### *Sanicula* L.—SANICLE

#### *Sanicula graveolens* Poepp. *ex* DC.—SIERRA SANICLE

Preferring dry habitats, this species is relatively common on the southeast side of the mountain. It grows from a heavy taproot with basal leaves and has a few reduced stem leaves, pinnately divided into 3 toothed lobes, each again lobed and toothed. The flowering stems are up to 30 cm in height and the umbels consist of 3-5 small, globe-shaped umbelets with yellow flowers. Oval fruits are 4 mm long and covered with hooked bristles.

Known from modern collections at Crofton Ridge, the DNR quarry, and northeast of Bench Lake, this species was also collected by Suksdorf at Bird Creek Canyon.

## Apocynaceae Juss.—DOGBANE FAMILY

### *Apocynum* L.—DOGBANE

#### *Apocynum androsaemifolium* L.—SPREADING DOGBANE

Opposite leaves with a tendency to droop distinguish this many-branched perennial that may reach 50 cm in height. The stems that exude a milky juice when cut. The 3-8 cm long leaves are opposite and oval. The bell-shaped, pink flowers are borne in cymes. The 5 free lobes of the 5-8 mm long corolla curve backwards. The slender follicles are 6-8 cm long, reminiscent of cultivated beans.

Found on the west and southeast aspects of the mountain, this species prefers dry sites up to about 5,500 feet. It has been located at the DNR quarry and collected at Hellroaring Canyon.

## Araliaceae Juss.—ARALIA FAMILY

### *Oplopanax* (Torr. & A. Gray) Miq.—DEVIL'S CLUB

#### *Oplopanax horridus* Miq.—DEVIL'S CLUB

Aptly named, the yellowish spines that line the 1-4 m tall, stout stems of this robust perennial are not something one wants to experience "first hand." The 10-30 cm broad leaves are palmately lobed with 5-7 major divisions, toothed at the margins and clustered toward the tops of the stems. Both leaves and stalks are spiny, as well as the stems. Small flowers, greenish yellow in color, each with 5 petals and 5 sepals fused at their bases, are configured in rounded umbels. The pistil is 5-parted and the umbels are borne in a tall, narrowly pyramidal raceme-like structure. The flowers mature to an elongated cluster of red berries.

Common in middle elevation forests at streamsides and on swampy ground up to a little over 4,000 feet, this striking plant may be seen at Council Lake and along Road 23.

## Aristolochiaceae Juss.—BIRTHWORT FAMILY

### *Asarum* L.—WILD-GINGER

#### *Asarum caudatum* Lindl.—WILD-GINGER

The common name is derived from the scent of the stout rootstocks (and to a lesser extent the leaves) of this spreading perennial. The 5-10 cm broad leaves are dark green and heart-shaped, made more noticeable by the 10-15 cm tall slender stalks. The solitary flowers nestle under the leaves on short stalks at the base of the plant. There are no petals but the distinctive 3 purplish-brown sepals are united into an urn-shaped cup. The free lobes of the sepals are "caudate" or "tailed;" that is, long and very slender.

A middle elevation species of forests and open areas along trails, wild-ginger is uncommon although may be present at most any forest location, sometimes forming extensive patches. It was collected along Road 8040 at 4,000 feet, and may also be seen along Road 070, below the Stagman trailhead.

## Asteraceae Dumort.—SUNFLOWER FAMILY, ASTER FAMILY

There are 49 genera and 102 sunflower family species at the mountain, making it the most numerous and diverse by far. Found in all habitats except perhaps the most shaded forests, the asters are particularly showy in open meadows, including sites that vary from wet and seasonally inundated areas to dry and rocky alpine slopes. They are an important part of the mountain's flora, and, particularly at high elevations, often the only highly visible flowers in the vicinity.

The genera are distinguished by unique features of the inflorescence. The flowers are actually a composite (hence the former name for the family, the Compositae) of many small, individual flowers borne on a common receptacle. In addition, the flower heads are cradled in one or more series of "involucral" bracts—the phyllaries. A phyllary may range in structure and thickness from leaflike to papery or even spiny. Within the head, there are small, individual flowers of two types.

Ray (ligulate) flowers each have a corolla with a strap-shaped ligule—these flowers resemble a conventional petal and the ray may be both colorful and of considerable length. Typically, the rays have small teeth at the tips. The ray flowers always lack stamens and may or may not have a fertile ovary. Heads composed of ray flowers only are called "radiate." Heads with both ray and disk flowers have the rays placed at the outer edge of the receptacle and the disk flowers arranged at the center.

The disk flowers are perfect, with stamens and ovary present. The corollas are tubular in shape and may have 5 small terminal lobes. There are 5 stamens and the inferior ovary develops into a single-seeded achene. The individual flowers may be subtended on the receptacle by chaffy bracts or scales. Flowers composed of disk flowers only are called "discoid."

The achene varies considerably in size, shape, and surface features. There may be a slender extension, called a "beak." In some genera, the sepals have evolved into a ring of hairs, bristles, awns, or scales at the top of the ovary and subsequently the developing achene—collectively these are the "pappus." The nature of the pappus, which is not always present, can be important in keying the asters.

A hand lens (10-power) is helpful in discerning the fine details of the phyllaries, pappus, and achenes, when keying the asters. Dissection of the flower heads may be necessary.

1 Plants thistlelike, the leaves and phyllaries spine-tipped ..... *Cirsium*
1 Plants not thistlelike; the leaves and phyllaries may be toothed or pointed, but not spine-tipped ........ 2

2(1) Head consisting of ray flowers only, the rays 5-toothed; sap milky ........ 3
2 At least some tubular disk flowers present; rays if present 2- or 3-toothed; sap watery, sometimes scant ........ 14

3(2) Pappus absent ........ *Lapsana*
3 Pappus present ........ 4

4(3) Flowers blue; pappus of minute scales ........ *Cichorium*
4 Flowers variously colored, not blue; pappus bristlelike to featherlike ........ 5

5(4) Flowers 5 per head; terminal leaf segment resembling an ivy leaf ........ *Mycelis*
5 Flowers more than 5 per head; terminal leaf segment not ivy-like ........ 6

6(5) Pappus brownish ........................................................ 7
6 Pappus white ........................................................ 8

7(6) Plant with basal leaves and well-developed stem leaves .............. ........................................................ *Hieracium*
7 Plant with basal leaves only ........................................ *Microseris*

8(6) Plant with basal leaves and well-developed stem leaves ........... 9
8 Plant with basal leaves only ........................................................12

9(8) Flowering stem grasslike, about 1 m tall ....................*Tragopogon*
9 Flowering stem not grasslike, less than 0.5 m tall ............10

10(9) Plant with basal, toothed or lobed leaves; flowering stem with small bracts ........................................................ *Hypochaeris*
10 Plant with basal leaves as well as well-developed stem leaves ... 11

11(10) Pappus of slender bristles ........................................... *Crepis*
11 Pappus bristles featherlike from a short scalelike base... *Microseris*

12(8) Phyllaries in 2 series, one long and one very short; achene minutely spiny at the upper end ........................................ *Taraxacum*
12 Phyllaries in several series (if apparently in 2 series, then not long and short as above); achenes not spiny ................................13

13(12) Achenes beaked .................................................... *Agoseris*
13 Achenes beakless ............................................. *Nothocalais*

14(2) Ray flowers absent or inconspicuous (less than 1 mm long); heads composed of disk flowers only ........................................... 15
14 Ray flowers present, generally conspicuous .......................... 29

15(14) Pappus absent ........................................................ 16
15 Pappus present, consisting of slender bristles ....................... 19

16(15) Phyllaries absent, the heads tiny and subtended by several leaves.. ........................................................ *Psilocarphus*
16 Phyllaries present ........................................................ 17

17(16) Phyllaries fringed with black hairs or sharply pointed at the tip ........ ........................................................ *Centaurea*
17 Phyllaries if hairy then not black ........................................ 18

18(17) Leaves pinnately dissected; weedy, generally odorous plants, heads yellow, many, in flat-topped clusters ............... *Tanacetum*
18 Leaves deltoid-ovate, sometimes broadly toothed; native; heads white, in an open few-flowered panicle .................. *Adenocaulon*

19(15) Phyllaries membranous, papery or transparent ........ 20
19 Phyllaries herbaceous, leaflike, green ........ 24

20(19) Leaves variously short-hairy or hairless, never white-wooly ........ *Artemisia*
20 Leaves with white, wooly hairs ........ 21

21(20) Plants with a taproot; short-lived perennial ........ 22
21 Plants fibrous-rooted, often with rootstocks or runners; annuals or perennials ........ 23

22(21) Heads small, involucre 2-4 mm high; clusters of heads leafy-bracted; plants less than 20 cm tall ........ *Gnaphalium*
22 Heads larger, involucre 4-7 mm high; clusters of heads not leafy-bracted; plants 20-90 cm tall ........ *Pseudognaphalium*

23(21) Basal leaf rosettes present at flowering time; stem leaves much reduced ........ *Antennaria*
23 Basal leaf rosettes absent at flowering time; stem leaves about equal to lower leaves ........ *Anaphalis*

24(19) Leaves opposite ........ *Arnica*
24 Leaves basal or alternate ........ 25

25(24) Heads yellow or yellowish ........ 26
25 Heads white to rose to purple ........ 28

26(25) Leaves palmate, deeply toothed; basal leaves at least 20 cm broad ........ *Cacaliopsis*
26 Leaves lanceolate to elliptic to oblanceolate (rarely lobed or toothed); basal leaves not more than 5 cm wide ........ 27

27(26) Appendages of style more than 0.7 mm long; leaves lanceolate to elliptical ........ *Heterotheca*
27 Appendages of style less than 0.5 mm long; leaves linear ........ *Erigeron*

28(25) Heads up to 5 mm high; phyllaries green ........ *Ageratina*
28 Heads 10-14 mm high; phyllaries dark-margined ........ *Saussurea*

29(14) Pappus absent ........ 30
29 Pappus present ........ 35

30(29) Ligules less than 4 mm long; leaves pinnately divided into linear segments ........ *Achillea*
30 Ligules more than 6 mm long; leaves, if pinnately dissected, then in broader segments ........ 31

31(30) Ray flowers yellow ........ 32
31 Ray flowers white ........ 34

32(31) Rays 10 or more; stout perennial, flowering stems 50-100 cm tall ... ........ *Balsamorhiza*
32(31) Rays 5 or fewer; slender annual, less than 10 cm tall .............. 33

33(32) Flower head 2-4.5 mm high; plants less than 10 cm tall ........ *Hemizonella*
33 Flower head larger, 5-12 mm high; plants more than 10 cm tall ...... *Madia*
34(32) Plants at least 30 cm tall in flower; rays 10-20 mm long ........ *Leucanthemum*
34 Plants less than 20 cm tall in flower; rays 6-12 mm long ........ *Anthemis*

35(29) Pappus of short awns or scales .......... 35
35 Pappus of slender bristles .......... 38

36(35) Leaves basal; heads on leafless stems .......... *Hulsea*
36 Stem leaves present .......... 37

37(36) Leaves pinnately lobed or three-toothed at the tips ...... *Eriophyllum*
37 Leaves even-edged, lanceolate .......... *Helianthella*

38(35) Rays yellow or cream-colored .......... 39
38 Rays white, blue, or purple .......... 46

39(38) Stem leaves opposite .......... *Arnica*
39 Stem leaves alternate or all basal .......... 40

40(39) Phyllaries of more or less equal length, in one series and not overlapping .......... 41
40 Phyllaries of unequal length, overlapping in two or more series .. 43

41(40) Stem leaves well developed, little reduced in size upwards ........ *Senecio*
41 Stems leaves much reduced upwards .......... 42

42(41) Plant pubescent at flowering time .......... *Senecio*
42 Plant hairless or becoming so by flowering time, or with small tufts in the axils .......... *Packera*

43(40) Phyllaries glandular-hairy; heads solitary .......... *Tonestus*
43 Phyllaries not glandular; heads several to many per stem ......... 44

44(43) Plant a low, branched shrub; pappus light brownish ...... *Ericameria*
44 Plant herbaceous; pappus white .......... 45

45(44) Head one per stem .......... *Erigeron*
45 Heads many, arranged in panicles .......... *Solidago*

46(38) Basal leaves round to ovate in outline, deeply lobed ....... *Petasites*
46 Basal leaves various but not both round and deeply lobed ......... 47

47(46) Rays many, not much longer than disk flowers ................ *Conyza*
47 Rays few to many, well developed, most often longer than disk flowers ........................................................................ 48

48(47) Phyllaries with a papery texture, generally not green; style branches blunt, to many, well developed, most often longer than disk flowers ........................................................ *Erigeron*
48 Phyllaries green and sometimes leaflike, at least at the tips; style branches pointed ........................................................... 49

49(48) Head solitary on leafless stem; leaves basal ........... *Oreostemma*
49 Heads several, on leafy stems ............................................ 50

50(49) Phyllaries glandular .......................................... *Canadanthus*
50 Phyllaries hairless or short-hairy but not glandular .................. 51

51(50) Phyllaries keeled; heads fewer than 10; leaves not toothed ................................................................ *Eucephalus*
51 Phyllaries not keeled; heads typically more than 10; leaves toothed or not ........................................................................ 52

52(51) Expanded terminal portion of the disk flower about as long as the slender tube; phyllaries usually purplish ......................... *Eurybia*
52 Terminal portion of the disk flower less than the slender tube; phyllaries rarely purplish ................................ *Symphyotrichum*

## *Achillea* L.—YARROW

### *Achillea millefolium* L—YARROW

Plant taxonomists have gone back and forth over the identity or identities of this species. The *Flora of North America* now considers *A. millefolium* to be a single highly variable species in which two morphological trends are seen: plants from higher elevations tend to have darker margins on the bracts of the involucre and have more wooly pubescence. At Mount Adams, these trends hold: plants from the lower reaches have greenish to light brown bracts and dark brown bracts at higher elevations. In addition, plants from higher elevations tend to be shorter: as short as 10 cm at timberline but 50 to 100 cm at middle elevations.

In all its guises at Mount Adams, the plants have basal and stem leaves that are finely divided into an easily recognizable fernlike or nearly featherlike blade that is grayish in tone. The small flowering heads, each about 5 mm high, are arranged in flat-topped clusters, with one cluster per flowering stem. Typically, there are 4 or 5 white or pinkish ray flowers along with several yellow disk flowers. The achenes are somewhat flattened and prominently veined. They lack a pappus.

At the lower limit of the study area, yarrow grows on disturbed sites, particularly along roadsides, and occasionally near trails and other middle elevation open areas, including alongside the road to King Mountain, near Road 115, and at Hellroaring Canyon. At and above timberline at elevations in excess of 6,300 feet, yarrow prefers dry soils at meadow edges and has been found growing at the saddle on the north side of Little Mount Adams and at Hellroaring River.

### *Adenocaulon* Hook.—TRAIL PLANT

#### *Adenocaulon bicolor* Hook.—TRAIL PLANT

The common name of this plant refers to the white undersides of the leaves, which, if turned over, would mark the trail. Smooth and green above, the white color beneath is due to densely packed, wooly hairs. The 5-10 cm long leaves are triangular in outline, and heart-shaped at the base with a lobed or wavy margin. The 30-100 cm tall stems are slender and bear open panicles of small heads. The involucres are approximately 3 mm high and 5 mm in diameter, while the heads are discoid and composed of 5-10 whitish flowers. The green, smooth phyllaries become refluxed at maturity. The achenes are glandular near the top and there is no pappus.

More common at lower elevations, but seen occasionally along forest trails up to 4,500 feet, this plant is most easily recognized by the leaves. It grows along the Riley Creek trail and on the Stagman Ridge trail, both on the west side of Mount Adams.

### *Ageratina* Spach—SNAKEROOT

#### *Ageratina occidentalis* (Hook.) King & H.E. Robins. WESTERN SNAKEROOT

From 15-70 cm tall, this perennial bears several stems, rising from a woody base; it spreads by slender rhizomes. The 1.5-6.5 cm long leaves are stalked, alternate on the stem, and triangular to ovate. They are toothed and bear small, stalkless glands on the underside. Composed of disk flowers only, the heads are slender and arranged in small groups at the ends of the branches of the inflorescence. The involucral bracts are narrow and typically overlap. The corollas vary from pink to light purple-red while the achenes are 5-angled and glandular.

This species is known from a single Suksdorf collection, made on the south side of the mountain, probably below 5,000 feet.

# Asteraceae

## *Agoseris* Raf.—MOUNTAIN-DANDELION

The leaves of these dandelion-like wildflowers are entirely basal and, when cut or broken they and the stems secrete a bitter, milky juice. Each leafless stem bears a solitary head composed of ray flowers only. The flowers of most species are bright yellow and highly visible; *A. aurantiaca* is a burnt-orange color. Attached to a short or long slender beak, the showy dandelion-like pappus consists of numerous soft, white bristles.

Two of the *Agoseris* species at Mount Adams are eastern Cascades plants—*A. retrorsa* is a species of dry habitats and *A. monticola* is at the northern end of its range at the mountain.

1 Delicate annual; flowering stem less than 10 cm tall .................................................................. *A. heterophylla* var. *heterophylla*
1 Perennials; stouter plants with stems at least 15 cm tall ............ 2

2(1) Achenes with short beak, half as long as body ..........................3
2 Achenes with long beak, 1-4 times as long as body .................. 4

3(2) Leaves, stems, and, especially, the involucre densely hairy ................................................................................ *A. monticola*
3 Plants less hairy overall, hairs mostly confined to the top of the stem and the edges of the bracts of the involucre ................................................................ *A. glauca* var. *dasycephala*

4(2) Beak of achene less than twice as long as the body ................. 5
4 Beak of achene 2-4 times as long as the body .......................... 6

5(4) Flowers orange ............................ *A. aurantiaca* var. *aurantiaca*
5 Flowers yellow .................................................... *A.* x *elata*

6(4) Achenes tapered to the beak; leaves with few, sharp forward pointing lobes ............................ *A. grandiflora* var. *grandiflora*
6 Achenes blunt; leaves with several, sharp, backward pointing lobes ........................................................................ *A. retrorsa*

### *Agoseris aurantiaca* (Hook.) Greene var. *aurantiaca*
### ORANGE MOUNTAIN-DANDELION

The 10-20 cm long leaves of this taprooted perennial are narrowly oblanceolate with a few teeth along the margins. The 2-3 cm broad head is borne at the top of a 10-30 cm tall stem. The rays are orange to reddish-orange; they usually turn pink to purple as they wither and dry. The 15-20 mm high involucre is wooly at its base, and the beak of the achene is shorter than the body.

In meadows along Hellroaring Creek, close to Bench Lake, plants with pink rays are found scattered among normally-colored plants. They show this color in bud, not just in age. An *Agoseris* from the Rocky Mountains of the northern U.S. and southern Canada, *A. lackschewitzii*, regularly has pink heads, but in no other features do the pink Mount Adams plants resemble that species.

Typically found as individual plants in open areas from middle to subalpine elevations, the flower color and solitary-head arrangement of this *Agoseris* serve to distinguish it from other aster family members. It grows around the mountain: in the meadow along Hellroaring Creek, at the DNR Quarry, in Midway Meadows, along 82 to the South Climb trailhead, in upper Bird Creek, and at Muddy River Canyon.

### ***Agoseris* x *elata* (Nutt.) Greene—TALL MOUNTAIN-DANDELION**

The stems of this stout perennial range from 20-70 cm in height. The 10-30 cm long, oblanceolate leaves may be even-edged or bear a few broad teeth. The yellow rays may turn pinkish when dried and the involucre is 2-3 cm high. The outer bracts are more blunt than the inner, and the 8-10 mm achene tapers to a beak nearly as long.

The unusual-looking form of the name indicates that this "species" is thought to represent a stabile, reproducing hybrid. According to the *Flora of North America*, "Specimens that belong to A. ×elata represent a complex assemblage that has relatively few defining features and appears to be of hybrid origin. Most specimens appear to be intermediate between *A. grandiflora* and *A. aurantiaca*; most also appear to have characteristics of *A. monticola* or *A. glauca* var. *dasycephala*. The exact parentage remains unclear."

This middle elevation to subalpine, uncommon species prefers open sites near trails or meadow edges. It is found at an elevation of 5,960 feet near the Pacific Crest Trail on the northwest side of the mountain, south of Road 56 close to Potato Hill, and at Avalanche Valley on the southwest.

### ***Agoseris glauca* (Pursh) Raf. var. *dasycephala* (Torr. & A. Gray) Jepson—PALE MOUNTAIN-DANDELION**

This *Agoseris* differs from the variety *monticola*, which is the most frequently seen variety at the mountain, chiefly by features of the pubescence, as outlined in the key. Leaf shape and size are not useful in separating the plants at Mount Adams.

This variety has not been documented previously from so far south in Washington. It is known from just one collection made at Mount Adams, by Sarah Gage and Sharon Rodman at Bird Creek Meadows, where it grew at a trailside in loose, sandy soil.

## Asteraceae

### *Agoseris grandiflora* (Nutt.) Greene var. *grandiflora*
### LARGE-FLOWERED MOUNTAIN-DANDELION

This taprooted perennial is distinguished by basal leaves that are deeply dissected into linear lobes that point towards the tip of the leaf. They are oblanceolate, 10-15 cm long, bright green, and finely hairy beneath. The 15-20 cm tall flowering stems bear a few loose hairs near the base and short, thick hairs beneath the head. The head is about 2 cm broad, widening as it matures. The phyllaries are overlapping in 2 series, with the outer ones shorter, ovate-lanceolate, and tinged reddish, while the inner ones are lanceolate and lengthen with age. The rays are yellow and approximately equal in length to the involucre. The pappus consists of slender white bristles, and the 4-5 mm long achene is ribbed, tapered to the tip, and has a slender, 10-15 mm long beak.

A middle elevation forest edge species, plants have been located on Trail 75 at Salt Creek and along Road 8040.

### *Agoseris heterophylla* (Nutt.) Greene var. *heterophylla*
### ANNUAL AGOSERIS

A small annual that grows from a slender taproot, the basal leaves of this delicate plant are thin, oblanceolate, short-hairy, and reach approximately 8 cm in length; the edges are typically not toothed, although in robust plants may be faintly toothed. Most often there is only one stem per plant, although occasionally, two; the 2-10 cm tall stems are very slender. The involucre varies to 1 cm tall, and is exceeded by the yellow rays. The beak is 2-3 times the length of the achene. The pappus is composed of white bristles.

Found alongside roads in middle elevation seasonally moist sites, this species grows alongside Road 8040, at the end of Road 100, at the DNR quarry, and near the gravel pit alongside Road 23 at an elevation of 4,000 feet.

### *Agoseris monticola* Greene— MOUNTAIN-DANDELION

Mostly less than 25 cm tall, this perennial bears lanceolate, sharply-tipped leaves that are for the most part hairless; the leaves are usually even-edged, but may also be broadly toothed. The 3-6 cm broad heads are composed of bright yellow rays.

Known from the southeast side of the mountain in subalpine meadows, this uncommon species is found in the upper part of Bird Creek Meadows at 7,200 feet and is also known from a Suksdorf collection at Hellroaring Canyon. Mount Adams is at the northern range limit of this variety.

### *Agoseris retrorsa* (Benth.) Greene
### SPEAR-LEAF MOUNTAIN-DANDELION

This perennial varies from 15 to 60 cm in height and is covered with soft, wooly hairs when young, becoming nearly smooth with age. The 10-40 cm long leaves are dissected into backward curved segments. This species is similar to *A. grandiflora,* but the heads are narrower and the achenes are abruptly beaked from a flattened summit. The involucre is 2.5-5 cm tall when in fruit. The yellow flowers turn pinkish with age. The beak is 2-4 times as long as the 5-7 mm long achenes.

A species of dry open sites, it is found alongside Trail 75 near Salt Creek (along with *A. grandiflora* here), at the gravel pit at 4,000 feet on Road 23, and at the DNR Quarry on the southeast side of the mountain.

## *Anaphalis* (L.) Benth. *ex* C.B. Clarke—EVERLASTING

### *Anaphalis margaritacea* Benth. & Hook.—PEARLY EVERLASTING

A common native perennial that frequently behaves as if it were an invasive weed, this plant forms loose clumps, spread from rootstocks. The stems are leafy and vary from 60-100 cm tall. The leaves are narrowly lanceolate, dark glossy-green on the top and white-wooly beneath. The flower heads are configured in dense flat-topped clusters, each head ranging from 5-6 mm in height. The dry and papery phyllaries are ovate and pearly white in hue. The dark yellow flowers are discoid, and the pappus consists of short, fine, white, bristles.

Common in middle elevation dry to moderate moist sites, often at roadsides and other disturbed and open places, this species has been noted alongside Roads 82 and 34 at elevations from 4,000 to 4,300 feet. It was collected at Hellroaring Canyon and is cosmopolitan at the mountain.

## *Antennaria* Gaertn.—PUSSYTOES

A genus represented by several species at the mountain, many spread by runners, often forming large colonies. The leaves and stems vary from short-hairy to wooly. The small heads are composed of disk flowers only, with male and female flowers borne on separate plants. Male plants are sometimes absent altogether; in such a case, the female plants produce seeds "apomictically," without fertilization of the ovules. The involucral bracts overlap and their shape, color, and texture, which may be papery or not, are important in distinguishing the species. The pappus is composed of fine bristles and differs between male and female plants: bristles of the female pappus are united at their bases into a ring, while in the male flowers they are separate, thickened, and barbed.

## Asteraceae

These species are locally common, typically in open sites, and often on disturbed ground. They range from middle elevation meadows to timberline.

*Antennaria geyeri* is strictly an eastern Cascades species of dry habitats, often in ponderosa pine forests. Likewise, *A. anaphaloides* also tends to have a more eastern distribution. Both are absent from Mount Rainier, as is *A. alpina*, a species with a circumboreal distribution.

1 Plants lacking runners and not forming mats .......... 2
1 Plants with runners, forming mats .......... 4

2(1) Largest leaves 1-3 cm long; female involucres narrow, pinkish; plants 5-15 cm tall .......... *A. geyeri*
2 Largest leaves 3-15 cm long; female involucres broad, rarely pinkish; plants more than 10 cm tall .......... 3

3(2) Plants 1-2 dm tall; involucre blackish, inner bracts white at the tip .......... *A. lanata*
3 Plants 2-5 dm tall; involucre white, with small dark spot at base of bracts .......... *A. anaphaloides*

4(1) Flowering stem glandular in the upper portion; heads in an open raceme .......... *A. racemosa*
4 Flowering stem not glandular; heads in more or less dense, flat-topped clusters .......... 5

5(4) Upper surface of the leaves green or sparsely long-hairy; leaves with 1-3 prominent veins .......... 6
5 Upper surface of the leaves densely long-hairy; leaves with only 1 prominent vein .......... 7

6 (5) Upper surface of the leaves sparsely long-hairy, at least when young .......... *A. howellii* ssp. *neodioica*
6 Upper surface of the leaves green and hairless, even when young .......... *A. howellii* ssp. *howellii*

7(5) Phyllaries pinkish .......... *A. rosea* ssp. *rosea*
7 Phyllaries at least in part greenish black to brownish black .......... 8

8(7) Tips of the involucral bracts rounded, the bracts whitish at the tips, dark brown or blackish brown on the lower portion, blunt .......... *A. umbrinella*
8 Tips of the involucral bracts pointed, the bracts greenish black or brownish throughout, sharp-tipped .......... *A. media*

### ***Antennaria anaphaloides* Rydb.—PEARLY PUSSYTOES**

A stout, tall pussytoes, this perennial varies from 20-50 cm in height. The basal leaves reach 15 cm in length and are 2 cm wide. The heads are numerous and borne in a broad inflorescence, and the membranous portion of the involucral bracts is completely white, or may have a small dark spot at the base.

This species differs from *A. umbrinella* in height and the whitish color of the bracts. It is a middle elevation species of hillsides and open woods. At Mount Adams, it is known from a single Thomas Howell collection at the Oregon State University herbarium, for which no other information is available on the label.

### *Antennaria geyeri* A. Gray—PINEWOODS PUSSYTOES

With several stems ascending from a woody base, this tiny plant varies between 3 and 15 cm in height. The plant is white-wooly throughout and the 3 cm long lower stem leaves are oblanceolate; the upper leaves are reduced in size. Pinkish, the female involucre bracts are 7-9 mm high, with the corollas ranging from 4.5-8 mm in length when dry. The male involucre is shorter. The pappus has short, stiff barbs.

An eastern Cascades species with a preference for open forests, it is rare at Mount Adams, known from a single Henderson collection in the Oregon State University herbarium, made at the "base of Mount Adams."

### *Antennaria howellii* Greene ssp. *howellii*—HOWELL'S PUSSYTOES

This plant differs from the subspecies *neodioica* in the absence of hairs from the upper surface of the leaf, those of *neodioica* often becoming nearly smooth with age. The 2 cm leaves of *howellii* are also a little longer.

This subspecies is known from the trail northwest of Bench Lake and also from a poorly-documented Henderson collection.

### *Antennaria howellii* Greene ssp. *neodioica* (Greene) Bayer FIELD PUSSYTOES

With ground-covering runners, this matted plant bears 1.5 cm long obovate leaves on tapering stalks. The slender flowering stems vary from 15-30 cm tall and are wooly but not typically glandular. The small stem leaves are stalkless and linear, while the 8-10 mm high heads are clustered at the top of the stem. Narrowly lanceolate phyllaries are brownish at the base and whitish at the papery, pointed tip.

Most typically a low elevation species of sunny, rocky slopes in forest openings and along road banks, it is rare at Mount Adams, being known from a subalpine collection at Hellroaring Canyon, made by Suksdorf.

## Asteraceae

### *Antennaria lanata* (Hook.) Greene—WOOLY PUSSYTOES

This species lacks runners or rootstocks and so is tufted rather than matted. The 10-15 cm long stems are single. The 4-10 cm long basal leaves are oblanceolate, loosely wooly, and prominently 3-veined, the stem leaves being much reduced in size. The heads are crowded into a rounded terminal cluster; the female heads are 6-8 mm high, with dark brown to blackish phyllaries.

Common, this species typically grows from the subalpine to the alpine regions on rocky slopes and flats. It is found at 6,300 feet of elevation in the upper meadow on Crooked Creek on the southeast side of the mountain. It also grows alongside the Killen Creek Trail on the northwest side of the mountain, and is known at Hellroaring River and near Bench Lake. It is found at lower elevation in the first major meadow along the Stagman Ridge trail at 5,300 feet.

### *Antennaria media* Greene—ROCKY MOUNTAIN PUSSYTOES

Forming densely leafy mats from runners, the stems of this species range from 3 to 8 cm tall and bear long hairs. The leaves are 5-12 mm long, oblanceolate to spoon-shaped and profusely white-wooly. The flowering stem leaves are linear, and the heads are crowded into a terminal cluster, with the individual heads ranging from 5-6 mm in height. Both the inner and the outer phyllaries are pointed; they are long-hairy below and greenish-black at the papery tip.

Very uncommon, this species is known from a Henderson collection, made in 1892. No further label information is given.

### *Antennaria racemosa* Hook.—HOOKER'S PUSSYTOES

The open, elongated inflorescence distinguishes this species. The heads are borne on slender stalks in a raceme or narrow panicle. This species is taller than other antennarias, reaching 50 cm in protected sites. The upper stem is short-hairy although not wooly and it is notably glandular. The 3-8 cm long basal leaves are densely hairy on the lower side and nearly smooth above; they are spoon-shaped to nearly round and borne on slender stalks. The stem leaves are linear. The 5-8 mm high heads have green or brown phyllaries.

A middle elevation species of open sites, it is known from Road 23 at a culvert south of the gravel pit, at the Horseshoe Lake campground, and from a Suksdorf collection west of Stagman Ridge.

### *Antennaria rosea* Greene ssp. *rosea*—ROSY PUSSYTOES

Very lovely with its pink heads on compact, mat-forming plants, this species bears leaves that are wooly on both surfaces, 2-3 cm long, and spoon-shaped to oblanceolate. The 10-30 cm tall flowering steams bear 7-12 heads in a compact, terminal cluster. The heads are 5-6 mm in height, and the phyllaries are dull to bright pink, although on occasion pale pink or whitish.

Locally common and easy to recognize from the pink color, this is a middle elevation to subalpine species of meadow edges and other openings. It is found at milepost 34 on Road 23, at Midway Meadows, Muddy Meadows, near Road 82, and at the DNR Quarry, as well as on the saddle on the north side of Little Mount Adams (elevation of 6,437 feet).

#### ***Antennaria umbrinella*** **Rydb.—DARK PUSSYTOES**

This species is distinguished from *A. media* by the phyllaries which in this case are rounded at the tip, while the papery portion of the inner phyllaries is typically whitish, although sometimes light brown.

Fairly common in subalpine openings and in meadows that become fairly dry, this species is known in the upper Bird Creek Meadows region at 7,200 feet and at Hellroaring Canyon. It has also been found at Horseshoe Lake.

### ***Anthemis*** **L.—DOG-FENNEL**

#### ***Anthemis arvensis*** **L.—CORN-CHAMOMILE**

A weed, the plants vary from 20-40 cm in height, although they sometimes sprawl along the ground on their branched steams. The leaves are finely divided and ill-scented when crushed. The heads are 2.5-3.5 cm across and the white rays are 7-12 mm long. There is no pappus.

This species is known from a collection at the Riley Creek trailhead.

### ***Arnica*** **L.—ARNICA**

Common species of the subalpine meadows, this genus is also represented in middle elevation forest openings and wet meadows. With the exception of two species (*A. discoidea* and *A. parryi*), the flowers have both ray and disk flowers. The flowers are typically bright yellow and showy. The stems bear opposite leaves, a key characteristic for these plants, with the number of paired stem leaves varying from 2-12. The inflorescence is headlike, with several heads borne in flat-topped inflorescences. The rays, when present, are typically blunt and toothed at the tip. The phyllaries are configured in 1 or 2 rows. There is a pappus of numerous, fine bristles.

*A. discoidea* is at the northern end of its range at Mount Adams and is known from a single collection made by the authors. *A. rydbergii* and *A. longifolia* are likewise uncommon, while the remaining species are well-represented. *A. gracilis* was formerly considered a variety of *A. latifolia;* it is a higher elevation, smaller plant.

1 Stem leaves in 5-12 pairs .................................................... 2
1 Stem leaves in 2-4 pairs, not including basal cluster ..................... 3

2(1) Involucre bracts blunt to slightly sharp; tuft of long hairs near tip ........ ........................................................... *A. chamissonis*
2 Involucre bracts sharply tipped, tip not particularly hairy .................. ............................................................ *A. longifolia*

3(1) Heads disk flowers only ........................................................ 4
3 Heads with rays and disk flowers ............................................ 5

4(3) Lower leaves ovate to more or less heart-shaped; involucral bracts slightly sharp-tipped to sharp-tipped; heads not nodding .............. ........................................................... *A. discoidea*
4 Lower leaves lanceolate; involucral bracts gradually tapered; young heads nodding ......................................................... *A. parryi*

5(3) Pappus slightly feathery, tawny colored; tufts of basal leaves lacking . ........................................................... *A. mollis*
5 Pappus with barbs or stiff hairs, white; basal leaves present ........... 6

6(5) Leaf blades narrower, 3-10 times as long as wide ........... *A. rydbergii*
6 Leaf blades broad, 1-2.5 times as long as wide .......................... 7

7(6) Achenes short-hairy to base; involucre with copious, long white hairs ........................................................... *A. cordifolia*
7 Achenes glabrous below; involucre without hairs ........................ 8

8(7) Small, tufted plants; heads 3-9, narrow, involucre 7-13 mm high ........ ........................................................... *A. gracilis*
8 Larger plants, lower elevations; heads 1-3, involucre 10-18 mm high ..........................................................*A. latifolia*

### *Arnica chamissonis* Less.—NARROW-LEAVED ARNICA

The solitary stems of this *Arnica* range from 20-100 cm tall and are hairy and glandular above. The stem leaves are borne in 5-10 pairs and are rather uniform in size, lanceolate to oblanceolate in shape, sometimes slightly toothed, and 5-30 cm long. Several heads are grouped in a hemispherical clump, the involucre is 8-12 mm high, and the bracts bear tufts of hairs at the tips. The rays are pale yellow and 1.5-2 cm long; the achenes are short hairy and the pappus is tawny to whitish, sometimes minutely barbed.

A subalpine wet meadow species, it is known from a single Henderson collection made in "alpine meadows" in 1892.

### *Arnica cordifolia* Hook.—HEARTLEAF ARNICA

This species is most easily distinguished by the toothed, heart-shaped leaves that are 4-10 cm long and borne on stalks of about equal length. The sparsely long-hairy stems reach 40 cm tall, with 1-3 flower heads borne on long, slender stalks. The involucre is about 15 mm tall and the phyllaries are densely hairy on the lower portion. The ligules are about 2 cm long. The pappus consists of white, slender, barbed bristles.

Fairly common, this middle elevation species grows in meadows, alongside roads and in dry sites as well. It is found at the DNR Quarry, at Midway and Hellroaring Meadows, and alongside Road 5603 close to Potato Hill.

### *Arnica discoidea* Benth.—RAYLESS ARNICA

Similar to *Arnica parryi*, this species also lacks ray flowers but the lower leaves are ovate to almost heart-shaped. The heads are erect in the inflorescence, not nodding.

A southern Cascades species of open areas and common in the Columbia Gorge, this species was found by the authors along Road 23 at milepost 34, where it may be only an accidental introduction.

### *Arnica gracilis* Rydb.—SMALLHEAD ARNICA

Similar to *Arnica latifolia* and once considered a variety of that species, this plant is smaller in all its parts, growing in small tufts with stems that vary between 10 and 30 cm in height. There are 3-9 narrow and small heads, and the involucre is 7-13 mm high.

This subalpine species is uncommon at Mount Adams, growing at higher elevations than *A. latifolia*. It has been located on the north side of Little Mount Adams at 6,500 feet and at Bird Creek Meadows as well.

### *Arnica latifolia* Bong.
### BROADLEAF ARNICA, MOUNTAIN ARNICA

Sometimes reaching 50 cm in height, the sparsely, finely hairy stems of this arnica may be single or clustered on spreading rootstocks. Borne in 2-4 pairs, the ovate, toothed leaves reach a length of 4 cm; they are stalked at the base but not in the middle stem. The 1-3 flowering heads are set on long stalks. The 10-18 mm high involucre is narrow and may be sparsely hairy with scattered glands, or nearly hairless. The bright yellow rays are approximately 1.5 cm long, and the pappus is white and barbed.

The most common arnica at the mountain and sometimes found in large colonies, this is a middle elevation to subalpine species of forest edges, meadows, and disturbed sites. Large clumps are found at the base of the South Climb trail and alongside Road 8040. It grows at Babyshoe and Muddy Meadows, and alongside the trail between

Horseshoe and Green Mountain Lakes. A very high elevation individual is found at nearly 8,300 feet on the South Climb trail.

### *Arnica longifolia* D.C. Eat. in S. Wats.—SPEARLEAF ARNICA

Untoothed leaves on several stems, with 3-5 flowering heads per stem, distinguish this arnica. Stems may reach 50 cm in height and rise from a heavy, somewhat woody base. The lanceolate leaves are in 5 or more pairs on the stem; both stems and leaves are minutely glandular-hairy. The heads are hemispherical, with glandular phyllaries. The 1.5 cm long ligules are bright yellow, and the pappus is yellowish-brown and featherlike.

This species grows from middle to subalpine elevations on moist sites, including seeps, river banks, and cliffs. It is rare at the mountain, known from a Suksdorf collection made in Hellroaring Canyon.

### *Arnica mollis* Hook.—HAIRY ARNICA

Single stems rising from a branched rootstock characterize this species. The stems vary widely, from 20 to 60 cm tall. The 2-4 pairs of leaves are either not stalked or short-stalked at the base of the stem; they vary from toothed to not toothed, oblanceolate to elliptical in shape, and reach 15 cm in length, with the longest leaves at the base of the stem. The large heads may reach 6 cm in breadth and are borne 1-3 heads on the stem. The involucres are 12-18 mm high, and the phyllaries and stalks are glandular and hairy. The pappus is light brown and featherlike.

Although less common than *A. latifolia* this species is frequently encountered in wet subalpine meadow habitats. At Foggy Flat, it grows at nearly 6,100 feet. It is found alongside Road 23 at the junction to Takhlakh Lake, at Bird Creek, and in the Muddy River Canyon.

### *Arnica parryi* A. Gray—NODDING ARNICA

Unusual among the arnicas for having only disk flowers, the 3-10 heads of this species typically nod on long-hairy, glandular stems that are 30-50 cm tall. The lanceolate to ovate leaves are hairy on both sides and are borne in 3-4 pairs. The 10-15 mm high involucres are covered with a few scattered hairs, and the pappus is featherlike and yellowish-brown.

A lower subalpine meadow species, regularly encountered in small numbers, this arnica grows in an open area near the Pacific Crest Trail south of Potato Hill. It is also found in Midway Meadows, as well as alongside the Snipes Mountain Trail north of the Pineway Trail at an elevation of 5,500 feet. It is found near Road 8040 (the South Climb approach), and in Hellroaring Meadows.

### *Arnica rydbergii* Greene—RYDBERG'S ARNICA

At most 30 cm in height and bearing 2 or 3 pairs of small leaves on the stem, this is a rare species at the mountain. The 10 cm long lower leaves are not toothed, and are lanceolate to oblanceolate in shape and tufted at the base of the stem. The 7-10 rays are 1-2 cm long, and the pappus is white and barbed.

This arnica has been found at just one place at the mountain, at an elevation of 4,800 feet in a wet meadow along Hellroaring Creek, north of Bench Lake. Elsewhere in the west, if is typically found in dry meadows and on open slopes.

## *Artemisia* L.—SAGEBRUSH

A complex genus with many species and subjected to much revision by botanists, the representatives at the mountain consist of a weed and four natives. They are perennial herbs or small shrubs, and include a smaller form of the common sagebrush of eastern Washington. The leaves and upper stems are finely white-hairy, even silvery, or clothed in matted, wooly hairs, an adaptation to the dry habitats often preferred by members of this genus. The heads are discoid and are borne in panicles or racemes of many flowers. The papery phyllaries overlap; there is no pappus. Most species have strongly scented foliage. The alternate leaves are entire to pinnatifid, that is, finely divided in a pinnate manner.

*A. tridentata* is rare at lower elevations on the southeast side of the mountain. More likely to be encountered are *A. douglasiana* at middle elevation sites or *A. michauxiana,* a much smaller species of subalpine habitats.

1 Shrub; flowers perfect .......................... *A. tridentata* ssp. *vaseyana*
1 Perennial herbs; marginal flowers female only ............................ 2

2(1) Receptacle with numerous long hairs between the flowers; rare roadside weed .................................................. *A. absinthium*
2 Receptacle not hairy; native plants .......................................... 3

3(2) Leaves small, finely divided, 2-5 cm long, twice pinnatifid, ultimate segments toothed again ....................................... *A. michauxiana*
3 Leaves larger and less divided, entire to pinnatifid ....................... 4

4(3) Involucre broad, many-flowered, wider than high ................ *A. tilesii*
4 Involucre narrower, higher than wide ....................... *A. douglasiana*

### *Artemisia absinthium* L.—ABSINTHE

The stems of this 4-12 dm tall perennial herb are silky-hairy, becoming smooth. The 3-9 cm long leaves are borne on long stalks and are divided

2-3 times, with oblong segments 1.5-4 mm wide; the upper leaves are less divided and on shorter stalks. The large inflorescence is leafy; the involucre is about 2-3 mm in height and finely silky-hairy. The achenes are smooth.

A weed of disturbed areas, this species was collected close to Road 321, near the Pacific Crest Trail trailhead.

#### *Artemisia douglasiana* Bess. in Hook—DOUGLAS'S MUGWORT

A stout perennial with rootstocks, this sage ranges from 5-15 dm in height. The 7-15 cm leaves are lanceolate to elliptic and may be unlobed or divided with coarse teeth or lobes; they are softly-hairy beneath and green above. The inflorescence is panicle-like, and the involucre is 3-4 mm high and short-hairy. There are 6-10 pistillate flowers and 10-25 disk flowers.

Growing in middle elevation wet environments, but avoiding meadows, this *Artemisia* is relatively common at the mountain. It is found alongside Trail 75 at Salt Creek, along the Island Springs trail, and next to Road 8040, uphill from Morrison Creek at 5,000 feet.

#### *Artemisia michauxiana* Bess. in Hook.—MICHAUX'S MUGWORT

This little, multiple-stemmed, perennial is 20-40 cm tall and rises from a woody rootstock. The stem leaves are covered with short, wooly hairs beneath and are typically dark green above; basal leaves are lacking. The lower leaves are 2-5 cm long and are twice pinnately divided, the end segments often being toothed. The involucre is 3.5-4 mm high and glabrous. The outer 9-12 flowers are pistillate, while the inner 15-35 are perfect.

A species of rocky sites, it is known from Muddy River Canyon on the east side of the mountain, and the Ridge of Wonders on the southeast. The crushed leaves have a strong, pleasant, lemon-like odor.

#### *Artemisia tilesii* Ledeb.—ALEUTIAN WORMWOOD

Several stems from a heavy, woody rootstock rise 50-100 cm tall in this stout wormwood. Both the stems and the tops of the leaves are long-hairy with white hairs. The leaves are green above and pinnately divided into a few, forward pointing, lanceolate lobes. A few heads are borne in a branched panicle. The involucre is 4-8 mm wide, the height being less at 3-5 mm. There are 20-40 disk flowers and fewer pistillate flowers.

The *Flora of North America* does not recognize varieties in this species; plants at Mount Adams would, formerly, have been called var. *unalaschcensis.*

Found on gravelly or rocky sites, this species is known from three Suksdorf collections, including one at Hellroaring Canyon.

### *Artemisia tridentata* Nutt. ssp. *vaseyana* (Rydb.) Beetle MOUNTAIN BIG SAGEBRUSH

An erect, branching shrub that varies from 4-20 dm in height, this is a common species of open steppes in eastern Washington. The leaves and twigs appear gray from a covering of short, fine hairs; the leaves persist throughout the winter. They are 1.5-5 cm long, 3-toothed at the tip, and wedge-shaped. The many heads are borne in a loose panicle-like inflorescence approximately 1.5-7 cm wide. The whitish involucre is 3-5 mm high, and the flowers number 3-5.

Rare at Mount Adams and occurring on dry, open slopes above 6,000 feet, this species is known from a Suksdorf collection at Hellroaring Canyon. It was also found by the authors on the south facing slope of the Ridge of Wonders.

## *Balsamorhiza* Nutt.—BALSAMROOT

### *Balsamorhiza careyana* A. Gray—CAREY'S BALSMAROOT

A deep, woody taproot and many-parted rootstock support this stout, wide perennial. The basal leaves are borne on long stalks, the blade triangular, or occasionally heart-shaped at the base, and up to nearly 30 cm long and 15 cm wide. The leaves have noticeable veins and are roughly hairy and sometimes glandular. The flowering stems range from 20-100 cm in height and bear smaller leaves. The yellow rays are 2-4 cm long and number 8 or 13; the disc of the head is up to 2.5 cm wide. The involucre is sparsely wooly.

A species of open, dry sites more typical of the eastern Washington desert, it has been found at the DNR Quarry on the southeast side of the mountain, where it grows on east and south facing slopes in a Garry oak woodland.

## *Cacaliopsis* A. Gray—SILVERCROWN

### *Cacaliopsis nardosmia* (A. Gray) A. Gray—SILVERCROWN

Growing from a woody rhizome, this 40-100 cm tall perennial is leafy at the base, with much reduced middle and upper stem leaves. The largest leaves are borne on long stalks, and are up to 20 cm long and palmately divided. The segments are coarsely toothed or lobed; the leaves green above and short-hairy beneath, becoming glabrous in age. Multiple heads form a large raceme-like inflorescence. Discoid flowering heads are yellow and 10-30 mm wide; the involucre is 10-17 mm high.

An eastern Cascades plant of meadows and open woods, formerly named *Luina nardosmia,* this species is found at the DNR Quarry at 4,000 feet on a logged ridgeline and is also known from a Flett collection along the upper Klickitat River.

## Asteraceae

### *Canadanthus* G.L. Nesom—MOUNTAIN ASTER

#### *Canadanthus modestus* (Lindl.) G.L. Nesom
#### TALL MOUNTAIN ASTER

This species is distinguished from the other aster-like species at Mount Adams by its toothed leaves and glandular phyllaries. The leafy stems vary from 40-90 cm in height. The 4-8 cm long stalkless leaves are lanceolate, with small teeth on the margins. The numerous heads are borne in a 1.5-2 cm broad, leafy, flat-topped cluster. The glandular phyllaries are green throughout and overlap little. The 10-12 mm long ray flowers are deep purple, and the pappus is brownish.

Formerly named *Aster modestus*, this is a common species of moist forest openings, meadow edges, and other open areas. It grows at Swampy Meadows, alongside Trail 75, and near the Big Klickitat River, and on the upper Lewis River.

### *Centaurea* L.—KNAPWEED

Knapweeds are invasive weeds that have become widely established across Washington. This aggressive genus is represented by two species at the mountain, both from modern collections taken alongside roads. The plants are branched many times and bear alternate leaves. The heads are discoid, although in some species (such as the "bachelor's buttons") the outer row of disk flowers is enlarged. The flowers are purplish to sometimes cream. The phyllaries are ornamented with fringelike hairs or spiny tips; the pappus is composed of short bristles or narrow scales.

1 Phyllaries spine-tipped ................................................ *C. diffusa*
1 Phyllaries fringed with black hairs, not spine-tipped ........... *C. stoebe*

#### *Centaurea diffusa* Lam.—DIFFUSE KNAPWEED

This diffusely branched biennial reaches 120 cm in height. The leaves are pinnately divided and the lower leaves are 10-15 cm long. The numerous heads are only about 1.5 cm wide, and the phyllaries are pale green and spine-tipped. Pale purple disk flowers are few in number; occasionally white flowers are found. The pappus is composed of short, narrow scales and is occasionally absent.

An invasive weed, this knapweed is known from the DNR quarry on the southeast side, growing in low numbers and confined to the roadside.

#### *Centaurea stoebe* L.—SPOTTED KNAPWEED

This biennial ranges to 1 m in height and bears pinnately divided leaves; in its first year, the plants consist of a low rosette of leaves. The numerous heads are 2-3 cm wide and configured in an open panicle. The "spotted" comes from the phyllaries which are fringed with black hairs. The disk flowers are a light reddish-purple, and the pappus is composed of short bristles.

Fortunately rare at Mount Adams, this weed is a roadside disturbance species that has been found alongside Road 23 near 4,000 feet. This species has also been named *C. biebersteinii* and *C. maculosa.*

## *Cichorium* L.—CHICORY

### *Cichorium intybus* L.—CHICORY

A perennial weed distinguished by its bright blue flowers, the stems are rigid and may reach 1 m in height, with spreading branches. Deeply divided into angular lobes, the basal leaves are configured in a rosette. The 3-4 cm broad, stalkless heads are borne on the upper branches and are composed of ray flowers only. The pappus is a low crown of scales formed in 2 or 3 series.

Uncommon at the mountain, this colorful species is known on the west side at middle elevations, mostly along logging roads.

## *Cirsium* Mill.—THISTLE

Three aggressive thistles, one a native and the other two weeds, inhabit disturbed sites at the mountain. The plants have spine-tipped leaves and phyllaries, and, in the case of *C. vulgare,* spiny wings on the stems. The leaves are alternate and coarsely toothed. The globular heads are purplish and composed of disk flowers; the pappus consists of white, feathery bristles.

1 Plants with male and female flowers on separate plants; phyllary spines to 1 mm long; flowers reddish-purple ................ *C. arvense*

1 Plants with stamens and pistils in the same flower; phyllary spines longer than 1 mm; flowers purple ........................................... 2

2(1) Margins of the leaf stalks running down the stem and thus the stem "winged"; weedy plant of roadsides and waste ground ... *C. vulgare*

2 Stems not winged; native, in open woods and on banks .............. ............................................................ *C. edule* var. *macounii*

### *Cirsium arvense* (L.) Scop.—CANADA THISTLE

Slender stems 1-2 m tall characterize this robust perennial. The involucres are 1-2 cm high and bear short thorns. The disk flowers are light reddish-purple, and male and female flowers are borne on separate plants.

A weedy thistle, colonizing roadsides and logged areas, this species is found alongside Road 23 on the overlook south of the Pacific Crest Trail crossing. It also grows along Trail 75 at Salt Creek on the southwest side of the mountain.

### *Cirsium edule* Nutt. var. *macounii* (Greene) D.J. Keil CAYUSE THISTLE, EDIBLE THISTLE

Typically a biennial, although occasionally persisting longer, this 50-200 cm tall thistle bears heavy, leafy stems. The leaves are wooly when young and smooth with age. The involucres are 3-4 cm high, and the phyllaries are spine-tipped and densely webbed with hairs. The flowers are purple.

The sole native thistle at Mount Adams and relatively uncommon at the mountain, it grows on the north side alongside the Pacific Crest Trail south of Potato Hill, as well as on the northwest at Babyshoe Meadow and at Howard Lake northeast of the mountain.

### *Cirsium vulgare* (Savi) Ten.—BULL THISTLE

Similar to Canada thistle but more robust, the leaves of this thistle are tipped with strong spines. Also distinctive is the manner in which the stem leaf bases run downwards as spiny wings. The 2.5-4 cm high involucres are short-hairy and heavily spiny. The flowers are purple.

A weedy thistle of middle elevation roadsides, it is known from Road 84 and Road 82.

## *Conyza* Less.—HORSEWEED

### *Conyza canadensis* (L.) Cronq. var. *glabrata* (A. Gray) Cronq. HORSEWEED

This annual rises 50-100 cm tall from a taproot. The stems bear numerous narrow, untoothed leaves. A large number of heads are borne in an open panicle, and the involucres are 3-5 mm high. The rays are whitish and very short and narrow. The pappus is composed of very fine bristles.

Native across much of North America this species was probably introduced at Mount Adams. It resembles the fleabanes of the genus *Erigeron* and is rare at the mountain, having been found at the DNR quarry on the southeast side.

## *Crepis* L.—HAWKSBEARD

One annual weed and two native perennial species comprise the hawksbeards at the mountain. The plant stems have a milky juice and the leaves are undivided to toothed or pinnate. The alternate stem leaves are much reduced in size. The yellow flowers are composed of rays only and are configured in a few to many-flowered head. The pappus is of numerous white slender bristles.

1 Annual weed; heads 20-60 per stem ........................ *C. capillaris*
1 Native perennials; heads 7-12 per stem .................................. 2

2(1) Stem and leaves smooth, or with stiff hairs .................... *C. nana*
2 Stem and leaves wooly, long-hairy, and sometimes bristly .......... 3

3(2) Involucre 8-15 mm high; achenes greenish ................................ ........................................................ *C. atribarba* ssp. *atribarba*
3 Involucre 10-15 mm high; achenes yellowish-brown .. *C. intermedia*

### *Crepis atribarba* Heller ssp. *atribarba*—SLENDER HAWKSBEARD

Very similar overall to *C. intermedia* in appearance and stature, this Crepis varies in parts of its floral anatomy: the involucres are 8-15 mm high and usually have stout, black hairs among the more numerous wooly hairs. The corollas are 10-18 mm long and the achenes are greenish.

Rare at Mount Adams, this hawksbeard was collected by Robert Goff, in 2001 on the west side of Smith Butte, at approximately 4,000 feet.

### *Crepis capillaris* (L.) Wallr.—SMOOTH HAWKSBEARD

Distinguished by a basal rosette of lanceolate, toothed leaves, the stem leaves of this 30-90 cm tall hawksbeard are progressively reduced in size upwards. These leaves clasp the stem with earlike lobes. A panicle, the inflorescence is characterized by spreading, curving branches, with a few heads. Each head is of ray flowers only, bright yellow in color, and 1-1.5 cm broad. The phyllaries are lanceolate and glandular, approximately 7-9 mm long. The pappus is composed of numerous very fine white bristles.

This roadside weed of middle elevations is found alongside Road 23 on the west side. It does not invade intact habitats at Mount Adams.

### *Crepis intermedia* A. Gray in A. Gray et al.—LIMESTONE HAWKSBEARD

This perennial bears 1 or 2 stems rising from a taproot, and ranges from 20-70 cm in height. The herbage is grayish with short, softly wooly hairs. The basal and lower stem leaves are 10-40 cm long and pinnately divided with toothed margins. The 10-60 bell-shaped flower heads are borne in a narrowly-branched inflorescence that is nearly flat-topped. The involucre is 10-15 mm high and is typically covered with short, wooly hairs. The corollas are 14-30 mm long, and the achenes are mostly yellowish-brown.

Rare at the mountain, this species is known from a Suksdorf collection at Hellroaring Canyon; the elevation is not specified but a meadow edge habitat seems likely.

#### ***Crepis nana*** **Richards.—DWARF ALPINE HAWKSBEARD**

This taprooted perennial ranges from 10-20 cm in height, and varies from hairless to glaucous. There are several, erect to curved stems, typically branched. The basal leaves are spoon-shaped to ovate, and range to 8.5 cm in length, including the stalk. The involucre is cylindrical and 8-13 mm in height, the outer bracts shorter than the inner ones. The achenes are brownish and 4-7 mm long.

The *Flora of North America* does not recognize varieties in this species; plants at Mount Adams would, formerly, have been called var. *ramosum*.

Rare, this species is known from a single Suksdorf collection, made at 7,550 feet on "sandy gravel." This was probably on the southeast side of Mount Adams.

### ***Ericameria*** **Nutt.—GOLDENBUSH**

#### ***Ericameria bloomeri*** **(A. Gray) J.F. Macbr.—RABBITBUSH**

A species of middle elevation dry habitats, the herbage of this 20-60 cm tall shrub is glandular to occasionally wooly-hairy and the twigs are brittle. The 2-6 cm long leaves are linear to narrowly oblanceolate and may be straight or twisted. The flowering heads are clustered at the ends of the twigs, or may form a raceme-like inflorescence. The involucre is 7-11 mm high, with overlapping scales. The yellow rays number from 1-5 (sometimes they are absent), and are 6-12 mm long. There are 4-12 disk flowers, 7-11 mm long.

Formerly named *Haplopappus bloomeri*, this species is most commonly found on the drier south and southeast sides of the mountain where it grows in forest openings, although it is known from Stagman Ridge on the west at an elevation of 7,200 feet. It is also found at the DNR quarry, alongside Pineway Trail, and at the Cold Springs trailhead.

### ***Erigeron*** **L.—DAISY, FLEABANE**

Similar in appearance to the asters and their related genera, the fleabanes at Mount Adams are biennial or perennial herbs. They bear opposite leaves, and the flowering heads are borne in panicles or flat-topped clusters, or occasionally solitary. The phyllaries are in 1 or 2 series (3-5 series is typical for the asters). The numerous rays are quite narrow, whereas in asters there tend to be fewer and broader rays. There are numerous yellow disk flowers. The pappus may be of simple bristles or may be double; in this case, it consists of bristles and an outer row of narrow scales.

1 Disk flowers only .............................. *E. inornatus* var. *inornatus*
1 Disk and ray flowers present .............................................. 2

2(1) Rays yellow ........................................................ *E. linearis*
2 Rays purple to pinkish ...................................................... 3

3(2) Ligules very short and inconspicuous, less than 4 mm long, erect ... ........................................................................................ 4
3 Ligules conspicuous, 6 mm or more long, spreading .................. 5

4(3) Plants 30-60 cm tall; heads several to many per stem .................. ............................................................ *E. acris* ssp. *politus*
4 Plants less than 30 cm tall; heads 1 to a few per stem.................. ............................................................ *E. acris* ssp. *debilis*

5(3) Leaves dissected into 3-5 lobes ........................... *E. compositus*
5 Leaves toothed or not, but not divided into lobes ....................... 6

6(5) Rays to 1 mm wide; phyllaries long-hairy ................................ .................................................. *E. speciosus* var. *speciosus*
6 Rays 2-3 mm wide; phyllaries glandular .... *E. glacialis* var. *glacialis*

### *Erigeron acris* L. ssp. *debilis* (A. Gray) Piper—BITTER FLEABANE

The short and inconspicuous pinkish rays compose the rather undistinguished flower head of this species. The 5-20 cm tall stems bear small, lanceolate leaves; the basal leaves are oblanceolate. The stalks and phyllaries are sparsely glandular-hairy and the pappus is brown. The heads are either solitary or number 2-3 per stem.

Found to about 5,000 feet in middle to subalpine elevations, typically in shallow soil in dry places, this species grows alongside the Pacific Crest Trail south of Potato Hill on the face of a lava flow. Suksdorf collected it at Hellroaring Canyon as well, on the west side of the mountain.

### *Erigeron acris* L. ssp. *politus* (Fries) Schinz & R. Keller BITTER FLEABANE

Growing at lower elevations than the above subspecies, plants vary from 30-60 cm tall. The numerous heads are borne in an open panicle; they tend not to open as widely as those of variety *debilis*.

This variety has been located at the Pacific Crest Trail parking area near Road 23, alongside Trail 75 at the Salt Creek debris flow, and in Hellroaring Canyon. It is more likely to be seen in disturbed habitats, in contrast to the variety *debilis*.

### *Erigeron compositus* Pursh—DWARF MOUNTAIN FLEABANE

The few stems of this dwarfed alpine plant rise from a stout, woody base. The leaves are mostly basal, hairy, with long and slender stalks, the blades divided into 3 segments, each divided again into 3 segments. There is usually just one head on each 5-10 cm-long stem. The rays are whitish to light pink, but are sometimes absent altogether.

A relatively common alpine plant at the mountain, it is found on the summit of Little Mount Adams at an elevation of 6,800 feet. One of the highest elevation plants located for this study, it was collected by Paul Dixon at over 9,200 feet on the South Climb route; the plants were just 2 cm tall. It also grows alongside the trail above Hellroaring Overlook at 6,600 feet, and is known from the Pacific Crest Trail, north of Trail 64.

### *Erigeron glacialis* (Nutt.) A. Nelson var. *glacialis* SUBALPINE FLEABANE

Formerly named *E. peregrinus* ssp. *callianthemus* var. *callianthemus,* unbranched short-hairy stems range from 30-60 cm tall on this common subalpine daisy. The 5-20 cm long alternate basal leaves are spoon-shaped and stalked. The smaller stem leaves are lanceolate. The 2.5-4 cm broad heads are borne 1 per stem; the rays are lavender to rose-purple. The narrow phyllaries are spreading and minutely glandular. The pappus is simple and composed of whitish to light brown, fine bristles.

Occasionally, as at High Camp, plants are found that are just 10 to 20 cm tall, with much reduced leaves on the flowering stems. Such plants were once named *E. peregrinus* ssp. *scaposus.*

This characteristic meadow dweller is cosmopolitan and common, even abundant in some places. It may be seen at Babyshoe, Bird Creek, and Midway Meadows. It is also known from a Suksdorf collection at Hellroaring Canyon. It is known to reach 7,000 feet on the east side of Mount Adams.

### *Erigeron inornatus* (A. Gray) A. Gray var. *inornatus* RAYLESS FLEABANE

This perennial rises from a root crown and stout taproot to a height of 20-90 cm. Often with spreading hairs on the lower stems, the leaves are constant in size along the stem and lack a basal tuft; they are up to 5 cm long and linear or linear-oblong. There are several heads, and the involucre is 3-7 mm high, mostly hairless, with strongly overlapping bracts. Rays are absent in this species: the 4 disk flowers in each head are less than 3 mm long. The pappus consists of numerous fine bristles.

Found on dry, rocky sites in middle elevations east of the Cascades, this is a rare species at Mount Adams, known from a Henderson collection made on the upper Klickitat River.

### *Erigeron linearis* (Hook.) Piper—DESERT YELLOW FLEABANE

A slender perennial, 5-30 cm tall that rises from a branched rootstock, this fleabane is distinctive for the color of its rays, yellow instead of the usual white to pink or purple. The linear, basal leaves are 1.5-9 cm long, less than 3 mm wide, and stiffly hairy. The stem leaves are much smaller. The disk is 8-13 mm wide and the involucre 4-7 mm high; the latter is stiffly hairy and sometimes glandular. There are 15-45 yellow rays, 4-11 mm long. The corolla is 3.5-5.3 mm long, and the pappus is composed of 10-20 bristles, with a few outer scales.

Found in dry, rocky habitats east of the Cascades, this species is known from a Cotton collection made at Snipes Mountain on the southeast side of the mountain.

### *Erigeron speciosus* (Lindl.) DC. var. *speciosus*—SHOWY DAISY

This hairless, tufted perennial ranges from 30-50 cm in height and bears lanceolate, untoothed leaves. Arranged in a flat-topped cluster, there are 3-5 heads per stem. The numerous rays are violet and the double pappus is composed of bristles and scales.

Certain plants found at Mount Adams and elsewhere at lower elevations in the Washington Cascades were once called *Erigeron subtrinervis* var. *conspicuous.* These were said to differ from *E. speciosus* in being short-hairy on the stems and ciliate on the leaf margins. The *Flora of North America* does recognize *E. subtrinervis* as a distinct species but says that the var. *conspicuous* is synonymous with *E. speciosus.*

Less common than *E. glacialis* var. *glacialis,* this species is found at Grand Meadow and alongside the road up Snipes Mountain.

### *Eriophyllum* Lag. – ERIOPHYLLUM

Two varieties of the showy "Oregon Sunshine" are found at Mount Adams. They differ in the size of the flowering heads, although there may be some overlap. Typically, variety *lanatum* has more rays. The flowers are bright yellow, and the leaves are somewhat wooly. The phyllaries are in 1 or 2 series. The fruit is an achene and the pappus is composed of thin scales. The leaves are alternate, deeply cut in variety *lanatum* and merely with small teeth in variety *integrifolium.*

1 Heads large, involucre 9-12 mm high; rays 1-2 cm long ........... ........................................................... *E. lanatum* var. *lanatum*

1 Heads small, involucre 6-10 mm high, rays 5-12 mm long .............. .................................................. *E. lanatum* var. *integrifolium*

### *Eriophyllum lanatum* (Pursh) Forbes var. *integrifolium* (Hook.) Smiley
### WOOLY YELLOW DAISY, OREGON SUNSHINE

With smaller heads than the next variety, the involucre is only 6-10 mm high and the rays 5-12 mm long in this variety. The rays are fewer in number, typically either 5 or 8. The leaves are 3-toothed at the tips, or may be undivided.

A middle elevation to subalpine plant at the mountain, this variety is seen in open, seasonally moist to dry places. It has been found on the Ridge of Wonders, the Muddy River Canyon, the summit of Little Mount Adams at 6,800 feet, at the DNR quarry, and alongside Road 2329 on the north side at 4,150 feet.

### *Eriophyllum lanatum* (Pursh) Forbes var. *lanatum*
### WOOLY YELLOW DAISY, OREGON SUNSHINE

Brightly showy along rocky banks and other open areas, this plant is distinguished by gray-green foliage and stems as well as the large, bright yellow flower heads. The tufted stems may reach 50 cm in height; both stems and leaves are loosely wooly. The leaves are pinnately lobed or divided. The 2.5-4.5 cm broad heads have 6-15 ligules and are borne one per stem. The involucre is 10-12 mm high and the pappus consists of 4-12 small, translucent scales.

Collected by Flett and Heidenreich, this is a variety more typical in moister habitats at middle elevations than var. *integrifolium*. Label data is not given for these collections, but they were probably made on the south and southeast sides of Mount Adams. It is also seen on rocky banks at 4,000 feet on Road 23, near the Pacific Crest Trail crossing.

### *Eucephalus* Nutt.—ASTER

Formerly included in the genus *Aster*, from a short distance these two *Eucephalus* species certainly have a conventional aster "gestalt." They are fibrous rooted and lack a taproot; there are multiple heads per stem and the phyllaries are keeled but not glandular. *E. ledophyllus* is common and wide-ranging while *E. glaucescens*, a strikingly beautiful plant, is found only on dry hillsides southeast of the mountain.

1 Leaves glaucous, narrow and 5-10 times longer than broad .............................................................................. *E. glaucescens*

1 Leaves not glaucous, wider and about 3 times as long as broad ................................................... *E. ledophyllus* var. *ledophyllus*

### *Eucephalus glaucescens* (A. Gray) Greene—KLICKITAT ASTER

The herbage of this 4-15 dm tall plant is glaucous and hairless. The lower leaves are scale-like, while the stem leaves are even-sized and narrowly lanceolate, 3.5-9 cm long. There are multiple heads, and the involucre is 7-9 mm high, with overlapping, sharply- tipped, keeled bracts. The rays are purple and number about 13, although occasionally flowers with as few as 8 rays are found; they are 12-20 mm long. The pappus has a few short bristles. Well-grown plants may have dozens of stems.

A species with limited distribution, from Mount Adams south to the Columbia River, it is found in middle elevation to subalpine sites, including the DNR Quarry, the Island Springs trail, and Hellroaring Canyon, where Suksdorf found it.

#### ***Eucephalus ledophyllus* (A. Gray) Greene var. *ledophyllus***
#### **CASCADE ASTER**

The stems are tufted on this common, 30-90 cm tall aster. The 2-5 cm long leaves are lanceolate-elliptical, hairless and dark green on the upper side but hairy or wooly beneath. The lower stem leaves are smaller, often withering by flowering time. The heads are configured in a loose, flat-topped cluster, and the 7-11 mm long phyllaries are narrowly lanceolate and keeled. The light to dark purple rays are up to 2 cm long. The pappus is of whitish bristles.

Found at elevations from 4,500 to nearly 7,000 feet, this species is common from middle elevation to the lower subalpine environments, preferring wet habitats, including meadows, streamsides, and slopes. It grows along Hellroaring Creek at the Island Springs Trail crossing, as well as at Bench Lake on the southeast side. It is found at Midway Meadows and is known from a Henderson specimen on the north side at 5,000 feet.

### ***Eurybia* (Cass.) S.F. Gray—ASTER**

#### ***Eurybia radulina* (A. Gray) G.L. Nesom—ROUGHLEAF ASTER**

This 10-70 cm tall perennial has a spreading rootstock. The stems and undersides of the leaves are sparsely to densely short-hairy. The leaves are firm and sharply toothed, and up to 10 cm long, with the largest just above the stem base; the upper leaves are wider than the lower. Numerous heads are borne in a flat-topped, short inflorescence. The involucre is 6-9 mm high, and the bract scales are overlapping; they are purple-margined and sometimes green-tipped. The rays are white to purple and 8-12 mm long, and the disk flowers 7-8 mm long. The pappus is composed of various length bristles.

Formerly named *Aster radulinus*, this is a middle elevation to subalpine species of dry forest, found between 5,000 and 6,500 feet. It grows in an oak grove at the DNR quarry and was found by Paul Slichter alongside the Island Springs trail. It is also known on Little Mount Adams.

## *Gnaphalium* L.—CUDWEED

### *Gnaphalium palustre* Nutt.—WESTERN MARSH CUDWEED

A small annual, typically ranging between 3 and 15 cm in height, this species bears multiple branches, covered with long, soft hairs. The 1-3.5 cm leaves are oblanceolate or oblong. The leafy bracted, densely-clustered heads are 3 mm high, with densely wooly hairs below. The bracts are brown, with whitish tips; they do not overlap. The pappus bristles are distinct.

Preferring moist, open habitats, this species is known from the DNR Quarry, where it grows only in a vernally moist spot, on a south-facing stony slope.

## *Helianthella* Torr. & A. Gray—HELIANTHELLA

### *Helianthella uniflora* (Nutt.) Torr. & A. Gray var. *douglasii* (Torr. & A. Gray) W.A. Weber—DOUGLAS'S HELIANTHELLA

Clustered stems from 20-120 cm tall, rising from a branched rootstock, characterize this species. The stems are hairy or sometimes smooth below, the leaves lanceolate to elliptic, 3-nerved, and up to 15 cm long. The lower leaves are smaller than the upper leaves and more oblanceolate in shape. There is one large, striking head per leafy stem, composed of 13 rays (occasionally as many as 21) from 2-4.5 cm long. The involucral bracts are hairy along the edges.

A species of open woods, this variety is an eastern Cascade plant, rare at Mount Adams. It is known from an open, south-facing slope among ponderosa pine along Hellroaring Creek on the trail to Island Springs.

## *Hemizonella* (A. Gray) A. Gray—TARWEED

### *Hemizonella minima* (A. Gray) A. Gray—SMALL TARWEED

Typically no more than 10 cm tall and softly short-hairy and very glandular above, this widely spreading annual bears linear, opposite leaves 1-2 cm long. The heads are borne both in the forks of the stems and in small cymes at branch ends. The involucre is 2-4 mm high and has viscous glands; the rays are very small, and the achenes have an incurved beak at the tip.

Formerly included with *Madia*, this species has been reassigned to the genus *Hemizonella* based upon differences in its cellular and molecular biology. One subtle difference is seen in the mature achenes: in *Hemizonella*, they are compressed.

Preferring dry, open woods, this uncommon species is found along the Pineway Trail at 4,900 feet and along Trail 71 near the Aiken Lava Flow on the south side of the mountain. It is found, as well, at the DNR quarry.

### *Heterotheca* Cass.—FALSE GOLDENASTER

#### *Heterotheca oregona* (Nutt.) Shinners var. *oregona*
#### OREGON GOLDENASTER

This is a perennial that may be somewhat woody at the base. One to several stems reach to about 40 cm high and bear numerous leaves that are 3-4 cm long, lanceolate to elliptical, and pointed at the tips. Three to 5 heads are borne in a flat-topped inflorescence. The involucre is about 1 cm high, composed of several series of slender, overlapping bracts that are violet-colored at their pointed tips. Ray flowers are absent and the disk flowers are yellow. The pappus is of slender bristles. An out ring of very small, bristle-like scales is often found. The achene is slender and short-hairy.

The authors collected a single stem of this plant: it had been broken at a height of 20 cm after which a subsidiary stem developed, bearing a single head. The description above is of a typical plant.

Found once, at Muddy Meadows on level ground above the moister part of the meadow, growing in deep soil that had become fairly dry.

### *Hieracium* L.—HAWKWEED

These perennial herbs exude a milky sap. All except for *H. albiflorum* bear yellow ray flowers; that common species has white flowers. There are no disk flowers. The phyllaries are in 1-3 series and are ornamented variously with hairs and glands (visible with a hand lens). The pappus is composed of stiff, brown bristles. One, *H. caespitosum*, is a weed found along meadow edges.

1 Flowers white ........................................................ *H. albiflorum*
1 Flowers yellow ........................................................ 2

2(1) Plants with runners ............................................ *H. caespitosum*
2 Plants without runners ........................................................ 3

3(2) Leaves hairless; stems leafless ...................................... *H. tristle*
3 Leaves short-hairy or hairy; stems with one or more leaves .......... ........................................................ *H. scouleri*

#### *Hieracium albiflorum* Hook.—WHITE HAWKWEED

The slender, unbranched stems of this perennial are long-hairy near the base, hairless or nearly so above, and 40-80 cm tall. The 10-15 cm long lower stem leaves are oblanceolate, and borne on slender stalks. The upper leaves are not stalked and are lanceolate to elliptical. Numerous heads with white ray flowers are grouped at the top of the stems; each is about 1 cm broad. The phyllaries are linear-lanceolate, hairless, or with a few simple hairs.

Common, this middle elevation species is found in open places in forests, including roadsides, drier wooded sites, and even old burn sites. It grows alongside Roads 034, 23, 82, and 8040. Specimens are also known from the Pineway trailhead, a small lava flow near King Mountain, and at Hellroaring Canyon.

### ***Hieracium caespitosum*** **Dumort.—MEADOW HAWKWEED**

Capable of spreading widely from its slender runners, the stems of this weedy perennial range from 30-60 cm in height. The roughly hairy leaves are lanceolate to oblanceolate; and there are typically two smaller leaves on the stem. The 10-20 heads are configured in a rather dense, flattish panicle. The yellow rays are about 8 mm long and only slightly exceed the involucre. The heads range to 1 cm broad and the phyllaries are covered with coarse, black, stalked glands and whitish hairs.

This weed grows on the gravelly roadside near Grand Meadow as well as at the borders of Babyshoe Meadow.

### ***Hieracium scouleri*** **Hook.—SCOULER'S HAWKWEED**

The 30-60 cm tall slender stems of this perennial are long-hairy below and short-hairy near the tops. The 4-12 cm long leaves are untoothed, long-hairy, and bristly but also glaucous. The lower leaves are lanceolate to oblanceolate and tapered at the base to the stalk, while the reduced upper leaves lack stalks and are lanceolate in shape. The 7-20 heads are 1.5-2 cm broad, and the phyllaries are glandular, long-hairy with white, minute, starlike hairs.

Plants with leaves that are not glaucous and with relatively smaller flower heads have been called *H. cynoglossoides* and are found at lower elevations within the plant's range; that species is not recognized as distinct in the *Flora of North America.*

Growing in dry open sites, often in middle elevation forests, this species is found on the Round-the-Mountain trail at 5,900 feet, at the gate at Bird Creek, and on the trail northeast of Bench Lake. It is also known from Babyshoe Meadow, from a Flett collection along the upper Klickitat River, and Suksdorf collections at Hellroaring Valley.

### ***Hieracium triste*** **Willdenow *ex* Sprengel —SLENDER HAWKWEED**

Less than 30 cm tall, this small hawkweed bears basal leaves only. The 3-8 cm long leaves are spoon-shaped to oval, even or minutely toothed, and mostly hairless. The 4-7 small heads are borne on slender stems in a racemelike inflorescence; each is composed of yellow rays and is about 1 cm high. The narrow, pointed phyllaries have black hairs and black hairlike glands. This species was formerly called *Hieracium gracile.*

A species of dry subalpine meadows and forest openings, this is a common hawkweed at the mountain. It grows along the South Climb trail at 6,800 feet, and is also found along the Killen Creek and Riley Creek trails, alongside Road 2329, and at Hellroaring Canyon.

### *Hulsea* Torr. & A. Gray

#### *Hulsea nana* A. Gray—DWARF ALPINEGOLD

Small, this taprooted perennial bears glandular-hairy stems and leaves. The thickened, gray-green, hairy to wooly leaves are up to 5 cm long, lobed, and arranged in a basal cluster. A single bright yellow head, up to 3 cm broad, is borne at the end of each stem. The phyllaries are lanceolate, and the pappus is composed of translucent scales, joined at their bases.

A very showy species when in flower and locally common in higher subalpine to alpine dry, rocky sites, plants are regularly seen on the higher portions of the South Climb trail at elevations from 7,300 to 8,300 feet. It is found on the summit of Little Mountain Adams, as well as on the trail above Hellroaring Overlook. On the north, it grows above High Camp. The plant is usually out in the open by itself and is, perhaps, intolerant of competition.

### *Hypochaeris* L.—CAT'S-EAR

#### *Hypochaeris radicata* L.—ROUGH CAT'S-EAR

A basal rosette of pinnately lobed leaves up to 15 cm long and a milky sap help distinguish this weedy perennial. The "rough" refers to the stiff hairs on the leaves. The stems are branched and leafless and may reach 50 cm in height. The 2-3 cm broad heads are numerous and composed of yellow ray flowers only. The nearly linear phyllaries overlap, and the achene bears a long beak topped with a pappus of feathery white hairs.

A common roadside weed, it is found alongside Road 8040 (the South Climb road) as well as near Road 23. It does not invade meadows or other intact habitats at Mount Adams.

### *Lapsana* L.—NIPPLEWORT

#### *Lapsana communis* L.—COMMON NIPPLEWORT

This taprooted annual consists of a tall, slender, branched stem with milky sap. The lower leaves reach 10 cm in length, are ovate and stalked, toothed, and mostly hairless. The upper stem leaves are narrower and stalkless. The numerous heads are of yellow ray flowers only. A pappus is lacking.

Found on the roadside near Swampy Meadows on the west side, this is an uncommon weed, typically of shady areas and amidst low brush; it does not move into undisturbed places.

### *Leucanthemum* Mill.—DAISY

#### *Leucanthemum vulgare* Lam.—OXEYE DAISY

Most easily recognized by the large white flower heads, this weedy perennial bears alternate leaves that are lobed, toothed, and spoon-shaped. The upper stem leaves are smaller. A single 3-6 cm-broad head per stem consists of a broad center of yellow disk flowers and numerous white rays. The phyllaries are ovate, greenish at the center, with papery margins. A pappus is lacking.

Found along roadsides and other disturbed areas, this showy species grows alongside Road 8040 (the South Climb road), near the Pacific Crest Trail at Potato Hill, at the edges of Muddy Meadows, and at the horse camp near Hellroaring Creek, northeast of Bench Lake.

### *Madia* Molina—TARWEED

These are small, slender annual species with opposite, untoothed, and softly to roughly hairy leaves. The stems, leaves, and involucre are glandular and pleasantly to unpleasantly scented. The phyllaries are curved to enclose the achenes of the ray flowers; both the ray and disk flowers are yellow. In *M. glomerata*, the flower heads are densely clustered. A pappus is absent. *Madia minima* has been renamed *Hemizonella minima*.

Both species are found at or close to the quarry maintained by the Washington Department of Natural Resources on Road K6900, at 4,000 to 4,100 feet on the southeast side of Mount Adams. While native, each of these species is a disturbance specialist and takes advantage of the roads and logged tracts here.

1 Heads spindle-shaped, densely clustered; rays inconspicuous ....... ........ *M. glomerata*
1 Heads ovoid or urn-shaped, barely clustered; rays 4-7 mm long ..... ........ *M. gracilis*

#### *Madia glomerata* Hook.—MOUNTAIN TARWEED

This glandular, hairy annual ranges from 10-80 cm in height, and bears simple or sometimes ascending branches. The 2-7 cm long leaves are linear to lancelike. The heads are densely clustered ("glomerate"), and the involucre is spindle-shaped. The 2 mm long rays number only 1-3, or are sometimes lacking. The fertile disk flowers are numerous.

A species of dry open habitat in moderate elevation, it is known from the DNR quarry, where it grows at 4,100 feet on an open, sunny slope in woods dominated by Garry oak.

### *Madia gracilis* (Sm.) D.D. Keck—SLENDER TARWEED

A roughly-hairy annual that is glandular near the top, the stems may vary from 10-100 cm tall. The leaves are 3-10 cm long, and the heads are borne in a racemelike inflorescence. The 3-9 ray flowers are 4-7 mm long. The involucre is ovoid or broadly urn-shaped and 6-11 cm high. The achenes are flattened.

Uncommon at the mountain and preferring dry, disturbed, sunny sites at middle elevations, this species is found on the southeast side at the DNR quarry and at the end of Road 170.

### *Microseris* D. Don—MICROSERIS

Another dandelion-like genus with milky sap, these species also have showy, bright yellow flowers. Both are middle elevation species of open habitats at the mountain. The basal leaves are narrowly lanceolate and untoothed. The flowers are composed of rays only and borne singly on the leafless stalks. The bracts of the involucre are overlapping. The achenes are prominently nerved, and the pappus is composed of slender bristles.

The definition of the genus *Microseris* has changed over the years: *M. borealis* was moved into the genus from *Apargidium*, while another plant, *Nothocalais alpestris*, was moved out.

1 Pappus brownish; plants of perennially moist meadows ........................................................................ *M. borealis*
1 Pappus white; plants of dry or seasonally moist places .............. ........................................................................ *M. nutans*

### *Microseris borealis* (Bong.) Schultz-Bip.—NORTHERN MICROSERIS

This taprooted perennial exudes a milky sap. The 6-15 cm long, narrowly lanceolate basal leaves are minutely toothed and hairless. The 2-3 cm broad solitary heads, borne on leafless stems, are composed of ray flowers only, and are bright yellow. Long-tapered and in 2-3 series, the phyllaries overlap to some degree. The pappus is composed of brownish, slender, barbed bristles.

Listed as "sensitive" by the Washington Natural Heritage Program, this species is most common in middle elevation wet meadows at Mount Adams. It is found at Muddy Meadows (elevation 4,400 feet), and

Bathtub Meadow, at 4,100 feet, as well as in large numbers at Takh Takh Meadow.

#### *Microseris nutans* (Hook.) Schultz-Bip.—NODDING MICROSERIS

Varying from smooth to covered in small hairs, this perennial has 1 to several thick roots and typically reaches only 10 cm in height but often bears several heads. The narrow basal leaves are divided into irregular lobes. The common name refers to the immature heads, which nod on their stems. The involucre is typically about 1 cm high, and the outer bracts are much shorter than the inner bracts. The achenes taper and are 5-8 mm long, and may be softly hairy. The pappus consists of 15-20 narrow scales, each topped with feathery bristles.

Primarily a middle elevation species in habitats ranging from seasonally moist meadows to dry roadsides and trail borders, this species is fairly common at the mountain. It grows alongside the Stagman Ridge trail at 5,000 feet, near the road up Snipes Mountain, at Crofton Butte, in meadows near the DNR quarry, and near Road 82 (at 4,000 and 4,800 feet), and Road 034 on the north side of the mountain.

### *Mycelis* Cass.—WALL-LETTUCE

#### *Mycelis muralis* (L.) Dumort.—WALL-LETTUCE

Slender spreading rootstocks enable this taprooted, weedy biennial to invade roadsides, as well as undisturbed areas. Reaching 30-70 cm in height, the stems of the plants exude a milky sap. The basal and stem leaves are deeply divided into wide pinnate lobes, with the broad terminal lobe resembling an ivy leaf. Starlike heads, 1.5 cm broad, are composed of 5 yellow ray flowers only. The 1.5-2 mm long slender phyllaries form a narrow tube. The achene has a short beak and a pappus of long white bristles.

One of the more common weeds at Mount Adams, wall-lettuce grows alongside Road 82 at the Pineway Trail trailhead, and east of Bunnell Butte near Road 070. Unusual among the weedy plants at Mount Adams, this species has the ability to grow away from disturbed areas, especially into open forests.

## *Nothocalais* (A. Gray) Greene—PRAIRIE DANDELION

### *Nothocalais alpestris* (A. Gray) Chambers
### SMOOTH MOUNTAIN DANDELION

Taprooted, this perennial bears basal leaves only, and exudes a milky sap. The 5-15 cm long leaves are spoon-shaped to lanceolate, hairless, and have a few slender teeth that may point toward the base of the leaf. The 2-3.5 cm broad heads are composed of numerous yellow ray flowers; disk flowers are absent. The phyllaries consist of 2 series, with the outer series ovate-lanceolate and overlapping; occasionally the phyllaries have small purple spots. The achene is slender and beakless, and the pappus consists of long white bristles.

A common, showy plant of moist subalpine meadows, it grows alongside the trail above Hellroaring Overlook at 6,600 feet. Plants are also found at the Cold Springs trailhead (elevation 5,600 feet), and at Muddy River Canyon, the latter a Suksdorf collection.

## *Oreostemma* Greene—ASTER

### *Oreostemma alpigenum* (Torr. & A. Gray) Greene var. *alpigenum*
### ALPINE ASTER

Distinguished by a single head on short stems (less than 20 cm tall), the showy, 3-4 cm broad flowers also set this plant apart. A few small, narrow, bractlike leaves line the stem, while the lower leaves are hairless, oblanceolate, and 3-8 cm long. The 5-12 mm long phyllaries are linear and overlapping and the pappus consists of white bristles.

Common in middle elevation wet to dry meadows and on rocky slopes, this species was formerly named *Aster alpigenus*. Among other locations, it grows in the saddle on the north side of Little Mount Adams at 6,400 feet, at Takh Takh Meadow (elevation 4,600 feet), and at Hellroaring Canyon.

## *Packera* Á. & D. Löve –RAGWORT

Formerly included in the genus *Senecio*, the characteristics of the representative species at the mountain are similar to the senecios. The leaves of *Packera* are typically shallowly lobed in two of the species or deeply toothed with lobes at the base of the leaves. They are alternate and reduced in size upwards on the stems. The flowers are yellow, with both disk and ray flowers present; they are borne in flat-topped clusters, again in two species, or as a single head, in *P. streptanthifolia.*

*P. bolanderi* is rare at the mountain, while the other two species are commonly seen in openings, including middle elevation meadows, and alongside trails. *P. streptanthifolia* grows in subalpine meadows as well, and to elevations of 6,500 feet.

1 Basal leaves thick, shallowly palmately lobed, stem leaves smaller, tending to be pinnate with a larger terminal lobe ........................................................... *P. bolanderi* var. *harfordii*

1 Basal leaves not thickened, or lobed; stem leaves not lobed, but may be sharply toothed ........................................................ 2

2(1) Basal leaves heart-shaped, sharply toothed; stem leaves somewhat pinnate, sharply toothed ............... *P. pseudaurea* var. *pseudaurea*

2 Basal leaves not heart shaped, elliptic to rounded, with rounded teeth, or somewhat lobed; stem leaves reduced, rounded ............ ........................................................... *P. streptanthifolia*

### ***Packera bolanderi*** **(A. Gray) W. A. Weber & Á. Löve var. *harfordii* (Greenman) Trock & T. M. Barkley—HARFORD'S RAGWORT**

From a branching rhizome, this perennial ranges from 10-60 dm in height; the herbage is for the most part hairless except for fine tufts of wooly hairs at the base and in the leaf axils. The 7 cm long and wide basal leaves are thickened, heart-shaped, palmately lobed, typically with teeth, and borne on stalks; there may be small leaf segments below the large terminal leaf. The stems bear smaller leaves. The yellow rays are 6-12 mm long, and the 5-7 mm high involucre is hairy.

Formerly named *Senecio bolanderi,* this species is rare at the mountain, known from a single Flett collection, made in Skamania County. It is more typically a southern plant, Mount Adams thus being at the northern end of its range.

### ***Packera pseudaurea*** **(Rydb.) W.A. Weber & Á. Löve var. *pseudaurea* FALSEGOLD GROUNDSEL**

A fibrous-rooted perennial rising from a spreading rootstock, this common wetland plant becomes hairless with age. The thin, basal leaves are borne on long stalks, and are truncated at the base and edged with sharp forward-pointing teeth. The stem leaves are typically stalked and pinnately divided at their bases. There are multiple flower heads, 8-13 mm wide; the involucre is 5-8 mm high. The yellow rays are 6-10 mm long.

Formerly named *Senecio pseudaureus,* this species grows in middle elevation wet meadows as well as open, moist places, below 5,000 feet. Plants are found alongside the Island Springs trail, at Midway Meadows, and near Road 115.

### ***Packera streptanthifolia*** **(Greene) W.A. Weber & Á. Löve ROCKY MOUNTAIN GROUNDSEL**

This species may reach 30 cm in height but is often much less. The blades of the lower leaves are 3-4 cm long, stalked, rounded to ovate in shape, and coarsely toothed. The 2-4 cm long upper stem leaves are oblong, lobed, and stalkless. The single heads are about 3 cm broad.

Formerly named *Senecio cymbalarioides*, this is a fairly common species at Mount Adams, growing in wet meadows from middle to subalpine elevations. It is found in Babyshoe and Grand Meadows. Plants growing at over 6,000 feet are common in the meadow at Foggy Flat; individuals also grow alongside the trail uphill from Muddy Meadows.

### *Petasites* Mill.—COLTSFOOT

#### *Petasites frigidus* (L.) Fries var. *palmatus* (Ait.) Cronq.
#### ARCTIC COLTSFOOT

An early season plant often was appearing as soon as the snow melts, the stems are clothed in short, wooly white hairs and many hairy bracts. The long-stalked rounded leaves are heart-shaped at the base and 10-40 cm broad; they are borne directly on the rootstock. The leaves appear after the 40 cm tall flowering stems. The heads bear both ray and disk flowers and are whitish to pinkish in color. The lanceolate phyllaries are hairy at the base and the pappus consists of white bristles.

The similar, high-elevation variety *nivalis* is absent from Mount Adams, although it is frequently seen at Mount Rainier and at the Goat Rocks.

Found along roadsides and moist banks, streams, and other wet places, the leaves alone distinguish this common, low to middle elevation species. It was collected by Suksdorf near both the White Salmon and Klickitat Rivers.

### *Pseudognaphalium* Kirp.—CUDWEED

Formerly included in the *Gnaphalium* genus, these species have disk flowers only. The flower heads are somewhat elongated and sometimes densely clustered at the top. The leaves are oblanceolate to linear. The pappus is composed of stiff bristles that fall separately.

These are middle elevations species of dry, open sites, preferring disturbed places.

1 Herbage glandular-hairy, sometimes with soft, wooly hairs on the lower surface ..................................................... *P. macounii*
1 Herbage not glandular, more or less covered with soft, wooly hairs . ........................................................................ *P. thermale*

#### *Pseudognaphalium macounii* (Greene) Kartesz
#### MACOUN'S CUDWEED

An annual or biennial, this simple to branched species ranges from 40-90 cm in height. The stem is glandular-hairy and the inflorescence is short hairy, or sometimes wooly and glandular near the base. The leaves extend down the stem at their bases; they are oblanceolate and 4-10 cm long while those near the top of the stem are linear-oblong. The heads are in compact clusters and the involucre is 5-7 mm high with yellowish to nearly white overlapping bracts. The pappus bristles are distinct.

Named *Gnaphalium viscosum* in Hitchcock, this is a species of forest openings. It is found at the DNR quarry, alongside Trail 75 at Salt Creek, and near Road 23.

### *Pseudognaphalium thermale* (E. E. Nelson) G. L. Nesom NORTHWESTERN CUDWEED

The slightly bowed stems number 1-4 and rise 20-70 cm from a taproot in this uncommon, dry habitat species. The stems and leaves are whitish with wooly hairs, the leaves are linear-oblong, 3-7 cm long below and shorter above. They run down the stem a short distance at their bases. Composed of disk flowers only, the heads are dull yellow in color. The phyllaries are papery and whitish and overlap in 3 distinct series. The pappus is composed of white bristles that are not united at their bases.

Formerly named *Gnaphalium microcephalum,* this native perennial is known from a single collection made by Beth Skaggs Ryan at Snipes Mountain.

## *Psilocarphus* Nutt.—WOOLYHEADS

### *Psilocarphus tenellus* Nutt. var. *tenellus*—SLENDER WOOLYHEADS

Erect when young, this slender annual transforms to a branched, prostrate, matted plant with age. It is sparsely hairy and the 4-15 mm long leaves are spatulate to oblong. There are 25-46 female flowers in the small, spherical heads, each of which is subtended by a 1.3-2.5 mm long bract. A true involucre of phyllaries is absent. The 0.6-1.2 mm long achenes are somewhat compressed, and oblanceolate to obovate in shape.

A species most typically found in dried or wet beds of vernal pools, it grows primarily south of Washington but was found at Mount Adams near Road 115 on the north side of the mountain at 4,450 feet.

## *Saussurea* DC.—SAWWORT

### *Saussurea americana* D.C. Eat.—AMERICAN SAWWORT

The common name refers to the closely-toothed leaf margins of this plant. The stems range from 50 to 120 cm tall and the lower leaves are ovate and about 15 cm long; they are reduced in size and more lanceolate further up the stem. The numerous purple heads are configured in a compact, flat-topped cluster composed of disk flowers only. The short-hairy phyllaries consist of several series and are ovate.

The double pappus has an inner ring of bristles united at the base, and an outer ring of shorter, scalelike bristles.

This common species grows from middle elevations to subalpine meadows on the southeast side of the mountain. It is found along the road to Bench Lake and on the lower part of the Island Springs Trail, and is also known from a Suksdorf collection at Muddy River Canyon.

### *Senecio* L.—GROUNDSEL

Tall, fibrous-rooted perennials, with leafy stems and flat-topped clusters of yellow or white-rayed flowers, these are most typically middle elevation species of open sites. The leaves are toothed and alternate on the stems and vary from ovate-lanceolate to triangular; basal tufts of leaves may be present. The phyllaries are slender and pointed. The pappus is composed of soft, white, slender bristles.

Both species are natives. Often growing on disturbed ground, the senecios also inhabit wet to dry meadows. The yellow-flowered plants are locally common.

1 Stem leaves not reduced upwards, narrowly triangular, the blade squared off at the base .......................................... *S. triangularis*
1 Stem leaves reduced upwards, ovate-lanceolate ...................... 2

2(1) Rays flowers yellow ...................... *S. integerrimus* var. *exaltatus*
2 Ray flowers white to cream ......... *S. integerrimus* var. *ochroleucus*

#### *Senecio integerrimus* Nutt. var. *exaltatus* (Nutt.) Cronq.
#### WESTERN SENECIO

A single flower on stems ranging from 10-60 cm in height, depending on the habitat, defines this perennial. The 3-15 cm long, oblanceolate lower leaves are tapered to a thick stalk and are covered with matted wooly hairs when young but become smooth with age; the stem leaves are much smaller. Numerous heads, each about 1 cm broad, with yellow rays make up a compact, flat-topped cluster. The phyllaries are black-tipped.

Common on middle elevation rocky slopes and open sites this species grows at Crofton Butte, the DNR Quarry, and alongside the trail at the end of Road 170.

#### *Senecio integerrimus* Nutt. var. *ochroleucus* (A. Gray) Cronq.
#### WHITE WESTERN SENECIO

Otherwise similar to variety *exaltatus*, the cream-colored or whitish ligules distinguish this less commonly found variety.

This somewhat unusual senecio, owing to flower color, grows near the trail at the end of Road 170 on an open slope in a logged area.

## Asteraceae

### *Senecio triangularis* Hook.—ARROWLEAF SENECIO

Tall and robust, the leafy stems of this senecio range from 50-100 cm in height. The narrowly triangular leaves are regularly toothed on the margins, heart-shaped or squared-off at the base, and borne on a short stalk. The numerous heads, each about 2 cm broad, are configured in a somewhat compact, flat-topped cluster.

A common species at the mountain, it is found in meadows, along stream banks, and in other open or brushy sites. It grows at Babyshoe Meadow, alongside the Muddy Meadows trail, and at Midway Meadows. Plants are also found near Road 23; Suksdorf collected specimens at Bird Creek Caves and Hellroaring Canyon.

### Solidago L.—GOLDENROD

These are perennial herbs, with alternate, undivided, toothed leaves. The leaves are fairly closely crowded on the stems. The flowers are yellow, with both disk and ray flowers. They are configured in pyramidal heads. The phyllaries are lanceolate, in several series, papery at the base, and greenish at the tip. The pappus is of slender, white bristles.

Late season flowers, the goldenrods are conspicuous and welcome wildflowers found throughout the region.

1 Middle elevation plants; basal leaves lacking; stems leaves lanceolate, about equally leafy above and below........................ ........................................................ *S. lepida* var. *salebrosa*

1 Subalpine to alpine plants: basal leaves obovate to oblanceolate; stem leaves reduced ...................................................... 2

2(1) Taller plants, to 30 cm; leaf stalks fringed with short hairs ............ ............................................. *S. multiradiata* var. *scopulorum*

2 Dwarf plants, to 10 cm tall; leaf stalks lacking hairs ...................... ......................................... *S. simplex* ssp. *simplex* var. *nana*

### Solidago lepida DC. var. salebrosa (Piper) Semple
### ROCKY MOUNTAIN CANADA GOLDENROD

The 50-200 cm tall stems of this goldenrod bear uniform leaves throughout the length of the stems. The leaves are 6-12 cm long, lanceolate, and toothed. There are many heads borne in an elongated, pyramid-shaped panicle. The heads have short ligules and are about 5 cm broad.

This tall native goldenrod has gone by the name *Solidago canadensis* for a very long time. A key difference is that the upper parts of *S. lepida* – leaves, stems, and involucres - bear short-stalked glands.

Relatively common alongside roads and in meadows, this species is known from Grand Meadow, Bench Lake, and Hellroaring Canyon.

### *Solidago multiradiata* Ait.—NORTHERN GOLDENROD

Up to 30 cm tall, this slender plant bears oblanceolate leaves that are gradually reduced in size and become more pointed at the tip near the top of the stem. The 2-8 cm long leaves are even or minutely toothed, and the stalks are fringed with short hairs. Composed of about 13 ray flowers, the heads are arranged in an open, flat-topped cluster. The phyllaries are in 2 overlapping series.

This uncommon species was collected at Devil's Garden, on the northeast flank of Mount Adams, by Beth Skaggs Ryan at 7,800 feet of elevation.

### *Solidago simplex* Kunth ssp. *simplex* var. *nana* (A. Gray) Ringius DWARF GOLDENROD

The leaves are reduced upward on this 10 cm tall goldenrod; they are spoon-shaped to oblanceolate, thickish, coarsely toothed, and up to 5 cm long. The margins of the leaf stalk are not fringed with hairs. A few heads (less than 10) are arranged in a short, compact, raceme-like inflorescence. The phyllaries barely overlap.

Relatively common in the subalpine to alpine regimes on talus slopes and ridge tops to about 7,000 feet, this tiny goldenrod is found alongside the trail above Hellroaring Overlook, at Hellroaring Canyon, and near High Camp on the north side.

### *Symphyotrichum* Nees—ASTER

The aster genus having been split by chromosomal and morphological considerations into several genera, *Symphyotrichum* species are characterized by multiple flower heads and phyllaries without glands or keels; the plants are without glands as well. They differ from *Eurybia,* a closely related genus, in the characteristics of the disk flowers, in which the terminal lobed portion is shorter than the tube. The flowers are purple to pinkish with many rays; the disk flowers are yellow.

Typically middle elevation meadow species, two are relatively common, while *S. foliaceum* (both varieties) is rare at the mountain.

1 Leaves toothed; outer involucral bracts membranous, thin, brownish ........................................ *S. subspicatum*

1 Leaves not toothed; outer involucral bracts not membranous, greenish ........................................ 2

2(1) Leaves and involucral bracts small, narrow and not leafy; the middle stem leaves less than 1 cm wide ........................................................................... *S. spathulatum* var. *spathulatum*

2 Leaves and involucral bracts relatively large and leafy; the middle stem leaves over 1 cm wide ............................................... 3

3(2) Plants less than 2.5 dm tall; involucral bracts with purple tips and margins ........................................... *S. foliaceum* var. *apricum*

3 Plants more than 2.5 dm tall; involucral bracts not purplish-tipped ... ........................................................ *S. foliaceum* var. *parryi*

### ***Symphyotrichum foliaceum*** **(DC.) G.L. Nesom var.** ***apricum*** **(A. Gray) G.L. Nesom—ALPINE LEAFY ASTER**

Fibrous-rooted from a spreading rootstock, this variety reaches as much as 25 cm in height. It may be prostrate or ascending, with stalked lower leaves that are oblanceolate to obovate, and sessile middle stem leaves, typically 5-12 cm long. The heads are solitary to sometimes many and the rose-purple to violet rays number 15-60 and are 1-2 cm long. The nearly leaf-like involucral bracts overlap and are most often purplish on the tips and margins, and the pappus is white to reddish.

A subalpine to alpine variety, and uncommon at the mountain, this was collected by Henderson on the "south slope" of Mount Adams.

### ***Symphyotrichum foliaceum*** **(DC.) G.L. Nesom var.** ***parryi*** **(D.C. Eat.) G.L. Nesom—LEAFY ASTER**

Typically with a few branches, this variety ranges from 20-60 cm in height. The 8-10 cm long lower stem leaves are oblanceolate, and have a winged stalk. The involucre typically is not purplish on the margins or tips.

A subalpine plant, as with var. *apricum*, this is an uncommon plant at the mountain. It was collected by Suksdorf at Hellroaring Canyon.

### ***Symphyotrichum spathulatum*** **(Lindl.) G.L. Nesom var.** ***spathulatum*** **WESTERN MOUNTAIN ASTER**

This fibrous-rooted perennial rises 20-50 cm tall from a creeping rootstock. The leaves are glabrous, the lower ones oblanceolate with stalks and the middle ones narrower and stalkless; they are 3-15 cm long. There are a few heads arranged in a leafy inflorescence, with the involucre 5-7 mm high, composed of narrow, overlapping bracts with sharp tips, purplish in color but green at the base. The blue to violet rays number 20-50 and are 6-15 mm long.

Formerly named *Aster occidentalis* var. *occidentalis*, this species inhabits middle elevation to subalpine meadows as well as open forests. Suksdorf collected it at Hellroaring Canyon. It also grows alongside Pineway Trail, and in the dry meadows alongside Road 5603, south of Potato Hill.

### *Symphyotrichum subspicatum* (Nees) G.L. Nesom
### DOUGLAS'S ASTER

This stout aster varies from 30-100 cm in height and bears branched stems with lanceolate leaves. The stem leaves are either short-stalked, or not clasping at the base if stalked; they are toothed and lanceolate to oblong. The numerous, 1.5-2.5 cm broad heads are composed of light purple ligules and yellow disk flowers. The phyllaries are firm, with papery margins, and the pappus is a light reddish-brown.

Formerly named *Aster subspicatus* var. *subspicatus,* this is an uncommon middle elevation species, collected by Suksdorf at an "island" in Bird Creek, and noted also by the authors at the Pacific Crest Trail crossing of Road 23.

## *Tanacetum* L.—TANSY

### *Tanacetum vulgare* L.—COMMON TANSY

With glandular leaves but otherwise hairless, the stout, branched stems of this robust weed range from 50-100 cm in height. The 10-20 cm long, fern-like leaves are short-stalked or sometimes stalkless and are divided into small, linear, sharp leaflets. The numerous heads are yellow, about 1 cm broad, and arranged in flat-topped clusters.

Found along middle elevation roadsides, this weed is, fortunately, rare at Mount Adams: it is likely that the study area is too high in elevation to suit the species. It grows along Road 23 near the Pacific Crest Trail crossing.

## *Taraxacum* F.H Wiggers—DANDELION

### *Taraxacum officinale* F.H. Wiggers
### COMMON DANDELION

A basal rosette of hairless, pinnately lobed, toothed leaves help to distinguish this familiar perennial weed. The stems exude a milky sap, and the bright yellow head is composed of ray flowers only. Solitary, it is 2-3.5 cm broad and borne on a naked stem. The phyllaries are in 2 series, with the outer series bent backward at the tips. The pappus, composed of a tuft of slender white bristles, is shaped like a parachute. The achene is typically olive-brown in color.

No native species of *Taraxacum* has yet been found at Mount Adams.

Well-known and a weed of disturbed areas along roadsides, trails, and openings in the forest, this middle elevation species grows in such habitats close to the roads at the mountain. It can be seen alongside Road 2329 close to Midway Meadows, at Swampy Meadows, Muddy Meadows, and near the DNR quarry.

### *Tonestus* A. Nels.—GOLDENWEED

#### *Tonestus lyallii* (A. Gray) A. Nels.—LYALL'S GOLDENWEED

With leafy stems up to 20 cm tall, this is a low-growing perennial herb of alpine habitats. The 1-5 cm long leaves are spoon-shaped to oblanceolate, and finely glandular-hairy. The 2-3 cm broad head is solitary, with numerous yellow ray and disk flowers. The phyllaries are lanceolate in shape, and glandular; the pappus is composed of hairlike white bristles.

Uncommon at Mount Adams, this species occurs on alpine ridges and slopes and was collected by Henderson on a rocky ridge "above the glaciers and Muddy Canyon." This probably points to a location between the Ridge of Wonders and Sunrise Camp, between 7,500 and about 8,000 feet.

### *Tragopogon* L.—SALSIFY

#### *Tragopogon dubius* Scop.—YELLOW SALSIFY

A lovely weed that exudes a milky sap, this species has pale yellow flowers, 5-10 cm broad, composed of ray flowers only. The stems range from 30-100 cm tall, and have long, grasslike leaves. Both stems and leaves are glaucous. The phyllaries are composed in 1 series, 4-6 cm long, and linear-lanceolate in shape. The 2 cm long pappus consists of feathery bristles that are united for a distance above the achene.

Fairly common, this middle elevation weed grows along roadsides and in other open, disturbed places. It is found near Road 23 south of the Pacific Crest Trail crossing, along Road 8040 and 82, alongside the road up Snipes Mountain, and at the DNR quarry.

## Berberidaceae Juss.—BARBERRY FAMILY

This family is represented by three genera and five species at the mountain. The genera are quite dissimilar in appearance; three species (*Berberis*) are "Oregon grapes," shrubs with spiny leaves, and the other two are herbs. All have a superior ovary consisting of 1 pistil. *Berberis* and *Vancouveria* flowers have 6 sepals, 6 petals, and 6 stamens. *Achlys* lacks petals and sepals altogether—the white flower color is attributed to the mass of 9-13 stamens and the single pistil.

1 Shrubs with woody stems; leaves pinnate and bearing marginal spines .......... *Berberis*
1 Herbs; leaves compound but not pinnate, the margins not bearing spines .......... 2

2(1) Leaves divided once; flowers in a spike, petals absent ........ *Achlys*
2 Leaves divided two or three times; flowers in a panicle, petals present ........................................................... *Vancouveria*

### *Achlys* DC.—VANILLA-LEAF

#### *Achlys triphylla* (Sm.) DC.—VANILLA-LEAF

The common name comes from the vanilla scent of the dried leaves. Growing from spreading rootstocks, this species may form extensive patches. The plants are 20-40 cm tall and distinguished by the roundish, large, light green leaves, each divided into 3 lobes. Each lobe is triangular to fan-shaped; in total 4-11 cm long and 4-8 cm wide, with the central leaflet the smallest and 3-toothed. Both sepals and petals are absent: the flowers are actually "balls" of 9-13 long, white stamens that are arranged in a tall slender spike. The fruit is a short, curved achene.

Common in middle elevation forests and alongside trails and roads, this cosmopolitan species is found near Road 82, Road 2329 at Trail 7B, and alongside Road 8040 (South Climb road).

### *Berberis* L.—OREGON-GRAPE

These are prostrate to upright, shrubby plants with woody stems and evergreen leaves. The leaves are sharply tipped and pinnately compound. They are palmately or pinnately veined, an important distinction to observe. A long raceme of bright yellow flowers is borne at or near the ends of the branches; each flower is composed of several whorls of perianth segments, difficult to distinguish as petals and sepals. The fruit is a glaucous, dark blue-purple berry.

1 Leaflets number 9-19, palmately veined ...................... *B. nervosa*
1 Leaflets number 5-9, pinnately veined .................................... 2

2(1) Typically upright shrubs; leaflets twice as long as broad, with prominent spine-tipped teeth, glossy on upper side ... *B. aquifolium*
2 Trailing shrubs; leaflets less than twice as long as broad, with small spines, dull to glossy on upper surface ........................ *B. repens*

#### *Berberis aquifolium* Pursh—OREGON-GRAPE

With erect stems, these 1-3 m tall plants are easily recognized by the dark green, spiny leaves. The leaflets number 5-9 and are oval to ovate, glossy on the upper surface, and widely spaced on the stems. The yellow flowers are numerous in a cluster of racemes, 5-8 cm long.

A middle elevation species of forests and open sites, it is found on the south aspects of the mountain along Road 8040, at the end of Road

170, and at "Cave Cliffs," a place whose location is unclear but that is in Bird Creek region, where it was collected by Suksdorf.

### *Berberis nervosa* Pursh—DWARF OREGON-GRAPE

Less than 50 cm tall, this species is much shorter than *B. aquifolium*, and is further distinguished by very stout, erect stems. The leaves ascend upward and are closely spaced. The 11-19 leaflets are spiny, glossy on both surfaces, and lanceolate to ovate in shape. The yellow flowers are borne in dense clusters of short racemes.

A middle elevation forest species, often of drier sites, it is locally common on the north and west sides of the mountain. It is found alongside Road 034 and Road 023, and the Pacific Crest Trail near Swampy Meadows.

### *Berberis repens* Lindl.—CREEPING OREGON-GRAPE

Similar to *B. nervosa* but more prostrate, this is a rare species at the mountain. The leaflets number from 5-7 and are usually less than twice as long as broad, with the lower surface glaucous and the upper surface glossy or dull.

Known from a single location along Island Springs trail at 5,050 feet, where it grows with ponderosa pine on a south-facing, grassy slope, it probably does not ascend into the study area elsewhere at Mount Adams.

## *Vancouveria* C. Morren & Decne.—INSIDE-OUT FLOWER

### *Vancouveria hexandra* (Hook.) C. Morren & Decne. INSIDE-OUT FLOWER

The common name is derived from the appearance of the flower, as the white sepals and petals are turned backwards (reflexed) from the pistil and stamens. This perennial herb rises from a slender rootstock and bears twice-compound leaves on slender stalks, 10-40 cm in length overall. The coarsely 3-lobed leaves are more or less round in outline and the fruit is a follicle.

This species is rare at the mountain, known from an observation on the west side and a Suksdorf collection on the northwest, probably along the Lewis River.

## Betulaceae Gray—BIRCH FAMILY

Well-represented by three genera, this is the family that includes a very common lowland tree species, red alder (*Alnus rubra*). Less common at middle elevations, like other birch family members, the alders are species of streamsides, wetlands, and other damp places. The alternate, toothed leaves of the birches have straight veins and are undivided. The trees and shrubs are most easily recognized in late winter by the long, hanging male catkins that are composed of many small flowers. The female alder catkins bear a few flowers, are rounded, and resemble a small woody cone when mature. The female flowers of the single hazelnut (*Corylus*) species are arranged in small clusters that develop into large nuts. Both male catkins and female flowers are borne on the same plants—birch family members are therefore monoecious species.

Although locally common, the two middle elevation alders (*Alnus viridis* ssp. *sinuata* and *Alnus incana* ssp. *tenuifolia*) do not tend to form the extensive thickets found in other higher elevation Cascade Mountain localities. This may be due to the relative dryness of Mount Adams and the scarcity of avalanche chutes in the lower elevations.

1 Flowers few, in small clusters; the fruit nutlike and enclosed in a papery husk .......................................................... *Corylus*
1 Flowers many, in catkins: the fruit flattened, winged or wingless ..... ........................................................................2

2(1) Main bracts of usually clustered male catkins hardened, persistent . ........................................................................ *Alnus*
2 Main bracts of usually single or paired male catkins not hardened, deciduous ............................................................ *Betula*

### *Alnus* Mill.—ALDER

Locally common at Mount Adams, in general, alders are easily recognized by the elliptic to ovate, pale green leaves and the long, narrow male catkins. These are borne on the same plants as the female catkins, which are rounded and develop into dark, woody "cones." The plants are shrubs or trees of moist habitats where they may form dense thickets and are most often seen along streams and rivers, as well as on debris flows where they are early colonizers.

1 Catkins flowering with leaves on current season's growth; fruits with thin, small wings; leaves not rolled under ...... *A. viridis* ssp. *sinuata*
1 Catkins flowering before the leaves, on previous season's growth; fruits with or without wings; leaves somewhat rolled under .......... 2

2(1) Fruits with narrow wings; leaves wavy and turned under at the margins, with a pale lower surface; new growth hairless .... *A. rubra*
2 Fruits without wings; leaves wavy or lobed but neither turned under at the margins nor markedly pale beneath; young growth densely short-hairy ......................................... *A. incana* ssp. *tenuifolia*

## Betulaceae

### *Alnus incana* (L.) Moench ssp. *tenuifolia* (Nutt.) Breitung
### THINLEAF ALDER, MOUNTAIN ALDER

Shrubs from 2-5 m tall, the bark of this alder is grayish-brown or reddish, and the young twigs, inflorescences, and petioles are typically clothed in soft short hairs. The 3-7 cm long leaves are elliptic or ovate-oblong, rounded at the base, and sometimes sharply tipped. The margins of the leaves are toothed and do not curl under; their upper surface is green and the lower surface is pale and short-hairy. The catkins develop on the previous season's growth and are 3-10 cm long. The female catkins are ellipsoid-ovoid and 9-13 mm long; the fruit is thin-margined and lacks a membranous wing.

Common in middle elevation moist habitats, this is a cosmopolitan species at the mountain, in places as prevalent as *A. viridis.* It is found alongside the trail from Muddy Meadows to the Pacific Crest Trail, near Road 2329 at the Trail 7B trailhead, at Hellroaring Canyon, and on "islands in Bird Creek," the last a Suksdorf collection.

### *Alnus rubra* Bong.—RED ALDER

The pinkish tone of the male catkins enlivens the late winter forest, as this species blooms early, sometimes before the snow melts. It is a tree that may reach 20 m. The bark is smooth, gray, and often splotched with whitish lichen. The 5-15 cm long oval leaves are singly-toothed and somewhat inrolled at the margins; they open well after the catkins. The male catkins are 10-15 cm long and the female "cones" are 15-25 mm long when mature.

Typically a low elevation tree of disturbed and wet habitats, it is found at the lower limits of the study area, on the west side, near 4,000 feet. A good place to see this tree is alongside Road 23 at Riley Creek.

### *Alnus viridis* (Vill.) Lam. & DC. ssp. *sinuata* (Regel) Á. & D. Löve
### SITKA ALDER, SLIDE ALDER

With multiple branches, this shrub may reach 5 m in height, although the stems are often bent, nearly lying along the ground on steep sites. The flowers appear in the spring with the leaves. The leaves are doubly toothed, with flat margins, and are rounded at the base. The male catkins are 12-15 cm long and the female "cones" are 12-15 mm long.

A common subalpine shrub of wet draws, open meadows, lakeshores, and rocky hillsides, this species is found at Big Muddy Creek at "6-7000 feet" (Suksdorf collection), along Road 034 at 4,050 feet, in Grand Meadow, and at Hellroaring Creek. "Slide" alder refers to the ability of this species to exploit openings in the forest created by landslides and avalanches.

### *Betula* L.—BIRCH

#### *Betula glandulosa* Michx.—DWARF BIRCH

Ascending or spreading, this small birch may reach 3 m in height. The bark is dark brown and smooth, the lenticels small and pale. The twigs are for the most part glabrous, although occasionally short-hairy, and are covered with large, resinous glands. The leaf blade is obovate to rounded with lateral veins and is 0.5-3 cm in length, the base wedge-shaped to rounded, and the margins toothed or wavy. The cones are cylindrical and 1-2.5 cm long.

A middle elevation and subalpine species of habitats varying from rocky slopes to wet meadows, this birch is a prominent species on slightly higher ground in the midst of the extensive meadows west and southwest of the mountain, such as Grand and Swampy Meadows. It is often found with bog huckleberry (*Vaccinium uliginosum*) and bog willow (*Salix pedicillaris*). It was also collected by Flett on the Little Klickitat River.

### *Corylus* L.—HAZELNUT

#### *Corylus cornuta* Marshall var. *californica* (A. DC.) Sharp CALIFORNIA HAZELNUT

A multiple-branched shrub composed of stems that reach 1-5 m tall, this is a deciduous species of middle elevation dry hillsides and open habitats. The doubly-toothed leaves are flat at the margins and somewhat heart-shaped at the base. The flowers open in early spring, before the leaves unfurl. The densely flowered male catkins are approximately 10 cm long, and the female flowers develop into a cluster of 2-3 rounded, edible nuts, approximately 20 mm long. The nuts are enclosed in papery husk.

Uncommon at the mountain, this species has been found on the southeast side at the end of Road 170 and on Snipes Mountain at 4,120 feet of elevation.

## Boraginaceae Juss.—BORAGE FAMILY

Tall bluebells, *Mertensia paniculata,* is the one significant wildflower among the small number of borages at Mount Adams. The plants are roughly hairy, especially in the calyx, with mostly alternate leaves and flowers in one-sided racemes that uncoil as the flowers open, technically called a scorpioid cyme. The flowers range from white to blue (the yellow- or orange-flowered amsinckias are not found Mount Adams); the 5 petals are fused to form a tube of varying length, with the free lobes spreading greatly or little. At the throat of the flower, where the lobes join the tube, are 5 crest-like structures called fornices which may be white or yellow, giving the flower an "eye." There are 5 stamens and a single style; the ovary is 4-parted and develops into 4 hard nutlets. Separating *Cryptantha* and *Plagiobothrys* requires examination of the nutlets under a handlens to determine the shape of the receptacle to which the nutlets attach and the position of the attachment scar, whether basal or lateral.

1 Corolla tube long, funnel-shaped, free lobes spreading slightly ....... ......................................................................... *Mertensia*
1 Corolla tube short, the lobes spreading widely at nearly right angles ......................................................................................... 2

2(1) Corolla reddish-purple; tall (to 100 cm), coarse biennial weed ........ ........................................................................ *Cynoglossum*
2 Corolla white or blue; seldom more than 70 cm tall, annual or perennial natives ................................................................. 3

3(2) Nutlets armed with prickles ........................................ *Hackelia*
3 Nutlets unarmed or with minute bumps .................................. 4

4(3) Flowers blue; receptacle flat; nutlet attachment basal ...... *Myosotis*
4 Flowers white; receptacle cone-shaped; nutlet attachment lateral ... ......................................................................................... 5

5(4) Wall of the nutlet grooved above the attachment scar ... *Cryptantha*
5 Wall of the nutlet keeled above the attachment scar .. *Plagiobothrys*

### *Cryptantha* Lehm. *ex* G. Don—CRYPTANTHA

Superficially similar to *Plagiobothrys,* the popcorn flowers, the key differences between the two requires an examination of the mature nutlets under high magnification to determine the nature of the attachment of the nutlet to the style. Both the species at Mount Adams are annuals, chiefly growing on disturbed ground. The flowers are white and the calyx is ornamented with stiff, sharp hairs.

1 Nutlets bearing tiny, low bumps; hairs of stems and leaves appressed ....................................................... *C. simulans*
1 Nutlets smooth; hairs of stems and leaves spreading ....... *C. affinis*

### *Cryptantha affinis* (A. Gray) Greene—SLENDER CRYPTANTHA

Less than 30 cm tall, this annual herb is bristly-hairy with opposite lower stem leaves and alternate, 1-3 cm long upper leaves. The leaves are linear to narrowly oblong. The whitish flower is tiny (just 1 mm across) and partially obscured by the calyx. The 4 nutlets are smooth and up to 2 mm long, with a scar near the margin.

Common on the southeast side of the mountain, this species is found at the DNR quarry, alongside Road 6900, at the horse camp on Hellroaring Creek, and along Road 8040 and Road 071. Historic collections include a Flett specimen at the Klickitat River and a Suksdorf plant from Hellroaring Canyon.

#### *Cryptantha simulans* Greene—PINEWOODS CRYPTANTHA

Taller than the previous species, this *Cryptantha* can reach 50 cm in height and has widely-spreading branches. The leaves and stems are strigose (that is, they are densely covered with stout hairs that lay flat against the leaf or stem surface). There are relatively few leaves for the size of the plant; these are linear-elliptical and up to 4 cm long. The flower is 1-2 mm across and the nutlets are 2-3 mm long, the surface with scattered low, rounded bumps.

This species grows on the ridge at the DNR quarry, where it was found in 2006 in large numbers in a clearcut.

### *Cynoglossum* L.—HOUND'S TONGUE

#### *Cynoglossum officinale* L.—HOUND'S TONGUE

This coarse, single-stemmed biennial is 3-12 dm tall, with stems leafy throughout. The entire plant is covered with long, soft hairs. The lower leaves are oblanceolate to elliptic and taper to a stalk; they are 1-3 cm in length overall. The upper leaves are oblong or lanceolate, stalkless, and not much reduced in size. The flowers are arranged singly along the curved pedicel. The corolla is reddish-purple with the limb, 1.5 cm wide. The ovate nutlets are 5-7 mm long and form a broad, bristly fruit.

A weed found along roadsides and other disturbed sites, it was collected alongside Road 170 near King Mountain.

### *Hackelia* Opiz.—STICKSEED

The white to blue flowers are borne on short branches of the flowering stem in a few-flowered "false raceme." At the center is a yellow "eye." The basal leaves are oblong to narrowly elliptic, and the stem leaves are sessile to clasping. The corolla is a short tube, with a spreading, flattened, 5-lobed face. The flowering stems turn down when the fruit develops, while the nutlets are ornamented with hook-like bristles.

As with other borage genera, the hairiness of the stems and leaves set these blue-flowered plants apart. Preferring dry habitats, this genus is apparently confined to the eastern and southeastern aspects of the mountain.

## Boraginaceae

1 Corolla limb blue; lower stem leaves stalked ............. *H. micrantha*
1 Corolla limb white; lower stem leaves stalkless .............. *H. diffusa*

### ***Hackelia diffusa*** **(Lehm.) I.M. Johnston var.** ***diffusa*** **SPREADING STICKSEED**

This perennial typically has several stems but occasionally is only single-stemmed; each stem is 2-7 dm tall. The stems are stiffly hairy with the upper hairs more flattened against the stem; the leaves also bear stiff, densely-packed hairs. The 6-18 cm long basal leaves are oblanceolate to narrowly elliptic, and the 5-12 cm upper leaves are sessile and lanceolate to elliptic in shape. The white corolla has a yellow eye; the limb is 8-18 mm wide.

This species is known from Suksdorf collections at Hellroaring Canyon and in the Big Muddy Creek Canyon.

### ***Hackelia micrantha*** **(Eastw.) J.L. Gentry—JESSICA'S STICKSEED**

Rising from a taproot and branched root crown, this 3-10 dm tall perennial has several stems covered with short, stiff hairs. The oblanceolate to narrowly elliptic leaves are also hairy, up to 35 cm long, and borne on stout stalks. The stem leaves are 5-20 cm long and more oblong and sessile than the basal leaves. Several blue flowers with a yellow or whitish eye are 7-11 mm wide. The marginal prickles of the nutlets are separated, giving a spiny appearance.

This species is known from a Flett collection made on the upper Klickitat River.

### ***Mertensia*** **Roth—BLUEBELLS**

### ***Mertensia paniculata*** **(Ait.) G. Don var.** ***borealis*** **(J.F. Macbr.) L.O. Williams—TALL BLUEBELLS**

Reaching 1 m in height, this perennial consists of several stems from a single rhizome that give the plants a tufted appearance. The plants are glaucous and mostly hairless, and the ovate-lanceolate to nearly elliptical leaves sometimes bear hairs on the underside. The lower leaves are stalked and 3-14 cm long, while the upper leaves are reduced and stalkless. The nodding, bell-shaped flowers are configured in a coiled cyme, resembling the tail of a scorpion. They are pinkish in the bud, but blue to blue-violet when open and 10-14 mm long. The glaucous sepals are about 4 mm long and bear a fringe of short hairs on the margins.

*Mertensia platyphylla* is very similar in appearance and has been reported from Mount Adams. All plants studied in the field, however, have proven to be *M. paniculata. M. platyphylla* can be distinguished by its larger anthers; its range is from the Puget Trough southwards, from the hills of the western Cascades to the coast.

A middle elevation species of open, moist sites in forests, at meadow edges, and along streams below 6,000 feet, this plant grows in Hellroaring Canyon, and has also been located along the Stagman Ridge trail as well as on the trail northeast of Bench Lake.

### *Myosotis* L.—FORGET-ME-NOT

#### *Myosotis discolor* Pers.—CHANGING FORGET-ME-NOT

Occasionally a biennial, this slender annual is 1-5 dm tall, with single or multiple branches, and stiffly hairy. The lower leaves are 1-4 cm long and oblanceolate, while the upper leaves are more oblong. Opening as whitish or yellowish, the 1-2 mm wide corolla changes to blue; the flowers are borne in short racemes. The nutlets are dark brown or blackish.

A weedy species, this plant was collected alongside Road 23, south of the overlook.

### *Plagiobothrys* Fisch. & C.A. Mey.—POPCORNFLOWER

#### *Plagiobothrys scouleri* (Hook. & Arn.) I.M. Johnston var. *hispidulus* (Greene) Dorn—SLEEPING POPCORNFLOWER

Occasionally single stemmed and erect, but more often with numerous and prostrate or ascending stems, this taprooted annual may reach 20 cm in length. The leaves are stiffly hairy and primarily on the stems only; they are linear, up to 6.5 cm long, with the lower few pairs opposite and the remainder alternate. The corolla is only 1-4 mm wide, the flowers borne in a spike.

A native species, this plant was found by the authors in Midway Meadows on the north side and near Road 6900 below the DNR quarry on the southeast. It prefers to grow below 4,500 feet on flats that are seasonally moist but become very dry by early summer.

## Brassicaceae Burnett—MUSTARD FAMILY

The mustards are most easily distinguished by the 4 distinct petals arranged at right angles to each other, accounting for the former name of the family, Cruciferae, meaning "bearing a cross." The family includes annual, biennial, and perennial herbs. It is widespread and numerous, represented by 14 genera and 34 species, 4 of which are weeds.

In addition to the 4 petals, there are 4 sepals, 6 stamens, and 1 pistil with 2 chambers; the pistil is podlike when mature. The petals are often distinctly clawed. The plants may be tufted with basal leaves only, or tall and leafy throughout. The leaves are typically slender and simple to toothed or lobed, often bearing simple to intricate hairs (the nature of which figures in the keys that follow). The flowers are arranged in inflorescences that vary from compact and headlike to simple or branched racemes. The fruits range from long, slender siliques to shorter, more rounded silicles.

Wide-ranging and including some members with pretty if not spectacular flowers, this family is also distinguished by having one of the higher ranging species, *Smelowskia calycina,* which is found at over 9,000 feet of elevation.

The key is based upon a preliminary examination of the mature fruit. The fruit may be determined sometimes, too, by the shape of the ovary. If the fruit is absent, comparing the results by starting at couplets 3 and 9 will aid in identification.

1 Fruit a silicle; oval, less than twice as long as wide ...................... 2
1 Fruit a silique; elliptic, more than twice as long as wide ................ 7

2(1) Petals yellow........................................................................... 3

2 Petals white, pink, or purplish (if pale yellow, then the silique strongly constricted between the seeds ................................ 5

3(2) Silicles roundish in outline, conspicuously inflated ....................... ........................................................................ *Physaria*
3 Silicles elliptical to nearly linear, flattened................................ 4

4(3) Silicles oblong, twice as long as broad; style to 1 mm long ....... ........................................................................... *Draba*
4 Silicles oval to obovate, not over twice as long as broad; style at least 2 mm long ................................................... *Lesquerella*

5(2) Flowering stems leafy; upper stem leaves clasping; seed 1 per chamber ........................................................... *Lepidium*
5 Stem leaves absent or present but not clasping; seeds 2 or more per chamber ............................................................. 6

6(5) Plants with basal as well as stem leaves ....................... *Capsella*
6 Plants with basal leaves only ..........................................*Draba*

7(1) Petals yellow or orange-yellow ............................................. 8
7 Petals white, pink, or purplish ...............................................11

8(7) Plants hairless .................................................... *Barbarea*
8 Plants short-hairy ...................................................................... 9

9(8) Petals more than 1 cm long; hairs on leaves flattened and forked ... ................................................................... *Erysimum*
9 Petals less than 1 cm long; hairs various, but not flattened ........ 10

10(9) Hairs on the leaves branched; stigma not divided ....... *Descurainia*
10 Hairs on the leaves simple, unbranched; stigma 2-lobed ............. ................................................................... *Sisymbrium*

11(7) Silicle strongly constricted between each seed; silicle of 2 chambers, the lower small and seedless, resembling a stalk .......... ................................................................... *Rhaphanus*
11 Silicle not at all constricted or, at most, slightly so ....................12

12(11) Leaves mostly hairless ........................................... *Cardamine*
12 Leaves short-hairy .......................................................... 13

13(12) Plants annual ................................................... *Arabidopsis*
13 Plants perennial ...............................................................14

14(13) Leaves partly to fully pinnate ................................ *Smelowskia*
14 Leaves smooth-edged to slightly toothed ............................ *Arabis*

### *Arabidopsis* Heynh.—ROCKCRESS

#### *Arabidopsis thaliana* (L.) Heynh.—THALE CRESS

The stems of this simple to freely-branched annual range from 10-40 cm in height and are softly short-hairy below to smooth above. The 1-4 cm long, slightly toothed oblanceolate leaves are borne in a basal rosette and are variously hairy with simple and forked hairs. The stem leaves are lanceolate, 5-20 mm long, and stalkless. The inflorescence is racemelike with many flowers on slender stalks. The white petals are about 3 mm long, and the linear siliques are 10-15 mm long.

This weed of middle elevation disturbed sites is known from a collection at the summit overlook on Road 23.

### *Arabis* L.—ROCKCRESS

The eleven species of rockcress at Mount Adams are biennials or perennials. Rising from a taproot, the plants are often branched above a short stem. The basal leaves typically form a rosette and have stalks; the unstalked stem leaves often have clasping auricles. The flowers are arranged in bractless racemes and range in color from white to rose-purple. The fruit is a long and slender silique, sometimes flattened.

1 Mature siliques pendulous on the stem .................................. 2
1 Mature siliques widely-spreading to ascending or erect ............. 4

2(1) Base of the plant woody; siliques 4-6 mm broad ........................................................................ *A. suffrutescens* var. *suffrutescens*

2 Base not woody; siliques to 2.5 mm broad ................................ 3

3(2) Plant to 15 cm tall; stalk of mature silique curved ......................................................................... *A. hoelboellii* var. *pendulocarpa*

3 Plants greater than 30 cm tall; stalk of mature silique straight .................................................. *A. holboellii* var. *retrofracta*

4(1) Stem leaves clasping; plants mostly taller than 40 cm from a basal tuft of leaves ........................................................................ 5

4 Stem leaves attached directly to the stem but not clasping; plants low, branched, mostly less than 40 cm tall ............................... 7

5(4) Basal leaves narrowly oblanceolate ..................... *A. drummondii*

5 Basal leaves widely oblanceolate to obovate ........................... 6

6(5) Flowers cream-colored; stem leaves glaucous ............... *A. glabra*

6 Flowers white; stem leaves not glaucous .... *A. hirsuta* var. *glabrata*

7(4) Seeds not winged ................................................. *A. nuttallii*

7 Seeds winged, the wing 0.2 mm broad or wider ....................... 8

8(7) Flowers white; basal leaves blunt ............... *A. furcata* var. *furcata*

8 Flowers colored; basal leaves pointed ................................... 9

9(8) Plants sometimes more than 30 cm tall; flower stalk hairy; petals deep rose-purple ........................... *A. sparsiflora* var. *subvillosa*

9 Plants less than 25 cm tall; flower stalk hairless; petals colored otherwise .....................................................................10

10(9) Mature siliques erect on the stem; silique 2-3 mm broad ............................................................................ *A. lyalli* var. *lyallii*

10 Mature siliques ascending to widely spreading; silique less than 2 mm broad .....................................................................11

11(10) Basal leaves few-toothed; siliques surrounding the stem ............................................................... *A. microphylla* var. *microphylla*

11 Basal leaves toothless; siliques tending to be on one side of the stem (secund) .............................. *A. lemmonii* var. *paddoensis*

### *Arabis drummondii* A. Gray—CANADIAN ROCKCRESS

Although most often a biennial, this species may flower in its first year. It bears a single stem 30-90 cm tall. The 2-4 cm long basal leaves are narrowly oblanceolate, tapered to the stalk, untoothed or with a few small teeth and sparse flattened short hairs. The smaller stem leaves are lanceolate in shape and clasping. The 8-10 mm long, white or pink flowers are numerous and the siliques are 4-10 cm long, erect, and held close to the stem.

Typically found on rocky banks and slopes at middle elevations, this species is known from Henderson collections on the Klickitat River.

### *Arabis furcata* S. Wats. var. *furcata*—CASCADE ROCKCRESS

This tufted perennial is configured as 1 or more stems that vary from 10-40 cm in height and are typically hairless. The 2-5 cm long basal leaves are spoon-shaped or obovate and also usually hairless; even if hairs are present, the leaves appear dark green. The 4-8 mm long, white flowers are held more or less erect.

Common and cosmopolitan at the mountain, this is a species of middle to subalpine meadows and other open areas. It grows at Hellroaring Canyon and Meadows, on the lower slope of the north side of Little Mount Adams, at Crofton Butte, and along the Round-the-Mountain trail at 6,300 feet. On the north it is known from Potato Hill alongside the Pacific Crest Trail. It grows high on the northeast side at Devil's Garden.

### *Arabis glabra* (L.) Bernh.—TOWER MUSTARD

Covered with spreading, forked or branched hairs, the typically single stem of this native biennial may reach 100 cm in height. The stems are glaucous or hairless near the top and hairy below. The 2-5 cm long basal leaves are oblanceolate, toothed or pinnately lobed, and short hairy, while the smaller stem leaves are lanceolate in shape and clasping. The 5-7 mm long flowers are cream-colored, and the erect fruits are 4-10 cm long.

This is a species of open places on gravelly soil. It is rare at the mountain, having been collected by Flett on the upper Klickitat River. The plant has a weed-like appearance, but is native throughout Washington, and is most often seen in disturbed places.

### *Arabis hirsuta* (L.) Scop. var. *glabrata* Torr. & A. Gray<br>HAIRY ROCKCRESS

Typically a biennial, this species bears simple or forked hairs; the single stem ranges from 15-50 cm in height. The 2-5 cm long basal leaves are oblanceolate, untoothed, or shallowly toothed. The stem leaves are stalkless, clasping, and lanceolate to obovate in shape. The 4-6 mm long flowers are white, and the 2-5 cm fruits are erect.

Rare at the mountain, this species is known from a Flett collection on the upper Klickitat River.

## Brassicaceae

### *Arabis holboellii* Hornem. var. *pendulocarpa* (A. Nels.) Rollins
### HOELBOELL'S ROCKCRESS

Quite distinctive from the variety *retrofracta* of lower elevations at Mount Adams, this plant reaches only about 15 cm in height. The stem leaves are not auriculate-clasping and the siliques hang straight down from very short, sharply curved stalks.

This variety has been collected in the Olympic Mountains and at scattered locations in the Wenatchee Mountains. This is evidently the first location reported in the Cascades. It was found by Paul Slichter at Devil's Gardens, in fruit on July 24, 2005. It grew on top of a sheer cliff with an eastern aspect, at 7,850 feet.

### *Arabis holboellii* Hornem. var. *retrofracta* (Graham) Rydb.
### HOLBOELL'S ROCKCRESS

Another biennial rockcress, this one bears both simple, short hairs, and flat, starlike hairs. The 30-60 cm tall multiple stems rise from a branched base. The 1-5 cm long basal leaves are narrowly oblanceolate and shallowly toothed; the stem leaves are oblanceolate and clasped at the base. The 7-8 mm long flowers are pale purple, and the 4-6 cm long fruits hang downward on straight stalks.

A species of gravelly sites at middle to lower subalpine elevations, it grows south of the overlook alongside Road 23. It was also collected by Howell in 1882 with only the specification of "Mount Adams," lacking other details but probably from the south side.

### *Arabis lemmonii* S. Wats. var. *paddoensis* Rollins
### MOUNT ADAMS ROCKCRESS

Densely tufted, this perennial has a branched rootstock from which several 5-20 cm tall, simple stems rise. The stems are typically densely hairy with short, branching hairs. The 1.5-2 cm long basal leaves are configured in a rosette and are oblanceolate to rounded or slightly sharp-tipped, shallowly toothed, and grayish with short, dense hairs. The many stem leaves may overlap, and are oblong to lanceolate, 0.5-2 cm long, sharply tipped, and usually hairless. The inflorescence is a sparsely-flowered raceme and the 4.5-7 mm long petals are light rose-purple. The siliques are 4.5-7 mm long and glabrous, tending to be arranged flag-like on one side of the stem.

A subalpine to alpine species of cliffs and talus slopes, it was collected by Suksdorf on the northwest side, and at the Klickitat Glacier (on the east) and Hellroaring Canyon. It was also collected by Henderson in the Muddy River Canyon. The variety name, paddoensis, commemorates the Native American name for Mount Adams, "Paddo."

### *Arabis lyalli* S. Wats. var. *lyalli*—LYALL'S ROCKCRESS

The stems of this tufted perennial range from 5-20 cm in height. The 1-3 cm long basal leaves are oblanceolate in shape, toothless, and short-hairy with branched hairs. The stem leaves are narrowly lanceolate and clasping. The 7-8 mm long flowers are rose to purplish and the 2-5 cm long pods are held erect.

Fairly common in rocky habitats, this species grows near the Round-the-Mountain trail on the southeast side at an elevation of nearly 6,300 feet. It is also known from Hellroaring Canyon and from a specimen on the northwest side of the mountain, both collected by Suksdorf.

### *Arabis microphylla* Nutt. var. *microphylla*
### LITTLELEAF ROCKCRESS

This tufted perennial bears several erect or slightly curved stems that range from 10-20 cm tall; they are slender and finely hairy although occasionally hairless at the base. The 2-3 cm long basal leaves are borne in a rosette and are narrowly oblanceolate with a sharp tip and a few teeth. The leaves typically bear many hairs, and are grayish. The stem leaves may be numerous and are stalkless, with ear-like lobes, 10-25 mm long and oblong to linear-lanceolate. The racemes may be few or many-flowered, and the pink to purplish petals are only 5-8 mm long. The siliques are hairless, and turned down; they are 2.5-6 cm long.

A subalpine to alpine species of the eastern Cascades, it is known from a single collection at Devil's Garden at 7,800 feet, made in 1983 by Beth Skaggs Ryan.

### *Arabis nuttallii* B.L. Robins.—NUTTALLS'S ROCKCRESS

A tufted plant that rises from a heavy rootstock, this rockcress has oblanceolate leaves 3-4 cm long and up to 1 mm wide. Pubescence is variable: the leaves may be hairless, especially the upper side; the leaf margin is ciliate and the underside may bear long hairs. There are several flowering stems, each with a few small leaves. The flowers are white to pale violet, with petals 6-8 mm long. The siliques are 1-2 cm long, very slender, and are held erect or on spreading stalks.

Found only once at Mount Adams by Don Knoke, on Road 8040 between Cold Springs and Morrison Creek camp; it grew in an opening in the ponderosa pine forest on a south-facing slope.

### *Arabis sparsiflora* Nutt. var. *subvillosa* (S. Wats.) Rollins
### HAIRYSTEM ROCKCRESS

Either a short-lived perennial or a biennial, the 1 to many stems of this species rise 3-10 cm from a branched rootstock. The stems are hairy with branched to starlike hairs, particularly on the lower parts. The 2-9 cm long, toothed basal leaves are borne in a rosette and are oblanceolate in shape and densely hairy. The leaf stalks are also densely hairy. The 2-8 cm long stem leaves are numerous and often overlapping with earlike lobes, and linear to oblanceolate in shape. The racemes are many-flowered, and the 6-14 mm long petals vary in color from white to deep purple. The 4-12 cm long siliques are glabrous, 1-veined, and curved.

An eastern Cascades variety (and southward), this is an uncommon species at Mount Adams. It grows at the DNR Quarry, and is also known from Suksdorf collections at Hellroaring Canyon.

### *Arabis suffrutescens* S. Wats. var. *suffrutescens*
### WOODY ROCKCRESS

Distinguished by the woody, branching base, this perennial ranges from 20-30 cm in height, with the many annual stems reaching as much as 40 cm. The 2-4 cm long leaves at the base of the stems and on the side branches are narrowly oblanceolate, while the many stem leaves (the upper ones are overlapping) are narrowly oblong to linear-lanceolate and 1-2 cm long. The petals are pink to purplish and 5-8 mm long. The 4-6 cm long siliques are glabrous and pendant, and are 1-veined.

Typically found in eastern Cascades habitats and southward, this uncommon species is actually known from the northwest side of the mountain, as well as at Hellroaring Canyon, both of these being Suksdorf collections.

## *Barbarea* Ait. f.—YELLOWROCKET

### *Barbarea orthoceras* Ledeb.—AMERICAN YELLOWROCKET

A hairless perennial or biennial that ranges from 30-90 cm tall, this species bears a few basal leaves that are pinnately lobed. Beneath the large terminal leaflet, which may reach 8 cm in length, there is a pair of smaller leaflets. The stem leaves are smaller, of a similar configuration as the basal ones, but stalked and somewhat clasping. The branched inflorescence is composed of many yellow flowers 4-5 mm long. The 2-4 cm long fruits are spreading or ascending.

Uncommon in middle elevations, this species is found at the summit overlook on Road 23, at the intersection of Roads 150 and 70, and is also known from a Flett collection at the Klickitat River.

## *Capsella* Medik.—CAPSELLA

### *Capsella bursa-pastoris* (L.) Medik.—SHEPHERD'S PURSE

The stems of this annual weed are branched and may reach 50 cm in height, but typically the plants are smaller when on poor soil. The plant is short-hairy with both simple and branched hairs. The 3-6 cm long, oblanceolate basal leaves are stalked and pinnately-toothed. The smaller stem leaves are lanceolate and somewhat clasping. The white flowers are about 2 mm long, and the 6-8 mm long fruits are flattened and heart-shaped.

A weed of roadsides and other waste ground, it grows at Keene's Horse Camp on the north side, and at the Stagman Ridge trailhead on the west.

### *Cardamine* L.—BITTERCRESS

The basal leaves of the delicate plants of this genus are quite often distinctive from the stem leaves. Two species are annual (or occasionally biennial).The flowers are pink or white, the flowers of the perennial species being quite showy. The plants are mostly hairless and the fruit is a silique.

1 Leaves all simple, merely toothed ............... *C. cordifolia* var. *lyalli*
1 Leaves all, or at least those of the upper stem, lobed or compound.. ........................................................................... 2

2(1) Petals 7-14 mm. long; style 3-8 mm. long .... *C. nuttallii* var. *nuttallii*
2 Petals 2-7 mm. long; style 0.5-2 mm. long .............................. 3

3(2) Perennial plants; petals 3-7 mm. long ......... *C. breweri* var. *breweri*
3 Annual plants; petals 2-4 mm. long ....................................... 4

4(3) Siliques 1.3-1.5 mm. broad; lateral stem leaflets ovate ................. ............................................ *C. oligosperma* var. *oligosperma*
4 Siliques 0.7-1 mm. broad; lateral stem leaflets linear or lanceolate .. .............................................................. *C. pensylvanica*

### *Cardamine breweri* S. Wats. var. *breweri*—BREWER'S BITTERCRESS

This perennial rises on unbranched, erect stems 15-45 cm tall from a very short rootstock. The 1-3 cm long simple basal leaves are few in number. Both the basal and stem leaves are stalked. The flowering stems are simple to freely branched, 20-60 cm tall, and are leafy; those leaves are wavy, with 3-8 lobes, and the terminal leaflet is rounded to wedge-shaped at the base. The numerous flowers have 3-4 mm long petals, and the fruits are erect and about 2 cm long.

Rare at the mountain, this species is known from an 1882 Howell collection, with no other habitat or location given; it was probably made on the south side. Elsewhere in the Cascades, it grows at low to middle elevations in wet places in forests.

**_Cardamine cordifolia_ A. Gray var. _lyallii_ (S. Wats.) A. Nels. & J.F. Macbr.—HEARTLEAF BITTERCRESS**

This erect bittercress rises from slender rhizomes, with simple flowering stems 20-60 cm tall; the stems are hairless near the top and hairy at the base. The leaves are kidney-shaped to heartlike, primarily on the stem; the basal leaf or leaves are long-stalked. They range from 3-10 cm in length overall and are shallowly toothed and hairless. The leafy racemes are few-flowered; the flowers with white petals are 7-9 mm long.

An attractive but rare species, found in wet meadow and at streamsides, it was collected near the Klickitat River by Flett.

**_Cardamine nuttallii_ Greene var. _nuttallii_**
**NUTTALL'S BITTERCRESS**

This species is distinguished by the small, 2-5 mm thick, elongated tubers on the rootstock. The basal leaves are long-stalked and rise directly from the rootstock and the leaf blades are round in outline and shallowly lobed. The stem is slender, less than 20 cm tall, and the stem leaves are divided into 3-5 more or less pointed lobes. A few pink flowers, with 10-13 mm long petals, are borne at the tops of the stems. The 2-3 cm long fruits are borne on ascending stalks.

A middle elevation species of moist woods, it is known from a collection made by the authors on the west slope of Smith Butte at 4,000 feet, on the southeast side of the mountain. It was observed close to *Calypso,* at the edge of a fairly recent lava flow northeast of Bunnell Butte, and from about 4,000 feet on Road K6000, on the southeast side.

**_Cardamine oligosperma_ Nutt. var. _oligosperma_**
**LITTLE WESTERN BITTERCRESS**

This annual or biennial species bears stems up to 30 cm tall. It has a basal rosette of leaves that are up to 8 cm long and pinnately divided into 7 or 9 rounded leaflets. The raceme is more than 3 cm tall, and the white petals are 2-3 mm long. The fruits are erect, crowded, and 1-2 cm long.

Found in disturbed areas, such as roadsides, campgrounds, or open woods, this variety prefers wet ground. It grows at Spring Creek Meadow at 4,200 feet, in a disturbed area at the meadow edge.

**_Cardamine pensylvanica_ Muhl. _ex_ Willd.**
**PENNSYLVANIA BITTERCRESS**

This annual or biennial bears 30-60 cm tall stems that are often branched. The few basal leaves fall early, and the leafy stems bear stalked leaves to about 6 cm in length; they are stalked and divided into 7-11 narrow leaflets. The white petals are 2-4 mm long, and the 2.5 cm long fruits are borne on spreading stalks. It is quite similar to *C. oligosperma.*

A species of seasonally wet ground in open forest and meadows of the lower elevations at the mountain, it grows at Midway Meadows on the north and was collected by Flett at the Klickitat River.

### *Descurainia* Webb & Berth.—TANSY-MUSTARD

#### *Descurainia incana* (Bernh. *ex* Fisch. & C.A. Mey.) Dorn ssp. *viscosa* (Rydb.) Kartesz & Gandhi—MOUNTAIN TANSY-MUSTARD

A branched annual, or sometimes biennial, with starlike hairs on the stems and leaves, the flowers are yellow and the siliques linear. The 30-90 cm tall stems are typically branched, short-hairy, and glandular, particularly in the inflorescence. The leaves are twice pinnately divided, up to 10 cm long, with linear segments. The upper leaves are once divided and smaller. The petals are about 2 mm long and the 1-2 cm long fruits are linear and straight.

Similar to the genus *Sisymbrium*, the 2-lobed stigma of *Descurainia* separates the genera. "Tansy" is in reference to the multiply-pinnate leaves, which resemble those of the aster family member *Tanacetum*.

Weedlike in appearance, this native grows in middle elevations on typically drier, open forest sites. It is found alongside the Pineway Trail, near Road 071, at Hellroaring Canyon, and near the DNR quarry.

### *Draba* L.—DRABA

Known only from the northeast and eastern sides, these are rare plants at the mountain. They are tufted or mat-forming perennials. The fruits are flattened silicles. The flowers are yellow or white in the case of *D. lonchocarpa*. The hairs on the leaves also distinguish the species, as with *D. incerta* they are "double pectinate."

1 Petals white .......................... *D. lonchocarpa* var. *lonchocarpa*
1 Petals yellow .......................................................... 2

2(1) Stems leafy; plant with a rosette of leaves, not matted or tufted ...... .................................................... *D. albertina*
2 Stems not leafy; plants matted or tufted ................................ 3

3(2) Stems up to 7 or 8 cm tall; hairs of undersides of leaves comb-like.. .................................................... *D. incerta*
3 Stems 10-15 cm tall; hairs of undersides of leaves starlike ........... .................................................... *D. paysonii* var. *paysonii*

### *Draba albertina* Greene—SLENDER DRABA

Occasionally flowering the first year, this 2-20 cm tall leafy biennial or perennial rises from a simple or branched rootstock. The leaves are in a basal rosette, and are 10-25 mm long, linear-spatulate to narrowly oblanceolate, with hairs on the margins. The lower surface of the leaves bears simple to starlike hairs, and the stems are leafless. The racemes are composed of 3-20 flowers, and the 2-3 mm long petals are yellow, although they fade to white. The 5-12 mm long silicles are narrowly elliptic.

Named *D. crassifolia* in Hitchcock, this is a species of subalpine to alpine talus slopes or dry meadows. It is known from a Flett collection on the Klickitat River.

### *Draba incerta* Payson—YELLOWSTONE DRABA

The old leaves of this perennial remain on the plant, so that in age it forms a dense tuft. The leaves are narrowly oblanceolate, short-hairy with complex, comb-like hairs (at least on the underside), and 5-10 mm long. The stems reach 10-15 cm in height and are leafless. The yellow flowers number 5-8 and arranged in a short raceme. The fruits are lanceolate, 4-8 mm long.

*D. incerta* is a plant of open, rocky ridges and was collected by both Flett and Suksdorf. The specimens are all poorly documented, although at least one seems to have come from Little Mount Adams.

### *Draba lonchocarpa* Rydb. var. *lonchocarpa*—SPEAR-FRUITED DRABA

The tufted stems of this little, high elevation draba are less than 10 cm tall. The 5-15 mm long leaves are oblanceolate, and short-hairy with starlike hairs. The white flowers are crowded into a short inflorescence and the 10-15 mm long fruits are linear and sometimes twisted.

Rare at the mountain, this is an upper subalpine species and was collected at the Klickitat Glacier and at "7-8,000 feet" by Suksdorf.

### *Draba paysonii* Macbr. var. *paysonii*—PAYSON'S DRABA

A cushion-forming perennial, the plants have closely arranged, short, oblanceolate leaves that are less than 1 cm long; the young leaves are grayish, with dense, forked hairs. The raceme of 6-10 yellow flowers rises about 8 cm on a slender, leafless stem. The fruits are nearly ovate, about 7 mm long and 4 mm broad; the 1 mm long style remains on the maturing fruit.

The variety *treleasii* has been collected widely in Washington, including at Mount Rainier. It is separated from *paysonii* by its shorter fruits, 3-5 mm long, and shorter style. The variety *paysonii* occurs in the Little Belt Mountains of Montana and Wyoming; the status of *paysonii* at

Mount Adams should be investigated more closely with additional material.

This species has been found at Devil's Gardens, on the northeast flank of Mount Adams at 7,850 feet, growing among small rocks on an open flat.

### *Erysimum* L.—WALLFLOWER

The showy flowers of this genus are borne in crowded racemes; the axis of the raceme lengthens as the fruits mature. The leaves are oblanceolate and vary from smooth on the edges to wavy-toothed; the leaf surfaces are hairy, sometimes enough to give the plant a grayish cast. The petals are yellow to orange-yellow and have a long claw with an expanded blade. The fruit is a flattened or 4-angled silique.

1 Petals lemon-yellow; plant multiple-stemmed; siliques flattened, pea-like ........................................ *E. arenicola* var. *torulosum*

1 Petals yellow to orangish; plant with one stem; silique 4-sided ....... ................................................... *E. capitatum* var. *capitatum*

#### *Erysimum arenicola* S. Wats. var. *torulosum* (Piper) C.L. Hitchc.
#### CASCADE WALLFLOWER

This biennial or short-lived perennial herb is easily recognized by its short raceme of large, bright yellow flowers. The first-year leaves are 3-8 cm long, coarsely toothed, and sparsely hairy. The stems may reach 40 cm in height; the stem leaves are reduced in size and lack teeth. The 15-18 mm long yellow petals are spread widely, and the flowers are up to 1.5 cm broad. The 6-8 cm long siliques are twisted and squarish in cross section.

Found on rocky slopes in the subalpine habitat regime, this species was collected by Suksdorf in Hellroaring Canyon, and in Bird Creek Canyon. It's of spotty occurrence – not rare, but few are seen in any one place.

#### *Erysimum capitatum* (Dougl. *ex* Hook.) Greene var. *capitatum*
#### WESTERN WALLFLOWER

The herbage is grayish to greenish on this 20-100 cm tall biennial or short-lived perennial. The rootstock is simple and the stems vary to simple or somewhat branched from the base or above. The basal leaves are typically in a rosette, are toothed, and vary from 3-12 cm in length, on slender stalks. The stem leaves are sometimes toothed and not much reduced in size. The petals are yellow to deep orange and 15-25 mm long, with stiff pedicels. The siliques are slightly flattened and squarish in cross section, ascending, and 3-10 cm long.

Typically an eastern Cascades species, this species is a very showy wallflower of middle elevation dry, open sites. It grows along Road 8040 and at Hellroaring Canyon, in open places in forests.

### *Lepidium* L.—PEPPERGRASS

#### *Lepidium heterophyllum* Benth.
#### PURPLE-ANTHER FIELD PEPPERWORT

Distinguished by the purple anthers, this weed bears 2-2.5 mm white petals. The leaves appear to encircle the stem; there are true auricles on the upper stem leaves. The basal leaves are entire to lobed—in the latter case the terminal lobe is larger than the small ones at the base of the leaf. The inflorescence is a raceme and lacks bracts. The 2-2.5 mm petals are white; the common name refers to the purple-colored anthers that are easily seen against the petals. The silicles are 5-6 mm long.

Introduced, this species was known in Oregon and California, but not recorded in Washington by Hitchcock. It is fairly common at Mount Adams, on disturbed ground. A collection was made by the authors on the southeast side of the mountain near Road 071. It is also known from Road K6900, Road 170 (at the end), at the horse camp on Hellroaring Creek, and at the summit overlook near Road 23.

### *Lesquerella* S. Wats.—BLADDERPOD

#### *Lesquerella occidentalis* S. Wats. ssp. *occidentalis*
#### WESTERN BLADDERPOD

Biennial or perennial, the simple stems of this species may vary from prostrate to erect and are 5-15 cm long. The herbage is silvery to greenish and the rootstock is branched. The basal leaves are in a rosette and are 1.5-8 cm long, and ovate to rounded in shape. There are a few 5-15 mm long stem leaves on erect to curved stems. The yellow petals are 7-10 mm long, and the silicles are ovate to elliptic, 4-6 mm long and flattened along the upper margins; the tip is tapered.

An eastern Washington species of rocky hillsides and sagebrush habitat, it is known from a single Flett collection, made at "Mount Adams," most likely on the east side of the mountain.

### *Physaria* (Nutt. *ex* Torr. & A. Gray) A. Gray—TWINPOD

#### *Physaria alpestris* Suksdorf—ALPINE TWINPOD

This perennial is configured as several short stems (5-15 cm in height) rising from a somewhat woody base. The 4-8 cm long spoon-shaped leaves are toothless and whitish in color from the dense, starlike hairs. The leaves of the flowering stems are small and lanceolate. The few flowers have 2-9 mm long yellow petals. The 2 fruit chambers are rounded and notched at the top and bottom where they join, hence "twinpod." They are about 15 mm high, flattened and inflated.

A high elevation species and rare at the mountain, it was collected by Suksdorf on the Ridge of Wonders and by Flett at Klickitat Meadows, both places on the east side of Mount Adams.

## ***Raphanus*** **L.—WILD RADISH**

### ***Raphanus sativus*** **L.—WILD RADISH**

This annual or biennial is stiffly-hairy, and has a fleshy, elongated taproot. The 40-120 cm tall stems are freely branched, and the purplish petals (although they may vary to white or yellow with dark veins) are 15-20 mm long. The siliques are 3-6 cm long and constricted between the seeds, with a conical beak.

A weed of disturbed places, wild radish was collected at the Morrison Creek trailhead on the south side of the mountain at 4,560 feet.

## ***Sisymbrium*** **L.—TUMBLE MUSTARD**

### ***Sisymbrium altissimum*** **L.—TUMBLE MUSTARD**

This coarse plant bears branched stems that range from 60-150 cm in height. The pale yellow petals are 6-8 mm long and the 6-10 cm long fruits spread widely.

A weed of dry, waste ground, it is rare at the mountain, having been collected by the authors on the Snipes Mountain trail, just north of Pineway Trail, at 4,900 feet.

## ***Smelowskia*** **C.A. Mey.—SMELOWSKIA**

These are low, cushion-forming perennials with tufted stems. The leaves are pinnately divided and clothed with whitish hairs. The stems are also hairy, and the flowers are in short racemes, the flowering stems less than 15 cm tall with 2 or 3 leaves. The petals are white and the fruit is a silique. Both are high elevation species, with *S. calycina* growing at over 9,200 feet on the south side of the mountain. *S. ovalis* has a more southerly distribution in the Cascades.

1 Basal leaves with long, stiff hairs on the stalk; siliques 5-10 mm long ............................................. *S. calycina* var. *americana*

1 Basal leaves lacking long, stiff hairs on the stalk; siliques to 5-6 mm long ........................................................ *S. ovalis* var. *ovalis*

### *Smelowskia calycina* (Steph. *ex* Willd.) C.A. Mey. var. *americana* (Regel & Herder) Drury & Rollins—ALPINE SMELOWSKIA

In addition to the characteristics noted in the key, this species is distinguished by petals that are 4-8 mm long.

A high elevation species, plants have been noted at over 9,020 feet elevation on the South Climb route close to the Lunchcounter. It was also collected at the White Salmon Glacier by Suksdorf.

### *Smelowskia ovalis* M.E. Jones var. *ovalis* SMALL-FRUIT SMELOWSKIA

The petals of this species are smaller than *S. calycina*, being only 4-5 mm long.

Found along rocky slopes and ridges in the higher subalpine to alpine habitats, this species grows along the South Climb route at 7,300 feet. It is also found on the moraine below the Mazama Glacier above Hellroaring overlook. Henderson also collected it in 1882, but the collection bears no location information.

## Callitrichaceae Link—WATER-STARWORT FAMILY

### *Callitriche* L.—WATER-STARWORT

### *Callitriche palustris* L.—SWAMP WATER-STARWORT

A perennial aquatic plant, the slender stems of this starwort are up to 45 cm long. The leaves may be floating or submerged and the plants sometimes become stranded on muddy sites late in summer. The leaves are opposite, the edges of their bases forming thin ridges circling the stem. The linear, submerged leaves are shallowly notched at the tip, 5-20 mm long with a single main vein; the floating leaves are shorter and up to 3 mm wide. They are more or less obovate, with 3 main veins. Shallowly notched at the top, the fruits are rectangular with rounded corners, giving a blocky appearance.

This species is known from a single modern observation at Mirror Lake on the southeast side of the mountain, where it grows in mud in shallow water at the inlet stream.

## Campanulaceae Juss.—BELLFLOWER FAMILY

### *Campanula* L.—BELLFLOWER

The bellflowers are herbaceous perennials, with mostly toothed, alternate leaves. The flowers, a few per stem, are arranged in a raceme-like inflorescence and are more or less bell-shaped, with 5 free lobes. The ovary is inferior and there are 5 stamens; the fruit is a fleshy capsule that later dries and opens by small, lateral pores at the tops of the sides.

1 Style exserted from the corolla; lobes wide spreading.................... ..................................................................... *C. scouleri*
1 Style as long as the corolla; lobes slightly spreading ................. 2

2(1) Dwarf plants, to 15 cm tall; few flowers; capsules erect ................ ..................................................................... *C. scabrella*
2 Plants to 10-80 cm tall; several to many flowers; capsules nodding ..................................................................... *C. rotundifolia*

### *Campanula rotundifolia* L.—SCOTS BLUEBELLS

Beautiful flowers distinguish this species. The basal leaves are ovate to roundish, 2-5 cm long, and borne on slender stalks. The stem leaves are quite different, being linear, 2-7 cm long, and not stalked. The flowers are borne in an open raceme on 10-40 cm tall, unbranched stems. They are light blue-purple, 2-3 cm long, and nod from long, slender stalks. The free lobes are relatively short and hide the style.

This species of subalpine talus slopes, crevices and streambanks is rarely seen at Mount Adams, although it is a common sight at mountains elsewhere in the Cascades. It is known from two Suksdorf collections, one on Little Mount Adams and one at Mazama Glacier.

### *Campanula scabrella* Engelm.—ROUGH BELLFLOWER

Small, stiff hairs cover the spreading stems that may reach 1 dm in length of this taprooted perennial. The 0.5-4 cm long basal leaves are oblanceolate, while the stem leaves are narrower and nearly the same size. The flowers are typically solitary and erect. The blue corolla is 6-12 mm long, with the lobes varying in relationship to the tube. The style equals the corolla in length.

A species of talus slopes and flats at high elevation sites, typically growing among small stones and cinders, it is known from the summit of Little Mount Adams at 6,700 feet and from Hellroaring Canyon.

### *Campanula scouleri* A. DC.—SCOULER'S HAREBELL

Sprawling on stems up to 30 cm long, this campanula has ovate leaves near the base of the stems and lanceolate leaves above. They are 3-8 cm long, sharply toothed, and stalked. The light blue to nearly white flowers are 1-1.5 cm long, and bell-shaped. The free lobes measure approximately half the length of the flower and spread widely, exposing the style.

Fairly common in middle elevations to the subalpine, from 4,000 to over 7,000 feet, plants have been found at the trailhead of Trail 75 on the southwest side, at Morrison Creek and alongside Road 8040. They also grow near Road 23 on the northwest, at Midway Meadows, and at Hellroaring Canyon.

## Caprifoliaceae Juss.—HONEYSUCKLE FAMILY

Of diverse forms, the honeysuckles at Mount Adams include plants that look like garden honeysuckles but many more besides. These are trees or shrubs with opposite leaves. The corolla is typically irregular, with 5 lobes above a tube of varying length. The ovary is inferior and the fruit is often fleshy, colorful, and conspicuous.

1 Flowers densely clustered in terminal cymes or umbels; flowers more or less flat .......... 2
1 Flowers in pairs or short racemes or in axillary clusters; flowers tubular or funnel-shaped .......... 3

2(1) Leaves pinnate .......... *Sambucus*
2 Leaves simple or lobed .......... *Viburnum*

3(1) Plants with slender, creeping stems and glossy, evergreen leaves... .......... *Linnaea*
3 Plants upright shrubs or true vines; leaves deciduous, not glossy ... .......... 4

4(3) Flowers nearly regular; berries white .......... *Symphoricarpos*
4 Flowers irregular; berries red or black .......... *Lonicera*

### *Linnaea*—TWINFLOWER

#### *Linnaea borealis* L. ssp. *longiflora* (Torr.) Hultén—TWINFLOWER

Distinguished by evergreen leaves and long, slender trailing stems 1 m or more in length, this beautiful plant forms carpeting mats along the forest floor. The leaves are borne on both the stems that run along the ground and on 6-10 cm tall upright stems; they are 1-2 cm long, glossy, bright green, and oval to obovate with shallow teeth. The twin pink flowers are showy at the top of a forked, glandular stalk. They are 12-16 mm long, slightly irregularly bell-shaped, and scented of almond. The dry nutlet is clothed with short, hooked hairs.

Cosmopolitan at Mount Adams and common in dense forest and open forest edges, this species has been noted on the road to King Mountain and at Trail 7B on Road 2329.

## *Lonicera* L.—HONEYSUCKLE

Vines or shrubs with untoothed, deciduous leaves, honeysuckles bear flowers that are irregular to slightly 2-lipped, with 5 partly fused petals and 5 sepals. The flowers are arranged in terminal inflorescences (*L. ciliosa*) or borne in the leaf axils. The enlarged purplish bracts beneath the inflorescence distinguish *L. involucrata*. Flowers vary from dark red to yellow; the corolla is 5-lobed, and often appears 2-lipped. The fruit is a small, several-seeded berry.

Mount Adams is at the northern range limit of one of the species, *L. conjugialis*. Known from Suksdorf collections at the mountain, according to Hitchcock *L. caerulea* is quite rare in the region.

| | | |
|---|---|---|
| 1 | Vine with twining stems; several flowers in terminal or axillary inflorescences; flowers orange .................................... | *L. ciliosa* |
| 1 | Shrubs; flowers paired in leaf axils; flowers white, yellow, or pink .... ........................................................................ | 2 |
| 2(1) | Bracts at top of the flower stem enlarged, outer pair 8-15 mm long or more; ovaries and fruits free, separate ................ | *L. involucrata* |
| 2 | Bracts at top of the flower stem narrow and inconspicuous, mostly less than 5 mm long; ovaries and fruits partly or wholly fused ...... | 3 |
| 3(2) | Flowers dark red or reddish-purple . ....................... | *L. conjugialis* |
| 3 | Flowers yellow ................................................................... | 4 |
| 4(3) | Bractlets of each flower pair long enough to overlap the tubes of the flowers ............................................. | *L. caerulea* var. *cauriana* |
| 4 | Bractlets short, not reaching above the bases of the flowers .......... ................................................................. | *L. utahensis* |

### *Lonicera caerulea* L. var. *cauriana* (Fern.) Boivin
### BLUEFLY HONEYSUCKLE

A shrub that can reach 2 m in height, this honeysuckle is a subalpine species at Mount Adams. The 2-6 cm long leaves are elliptic to somewhat oblong, borne on short stalks, and rounded at the tip. They are short-hairy beneath. The 10-13 mm yellow corolla is scarcely 2-lipped, with the lobes often a little shorter than the tube, which is slightly spurred at the base and hairy within and without. The 1 cm long fruit is red.

This species is known from two Suksdorf collections, with an elevation of "6-7,000 feet" specified for one of them. These were probably made on the southeast side of the mountain, to judge from other collections made around the same dates. Variety *cauriana* was originally named by Fernald from a Suksdorf collection made at Mount Adams.

## Caprifoliaceae

### *Lonicera ciliosa* (Pursh) DC.—ORANGE HONEYSUCKLE

The slender vines of this shrub reach 8 m in length, and tend to clamber and twist over other plants. The 2-6 cm long leaves have short hairs on the margins; they are hairless and somewhat glaucous on the underside. The 2-2.5 cm-long orange flowers are borne in small clusters on the ends of the stems, above a pair of joined leaves. The berry is red.

A middle elevation species of open forest, and rare at the Mount Adams above 4,000 feet, this species was collected by the authors along Road 170 on the southeast side, close to King Mountain, where it clambered through a willow thicket.

### *Lonicera conjugialis* Kellogg—PURPLEFLOWER HONEYSUCKLE

A tall honeysuckle, varying from 6-15 dm, the leaves are borne on short petioles and vary in shape from elliptic to broadly ovate. They are 2.5-7.5 cm long and stiffly hairy beneath. The flowers are paired, and the corolla is dark reddish-purple, 8-11 mm long, strongly 2-lipped, and long-hairy within. The upper lip is shallowly 4-lobed, and the lower lip is entire. Nearly 1 cm long, the fruits are reddish-black and divided into 3 parts, mostly united.

Fairly common in middle elevations on moist sites, this species is found along the Stagman Ridge trail on the southwest side of the mountain. It grows along the Island Springs trail on the southeast, and on the west side as well. It was historically collected at Big Klickitat River (a Henderson collection), and by Suksdorf at Hellroaring Canyon and at "5-6,000 feet" (location unspecified).

### *Lonicera involucrata* (Richardson in Franklin) Banks var. *involucrata* TWINFLOWER HONEYSUCKLE

This is an upright honeysuckle, with stems up to 3 m tall. The 5-15 cm long leaves are oval to broadly lanceolate, typically somewhat hairy on the underside. The yellow-orange flowers are paired in the axils of the upper leaves; they are cupped by a pair of broad reddish-purple bracts. The black berries are conspicuous against the colorful bracts.

Preferring wet habitats, this is the most frequently-seen honeysuckle at Mount Adams in the middle elevation forest. It has been located along the Island Springs trail, on the road to Bench Lake, alongside the trail from Muddy Meadows to the Pacific Crest Trail, at Killen Creek Meadow, and on Road 23 at the Pacific Crest Trail crossing.

### *Lonicera utahensis* S. Wats.—UTAH HONEYSUCKLE

From 1-2 m tall, this honeysuckle is similar to *L. conjugialis* in being an erect shrub with distinct leaves. It differs in the creamy to yellow color of the flowers, and in the divergent fruits.

Uncommon at the mountain, this species was collected by the authors at Killen Creek meadows on the north side.

### Sambucus L.—ELDERBERRY

Easily recognized by their berries, these are tall, erect shrubs with weak stems and long leaves. The leaves are pinnately divided into large, sharply toothed lobes. The small, white- to cream-colored flowers are regular and configured in large, terminal, flat-topped (*S. nigra*) or pyramidal cymes (*S. racemosa*). The flowers are flat-faced and regular, with 5 partly-united petals, 5 sepals, and 5 exserted stamens. The fruit is a berry with 3-5 nutlets.

Never really common, these shrubs grow in middle elevation, open, often disturbed, rocky sites. The most commonly encountered elderberry at the mountain is *S. racemosa* var. *melanocarpa,* a variety with purplish rather than the typical red berries of red elderberry. Blue elderberry (*S. nigra*), the typical eastern Washington species, grows in dry places on the southeastern side of the mountain; the berries of this species are palatable.

| | | |
|---|---|---|
| 1 | Inflorescence flat-topped; fruits glaucous ....... | *S. nigra* ssp. *cerulea* |
| 1 | Inflorescence pyramidal; fruits not glaucous ............................ | 2 |
| 2(1) | Fruit red ........................................ | *S. racemosa* var. *racemosa* |
| 2 | Fruit purple ............................... | *S. racemosa* var. *melanocarpa* |

#### *Sambucus nigra L.* ssp. *cerulea* (Raf.) R. Bolli—BLUE ELDERBERRY

Occasionally a small tree up to 10 m tall, this shrub bears multiple glaucous stems. The 5-9 lanceolate to elliptic, hairless leaves are 8-12 cm long, sharp-tipped, and sharply toothed. Borne in a flat-topped, umbel-like cyme, the white to creamy flowers are 4-5 mm broad. The blue-black berries have a whitish bloom on the surface.

Most easily distinguished from red elderberry by the flat-topped blooms, this eastern Cascades species of dry habitats is rare at the mountain. It is found near Road 6000 on the southeast side, and along Road 23 on the southwest, just east of the Cascade crest.

#### *Sambucus racemosa* L. var. *melanocarpa* (A. Gray) McMinn BLACK ELDERBERRY

A shrub, ranging from 1-3 m tall, and characterized by purplish-black fruit, this is the most common elderberry at the mountain. There are 5-7 leaflets per leaf, each 5-15 cm long, and short-hairy on the underside. The 5-6 mm broad flowers are borne in an elongated, pyramidal cyme. The fruits are purplish-black.

Hitchcock reports this variety as coming north, "even as far as Mount Adams," but it is certainly the most common elderberry at the mountain. Found in middle elevation openings, rocky slopes, and disturbed sites, this variety is most easily recognized by the dark fruit. It grows along the Pineway trail, on Snipes Mountain, alongside Road 6000, and along slopes near Bench Lake on the southeast. It is also found alongside Road 2329 and near the Pacific Crest Trail north of Trail 64.

### ***Sambucus racemosa* L. var. *racemosa*—RED ELDERBERRY**

Similar to *S. racemosa* var. *melanocarpa* but generally taller (up to 5 m), this variety also differs in the red color of the berries. The leaves are markedly hairy beneath.

Uncommon at the mountain, this variety is found alongside Road 2329, near the Snipes Mountain trail, and at Hellroaring Canyon.

### ***Symphoricarpos* Duhamel—SNOWBERRY**

The common name refers to the white berrylike fruit, palatable to some animals but not humans. The fruit often persists through the fall and winter, long after the leaves have fallen. Shrubby species, the plants range in size from the trailing *S. hesperius* to the erect, branching *laevigatus* variety of *S. albus*, which may reach 2 or more meters in height (variety *albus* is much reduced in stature). In the spring, small bell-shaped flowers that vary from long to compact are borne in terminal or axillary racemes. The flowers are white to pinkish and composed of 5 sepals and 5 mostly-fused petals. The deciduous leaves are oval, 1-5 cm long, and short-hairy.

Two of the four *Symphoricarpos, S. oreophilus* and *S. albus* var. *albus,* are rare at the mountain, while *S. albus* var. *laevigatus* is the most common. These are middle elevation shrubs, of open habitats, such as forest boundaries and trail borders.

1 Corolla long and narrow, lobes ¼ - ½ as long as the tube ........................................................................ *S. oreophilus* var. *utahensis*

1 Corolla short and broad, lobes mostly equal in length to the tube ........................................................................ 2

2(1) Trailing or creeping shrub, less than .5 m tall; corolla 3-5 mm ........................................................................ *S. hesperius*

2 Erect shrub, taller than .5 m; corolla 5-7 mm .............................. 3

3(2) Plant less than 1 m tall; fruits to 1 cm; twigs hairy ........................................................................ *S. albus* var. *albus*

3 Plants greater than 1 m tall; fruits to 1.5 cm; twigs smooth ........................................................................ *S. albus* var. *laevigatus*

### *Symphoricarpos albus* (L.) Blake var. *albus*—SNOWBERRY

A shrub that reaches about 1 m in height, this snowberry has oval leaves 2-5 cm long. The stout stems often have wavy or lobed margins. The 4-5 mm long flowers are hairy on the inside. The berries are mostly 8-10 mm broad.

This variety is rare at the mountain, having been located on the west side at 4,200 feet on the Stagman Ridge trail.

### *Symphoricarpos albus* (L.) Blake var. *laevigatus* (Fern.) Blake COMMON SNOWBERRY

Similar to var. *albus*, this variety differs in the larger fruits (1-1.5 cm long) and in the size. Reaching 1-2 m tall, the twigs and lower surfaces of the leaves are sparsely hairy.

The most common variety at the mountain, it is found at the DNR Quarry, at the end of Road 170 on the southeast, and on Stagman Ridge on the southwest.

### *Symphoricarpos hesperius* G.N. Jones—CREEPING SNOWBERRY

Although sometimes erect, this is typically a trailing shrub with stems up to 1.5 m long. The 1-3 cm long oval leaves are entire or sometimes lobed. The 4 mm long flowers may have a few short hairs inside. The berry is about 6-8 mm long.

Found by the authors near Morrison Creek on Road 8040, this species is also known from a historical Henderson collection made in 1892 at an unrecorded location at Mount Adams.

### *Symphoricarpos oreophilus* A. Gray var. *utahensis* (Rydb.) A. Nels. MOUNTAIN SNOWBERRY

Erect shrubs ranging between .5-1.5 m tall, this snowberry is an east side forest species, rare at the mountain. The elliptic to elliptic-ovate leaves are 1-3.5 cm long, and are borne on 1-4 mm long stalks. The flowers droop from the upper leaf axils, or in few-flowered terminal racemes. The white corolla is bell-shaped, 7-10 mm long, with the lobes up to ½ as long as the tube. The 7-10 mm fruits are ellipsoid.

This species is known from a single site near the start of the Island Springs trail, close to Bench Lake on the southeast side of the mountain.

## *Viburnum* L.—VIBURNUM

### *Viburnum edule* (Michaux) Raf.—HIGHBUSH CRANBERRY

This multi-stemmed shrub ranges between 1-2 m tall and is distinguished by its rounded leaves. They are sharply toothed, palmately veined, and often 3-lobed at the end. The 3 mm broad white flowers are borne in small cymes. The petals spread widely above the tube; the 5 stamens are shorter than the petals. The bright red, berrylike drupes persist on the bushes through the winter.

Cosmopolitan at the mountain, this species grows in wet places in open forests and at meadow edges and is found at Swampy Meadow, along Road 115 at Midway Meadows, and in the meadow alongside Road 2329.

## Caryophyllaceae Juss.—PINK FAMILY

Consisting of 15 native and 7 weedy species at Mount Adams, most pinks bear small flowers, although the intricate flowers of the *Silene* species are quite showy. They are found from middle elevations to the higher subalpine regime, typically in open, somewhat dry habitats. There are both annual and perennial herbs present, each with opposite, untoothed leaves. The flowers vary widely: there are typically 4 or 5 petals, although the petals may be absent altogether. The petals may be "clawed," with a broad blade above and a slender attachment below. There are 4 or 5 sepals, either separated or united into a tube. Most species have 10 stamens and the ovary is superior, with 2-5 styles. The fruit is a capsule.

| | | |
|---|---|---|
| 1 | Sepals united | 2 |
| 1 | Sepals distinct or almost distinct | 3 |
| 2(1) | Flowers with conical, close, but not overlapping bracts | *Dianthus* |
| 2 | Flowers without bracts | *Silene* |
| (1) | Papery stipules present at base of leaves | *Spergularia* |
| 3 | Stipules absent | 4 |
| 4(3) | Capsule cylindrical, curved near the tip | *Cerastium* |
| 4 | Capsule egg-shaped to elliptical or nearly cylindrical, but never curved at the tip | 5 |
| 5(4) | Styles 5, alternating with the sepals | *Sagina* |
| 5 | Styles mostly 3, opposite the sepals | 6 |
| 6(5) | Petals deeply divided at the tip | *Stellaria* |
| 6 | Petals not notched, rounded at the tip | 7 |
| 7(6) | Mature capsule opening with 3 teeth | *Minuartia* |
| 7 | Mature capsule opening with 6 teeth | 8 |

8(7) Styles 2-3 mm long; leaves 3-10 mm wide .................. *Moehringia*
8 Styles 0.5-2 mm long; leaves up to 1 mm wide ................ *Arenaria*

## *Arenaria* L.—SANDWORT

### *Arenaria capillaris* Poir. ssp. *americana* Maguire
### SLENDER MOUNTAIN SANDWORT

With short branches creating dense mats, this perennial bears linear, sharply pointed, and sometimes curved leaves 1.5-6 cm long. The numerous flowering stems can reach 30 cm tall, and bear a few pairs of leaves. The flowers are borne in few-flowered, flat-topped clusters.

A subalpine to alpine plant of rocky sites, including talus slopes, this species is common at the mountain. Locations include the north side of Little Mount Adams, the Island Springs trail, the Round the Mountain trail north of the Stagman Ridge trail, the Cold Springs trailhead, and Road 82 at the gate to Bird Creek.

## *Cerastium* L.—MOUSE-EARRED CHICKWEED, CHICKWEED

These annual or perennial herbs are distinguished from other pink family members by the 5 distinct sepals and 5 petals that are shallowly to deeply notched at the tips. The fruit is a cylindrical capsule that curves at maturity. There is a single native species at Mount Adams; the other three are introduced.

1 Native perennial; petals at least 1.5 times longer than the sepals ........................................................ *C. arvense* ssp. *strictum*
1 Annual weeds; petals less than 1.5 times as long as the sepals .......................................................................... 2

2(1) Flowers clustered in heads; petals obscure, not exceeding the sepals ........................................................ *C. glomeratum*
2 Flowers in cymes; petals usually as long as or longer than the sepals .......................................................................... 3

3(2) Flower stalks longer than the sepals; petals shallowly notched ....... ........................................................ *C. semidecandrum*
3 Flower stalks as long as or shorter than the sepals; petals 2-lobed .. ........................................................ *C. nutans* var. *nutans*

### *Cerastium arvense* L. ssp. *strictum* (L.) Ugborogho
### FIELD CHICKWEED

A native perennial, this species is distinguished by its showy white flowers. The 15-40 cm tall stems are somewhat matted and hairy. The 2-3 cm long leaves are linear to lanceolate, and there are small bundles of leaves in the axils of the upper stem leaves. The bracts of the inflorescence are characterized by papery margins. The stalks and the sepals are minutely glandular. The deeply notched petals are 12-15 mm long and 1 cm wide.

Known from a Suksdorf collection at Hellroaring Canyon, and also from Flett and Henderson collections on the east side, this middle elevation to alpine elevation species of dry or rocky sites is uncommon at Mount Adams, but where present is sometimes abundant. It is known from as high as 8,300 feet.

### *Cerastium glomeratm* Thuill.—SLENDER CHICKWEED

With 10-20 cm tall erect stems, this weedy middle elevation annual is glandular-hairy throughout. The 5-20 mm long leaves are oval to narrowly ovate. The flowers are borne in small heads at the tops of the stems and the flower stalks are shorter than the sepals. Both petals and sepals are approximately 5-6 mm long.

Rare at Mount Adams, this weed was collected by the authors alongside Road 115 at Midway Meadows at an elevation of 4,500 feet.

### *Cerastium nutans* Raf. var. *nutans*—NODDING CHICKWEED

A glandular-hairy annual that bears 1 to many simple or branched stems 5-20 cm long, this species has basal and lower stem leaves that are oblanceolate to spoon-shaped and 7-25 mm long. The 5-20 mm long stem leaves are linear-lanceolate to ovate and stalkless. The flowers are configured in a loose and leafy cyme; the pedicels are over twice as long as the calyx. The sepals are 3-5 mm long, and the petals are usually shorter than the sepals.

A species of middle elevation dry to moist sites, this plant grows at Muddy Meadows on the southwest side and at Midway Meadows on the north. It is found on disturbed, drier parts of each meadow, in small numbers.

### *Cerastium semidecandrum* L.—FIVE-STAMEN CHICKWEED

This is an annual weed, branched at the base with several erect or ascending sticky stems, reaching 20 cm in height. The leaves are stalkless, 5-18 mm long, and covered with short, white hairs. The basal leaves are narrowly oblanceolate, and the stem leaves are ovate to elliptic. The inflorescence is configured as a 3 to 30 flowered cyme. The petals are white and notched, while the sepals are greenish. There are 5 stamens instead of 10 as is usual for *Cerastium*; hence, "semi-deca" in the name.

A weed more commonly found south of Mount Adams (in Oregon), it is known from a single collection made by the authors at Midway Meadows at the end of Road 115, at 4,500 feet.

### *Dianthus* L.—PINK

#### *Dianthus armeria* L.—GRASS PINK, DEPTFORD PINK

A single stem 30-60 cm tall characterizes this annual that may live two years. There is a tuft of linear, basal leaves up to 10 cm long, with the stem leaves progressively smaller. The 3-6 flowers are borne in a crowded cyme, and the blade of the dark pink petal is about 3 mm long; it is slightly wider than the claw.

This weedy species is known from a single site alongside Road 23, ½ mile south of the intersection with Road 8860, on the north side of Grand Meadow.

### *Minuartia* L.—SANDWORT

Subalpine to alpine perennials with short linear leaves, these species were formerly included in *Arenaria*. The capsules open by 3 valves—in *Arenaria*, as now defined, they open by 6 valves. Prior to the maturity of the fruit, close examination of the developing ovary will reveal 3 sutures in *Minuartia*; *Arenaria* has 6.

1 Stems very fragile, easily broken; sepals blunt ......... *M. obtusiloba*
1 Stems not fragile; sepals sharp-tipped ........ *M. nuttallii* var. *nuttallii*

#### *Minuartia nuttallii* (Pax) Briq. var. *nuttallii*—BRITTLE SANDWORT

The 10 cm long stems of this spreading perennial are glandular-hairy and prone to breaking at the nodes of the leaves. The 3-10 mm long leaves are linear and sharply pointed. The sepals are 3-veined, with a long point and approximately 4-5 mm long. The petals are usually a bit shorter than the sepals. The sepals are also longer than the mature capsule.

An alpine plant, this species has been found on the lower slope on the north side of Little Mount Adams at 6,600 feet and at "7-8,000 feet" by Suksdorf at an unspecified location, most likely close to the Mazama Glacier.

#### *Minuartia obtusiloba* (Rydb.) House—ALPINE SANDWORT

The 10 cm long densely tufted stems of this perennial form mats as they trail along the ground. The 4-7 mm long leaves are linear and minutely glandular-hairy. Each slender flowering stem bears a single flower. The petals are approximately 10 mm long, and the sepals are short and tend to curve inwards, covering the petals. The capsule is approximately as long as the sepals.

A subalpine to alpine species, this sandwort is known from the summit of Little Mount Adams at 6,700 feet and from Hellroaring Canyon (a Suksdorf collection with no other specific information).

### *Moehringia* L.—GROVE SANDWORT

#### *Moehringia macrophylla* (Hook.) Torr.
#### LARGE-LEAF SANDWORT

Several 5 to 15 cm-tall stems densely clothed in 1-6 cm long lanceolate to oblanceolate pairs of leaves rise from a slender, spreading rootstock. Both stems and leaves are typically finely hairy. The stems bear 2-6 long-stalked white flowers in an open cyme. The 4-5 mm long sepals are somewhat longer than the petals.

Found in moist, disturbed roadside locations as well as woods and shady meadows, this species grows alongside Road 23 and at the intersection of Road 782 and Road 8040 on the south side. It is also known from a Suksdorf collection made "above Bird Creek."

### *Sagina* L.—PEARLWORT

These annual or perennial plants grow as compact or spreading mats. The leaves are linear and sharply pointed; there may be secondary bundles of leaves in the axils of the main leaves. The flowers are borne on threadlike stalks and are white. The sepals and petals number 4 or 5 and are typically less than 2 mm long. The 3 mm long mature capsule is conical to egg-shaped and opens by 4 or 5 valves.

1 Plant annual, with very slender stems, without a basal rosette of leaves .................................... *S. decumbens* ssp. *occidentalis*
1 Plant perennial, with stems more stout and with a basal rosette of leaves ........................................................................ 2

2(1) Stem leaves with bundles of secondary leaves in the axils; sepals mostly 4 ....................................................... *S. procumbens*
2 Stem leaves merely paired; sepals 5 ...................... *S. saginoides*

#### *Sagina decumbens* (Elliott) Torr. & A. Gray ssp. *occidentalis* (S. Wats.) G.E. Crow—WESTERN PEARLWORT

This native annual bears slender, weak stems up to 15 cm tall. It lacks a basal rosette of leaves as well as the leaf bundles in the axils. The leaves are 5-20 mm long, and the flower stalks are typically glandular-hairy and tend to remain straight after flowering. There are 5 petals and sepals, and 5 or 10 stamens. The capsule is conical.

This species is known from a collection made by the authors near Trail 75 at Salt Creek on the southwest side.

### *Sagina procumbens* L.—CREEPING PEARLWORT

This is a matted, weedy species, with slender stems approximately 15 cm long. The plants have a basal rosette of leaves, the largest 3-10 mm long; the stem leaves bear bundles of smaller leaves in the axils. The flowers are borne in the leaf axils on hairless stalks 5-20 mm tall. The stalks curve at the top when mature. There are typically 4 sepals, petals, and stamens; occasionally a plant will bear flowers without petals. The capsule opens by 4 valves.

This weed is known from a collection along Road 115 on the northwest side of the mountain, where it grows in a highly disturbed dry meadow.

### *Sagina saginoides* (L.) H. Karst.—ALPINE PEARLWORT

This hairless, matted perennial bears basal leaf rosettes, and has slender, ascending stems. The 5-15 mm long leaves are linear. The flowering stems may reach 10 cm in height, and the slender, hairless stalks are 1-3 cm long. There are 5 sepals and petals and 10 stamens. The capsule is conical.

A subalpine to alpine plant known from a Suksdorf collection made at Hellroaring Canyon, specific information is not given on the label. Elsewhere in the Washington Cascades, the species grows on moist ground among small rocks.

### *Silene* L.—CAMPION, CATCHFLY

This large genus is represented by three native perennial species at the mountain. These include a low, matted species (*S. suksdorfii*) and two tufted species. The flowering stems are glandular-hairy, at least on the upper half. One of these, *S. oregana,* bears intricate flowers with deeply divided and forked lobes. The ribbed calyx is formed from the 4 fused sepals and may be somewhat inflated, although not so much as with weedy *Silene* species. The petals are longer than the calyx and consist of a slender claw and broader blade. At the junction of the claw and blade are paired scalelike or pointed auricles and, in the case of two species, lateral lobes, resulting in an ornate flower. There are 10 stamens and 3 styles; the capsule is egg-shaped.

1 Introduced plant found at low elevation roadsides; calyx hairless, becoming inflated at maturity ...................................... *S. vulgaris*
1 Native plants; calyx short-hairy and often glandular, not becoming markedly inflated at maturity ................................................... 2

2(1) Alpine plants, typically much less than 15 cm tall ........ *S. suksdorfii*
2 Middle elevation and subalpine plants, more than 20 cm tall ........ 3

3(2) Each stem with 2-4 flowers, typically borne singly; auricles 2, blunt; petal tips divided into 4 blunt lobes .............................. *S. parryi*

3 Each stem with 8-10 flowers, often paired; auricles 4, pointed; petal tips divided into 4 to 6 pointed lobes .......................... *S. oregana*

### *Silene oregana* S. Wats.—OREGON CATCHFLY

This tufted plant is characterized by 15-25 cm tall stems that are short-hairy and glandular above. The 3-5 cm long basal leaves are narrowly obovate and hairless. There are 2-3 pairs of smaller, short-hairy stem leaves. The 15 mm long calyx is glandular and cylindrical before the capsule expands. The 14-15 mm long petals are white and are elaborately formed. The 2-lobed blades are deeply divided, and each lobe is forked at about its midpoint. There are 2 linear side lobes and 4 pointed auricles at the point where the blade meets the claw.

Fairly common on the southeast side of the mountain, this species has also been noted on the west. Typically it is found in drier habitats, up to about 6,900 feet, including the DNR quarry, Pineway Trail, the trail northeast of Bench Lake, and at the gate at Bird Creek on Road 82. It is also known from a Suksdorf collection at Hellroaring Canyon.

### *Silene parryi* (S. Wats.) C.L. Hitchc. & Maguire—PARRY'S CATCHFLY

This tufted perennial bears mostly basal leaves. The 20-50 cm tall stems are finely short-hairy below and glandular above. The 3-7 cm long basal leaves are narrowly oblanceolate, with the stems leaves much reduced and narrower. The flowers are in groups of 2-4 in a narrow, loose, and unbranched inflorescence. The ribs of the calyx are glandular and the 12-15 mm long petals are white. The blade of the petal is deeply divided into 2 narrow lobes, each with a narrower lateral lobe nearly as long; thus the flower appears 4-lobed. There are 2 blunt auricles that range from 1-2 mm long.

A fairly common subalpine to alpine plant on the southeast side of Mount Adams, Parry's catchfly is known from collections along Trail 20 near Island Springs, at the head of Hellroaring River, and close to the terminus of the Mazama Glacier. It can grow in light shade with subalpine fir.

### *Silene suksdorfii* B.L. Robins.—CASCADE CATCHFLY

Low and tufted, this is a mat-forming perennial of subalpine to alpine environments. The basal leaves are linear, blunt at the tip, and less than 2 cm long. There are 1 or 2 pairs of stem leaves. The flowering stems are approximately 10 cm high and the flowers are borne on glandular stalks, 2 or 3 per stem. The ribs of the calyx are densely clothed with purplish hairs. The white petals are 15-20 mm long and the blade is deeply divided. There are 2 nearly linear auricles at its base, but lateral lobes are lacking.

This species is known from the summit of Little Mount Adams, from a Suksdorf collection at the head of Hellroaring Canyon, and from a Henderson collection designated as "at and above glaciers" —probably on the south side. It reaches almost 8,000 feet. According to Hitchcock, it is primarily a "peak" species known at selected mountains from Mount Baker in northern Washington to Mount Thielson in Oregon.

#### *Silene vulgaris* (Moench) Garcke—BLADDER CAMPION

Branched, hairless stems up to 50 cm long define this weedy perennial. The 3-5 cm long leaves are ovate-lanceolate, while the stem leaves are narrower and shorter. The calyx is clothed with a few hairs and the white flowers are numerous in open cymes. The petals are 15 cm long and the blade is deeply divided into 2 divergent lobes. There are 2 very small auricles at the base of the blade.

This weed is known from a single collection made by the authors at the trailhead at Morrison Creek, at 4,560 feet on highly disturbed ground. It seems likely that the plant will not persist here.

### *Spergularia* (Pers.) J. Presl & C. Presl—SANDSPURRY

#### *Spergularia rubra* (L.) J. Presl & C. Presl—RED SANDSPURRY

Distinguished by prostrate stems that reach 20 cm in length but may be much shorter, this matted annual may persist for more than a year. The 5-10 mm long leaves are borne in bundles of 2 or more in the axils of the stem leaves. The solitary flowers are borne on short, threadlike, glandular stalks at the tops of the stems, and are pink to reddish-pink. There are 6-10 stamens.

One of the most common weeds at Mount Adams, reaching at least 4,500 feet, it has been found on the southeast side on Road K6900, at the wet meadows on Road K6000, and at the Hellroaring Creek trailhead parking lot. It is also known from the Road 23 overlook and from a Suksdorf collection made at Bird Creek Meadows, an indication that this weed has been present for a long time.

### *Stellaria* L.—STARWORT

Perennial natives, these species differ from other pink family members in *not* having features that distinguish the other genera: they lack stipules, clawed petals, bundles of leaves in the leaf axils, and curved capsules. The stems tend to be lax and the flowers are solitary or in small cymes. There are 5 free sepals; when present, the 5 petals are shallowly or deeply divided into 2 lobes. The capsule is egg-shaped or somewhat cylindrical, with six valves.

## Caryophyllaceae

1 Petals longer than the sepals .................................. *S. longipes*
1 Petals shorter than the sepals, or petals absent ........................ 2

2(1) Flowers solitary in the axils; leaf margins crisped ........... *S. crispa*
2 Flowers few to many in clusters; leaf margins even .................. 3
3(2) Flowers in false umbels; bracts of the inflorescence small, papery .. ................................................................ *S. umbellata*
3 Flowers in open, branched cymes, not appearing umbel-like; bracts of the inflorescence leafy, at least in the lower branches ........... 4

4(3) Stem leaves lanceolate, mostly more than 2 cm long; sepals 3 to 3.5 mm long ..................................... *S. borealis* ssp. *sitchana*
4 Stem leaves elliptic to ovate, mostly less than 2 cm long; sepals less than 3 mm long ......................................... *S. calycantha*

### *Stellaria borealis* Bigelow ssp. *sitchana* (Steudel) Piper BOREAL SANDWORT

This sprawling perennial bears hairless stems that vary widely—from 15-50 cm long. The 2-8 cm long leaves are narrowly lanceolate to ovate. The flowers may vary from a few to several in small cymes at the tops of the stems. As the capsule ripens, the stalks bend downwards. Typically there are 5 petals that are shorter than the 3.5-.4.5 mm long sepals; occasionally, petals are absent. There are 5 stamens.

Rare at the mountain, this species is known only from a Suksdorf collection made on the northwest side, probably at the Lewis River at around 4,000 feet.

### *Stellaria calycantha* (Ledeb.) Bong.—NORTHERN SANDWORT

This perennial is configured with prostrate or weakly ascending stems that are 5-25 cm long and short-hairy above. The 3-25 mm long leaves are elliptic to ovate (occasionally lanceolate). The flowers may be borne singly in the leaf axils, or sometimes grouped in a few-flowered cyme. The 1.5-3 mm long sepals are longer than the petals, which are frequently absent altogether. There are 5 stamens.

Known from Suksdorf collections at Hellroaring Canyon and at "6-7,000 feet" (location unspecified although probably the southeast side), elsewhere in the Cascades, this species favors moist, open places in the subalpine regime.

### *Stellaria crispa* Cham. & Schltdl.—CRISPED SANDWORT

Up to 40 cm long, the weak, prostrate stems of this perennial occasionally become matted. The 5-25 mm long leaves are ovate, with the lower leaves on short stalks and the upper ones stalkless. The leaf margins are wavy but not toothed, hence the common name of "crisped." The 1-2 cm long, solitary flowers are borne on slender stalks in the leaf axils. The 2.5-4 mm long sepals have papery margins; the petals are usually absent. There are 10 or fewer stamens.

Moisture-loving, this common, unobtrusive plant has been observed at many locations, including the meadow of Hellroaring Creek at 6,000 feet, the culvert at Road 23 close to the overlook, the roadside near Grand Meadow, Bathtub Meadow, and along the trail from Muddy Meadows to the Pacific Crest Trail. It tolerates both sun and shade.

#### ***Stellaria longipes*** **Goldie—LONG-STALKED SANDWORT**

This erect perennial has stems 10-20 cm tall, clothed with 1-4 cm long linear to narrowly lanceolate, sharply pointed leaves. The flowers are numerous on erect branches in a narrow inflorescence. The sepals are 3-5 mm long, and the petals are somewhat longer. The capsule is longer than the calyx.

Rare at the mountain, this species is known from a single observation by Paul Slichter in the saddle on the north side of Little Mount Adams, at about 6,500 feet.

#### ***Stellaria umbellata*** **Turcz. *ex* Kar. & Kir.—UMBRELLA STARWORT**

A slender, weakly ascending plant with stems that reach about 25 cm in length, the leaves are about 15 mm long, rarely to 20 mm and lanceolate to oblong. The branches of the cyme are threadlike and give the appearance of being arranged in an umbel. The flowers often lack petals; if present, they are much shorter than the 2-3 mm long sepals.

This species is known from just one collection made by Elroy Burnett, close to Foggy Flat at about 5,800 feet on the north side of Mount Adams.

## Celastraceae R. Br.—STAFF-TREE FAMILY

### ***Paxistima*** **Ref.—MOUNTAIN-BOXWOOD**

#### ***Paxistima myrsinites*** **(Pursh) Raf.—MOUNTAIN-BOXWOOD**

Rounded and typically not more than 50 cm tall, this shrub bears opposite, evergreen leaves. Elliptical to ovate and toothed on the margin above the midpoint, they are dark green and on short stalks. The tiny maroon flowers are configured in small clusters in the leaf axils. They consist of 4 sepals, 4 petals, and 4 stamens, the stamens borne on a disk that curves half-way around the ovary. The fruit is small and asymmetrical.

Relatively common in middle elevation forests and openings, this sole member of its family at Mount Adams is found on the road to King

Mountain, along Road 2329, and at Snipes Mountain. Another spelling of the name is *Pachistima*.

## Chenopodiaceae Vent.—GOOSEFOOT FAMILY

### *Chenopodium* L.—GOOSEFOOT

#### *Chenopodium album* L. var. *album*—LAMB'S QUARTERS

This annual herb ranges from 50-100 cm tall and is branched. The 2-4 cm long, opposite leaves are stalked, ovate to diamond-shaped, and irregularly toothed. The underside of the leaves is covered with grayish, mealy particles. The 2 mm broad, stalkless, greenish flowers are in terminal or axillary spikes; they consist of 5 short sepals and 5 stamens. There are no petals.

A sparingly naturalized weed, this species is found at the DNR quarry, at the Morrison Creek trailhead, along the Pineway Trail, and at the horse camp at Hellroaring Creek, above Bench Lake.

## Clusiaceae Lindl.—MANGOSTEEN FAMILY

### *Hypericum* L.—ST. JOHNSWORT

These are perennial herbs with opposite, attached leaves, often dotted with glands. The flowers are composed of 5 broad, rounded, yellow petals and 5 lanceolate sepals. The stamens number from 15-50 and may be united at their bases in several groups. The fruit is a capsule.

1 Matted plant of bogs and meadows; petals less than 6 mm long; leaves not black-dotted along margins ................ *H. anagalloides*

1 Upright plants of open areas; petals more than 6 mm long; leaves black-dotted along margins ................................................ 2

2(1) Sepals 3-5 times as long as broad, sharply-tipped; leaves oblanceolate; weed .......................................... *H. perforatum*

2 Sepals less than 3 times as long as broad, rounded to sharply-tipped; leaves ovate; native perennial ..... *H. scouleri* ssp. *nortoniae*

#### *Hypericum anagalloides* Cham. & Schltdl.—TINKER'S PENNY

This species spreads from runners as a matted groundcover, with stems 5-25 cm long. The 3-10 mm long leaves are rounded and clasp the stems; they are marked with greenish glandular dots. Several flowers are configured in a cyme. The 2-4 mm long yellow petals may be shaded a salmon or orange color. The fruit is 1-chambered.

A middle elevation native of wet ground in meadows and boggy habitats, this is a relatively common species at the mountain. It grows at

Swampy and Babyshoe Meadows, as well as alongside Road 6900. It is also abundant in the meadow at the intersection of Road 23 and 2329.

### *Hypericum perforatum* L.—COMMON ST. JOHNSWORT

The erect plants of this roadside weed have numerous, 30-100 cm tall branched stems from a heavy taproot; it also spreads by runners. The 1.5-2.5 cm long leaves are linear to oblong, with dark glandular dots; the sepals and petals bear similar dots. The numerous flowers are borne on stiff branches in a leafy cyme. The bright yellow petals are 8-12 cm long, and the fruit is 3-chambered.

A noxious species, it is most common on the west side, particularly along Road 23. It is, as yet, scarce elsewhere.

### *Hypericum scouleri* Hook. ssp. *nortoniae* (M.E. Jones) J. Gillett WESTERN ST. JOHNSWORT

Rising from widely-spreading slender stolons and rhizomes this perennial bears erect stems that range from 10-80 cm in height. The stems vary from simple to freely branched, and the 1-3 cm long leaves are ovate to obovate in shape. The cymes are few-flowered, and leafy, the 4-5 mm long sepals are dotted a purplish-black; the petals are twice as long and yellow with purplish-black dots on the margins. There are numerous stamens and the 3-celled capsule is 6-9 mm long.

A wet habitat species from above 5,000 feet, it was collected at Hellroaring Canyon by Suksdorf. It is also known from a collection made by Elroy Burnett on the southeast side, in the area near Bird Creek Meadows.

## Convolvulaceae Juss.—MORNING GLORY FAMILY

### *Calystegia* R. Br.—BINDWEED

Reminiscent of both morning glories of the garden and the weedy bindweeds, the two species in this family at Mount Adams are uncommon native perennial vines that prefer dry slopes below about 5,000 feet, where they twine among low shrubs or sprawl on the ground. Each has a 5-lobed, funnel-shaped flower with 5 stamens, 1 pistil with 2 stigmas, and a capsule bearing a few large seeds.

1 Plants truly climbing vines; stems mostly short-hairy .................... *C. sepium* ssp. *angulata*

1 Plants trailing or sprawling; stems hairless ............................. C. *atriplicifolia* ssp. *atriplicifolia*

**_Calystegia atriplicifolia_ Hallier f. ssp. _atriplicifolia_**
**NIGHTBLOOMING FALSE BINDWEED**

Trailing to more or less erect stems that may vary between 1-6 dm, depending on their configuration, this low plant rises from slender rootstocks. Long stalked, the leaves are triangular to heart-shaped, 4-5 cm long, and thickened. The white to pinkish flowers are borne singly, the corolla funnel-shaped and flared, and 3-5 cm long. The capsule is about 1 cm long.

Preferring rocky, open sites, this middle elevation species is found on the south and east side of Mount Adams. Historic collections were made at Bird Creek Meadows, along the Big Muddy River, and at Morrison Creek. It was formerly named *Convolvulus nyctagineus* Greene.

**_Calystegia sepium_ (L.) R. Br. ssp. _angulata_ Brummitt**
**HEDGE FALSE BINDWEED**

Trailing stems 2-3 m long from slender, elongate rhizomes distinguish this sprawling, clambering species. The 5-12 cm long leaves are arrowhead-shaped with the rounded basal lobes varying between directed outward or downward. The flowers are borne singly in the leaf axils. A white to deep pink corolla 4-7 cm long is funnel-shaped. The capsules are ovoid to rounded, and are 1 cm long.

Preferring moist soil in open habitats, but tolerating drier places, this species also grows in disturbed areas along roadsides. It has been found near Snipes Mountain, at the junction of Road 8040 and Road 781, near Morrison Creek, and at the gate at Bird Creek on Road 82. It is also known from the Island Springs trail in the Bird Creek area and from a Henderson collection at Muddy River Canyon.

## Cornaceae (Dumort.) Dumort.—DOGWOOD FAMILY

### *Cornus* L.—DOGWOOD

Three species occur at Mount Adams, but only the herbaceous perennial bunchberry (*C. unalaschkensis*) is frequently seen. The leaves are simple (neither toothed nor lobed) and opposite, or whorled in the case of bunchberry. The small flowers are crowded into flat-topped clusters or hemispherical heads. The "flower" of bunchberry appears very different: a whorl of large, white bracts setting off the cluster of true, but individually insignificant, flowers at the center. Petals and sepals are in fours and the fruit is a drupe (like a cherry in structure, but with 2 stones)

1 Perennial herb, with whorled leaves; flowers subtended by large white bracts .............................................. *C. unalaschkensis*
1 Shrubs, with opposite leaves; flower clusters lacking bracts ........ 2

2(1) Petals 2-3 mm long; styles 1-2 mm long ..... *C. sericea* ssp. *sericea*
2 Petals more than 3 mm long; styles 2-3 mm long ........................ ................................................... *C. sericea* ssp. *occidentalis*

### *Cornus sericea* L. ssp. *occidentalis* (Torr. & A. Gray) Fosberg WESTERN DOGWOOD

A spreading shrub 2-4 m tall, this dogwood is distinguished by the bright red to reddish-purple bark of young branches. The color of the mature branches is gray. The leaves are oval to ovate and 4-8 cm long, with heavy veination. They are typically hairy on the underside; in this subspecies the hairs lie flat against the leaf surface. The white flowers are in terminal clusters, up to 10 cm broad and nearly flat. The fruits are white and the stones are grooved lengthwise.

Evidently rare at Mount Adams, this subspecies is known from a Suksdorf collection made in the valley of Big Muddy Creek, without other details on the label.

### *Cornus sericea* L. ssp. sericea—REDOSIER DOGWOOD

Very similar to ssp. *occidentalis*, to such a degree that the best features to separate them are those given in the key. In addition, the hairs of the leaves are likely to be spreading or wooly. The stones are smooth, not grooved.

Another plant collected by Suksdorf in the valley of Big Muddy Creek, no other details of its habitat are given.

### *Cornus unalaschkensis* Ledeb.—BUNCHBERRY

Widely spreading rootstocks allow this attractive perennial herb to form large patches in favorable areas. The individual stem is 10-20 cm tall, at the top of which 4-7 leaves form a whorl; 1 or 2 small, leaflike bracts are usually present near the midsection of the stem. The leaves are oval, pointed at the ends, and 2-8 cm long. The greenish flowers form a compact head on a short stalk. Beneath the head is another whorl of 4 white bracts, each about 3 cm long. The fruit is bright orange-red.

## Crassulaceae DC.—STONECROP FAMILY

Found primarily on the southeast side of the mountain, the stonecrops are not particularly widespread, unusual given their tendency to grow in open, dry places. They are represented by two genera and four species, with two of the three sedums very uncommon. The flower color ranges from yellow to pinkish or purple. The flowers are borne in open, freely branching cymes. The stems are typically thickened and the leaves oval to rounded, simple, stalkless, and succulent, although flattened in some species. The 5 sepals are united at their bases; the petals may be fused as well. There are typically 10 stamens. The fruits are follicles.

*Rhodiola integrifolia* was formerly included in the *Sedum* genus. It is distinguished by flower color and the fact that male and female flowers are borne on separate plants.

1 Leaves flattened; flowers pink to reddish-purple ............ *Rhodiola*
1 Leaves not flattened; flowers yellow .............................. *Sedum*

## *Rhodiola* L.—STONECROP

### *Rhodiola integrifolia* Raf. ssp. *integrifolia*
### KING'S CROWN, LEDGE STONECROP

Lacking a basal rosette, this perennial is distinguished by very thick, 5-10 cm tall branched stems. The stem leaves are obovate, flat, and are borne alternately; they are sometimes toothed above the middle. The 3 mm long petals are pinkish to reddish-purple, as are the 2 mm long sepals. The follicles are erect and curved outward at the tips.

Known from Suksdorf collections, one made at Hellroaring Canyon and another at "7-8,000 feet," this is a rare stonecrop at the mountain.

## *Sedum* L.—STONECROP

These are perennial herbs with short, thick stems and succulent, stalkless leaves. Typically, there is a basal rosette of leaves as well as leafy stems. The yellow flowers are borne in cymes. The 5 sepals are united at the base and the petals may also be partially fused. There are 10 stamens. The pistils develop into erect or divergent follicles.

1 Leaves on the flowering stems opposite, oval to spatulate, less than 1 cm long ...................................................... *S. divergens*
1 Leaves on the flowering stems alternate, various shapes, more than 1 cm long ....................................................................... 2

2(1) Leaves broadest below midlength, tapering, strongly keeled; petals 6-8 mm long ................................................ *S. stenopetalum*
2 Leaves broadest above midlength, flattened but succulent; petals 10-13 mm long ................................................. *S. oreganum*

#### *Sedum divergens* S. Wats.—SPREADING STONECROP

*Divergens* refers to the follicles, which spread widely as the seeds mature, although the plant spreads as well from horizontal stems. The 10 cm tall flowering stems are leafy, with the leaves borne in opposite pairs. The basal leaves are bright green, sometimes tinged reddish, widest above the middle, broadly obovate in shape, and very thick. The stem leaves are shorter and flatter. The 6-7 mm long yellow petals have a lengthwise groove and are not fused.

A middle elevation to subalpine species of cliffs and rocky sites, it is locally common at Mount Adams although never really abundant. It is found on the ridge above Muddy River Canyon, at Hellroaring Canyon, and alongside Road 23.

#### *Sedum oreganum* Nutt. ssp. *oreganum*—OREGON STONECROP

Growing from robust rootstocks, this perennial has basal rosettes, with flowering stems that range from 10-20 cm tall. The 6-18 mm long leaves are obovate to spoon-shaped, flattened, and bright green. The flowering stem leaves are borne in an alternate configuration. The 8-10 mm long yellow petals are fused slightly at their bases. The follicles are erect.

Very uncommon at the mountain, this species is known from a Flett collection at "Hellroaring River" – no other location information is given on the herbarium label.

#### *Sedum stenopetalum* Pursh—WORMLEAF STONECROP

The tall stems of this stonecrop rise to 20 cm from rootstocks. The 5-15 mm long leaves are alternate, linear to linear-lanceolate in shape, strongly keeled beneath, and sharply tipped. (The dried midrib of the leaf often persists on the stem.) The 6-8 mm long yellow petals are narrowly lanceolate and the follicles are widely divergent.

This species is known from a single Flett collection, made at "Mount Adams."

## Droseraceae Salisb.—SUNDEW FAMILY

### *Drosera* L.—SUNDEW

#### *Drosera anglica* Huds.—ENGLISH SUNDEW

The thickened, sticky basal leaves, configured in a rosette, distinguish this insectivorous species. The leaf blades are typically twice as long as broad, oblanceolate to spoon-shaped, and 1-3 cm long. The leafless stems are 6-18 cm tall. The inflorescence is raceme-like, occasionally with 2 racemes, and has 2-7 flowers. The 5-6 mm long calyx is conelike for about 1/3 of its length, with ovate-oblong lobes. The white, oblong petals are longer than the calyx. The 4-5 styles are split for 2/3 of their length.

Found in wet sphagnum meadows at middle elevations, this interesting species is locally common, primarily on the west and northwest sides of Mount Adams. It grows at Swampy Meadows and was collected by the authors at Babyshoe Meadow.

## Ericaceae Juss.—HEATH FAMILY

As used in this flora, the Ericaceae excludes the Monotropaceae, herbaceous plants that lack chlorophyll, and the Pyrolaceae, herbs with green leaves and separate petals. Nevertheless, the Ericaceae is a diverse group. All that occur at Mount Adams are shrubs or sub-shrubs. Madrone (*Arbutus menziesii*), a common tree in the Northwest, is absent.

All have 5 free or partly fused sepals and 5 partly or nearly fully fused petals; the corolla varies from nearly flat to deeply urn-shaped. An exception is *Vaccinium oxycoccos*, the cranberry: the latter has 4 free sepals and 4 free petals that turn backwards. The ovary is superior, except in *Vaccinium*. Stamens number 8 or 10. The fruit is a capsule, sometimes dry but more often berry-like.

1 Ovary inferior; lobes of the calyx dry and persistent on top of the berry (huckleberries) ............ *Vaccinium*

1 Ovary superior (or apparently inferior in *Gaultheria* which has a fleshy calyx lobes at maturity); lobes of the calyx, if persisting, at the base of the fruit ............ 2

2(1) Fruit fleshy, berrylike ............ 3

2 Fruit a dry capsule ............ 4

3(2) Bark reddish, smooth, peeling ............ *Arctostaphylos*

3 Bark gray to gray-brown, not peeling ............ *Gaultheria*

4(2) Leaves less than 5 mm long, scale-like, closely overlapping on the stem ............ *Cassiope*

4 Leaves more than 6 mm long, not scale-like, not closely overlapping ............ 5

5(4) Corolla saucer-shaped ............ *Kalmia*

5 Corolla bell-shaped to urn-shaped ............ 6

6(5) Plants heather-like, less than 1 m tall; leaves less than 5 mm wide . ............ *Phyllodoce*

6 Plants upright shrubs, more than 1 m tall; leaves more than 10 mm wide ............ 7

7(6) Flowers white, bell-shaped ................................ *Rhododendron*
7 Flowers pinkish to salmon-colored ............................ *Menziesia*

## ***Arctostaphylos*** **Adans.—MANZANITA**

Distinguished by shiny reddish-brown bark on the older branches, these shrubs bear stiff evergreen leaves. The bell-like flowers are nearly pinched closed at the mouth and are arranged in short racemes. There are 5 partly fused sepals and 5 fused petals, united except for the small free tips at the mouth of the flower. There are 10 stamens and the fruit is a dryish berrylike drupe; within are several stony nutlets. *A. nevadensis* is common along dry banks on middle elevation roadsides; *A. uva-ursi* is rare at Mount Adams in the subalpine zone.

1 Leaves rounded to shallowly notched at tips; flowers usually pinkish; berry bright red; plant prostrate ..................... *A. uva-ursi*
1 Leaves with a distinct point at the tip; flowers white; berry dull red; plant low and mounded .................................... *A. nevadensis*

### ***Arctostaphylos nevadensis*** **A. Gray—PINEMAT MANZANITA**

Finely short-hairy branches upwards of 100 cm long form a mounded shrub that may reach 50 cm in height but is usually much less. The leaves are oblanceolate to obovate and 1-3 cm long, pointed at the tip, and bright green and shiny on both sides. The white flowers are borne in very short racemes, giving a rounded appearance to the inflorescence. The corolla is 5-6 mm long while the red fruit is 7 mm broad and globose in shape.

The most common manzanita at Mount Adams, this middle elevation species forms very large mats, often covering roadcuts. It is common, being found, among other places, at the Lewis River bridge on Road 23, and along the Island Springs trail. At the DNR quarry on the southeast side, plants reach an unusual height; however, these appear to be "pure" *A. nevadensis,* not involving any hybridization with the shrubby *Arctostaphylos columbiana* of lower elevations.

### ***Arctostaphylos uva-ursi*** **(L.) Spring.—KINNIKINNICK, BEARBERRY**

Nearly prostrate, this shrub has 100 cm branches that root as they spread, creating extensive mats of foliage. Oblanceolate to obovate and rounded at the tip, the mostly hairless leaves are 1-3 cm long, dark green on the upper side, and pale green below. The white or pinkish flowers are borne in short, dense racemes. The corolla is 4-5 mm long. The 8-10 mm broad fruit is globose and bright red.

Uncommon at the mountain, this species has been located at High Camp on the north side at an elevation of more than 6,500 feet, where it grows on loose soil on flat ground.

# Ericaceae

## *Cassiope* D. Don—CASSIOPE

### *Cassiope mertensiana* (Bong.) G. Don var. *mertensiana* WHITE MOUNTAIN HEATHER

A subalpine to alpine shrub, this heather is less common than pink heather at the mountain. Low and spreading, the branches reach 20-40 cm tall and are densely covered with opposite, dark green scalelike leaves 2-4 mm long. The solitary flowers rise from the axils of the upper leaves on slender, nodding stalks. The sepals are reddish, in striking contrast to the bright white, bell-shaped corolla, itself 5-6 mm long. The 2-3 mm long fruit is a rounded capsule.

Growing above 6,000 feet, this heather is found in meadows at the bottom of the White Salmon Glacier and at Horseshoe Meadow on the west and southwest sides. This species is also found at Killen Creek on the north side.

## *Gaultheria* L.—WINTERGREEN

Both *Gaultheria* species at Mount Adams are prostrate, creeping shrubs, seldom more than 10 cm tall. The leaves are evergreen, tough and leathery. The bell-shaped flowers are solitary in the axils of the leaves; they have 5 partly fused sepals, 5 united petals, and 10 stamens. The fruit is a capsule, surrounded by the fleshy, berrylike calyx. Neither species has the familiar taste of true wintergreen. Salal, *G. shallon*, a common and abundant shrub in the lowlands of western Washington, is absent above 4,000 feet at Mount Adams.

1 Leaves 1–2 cm long, smooth or inconspicuously toothed; calyx smooth ........................................................ *G. humifusa*
1 Leaves 2.5–4 cm long, toothed; calyx hairy .............. *G. ovatifolia*

### *Gaultheria humifusa* (Graham) Rydb.—ALPINE WINTERGREEN

Trailing, mostly hairless stems from a stout rootstock reach 10-15 cm long on this sub-shrub. The 15 mm long oval leaves are rounded at the tip and usually toothless but occasionally have small teeth near the tip. The white flowers are about 4 mm long, borne singly on short, leafy, vertical stems. The hairless sepals equal the corolla in length. The 5-6 mm broad red fruit resembles a round berry.

Collected by Suksdorf in the 1880s at elevations up to 7,000 feet, presumably on the south and southeast sides of Mount Adams, this is a relatively uncommon species at the mountain.

#### *Gaultheria ovatifolia* A. Gray—SLENDER WINTERGREEN

Creeping along on prostrate branches that may be up to 30 cm long, this unobtrusive shrub is relatively common at the mountain. The stems have spreading hairs and the ovate leaves are 2-4 cm long, toothed on the margins and pointed at the tip. Pinkish flowers about 4 mm long are borne singly on leafy stems 10-15 cm tall. The reddish-hairy sepals are much shorter than the corolla and the red, berrylike fruit is 5-6 mm broad.

This middle elevation species grows in open forests, typically below 4,500 feet, and has been found by the authors at the Lewis River crossing of Road 23 and just north of Midway Meadows on Road 2329.

### *Kalmia* L.—LAUREL

#### *Kalmia microphylla* (Hook.) A. Heller—ALPINE LAUREL

While plants found in cold subalpine zones are mounded and prostrate, individuals growing at lower elevations may reach 40 cm in height. The evergreen leaves vary as well: the lower elevation plants have relatively narrow, oblong 2-3 cm leaves with incurved margins, while the matted subalpine plants bear broad leaves less than 2 cm long. Common to all plants are the saucer-shaped pink flowers borne at the top of the stem in a loose rounded cluster. They vary from 12-20 mm broad in lower elevation plants and 10-12 mm broad in the subalpine ones. Each of the 10 stamens is tucked into a small pocket in a lobe of the corolla; they snap up to release pollen when touched by an insect. The reddish fruit is a 5-chambered capsule.

Formerly considered as two separate species or varieties, depending on stature and elevation, current nomenclature puts both variations into *K. microphylla*. Relatively common at the mountain, alpine laurel is found in the middle elevations at Grand Meadow, Swampy Meadows, and at Takh Takh Meadow among others, showing a preference for meadows with sphagnum underpinnings. At higher elevations, it grows along the trail above Hellroaring Overlook and at Hellroaring Canyon.

### *Menziesia* Sm.—MENZIESIA

#### *Menziesia ferruginea* Sm.—FOOL'S HUCKLEBERRY

The fruit distinguishes this plant from the true huckleberries (genus *Vaccinium*), even if the foliage does not on this medium-sized to tall shrub. Widely spreading branches define a shrub that may reach 2-3 m tall. The toothed leaves are oblanceolate in shape, deciduous, and sparsely hairy. Borne along the upper stems in umbel-like clusters, the flowers are urn-shaped and also huckleberry-like. The pinkish to reddish-yellow corolla is about 8 mm long and nods from the end of a glandular-hairy stalk. The fruit is a dry capsule, hardly palatable.

A middle elevation forest species, and fairly common, this shrub is cosmopolitan at the mountain. Located at Bathtub Meadows, it is also known from a Flett collection on the south side and an unspecified Suksdorf collection ("base of mountain").

### *Phyllodoce* Salisb.—MOUNTAIN HEATHER

Classic components of the subalpine meadows at Mount Adams, these are matted, ground-covering shrubs with upright stems. The needlelike evergreen leaves densely clothe the upper stems and are about 1 cm long. The leaf edges curve back, making the underside appear channeled. The flowers cluster attractively on glandular stalks at the tops of the stems. The fruit is a dry capsule.

1 Corolla pink, smooth externally ........................ *P. empetriformis*
1 Corolla yellow, glandular externally ..................... *P. glanduliflora*

#### *Phyllodoce empetriformis* (Smith) D. Don—PINK HEATHER

This heather is best distinguished by the rose-pink, 6-8 mm long bell-shaped flowers. The free lobes of the petals are turned back. The flowers are borne in small umbel-like clusters or as individual blooms. The style is prominently exserted and the capsule is 2-4 mm long.

A subalpine, open habitat species, occasionally found at forest edges, this is the most common heather at the mountain. It grows in middle elevation forest habitat at Stagman Ridge as well as in the lower meadows at Killen Creek. Subalpine plants are found in Bird Creek Meadows, Hellroaring Canyon, the White Salmon Glacier, and along the South Climb trail.

#### *Phyllodoce glanduliflora* (Hook.) Coville—YELLOW HEATHER

A narrow mouth at the top of an urn-shaped pale yellowish-green flower helps to distinguish this heather. The flowers are 6-8 mm long and are made sticky by many small glands. The capsule is approximately 4 mm long.

Typically preferring higher elevation habitats than *P. empetriformis,* this heather grows in meadows and open, rocky places above Hellroaring Overlook, along the South Climb trail at 7,300 feet elevation, near the White Salmon Glacier, and on the north side of Little Mount Adams.

## *Rhododendron* L.—RHODODENDRON

### *Rhododendron albiflorum* Hook. var. *albiflorum*
### CASCADE AZALEA, WHITE RHODODENDRON

Widely spreading branches form a relatively dense, deciduous shrub 1-2 m tall. Young branches are covered in coarse reddish hairs. The 3-8 cm long leaves are elliptical to ovate, sparsely short-hairy, deep green on the top, and lighter beneath. The small clusters of slightly irregular white flowers are borne beneath the leaves at the top of the previous year's growth; the 2 cm broad flowers are shallowly bell-shaped and the 10 stamens are curved. The fruit is an oblong capsule that splits lengthwise.

A large number of plants form an extensive patch near the summit of Potato Hill on the north side of the Mount Adams, a somewhat surprising location given the dry, open environment found there. More typical habitat is found at meadow edges above 4,000 feet, as at Babyshoe Meadow, Bench Lake, and in the canyon of Hellroaring Creek. In such places, this species can form dense thickets.

## *Vaccinium* L.—HUCKLEBERRY, WHORTLEBERRY

A highly diverse group of plants that range from threadlike creepers to tall and vigorous shrubs, vacciniums can be found in virtually all habitats at Mount Adams. All are deciduous except for the cranberry. (*Vaccinium ovatum*, the evergreen huckleberry that is very common in lowland forests, is absent above 4,000 feet at Mount Adams). The flowers, with the exception again of the cranberry, are bell-shaped or urn-shaped, white to pink, and solitary on short stems in the axils of the leaves. The fruit is a fleshy berry, from red to blue to almost black in color, and, in most species, of good flavor.

Huckleberry fields drew large numbers of Native Americans to the slopes of Mount Adams and do so to this day, along with recreational and commercial pickers. Thinleaf huckleberry, *V. membranaceum*, provides the greatest volume of the harvest.

1 Trailing, vinelike; petals 4, separate, turned backward ........................................ *V. oxycoccos*
1 Upright shrub; petals 5, united, joined to form a urn-shaped or bell-shaped corolla ........................ 2

2(1) Leaves not toothed, glaucous; restricted to sphagnum bogs ........................................ *V. uliginosum*
2 Leaves toothed, glaucous only in *V. deliciosum*; plants of meadows and forests ........................ 3

3(2) Twigs strongly angled, green; berry red ........................ 4
3 Twigs not strongly angled, greenish or not; berry blue or purple ....6

| | | |
|---|---|---|
| 4(3) | Tall shrub, more than 1 m tall .............................. | *V. parvifolium* |
| 4 | Low shrub, not more than 40 cm tall ...................................... | 5 |
| 5(4) | Twigs numerous and oriented vertically, broomlike; leaves with fine, small teeth, to 15 mm long .................................. | *V. scoparium* |
| 5 | Twigs fewer, more or less spreading; leaves sharply toothed, 10–30 mm long ............................................................ | *V. myrtillus* |
| 6(3) | Plants typically at least 1 m tall ............................................ | 7 |
| 6 | Plants typically less than .5 m tall .......................................... | 8 |
| 7(6) | Leaves thin, finely toothed along their entire length ...................................................................... | *V. membranaceum* |
| 7 | Leaves thickish, finely toothed only towards the tips ... | *V. ovalifolium* |
| 8(6) | Young twigs smooth; leaves glaucous; corolla spherical ................................................................................ | *V. deliciosum* |
| 8 | Young twigs short-hairy or glandular; leaves green; corolla elongated urn-shaped ...................................... | *V. caespitosum* |

### *Vaccinium caespitosum* Michx.—DWARF HUCKLEBERRY

A widely-spreading plant, rising from woody rootstocks, this species forms mats 1.5-3 dm tall. The twigs are somewhat angled and clothed in yellowish-green to reddish bark, covered with short hairs. The 1-3 cm long leaves are oblanceolate, with the tip varying from acute to blunt, light green on the upper surface, paler and glandular beneath. Gland-tipped, fine teeth are borne above the middle to the tips of the leaves. The 5-6 mm long whitish to pinkish flowers are borne singly in the leaf axils; the corolla is tubular and twice as long as broad. The 5-8 mm rounded berry is glaucous-blue and palatable.

Growing in middle elevations, this is a species of meadows and open slopes. It has been located at King Mountain, Muddy River Canyon, and at Hellroaring Creek. It is found on the northwest side of the mountain and was collected by Eugene Hunn above Howard Lake at 4,700 feet, on the northeast.

### *Vaccinium deliciosum* Piper
### RAINIER BLUEBERRY, CASCADE HUCKLEBERRY

Less than 30 cm tall, this low, rounded and matted huckleberry has widely spreading branches. The 2-3 mm long, oval to obovate leaves are toothed above the middle and are somewhat glaucous on the underside. The nearly round pinkish flowers are 5-6 mm long and the black, glaucous berries are 6-8 mm across.

"Rainier" in the name of this plant honors the fact that the species was first described in the scientific literature from material collected by Charles Piper at Mount Rainier.

Appropriately named, the fruit of this berry is the sweetest and most flavorful of all the huckleberries. It is a subalpine meadow species with a wide distribution at Mount Adams, although typically not in large numbers at any specific location. Small plants are found on a dry flat at the foot of Potato Hill. More typical locations include upper Stagman Ridge, Bird Creek, and Hellroaring Canyon, where the species favors open, well-watered meadows, reaching 6,500 feet.

### *Vaccinium membranaceum* Dougl. *ex* Hook.
### THINLEAF HUCKLEBERRY

Angled twigs and spreading branches give a somewhat open appearance to this 0.5-1.5 m tall huckleberry. The 1-4 cm long ovate to oblong-ovate leaves terminate in a long, tapered tip, and are light green, although not glaucous. They are finely toothed along the whole margin (a useful point of difference with *V. ovalifolium*). The 4-5 mm long, rounded flowers are wider than long and are pink to greenish-pink. Within the flowers is a sweet drop of nectar. The 7-10 mm berries are black.

The most common huckleberry of middle elevation forests and much sought after for its fruit which is picked commercially, this species can dominate the understory in favored locations. It is cosmopolitan with modern observations throughout the region but seems to reach its greatest abundance in the lodgepole pine forests in the north. Old Suksdorf specimens collected at Hellroaring Canyon came from an elevation of over 6,000 feet.

### *Vaccinium myrtillus* L. var. oreophilum (Rydb.) Dorn
### DWARF BLUEBERRY

Sharply angled, greenish twigs construct a low plant that is matlike. The stems are at most 20-30 cm tall. The thick, dark green leaves are more or less ovate, 1-3 cm long, and sharply toothed. The pinkish flowers are rounded and 5 mm long. The 5-8 mm broad berry varies from dark red to bluish in color.

Not always easy to tell apart from *V. scoparium*, this is a middle elevation to subalpine species that has been found on the Pacific Crest Trail south of Potato Hill at an elevation of 4,500 feet. It has also been observed on Road 82 west of Bird Creek, at Takh Takh Meadow, and was collected at Hellroaring Canyon by Suksdorf. It is also known from a Henderson collection, for which precise location information is absent.

### *Vaccinium ovalifolium* Sm.—OVAL-LEAF HUCKLEBERRY

Another huckleberry with sharply angled twigs, this upright shrub may reach 1-2 m tall. The ovate-elliptic leaves are 2-4 cm long, glaucous on the underside, and typically not toothed, although there may be a few fine teeth on the margins near the tip. The 6-8 mm long pink flower is egg-shaped, and the black and glaucous berries are 6-9 mm broad.

Another edible huckleberry, this is a middle elevation species of meadow edges and forest openings, occasionally as locally common as *V. membranaceum*. It is cosmopolitan at Mount Adams, with locations including Swampy Meadows, Chain of Lakes, and the White Salmon River. Eugene Hunn collected it at nearly 5,000 feet at Howard Lake, northeast of the mountain.

### *Vaccinium oxycoccos* L.—CRANBERRY

A prostrate shrub with slender stems and evergreen leaves, this small *Vaccinium* is a wetland species. The leaves are 5-15 mm long, ovate to lanceolate, acute, and deep green on the upper side, more pale beneath. The margins of the leaves curve back. The deep pink flowers are single or in several-flowered clusters; they are borne on 2-4 cm long pedicels. Unusual for plants in the Ericaceae, there are 4 petals that are not united; each is 5-8 mm long and curved backward, rather like shooting stars (which belong to the unrelated genus *Dodecatheon*). The fruit is a red berry 5-10 mm broad, the classic cranberry.

Restricted to sphagnum bogs and requiring near inundation in places along streamlets and pools, this species is known only from Grand Meadow. We know of no other location in Washington where cranberry grows at so high an elevation.

### *Vaccinium parvifolium* Sm.—RED HUCKLEBERRY

Light green branches and leaves distinguish this 1-2 m tall, erectly configured huckleberry. The branches are sharply angled and the toothless leaves are more or less oval and 5-20 mm long. The round, pink flowers are about 5 mm long. The red berries are 6-8 mm broad. They have a tart taste, but are edible.

More typically a lowland species found west of the Cascades in Washington, and thus below the study area elevation, this huckleberry is known to us only from a Suksdorf collection made in 1885 on the northwest side of Mount Adams, perhaps along the upper Lewis River.

### *Vaccinium scoparium* Leiberg ex Coville
### GROUSE WHORTLEBERRY

Erect stems and branches that diverge little distinguish this "broomlike," 15-40 cm tall shrub. Both branches and the narrowly ovate leaves are light green in color. The 8-15 mm long leaves are toothed on the margins. The urn-shaped flowers are about 4 mm long, and the bright red berries measure 3-5 mm across. The fruit is tart but flavorful.

More common than the similar *V. myrtillus* and favoring comparable habitats, this species grows in open places from middle elevations to the subalpine. It ranges from dry sites, such as the foot of Potato Hill to Grand Meadow, a large, very wet expanse on the southwest side. It is relatively common along trails on the north side.

#### *Vaccinium uliginosum* L.—BOG HUCKLEBERRY

This stout, woody shrub ranges from 2-5 dm tall, freely branched with rigid but not angled stems. The young branches are yellowish-green and short-hairy, while the old bark turns grayish-red. The 1-3 cm long leaves are untoothed, oblanceolate to obovate, glaucous, and veined on the lower surface. The 1-4 flowers are borne in the axils, with prominent bud scales. They are pink and 5-6 mm long. The sepals are persistent on the 6-8 mm broad, glaucous blue berry.

Forming thickets at wet meadow edges and on higher ground within meadows, this middle elevation wetland species is found at Mirror Lake, Babyshoe Meadow, Grand Meadow, Chain of Lakes, Hellroaring Canyon, and Takh Takh Meadow. It is most frequently found on well-developed sphagnum soils. The berry is not particularly tasty nor does the plant fruit heavily.

### Fabaceae Lindl.—PEA FAMILY

The pea flowers are composed of 5 sepals fused into a tube with free tips and 5 free petals that differ in both size and shape. The upper petal is broad, forming a banner, and the 2 lateral petals are narrow and wing-like. They enfold 2 lower petals, which in turn form a keel that enfolds a single pistil and 10 stamens. The fruit is distinctive, consisting of a beanlike pod that is usually straight although sometimes coiled.

The family includes annual or perennial herbs or shrubs with compound leaves that bear stipules; the leaves are mostly pinnate, although palmate in some important genera, such as the lupines (*Lupinus*).

The peas are found in a variety of habitats, from middle elevation forest edges and open, disturbed ground, to alpine meadows. There are 5 genera and 22 species at the mountain; 5 species are weeds. The lupines in particular are widespread, and represented by 8 species, the most for any of the genera.

1 Leaves trifoliate or palmately divided .................................... 2

1 Leaves pinnately divided (sometimes falsely trifoliate in *Lotus*, the lower pair of leaflets mimicking stipules) ............................. 3

2(1) Flowers in racemes; leaflets 5 or more .......................... *Lupinus*

2 Flowers in heads; leaflets 3 (5-9 in *T. macrocephalum*) .... *Trifolium*

3(1) Midrib of most leaves terminating with a bristle or tendril (thus an even number of leaflets) ............................................... *Lotus*
3 Most leaves with a terminal leaflet (thus an odd number of leaflets).. .................................................................................... 4

4(3) Style flattened, hairy along one side ............................ *Lathyrus*
4 Style round and slender, hairy only surrounding the tip .......... *Vicia*

### *Lathyrus* L.—PEAVINE, WILD PEA

As with the vetches, *Lathyrus* species bear pinnately compound leaves that terminate in a tendril, although in some plants the tendril may be reduced in size to a bristle. With this tendril, they are able to clamber through low vegetation but just as often sprawl on the ground. *Lathyrus* can be most reliably distinguished from vetches (*Vicia*) by having a style that is hairy only on its upper side. The flowers are borne in racemes in the axils of the upper leaves. The stipules are often prominent and leaflike. The keels of the flowers in the species at Mount Adams are about equal length to the wings.

1 Leaflets oval to elliptic; flowers more than 16 mm long .................. ........................................... *L. nevadensis* var. *nevadensis*
1 Leaflets very narrow oblong ................................................2

2(1) Tendrils lacking; flowers 8-12 mm long, white ............................ ....................................................... *L. lanszwertii* var. *aridus*
2 Tendrils well-developed; flowers 13-16 mm long, pink to lavender ... ................................................ *L. lanszwertii* var. *lanszwertii*

#### *Lathyrus lanszwertii* Kellogg var. *aridus* (Piper) Jepson—DESERT PEA

With clambering to erect stems ranging between 15 and 80 cm in length, this perennial has 2-lobed stipules that are shorter than the leaflets. The linear to oblong leaflets number 4-10 and are 3-10 cm long. Subspecies *aridus* lacks tendrils. The flowers are 8-12 mm long, and white; the calyx is 5-8 mm long with lanceolate teeth. The pod is glabrous, 4-6 cm long and 3-6 mm broad.

Found on the north and northeast sides of Mount Adams, this is more typically an eastern Cascades species that finds suitable habitat in the open, dry, lodgepole pine forests at the mountain.

#### *Lathyrus lanszwertii* Kellogg var. *lanszwertii*—LANSZWERT'S PEA

This variety is distinguished from the variety *aridus* in having well-developed tendrils and flowers between 13-16 mm long that are pinkish to lavender.

This subspecies is known from a single collection made at the Mazama Glacier by Suksdorf, most likely from a point well below the terminal moraine.

***Lathyrus nevadensis* S. Wats. var. *nevadensis*—NUTTALL'S PEAVINE**

This native species has angled but wingless stems that clamber or climb and are about 1 m long. The leaves, 8-12 cm long, are composed of 4-10 lanceolate to oval leaflets, with a branched tendril; each leaflet is 2-3 cm long. The slender stipules are about 1 cm long, and the racemes consist of 4-6 light bluish violet flowers 10-16 mm long. The pod is straight, hairless, and 3-4 cm long.

A middle elevation species fairly common in moist environments, this pea is found on the north side of the mountain at Muddy and Midway Meadows, and on the south at Hellroaring Canyon and the DNR quarry, where it grows with Garry oak.

## *Lotus* L.—BIRDSFOOT-TREFOIL

One annual and two perennials, one invasive, comprise the *Lotus* genus at Mount Adams. They grow chiefly in disturbed areas near trailheads and roads. There are 3-5 leaflets as well as a terminal leaflet (rather than a tendril). The stipules consist of small dark glands. The flowers, solitary or in umbels, are borne in the axils of the upper leaves on short to long, bracted stalks. The pod is straight and slender.

1 Plants annual; flowers solitary ....... *L. unifoliolatus* var. *unifoliolatus*
1 Plants perennial; flowers in umbels ........................................ 2

2(1) Leaves not stalked; flowers 10-12 mm long, yellow .. *L. corniculatus*
2 Leaves short-stalked; flowers 8-10 mm long, yellow marked with red lines ...................................... *L. nevadensis* var. *douglasii*

***Lotus corniculatus* L.—BIRDSFOOT-TREFOIL**

An introduced species, with spreading stems 40-80 cm long, this hairless perennial forms broad clumps. The 5 obovate leaflets, 10-15 mm long, include a pair that is tightly appressed against the stem giving the appearance of stipules. The actual stipules are reddish-brown and glandlike. Bright yellow, the flowers are borne in umbels of 3-8 on stalks 6-8 mm long in the leaf axils. Each flower is 10-12 mm long.

A common, showy, and aggressive weed, this lotus may be seen in late spring along roadsides and at trailheads, including the approach along Road 23 from the north and on the road to Takhlakh Lake.

## Fabaceae

### *Lotus nevadensis* (S. Wats.) Greene var. *douglasii* (Greene) Ottley
### DOUGLAS'S BIRDSFOOT-TREFOIL

This is a sprawling plant, with slender stems that reach 30-40 cm in length, superficially resembling the weedy *L. corniculatus*. The leaves are on stalks about 5 mm long and there are typically 5 elliptical leaflets, each 5-15 mm long. The flowers are borne in umbels, 8-10 mm long, and are yellow, marked with fine red lines at the throat. The fruit is a sickle-shaped pod about 10 mm long.

A native perennial, this species nevertheless is found on disturbed ground, and was collected by the authors along roadsides near the DNR quarry and at the quarry itself, on the southeast side of Mount Adams.

### *Lotus unifoliolatus* (Hook.) Benth. var. *unifoliolatus*
### SPANISH-CLOVER

The stems of this delicate plant reach 10-20 cm in height, but are often less on poor ground. The plant is hairy, with leaflets 1-2 cm long that are lanceolate to elliptical. The yellow to pink flowers are 5-9 mm long, with an erect banner.

Found in the study area as a disturbance species, this native annual lotus behaves as if it were a weed. It is known from three collections made for this study at Grand Meadow, in an open parking area along Road 23 near the Pacific Crest Trail crossing, and on Road 170 on the north side.

### *Lupinus* L.—LUPINE

A variable genus with many species, the lupines are attractive and often very showy wildflowers of purple to blue-purple shades, or occasionally, as in the case of *L. arbustus*, pale cream. The flowers are pea-shaped and borne in a raceme. The pods are oblong, flattened, and short-hairy. The leaves are palmately divided into slender leaflets, varying in number from 5 to 13. Careful examination of the flowers is essential in determining the species: look for hairs on the back of the banner, whether the upper lobe of the calyx is spurred, and the degree to which the banner margins turn back (reflex) from the wing petals. (When viewed from the side, a banner that is slightly reflexed gives the flower the appearance of having a small distance from the tip of the wings to the tip of the banner.)

Commonly observed in most open habitats on up to the upper subalpine meadows, lupines also grow as disturbance species along roadsides and around trailheads. The many species at the mountain range from the lowest elevations to nearly 7,000 feet. Most species are easily seen although one small member, *L. sellulus*, is diminutive and most likely to be noticed in large groups.

1 Banner hairy ........................................................................ 2
1 Banner glabrous .................................................................. 3

2(1) Calyx not spurred ........... *L. sericeus* ssp. *sericeus* var. *flexuosus*
2 Calyx spurred .................................... *L. arbustus* ssp. *silvicola*

3(1) Banner slightly reflexed ..................................................... 4
3 Banner strongly reflexed ................................................... 5

4(3) Leaves present at the base of the stalk at flowering time .............. ............................................ *L. bingenensis* var. *subsaccatus*
4 Basal leaves withered at flowering time ........................... ................................................... *L. argenteus* ssp. *argenteus*

5(3) Stems branched, ending in racemes, many stem leaves; pedicels at least 5 mm long ........................................................................ 6
5 Stems unbranched, plants grayish, pedicels less than 5 mm long ... ........................................................................................ 7

6(5) Plants with stiff hairs, more than 25 cm tall ................................ ...................................................... *L. latifolius* ssp. *latifolius*
6 Plants with soft, unmated hairs, 10-25 cm tall ............................ ................................................ *L. arcticus* ssp. *subalpinus*

7(5) Plants low and spreading, less than 30 cm tall ......................... ........................................... *L. sellulus* ssp. *sellulus* var. *lobbii*
7 Plants more than 30 cm tall ................................................ 8

8(7) Plants more than 60 cm tall; stems hollow ................................ ............................................ *L. polyphyllus* ssp. *polyphyllus*
8 Plants less than 60 cm tall; stems not hollow .............................. .......................................................................*L. burkei* ssp. *burkei*

### ***Lupinus arbustus* Dougl. *ex* Lindl. ssp. *silvicola* (Heller) D. Dunn—LONGSPUR LUPINE**

Erect to spreading, sometimes branched, the 2-5 dm tall stems create a broad, robust lupine of dry places. The stem leaves are composed of 7-11 oblanceolate to oblong leaflets 3-5 cm in length borne on long petioles at the base and reduced upwards, they have long, flattened hairs. The 7-20 cm long raceme is generally open and consists of many flowers 9-14 mm in length with 3-7 mm pedicels. The calyx is 1-3 mm long and notably spurred on the upper portion; the lower lip of the calyx is much longer than the upper. The petals are white to cream, with a blue to purple tinge; they may vary widely. The banner is hairy and not much reflexed.

Collected at the DNR quarry, where it grows in light shade under ponderosa pine and Garry oak at 4,000 feet, this lupine is typically a species of lower elevations to the east and south.

### *Lupinus arcticus* S. Wats. ssp. *subalpinus* (Pier & B.L. Robins.) D. Dunn—SUBALPINE LUPINE

This is a 15-40 cm tall, unbranched perennial lupine, with hairy stems and leaves. The leaves are on long stalks, each with 5-7 oblanceolate, 1.5-3.5 cm long leaflets. The tall raceme of many blue to blue-violet flowers, 10-16 mm long, blooms in mid-summer. The pod is about 4 cm long.

The most common lupine in the subalpine zone on the north and west sides of the mountain, this species is "replaced" by *Lupinus sericeus* on the drier south slopes, although it does reappear in the wet meadows of Hellroaring Canyon and Bird Creek on the southeast.

### *Lupinus argenteus* Pursh ssp. *argenteus*—SILVERY LUPINE

Silvery lupine is named for the short, shiny hairs that densely cover the stem and leaves. Each plant typically has several stems that are up to 50 cm tall. The basal and lower stem leaves are usually withered and fallen by the time the plant flowers. The 7-9 leaflets are 2-3 cm long and narrowly lanceolate to slightly oblanceolate. The flowers are arranged in a series of 5-7 whorls in a slender raceme. Each is about 10 mm long, medium blue, with a white spot on the banner.

With a distribution covering most of the western United States, this lupine is known at Mount Adams from only one collection made at almost 4,000 feet on the west slope of "a small butte off of Smith Butte." This is a gently sloping area, with a south aspect, and mostly brushy.

### *Lupinus bingenensis* Suksdorf var. *subsaccatus* Suksdorf BINGEN LUPINE

This 4-8 dm tall perennial has multiple, unbranched stems covered in short to longish hairs. The basal leaves are persistent, with the petioles 3-5 times as long as the 2.5-4 cm blades. The leaflets number 9-11 and are narrow and pubescent on both surfaces. The numerous 9-12 mm long flowers are blue to purple and are loosely arranged in a raceme less than 10 cm long.

Bingen, a town on the Columbia River across from The Dalles, Oregon, was home to the Suksdorf family.

This is another eastern Cascades species and is known from a single collection made at Bird Creek Meadows near Hellroaring Overlook by Sarah Gage and Sharon Rodman on their "Henderson Centennial" collecting trip.

### *Lupinus burkei* S. Wats. ssp. *burkei*—LARGELEAF LUPINE

Considered by Hitchcock as a subspecies of *Lupinus polyphyllus*, this species differs in having solid stems that reach a height of 60 cm, shorter than *polyphyllus*. The flowers, at least at Mount Adams, appear more true blue in color.

This eastern Cascades species is found at middle elevations in habitats somewhat drier than *L. polyphyllus* on the southeast side of Mount Adams. It grows at Mirror Lake near Bird Creek Meadows and at the DNR quarry south of Bench Lake, where it is especially abundant in moist areas in clearcuts.

### *Lupinus latifolius* Lindl. *ex* J. G. Agardh ssp. *latifolius* BROADLEAF LUPINE

Tall and vigorous, this 30-60 cm perennial bears hairy, typically branched stems. Oblanceolate leaflets in groups of 7 or 8 are most often 3-6 cm long although not uncommonly longer. The flowers are blue to blue-violet and about 20 mm long. They are more or less whorled in their tall raceme. The hairy pod is 4 cm long.

A middle elevation species, growing to about 5,000 feet, this is a common lupine along roadsides, in meadows, on riverbanks, and other open sites where it may enjoy an extended blooming period. It grows along the roadside near King Mountain and at Hellroaring Creek on the southeast side, at Potato Hill on the north, and along Road 23 on the west.

### *Lupinus polyphyllus* Lindl. ssp. *polyphyllus*—BIGLEAF LUPINE

Lush, tall - to 1 m or sometimes more - and branched, this large lupine is a showy, wetland plant. The stout stems are hairless and hollow at the base. The basal leaf stalks are 3-6 times as long as the leaflets, with the stem leaves on shorter stalks. Each of the 9-13 elliptic to oblanceolate leaflets is 4-10 cm long and 1-2.5 cm broad. The leaflets are smooth on the upper surface and hairy beneath. Dense racemes of violet flowers are 15-40 cm tall; the flowers are 10-15 mm long, borne on 4-8 mm stalks. The pods are 3-5 cm long and hairy.

A spectacular lupine, this species is most common in wet meadows or along stream banks, places that are well-watered all year, and is apparently confined to the north and west sides of the mountain; on the south *Lupinus burkei* ssp. *burkei* seems to occupy its niche. Bigleaf lupine may be found at Spring Creek, Muddy Meadows, and Midway Meadows where it grows in considerable numbers.

### *Lupinus sellulus* Kellogg ssp. *sellulus* var. *lobbii* (A. Gray *ex* S. Wats.) Cox—DWARF LUPINE

Tiny and grayish from the effect of its long, silvery hairs, this beautiful lupine makes up for size with a covering of seasonal flowers. Less than 15 cm tall, it grows in a matlike fashion from a woody base. Basal leaves are divided into 5-7 parts, with the individual leaflets oblanceolate in outline, 5-10 mm long, and borne on slender stalks. The densely flowered inflorescence forms a short, headlike raceme. The flowers are blue with a showy white patch on the banner, 10-12 mm long, and very fragrant. On occasion, white flowered plants are seen.

Previously this species was named *Lupinus lepidus* var. *lobbii*. It is a common subalpine to alpine plant, but may also be found as a disturbance species at middle elevation roadsides. Large patches grow at High Camp on the north side of Mount Adams and it reaches nearly 8,000 feet along the South Climb route. It grows on the northeast side at Devil's Garden and small numbers are found at the summit of Potato Hill.

### ***Lupinus sericeus*** **Pursh ssp.** ***sericeus*** **var.** ***flexuosus*** **(Lindl.** ***ex*** **J.G. Agardh) C.P. Sm.—SILKY LUPINE**

Silvery leaves and stems distinguish this 2-5 dm tall, multiple-stemmed perennial. The lower leaf stalks are as much as 3 times as long as the 3-6 cm oblanceolate leaflets while the stem leaf stalks are shorter. There are 7-9 leaflets; at flowering time most leaves are on the stems only. The loose, narrow racemes are 10-15 cm long and the 10-12 mm flowers are often arranged in whorls and are lavender or blue. The calyx is silky and not spurred. The banner is sparsely hairy on the back.

Similar to *L arbustus* but lacking the spur, this is the common subalpine to alpine lupine of the south and southeast sides of Mount Adams, particularly along the South Climb trail to over 7,000 feet where it often grows with the brilliant yellow sulphur buckwheat (*Eriogonum umbellatum*). It is also found on the slopes of Potato Hill and, surprisingly, on the west side along the Around-the-Mountain trail in dry, rocky places between 6,000 and 6,200 feet.

### ***Trifolium*** **L.—CLOVER**

With the exception of *T. macrocephalum*, this genus bears leaves composed of 3 leaflets, with prominent stipules. Four of the 7 species at the mountain are weeds, one (*T. dubium*) an annual. The stems are creeping or erect and the flowers are borne on naked stalks, arranged in more or less dense heads which may be terminal (3 species) or borne in the leaf axils. The flower stalks vary from short to long. The flowers turn sharply downward as the pod develops.

*Trifolium longipes* is the only common native at the mountain and is found primarily in wet to seasonally dry meadows.

1 Plants annual; flowers yellow .................................... *T. dubium*
1 Plants perennial; flowers white to pink or red .......................... 2

2(1) Leaflets typically 5-9; flowers 30-100 per head, more than 18 mm long ....................................................... *T. macrocephalum*
2 Leaflets 3; flowers less than 30 per head, less than 15 mm long ... 3

3(2) Calyx pubescent .......................................... *T. pratense*
3 Calyx glabrous.......................................................... 4

43) Flowers at least 10 mm long; heads terminal and solitary .............
.................................................. *T. longipes* ssp. *longipes*
4 Flowers 5-9 mm long; heads axillary ......................................... 5

5(4) Corolla white to pinkish; leaflets notched, wider at tip ...... *T. repens*
5 Corolla pinkish to red; leaflets rounded .................... *T. hybridum*

### *Trifolium dubium* Sibth.—LITTLE HOP-CLOVER

With slender stems 5-30 cm long, this introduced annual clover bears pinnately compound leaves. The terminal leaflet is on a short stalk, and the untoothed stipules are lanceolate. The leaflets are obovate, 5-12 mm long, and toothed. The flowers are yellow, the heads small (less than 8 mm across), and the flowers only 3 mm long. The egg-shaped pod is about 3 mm long.

This weed is known from a single collection made by the authors at Keene's Horse Camp on the north side of the mountain.

### *Trifolium hybridum* L.—ALSIKE CLOVER

This weedy clover has spreading or erect, 30-60 cm tall stems. The obovate leaflets are 1-3 cm long; they may be blunt or notched. The stipules are ovate-lanceolate. The rounded inflorescence on a terminal stalk is 1.5-3 cm broad and composed of slender, pink, 6-10 mm long flowers.

Known from Muddy Meadows and alongside Road 23 on the west side of the mountain; at both locations it grows at about 4,000 feet. Except as an occasional weed along trails used by horses, it is unlikely to be seen any higher.

### *Trifolium longipes* Nutt. ssp. *longipes*—LONGSTALK CLOVER

This clover is distinguished from *T. hybridum* by its height, which is less than 30 cm, the few slender stems, and the narrowly elliptical leaves that are blunt at the tips. The head is oblong rather than rounded, and the whitish flowers are 11-18 mm long.

Fairly common at the mountain, this native species grows at Midway Meadows, Killen Creek Meadow, and Muddy Meadows. It was found at Foggy Flat at 6,050 feet and was collected by Suksdorf at Hellroaring Canyon. Henderson collected it near the White Salmon River. It seems to favor meadows that become rather dry late in the summer.

## Fabaceae

### *Trifolium macrocephalum* (Pursh) Poir.—LARGEHEAD CLOVER

With thick roots and stems 1-3 tall, this hairy perennial is a native clover of dry habitats. It is unique in having 5-9 leaflets rather than the usual 3 (leading to the possibility of confusion with the lupines). The leaflets are oblanceolate, thick, and .5-2.5 cm long. The round, terminal, solitary heads are showy, measuring 3-5 cm in diameter and pinkish to rose-pink in color. The individual flowers are 22-28 mm; an involucre is lacking. The calyx is plumose and hairy, nearly as long as the flower, with the teeth nearly as long as the wing.

This species is known from a collection made by Flett "near Mount Adams," on a date when he was on the upper reaches of the Klickitat River.

### *Trifolium pratense* L.—RED CLOVER

Another introduced clover, this one is a 30-50 cm perennial with short-hairy, erect stems. The obovate leaflets bear small teeth and are 1-4 cm long. A bright red-pink round head is about 2 cm across and essentially stalkless. The flowers are 13-20 mm long with shorter sepals that are covered with long, silky hairs. There is a false involucre of leaflike bracts, set just below the flower head.

Found at Midway Meadows on the north side, this weed is relatively uncommon.

### *Trifolium repens* L.—WHITE CLOVER

An introduced species, this prostrate, glabrous perennial roots from creeping stems that are as much as 60 cm long. Obovate and toothed, the 1-2 cm long leaflets are sometimes notched at the tips and feature a white chevron on the upper surface. The petioles are longer than the leaves. Rounded heads approximately 1.5 cm broad are composed of tubular, 6-10 mm white flowers.

A middle elevation, roadside plant, this is among the most common of the weeds at Mount Adams. It is found at the horse camp on Hellroaring Creek as well as at Midway Meadows on the north side and here and there along Road 23. It will occasionally inhabit damaged parts of meadows, as at Horseshoe Lake.

### *Vicia* L.—VETCH

### *Vicia americana* Muhl. *ex* Willd. ssp. *americana*—AMERICAN VETCH

Stems that may reach 100 cm in length characterize this spreading perennial with sparsely hairy stems and grasping tendrils. Notched to blunt or pointed on the tip, the oval to linear-oblong leaflets are 1-3 cm long and short-hairy. The stipules are about 1 cm long and have several sharp lobes. From early to mid summer the 1-sided racemes of 4-9 blue-purple flowers, 1.5-2 cm long, are a common sight. The hairless, narrow pods are 2-4 cm long.

This cosmopolitan, native species at the mountain grows at middle elevations in habitats ranging from meadows to roadsides, reaching about 4,500 feet. It grows at Muddy Meadows, on the road to the South Climb route, and near the DNR quarry.

Several weedy species of vetch grow in Washington, but none has been found at Mount Adams.

## Fagaceae DuMort.—BEECH FAMILY

### *Quercus* L.—OAK

#### *Quercus garryana* Dougl. *ex* Hook. var. *garryana* OREGON WHITE OAK, GARRY OAK

A deciduous tree from 10-20 m tall (occasionally taller), and a trunk diameter up to 1 m, this is a species of open habitats, including lowland prairies to the west, and rocky outcrops east of the Cascades. The bark is thick, furrowed, and scaly. The young growth is reddish and short hairy. The leaves are stalked, 1-2 cm long or more, with the blades oblong to obovate in outline, bright green on the upper surface, and somewhat reddish to yellowish and softly hairy beneath. The leaves are deeply pinnately lobed. The male flowers are catkins, borne on the current season's growth, while the female flowers are single to clustered, and surrounded by a cuplike involucre. The acorns mature in one season; they are 2-3 cm long with a shallow cup and ovoid to round in shape.

Typically found in Washington at lower, drier elevations, this oak occurs in open groves above 4,000 feet at the DNR quarry on the southeast side of the mountain.

## Fumariaceae L.—FUMITORY FAMILY

### *Dicentra* Bernh.—BLEEDING-HEART

Unusual-shaped flowers that vary from pink to purplish distinguish this genus of attractive perennials. The outer petals are united, sac-like or pouched, with distinctive spurs. There are 2 narrow to oval sepals, much shorter than the petals. The common name suggests the shape of the flowers. The leaves are fern-like, blue-green and glaucous.

The related genus *Corydalis* is absent from the Mount Adams study area.

1 Flowers one per stem; subalpine plant ........................ *D. uniflora*
1 Flowers several per stem; mid-elevations *D. formosa* ssp. *formosa*

### *Dicentra formosa* (Haw.) Walp. ssp. *formosa*
### WESTERN BLEEDING-HEART

Strongly spreading rootstocks enable this species to form extensive colonies. The basal leaves rise on long stalks and are 2 or 3 times divided into angular segments, with a 20-50 cm overall length. The heart-shaped, pink to rose-purple flowers are in groups of 4 or more, and nod in loose racemes on arching stems. Each is 14-18 mm long, with the outer petals spurred at the base and spreading at the tips. The 15-20 mm long capsule is narrow.

Uncommon, probably because the study area is above the more typically lowland habitat of this lovely species, it is, however, known from the northwest side of the mountain, at 4,400 feet near the Stagman Ridge trailhead.

### *Dicentra uniflora* Kellogg—STEER'S-HEAD

Less than 10 cm high, this small plant forms patches from clusters of tuber-like rootstocks. The leaves are 2 or 3 times divided into slender, oblong segments. The pinkish flower is 15 mm long and borne singly on short stems. The outer petals curve back strongly, making "horns" and the spurs are saclike. The 10 mm long capsule is ovate.

A large patch of this species grows on an open slope above the Round-the-Mountain trail at an elevation of nearly 6,100 feet on the southwest side of the mountain. It is also known from Bird Creek Canyon (a Suksdorf collection), and from below Avalanche Glacier. The plants flower very early in the season and fade rapidly to the rootstocks, making it easy to miss or overlook.

## Gentianaceae Juss.—GENTIAN FAMILY

One common and one rare species comprise the gentians at Mount Adams. Both are perennial herbs with opposite or whorled leaves. The 4 or 5 petals are at least partly united into a tube and the fruit is a capsule.

| | | |
|---|---|---|
| 1 | Flowers one per stem, 5-lobed .................................... | *Gentiana* |
| 1 | Flowers numerous in a panicle, 4-lobed ......................... | *Frasera* |

### *Frasera* Walt.—GREEN GENTIAN

### *Frasera albicaulis* Dougl. *ex* Griseb. var. *columbiana* (St. John) C.L. Hitchc.—WHITESTEM FRASERA

Several flowering stems 1-7 dm tall rise from the branched root crown of this perennial herb. The 5-30 cm long basal leaves are linear-oblanceolate to spatulate, 3-nerved, and white along the margins. They are configured in a whorl, while the smaller stem leaves are opposite. The inflorescence is a compact panicle. The petals are pale to dark blue or purplish, with lobes 5-11 m long, often scalelike on the inner surface. The filaments are united at the base. The 10-15 mm long capsule is somewhat compressed.

This is a species of dry, middle elevation habitats, known in the study area from a single Flett collection on the Klickitat River east of Mount Adams. It is also found at about 3,500 feet in oak woodlands on the road to Bird Creek Meadows.

### *Gentiana* L.—GENTIAN

#### *Gentiana calycosa* Griseb.—MOUNTAIN BOG GENTIAN

With stems that vary from 5-30 cm, this perennial herb bears opposite leaves. The stems are unbranched, and the 1.5-3 cm long ovate leaves are toothless and hairless. On top of each stem a 3-4 cm long single flower is dark blue, dotted with green on the interior. Rarely, plants will have 2 or 3 flowers per stem. The petals are united most of their length; the free lobes slightly spreading. The fruit is a capsule.

When in flower, this subalpine meadow plant often forms spectacular patches, best-developed between 5,500 and 6,500 feet. The flowers tend to close at dusk and pink flowers are occasionally encountered. This gentian was collected at "snowline" by Henderson and at Hellroaring Canyon by Suksdorf. It is known on the Round-the Mountain trail on the southeast side, on the trail above Hellroaring Overlook and at Killen Creek. It is also found as low as Takh Takh Meadow.

## Geraniaceae DC.—GERANIUM FAMILY

### *Erodium* L'Her.—CRANE"S BILL, FILAREE

#### *Erodium cicutarium* (L.) L'Her. *ex* Ait. ssp. *cicutarium*—FILAREE

This weedy species is a short-hairy annual with basal leaves that are oblanceolate in outline and pinnately divided into toothed leaflets. The 10-30 cm long stems are leafy and typically sprawl on the ground. The flowers are borne in umbels of 2-4 on long stalks in the axils of the upper stem leaves. They are about 1 cm broad and composed of reddish-purple petals. The style is 4-5 mm long at maturity and coiled like a spring.

This species is found at the DNR quarry on the southeast side of the mountain, at 4,000 feet, growing in small numbers around a parking area.

# Grossulariaceae

## Grossulariaceae DC.—GOOSEBERRY FAMILY

### *Ribes* L.—CURRANT, GOOSEBERRY

Formerly included in the Saxifragaceae, this genus consists of many shrubby species. The gooseberries bear prickles or spines on the branches, while the currants lack prickles or spines. The leaves are alternate, palmately lobed and toothed, often short-hairy and glandular. The flowers are borne in racemes in the axils of the leaves. They are saucer-shaped to tubular, while the calyx is partly united with the ovary. The petals are shorter than the sepals; the latter are often colored, resembling petals. The ovary is inferior and develops into a berry that may be covered with prickles. The berries are juicy and edible, although not particularly flavorful in the species at Mount Adams. The berry may be glaucous, the white bloom imparting a bluish color. Close examination of the glands on the surface of the berry aids in identification.

1 Spines present at the leaf nodes and sometimes along the stems (gooseberries) .......... 2
1 Spines absent from the leaf nodes of the stems (currants) .......... 4

2(1) Calyx tube cylindrical to bell-shaped, the free lobes slightly spreading; flower stalk not jointed just below the ovary .......... *R. watsonianum*
2(1) Calyx tube saucer-shaped, the lobes spreading widely; flower stalk jointed just below the ovary .......... 3

3(2) Leaves short-hairy and glandular; berry reddish ..... *R. montigenum*
3 Leaves typically hairless, not glandular; berry purple ..... *R. lacustre*

4(1) Glands on the ovary and berry flat; flowers greenish; leaves with a foul smell .......... *R. bracteosum*
4 Glands on the ovary and berry stalked; flowers greenish to white or reddish; leaves with mild smell .......... 5

5(4) Calyx tube wider than long, nearly flat to broadly saucer-shaped .......... *R. acerifolium*

5 Calyx tube longer than wide, bell-shaped to cylindrical .......... 6

6(5) Calyx tube cylindrical; berry red .......... *R. cereum* var. *cereum*
6 Calyx tube bell-shaped; berry bluish to black ...... *R. viscosissimum*

#### *Ribes acerifolium* Koch—MAPLELEAF CURRANT

With spreading branches this 1 m tall currant is distinguished by its "maplelike" broad leaves. There are 5-7 wide, finely toothed lobes, 3-7 cm broad. A drooping raceme consists of approximately 10 greenish flowers, each tiny (less than 10 mm across) and saucer-shaped, with small, reddish petals. The filament of each stamen also distinguishes this species—it is broad at the base. The berry is black, glaucous, 6-10 mm broad, and bears a few stalked glands on the surface.

Fairly common on the south side, this species is also known from a Suksdorf collection at Hellroaring Canyon. It typically grows in open woods at meadow edges, reaching the subalpine zone.

### *Ribes bracteosum* Dougl. *ex* Hook.—STINK CURRANT

As the common name implies, this species announces its presence with a strong smell. The plants are 2-3 m tall, with erect, thornless stems. The 5-20 cm broad leaves are primarily 7-lobed; the lobes are toothed and sharply pointed. The leaves are glandular on the underside and extrude a skunklike odor when crushed. The whitish flowers number 20-40 and are borne in an erect raceme that measures 5-25 cm long. They are small and saucer-shaped. A blackish, glaucous berry adds to the unpleasantness with an unappealing flavor. It is about 1 cm across.

Found at Council Lake on the west side, along Road 23 at Twin Falls Creek, and known also from a Suksdorf collection of unspecified location, this is a relatively common species of middle elevation forests, where it is found at streamsides.

### *Ribes cereum* Dougl. var. *cereum*—WAX CURRANT

An unarmed shrub 0.5-1.5 m tall, with a spreading to erect configuration, the new branches of this species are short-hairy and glandular. The 1.5-2.5 cm broad leaves are kidney-shaped to fan-like and are typically glandular on both surfaces; they are shallowly lobed. There are 2-8 flowers in a headlike cluster much shorter than the leaves. The inflorescence is short-hairy and glandular. The calyx is greenish white to white, sometimes almost pink, hairy and glandular, and 6-8 mm long with spreading lobes. The spatulate petals are 1-2 mm long. The inedible fruit is ovoid, 6-8 mm long and red.

A middle elevation species, sometimes of disturbed sites, this currant was found by the authors at Snipes Mountain, on Road 82 at the gate to Bird Creek, in the vicinity of Bunnell Butte, at the Aiken Lava Flow, and on the road to King Mountain at the Tract D boundary.

### *Ribes lacustre* (Pers.) Poir.—SWAMP GOOSEBERRY

Ascending stems armed with short spines form a plant 1-2 m tall with bristly young branches. The 3-5 cm broad leaves are lobed 3-7 times and are toothed and hairless. The leaf stalks and flower stalks are glandular and 5-15 flowers are borne in each erect raceme. The flowers are greenish and 7-8 mm broad. The 5 mm broad black fruit is sparsely covered with stalked glands.

Found from the north to the southwest sides at middle elevations, this gooseberry grows on the lava flow south of Potato Hill, along the Snipes Mountain trail, and on Road 2329 at the lava flow near Takh Takh Meadow.

### *Ribes montigenum* McClatchie—MOUNTAIN GOOSEBERRY

Covered with fine, short hairs and minute bristles, this low, spreading shrub is 20-50 cm tall. The branches also bear spines 4-6 mm long. The leaves are 1-2.5 cm broad, and divided into 5 segments about 2/3 of their length; they are also toothed and lobed. The pendant racemes are borne in the leaf axils, and are barely longer than the leaves; there are 4-to-7 flowers. The ovate sepals are green to pinkish and 2.5-3 mm long. The petals are broad and only half as long as the sepals. The reddish, rounded berry is 5-7 mm long.

This species was collected on the east side at Hellroaring Canyon by Suksdorf and at high elevations in the Muddy River Canyon by Henderson. Even at high elevations, it is less frequently seen than *R. lacustre.*

### *Ribes viscosissimum* Pursh—STICKY CURRANT

A low shrub of spreading stems 1-2 m long, the toothed leaves are 5-8 cm broad with 5 rounded lobes that are glandular-hairy on each side. The 6-12 flowers are narrow tubes, borne in an open raceme and are whitish or greenish white, with small, erect petals, and spreading sepals. The 10 mm broad black berry is sticky and bears many glandular bristles.

Fairly common in dryish, rather open, middle elevation forests to about 5,000 feet, this currant has been found on Stagman Ridge, along the Klickitat River, and along Road 8040.

### *Ribes watsonianum* Koehne—SPINY GOOSEBERRY

As the common name implies, this is a spiny-stemmed shrub. The stems are 1-2 m long and erect to spreading. The leaves have 3-5 lobes with shallow, coarse teeth, are 3-6 cm broad and glandular-hairy on both sides. The 2-4 flowers, borne in short, nodding racemes, have greenish white sepals 6-8 mm long, united below into a short tube and flared above. The white petals are shorter than the sepals. Both the immature ovary and the purplish berry bear dense bristles, with some gland-tipped.

The range of this currant reaches the subalpine, with specimens found along the trail above Hellroaring Overlook, at Bird Creek, at Big Muddy Creek, and at lower elevations on Road 040.

## Hydrangeaceae Dumort.—MOCK-ORANGE FAMILY

### *Philadelphus* L.—MOCK-ORANGE

#### *Philadelphus lewisii* Pursh—LEWIS'S MOCK-ORANGE

This tall shrub ranges from 2-4 m in height and is further distinguished by the flaking, grayish bark. The 3-5 cm long deciduous leaves are borne opposite and are ovate with a tapered point and typically toothed on the margins. The white, fragrant flowers do resemble those of an orange and are borne in a raceme. They are about 3 cm broad and are composed of 4 sepals and 4 petals, numerous stamens, and a half-inferior ovary. The fruit is a woody capsule.

Found on moist, rocky hillsides below 5,000 feet at Mount Adams, mock-orange is an uncommon, showy shrub. Fine plants grow near Bench Lake alongside the trail to the horse camp on Island Springs Creek.

## Hydrophyllaceae R. Br.—WATERLEAF FAMILY

Delicate annuals to tall and coarse perennials, members of the family are united by features of the floral parts. The 5 sepals are fused to about the midpoint or less and are coarsely hairy. The 5 petals are mostly fused, with the free lobes spreading or not. The inflorescence varies greatly, from single, axillary flowers in *Nemophila* to coiled cymes in *Phacelia* to headlike clusters in *Hydrophyllum*. In the latter two genera the 5 stamens are conspicuously exserted from the corolla. The fruit is a dry capsule.

1 Delicate annual; flowers solitary in the axils of the leaves ............................................................................... *Nemophila*
1 Perennials, often coarse; flowers in cymes or on stems that rise directly from the crown of the rootstock .................................. 2

2(1) Flowers in elongated, coiled cymes ............................. *Phacelia*
2 Flowers in congested, headlike cymes .................. *Hydrophyllum*

### *Hydrophyllum* L.—WATERLEAF

None of the three waterleaf species is common at Mount Adams. These are low-growing perennials, with succulent stems and alternate, pinnately lobed leaves. The flowers are bell-shaped, white to purplish, with conspicuously exserted stamens and arranged in compact to headlike cymes.

1 Leaflets not toothed along the margins; flowering stems typically shorter than the leaves .................... *H. capitatum* var. *capitatum*

1 Leaflets toothed along the margins; flowering stems typically taller than the leaves ................................................................ 2

2(1) Leaves longer than wide with 7-11 leaflets ................ *H. tenuipes*

2 Leaves about as long as wide, with 7 or fewer leaflets ................. ....................................................... *H. fendleri* var. *albifrons*

### *Hydrophyllum capitatum* Dougl. *ex* Benth. var. *capitatum* BALLHEAD WATERLEAF

Attached to a short rhizome with fleshy roots, the 1-4 dm tall stems of this perennial are covered with short, stiff hairs. The large (1.5 dm) pinnate leaves are borne on long petioles and are divided into 7-11 leaflets, cleft to the midpoint. The leaflets are rounded with a sharp tip; the central lobe often has two teeth. The ball-shaped head (a compact cyme) is borne below the leaves on short stalks. The lavender corolla is 5-9 mm long

The most abundant hydrophyllum at Mount Adams but nevertheless not common, this species is found in moist sites in open middle elevation forests. Suksdorf collected the plant at Bird Creek Meadows.

### *Hydrophyllum fendleri* (A. Gray) A. Heller var. *albifrons* (Heller) J.F. Macbr.—WHITE WATERLEAF

Succulent, leafy stems with downward pointing, soft hairs rise from a short rootstock in this 20-30 cm tall waterleaf. The pinnately-lobed leaves are primarily basal, 10-20 cm long overall, and bear white hairs beneath and stiffer hairs above. There are 7-11 leaflets, sharply toothed with 4-8 teeth on a side. The upper leaves are smaller than those near the base. The white to lavender or purplish corolla is 6-10 mm long, and the calyx lobes are half that size.

Preferring moist open places, this middle elevation species is known at Mount Adams from a Suksdorf specimen made at Hellroaring Canyon.

### *Hydrophyllum tenuipes* A. Heller—PACIFIC WATERLEAF

This species is distinguished from *H. fendleri* by the more rounded leaves that are about as wide as they are long and less distinctly pinnate, with fewer than 7 lobes. The leaves are 10-15 cm long, softly hairy on both sides, and sharply toothed. The greenish white flowers are approximately 7 mm long.

A species of low to middle elevation moist habitats in open forests, it is known at the mountain from a Suksdorf collection at Hellroaring Canyon.

### *Nemophila* Nutt.—BABY BLUE EYES

#### *Nemophila breviflora* Gray—SHORT-FLOWERED BABY BLUE EYES

A branched annual 1-3 dm tall with loosely erect or ascending weak stems, this species is armed with downward oriented short prickles. The alternate leaves are thin and covered with stiff hairs, with a fringe of hairs on their margins. The leaf has 2 pairs of spreading lateral lobes approximately 2 cm long, with a sharp tip. The lavender corolla is only about 2 mm long; the lobed, stiffly hairy calyx extends past the corolla, hence "short-flowered."

This plant grows in middle elevations in forests or thickets. It was found by Flett on the Klickitat River just east of Mount Adams.

### *Phacelia* Juss.—PHACELIA

*Phacelia* is a diverse genus, ranging from annuals to tall perennials fit for the garden border to low, semi-woody alpine plants. They have alternate, often lobed leaves and the plants are usually roughly hairy. The inflorescence is composed of coiled cymes, appearing spikelike or racemelike. The bell-shaped flowers vary in color and slightly exceed the sepals; the stamens are prominently exserted.

Of the six species at Mount Adams, three are easily recognized: both *Phacelia nemoralis* and *P. procera* are tall and robust, and *P. sericea* has stunning violet-blue flowers set against silver leaves. The remaining three resemble each other in many respects and overlap in their elevational ranges as well.

| | | |
|---|---|---|
| 1 | Plant robust, 1-2 m tall | 2 |
| 1 | Plant erect and slender to compact, rarely more than 70 cm tall | 3 |
| 2(1) | Stems coarsely bristly | *P. nemoralis* |
| 2 | Stems with sparse, appressed hairs if any | *P. procera* |
| 3(1) | Lower leaves pinnately lobed; corolla blue-purple | *P. sericea* ssp. *sericea* |
| 3 | Lower leaves undivided or with a pair of small lobes at the base; corolla white to pale lavender | 4 |
| 4(3) | Low, compact plants of open subalpine to alpine places; leaves densely hairy and silvery | *P. hastata* var. *compacta* |
| 4 | Mid-elevation plants, typically over 40 cm tall; leaves hairy to bristly, but not silvery | 5 |

5(4) Lower leaves usually with 1 pair of lobes at the base .................... *P. leptosepala*

5 Lower leaves usually with 2 or more pairs of lobes .................... *P. heterophylla* var. *virgata*

### ***Phacelia hastata*** **Dougl. *ex* Lehm. var. *compacta* (Brand) Cronq.** **SILVERLEAF PHACELIA**

The ascending stems on this low, tufted species are 10-30 cm long. The lanceolate leaves are primarily basal and 10-20 cm long, including the stalks; the stem leaves are reduced in size, while the larger basal leaves have a small pair of lobes. Both the stems and leaves are densely clothed with stiff, straight hairs, giving a silvery appearance. The bell-shaped flowers are whitish to pale lavender, 4-7 mm long.

Preferring dry, rocky habitats, this species is uncommon at Mount Adams, known from a collection made by Eugene Hunn at Howard Lake, northeast of the mountain at 5,000 feet.

### ***Phacelia heterophylla*** **Pursh ssp. *virgata* (Greene) Heckard** **VARILEAF PHACELIA**

Often found growing as a single flowering stem, this species typically reaches 50-100 cm in height. The lower stem leaves are about 5 mm long, most with a pair of narrow, basal lobes; the upper leaves are smaller and may lack the lobes. Whitish flowers are arranged in short, lateral cymes on the upper portion of the stem.

This biennial or perennial *Phacelia* grows at lower elevations in forest openings. It was found by Robert Goff on the west side of a small hill just north of Smith Butte. Most of the study area does not provide suitable habitat

### ***Phacelia leptosepala*** **Rydb.—NARROW-SEPALED PHACELIA**

Similar to *P. hastata*, with 30-50 cm tall stems, this species is not only taller but is also not tufted; the multiple stems curve near the base and spread as they rise. The stem leaves are not as reduced in size while the basal leaves may have a pair of lobes at the base. The leaf surface is roughly hairy but not silvery. The bell-shaped flowers are whitish to purplish, and 5-7 mm long.

A dry habitats species of lower elevations than *P. hastata*, this species was found by the authors on the south and southeast sides of the mountain. It grows along the Snipes Mountain road, and at King Mountain.

### ***Phacelia nemoralis*** **Greene—SHADE PHACELIA**

Distinguished by its size, the thick, erect stems of this *Phacelia* vary from 50-150 cm tall and are clothed with dense, stiff hairs. The ovate to lanceolate lower leaves are pinnately compound and 5-25 cm long. They are divided into 3-7 lobes. The bell-shaped flowers are configured in short, bracted cymes, yellowish in color, and 4-6 mm long.

More typically a low to middle elevation species of open meadows elsewhere in the southern Cascades, specimens of this plant were collected by Suksdorf in Hellroaring Canyon at unspecified elevations. It is surprising to see the species at Mount Adams.

### *Phacelia procera* A. Gray—TALL PHACELIA

Conspicuously black-glandular in and near the inflorescence (but otherwise nearly hairless), this perennial ranges from 50-220 cm tall. The leaves are commensurate with the size, reaching 12 cm long and 7 cm wide. They are pinnately divided into a few lobes or are merely cleft or coarsely toothed. The largest leaves are above the base, with basal leaves lacking, and stem leaves reduced in size. The inflorescence is distinguished by several rounded cymes clustered into a corymb. The bell-shaped corolla is greenish-white, 5-7 mm long and 5-9 mm wide.

Growing in meadows or open forests in the middle elevations, this species is often encountered up to about 5,000 feet on the south side of the mountain. It is known from Road 6900 below the DNR quarry, at Crofton Butte, and along the road to Snipes Mountain, and on Snipes Mountain itself.

### *Phacelia sericea* (Graham) A. Gray ssp. *sericea*
### SILKY PHACELIA, ALPINE PHACELIA

This tufted species rises from a woody base, reaching 10-20 cm tall. The stems and leaves bear silky hairs. The leaves are narrowly oblanceolate in outline; they are cut deeply into slender, 2-6 cm long pinnate lobes. The bluish-violet flowers are 5-6 mm long and borne in dense, oblong, headlike clusters. The stamens are much longer than the corolla.

A subalpine to alpine species of rocky habitats, found at Hellroaring Canyon and at Muddy River Canyon "above the glacier," this latter a Henderson collection. It is also known at a "moraine, NE side" from a Suksdorf collection.

## Lamiaceae Lindl.—MINT FAMILY

Mints are few in number at Mount Adams; just four native perennials are found. Most are attractive wildflowers with stems that are square in cross-section; they bear opposite leaves, and flowers in whorls on tall stems. All are more or less odorous, but none especially pleasant and none resembling true mint (*Mentha* species). The calyx is 5 lobed and the 5 lobed corolla is "bilabiate" – irregular and two lipped, with the upper

2 lobes more or less fused and the lower 3 forming a flattish lip. There are 4 stamens and the ovary develops into 4 nutlets.

| | | |
|---|---|---|
| 1 | Corolla nearly regular .......... | *Monardella* |
| 1 | Corolla clearly bilabiate .......... | 2 |
| 2(1) | Upper lip of the corolla not hoodlike, thus the stamens exserted .......... | *Agastache* |
| 2 | Upper lip of the corolla hoodlike, the stamens not exserted .......... | 3 |
| 3(2) | Calyx 2-lipped, with unequal lobes, the upper lip 3-toothed, the lower with 2 narrow segments .......... | *Prunella* |
| 3 | Calyx more or less equally 5-toothed .......... | 4 |
| 4(3) | Flowers in a dense head, white .......... | *Nepeta* |
| 4 | Flowers in open whorls, rose-purple .......... | *Stachys* |

### ***Agastache*** **Clayton *ex* Gronov.—GIANT HYSSOP**

#### ***Agastache occidentalis*** **(Piper) Heller—WESTERN GIANT HYSSOP**

Simple or often branched, stiffly hairy stems rise 4-8 dm from fibrous roots in this rangy perennial. The 6 cm long leaves bear rounded teeth on the margins and are triangular to heart-shaped; they are borne on 1-5 cm long petioles and are often roughened above and finely hairy beneath. The inflorescence is 3-15 cm long, the toothed calyx tinged purplish, and the corolla whitish and 10-14 mm long.

A species of the eastern Cascades, often found on rocky sites, it is relatively common in the middle elevations in forest openings below 5,000 feet on the southeast side of the mountain. It has been found on Road 6900, below the DNR quarry, alongside Pineway Trail, near the road up Snipes Mountain, northeast of Bunnell Butte, and is also known from a Suksdorf collection.

### ***Monardella*** **Benth.—BEE-BALM**

#### ***Monardella odoratissima*** **Benth. ssp. *discolor*** **(Greene) Epling MOUNTAIN MONARDELLA**

This compact, shrublike plant bears tufted stems that are woody at the base. The stems are 10-30 cm tall and short-hairy. The 5-20 mm long ovate to lanceolate leaves are whitish-hairy and borne on short stalks. Pale violet flowers are crowded into a headlike inflorescence about 2 cm wide set above purplish, oval bracts. The upper lip of the 7 mm long corolla is erect and 2-lobed; the lower lip has 3 linear lobes and is somewhat spreading. The scent of the crushed leaves is pleasant, a mix of mint and citrus.

A subalpine species this plant is known from an 1882 Henderson collection made on the east side of the mountain on "sunny cliff slopes" and a Lila Leach collection with no specific details. At Mount Rainier, it reaches 7,000 feet, and so it seems a possibility at high elevations on the east side of Mount Adams.

### *Nepeta* L.—CATNIP

#### *Nepeta cataria* L.—CATNIP

A perennial with creeping rootstocks, this member of the mint family has grayish-green leaves, tinted with purple, on stems that may reach 1 m in height. The margins of the ovate leaves have rounded teeth and are 2-6 cm long. The flowers are in head-like spikes at the tops of the stems. The flowers are white, with tiny purple spots on the lower lip. The upper lip is rounded and hoodlike, hiding the stamens.

A single plant was found by the authors in the parking area at the DNR quarry.

### *Prunella* L.—SELF-HEAL

#### *Prunella vulgaris* L. ssp. *lanceolata* (W.P.C. Barton) Hultén SELF-HEAL

Spreading by short rootstocks, this species may have erect stems as well as prostrate ones and often forms patches. The flowering stems are short-hairy and topped with a dense, oblong, headlike spike of blue-violet flowers. At the base of the flower head are a set of leaflike bracts. The lanceolate to ovate leaves are primarily basal, dark green, and 2-6 cm long. The leaves on the middle of the stem are 3 times as long as wide. The 10-14 mm long corolla is 2-lipped, the upper lip consisting of 2 lobes that arch and cover the stamens. The lower lip is formed of 3 spreading lobes.

The weedy *Prunella vulgaris* ssp. *vulgaris* has not been found at Mount Adams. Its stems tend to lie flat on the ground and the middle stem leaves are narrower, only about twice as long as wide.

Found at the edges of middle elevation forests and in disturbed areas such as roadsides, this native self-heal is relatively uncommon at the mountain. It has been located by the authors along Road 8040 (the South Climb Road), at Swampy Meadows, and on Trail 75 on the southwest side.

### Stachys L—HEDGE-NETTLE

#### *Stachys chamissonis* Benth. var. *cooleyae* (Heller) G. Mulligan & D. Munro—COOLEY'S HEDGE-NETTLE

The stems of this 1-2 m tall unpleasantly-scented perennial are occasionally purplish. The narrowly triangular to ovate leaves are stalked, coarsely toothed, and 5-15 cm long. The flowers are borne in loose, terminal clusters, and the rose-purple corolla is 2-3.5 mm long, 2-lipped, and spotted with white on the lower lip.

A middle elevation species of wet ground, stream banks, and other moist sites, this plant is fairly common at Mount Adams below 4,500 feet. It has been located on Trail 75 at Salt Creek on the southwest side, at Council Lake, and on Road 6900 near the DNR Quarry. On the northwest, it grows alongside Road 23 at milepost 31. It is also found on the north side.

## Lentibulariaceae Rich—BLADDERWORT FAMILY

### *Utricularia* L.—BLADDERWORT

These submerged, aquatic plants are carnivorous, employing small, hollow bladders which trap and digest small crustaceans, insect larvae, and other organisms. The leaves are finely dissected. At flowering time, a slender stalk rises above the surface, carrying a few bright yellow flowers in a raceme. The corolla is 2-lipped, sometimes featuring a broad palate that nearly closes the throat; the floral tube projects backwards into a short spur.

Plants at Mount Adams do not flower every year and no pattern to their flowering has yet been observed by us.

1 Bladders borne on short branches separate from leaves; corolla spur as long as lower lip; lower lip 8-12 mm ............. *U. intermedia*

1 Bladders borne on leaves; corolla spur shorter than lower lip; lower lip 4-8 mm ............................................................ *U. minor*

#### *Utricularia intermedia* Hayne—FLATLEAF BLADDERWORT

The leaves are 3-parted at the base and then are forked 1-3 times again; the segments are flat. The tips of the leaflets are blunt to rounded. The bladders are borne "raceme-like" on specialized, leafless branches. The lower lip of the corolla is 8-12 mm long and the spur is nearly the same length. The fruiting stalk is erect.

This species grows in middle elevation ponds and wetlands, and was found by the authors at Swampy Meadows and Grand Meadow on the southwest side of Mount Adams.

#### *Utricularia minor* L.—LESSER BLADDERWORT

This species is similar to *U. intermedia,* except that the bladders are borne on normal leaves that are shorter (0.3-1 cm long) and have pointed tips. The lower lip of the corolla is 4-8 mm long, and the spur is much shorter. The palate is small or obsolete. The fruiting stalk is curved.

Also growing in middle elevation meadows, this species was found by the authors at Bathtub Meadow and at the meadow at the intersection of Road 23 and Road 2329. It seems to prefer deeper pools than *U. intermedia.*

## Limnanthaceae R. Br.—MEADOWFOAM FAMILY

### *Floerkea* Willd.—FLOERKEA

#### *Floerkea proserpinacoides* Willd.—FALSE-MERMAID

A fleshy herb that ranges from 2-10 cm in height, the stems are glabrous, and sprawling to weakly erect. Borne on stalks 1-4 cm long, the leaflets are 3-20 mm long and oval to narrowly oblanceolate in shape. The 3 mm long sepals are twice as long as the white, spatula-shaped petals, the latter sparsely hairy with long, straight hairs. There are typically 3 stamens that alternate with the petals and are fused with a scalelike gland, or, occasionally twice as many stamens with those opposite the petals being glandless. The fruit is 2-lobed, 2.5 mm long, rounded, bumpy, and closed at maturity.

This lowland plant of vernally wet places was found once at Mount Adams, by Flett on the Klickitat River northeast of the mountain.

## Loasaceae Juss.—BLAZING-STAR FAMILY

### *Mentzelia* L.—BLAZING-STAR

Two inconspicuous plants comprise this family at Mount Adams; the spectacular wildflower blazing-star, *M. laevicaulis,* occurs at lower elevations nearby in the Klickitat River Canyon. The two species are annuals, with 5 small, yellow flowers and numerous stamens; the ovary is inferior and produces many small seeds in a brittle capsule. The leaves are alternate and pinnately divided or not; all parts of the plants are roughly hairy.

1 Leaves pinnately lobed; flowers in a loosely-branched cyme; capsule widened towards the top ............................ *M. albicaulis*

1 Leaves wavy margined but typically not lobed; flowers congested at the top of the stem; capsule straight-sided ................. *M. dispersa*

### *Mentzelia albicaulis* (Hook.) Torr. & A. Gray
### WHITE-STEMMED BLAZING-STAR

An annual, usually with 1 flowering stem that reaches about 20 cm in height, "white-stemmed" refers to the shining white color of the surface of the stem. The leaves are usually pinnately divided and up to 5 cm long. They are arranged in a loose cyme consisting of 3-5 branches; the bracts of the cyme are distinctive in being nearly linear. The flowers are 2-5 mm long.

A characteristic plant of the foothills on the east side of the Cascades, this species was collected by Flett on the upper Klickitat River, east of the mountain.

### *Mentzelia dispersa* S. Wats.—BUSHY BLAZING-STAR

Well-grown plants of this *Mentzelia* may be "bushy," but are more typically seen at Mount Adams as a single-stemmed plant. This species is similar in stature to *M. albicaulis* but bears undivided leaves. The surface of the stem is green. The flowers are also yellow and 3-6 mm long, arranged in a contracted cyme.

Evidently collected at the same place by Flett as *M. albicaulis*, for both are mounted on the same herbarium sheet, this is also a plant of the east Cascades foothills.

## Malvaceae Adans.—MALLOW FAMILY

An unexpected family to find at Mount Adams, two species barely reach the study area on the southeast side of the mountain. Both are perennials with alternate, palmately-veined leaves, and slender stipules. The flowers are in racemes or raceme-like cymes and have 5 petals and 5 sepals; there are numerous stamens that are grouped together surrounding the style. The ovary is superior and the fruit is a capsule.

1 Leaf blades 5-7 lobed, sharply-toothed, 5-10 cm long; petals at least 2 cm long .................... *Iliamna*

1 Leaf blades rounded in outline, up to 5 cm long; petals 1-2 cm long .................... *Sidalcea*

### *Iliamna* Greene—WILD HOLLYHOCK

### *Iliamna rivularis* (Dougl. *ex* Hook.) Greene var. *rivularis*
### STREAMBANK WILD HOLLYHOCK

Borne on hairy stems 1-2 m tall this showy perennial grows on the eastern Cascade slopes. The leaves are 5-to-7 lobed, resembling maple leaves, and 4-10 cm long. The flowers grow in short racemes or raceme-like cymes, with 2 cm long, pinkish to lavender petals on stout pedicels about 1 cm long. The sepals are bluntly pointed and 3-5 mm long.

This species of dry middle elevation habitats is known from the DNR quarry on the southeast side of the mountain.

#### ***Sidalcea*** **A. Gray—OREGON CHECKERBLOOM**

#### ***S. oregana*** **(Nutt. *ex* Torr. & A. Gray) A. Gray ssp. *oregana* var. *procera* C.L. Hitchc.—OREGEON CHECKERBLOOM**

Typically with several flowering stems rising up to 1.5 m from a thickened root crown, this species has somewhat glaucus leaves. The racemes are tall and slender, with numerous pink to dark pink flowers on short pedicels. The sepals are 4-9 mm long.

As in the above, Oregon checkerbloom is typically seen at lower elevations east of the Cascades in Washington. It is known from a single Flett collection, made on the upper Klickitat River in 1899.

### Menyanthaceae (Dumort.) Dumort.—BUCKBEAN FAMILY

#### ***Menyanthes*** **L.—BUCKBEAN**

#### ***Menyanthes trifoliata*** **L.—BUCKBEAN**

The common name is taken from "bog-bean," in reference to the similarity of the 3-parted leaves to those of a cultivated bean plant. This is a clump-forming perennial with leaves that rise directly on long stalks from thick rootstocks. The 5-10 cm long leaflets are elliptical to lanceolate. The flowers are bright white, pink on the outside of the petals and bear long white hairs on the inner surface. They are borne several in a raceme on a leafless stem. They are about 2 cm broad, with the 5 petals united below and spreading above. The ovary is partly inferior and the fruit is an oval capsule.

Found along the edges of ponds and lakes in standing water, often forming extensive patches, this species is relatively common on the north and northwest sides of the mountain. Occasionally, it may be found among other vegetation in very wet meadows. It was collected by the authors at Bathtub Meadow and is also known from Horseshoe Lake, Muddy Meadows, Ollalie Lake and Takhlakh Lake.

### Monotropaceae Nutt.—MONOTROPA FAMILY

Formerly included in the Ericaceae, or Heath Family, the Monotropaceae are distinctive in the landscape: they are herbaceous plants that lack chlorophyll and bear leaves that are reduced to scales. Only two species are found at Mount Adams, many fewer than occur in lower elevation forests in Washington. Both have 5 petals that are free in *Monotropa*, fused in *Pterospora*. The fruit is a dry capsule.

1 Petals distinct; flower stalks becoming erect with age .... *Monotropa*
1 Petals united; flower stalks remaining curved downwards with age .. ........................................................................ *Pterospora*

## *Monotropa* L.—MONOTROPA

### *Monotropa hypopithys* L.—PINESAP

Typically growing in clumps of several 10-40 cm tall stems, this species bears insignificant, scalelike leaves. Plants most often are a muddy yellowish-brown in color, although individuals, mixed with duller plants, may be red, a clear yellow-brown, or occasionally a cream color. The raceme is composed of 3-20 flowers, each elongated-oblong, 1-2 cm long, with free petals.

A middle elevation plant of old forests, this is an uncommon species at the mountain. It was collected by Suksdorf at Hellroaring Canyon, and was also found on the northwest side, collected there by Beth Skaggs Ryan.

## *Pterospora* Nutt.—PINEDROPS

### *Pterospora andromedea* Nutt.—PINEDROPS

Pinedrops is an arresting plant with reddish-brown stems that vary from 30 to nearly 100 cm tall, sturdy enough that they often persist through the winter. They are glandular-short-hairy with numerous, small, scale-like leaves on the lower half. Green leaves are lacking. Urn-shaped flowers on short, nodding stalks, in a raceme, clothe the upper half of the stem; they are 6-7 mm long, whitish when young but soon turn reddish brown. There are 10 stamens included within the flower. The fruit is a dry capsule.

Found in open coniferous woods on dryish ground at lower to middle elevations on the south and east sides of Mount Adams, this species grows in the meadows near the DNR quarry with ponderosa pine. It is also found alongside the trail northeast of Bench Lake at 4,600 feet elevation, presumably a high elevation for this species.

## Nymphaeaceae Salisb.—WATER LILY FAMILY

### *Nuphar* J.E. Smith—POND-LILY

#### *Nuphar lutea* (L.) Sm. ssp. *polysepala* (Engelm.) E.O. Beal YELLOW POND-LILY

This aquatic herb rises from on a stout, heavy rootstock. The 10-30 cm long, heart-shaped leaves are borne on thick, hollow stalks and float on the water's surface. The 10 cm broad flowers are cup-shaped, with the bright yellow sepals providing the eye-catching color. There are 6-12 sepals, but the petals are only about 1 cm long, hidden by the many reddish stamens. These surround a broad, bright yellow, disklike stigma. The fruit is a large, oval, leathery capsule, easily seen.

Fairly common in ponds and lakes below 4,500 feet, this species forms patches on Olallie Lake (near the boat launch), at Horseshoe Lake, and is found in small ponds alongside the trail between Muddy Meadows and the Pacific Crest Trail. It also grows at Bathtub Meadows. No herbarium collections of this plant were located.

## Onagraceae Juss.—EVENING-PRIMROSE FAMILY

Well-represented at Mount Adams, this is a diverse family that includes the numerous epilobiums or willow-herbs. Members of the Onagraceae are annual and perennial herbs, with simple, mostly opposite leaves and slender stems. The flower parts are in 4s (2s in the case of *Circaea*) and are borne in spikes or racemes. The ovary is inferior and the fruit is a slender, elongated capsule, again with the exception of *Circaea*.

All of the 23 species at Mount Adams are natives and many are showy wildflowers. Some species are found in disturbed, open areas. They occupy streamsides and meadows as well as dry ground. Most common in middle elevations, some are found in subalpine meadows as well. Enchanter's nightshade (*Circaea alpina* ssp. *pacifica*) is unique in being a deep forest inhabitant.

| | | |
|---|---|---|
| 1 | Flowers yellow | *Camissonia* |
| 1 | Flowers white to pink or deep rose | 2 |
| 2(1) | Sepals, petals, and stamens in 2s | *Circaea* |
| 2 | Sepals, petals, and stamens in 4s or 8s | 3 |
| 3(2) | Seeds with a tuft of hairs at one end; sepals erect to spreading | 4 |
| 3 | Seeds lacking such a tuft of hairs; sepals turned back | 5 |

4(3) Leaves alternate, more than 7 cm long ...................... *Chamerion*
4 Leaves opposite, at least on the lower stem ................ *Epilobium*

5(3) Petals large and showy, at least 5 mm long ..................... *Clarkia*
5 Petals small, no more than 2 mm long .................... *Gayophytum*

## *Camissonia* Link.—EVENING-PRIMROSE

### *Camissonia subacaulis* (Pursh) Garrett
### LONG-LEAF EVENING-PRIMROSE

This plant, rare at Mount Adams, has a deep taproot and leaves arranged in a basal tuft; each leaf is 5-15 cm long, narrowly obovate, and mostly hairless, with a wavy margin. The several flowers rise on slender floral tubes from the crown of the plant - there is no flowering stem. The flowers are yellow, 10-12 mm long, and notched; they do not turn reddish or purplish in age, as do the petals of some related species.

This foothills plant is known for Mount Adams from one collection, made in 1899 by Flett on the upper Klickitat River.

## *Chamerion* Raf. *ex* Holub—FIREWEED

### *Chamerion angustifolium* (L.) Holub ssp. *angustifolium*—FIREWEED

Leafy stems that reach 1-2 m in height characterize this robust species, which may grow in broad clumps in certain locations but tends towards few stems at the mountain. The stems are grayish-hairy on their upper portion. Alternate, stalkless or short-stalked leaves are lanceolate in shape and 8-15 cm long. The stigma is prominent and 4-lobed; the bright pink flowers measure 2-3 cm across. The 4-9 cm capsule may be silvery-gray on the upper side and purplish on the lower.

A plant more typically seen at low to middle elevations, fireweed is relatively uncommon at Mount Adams. It has been found at Hellroaring Creek, along Road 23 near the junction of the road to Cougar, at Bench Lake, and as high as 6,800 feet on the summit of Little Mount Adams. The species was previously named *Epilobium angustifolium* L. ssp. *angustifolium*.

## *Circaea* L.—ENCHANTER'S NIGHTSHADE

### *Circaea alpina* L. ssp. *pacifica* (Asch. & Magnus) P.H. Raven
### ENCHANTER'S NIGHTSHADE

This low perennial rises from tuberous roots and may form extensive patches. The 10-50 cm tall leafy stems are short-hairy near the top. The 3-6 cm long leaves are opposite and borne on short stalks, finely toothed on the margins, and short-hairy beneath. The white flowers are borne in a terminal raceme. Each has two notched petals, tiny at 2.5 mm long;

there are 2 turned-back sepals. The pair of nutlets, covered in hooked hairs, is distinctive.

A lower elevation species of moist forests, this species is known from a Suksdorf collection at the Lewis River on the west side. It is unlikely to occur elsewhere in the study area.

### *Clarkia* Pursh—CLARKIA

#### *Clarkia rhomboidea* Dougl. *ex* Hook.—DIAMOND CLARKIA

This species is a simple-branched annual, 1.5-10 dm tall, with stem leaves. The petioles are slender and 1-3 cm long and the 2-7 cm blades are lanceolate to elliptic. They occasionally bear small teeth. The flowers form a loose raceme; the petals are rhomboid, rose-purple, 5-10 mm long and 3-6 mm broad. There are 8 stamens.

This species is known from the DNR Quarry at 4,100 feet on the southeast side of the mountain, where it grows in open, grassy areas with Garry oak.

### Epilobium L.—WILLOW-HERB

No genus among the dicotyledonous plants contains more species at Mount Adams than *Epilobium*. These are small to large annuals or perennials. They bear mostly opposite leaves. The flowers have 4 sepals, 4 petals, and 8 stamens; the stigma is nearly unlobed (but 4-lobed in *E. luteum*). The long, slender capsule is 4-celled and the seeds bear a tuft of hairs at the end, an aid to wind dispersal. A number of species are distinguished by being "hairy in lines" — that is, from each side of the base of the leaf stalk a thin line of small hairs running down the stem is visible.

Two hybrids have been identified from Mount Adams. These may be hard to place in the key and are rare enough that they are only mentioned here. They are:

*Epilobium* x *treleasianum* is a fertile hybrid between *E. luteum* and *E. ciliatum* ssp. *glandulosum*, with pink petals about 10mm long and a 4-parted stigma.

*Epilobium luteum* Pursh x *?hornemannii* ssp. *hornemannii*

Fireweed, formerly included in this genus, has been assigned to *Chamerion* based upon characteristics of floral anatomy.

1 Flowers yellow; petals 10-15 mm long .......................... *E. luteum*
1 Flowers white, pink, or purple; petals rarely as much as 10 mm.... 2

2(1) Plants annual; the skin of the lower stem dry and peeling away at maturity .......................... 3
2 Plants perennial; the skin of the lower stem not peeling .............. 4

| | | |
|---|---|---|
| 3(2) | Plants 40-100 cm tall; leaves hairless ................ *E. brachycarpum* | |
| 3 | Plants to 30 cm tall; leaves with fine, short hairs .......... *E. minutum* | |
| 4(2) | Turions (small, below-ground winter buds formed of fleshy, overlapping scales at the base of the stem) or basal rosettes of leaves present ................ | 5 |
| 4 | Turions or basal rosettes absent ................ | 7 |
| 5(4) | Stems mostly branched above the midpoint; petals 5-10 mm long ... .......... *E. ciliatum* ssp. *glandulosum* | |
| 5 | Stems mostly unbranched; petals 3-5 mm long ........................ | 6 |
| 6(5) | Leaves not stalked or short-stalked; capsule glandular ................ .......... *E. halleanum* | |
| 6 | Leaves stalked; capsule hairy but not glandular .......................... .......... *E. ciliatum* ssp. *ciliatum* | |
| 7(4) | Plants almost hairless; leaves glaucous . ................................ | 8 |
| 7 | Plants more or less short-hairy throughout; leaves not glaucous .......... | 9 |
| 8(7) | Stems 30-80 cm tall; upper leaves lanceolate, well-spaced and not overlapping . .......................... *E. glaberrimum* ssp. *glaberrimum* | |
| 8 | Stems less than 35 cm tall; upper leaves ovate, closely-spaced and overlapping .............................. *E. glaberrimum* ssp. *fastigiatum* | |
| 9(7) | Flowers white ................................................ *E. lactiflorum* | |
| 9 | Flowers pink, rose, or purple ............................................ | 10 |
| 10(9) | Flowering stems erect, solitary or a few per plant ...................... | 11 |
| 10 | Plants tufted or matted, with numerous flowering stems ........... | 12 |
| 11(10) | Leaves 2-4 cm long; petals 4-8 mm long. .................................. .......... *E. hornemannii* ssp. *hornemannii* | |
| 11 | Leaves 5-7 cm long; petals 3-5 mm long ... *E. ciliatum* ssp. *ciliatum* | |
| 12(10) | Plants hairless or with a few hairs in the inflorescence ................ .......... *E. oregonense* | |
| 12 | Plants short-hairy, the hairs often in lengthwise lines on the stem ... .......... | 13 |
| 13(12) | Leaves pale green; flower buds erect; capsule club-shaped .......... .......... *E. clavatum* | |
| 13 | Leaves bright green; flower buds nodding; capsule linear ............. .......... *E. anagallidifolium* | |

### *Epilobium anagallidifolium* Lam.—ALPINE WILLOW-HERB

With tufted and matted stems, this diminutive species may reach 10 cm in height. The stems bear tiny hairs in lines and nod at their tops. Light green, hairless leaves measure 6-15 mm long and are oval to lanceolate, with a few small teeth. The inflorescence is sometimes sparsely glandular, and the pink to rose- purple petals are 3-5 mm long. The 15-30 mm long capsule has a few small hairs.

An uncommon middle elevation to subalpine species, there are Suksdorf and Henderson collections from the north and south sides of Mount Adams.

### *Epilobium brachycarpum* C. Presl—AUTUMN WILLOW-HERB

Tall and diffuse, this annual has branched stems 30-80 cm in length. At the base of aging stems, the skin dries and peels. The 2-5 cm, almost hairless leaves are alternate lower on the stem and opposite above, narrowly lanceolate with a fold along the midvein. White to rose-pink flowers are borne in loose racemes on panicle-like upper branches. The petals vary from 2-8 mm long and the capsule is slender, somewhat club-shaped and 10-15 mm long.

This middle elevation species is known from collections on the south and southeast sides of the mountain, reaching about 4,600 feet, where it grows on open slopes that become quite dry late in the season. Elsewhere at Mount Adams, it finds little suitable habitat.

### *Epilobium ciliatum* Raf. ssp. *ciliatum*—COMMON WILLOW-HERB

The basal rosette of leaves of this perennial *Epilobium* usually persists through the winter. The slender stems may reach 100 cm in height and are glandular-hairy on the upper parts, the hairs configured in lines as well as scattered. Lanceolate to elliptical, the leaves are 1-10 cm long with pronounced veins. The pink to rose-purple petals are 2-6 mm long. The hairy fruit is very slender and 15-100 mm long.

This species is known from collections at Bird Creek Meadows on the southeast and the Lewis River on the west. It can also be found in wet, open, disturbed places, as alongside roads.

### *Epilobium ciliatum* Raf. ssp. *glandulosum* (Lehm.) Hoch & P.H. Raven—COMMON WILLOW-HERB

Short, fleshy offshoots at the base of the stem ("turions") characterize this subspecies. The leaves are ovate with 8-14 mm long petals and the inflorescence is leafy.

This subspecies has been found on the north side of Mount Adams at Midway Meadows and on the south at Hellroaring Creek, close to Bench Lake.

## Onagraceae

### *Epilobium clavatum* Trel.—CLUB-POD WILLOW-HERB

The 20 cm tall, leafy, ascending stems of this tufted plant bear flattened hairs. The 10-25 mm long leaves are elliptical to ovate and the petals are 3.5-6 cm long; the flowers are erect in bud. The 2-4 cm long capsule is hairy, club-shaped, and widest at the tip

The most common willow-herb species of the subalpine to alpine habitats, with a preference for wet sites, this species has been found at Hellroaring Canyon, Killen Creek, and at the Pacific Crest Trail/Trail 64 junction, as high as 6,200 feet.

### *Epilobium glaberrimum* Barbey in Brewer & S. Wats. ssp. *fastigiatum* (Nutt.) Hoch & Raven—GLAUCOUS WILLOW-HERB

Clumped, erect stems that may reach 35 cm in height characterize this perennial willow-herb. The unbranched stems are hairless and glaucous, with clasping, lanceolate-ovate leaves that are 1-3.5 cm long. The leaves are crowded and overlap, at least in the upper portion of the stem. The pink to rose-purple petals are 3-7 mm long. The capsule is 2-7 cm long; it is sometimes sparsely hairy.

This is the more common of the two varieties of *E. glaberrimum* at Mount Adams, found in habitats ranging from roadsides to subalpine cliffs and slopes, often on seasonally dry ground. This subspecies has been located at Road 23 near the summit overlook and in the meadow along Hellroaring Creek at 4,500 feet. A Henderson collection specifies a plant on the south side, "below the snowline."

### *Epilobium glaberrimum* Barbey in Brewer & S. Wats. ssp. *glaberrimum*—GLAUCOUS WILLOW-HERB

The stems of this subspecies may reach 80 cm and are often branched, distinguishing it from variety *fastigiatum*. The well-spaced lanceolate leaves are 2-7 cm long. The petals measure 5-12 mm in length.

Less common at Mount Adams, this subspecies is found at middle elevations on the west side, as alongside Road 23, where it may occur in proximity to the variety *fastigiatum*.

### *Epilobium halleanum* Hausskn.—GLANDULAR WILLOW-HERB

This is a 40 cm tall perennial, sparsely hairy, usually short-hairy in lines on the upper stem. The ovate to oblong leaves are stalkless or on very short stalks. The pink petals are about 4 mm long and the flowers nod when in bud. The sparsely glandular capsule is 3-5 cm long.

A common species of moist, middle elevation to subalpine sites, it has been found at Muddy Meadows and on the north slope of Hellroaring Canyon at 6,500 feet.

### *Epilobium hornemannii* Reichenb. ssp. *hornemannii*
### HORNEMANN'S WILLOW-HERB

Leafy, unbranched stems are configured in a loosely clumped plant 10-40 cm tall; it may form extensive patches. Ovate and short-stalked, the hairless leaves have spreading teeth and are 2-4 cm long. The inflorescence nods at the top of the stem and is composed of a few flowers. The pink petals are 4-8 mm long and the 4-7 cm long capsule is slender and sparsely hairy.

This common species was found by the authors on sphagnum in Foggy Flat meadow on the north side of Mount Adams at 6,000 feet, as well as at High Camp Meadows at over 6,800 feet, and at Hellroaring Canyon.

### *Epilobium lactiflorum* Hausskn.—WHITE WILLOW-HERB

Slender, tufted stems, 10-30 cm tall, distinguish this perennial. The stems are typically hairless but occasionally are minutely hairy in lines on the upper part. Narrowly ovate-lanceolate, the leaves bear widely-spaced teeth, and are 2-5 cm long. The inflorescence is glandular, nodding or erect, and the petals are white and 3-7 mm long. The 5-10 cm long slender capsule is hairy.

A common species from middle elevations to the subalpine, white willow-herb has been collected in wet, sunny places at Hellroaring Canyon, along Bird Creek, below the White Salmon Glacier, and at Babyshoe Meadow.

### *Epilobium luteum* Pursh—YELLOW WILLOW-HERB

Simple stems 20-70 cm tall rise from the widespread rootstocks of this perennial. The stems are short-hairy in lines. The opposite, nearly stalkless leaves are ovate-lanceolate to lanceolate in shape, hairy on the margins, and 3-8 cm long. The flowers are borne in the axils of the reduced upper leaves; the yellow petals are 14-18 mm long and obcordate. The style extends beyond the petals and the linear-lanceolate sepals are 8-13 mm long.

A wetland species, distinguished by the large, yellow flowers, this *Epilobium* has been found at the confluence of Cascade Creek and Salt Creek on the southwest side of Mount Adams, where it grows in seeps on the debris flow. More typically, it grows in moist subalpine meadows, as in Hellroaring valley, where it was collected by Suksdorf.

### *Epilobium minutum* Lindl. *ex* Lehm. in Hook.
### SMALL-FLOWERED WILLOW-HERB

Short-hairy, this slender annual reaches 30 cm in height. The 10-20 mm long opposite leaves are lanceolate and toothed. The inflorescence is a bracted raceme, composed of a small number of flowers, each with pink petals 3-4 mm long. The slender, curved capsule is 2-2.5 cm long.

More typically a lowland plant of open, dry places, this species is common at 4,100 feet at the DNR quarry on the southeast side of Mount Adams, but has also been located by the authors on Stagman Ridge at 5,700 feet on the southwest side, where it grows on a west-facing rocky outcrop in an open Pacific silver fir forest.

### *Epilobium oregonense* Hausskn.—OREGON WILLOW-HERB

This perennial consists of matted, slender, hairless stems 5-20 cm tall. The ovate-lanceolate leaves are stalkess, widely spaced, and 10-20 mm long. They are marked with reddish veins. There are 1-3 flowers per stem. The pink petals are 3-5 mm long and the capsule is 2-4 cm long, glandular-hairy, and slender.

An uncommon wet meadow plant, this species is known from two Suksdorf collections, one made at Hellroaring Canyon and the other from the canyon of the upper Klickitat River.

### *Gayophytum* A. Juss.—GROUNDSMOKE

Similar to the epilobiums, the species are typically more diffusely branched and bear alternate leaves. The flowers are small, regular, with leafy bracts; the sepals are turned back. The capsules are slender to somewhat club-shaped. The hairless seeds help distinguish *Gayophytum* from *Epilobium*. These plants are superficially similar and careful measurements of the flower parts and observation of the maturing fruits are essential to differentiate the species at Mount Adams.

| | | |
|---|---|---|
| 1 | Petals typically 4-8 mm long, rarely as short as 1.5 mm .................................................... | *G. diffusum* |
| 1 | Petals 0.5-3 mm long .................................................... | 22 |
| 2(1) | Fruits irregular due to aborted seeds .................. | *G. heterozygum* |
| 2 | Fruits regular; seeds maturing .................................... | 3 |
| 3(2) | Petals 0.8-1.5 mm .................................................... | *G. humile* |
| 3 | Petals 1.3-1.8 mm .................................................... | *G. racemosum* |

### *Gayophytum diffusum* Torr. & A. Gray
### SPREADING GROUNDSMOKE

Diffusely branched in the inflorescence, this annual is 15 to 60 cm tall, with long, scattered hairs on the stems. The leaves are linear to oblanceolate, 1.5-5 cm long. The pedicels are threadlike and 1-2 mm long and the petals are white to pinkish, 1-5 mm long. The capsules are erect and 4-12 mm long.

Found on dry, loose soil on the southeast side of the mountain, this species has been collected at Bird Creek Meadows, Hellroaring Creek, on the road to Bird Creek Meadows, and at the summit of Little Mount Adams at 6,800 feet.

### *Gayophytum heterozygum* Lewis & Szweykowski ZIGZAG GROUNDSMOKE

A stabile hybrid of *G. oligospermum* and *G. eriospermum*, this species resembles *G. diffusum* except for the appearance of the fruit. It is irregularly "beaded" with seed, since many of the seeds in each capsule tend to be aborted. The species is self-fertile and does not appear to cross with other species at Mount Adams. The common name refers to the angular branching of the inflorescence.

Hitchcock called this hybrid *G. diffusum* var. *villosum*. It is interesting that the parents of this hybrid are both species restricted to California.

This species is known from Suksdorf collections at Hellroaring Canyon and Bird Creek. Habitat and elevation information is not given for these collections.

### *Gayophytum humile* Juss.—DWARF GROUNDSMOKE

This low plant is a diffusely-branched annual, 5-20 cm tall. It bears many linear to spoon-shaped leaves 5-30 mm long and 1-2 mm broad. The flowers are stalkless or short-stalked; they are borne in dense spikes with the bracts nearly as long as the stem leaves that nearly conceal the flowers and fruits. The capsules are 7-15 mm long.

This small plant is known from Hellroaring Canyon, Bird Creek Island, and the upper White Salmon River, where it grows in open, seasonally moist places.

### *Gayophytum racemosum* Torr. & A. Gray BLACKFOOT GROUNDSMOKE

Similar to *G. humile,* the primary difference between the two species is in the seeds. They are slightly longer in this species (1 mm) and held erect in the capsule rather than obliquely set.

This uncommon species is known from two collections on the southeast side of the mountain—one made by Kruckeberg between Bluff Lake and Bird Lake in an open, conifer forest, and the second by Suksdorf at Hellroaring Canyon.

## Orobanchaceae Vent.—BROOMRAPE FAMILY

### *Orobanche* L.—BROOMRAPE

Two species of this parasitic group of plants are found at Mount Adams. Both lack chlorophyll and instead gain nutrients through attaching their roots to the roots of host plants. The flowers resemble those of many members of the figwort family, the Scrophulariaceae; they are 2-lipped, with a long tube. The ovary is superior and composed of 2 chambers that develop into a dry capsule with numerous, tiny seeds.

1 Flower stalks numbering 4-10, equal in length to the inflorescence stem; calyx lobes equaling or shorter than the tube ........................................................................................ *O. fasciculata*
1 Flower stalks 1-3, much longer than the short inflorescence stem; calyx lobes longer than the tube . ............................. *O. uniflora*

### *Orobanche fasciculata* Nutt.—CLUSTERED BROOMRAPE

The uniquely yellow to purple stems of this parasitic plant are 3-15 cm long and slender to sometimes stout. The plants are finely short-hairy and glandular throughout. The inflorescence is a dense, short corymb, with the flowers borne on pedicels up to 3 cm long, or occasionally stalkless. The 22-28 mm long corolla is purplish, the 4-6 mm long lower lip barely spreading. The anthers are wooly.

This is a rare species at the mountain, known from a Suksdorf collection made at "Donner's Glacier," a name he used for the Klickitat Glacier, which lies at the head of Big Muddy Creek. Elsewhere in Washington, *O. fasciculata* frequently parasitizes *Artemisia* species, so it makes some sense to think that Suksdorf's collection was made on the Ridge of Wonders, which forms the south wall of "Donner's Vale" below Donner's Glacier, a place where *Artemisia tridentata* grows.

### *Orobanche uniflora* L.—NAKED BROOMRAPE

Attached to its host's roots, this is a leafless, parasitic plant. A purplish, stemlike stalk, 5-10 cm tall and glandular-hairy supports a single flower at the top. The purplish, tubular flower is white at the throat, curved, and 2-lipped. The upper lip has 2 lobes and is erect, while the lower lip is divided into 3 spreading lobes. The 6-8 mm long fruit is an egg-shaped capsule.

Rare at the mountain, this small plant is known from the DNR quarry on the southeast side, where it was found by Paul Slichter in 2005. Its host here is not known, but at Mount Rainier the plant parasitizes *Montia parvifolia*, *Sedum* species, and some saxifrage species, especially *Suksdorfia*.

## Oxalidaceae R. Br.—WOOD-SORREL FAMILY

### *Oxalis* L.—WOOD-SORREL

#### *Oxalis triliifolia* Hook.—THREE-LEAF WOOD-SORREL

This delicate perennial herb has short, vertical rootstocks. The 3-5 cm long leaflets are borne on hairy, leafless stalks that may reach 30 cm in height. The 3-5-lobed leaflets are heart-shaped. The flowers are borne in groups of 6-8 in umbels and each has 5 free sepals and 5 petals, with 10 stamens and a superior ovary. The 8-14 mm long petals are white and the 2-3 cm long capsule is straight and slender.

A middle elevation forest species, it is uncommon at the mountain. It was collected by the authors alongside Road 23 on the west side, in a low, wet bank where it grew in a devil's club thicket.

## Plantaginaceae Juss.—PLANTAIN FAMILY

### *Plantago* L.—PLANTAIN

No native plantains occur at Mount Adams and the two weedy species are not common, mostly restricted to roads and trailsides, campgrounds, but occasionally moving into dry meadows. Both species are perennials, with heavily-veined basal leaves. The flowers are in spikes on leafless stems. They are obscure, consisting of 4 separate sepals and 4 mostly united petals; the free lobes of the petals are brownish and papery.

1 Leaves lanceolate, tapered to an indefinite stalk ....... *P. lanceolata*
1 Leaves elliptic to ovate, with a slender stalk .................. *P. major*

#### *Plantago lanceolata* L.—ENGLISH PLANTAIN

Held erect, the 5-20 cm long, lanceolate leaves of this species surround the 25-45 cm tall flowering stem. The slender spike is up to 5 cm long.

A weedy species found alongside roads and other disturbed sites, it grows at middle elevations and has been located by the authors at the horse camp on Hellroaring Creek and at the intersection of Road 8040 and Road 781, on the south side.

#### *Plantago major* L.—COMMON PLANTAIN

The 5-20 cm long leaves of this plantain tend to lie close to the ground, forming a loose rosette. The flowering stem may reach 50 cm in height, and the spike is up to 20 cm long.

Preferring wetter habitats than *P. lanceolata*, this weed grows at the edges of Swampy Meadows and at the horse camp at Hellroaring Creek.

## Polemoniaceae

### Polemoniaceae Juss.—Phlox Family

Avoiding only the deepest lowland forests, members of the Phlox family can be found in all habitats at Mount Adams, from dry lodgepole pine forests on the north to swampy lake margins on the west, to alpine scree on the south. A few are annuals but most are perennial. All have 5 sepals, 5 partly-fused petals, with a slender tube and spreading lobes, and 5 stamens. The female portion of the flower is in 3s: 3 separate stigmas atop 3 united styles and a 3-parted ovary that develops into a capsule that splits at maturity into 3 sections.

1 Calyx tube eventually rupturing as the capsule matures; at least the lower leaves opposite ........ 2
1 Calyx tube expanding with the maturing capsule and not rupturing; leaves alternate ........ 6

2(1) Stamens attached at different levels in the tube; leaves not toothed ........ 3
2 Stamens attached at or about at the same level in the tube; leaves mostly divided ........ 4

3(2) Plants annual ........ *Microsteris*
3 Plants perennial ........ *Phlox*

4(2) Leaves all opposite and palmately divided ........ *Leptosiphon*
4 At least the upper leaves alternate, undivided or pinnately divided... ........ 4

5(4) Calyx lobes more or less unequal; sharp-tipped leaves .. *Navarretia*
5 Calyx lobes equal; leaves soft, not sharp-tipped ........ *Ipomopsis*

6(1) Leaves pinnately compound, the individual leaflets distinct on the midvein of the leaf ........ *Polemonium*
6 Leaves pinnately to palmately divided, the lobes often toothed but not clearly distinct as leaflets ........ *Collomia*

### *Collomia* Nutt.—COLLOMIA

Showy wildflowers, the 5 species of *Collomia* at Mount Adams include just one perennial, the sprawling alpine *C. larsenii*. The annuals grow in forest openings, dry meadows, and disturbed places, such as alongside trails and roads. The flowers are arranged in heads at the tops of the stems and the leaves are alternate. Among the Polemoniaceae, the calyx in this genus is unique: the sepals are fully fused and lack membranous sutures between them. The flowers feature a long tube with 5 free lobes.

1 Sprawling perennial of open alpine slopes .................... *C. larsenii*
1 Annuals with upright stems, middle elevation to subalpine .......... 2

2(1) Leaves pinnately lobed and toothed ..................... *C. heterophylla*
2 Leaves neither lobed not toothed ........................................... 3

3(2) Flowers salmon-colored ...................................... *C. grandiflora*
3 Flowers pink ..................................................................................... 4

4(3) Plant unbranched; flowers in well-defined, terminal heads .............
....................................................................................... *C. linearis*
4 Plant branched; flowers in small aggregations in the forks of the upper branches .................................................... *C. tinctoria*

**_Collomia grandiflora_ Dougl. _ex_ Lindl.—GRAND COLLOMIA**

Beautiful salmon to yellowish flowers top the robust stems of this large annual. The plants may reach 1 m tall, and the leaves are broadly lanceolate to linear, alternate, and 1-7 cm long. The flowers are 2-3 cm long and the lobes are 5-10 mm.

Growing on dry or disturbed sites in middle elevations, reaching 5,500 feet, this lovely plant was found by the authors alongside Road 8040, at the junction of Road 071 and Road 150, not far from the Aiken Lava Bed. It was also collected by Suksdorf at both Hellroaring Canyon and on the "east side."

**_Collomia heterophylla_ Hook.—VARIABLE-LEAF COLLOMIA**

This is a low, easily overlooked, branched annual no more than 20 cm tall that differs from the other collomias in having pinnately lobed leaves. The leaves are irregularly toothed and as much as 3.5 cm long; the upper stem leaves are often undivided. The light to dark pink flowers are configured in small terminal clusters or are borne in the axils of the upper stem leaves. The flower tube is 10-14 mm long, the free lobes an additional 3-4 mm long, and there is a white "eye" at the throat.

A middle elevation, disturbance habitat species, it is known from a Suksdorf collection on the northwest side of the mountain. It has been observed along the side of Road 23 west of Mount Adams and at the DNR quarry on the southeast at 4,000 feet.

**_Collomia larsenii_ (A. Gray) Payson—ALPINE COLLOMIA**

This perennial rises from a deep taproot, and consists of sprawling, single or sometimes slender branched stems that form patches several dm across. The stem branches are typically covered by sand and small stones, so that the appearance is of clustered but separate plants. The leaves are alternate, sometimes crowded, and up to 3 cm long; they are deeply cleft into 3-7 segments, sometimes divided again. The flowers are borne in leafy clusters at the ends of the stems. The 12-35 mm corolla is tubular and ranges from blue to pink to white in color.

Formerly named *C. debilis* var. *larsenii* (A. Gray) Brand, this is a timberline and alpine species, reaching nearly 8,000 feet, that has been found on the north side of Little Mount Adams. It has been collected along the South Climb route, at Stagman Ridge, and on the moraine below the Mazama Glacier. It is also known from a Henderson collection on the east side of the mountain.

#### *Collomia linearis* Nutt.—NARROWLEAF COLLOMIA

Another annual plant, in this species the stems are unbranched and up to 30 cm tall. The 2-5 cm long, linear to lanceolate leaves are stalkless, and untoothed, except occasionally for small teeth on the largest lower leaves. A crowded head of 10-20 pink flowers at the top of the stem consists of individual flowers 8-10 mm long.

A middle elevation species, this *Collomia* was collected by the authors at Midway Meadows, and was also found at 4,000 feet on Road 8040, and at 4,700 feet on the Stagman Ridge trail.

#### *Collomia tinctoria* Kellogg—STAINING COLLOMIA

This plant is a slender, freely-branched annual up to 1.5 dm tall. It is glandular and short-hairy, with flowers borne from near the base to the top in the forks of the branches. The 1.5 cm long leaves are linear, with the lower leaves sometimes borne opposite. The corolla is a pinkish or lavender slender tube, 8-14 mm long, with short (1.5-2.5 mm) lobes.

A species of dry habitats, it is known from a single Flett collection on the Klickitat River, northeast of Mount Adams where it is probably at its upper reach.

### *Ipomopsis* Michx.—IPOMOPSIS

#### *Ipomopsis aggregata* (Pursh) V. Grant ssp. *aggregata*<br>SCARLET GILIA, SKYROCKET

A 2-10 dm tall biennial or short-lived perennial, this showy species typically blooms only once. The first-year plant consists of a tight rosette of pinnate leaves. The plants have 1 to several stems, covered with glands or long white hairs. The malodorous leaves are up to 1 dm long, pinnately divided to the midpoint of each leaflet, with narrow stems. The inflorescence is a cyme composed of bright orange to red, downward-facing tubular flowers, 1.5-3.5 cm in length. The lobes are 6-13 mm long with the filaments attached above the middle of the corolla tube.

This hummingbird plant is found in middle elevation dry and open habitats, including roadsides. It has been located along the Island

Springs trail, on the Snipes Mountain Trail north of the Pineway Trail, and at the intersection of Roads 8040 and 781. It is abundant along the east flank of the Aiken Lava Bed. There is also a Suksdorf collection from the northeast side.

## *Leptosiphon* Benth.—LEPTOSIPHON

Delicate annual plants, the two flaxflower species at Mount Adams are both more commonly found in open forests and brushy slopes. Each has slender branches and opposite, thread-like, lobed leaves. The tiny flowers are arranged in diffuse panicles, held on very slender stems, and are white to pale blue in color, usually with yellow at the throat of the flower. The fruit is a small capsule. These plants were formerly included in the genus *Linanthus*.

1 Corolla slightly if at all longer than the calyx .............. *L. harknessii*
1 Corolla 1.5-2 times longer than the calyx ............ *L. septentrionalis*

### *Leptosiphon harknessii* (Curran) J.M. Porter & L.A. Johnson HARKNESS'S FLAXFLOWER

A tall annual that may reach 2.5 dm but is frequently shorter, this species is freely branched and for the most part glabrous. The leaves are divided into 3-7 linear segments up to 1. 5 cm long; the uppermost leaves may be entire. Single flowers on long pedicels are white and 1.5-2.5 mm long, only slightly longer than the calyx. The floral tube is quite short.

Preferring open, often disturbed, dry habitats, this species is known from the ridge above the DNR Quarry, at 4,000 feet on the southeast side of Mount Adams.

### *Leptosiphon septentrionalis* (Mason) J.M. Porter & L.A. Johnson NORTHERN FLAXFLOWER

This species is best distinguished from *L. harknessii* by the length of the corolla relative to the calyx. The petals are also longer, reaching about 5 mm.

Also rare in the region, this species is known from a Flett collection made at Klickitat Meadows.

## *Microsteris* Greene—ANNUAL PHLOX

Until recently, this small genus has been included in *Phlox*, where it was distinguished from the other members of that genus in the Northwest by its annual habit. These are easily overlooked plants, but for the fact that they often are found in large numbers, flowering early in the year, often seen in disturbed places.

1 Stems unbranched, to 5-7 cm tall .............. *M. gracilis* var. *gracilis*
1 Stems branched, to 3 cm tall ..................... *M. gracilis* var. *humilis*

**_Microsteris gracilis_ (Hook.) Greene var. _gracilis_—SLENDER PHLOX**

A branched annual with a primary stem 8-25 cm in length, this phlox is taller than wide and sometimes unbranched. The 1-3 cm long leaves are oblanceolate and opposite on the lower portion of the stem and narrower and alternate toward the top. The pink flowers are solitary in the axils of the upper leaves and 8-10 mm long.

Relatively common in middle elevation meadows, this species has been found at Muddy Meadows, Midway Meadows, and at Potato Hill. It was collected by Suksdorf at Hell-roaring Canyon and also grows in a wet meadow at 4000 feet along Road 6000. It also grows as a disturbance species at roadsides.

**_Microsteris gracilis_ (Hook.) Greene var. _humilis_ (Greene) Mason SLENDER PHLOX**

Differing from *P. gracilis* ssp. *gracilis* in height, this species of drier habitats is more branched and varies from 1-5 cm in height, often as broad as tall. The corolla measures 5-8 mm with the lobes 1-2 mm.

More common in drier habitats, this subspecies is known from King Mountain and Hellroaring Canyon on the southeast side of Mount Adams and from Road 23, south of the overlook.

**_Navarretia_ Ruiz & Pavón—PINCUSHION-PLANT**

**_Navarretia divaricata_ (Torr. _ex_ A. Gray) Greene ssp. _divaricata_ SPREADING NAVARRETIA**

The flowering head barely reaching 5 cm, this low annual is often glandular, with an inflorescence characterized by long, sticky hairs. Multiple heads to the side of the primary head produce a broad plant. The leaves are few and are barely 2.5 cm long; they are pinnately divided to the midpoint and borne on slender stems. The calyx is 5-10 mm long, with some of the lobes greater in length than the corolla. The corolla is 3.5 mm long, with short lobes and white to pale pink or lavender in color.

Reaching its northern limit in Washington at Mount Adams, this species has been found near King Mountain, alongside Road 6900 on the southeast side, at Grand Meadow, and on Road 23, south of the overlook.

## *Phlox* L.—PHLOX

*Phlox* at Mount Adams is a genus of very showy perennial wildflowers, often found on rocky slopes above timberline. The plants have opposite, untoothed leaves on spreading branches. The flowers are typically solitary in the axils of the upper leaves (but in a cyme in *P. speciosa*). The flowers are large, with long, slender tubes and lobes that spread to form a flat face. Inside the tube, the stamens are attached at different levels.

1 Plants erect, typically 30-40 cm tall; petals notched .................................................................... *P. speciosa* ssp. *nitida*
1 Plants tufted or matlike, less than 20 cm tall; petals rounded ....... 2

2(1) Most leaves about 0.5 mm wide; stems rather upright, to 15 or 20 cm ............................................................ *P. caespitosa*
2 Most leaves 1-2.5 mm wide; stems somewhat spreading, 10-15 cm long ......................................................................... 3

3(2) Leaves glandular-hairy; style 1-2 mm long ............ *P. hendersonii*
3 Leaves smooth or hairy on the margins, not glandular; style 5-10 mm ................................................ *P. diffusa* ssp. *longistylis*

### *Phlox caespitosa* Nutt.—TUFTED PHLOX

A subalpine to alpine species, this taprooted, compact perennial consists of ascending, slender stems, 5-15 cm tall. The upper parts are glandular or glandular-hairy. The 5-13 mm long, narrow, linear leaves are thickened. Small hairs line the margins near the base of the leaves. Single flowers on short pedicels, or sometimes without, are white, with the corolla tube 8-14 mm long and the lobes 7-10 mm long.

Reported by Hitchcock as a species of open habitats in ponderosa pine forests, at Mount Adams this *Phlox* occurs at higher elevations. It is found in the highest reaches of Bird Creek Meadows, on the Ridge of Wonders above Hellroaring Canyon, and was reported by Suksdorf at Mazama Glacier and by Henderson as "above glaciers."

### *Phlox diffusa* Benth. ssp. *longistylis* Wherry—SPREADING PHLOX

The scientific and common names refer to the configuration of this species. The leafy stems spread widely, and old plants are often matlike. The 10-15 mm long leaves are linear, while the solitary flowers are stalkless and borne on the branch ends. When the flowers open they are white to lavender, with a single plant often showing variation in color. The corolla tube is approximately 10 mm long and the lobes are 6-8 mm long.

Relatively common in lower subalpine, dry habitats, this species extends its range into middle elevations and is cosmopolitan at the mountain. Large clumps are found on Potato Hill on the north; it is also known on the southwest along Road 23 near the summit overlook, as well as on the Stagman Ridge trail. It grows at Cold Creek on the south and at the gate to Bird Creek on Road 82. It was reported by Suksdorf at the upper reaches of Hellroaring Canyon, probably at about 6,000 feet.

### *Phlox hendersonii* (E. Nels.) Cronq.—HENDERSON'S PHLOX

Tufted and matlike, this low perennial has 3-parted, crowded leaves that are 5-10 mm long and very narrow. They are glandular-hairy with thickened margins. The solitary flowers are borne at the ends of the stems; they often have 6 petals. The calyx and corolla tube are nearly equal in length and measure approximately 1 cm long. The lobes are about 5 mm long, and the style 1-2 mm long.

This compact, attractive but relatively uncommon species is known from a Flett collection in a "small crater" (probably on the east side and perhaps from Little Mount Adams, where the authors have found large numbers of plants at the summit.) It grows on stony flats and should be expected only above 6,500 feet.

### *Phlox speciosa* Push ssp. *nitida* (Suksdorf) Wherry—SHOWY PHLOX

A spreading perennial from a woody taproot, this shrubby plant is 1.5-4 dm tall and typically glandular or glandular-hairy above. The linear to lanceolate leaves reach 7 cm in length and are widely spaced. The malodorous flowers are configured in terminal cymes. They are pink or purple (occasionally white) with 11-15 mm long tubes and 8-14 mm long lobes; the ends are frayed in appearance. The filaments are attached above the middle of the tube.

The study area at Mount Adams is barely within elevational range of this more typically lower elevation, dry habitat species. It was found by the authors along Road 80 on the southeast side and is also known from a Henderson collection simply labeled as "near Mount Adams".

## *Polemonium* L.—SKY-PILOT, JACOB'S LADDER

Four species of this attractive group of wildflowers grow at Mount Adams, providing some of the truest blues to be found. Although they vary greatly in stature and habitat, all have pinnately compound leaves, with the flowers arranged in loose to compact cymes. The flower has a shorter tube than is typical for the family and the lobes spread widely, becoming bell-shaped to funnel-shaped.

1 Corolla tubular, longer than wide, lobes shorter than the tube ......... ........................................................................ *P. elegans*

1 Corolla bell-shaped, as wide as long, lobes as long as the tube ... 2

2(1) Stems solitary, from short rhizomes; plants erect, 4-10 dm tall ....... ............................................. *P. occidentale* ssp. *occidentale*

2 Stems clustered from branched rootstock above a taproot; plants lax, to 3 dm. tall .................................................................... 3

3(2) Compact, less than 2 dm tall; leaflets less than 1 cm long, distinct; calyx lobes shorter than tube ................................................ .......................................... *P. pulcherrimum* ssp. *pulcherrimum*

3 Larger, to 3 dm tall or more; leaflets 1-3.5 cm long, terminal leaflets joined; calyx lobes longer than tube .................... *P. californicum*

### *Polemonium californicum* Eastw.—SHOWY JACOB'S LADDER

Lax, sparsely glandular-hairy, spreading stems 15-30 cm tall distinguish this loosely tufted perennial. The 10-20 cm long leaves have oval leaflets 1-3 cm long. The 3 terminal leaflets most often are merged at their bases. Bell-shaped flowers 9-12 mm long are configured in open cymes. The throat and tube are yellow, while the lobes are blue to blue-violet, a distinctive color combination found in *Polemonium* species. The calyx lobes are longer than the tube.

Common in open subalpine forests, this species also grows at high elevations near timberline, often under the "skirts" of subalpine fir. It grows alongside the trail to Lookingglass Lake above Stagman Ridge, on Little Mount Adams, in the meadows at 6,880 feet at Killen High Camp, and at 4,500 feet along Morrison Creek.

### *Polemonium elegans* Greene
### SKY-PILOT, ELEGANT JACOB'S LADDER

More compact than *P. californicum*, this tufted plant is 5-12 cm tall and is heavily glandular-hairy on both stems and leaves. The leaves are 4-7 cm long, bearing many rounded leaflets, the latter 2-5 mm long. The leaflets overlap on the midvein, a point of differentiation with *P. pulcherrimum*. The flowers are arranged in dense clusters, with 12-15 mm long corollas that are funnel-shaped and blue-violet in color. As with other genus members, they are yellow at the throat. The calyx is longer than the tube.

A showy, distinctively blue species of open subalpine environments, it is locally common, with plants observed at Hellroaring Canyon, on the summit of Little Mount Adams at 6,800 feet, and at the Mazama Glacier. It was noted in a "small crater" by Flett, probably, again, at the summit of Little Mount Adams.

### *Polemonium occidentale* Greene ssp. *occidentale*
### WESTERN JACOB'S LADDER

Solitary stems that rise 4-10 dm tall from horizontal rhizomes distinguish this species from the spreading or tufted polemoniums. The leaves consist of 11-27 lanceolate, sharply tipped leaflets that are 1-4 cm long. The 3 terminal leaflets are sometimes fused into one. The inflorescence is glandular or short-hairy. The flowers are crowded in a somewhat elongated, few-flowered panicle. The calyx lobes are typically shorter than the tube. The light blue corolla is 1-1.6 cm long and equally as wide, with longer lobes.

Found in middle elevation to subalpine locations, this species prefers wet sites and is sometimes found on floating mats in sphagnum bogs. It grows on the north side of the mountain at Foggy Flat and lower Midway Meadows. It is found at Mirror Lake, at Hellroaring Creek near the crossing of Island Springs trail, and near Bench Lake in the lower Hellroaring Meadows. There is also a Suksdorf collection from "northeast of Little Mount Adams" as well as Flett collections.

### *Polemonium pulcherrimum* Hook. ssp. *pulcherrimum*
### LOW JACOB'S LADDER

Low and tufted, with erect to spreading stems less than 10 cm high, this perennial is the smallest of the *Polemonium* species. The plant is sparsely hairy and glandular, and the leaves are primarily basal; they are about 5 cm long with ovate to rounded leaflets 4-8 mm long. The terminal leaflet is separated from those below. A crowded inflorescence makes the plant easily visible when in flower. The flowers are white to blue, with an 8-10 mm, bell-shaped corolla, and a yellow throat. The calyx lobes are equal in length to the tube or sometimes shorter.

Most easily recognized by size and the compact flower heads, this is a middle elevation to subalpine species of relatively dry and open sites, often occupying crevices between rocks and other protected places. It is found on Potato Hill on the north and at Little Mount Adams, Bench Lake, and Bird Creek Meadows on the south. It was also found "13 miles north of Trout Lake" by Zuberbuhler in 1936. This may be an anomalous forest site or an error in the collector's label.

## Polygonaceae Juss.—BUCKWHEAT FAMILY

A large family including many members that are weedy, obscure, or easily overlooked, the Polygonaceae does contain some notable wildflowers, including mountain-sorrel, the buckwheats, and American bistort. These are perennial or annual herbs, with simple, alternate leaves and, in most genera, leaf stipules that sheathe the stem. Flowers are in clusters that may be large or small, terminal or axillary. They have in common the absence of petals: the perianth consists of 4, 5 or 6 small tepals that are commonly greenish but may be colorful and petal-like. Stamens number 3-9 and the superior ovary bears 3 styles. The fruit is a hard seed called an achene that is typically enfolded in remnants of the perianth.

In the *Flora of North America,* species previously lumped in the genus *Polygonum* have been separated into a number of segregate genera, accounting for three names that may be unfamiliar to many -- *Aconogonon, Bistorta,* and *Fallopia.*

1 Plant a twining, vinelike perennial; leaves heart-shaped .... *Fallopia*
1 Plant not vinelike; leaves various, but not heart-shaped .............. 2

2(1) Flowers white, in a dense, spikelike raceme ................... *Bistorta*
2 Flowers greenish or colored, not white; inflorescence various ...... 3
3(2) Leaves lacking stipules; flowers clustered, in a "cup" formed of the fused involucral bracts .......................................... *Eriogonum*
3 Leaves with sheathing stipules; flowers, if clustered, lacking fused involucral bracts ................................................................ 4

4(3) Leaves kidney-shaped; lobes of the perianth 4 ................. *Oxyria*
4 Leaves various but not as above; lobes of the perianth 5 or 6...... 5

5(4) Lobes of the perianth 6 .............................................. *Rumex*
5 Lobes of the perianth 5 ...................................................... 6

6(5) Plant perennial and robust; leaves more or less ovate ................. ................................................................. *Aconogonon*
6 Plant annual, usually slender; leaves linear, lanceolate, or oval ...... .............................................................. *Polygonum*

## *Aconogonon* Meisner—KNOTWEED

The giants of the Polygonaceae, the two species here were segregated from the genus *Polygonum* based, partly, upon the fact that they are perennials which grow from woody rootstocks. The stems are leafy and the leaf blades are typically ovate. An important character is the nature of the sheathing stipules – in *Aconogonon* they are papery and tan to brownish or reddish while in *Polygonum* they are thin and transparent or silvery. There are 5 petal-like tepals that are slightly dissimilar: the outer 2 are smaller than the inner 3. There are 8 stamens.

1 Stems to 30-40 cm long; flowers in axillary racemes.................... ................................................... *A. davisiae* var. *davisiae*
1 Stems 1-2 m tall; racemes both axillary and terminal ................... ................................ *A. phytolaccifolium* var. *phytolaccifolium*

## Polygonaceae

### *Aconogonon davisiae* (W.H. Brewer *ex* A. Gray) Sojak var. *davisiae* FLEECEFLOWER

Rising from heavy roots, this perennial has stems that break easily. This characteristic enables the plant to spread when the broken pieces take root. Typically short-hairy, although sometimes hairless, the unbranched stems may reach 30 cm in length. The 1-5 cm long pale green leaves are ovate-lanceolate. The 1-2 cm long, obscure inflorescence is borne in the axils of the leaves. The greenish flowers are approximately 3 mm long.

A subalpine plant of open, dry meadows, and rocky sites, and seen very frequently at trailsides and other disturbed places, it is found on the north side of Little Mount Adams, at the Cold Springs trailhead, though the drier parts of Bird Creek Meadows, and in Hellroaring Canyon. Formerly named *Polygonum newberryi*, it is a common plant.

### *Aconogonon phytolaccifolium* (Meisner *ex* Small) Rydb. var. *phytolaccifolium*—POKE KNOTWEED

This perennial is distinguished by several stout and erect branches, often branched, 1-2 m tall, rising from a thick root, and altogether resembling in stature the noxious Japanese knotweed. The 6-12 cm-long lanceolate to ovate-lanceolate leaves are borne on the stems only, with the lower ones reduced in size. The flowers are borne in large panicles in the leaf axils and at the top of the stem. They are greenish-white, 2.5-3 mm long and fused at the base.

Formerly included in the *Polygonum* genus, this is a native subalpine to alpine species, often found on talus slopes. It occurs at lower elevations at Mount Adams as well, having been found alongside the road to Bench Lake. It is also known from a Suksdorf collection at Hellroaring Canyon and a Henderson collection on "alpine bluffs and bases."

### *Bistorta* (L.) Scop.—KNOTWEED

### *Bistorta bistortoides* (Pursh) Small—AMERICAN BISTORT

This perennial rises from a short, thick rootstock and is distinguished by the mostly basal leaves and an unbranched, 30-60 cm tall flowering stem. The 10-20 cm long leaves are narrowly oblong, prominently marked by a light green midrib, and long-stalked. The smaller stem leaves (sometimes stem leaves are lacking) are narrower, shorter, and not stalked. The flowers are borne in a compact, oblong spikelike raceme. The 4-5 mm long perianth is white and the lobes are united only at the base. There are 8 stamens.

This is a relatively common subalpine species, formerly part of *Polygonum*. It is found chiefly on the north and northwest sides of the mountain, and is also known from a Suksdorf collection at Hellroaring Canyon.

### *Eriogonum* Michx.—WILD BUCKWHEAT

These are native perennials rising from woody rootstocks or taking the form of low shrubs. The leaves are tufted, basal, and stalked; there are no stipules. The arrangement of the flowers is complex with the few to several flowers on short stalks held in an involucre. The involucres themselves may be solitary at the ends of the branches of the inflorescence, or more commonly are in small to large umbel-like heads. These heads may be solitary or themselves combined in secondary umbels. The perianth is typically 6-lobed and narrow at the base; it is often tinged with pink but is bright yellow in the very common sulphur buckwheat. There are 9 stamens.

1 Inflorescence subtended by 2 bracts; perianth glandular .............. ............................................ *E. pyrolifolium* var. *coryphaeum*
1 Inflorescence subtended by 3 bracts, or bractless; perianth not glandular ........................................................................ 2

2(1) Perianth narrowed to a stem-like base .................................... 3
2 Perianth rounded at base ........................................................ 6

3(2) Leaves linear, to 3 or 4 mm broad; flowering stems with a whorl of 5-8 leaflike bracts ................................................ *E. douglasii*
3 Leaves ovate, over 6 mm broad; flowering stems without bracts ..........................................................................................4

4(3) Leaves 7-25 cm long, triangular; flowering stems 20-50 cm tall ...... ........................................... *E. compositum* var. *compositum*
4 Leaves to about 3 cm long, oval to obovate; flowering stems less than 30 cm tall ..................................................................... 5

5(4) Prostrate; flowering stems less than 1 dm; flowers cream to yellow; leaves green above, white beneath ........................................ ......................................... ... *E. umbellatum* var. *hausknechtii*
5 Upright; flowers yellow; flowering stems greater than 1 dm; leaves grayish above and below ............. *E. umbellatum* var. *umbellatum*

6(2) Flowering stem stiffly branched, with numerous small heads ......... ........................................................................ *E. nudum*
6 Stem unbranched, with a single head ...... *E. ovalifolium* var. *nivale*

### *Eriogonum compositum* Douglas *ex* Benth. var. *compositum* ARROWLEAF BUCKWHEAT

The 3-10 cm long leaves of this buckwheat are ovate, and heart-shaped or arrowhead-shaped where the leaf meets the stalk. They are deep green and more or less hairless above but densely wooly beneath. The 15-40 cm tall stems are unbranched and long-hairy. The inflorescence is a compound umbel with leaflike bracts, and the involucre is more or less wooly. The 4-6 mm long creamy white flowers are borne on very long stalks. Plants with bright yellow flowers are found occasionally.

A subalpine to alpine species, but also found on drier, rocky sites at lower elevations, this species is known from the DNR quarry and from Trail 20 to Island Springs on the southeast side. It also was found west of Stagman Ridge by Suksdorf and was collected on the northeast as well.

### *Eriogonum douglasii* Hook.—DOUGLAS'S BUCKWHEAT

Low and matted, this subshrub is less than 1 dm tall, with many leaves. The 5-20 mm long linear to spoon-shaped leaves are whitish from the long and tangled hairs typically growing on both surfaces. The 5-10 cm tall flowering stems have a whorl of several leaves in the middle, and a rounded flower head. The flowers are lemon to pale yellow or pinkish, clothed in long, tangled hairs, and 5-6 mm long. The achenes are short-hairy at the tip.

A species of the southern Cascades east of the crest, extending south and east to California and the Great Basin, Mount Adams is apparently near the northern limits of its range. It is known from a single location at the DNR quarry on the southeast side.

### *Eriogonum nudum* Dougl. *ex* Benth.—NAKED BUCKWHEAT

This buckwheat does not form mats but rather rises from a simple or branched crown. The 1.5-3 cm leaves form a basal rosette and are oblong-lanceolate to oval in shape, wooly with untangled hairs beneath and greenish above. The flowering stems are 1-3 dm tall and leafless, with a whorl of 5-8 leaflike leaves at the base, and the inflorescence is branched 2 or 3 times with long stems. The white to pinkish (and occasionally yellow) flowers are interspersed with bracts that protrude from the involucre; they are soft-hairy and 3-4 mm long.

Preferring sandy or gravelly soil, this is another *Eriogonum* that occurs near the northern end of its range at the mountain. It has been found on the north side of the mountain at Midway Meadows and is also known from a Henderson collection, without location information.

### *Eriogonum ovalifolium* Nutt. var. *nivale* (Canby) M.E. Jones<br>CUSHION BUCKWHEAT

This matted, dwarfed buckwheat bears flowering stems 3-15 cm tall. The leaves are basal only, the 2-8 mm leaf blade ovate to round, thick, and densely white-hairy on both sides. The 3-5 mm long creamy yellow flowers are borne in a single small umbel.

A subalpine species, at the mountain it was found at "7-8000 feet" by Suksdorf and at the Muddy River by Henderson. There is also a Flett collection of unspecified location.

### *Eriogonum pyrolifolium* Hook. var. *coryphaeum* Torr. & A. Gray
### ALPINE BUCKWHEAT, DIRTY SOCKS

This tufted plant forms small cushions 20-30 cm across. Occasionally sparsely hairy above and densely white-wooly beneath, the green, 1-4 cm leaves are lanceolate to ovate. The flowering stem is 5-10 cm tall, and the 4-6 mm long whitish flowers are borne in a single umbel subtended by 2 narrow bracts.

Growing on rocky slopes from the subalpine to the alpine zones, this relatively common buckwheat is found all around the mountain, as at Devil's Garden on the northeast side, along the South Climb trail, and at Hellroaring Canyon. The second common name refers to the scent of the flowers, easily noticeable on a warm, windless day.

### *Eriogonum umbellatum* Torr. var. *hausknechtii* (Dammer) M.E. Jones
### HAUSKNECHT'S BUCKWHEAT

A typically prostrate plant from a strong taproot, the branches of this perennial form flat broad mats. The 1-1.5 cm long leaves are oblong-elliptic, and narrowed to a slender petiole. They are long-hairy below, with the upper surface green. The 2-30 cm tall flowering stems are more or less leafless (sometimes bearing small leaflike bracts), the inflorescence a simple to multiple-headed umbel. The cream to yellow flowers (sometimes tinged rose or purple) have 2.5-4 mm long lobes and a slender base from 1.5-2 mm long. The flowers enlarge with age.

This is the variety of the widespread Sulphur-flowered buckwheat found at high elevations in the Cascades and is common in subalpine habitats on the southeast side of the mountain. It is known from the summit of Little Mount Adams at 6,800 feet and in upper Hellroaring Canyon.

### *Eriogonum umbellatum* Torr. var. *umbellatum*
### SULPHUR-FLOWERED BUCKWHEAT

Bearing yellow flowers, this variety is upright rather than prostrate, with flowering stems at least 1 dm tall. The umbel is simple and the leaves grayish-wooly beneath.

Common in the subalpine regime on the southeast and east sides of the mountain, this species reaches about 6,200 feet. It is known at the Hellroaring Creek trailhead, alongside Trail 20, at Big Muddy Creek, and at Hellroaring Canyon.

## Polygonaceae

### *Fallopia* Adans.—FALSE BUCKWHEAT

#### *Fallopia convolvulus* (L.) Á. Löve—BLACK BINDWEED

This annual is distinguished by its unusual twining, vinelike stems that may reach 20-100 cm long. The stalked leaves are shaped like arrowheads, and are 2-6 cm long. The slender inflorescence is raceme-like and borne in leaf axils. The greenish-white 5-lobed flowers are approximately 4 mm long.

Formerly included in the *Polygonum* genus, this weed is known from a collection made by the authors alongside Road 23 at the Riley Creek trailhead on the northwest side of the mountain, a place frequented by equestrians.

### *Oxyria* Hill—MOUNTAIN-SORREL

#### *Oxyria digyna* (L.) Hill—ALPINE MOUNTAIN-SORREL

This hairless perennial bears 1.5-5 cm-broad, long-stalked, kidney-shaped leaves. They are basal only, have sheathing stipules, and turn reddish with age. The inflorescence is a compact panicle on a leafless stem 10-30 cm tall. The reddish-brown flowers nod on slender stalks; they are approximately 2 mm long and 4-lobed. The 4 mm long achenes are surrounded by a thin wing.

Common in the subalpine to alpine dry habitats, this species is cosmopolitan at the mountain. It is found at Hellroaring Canyon, at Devil's Garden, on the Pacific Crest Trail north of Trail 64 (elevation 5,800 feet), and at Hellroaring Overlook (6,500 feet).

### *Polygonum* L.—KNOTWEED

Much reduced in number after splitting out the segregate genera *Aconogonon, Bistorta,* and *Fallopia,* the remaining *Polygonum* species at Mount Adams are all annuals, often inconspicuous. They have branched stems and narrow to oval leaves with short, sheathing stipules that with age become fringed on the upper margin. The flowers are solitary or more often in small numbers in the axils of the upper leaves but occasionally appear to be in spikes. The perianth has 5 lobes that are greenish to white or reddish; stamens number 3-9 and there are 3 styles. The color and size of the achene is significant in identifying members of the genus.

1 Stems prostrate; uncommon roadside weed .............. *P. aviculare*

1 Stems erect to spreading; natives, although sometimes growing in disturbed places .............................................................. 2

2(1) Flowers in spikelike racemes at the tops of the stems; leaves linear to lanceolate .................................................................. 3
2 Flowers in the axils of the stem leaves; leaves typically elliptical to oval ................................................................................ 4

3(2) Flowers on recurved pedicels, 1-3 per axil ................ *P. douglasii*
3 Flowers on erect pedicels in densely crowded spikes .................. ................................................ *P. polygaloides* ssp. *kelloggii*

4(2) Plants to about 25 cm tall; leaves 15-25 mm long; flowers in the upper axils easily seen ........... *P. sawatchense* ssp. *sawatchense*
4 Plants to about 10 cm tall; leaves to 10 mm long; flowers in the upper axils hidden by the leaves ............................. *P. minimum*

### *Polygonum aviculare* L.—YARD KNOTWEED

This mat-forming annual has prostrate stems 10-20 cm long that may bend up at their tips. The 5-30 mm long, dull green leaves are lanceolate or sometimes wider, pointed at the tip, and stalked. The 2-8 white or pink flowers are borne in the axils of the leaves. There are 8 stamens and each flower is 2-3 mm long.

This weedy knotweed is known from a Suksdorf collection at Bird Creek Island and from observations made along Road 23 and Road 115, on the west and north sides, respectively.

### *Polygonum douglasii* Greene—DOUGLAS'S KNOTWEED

This slender plant is characterized by branched, 20-40 cm erect stems. The 3-4 cm long leaves are nearly linear to oblanceolate, reduced in size toward the top of the stem. The white to pinkish flowers are about 3 mm long, with a green midrib, and are borne in loose spikes. The achenes are black, shiny, and 3-3.5 mm long.

Following Hitchcock and Cronquist, one would cite two varieties from Mount Adams, based upon leaf size and shape. These are combined in the *Flora of North America*.

A middle elevation species of habitats that vary from dry to wet, and often disturbed sites, this knotweed is fairly common and cosmopolitan at the mountain. It is found on the southeast side at Hellroaring Canyon and at the end of Road 170. On the southwest it grows in the wetter Muddy Meadows area. It also is found at the Morrison Creek trailhead.

### *Polygonum minimum* S. Wats.
### BROADLEAF KNOTWEED, REDSTEM KNOTWEED

Branched reddish stems that range from 5-15 cm long define the configuration of this small annual. The 5-15 mm long leaves are oval to ovate, and, for the most part, stalkless. The pinkish flowers are about 2 mm long, with 5-8 stamens and are borne solitary in the leaf axils on erect stalks. Those at the tops of the stems are hard to see because of the overlapping leaves. The achenes are dark greenish-black and about 2 mm long.

Uncommon at the mountain, this plant is said by Hitchcock to be a subalpine to alpine species. However, at Mount Adams it was found by the authors on Road 6900 on the southeast at an elevation of approximately 4,100 feet. It is also known from a Henderson collection, probably on the Lewis River. More typically, it is seen at such places as the upper part of Hellroaring Canyon.

### *Polygonum polygaloides* Meisner ssp. *kelloggii* (Greene) J.C. Hickman
### KELLOGG'S KNOTWEED

Sometimes unbranched, this small, 2-7 cm tall, slender plant bears stalkless, linear leaves a mere 5-10 mm long. The greenish to whitish flowers are 1.5-2 mm long, typically with 3 stamens, and borne in small clusters in the axils of the crowded upper leaves. There are 8 stamens and the achene is brownish and 1.5-2 mm long.

This species is found on both the north and south sides of the mountain. It prefers seasonally moist ground at middle elevations, and has been located at Road 115 and at Hellroaring Canyon (a Suksdorf collection). It is also known from a Henderson collection of unspecified location.

### *Polygonum sawatchense* Small ssp. *sawatchense*
### SAWATCH KNOTWEED

An erect, sparingly branched annual 5-25 cm tall, the branches are roughened and 4-angled. The 15-25 mm leaves are lanceolate to elliptic-oblanceolate at the base; the reduced upward leaves are oblong, narrowing finally to linear bracts that are shorter than the flowers. The 1-4 greenish flowers are borne in the axils along the full length of the stem. The achene is 3 mm long, shiny, and black.

A species of dry to moist areas at lower elevations elsewhere in Washington, it is known for Mount Adams from a single collection made by the authors at the DNR Quarry on the southeast side.

## *Rumex* L.—DOCK

Weedy perennial herbs, uncommon at Mount Adams, the three species have stalked leaves and reddish-brown flowers arranged in tall, narrow panicles. The perianth is 6-lobed and the flowers are arranged in whorls. There are 6 stamens, 3 styles, and the ovary at maturity is a hardened achene enfolded by the 3 inner perianth segments. In some species, the midrib of the inner perianth lobes may swell, forming a tubercule on the mature achene.

1 Leaves arrowhead-shaped .................................. *R. acetosella*
1 Leaves narrowly elliptical to oblong or ovate ............................ 2

2(1) Leaves narrowly elliptical, crisped or distorted on the margins ........ ........................................................................ *R. crispus*
2 Leaves oblong to ovate, with flat margins ............... *R. obtusifolius*

### *Rumex acetosella* L.—SHEEP-SORREL

The slender, widely-spreading rootstocks of this perennial enable it to colonize large patches of ground. The 10-30 cm tall stems bear sour-tasting, stalked leaves that are arrowhead in shape and 3-10 cm long. The upper leaves are short, stalkless, and narrow to linear. The male and female flowers are borne on separate plants, and the inflorescence is a narrow, branched panicle. The 2 mm long flowers are reddish or reddish-brown. Tubercules are absent.

One of the most common weeds at Mount Adams, this species prefers wetter sites alongside roads and in other disturbed areas of middle elevations. It is cosmopolitan at the mountain, with locations including the horse camp at Hellroaring Creek, the intersection of Road 8040 and Road 781 on the south side, and on Road 034 on the north.

### *Rumex crispus* L.—CURLY DOCK

A robust perennial ranging from 50-150 cm tall, the common name "curly" refers to the waviness of the margins of the leaves, particularly at their bases. The 15-30 cm long basal leaves are dark green and narrowly oblong; the stem leaves are shorter and more narrow. The tall inflorescence is a dense, leafy panicle. The 5 mm long perianth is reddish-brown; the valves are not toothed, each has a tubercule.

Another weedy *Rumex*, this species is known from a single patch of plants at the horse camp on Hellroaring Creek, close to the Island Springs trail.

### *Rumex obtusifolius* L.—BITTER DOCK

A robust perennial with stems 50-60 cm tall, heavier than those of *R. crispus*, this species is best identified by the size and shape of the leaves; they are 15-30 cm long and up to 10 cm wide; the leaf margin is flat. The flowers are 3-5 mm long, arranged in loose whorls on the branches of a dense, somewhat spreading panicle. The valves are toothed but only one bears a tubercule.

This is an aggressive weed, but known only from the overlook on Road 23, where it was collected by the authors in 2006.

## Portulacaceae Juss.—PURSLANE FAMILY

All native species at Mount Adams, the purslane family is represented by four genera and 12 species at the mountain. There are four annuals and all of the species are either succulent or bear thickened leaves. The leaves are untoothed and may be alternate or opposite. The flowers have 2 sepals, 3-16 petals, and 2 to many stamens. The superior ovary has 2-8 styles and develops into a dry capsule. The showiest *Lewisia* species are absent; this genus being represented by 3 diminutive species. Two *Claytonia* members, western springbeauty (*Claytonia lanceolata* var. *lanceolata*) and heartleaf springbeauty (*Claytonia cordifolia*) bear flowers with petals that may be more than a centimeter in length. Pussypaws (*Cistanthe umbellata* var. *caudicifera*) also bears attractive flowers arranged in dense heads.

1 Flowers in headlike clusters; petals 4, stigmas 2 ............ *Cistanthe*
1 Inflorescence various, but not headlike; petals 5 to many, stigmas 3-8 ........................................................................ 2

2(1) Capsule circumsessile at the base, the top popping off like a lid; sepals 2-8 ............................................................ *Lewisia*
2 Capsule opening from the top down along 2 or 3 joints; sepals 2 .... ........................................................................ 4

3(2) Leaves mostly basal; the stems leaves only 2, often fused together at their bases ........................................................ *Claytonia*
3 Stems leafy along their lengths .................................... *Montia*

### Cistanthe Spach—CISTANTHE

#### *Cistanthe umbellata* (Torr.) Hershkovitz var. *caudicifera* (A. Gray) Kartesz & Gandhi—PUSSYPAWS

Growing as a prostrate mat from a deep taproot, this alpine plant is distinguished by basal rosettes of 1-3 cm long, spoon-shaped and hairless leaves. The 2-6 cm long flowering stems vary from prostrate to erect, and the inflorescence is a dense, rounded head. The 4-6 mm long sepals are papery and rounded and colored white to pinkish. The petals are of similar size and color.

This plant is also known as *Spraguea umbellata*.

Pussypaws is a very common resident of open, sandy or gravelly slopes and flats in the subalpine and alpine, all around the mountain, reaching 9,000 feet on the South Climb trail.

## *Claytonia* L.—SPRING BEAUTY

Perennial or annual herbs, *C. lanceolata* is distinguished from the rest by having tubers; the other perennials have short rootstocks. The plants are hairless and fleshy, with mostly basal leaves; the stem leaves consist of a single pair beneath the inflorescence. The inflorescence is a 1-sided raceme at the top of the stem. There are 5 pink or white petals, and 5 stamens. The ovary is 1-chambered, with a single style and 3 stigmas.

1 Plants perennial, from a round tuber; stem leaves lanceolate to ovate .......................................... *C. lanceolata* var. *lanceolata*
1 Plants annual, or if perennial then from a short rootstock; stem leaves more or less rounded .............................................. 2

2(1) Stem leaves partly or fully united at their bases, forming a disk on the stem .............................................................................. 3
2 Stem leaves not united ......................................................................... 4

3(2) Stem leaves united on both sides of the stem, the disk 2-5 cm across; widest basal leaf blades 1-4 cm across .......................... .................................................. *C. perfoliata* ssp. *perfoliata*
3 Stem leaves united only on one side of the stem, the disk less than 2 cm across; widest basal leaf blades to 1 cm across .................. ............................................................ *C. rubra* ssp. *rubra*

4(2) Petals 8-13 mm long; bracts absent from the inflorescence ........... .................................................................... *C. cordifolia*
4 Petals 6-8 mm long; each flower with 1 or 2 bracts ...................... ........................................................ *C. sibirica* var. *sibirica*

### *Claytonia cordifolia* S. Wats.—BROAD-LEAVED SPRINGBEAUTY

This perennial rises from a short rootstock and has basal leaves that are broadly ovate or heart-shaped, 5-20 cm long overall, with a 2-6 cm wide blade. The 10-30 cm tall stem bears 2 leaves just above the middle; these are stalkless and not fused, broadly lanceolate, and 2-5 cm long. The 3-10 cm long raceme is stalked and open; the flowers are bractless. The white petals are 10-13 mm long.

Preferring wet places at middle elevations, this species is both common and cosmopolitan at the mountain. It is found on the southeast side of the mountain in the Hellroaring Creek meadows just north of Bench Lake, along the Klickitat River, and on Road K6900 at 4,000 feet of elevation. It is also known along Road 23 on the west and at Killen Creek Meadow on the northwest side.

## Portulacaceae

### *Claytonia lanceolata* Pursh var. *lanceolata*
### WESTERN SPRINGBEAUTY

A perennial with one to several stems, 5-20 cm tall, this species is distinguished by having a deeply buried tuber. There may be 1 or 2 narrowly oblanceolate basal leaves on non-flowering plants. Flowering plants bear only 2 opposite, stalkless leaves, 2-5 cm long and lanceolate in shape; they are not fused. The inflorescence is a compact raceme with a small bract at its base. The white petals are lined with pink veins and are 5-12 mm long.

An early blooming, middle elevation to subalpine species of wet places, most often seen in forest openings that become dry by midsummer, this *Claytonia* was found by the authors at the end of Road 170 on the southeast side, and on Road 782 and Road 8040 on the south. It was also collected by Flett near the Klickitat River.

### *Claytonia perfoliata* Donn *ex* Willd. ssp. *perfoliata*
### MINER'S LETTUCE

This annual "lettuce" consists of spoon-shaped or occasionally long-stalked elliptical leaves that are 3-15 cm in length. The 10-20 cm tall flowering stem bears 2 opposite leaves that are fused at their bases on each side of the stem, thus forming a disk 2-5 cm broad. The 1-sided raceme is open, loosely-flowered, and has a single bract at the base. The 2-4 mm long white petals are lined with pink veins.

Preferring moist, middle elevation forested sites, this species is known from a collection by the authors at the junction of Road 071 and Road 150 on the southeast side at an elevation of 4,000 feet. Otherwise, the study area is too high to expect the species elsewhere.

### *Claytonia rubra* (T. Howell) Tidestr. ssp. *rubra*
### RED MINER'S LETTUCE

The common name refers to the reddish cast of the stems and leaves of this annual. Seldom more than 6-8 cm tall, the plant resembles *C. perfoliata*, except for the smaller size. The largest basal leaf blades are less than 1 cm broad, while the pair of stem leaves is fused on one side of the stem, forming a disk that is less than 2 cm broad.

Relatively common in middle elevation dry to moist, open habitats, this species was observed by the authors on the southeast side of Mount Adams in seasonally wet meadows alongside Road K6900 and at the end of Road 170 on the west side of King Mountain. It also grows along Road 782 at 4,000 feet.

### *Claytonia sibirica* L. var. *sibirica*—CANDYFLOWER

Although this species is common in the western Cascades, it is rare at Mount Adams, perhaps because of the 4,000 foot limit to the study area.

It is a perennial, growing from short rootstocks, with ovate, long-stalked basal leaves up to 25 cm long. The 1-6 cm long pair of stem leaves are ovate, stalkless, and not fused into a disk. The branched inflorescence has a bract beneath each flower. The white to pinkish petals are lined with pink veins and are 6-8 mm long.

This species is known from one collection made by the authors alongside Road 23 just south of the Lewis River, where the plant grows in a wet, partly shaded ditch.

### *Lewisia* Pursh—LEWISIA

Each of these species is a small perennial, easily overlooked. The petals range from white to rose and number from 5-11; there are 2 sepals, toothed in two of the species, and not united at their bases. The capsules open lidlike from near the base. One, *L. nevadensis,* is quite rare at the mountain and all have been found only on the southeast side.

1 Leaves 2 or 3, on a slender stem that rises from a deeply buried tuber .............................................................. *L. triphylla*
1 Leaves many, from a heavy rootstock .................................. 2

2(1) Sepals rounded, 2-5 mm long; leaves less than 8 cm long ........... .............................................................. *L. pygmaea*
2 Sepals pointed, 5-10 mm long; leaves to 15 cm long .................. .............................................................. *L. nevadensis*

#### *Lewisia nevadensis* (A. Gray) B.L. Robins.—NEVADA LEWISIA

Similar to and formerly considered a subspecies of *L. pygmaea,* this species is larger and has more sharply tipped sepals that are untoothed on their margins and 5-10 mm long. The narrowly oblanceolate leaves are up to 15 cm long.

This species has a more western geographical range than *L. pygmaea,* rarely being found in Idaho or the Rocky Mountains. It is known at Mount Adams from a single Flett collection on the upper Klickitat River.

#### *Lewisia pygmaea* (A. Gray) B. L. Robins.—DWARF LEWISIA

This tufted plant bears 2-5 cm long, fleshy, linear to linear-oblanceolate leaves from a thick, short rootstock. There are several 1-5 cm tall 1-flowered stems, often shorter than the leaves and sometimes prostrate. Rarely, plants have several flowers per stem. The rose-purple, (less frequently white with rose veins) petals are 6-7 mm long. The sepals most often bear gland-tipped teeth.

Preferring stony subalpine habitats that are seasonally wet, this species is rare at the mountain. It is known from two Suksdorf collections, one at Hellroaring Canyon, and the other at "5-6,000 feet" at an unspecified location.

### *Lewisia triphylla* (S. Wats.) B.L. Robins.—THREE-LEAF LEWISIA

This perennial consists of a 2-10 cm long threadlike stem rising from a small tuber. There is a whorl of 2 or 3 linear leaves 1-5 cm long, and a slender basal leaf may be present in younger plants. The 1 to several flowers are borne in an open cluster on a short stalk above the stem leaves. The white petals are about 4 mm long. The sepals lack teeth.

Uncommon, this subalpine species grows on seasonally moist, stony slopes. It is known from Klickitat Meadows, near Mazama Glacier at 7,545 feet, and along Crooked Creek, at 6,300 feet.

## *Montia* L.—MONTIA

The presence of more than 2 leaves on the stems separate this genus from *Claytonia*. The petals are often of unequal lengths in *Montia*. The two genera otherwise are quite similar.

| | | |
|---|---|---|
| 1 | Stem leaves opposite | *M. chamissoi* |
| 1 | Stem leaves alternate | 2 |
| 2 | Plant annual; petals less than 5 mm long | *M. linearis* |
| 2 | Plant perennial; petals more than 5 mm long | *M. parvifolia* |

### *Montia chamissoi* (Ledeb. *ex* Spreng.) Greene<br>WATER MINER'S LETTUCE

A widely spreading perennial from slender rhizomes and rooted horizontal stems, both of which bear bulbletlike protrusions, the 5-20 cm flowering stems are erect and simple to branched. The 2-5 cm long, opposite leaves are oblanceolate to diamond-shaped and narrow to a petiole base. The 3-10 flowers are borne in racemes in the leaf axils or at the ends of the stems. There are 5 white or pinkish petals 5-8 mm long and 5 stamens.

A middle elevation species of wet open places, this species is known from Flett collections at Klickitat Meadows and along the upper Klickitat River, at about 4,000 feet.

### *Montia linearis* (Dougl. *ex* Hook.) Greene<br>NARROW-LEAVED MONTIA

This species is easily distinguished from the other annual *Montia* at Mount Adams by its upright stems and very narrow leaves. The stems may reach 25 cm in height and the leaves 10 cm in length, although usually less. The white flowers are arranged in a 1-sided raceme, with petals about 3 mm long.

Like *M. fontana,* this is a scarce plant, found at seasonally moist, open places on the east and southeast sides of Mount Adams; it is known from a collection made by Flett on the upper Klickitat River.

**_Montia parvifolia_ (Moc. _ex_ DC.) Greene—LITTLELEAF MONTIA**

This perennial is often matted from a branching rootstock or runners. The 2-6 cm long basal leaves are oblanceolate to narrowly spoon-shaped; they are clustered and less than 5 mm wide. The 5-10 mm long stem leaves are ovate, thinner than the basal leaves, and alternate. The umbel-like (or short raceme) inflorescence is bracted, and the pinkish flower petals are 7-12 mm long, and of equal length. There are 5 stamens.

A common middle elevation species of moist sites, including mossy rocks, cliffs, slopes, and stream banks, it is known from a Flett collection at Klickitat River. Modern collections include Trail 75 at Salt Creek, near the junction of the Stagman Ridge and the Around the Mountain Trail at 5,700 feet, on Trail 20 near Bench Lake, and alongside Road 23.

## Primulaceae Vent.—PRIMROSE FAMILY

There are only two native genera of these showy wildflowers at Mount Adams, the shooting stars, *Dodecatheon,* and the starflowers, *Trientalis.* An attractive weed, *Lysimachia,* is also present.

There are few superficial similarities between these plants. There are 5 partly-united petals, although *Trientalis* not infrequently has 6 or 7, and a superior ovary. The truly distinguishing feature of this family is that the stamens are placed opposite the petals (alternate placement is more common).

It has not been possible to locate at Mount Adams the beautiful *Douglasia laevigata.* This rose-colored perennial was collected by Lois Kemp south of Mount Adams "on shear basaltic outcrops" at 2,120 feet on Dog Mountain, overlooking the Columbia River near Stevenson as well as on Mount Hood. It also occurs at Mount Rainier.

1 Leaves basal; petals turned back .......................... *Dodecatheon*
1 Stems leafy; petals spreading .......................................... 2

2(1) Leaves alternate, clustered at the top of the stems; flowers pink ..... ........................................................................ *Trientalis*
2 Leaves opposite, not clustered at stem tips; flowers yellow ........... ...................................................................... *Lysimachia*

## Primulaceae

### *Dodecatheon* L.—SHOOTING STAR

Uniquely attractive among the wildflowers at Mount Adams, the shooting stars have basal leaves and leafless flowering stems that terminate in small umbels. Each flower has 5 petals (rarely 4) that are united into a short tube; the free lobe of each petal is turned sharply backwards, resembling a cyclamen. The petals are pink to deep rose to purplish, although albino plants are known. The stamens are exserted and pressed against the style, giving a "beak" to the flower. The fruit is a thin-walled capsule that ruptures at the top.

1 Stigma slender, about the width of the style .............................................................................. *D. conjugens* ssp. *conjugens*

1 Stigma enlarged, headlike, about twice the width of the style ..... 2

2(1) Sepals and stems of the flowers glandular-hairy; flowers typically with 5 petals ....................................................... *D. jeffreyi*

2 Sepals and stems of the flowers hairless, not glandular; flowers typically with 4 petals ........................................... *D. alpinum*

#### *Dodecatheon alpinum* (A. Gray) Greene—ALPINE SHOOTING STAR

Very similar in appearance to small specimens of *D. jeffreyi*, this species can be recognized by the absence of glandular hairs in the inflorescence and the strong tendency of the flower to have just 4 petals. Its leaves are up to 10 cm long and only about 1.5 cm broad, much smaller than the average for Jeffrey's shooting star.

Evidently very rare at Mount Adams and distant from its typical California to northeastern Oregon range, the species is included based upon a collection made in 1954 by Carl Nelson at Mirror Lake, on the southeast side of Mount Adams. It was not seen there during the present study.

#### *Dodecatheon conjugens* Greene ssp. *conjugens*
#### DESERT SHOOTING STAR

Lacking rootstocks, this species is also distinguished from *D. jeffreyi* by a stigma that lacks a head-like structure and is less than twice as thick as the style. The filaments are more than 1 mm in length and united into a tube.

Rare at Mount Adams, this is predominantly a sagebrush species that comes up to the mountain along ridges that run to the east and southeast. J.B. Flett made a collection at Klickitat Meadows.

#### *Dodecatheon jeffreyi* Van Houtte—JEFFREY'S SHOOTING STAR

Usually growing in clumps, this herbaceous plant rises from a short rootstock and has basal leaves 15-40 cm long. They are narrowed at the base and occasionally stalkless. The flowers nod in an umbel on a 15-50 cm tall stem. The 5 rose-purple petals are sharply reflexed from the stamens and style, the lower portion being united into a short tube. The tube is white or yellow with a reddish ring at the throat, contrasting with the dark purple stamens that are pressed closely to the style. The stigma, the expanded tip of the style, is the clearest feature distinguishing this shooting star from the much less frequently seen *D. conjugens.*

Found in wet meadows and often near streams in middle to subalpine sites on all sides of the mountain, this showy flower is quite unmistakable and the color eye-catching. It grows at Grand Meadow, Takh Takh Meadow, and Takhlakh Lake, among other wetland sites.

## Lysimachia L.—YELLOW LOOSESTRIFE

### *Lysimachia nummularia* L.—CREEPING JENNY

This is a prostrate herb that roots at the nodes and spreads on creeping stems. The 1-3 cm long, dark green leaves are rounded to oblong-oval. The flowers are borne singly in the axils on 1-3 cm long pedicels. The lobes of the yellow corolla are 8-12 mm long and are glandular near the base on the upper surface.

A weed sparingly naturalized in Washington, creeping Jenny was collected by the authors at the Morrison Creek trailhead, where it grows on highly disturbed ground with a number of other weedy species.

## *Trientalis* L.—STARFLOWER

These delicate perennial herbs grow from deeply buried, potato-like tubers. The principle leaves are lanceolate to oblanceolate and arranged in a whorl at the top of the slender stem. Smaller leaves may be scattered on the stem below the main whorl. The 2-6 pink or white flowers are borne singly on threadlike stalks at the top of the stem. There are 5 (but occasionally 6 or 7) petals, forming a flat-faced blossom.

1 Leaves whorled at the top of the stems only ............................... *T. borealis* ssp. *latifolia*

1 Leaves whorled as well as scattered on the lower stem ............................... *T. europea* ssp. *arctica*

### *Trientalis borealis* Raf. ssp. *latifolia* (Hook.) Hultén
### BROADLEAF STARFLOWER

The lovely flowers of this species form small colonies of slender stems 10-30 cm tall. At the top of the stem there are 4-7 major leaves that are broadly lanceolate to oblanceolate, untoothed, and 3-8 cm long. The 10-15 mm wide flower varies from light to dark pink.

Relatively common in lower middle elevation forests and at meadow edges, this cosmopolitan species is found along Road 23, on the South Climb road (Road 8040), and at Big Muddy River.

### ***Trientalis europaea*** **L. ssp.** ***arctica*** **(Fisch.** ***ex*** **Hook.) Hultén**<br>**ARCTIC STARFLOWER, NORTHERN STARFLOWER**

This wetland species varies from 5-15 cm in height and bears mostly oblanceolate, 1-4 cm long leaves. There is a whorl of larger leaves at the top of the stem, with smaller leaves scattered along the stem. The white flowers, borne on long petioles, are 12-16 mm wide, with 7 lobes.

Found on the northwest and north sides of the mountain and limited to well-watered sphagnum meadows, this species was collected at Babyshoe Meadow and at the intersection of Road 23 and Road 2329. It is also known from Killen Creek and Muddy Meadows.

## Pyrolaceae Lindl.—WINTERGREEN FAMILY

Formerly included in the Ericaceae, this is a group of attractive evergreen perennials. The leaves are basal or arranged in whorls on short, upright stems. Flowers are solitary or in racemes at the tops of the stems, with 5 free petals. Some *Gaultheria* species, members of the Ericaceae that might be sought in the Pyrolaceae have united petals. The fruit is a dry capsule.

These plants all lack the characteristic taste of true wintergreen, *Gaultheria procumbens*, a member of the Ericaceae family.

| | | |
|---|---|---|
| 1 | Plants lacking green leaves | *Pyrola* |
| 1 | Plants with green leaves | 2 |
| 2(1) | Flowers solitary, white | *Moneses* |
| 2 | Flowers 2 to many, in racemes or flat-topped clusters | 3 |
| 3(2) | Flowers arranged along one side of the stem | *Orthilia* |
| 3 | Flowers disposed about the stem | 4 |
| 4(3) | Leaves basal; flowers in racemes | *Pyrola* |
| 4 | Leaves more or less whorled on the upper part of the stem; flowers in flat-topped clusters | *Chimaphila* |

### ***Chimaphila*** **Pursh—PIPSISSEWA**

The two *Chimaphila* species found at Mount Adams are common throughout the mountains of the northwest, favoring middle elevation forests. Each is a low-growing evergreen perennial, with somewhat woody stems. The leaves are tough and leathery, and arranged in whorls. The fragrant, open-faced flowers nod in a small raceme at the top of the stem; each has 5 sepals, 5 separate petals, and 10 stamens that lie flat against the petals. The fruit is a capsule.

1 Flowers 1-3 per stem; leaves dark green, dull ............ *C. menziesii*
1 Flowers 5-10 per stem; leaves bright green, shiny ........................................................................ *C. umbellata* ssp. *occidentalis*

**_Chimaphila menziesii_ (R. Br. _ex_ D. Don) Spreng.—LITTLE PIPSISSEWA**

The 8-15 cm tall stems bear 1 to a few leaves per node. The 1-3 cm long leaves are lanceolate to ovate, and are dull dark green in color. There are 1-3 white flowers that nod on slender stalks; with age the petals spread and curve backwards and become pinkish. The capsule is 5-7 mm broad.

Locally common in dense forests, most often associated with Pacific silver fir (*Abies amabilis*) this cosmopolitan species grows on Crofton Ridge on the southwest side, along trail edges at the end of Forest Service Road 170 on the southeast, on the west up Stagman Ridge and on the north near the Pacific Crest Trail.

**_Chimaphila umbellata_ (L.) W. Bart. ssp. _occidentalis_ (Rydb.) Hultén PIPSISSEWA**

Taller than *C. menziesii*, the 15-25 cm stems of this species are also more leafy, typically with two well-defined whorls of leaves that are elliptical to oblanceolate, and bright green and shiny, another contrast with *C. menziesii*. The pink flowers are 10-15 mm broad, broadly bowl-shaped and borne in groups of 5-10 on nodding stalks. The capsule is 6-8 mm broad.

A species of middle elevation forests, also found at meadow edges, pipsissewa grows alongside Trail 7B (at Road 2329) on the north side and alongside roads 50 and 8040 on the southwest and south. It also is found at Swampy Meadows and in Hellroaring Canyon.

**_Moneses_ Salisb. _ex_ S.F. Gray—SINGLE DELIGHT**

**_Moneses uniflora_ (L.) A. Gray—WOOD NYMPH, SINGLE DELIGHT**

This small perennial herb bears flowering stems 5-15 cm long that rise from a creeping rootstock. The 5-25 mm long leaves are roundish with a sharp tooth and borne on short stalks on the lower portion of the stem. The single nodding blossom is highly fragrant. The 8-12 mm long petals are waxy white, and the 4 mm long style is straight and has an enlarged stigma. The green ovary forms a center to the flower. The 6-10 mm broad fruit is a rounded, dry capsule. When not in flower, the plant resembles *Pyrola minor*, which may sometimes be separated by its larger leaves.

## Pyrolaceae

Formerly placed in the *Ericaceae* family, this species is uncommon and found in middle elevation, deep forests. It has been located alongside Trail 75 at Cascade Creek on the southwest side of Mount Adams and along the outlet stream that drains Swampy Meadows on the west side. The plant seems to have an affinity for well-rotted, buried wood that perhaps helps to provide a lasting source of moisture into the summer.

### *Orthilia* Raf.—SIDEBELLS

#### *Orthilia secunda* (L.) House—SIDEBELLS WINTERGREEN

The one-sided inflorescence distinguishes this appropriately named species from the similar pyrolas. Often forming small patches from spreading rootstocks, the 1-3 cm leaves of each plant are mostly basal, toothed, light green in color, and roundish to oval in shape. The 8-20 cm tall stem is slender and bears 5-15 flowers in a raceme near the top. The 6-8 mm long, bell-shaped flowers are pale green, the blooms quite ephemeral. The straight style is longer than the corolla and the fruit is a round, dry capsule.

Locally common in middle elevation forests throughout the region, reaching nearly 6,000 feet, this species may be found alongside Road 115 near Midway Meadows and Road 8040 close to Gotchen Creek, on the way to the South Climb trailhead. It is also found near Bathtub Meadow.

### *Pyrola* L.—WINTERGREEN

Attractive evergreen perennials, the pyrolas are found throughout the Mount Adams region below about 6,500 feet. They are plants of forests and groves, although *Pyrola asarifolia* may also be found at meadow edges. The leaves are mostly basal and rounded in outline. Five to 10 saucer-shaped flowers are in a raceme, with 5 sepals, 5 petals, and 10 stamens; the style may be straight or curved. The fruit is a capsule.

Several pyrolas are known to occur in forms lacking green leaves and these might be taken for members of the Monotropaceae. At Mount Adams, only *P. picta* is known to occur in this condition.

| | |
|---|---|
| 1 | Leaves more or less round, less than 5 cm long; style straight ....... ........................................................................ *P. minor* |
| 1 | Leaves ovate, if roundish more than 6 cm long; style curved ....... 2 |
| 2(1) | Leaves dark green with white veins; bract of the flower shorter than the pedicel ........................................................... *P. picta* |
| 2 | Leaves medium green, unmarked; bract of the flower much longer than the pedicel ........................................................... 3 |

3(2) Leaves with at least small teeth, truncate at the base; sepals at least 3.5 mm long ............................... *P. asarifolia* ssp. *bracteata*

3 Leaves untoothed, heart-shaped at the base; sepals less than 3.5 mm long ........................................... *P. asarifolia* ssp. *asarifolia*

### *Pyrola asarifolia* Michx. ssp. *asarifolia*—PINK WINTERGREEN

This and subspecies *bracteata* are the largest of the pyrolas at Mount Adams, with 10-40 cm tall flowering stems and thick basal leaves 3-8 cm long. The flowers are also large, up to 1.5 cm across. The 7-9 mm long petals are pink to rose-red, and the style is curved downward. The fruit is a dry, rounded capsule. This subspecies is distinguished by dull leaves that are heart-shaped at the base and not marginally toothed. The flowers tend to be lighter in color than subspecies *bracteata*.

Uncommon in moist forests, this subspecies was found by the authors in the meadow alongside Hellroaring Creek at 4,800 feet, close to Bench Lake.

### *Pyrola asarifolia* Michx. ssp. *bracteata* (Hook.) Haber PINK WINTERGREEN

The base of the leaves in this subspecies is more or less square or truncate; the margins are shallowly toothed and there is a glossy luster on the upper surface. The flowers are brighter than subspecies *asarifolia*, varying from light to deep rose-red.

Much more frequently seen than subspecies *asarifolia*, subspecies *bracteata* is nevertheless not as abundant at Mount Adams as it is in moister forests to the north. It is found both in middle elevation forests and in moist places at meadow edges, as near Bench Lake. This subspecies has been located alongside Road 5603 northwest of Potato Hill and at Trail 7B on 2329, locations on the north and northwest sides of the mountain.

### *Pyrola minor* L.—LESSER WINTERGREEN

Only 10-20 cm tall, this small species bears 1-4 cm long, small basal leaves that are oval to rounded and finely toothed. There are 5-20 white to pink flowers about 1 cm broad, and the style is straight and shorter than the petals, a useful feature in distinguishing this from the other pyrolas. When not blooming, the plants resemble *Moneses uniflora*; leaves in *Pyrola minor* are larger, on the average.

Typically considered a lower elevation species of dense forests, it is known from Bird Creek, where Suksdorf found it in a "small sphagnum swamp." The authors found it, again associated with sphagnum, at Foggy Flat at 6,050 feet on the north side of Mount Adams. It also grows under *Vaccinium membranaceum* in the campground at Horseshoe Lake.

### *Pyrola picta* Sm.—WHITE-VEIN SHINLEAF

The whitish markings outlining the major veins of the 2-6 cm long ovate to oval leaves of this species set it apart from other family members. The leaves are dark green, and the brightness of the veins varies from plant to plant, sometimes resembling rattlesnake orchid, *Goodyera oblongifolia,* in brightness. The 15-30 cm tall stems bear numerous, 1-1.5 cm broad flowers. The petals are greenish-white and the curved style is somewhat longer than the petals. Occasionally, reddish plants are found that lack leaves and any green coloration.

Another middle elevation forest dwelling pyrola, this species is locally common at the mountain below 5,000 feet. It is found alongside the Big Klickitat River on the east, near the trail at the end of Road 170 on the flank of King Mountain, on Crofton Ridge, and in the forest off Road 8040 on the way to the South Climb trailhead.

## Ranunculaceae Juss.—BUTTERCUP FAMILY

An ancient family characterized by numerous stamens and petals, when present, that vary from 3-15 in number, the buttercups are widespread and numerous in terms of species and genera. The flowers vary in color from the purple-blue of the delphiniums and anemones to the yellow buttercups (*Ranunculus*). Many of the flowers are very showy—such is the case with orange columbine (*Aquilegia formosa* var. *formosa*), and the large white-blossoms of the streamside marsh-marigolds (*Caltha*) As with the range in number of other floral parts, the pistils also range from 1 (in *Actaea*) to many. They develop into achenes, follicles, or, in the case of red baneberry (*Actaea rubra*), berries.

Widespread, the buttercups for the most part occupy open habitats that are wet to dry. They range from middle elevation meadows to the lower subalpine, the family providing many of the mountain's most colorful flowers. The buttercups are represented by 24 species in 9 genera.

1 Flowers irregular, the upper sepal spurred or hoodlike; flowers blue or purplish .......... 2
1 Flowers regular, the sepals all alike; flowers yellow, white, or red, or petals absent .......... 3

2(1) Upper sepal spurred; leaves deeply divided .......... *Delphinium*
2 Upper sepal hoodlike; leaves lobed and toothed, but not deeply divided .......... *Aconitum*

3(1) Flowers red and yellow, spurred, nodding on the stems ... *Aquilegia*
3 Flowers not colored red and yellow, lacking spurs, erect on the stems ........................................................................................ 4

4(3) Pistil 1, developing into a berrylike fruit; tall, coarse plants with compound leaves ................................................................ *Actaea*
4 Pistils 2 to several; fruit developing into an achene or follicle ........ 5

5(4) Fruit a several-seeded follicle; leaves simple and toothed or scalloped ........................................................................... *Caltha*
5 Fruit a 1-seeded achene ............................................................ 6

6(5) Petals and sepals present, the petals yellow ................ *Ranunculus*
6 Petals absent; sepals present, green or colored, but not yellow .... 7

7(6) Sepals colored, white to bluish, persistent; leaves whorled at the top of low stems (or both basal and whorled) .................. *Anemone*
7 Sepals greenish, soon falling; leaves basal and along stems ........ 8

8(7) Leaves alternate and compound on tall stems; inflorescence a raceme; stamens purplish ............................................... *Thalictrum*
8 Leaves simple, palmately lobed, chiefly basal; inflorescence a flattish cluster; stamens white ..................................... *Trautvetteria*

## *Aconitum* L.—MONKSHOOD

### *Aconitum columbianum* Nutt. var. *columbianum*
### COLUMBIAN MONKSHOOD

This 50-100 cm tall perennial is easily identified by the large (5-15 cm broad), dark green, toothed, palmately lobed leaves. It is distinguished by the flowers, too. The inflorescence is a tall, open raceme of dark blue to purple flowers on upcurved stalks. The 1.5-2 cm flowers are helmetlike in shape, with the uppermost of the 5 sepals arching over the lateral, smaller sepals. Beneath the "hood" are 2 small, spurred petals, as well as the stamens and 3-5 pistils. The pistils develop into follicles 1-2 cm long.

Although not common, this distinctive species is easily seen in wet meadows at middle elevations. On the north it grows at Midway Meadows and on the southwest at the crossing of the Island Springs trail over Hellroaring Creek and alongside the small stream on Road 82 close to the gate to Bird Creek. It was collected by Suksdorf at Hellroaring Canyon at an unspecified elevation.

# Ranunculaceae

## *Actaea* L.—BANEBERRY

### *Actaea rubra* (Ait.) Willd.—RED BANEBERRY

This robust species bears 30-90 cm-tall multiple branches and has long-stalked leaves. The 20-70 cm long leaves are ovate in outline; they are divided into 3 major lobes, each pinnately divided into 3-5 smaller, coarsely toothed leaflets. The inflorescence consists of a 2-3 cm long terminal raceme. The white flowers are approximately 5 mm broad, and the 4-10 petals are very small. The many stamens are also white. The 5-10 mm broad fruit is most often a bright red berry.

This is a middle elevation species of dry sites to moist woodlands. It is found at the DNR quarry, along Road 070 below the Stagman trailhead, at Rusk Creek, and at Hellroaring Canyon.

## *Anemone* L.—WINDFLOWER

The showiness of the bright flowers of this genus comes from the petal-like sepals, as the plants lack petals altogether. Instead, the sepals are white to purplish in color. The plants are perennials and typically produce only one stem; the stem leaves are whorled at the top of the stem, forming an involucre below the flower. The basal leaves may be few in number to several, as in the case of *Anemone multifida.* Typically 1-flowered, there are five sepals and numerous stamens. The many pistils are clustered in heads, and the fruit is a more or less hairy achene.

The distinctive western anemone (*Anemone occidentalis*), so common and abundant in subalpine meadows elsewhere in the Cascades, is nearly absent from Mount Adams.

1 Stem leaves simple, toothed but not divided; plants of lowland forests ........ *A. deltoidea*
1 Stem leaves compound or very deeply divided; habitats various ... 2

2(1) Achenes wooly; several basal leaves ........ 3
2 Achenes short-hairy but not wooly; few basal leaves ........ 5

3(2) Flowers two-to-three per stem; leaves not completely divided ........ *A. multifida* var. *multifida*
3 Flowers one per stem; leaves divided three times three or finer ... 4

4(3) Style at maturity 2-3.5 cm long, silky-feathery ........ *A. occidentalis*
4 Style less than 0.5 cm long, hairless........ *A. drummondii* var. *drummondii*

5(2) Stamens more than 35; sepals greater than 10 mm long ........ *A. oregana* var. *oregana*
5 Stamens fewer than 35; sepals less than 10 mm long ........ *A. lyallii*

### *Anemone deltoidea* Hook.
### COLUMBIAN WINDFLOWER, THREE-LEAVED ANEMONE

The mostly hairless stems, ranging from 10-25 cm tall, create a delicate plant that rises from a slender, creeping rootstock. The 3-parted basal leaf consists of ovate, toothed leaflets that are shorter than the flowering stem. The 3 stem leaves are whorled, stalkless, and toothed; they are 3-8 cm long and undivided. The flower is borne on a slender stalk and consists of 5 sepals, each 1-2 cm long. The egg-shaped achenes are few and are hairy on the lower half.

A low and middle elevation species elsewhere in the Cascades, this species is known at Mount Adams only from a Flett collection at Klickitat Meadows.

### *Anemone drummondii* S. Wats. var. *drummondii*
### DRUMMOND'S ANEMONE

This 5-25 cm tall plant rises from a branched, woody rootstalk. The stems are slender, and the plant is softly hairy. Several basal leaves, 5-15 cm long overall, are divided multiple times into long, slender segments. The stem leaves are borne on short stalks and are also divided many times. The 5 white sepals are 8-12 mm long and tinged bluish on the outside. The rounded achene is wooly.

Rare at the mountain, this middle elevation to alpine species shows a preference for crevices and rocky sites; it is known from a Suksdorf collection on the Big Muddy Creek on the east side of Mount Adams.

### *Anemone lyallii* Britton—LYALL'S ANEMONE

Much like *A. deltoidea,* this species differs in the stem leaves, which are divided into 3-5 leaflets and are on short stalks. Additionally, the short rootstock dictates that the plant will not form large clumps as does *A. deltoidea.* The 5-18 mm long sepals are whitish to bluish white. The hairy achene is elliptical in shape.

More common than most other anemones at Mount Adams, this middle elevation species inhabits sites ranging from wet to dry. It was found by the authors on the Stagman Ridge trail at 4,500 feet, along Road 070, and at Midway Meadows on the north side.

### *Anemone multifida* Poir. var. *multifida* DC.—GLOBE ANEMONE

This sturdy anemone is configured with 15-40 cm tall stems rising from a woody rootstock. Both stems and leaves are silky-hairy. The basal leaves are long-stalked, and the stem leaves are stalkless; both are finely divided 2-3 times into narrowly lanceolate segments. Typically there is 1 flower per stem, although on occasion 2-3 flowers are present. The upper side of the petals is whitish to cream-colored, and the underside is most often bluish. The rounded achene is densely clothed with long hairs.

A rare species known from a Suksdorf collection of unspecified location, it is most likely that he found it in a seasonally moist, stony location at or above timberline.

### *Anemone occidentalis* S. Wats.
### WESTERN ANEMONE, WESTERN PASQUEFLOWER

Western anemone is a sturdy plant with thick stems that can reach 50 cm tall. The leaves, 10-20 cm long, are pinnately divided into many small leaflets, altogether fernlike, and all parts of the plant are covered with soft hairs. There is one large, striking flower per stem, with 6 or 7 whitish sepals, each 2-3 cm long and surrounding the dense yellow stamens at the center of the blossom. The flower matures into an elongated head, with numerous achenes. The achene is 3-4 mm long, densely wooly; the style becomes very long, up to 3 cm, and is silky-feathery, a feature that assists in dispersal of the seeds by the wind.

It is surprising that this species, so common in subalpine meadows at Mount Rainier and the Cascade Mountains of Oregon, is virtually absent from Mount Adams. Perhaps the meadow habitats at higher elevations at Mount Adams are simply too dry to support the species. One collection is known, made by Eugene Hunn in 1977 at Howard Lake, northeast of the mountain, where it grew in a wet meadow at 4,850 feet.

### *Anemone oregana* A. Gray var. *oregana*—BLUE WINDFLOWER

A perennial with distinctive bluish-purple flowers, rising from a scaly, horizontal rhizome, this *Anemone* may form large patches in open forests. The plants are more or less stiff-hairy, with single flowering stems 1-3 dm tall. The leaves are 3-parted, with the basal leaflets, when present, 1-2 times lobed. The involucre leaves may reach 8 cm in length, with the lateral pair divided half their length; there are 2-5 teeth per side. There are 5 ovate to oblong-elliptic sepals, light blue, bluish-purple, or, rarely, pink in color. The 4 mm achenes are narrowly oblong, and there are 35-100 stamens.

The most common *Anemone* at the mountain, this species shows a preference for open, moist habitats in forests. It grows alongside Trail 73 near Crofton Ridge (elevation 4,400 feet) and at Grand Meadow on the southwest side. On the north, it is found at Midway Meadows, Killen Creek, and Muddy Meadows. Along Road 23 on the west side it may be found at milepost 41. Suksdorf collected this species at Bird Creek Island on the southeast, where it also abundant on the north side of King Mountain.

## *Aquilegia* L.—COLUMBINE

### *Aquilegia formosa* Fisch. *ex* DC. var. *formosa*—WESTERN COLUMBINE

The red and yellow blossoms of this species are strikingly beautiful. They nod in an open raceme, borne on branched stems that occasionally reach 90 cm in height. The 5 red sepals spread from the tubular petals and are 10-20 mm long. There are 5 yellow petals, 15-20 mm long, each consisting of a downward-projecting yellow blade beneath a long red spur. Each spur is tipped with a small sack of nectar, a treat for hummingbirds. There are numerous yellow stamens and styles that project downward from the face of the flower. The bluish-green leaves are primarily basal; they are divided into 3 main lobes, each again 3-times divided, and may be up to 30 cm long. The stalk straightens to hold the 5 slender follicles erect after the dropping of the petals and sepals.

A middle elevation species, typically of wet, open sites, this species is relatively common and cosmopolitan at the mountain. It is found alongside Road 8040, close to Gotchen Creek, on the south. It grows in lower Midway Meadows on the north and alongside Road 071 at Bunnell Butte. It is also found alongside the road up Snipes Mountain, and on Road 82 at an elevation of 4,000 feet.

## *Caltha* L.—MARSH-MARIGOLD

Hairless perennials, the two subspecies bear somewhat succulent, dark green leaves and stems. The basal leaves are broadly toothed, and a smaller stem leaf is typically present. The subspecies are separated by the shape of the leaves. The flowers are composed of sepals only; these number 5-10 and are very showy, bright white, with an occasional blue tinge on the backsides. The flowers are 2-4 cm broad and are borne 1 or 2 on tall stems. There are many stamens, giving the flower a bright yellow center. The clustered fruits are each a short follicle.

1 Leaves round, nearly as broad as long .......................................
........................................................ *C. leptosepala* ssp. *howellii*

1 Leaves oval, longer than broad...............................................
.......................... *C. leptosepala* ssp. *leptosepala* var. *leptosepala*

### *Caltha leptosepala* DC. ssp. *howellii* (Greene) Smith
### WHITE MARSH-MARIGOLD

The 5-10 cm long leaves of this subspecies are rounded in outline, and have a heart-shaped base where the stalk joins the blade. There are usually 2 flowers per stem, and the follicles are borne on short stems.

Often growing near standing water, including ponds and streambanks, this common subspecies blooms early in the season. It is found on the west shore of Council Lake and at Babyshoe Meadow, Takhlakh Lake, and Bathtub Meadow on the northwest side. It grows in Killen Creek Meadow, alongside the trail from Muddy Meadows to the Pacific Crest Trail, and as a roadside species along Road 23. Grand Meadow is another good location to find this plant.

### *Caltha leptosepala* DC. ssp *leptosepala* var. *leptosepala* ELKSLIP MARSH-MARIGOLD

This subspecies differs in having 1 flower per stem and more elongated leaves. These are 6 cm long, more or less oval, and heart-shaped to arrowhead-shaped at the base. The stalkless follicles are borne in a cluster.

Found in similar environments as subspecies *howellii* at the mountain, this subspecies grows at Takh Takh Meadow and at Chain of Lakes on the northwest. It is also found at Grand Meadow on the southwest and in the Hellroaring Creek meadow near Bench Lake.

## *Delphinium* L.—LARKSPUR

Striking for the color of their flowers, the 5 blue to blue-purple, large sepals are spread, with one extended backwards as a narrow spur that varies from slightly less than to twice as long as the other sepals. There are 4 smallish petals that are whitish to light blue in color and form an "eye" at the throat of the flower. The inflorescence is a terminal raceme of few to as many as 20 flowers; the flowering stems are erect. The leaves are palmately divided. There are 1-5 follicles with many winged seeds.

1 Stems not glandular; upper stem and pedicels smooth .................... .................................................. *D. menziesii* ssp. *menziesii*

1 Stems glandular; upper stem and pedicels short-hairy .................. ............................................ *D. nuttallianum* var. *nuttallianum*

### *Delphinium menziesii* DC. ssp. *menziesii*—MENZIES'S LARKSPUR

Growing from elongated or rounded tubers, the occasionally hollow single stems of this species are 1-5 dm tall and simple to branched. They may be hairy and glandular, particularly in the inflorescence. The 3-7 cm broad basal leaves are 2-3 times divided and borne on long petioles. The open racemes are 3-20 flowered and the 12-18 mm long sepals are deep blue. The spur is 13-15 mm long. The lower petals are blue, shallowly notched and lined with light veins, while the upper petals are pale blue. The 9-16 mm long follicles are densely hairy and spreading.

Much more common than *D. nuttallianum*, this species grows in open, middle elevation forests up to 5,000 feet, sometimes in groups, chiefly on the south and southeast sides of the mountain. It is found alongside Trail 73, Road 070, and the Snipes Mountain trail.

#### ***Delphinium nuttallianum*** **Pritz. *ex* Walp.—NUTTALL'S LARKSPUR**

Very similar to *D. menziesii* in appearance, the sepals spread less and are usually less than 12 mm long. The spur, too, is shorter in this species. The pedicels are typically shorter than the flowers, and the racemes are many-flowered.

Uncommon, this larkspur grows alongside Trail 73 near Crofton Butte at about 4,500 feet, and near Road 839.

### ***Ranunculus*** **L.—BUTTERCUP**

This is a well-represented genus at the mountain of perennials characterized by yellow petals perennial wildflowers, each with 5 petals and sepals. There are numerous yellow stamens and several pistils, arranged in small heads. The fruit is an achene. (The shape of the beak of the achene is significant at one point in the key; this feature may be observed in immature achenes with a handlens.) Most of the plants are perennials. The leaves are basal, and the short to tall stems are branched, leafy, or sometimes with bracts.

1 Leaves broadly lanceolate, not toothed or divided; plants of wet ground .......................................... *R. alismifolius* var. *alismellus*

1 Leaves divided and usually toothed; habitat various .................. 2

2(1) Plants hairless; leaf segments mostly rounded or blunt at the tips.... ............................................................................ 3

2 Plants more or less hairy, at least on the stems and basal leaves; leaf segments sharp-tipped . ............................................... 5

3(2) Petals 3-5 mm long, bright yellow ........................ *R. verecundus*

3 Petals more than 8 mm long, dark yellow to orange-yellow ......... 4

4(3) Middle lobe of leaf smooth or shallowly 3-lobed; tips of leaf segments rounded ................... *R. eschscholtzii* var. *eschscholtzii*

4 Middle lobe of leaf deeply lobed; tips of leaf segments somewhat tapered ........................................................ *R. suksdorfii*

5(2) Stems creeping and rooting at the leaf nodes ............................ .......................................................... *R. repens* var. *repens*

5 Stems erect, not rooting at the nodes ..................................... 6

6(5) Achene beak straight, basal leaves pinnately lobed .................... ........................................... *R. orthorthyncus* var. *platyphyllus*

6 Achene beak curved; basal leaves palmately lobed or compound ... ............................................................................ 7

7(6) Basal leaves pentagon-shaped in outline, deeply lobed ................................................................................ *R. acris* var. *acris*
7 Basal leaves rounded to egg-shaped in outline, deeply lobed to compound ........................................................................ 8

8(7) Petals 2-3 mm long ......................... *R. uncinatus* var. *parviflorus*
8 Petals 9-12 mm long .................. *R. occidentalis* var. *occidentalis*

### *Ranunculus acris* L. var. *acris*—TALL BUTTERCUP

This weedy species lacks the runners that are characteristic of the other weedy buttercup, *R. repens*. It has tall, leafy stems and is roughly hairy on both stems and leaves. The basal leaves are pentagon-shaped, deeply cut into sharp-pointed segments, and stalked, with an overall length of 10-15 cm. The branched stems, each with several flowers, may reach 100 cm in height. The petals are 7-15 mm long, and the 2-2.5 mm long achene has a tiny, hooked beak.

Uncommon in wet, middle elevation habitats in disturbed places, this species grows at Muddy Meadows as well as on the west side of the mountain.

### *Ranunculus alismifolius* Geyer *ex* Benth. var. *alismellus* A. Gray WATER-PLANTAIN BUTTERCUP

Mostly hairless, this tufted plant bears toothless (or sometimes minutely toothed) basal leaves. They are 5-8 cm long and tapered to the stalk. The 15-20 cm tall flowering stems may be single-flowered and leafless, or may bear 2 or 3 flowers on stalks above a pair of small leaves. The 8-10 mm long petals are yellow; the 1.5-2.5 mm long achene has a straight beak that is 0.5-1 mm long.

A common species of middle elevations, but found as high as 6,500 feet, this buttercup prefers wet sites, growing in several meadows, including Spring Creek, Takh Takh, and Babyshoe on the northwest. It is also found at Muddy Meadows, Midway Meadows, and Takhlakh Lake. On the southeast, it grows near Road K6000 in a wet meadow and in the upper meadow at Crooked Creek.

### *Ranunculus eschscholtzii* Schlecht. var. *eschscholtzii* ESCHSCHOLTZ'S BUTTERCUP

This perennial rises from fibrous roots with 1 to several erect stems and occasionally has yellow-to brown long hairs in the inflorescence. The flowering stems are leafless and the basal leaves are oval to obovate, 1-3 cm long and shallowly 3-lobed or sometimes 2 or 3 times dissected. The 3-8 mm long sepals are spreading, and purplish-tinged. The 7-15 mm long yellow petals are obovate, often as broad as long. There are 40-125 stamens and the 1.5-2 mm long achenes are numerous in a cluster.

This species is known from a Suksdorf collection at Hellroaring Canyon.

### *Ranunculus occidentalis* Nutt. var. *occidentalis*
### WESTERN BUTTERCUP

Stiffly hairy, this buttercup bears typically erect stems, freely branched, and 1.5-4 dm tall. The basal leaves are long-stalked and 2-3.5 cm long. They are lobed into 3 main segments, each deeply toothed into 3 parts, with the lateral leaves sometimes divided again. The stem leaves are deeply dissected and alternate on the stems. The 4.5-8 mm long sepals are greenish or pinkish-tinged, and the 5 yellow petals are oblong to narrowly obovate and 9-12 mm long, but much less broad.

Rare at the mountain, this species was collected by the authors at the junction of Spring Creek and Road 2329 on the northwest side of the mountain, under young Douglas-fir in an area used by campers and horses. Probably inadvertently introduced, it would not otherwise be expected in the study area.

### *Ranunculus orthorhynchus* Hook. var. platyphyllus A. Gray
### STRAIGHTBEAK BUTTERCUP

Sometimes stiffly hairy, this perennial bears several, erect to spreading, somewhat hollow stems that are usually branched; they are 2-6 dm tall and typically leafless. The 3-8 cm long basal leaves are borne on thick petioles up to 2.5 dm long. They are divided 2 or 3 times, with the central leaflet long-stalked, and the division toothed and lobed. The purplish-tinged sepals are 6-9 mm long and softly hairy, and the 5 yellow petals are 9-18 mm long. There are 50-70 stamens and 20-50 compressed achenes in a headlike cluster, approximately 3.5 mm long.

This is a rare species at the mountain, known from a Flett collection on the upper Klickitat River.

### *Ranunculus repens* L. var. *repens*—CREEPING BUTTERCUP

Spreading widely on long runners and rooting as it goes, this weedy perennial has short-hairy stems and leaves. The 2-8 cm long leaves are triangular in outline and deeply cut into 3 major lobes, each toothed. The stem leaves are reduced in size and the leaves are typically marked with irregular, light-colored patches. Several flowers on erect stems have dark yellow petals 10-13 mm long. The 2-3 mm long achene has a curved beak approximately 1 mm long.

A middle elevation weed of moist sites, it has been found at Muddy Meadows, alongside Road 5603, and at Horseshoe Lake.

### *Ranunculus suksdorfii* A. Gray
### SUBALPINE BUTTERCUP, SUKSDORF'S BUTTERCUP

Low and tufted, and occasionally forming small clumps, the flowering stems of this buttercup are 5-10 cm tall. The plants are hairless and the basal leaves are divided into 3 major lobes, each deeply toothed. The stems bear 1-3 dark yellow or yellow-orange flowers with 8-12 mm long petals. The 1.5-2 mm long achenes have a straight beak 0.5-1 mm long and are borne in a dense and elongated head.

A subalpine species of wet meadows and streamsides, it is found on the Pacific Crest Trail at 5,700 feet on the north side of the mountain and is also known from a Suksdorf collection on the northwest, probably on the upper Lewis River.

### *Ranunculus uncinatus* D. Don var. *parviflorus* (Torr.) L.O. Benson
### WOODLAND BUTTERCUP, SMALL-PETALED BUTTERCUP

This tall native perennial may reach 60 cm in height, with branching stems. It is lightly to moderately short-hairy, and the deeply 3-5 lobed leaves are broadly ovate and sometimes marked with purple. The lobes are toothed, and the total length of leaf and stalk is approximately 10 cm. The 2-3 mm long pale yellow petals are shorter than the sepals. The 2-2.5 mm long achene is hairy on the upper part, with a stout, curved beak 1-2 mm long.

Relatively common in middle elevation wet meadows, this species grows at Babyshoe Meadow on the northwest side. It is found at Midway Meadows, along the trail between Muddy Meadows and the Pacific Crest Trail on the north, and in the Hellroaring Creek meadow near Bench Lake on the southeast.

### *Ranunculus verecundus* B.L. Robins. *ex* Piper—MODEST BUTTERCUP

Hairless except for the short-hairy sepals that are quickly deciduous, this 10-20 cm tall perennial bears a few basal leaves and typically a single flowering stem. The rounded basal leaves have a heart-shaped base, 3 major lobes, and even teeth. The stem is bracted, with 1-3 flowers composed of 4-5 mm long, yellow petals that are longer than the sepals. The 1-5 mm long achenes have a short, hooked beak.

A species of rocky habitats, it is rare at the mountain and is known at Big Muddy Creek from a Suksdorf collection, made at 7,800 feet. Suksdorf collected the type specimen of this species there in 1883.

## *Thalictrum* L.—MEADOWRUE

### *Thalictrum occidentale* A. Gray—WESTERN MEADOWRUE

With bluish-green, mostly 3 times divided leaves, this plant resembles a columbine until it flowers. The leaf segments are 1-2 cm long with rounded teeth or lobes. The 30-90 cm tall stems rise from a stout rootstock. The inflorescence is an open raceme. Male and female flowers are borne on separate plants; petals are absent. In the male flowers, the stamens hang down and have purplish anthers. The female flowers have short pale green sepals surrounding numerous styles. The fruit is a rounded achene with prominent veins on the sides.

A middle elevation to subalpine species of open habitats, it is cosmopolitan and fairly common at the mountain. It grows alongside Road 2329 close to Midway Meadows, along the Snipes Mountain trail, at Big Muddy Creek, and in Hellroaring Canyon,

### *Trautvetteria* Fisch. & C.A. Mey.—TASSEL-RUE

#### *Trautvetteria caroliniensis* (Walter) Vail. var. *occidentalis* (A. Gray) C.L. Hitchc.—TASSEL-RUE, FALSE BUGBANE

Typically hairless, with stems 50-90 cm tall, this conspicuous perennial rises from spreading rootstocks. The 10-12 cm broad leaves are kidney-shaped, deeply lobed, toothed, and borne on long stalks. There are a few reduced stem leaves that may lack stalks altogether. The flat-topped clusters consist of numerous, tiny flowers lacking petals and with 4-8 quickly-deciduous sepals. As they fall, the "flower" becomes a ball of white stamens and styles. The fruit is a rounded achene.

Fairly common and cosmopolitan in middle elevation wet habitats, this species grows alongside Road 115 and Road 2329, close to Midway Meadows, on the north side of the mountain. It is found at Swampy Meadows on the southwest and is known from a Suksdorf collection at Hellroaring Canyon.

## Rhamnaceae Juss.—BUCKTHORN FAMILY

The buckthorns are shrubs or small trees with small flowers borne in dense clusters. There are 5 sepals, petals and stamens. The ovary is partly inferior, surrounded by a disk upon which the flower parts are borne. The fruit is a lobed, leathery capsule or berry-like fruit.

Cascara (*Frangula purshiana*) is uncommon at the mountain, found mostly on lava flows and other rocky outcroppings. There are two *Ceanothus* species, one very uncommon, and the other (*Ceanothus velutinus* var. *velutinus*) found at the lower elevations in dry openings.

1 Flowers showy, white, in large clusters; fruit a dry capsule.......................................................................................... *Ceanothus*

1 Flowers inconspicuous, greenish, in small clusters; fruit berrylike, black .................................................................... *Frangula*

## Rhamnaceae

### *Ceanothus* L.—BUCKBRUSH, CEANOTHUS

One evergreen and one deciduous member of this genus are present at the mountain. The shrubs are densely branched and bear small (3-5 mm broad), white, sweet-scented flowers in dense, narrowly pyramidal panicles at the ends of the short, lateral branches. The leaves are glossy green and palmately 3-veined. The fruit is a rounded, dry, 3-lobed capsule.

1 Leaves evergreen, sticky and sweet-smelling, short hairy beneath ................................................ *C. velutinus* var. *velutinus*

1 Leaves deciduous, not sticky nor sweet-smelling; hairy on veins beneath ................................................ *C. sanguineus*

#### *Ceanothus sanguineus* Pursh
#### REDSTEM CEANOTHUS, OREGON TEA TREE

This 1-3 m tall, spreading shrub bears leaves that are mostly oval, toothed, and 3-8 cm long. The common name "redstem" refers to the reddish color of the short branches; the 6-10 cm long flower clusters are borne on these branches.

A middle elevation, dry, open habitat species, it is known from the DNR quarry on the southeast side and probably doesn't reach much higher than 4,000 feet elsewhere at the mountain.

#### *Ceanothus velutinus* Dougl. *ex* Hook. var. *velutinus*
#### SNOWBRUSH, TOBACCO BRUSH

The sweet, resinous smell of the leaves helps to distinguish this shrub. Robust and spreading, the branches may reach 2 m in height and twice that across. The glossy appearance of the leaves (they are sticky to gummy) also sets the species apart. The leaves are 6-8 mm long, oval, and bear fine glandular teeth on the margins. The white to creamy white flowers are borne in showy clusters 5-10 cm long.

Common in dry middle elevation sites, particularly on the south side of the mountain, this species is a roadside shrub there. It grows near the Stagman Ridge trail, as well as alongside the road to King Mountain at the Tract D boundary. On the north, it is found at Potato Hill. Suksdorf located this species in Hellroaring Canyon as well, probably on south-facing slopes above the creek.

### *Frangula* P. Mill.—BUCKTHORN

#### *Frangula purshiana* (DC.) Cooper—CASCARA

A small tree or shrub from 3-12 m tall, this species is most easily recognized by the prominently veined leaves. These are oval to slightly obovate, 5-15 cm long, glossy green, finely toothed on the upper side, and short-hairy beneath. The 3 mm long greenish flowers are quite inconspicuous and are borne in small umbels in the axils of the leaves. The seed is a blackish, berrylike drupe.

Typically a lowland forest dweller, the most common habitat observed for this species at the mountain is, surprisingly, on the tops and sides of recent lava flows, between 4,500 and 5,500 feet. It was collected by the authors near the Snipes Mountain Trail, where it grows on the Aiken Lava Bed, as well as on top of Crofton Butte. A Suksdorf collection was made on a "south slope" in Hellroaring Canyon, at an unnoted elevation. This plant once was known as *Rhamnus purshiana*.

## Rosaceae Juss.—ROSE FAMILY

From prostrate alpine perennials to thorny trees, the members of the rose family at Mount Adams show a wide range of forms and occupy every habitat type, with 40 species in 20 genera. The structure of the flower is distinctive: the 5 or 10 sepals are partly fused to form a hypanthium, a bowl that partly or wholly surrounds the ovary; the petals and stamens are emplaced upon the rim of the bowl. In some genera, including the familiar apple, the fruit itself is the much-expanded hypanthium. In other genera, the fruit may be an achene, a follicle, a hip, or a drupe. There are 5 or 10 petals and sepals and each flower has numerous stamens and 1 or more pistils. The leaves are basal or alternate and pinnately-divided in many genera.

| | | |
|---|---|---|
| 1 | Trees or shrubs | 2 |
| 1 | Herbaceous plants, annuals or perennials (at most slightly woody at the base of the stems) | 13 |
| 2(1) | Ovary inferior; fruit an applelike pome | 3 |
| 2 | Ovary superior; fruit a drupe, follicle, hip, or achene | 5 |
| 3(2) | Flowers numerous in flat-topped clusters; leaves pinnate | *Sorbus* |
| 3 | Flowers not in flat-topped clusters; leaves simple or sometimes shallowly lobed | 4 |
| 4(3) | Plants with sharp thorns; flowers in corymbs | *Crataegus* |
| 4 | Plants unarmed; flowers in racemes | *Amelanchier* |
| 5(2) | Leaves pinnately compound; flowers showy, pink to deep rose | *Rosa* |
| 5 | Leaves simple or compound (if pinnately compound, then the flowers not pink) | 6 |
| 6(5) | Leaves simple, unlobed and untoothed | *Oemleria* |
| 6 | Leaves lobed or compound, often toothed | 7 |

7(6) Flowers yellow ........................................................................ 8
7 Flowers white to pink or red ................................................ 9

8(7) Leaves pinnately compound; flowers bright yellow ......... *Dasiphora*

8 Leaves with 3 teeth at the apex; flowers creamy-yellow ..... *Purshia*

9(7) Leaves palmately veined, lobed or divided ............................ 10
9 Leaves pinnately veined, lobed or divided .............................. 11

10(9) Fruit of compound fleshy drupelets (blackberries, raspberries) ....... ........................................................................ *Rubus*
10 Fruit an achene, dry ................................................ *Luetkea*

11(9) Leaves pinnately lobed and toothed; fruit a 1-seeded achene ...... ........................................................................ *Holodiscus*
11 Leaves simple, serrate; fruit a multiple-seeded drupe or follicle ...... ........................................................................ 12

12(11) Pistil 1; fruit a fleshy drupe ........................................... *Prunus*
12 Pistils 5; fruit a dry follicle ............................................ *Spiraea*

13(1) Plant 1-2 m tall; fruit an achene .................................... *Aruncus*
13 Plant shorter, seldom more than 0.5 m tall ............................ 14

14(13) Stamens 5; petals yellow .................................................. 15
14 Stamens 10 or more; petals white to reddish (yellow in *Potentilla* ... ........................................................................16

15(14) Leaves 3-parted; petals much shorter than sepals .......... *Sibbaldia*
15 Leaves pinnate with many lobed leaflets; petals about equal to the sepals .................................................................. *Ivesia*

16(14) Flowers white .................................................................. 17
16 Flowers yellow, reddish, or purplish ..................................... 18

17(16) Leaflets 3; achenes set on the surface of a fleshy receptacle (strawberries) ...................................................... *Fragaria*
17 Leaves compound with mostly linear segments .............. *Horkelia*

18(15) Styles persistent on the achenes at maturity ...................... *Geum*
18 Styles soon deciduous from the achenes .............................. 19

19(18) Flowers reddish-purple; trailing plants of swamps and shallow water ........................................................................ *Comarum*
19 Flowers yellow; erect plants of dry to moist places, but not of swamps or shallow water ........................................... *Potentilla*

## *Amelanchier* Medik.—SERVICEBERRY

### *Amelanchier alnifolia* (Nutt.) Nutt *ex* M. Roemer var. *semiintegrifolia* (Hook.) C.L. Hitchc.—WESTERN SERVICEBERRY, SASKATOON

A tall shrub that may reach 5 m in good habitat, with its loose racemes of pure white flowers borne at the branch tips, this species is easily recognized. Even without flowers, the oval, blue-green, deciduous 2-4 cm leaves are distinctively toothed along the top half. The triangular sepals remain on the fruit and are 3-4 mm long, while the 5 slender petals reach 10-15 mm. An inferior ovary with 5 styles matures to a bluish-black, 1 cm broad, glaucous pome. Applelike in shape, the fruit lacks sweetness.

Relatively uncommon at Mount Adams, serviceberry was found by the authors at Takhlakh Lake, Muddy Meadows, and alongside the road on the approach to King Mountain. Occasionally, it may be found as individual shrubs in the open grand fir – Pacific silver fir forest along Road 8040, near Morrison Creek. It is newly reported for the region in this study.

## *Aruncus* L.—GOAT'S BEARD

### *Aruncus dioicus* (Walter) Fernald var. *acuminatus* (Rydb.) H. Hara GOAT'S BEARD

Shrublike in appearance, this herbaceous perennial bears stems up to 2 m in length with leaves 5-10 cm long. The 2 or 3 times pinnately divided leaves are composed of lanceolate to ovate leaflets, each marginally toothed and terminating in a long, tapered point. The species is dioecious: male and female flowers consist of 5 petals approximately 1 mm long and are borne on separate plants. The creamy flowers are borne in panicles up to 40 cm long. A short, brownish follicle follows flowering.

Since the study area at the mountain begins at 4,000 feet, this more typically lowland species is rare, being known from a single Suksdorf collection at Hellroaring Creek.

## *Comarum* L.—MARSHLOCKS

### *Comarum palustre* L. PURPLE CINQUEFOIL, MARSH CINQUEFOIL

The unusual purplish-brown to reddish-brown flowers distinguish this species from the closely related yellow to orange potentillas. The water-loving, mat-like plants consist of creeping or sometimes floating stems. Pinnately divided leaves composed of 5-7 oblong, toothed leaflets also resemble their relatives; they are short-hairy on the underside and 5-8 cm long. Leafy stems that range from 30-90 cm tall bear several flowers.

The petals, 2-6 mm long, are shorter than the pointed sepals. The fruit is an achene.

Found in the large wet sphagnum meadows on the west side (Grand and Swampy Meadows), the unusual and striking flowers make the risk of wetting one's feet to see them worthwhile.

This species is also known by the name *Potentilla palustris.*

### *Crataegus* L.—HAWTHORN

#### *Crataegus suksdorfii* (Sarg.) Kruschke—SUKSDORF'S HAWTHORN

Ranging from a low shrub to a tree up to 8 m tall, and armed with straight or slightly curved 1-2 cm thorns, this species bears elliptic, serrate or twice-serrate leaves up to 9 cm long. The flowers have 20 stamens and the sepals are triangular, glandular and turned back. Rounded white petals measure 5-7 mm in length and have small rounded teeth along the margins. The apple-like, black fruit is 1 cm broad.

Uncommon, this hawthorn prefers wet areas and is new to this study. It is found on the west side of Grand Meadow, at the forest-meadow margin.

### Dasiphora Raf.—SHRUBBY CINQUEFOIL

#### *Dasiphora floribunda* (Pursh) Kartesz, comb. nov. ined. SHRUBBY CINQUEFOIL

Similar to *Potentilla* species, but differing in the hairy achene, this low shrub has 30-90 cm tall woody stems with shredded bark. The pinnate leaves consist of 5-7 narrowly oval, silky-hairy, 8-18 mm long leaflets. The leaflets have incurved margins, lack teeth, and are grayish. Flowers are borne in 1s or 2s in the leaf axils near the branch ends. Each has 5 bright yellow, 8-13 mm long, oval petals. The hairy achene is approximately 1.5-1.8 mm long.

This is a subalpine species found at Bird Creek Meadows, Little Mount Adams, and Hellroaring Creek. It grows in open places on stony slopes and in crevices, avoiding wet places, up to 7,000 feet.

The species is better known by the name *Potentilla fruticosa.*

### *Fragaria* L.—STRAWBERRY

Strawberries are common at Mount Adams in a variety of middle elevation habitats. The plants are tufted and bear showy white flowers, 1 to several per stem, followed by edible (although small) red fruits, classically strawberry-like in appearance. Each flower has 5 slender sepals and 5 broader bractlets. The leaves are divided into 3 leaflets that are toothed and variously hairy. The actual seeds are tiny achenes that are embedded upon the surface of the fleshy fruit.

1 Leaves bluish green, the upper surface typically somewhat glaucous; the central tooth of each leaflet much smaller than the two teeth flanking it ........................ *F. virginiana* ssp. *platypetala*

1 Leaves yellow-green to medium green; the central tooth at the tip about the same size as the two teeth flanking it .......................... ....................................................... *F. vesca* ssp. *bracteata*

### ***Fragaria vesca*** **L. ssp.** ***bracteata*** **(A. Heller) Staudt**
### **MOUNTAIN STRAWBERRY, GREENLEAF STRAWBERRY**

Distinguished from the other Mount Adams strawberry by leaves that are green on both surfaces, the central tooth of the 15-50 mm long, obovate and coarsely toothed leaflets is approximately the same size as the two flanking it. Flowering stems up to 30 cm tall rise above the leaves; each bears 2-5 flowers. The showy white petals are 5-8 mm long, and the bright red and tasty strawberry reaches 8 mm. Although brighter red in color, the flavor is more tart and the berries less juicy than those of *F. virginiana*.

A species of middle elevation forests, this strawberry also may populate meadow edges but is more likely to be found in shadier places. Less common than blueleaf strawberry, it is cosmopolitan at the mountain.

### ***Fragaria virginiana*** **Duchesne ssp.** ***platypetala*** **(Rydb.) Staudt**
### **VIRGINIA STRAWBERRY, BLUELEAF STRAWBERRY**

As the name implies, the 15-50 mm long leaves of this species are bluish-green, glaucous, with short-hairs below and hairless above. Obovate, the leaves are toothed with 7-11 teeth from the middle to the tip, the central tooth much smaller than the two flanking it. Short flowering stems bear a single flower with 5-9 mm long white petals. A pinkish or mottled white-and-pink fruit is 10-12 mm long.

The most common strawberry at the mountain, as well as the tastiest, this species shows a liking for disturbed areas as well as open forest settings. It tolerates a good amount of sunshine and its blooms brighten roadsides in middle elevations from spring to summer.

## ***Geum*** **L.—AVENS**

The flowers of the two *Geum* species at the mountain are quite different from one another, with the first being a more classic open-faced, yellow flower, and the other a vaselike or bell-like bloom with purplish petals. The leaves are pinnately compound, with somewhat to greatly enlarged terminal leaflets; in the case of *G. triflorum*, the leaflets are deeply lobed.

The sepals are nearly the size of the petals. In the achene, the persistent styles are elongated, often bent, and whiskered in *G. triflorum*, giving a soft, fuzzy appearance to the fruit. The plants are tall, the flowering stem upwards of 30 cm.

1 Sepals curved back; flowers yellow; leaves pinnately divided into round leaflets ...................... *G. macrophyllum* var. *macrophyllum*
2 Sepals erect; flowers pinkish; leaves pinnately dissected ............. ........................................................ *G. triflorum* var. *ciliatum*

### *Geum macrophyllum* Willd. var. *macrophyllum*—BIGLEAF AVENS

In favorable locations, the terminal leaflet of the pinnately divided leaves reaches 8 or more cm in breadth. It is kidney shaped, 3-lobed and blunt. The diminished side leaflets are rounded, while the smaller stem leaves are sharply toothed and without stalks. Flat-topped clusters of 5-petaled flowers set on tall stems; the bright yellow flowers have turned-back sepals. The fruit is a bristly achene with a long, hooked tip. Superficially resembling *Potentilla* species, the leaves help distinguish this species.

A middle to lower subalpine elevation species, bigleaf avens prefers habitats ranging from open, disturbed sites to forest edges and wet meadows, up to about 4,500 feet. It grows at Horseshoe Lake, Muddy Meadows, and Hellroaring Creek.

### *Geum triflorum* Pursh var. *ciliatum* (Pursh) Fassett<br>PRAIRIE-SMOKE

Pinnately divided leaves of hairy and grayish leaflets, the larger leaflets cleft into three lobes and these deeply toothed, distinguish this *Geum*. The flowering stems reach 40 cm in height, with small leaves at midlength, and 1-9 flowers at the top. The sepals are 8-12 mm in length and the reddish-purple petals are typically shorter. A 3 mm long pear-shaped achene matures on a 3-5 cm long straight or twisted, feathery style.

Very rare at the mountain, this is a species typical of dry sites east of the Cascades. It is known from one collection at Klickitat Meadows on the east side of Mount Adams, made by Flett at about 6,000 feet.

## *Holodiscus* K. Koch—OCEAN-SPRAY, CREAMBUSH

### *Holodiscus discolor* (Pursh) Maxim.—OCEAN-SPRAY

Broad, with arched branches, the young branches of this 2-5 m tall shrub bear short hairs. Blunt-tipped, the slightly lobed ovate leaves are 2-5 cm long, short-hairy on the underside, slightly hairy on top, and toothed above the middle. Young shoots bear wide leaves that reach 10 cm in length and may be lobed. Tiny, 4 mm broad, creamy flowers, with 5 petals and 5 sepals, form long and dense drooping panicles. Short follicles develop from the 5 pistils.

When in flower, this showy shrub is most obvious along open, lower elevation roadsides where it behaves as a disturbance species. The road to Bird Creek Meadows provides an excellent display arena.

### *Horkelia* Cham. & Schlecht.—HORKELIA

#### *Horkelia fusca* Lindl. ssp. *fusca*—PINEWOODS HORKELIA

A basal cluster of pinnate leaves on long petioles distinguish this multi-stemmed perennial. The leaflets are 1-2 cm long, divided at least half of their length, pubescent and greenish; the stem leaves are much reduced in size. Flowering stems range in height from 1.5-6 dm; the sepals are purplish, and 2-4.5 mm long. The rounded to obcordate petals are 2.5-6 mm long, white to pinkish and marked with fine reddish lines. The fruit is an achene approximately 2 mm long.

This species is common between 4,000 and 5,000 feet on the southeast side of Mount Adams, growing at roadsides in open forests on dry ground; it is often seen with lodgepole pine and was collected by the authors at Smith Butte.

### *Ivesia* Torr. & A. Gray—MOUSETAIL

#### *Ivesia gordonii* (Hook.) Torr. & A. Gray—GORDON'S IVESIA

Growing as a low clump, the leaves of this perennial are mostly basal, less than 10 cm in length, once-pinnate, and short-hairy and glandular. The flowers, less broad than deep, are borne in a flat-topped cyme. The 3 mm yellow petals are equally as long as the sepals. There are many stamens, 2-5 pistils, and the fruit is an achene with a deciduous style.

A subalpine to alpine species with a range from the Cascades to the Rockies and Sierra Nevada, this species is known from two collections at Mount Adams, both made at High Camp on the north side, where it is rather common.

### *Luetkea* Bong.—PARTRIDGEFOOT

#### *Luetkea pectinata* (Pursh) Kuntze—PARTRIDGEFOOT

From creeping, woody stems, this tiny evergreen shrub forms extensive, low mats. Palmately divided leaves with narrow, sharp 1-2 cm long segments are tufted and bright green. Set on 10-15 cm flowering stems are rounded and dense racemes of white flowers. The 3-mm long petals and sepals surround 20 long stamens that give a yellow cast to the flowers. Short follicles develop from the 5 pistils.

Most common in the subalpine region, typically above 5,000 feet in dry meadows, this species also grows on favorable sites at lower elevations, often behaving as a disturbance species. It is found in Hellroaring Meadows, on Stagman Ridge, and alongside the Killen Creek trail.

### *Oemleria* Rchb.—OSOBERRY

#### *Oemleria cerasiformis* (Hook. & Arn.) Landon—OSOBERRY

Reaching a height of 4 m, and sometimes treelike, this multi-stemmed shrub bears male and female flowers on separate plants. The toothless, deciduous leaves are oblanceolate and 5-10 cm long. Hanging racemes of 4-6 mm long, bell-shaped white flowers have a disagreeable odor and bloom very early in the spring. There are 15 stamens and 5 pistils; a berrylike, purplish black drupe is glaucous, approximately 1.5 cm long, and a food source for birds.

Very rare at the mountain, this low to middle elevation species was observed by the authors growing on the Aiken Lava Bed on the southeast side of Mount Adams and is also known from a Suksdorf collection made on the White Salmon River, to the southwest.

### *Potentilla* L.—CINQUEFOIL

Although this genus includes both annuals and perennials, those present at Mount Adams are all perennial herbs. The leaves are compound and the yellow flowers are arranged in cymes. There are 5 sepals that alternate with 5 bractlets, 5 petals, and 10 or more stamens. There are numerous pistils and the fruit is an achene.

This genus formerly included species now called *Comarum, Dasiphora,* and *Sibbaldia.*

1 Leaves pinnately divided .......... 2
1 Leaves trifoliate or palmately divided .......... 6

2(1) Leaves long and narrow, the leaflets toothed .......... 3
2 Leaves about half as wide as long, the leaflets deeply cut .......... 5

3(2) Petals shorter than the sepals .......... *P. glandulosa* ssp. *reflexa*
3 Petals as long as or longer than the sepals .......... 4

4(3) Flower stems greater than 20 cm .......... *P. glandulosa* ssp. *nevadensis*
4 Flower stems less than 20 cm .......... *P. glandulosa* ssp. *pseudorupestris*

5(2) Leaf stalk less than the blade, hairy; leaflet lobes overlapping ........ ................................................ *P. drummondii* ssp. *breweri*

5 Leaf stalk longer than the blade; leaflets pinnately toothed ½ to midvein, separated .................... *P. drummondii* ssp. *drummondii*

6(1) Leaflets 5 ............................................ *P. gracilis* var. *gracilis*

6 Leaflets 3 ...................................................... *P. flabellifolia*

### *Potentilla drummondii* Lehm. ssp. *breweri* (S. Wats.) Ertter
### BREWER'S CINQUEFOIL

Consisting of a few branches from a rootstock, this perennial is covered with silky hairs and sometimes with tangled hairs on the lower surfaces of the leaves, giving it a silvery-gray appearance. The flowering stems are 1-2.5 dm tall, and the basal leaves are pinnate, with 9-11 obovate leaflets. These are cleft more than half of their length and 1-2 cm long; the 2-3 stem leaves are much smaller. The flowers are arranged in a cyme; the petals are yellow and longer than the sepals. There are 20 stamens and numerous pistils with the style longer than the 1.3 mm achene.

Less common than the *drummondii* subspecies, this plant is found at middle to subalpine elevations on the east and south sides, including Little Mount Adams and the Klickitat River. It is considered a "sensitive" plant in the state of Washington and reaches its northern limit of distribution at Mount Adams.

### *Potentilla drummondii* Lehm. ssp. *drummondii*
### DRUMMOND'S CINQUEFOIL

Tufted and short-hairy with long-stalked basal leaves, this plant is composed of a few branches rising from a heavy rootstock. The pinnately divided leaves appear nearly palmate owing to a short midrib and are shorter than the stalks. Each of the 5-11 obovate leaflets are coarsely toothed and 10-50 mm long. An open cyme consists of 10-20 flowers with petals 5-10 mm long and sepals half that size.

Found in middle to subalpine elevations, this subspecies is quite common in meadows, including those near Horseshoe Lake, at Hellroaring Creek, and along the west side.

### *Potentilla flabellifolia* Hook. *ex* Torr. & A. Gray
### FAN-LEAF CINQUEFOIL

Hairless and low, this perennial has 10-12 cm long basal leaves with 3 leaflets, each 1-3 cm long, coarsely toothed and broadly obovate to fan-shaped. The 10-30 cm tall flowering stems are topped with 1-5 orangish-yellow flowers; the broadly notched petals are 6-10 mm long.

Showing a preference for middle to subalpine meadows, this species is common at the mountain to elevations of almost 6,500 feet. It is found near the Mazama Glacier on the southeast side, at Stagman Ridge on the southwest, at Takh Takh Meadow, Howard Lake, and alongside the Killen Creek trail on the north.

### *Potentilla glandulosa* Lindl. ssp. *nevadensis* (S. Wats.) Keck
### NEVADA CINQUEFOIL

Similar to variety *pseudorupestris*, the hairs of the leaves of this subspecies lack glands; it is found on drier sites.

This subspecies is known from a single Flett collection, probably made at the Klickitat River.

### *Potentilla glandulosa* Lindl. ssp. *pseudorupestris* (Rydb.) Keck
### STICKY CINQUEFOIL

A glandular, short-hairy perennial, this species bears simple or sparingly branched stems 15-30 cm tall. The pinnate leaves are divided into 5 or 7 lobes consisting of roundish to obovate, deeply toothed, hairy leaflets. The few stem leaves are reduced in size. Oval to obovate, the 0.5-1.5 mm petals vary from white to cream and are longer than the sepals; there are numerous pistils. The flowers are arranged in an open cyme.

This species populates meadows from middle to subalpine elevations on the south and east sides of the mountain. Suksdorf collected it at Hellroaring Canyon and on King Mountain, and Henderson found it "above the glacier" at Muddy River Canyon, most likely between 6,500 and 7,000 feet. It also grows in a meadow near the DNR quarry.

### *Potentilla glandulosa* Lindl. ssp. *reflexa* (Greene) Keck
### STICKY CINQUEFOIL

This variety is distinguished by cream-colored petals that are shorter than the sepals. Otherwise, it is similar in stature to variety *nevadensis* but has numerous glandular hairs on the stems and leaves.

This subspecies is known from just one collection made during this study on Road 200, at 4,100 feet, northwest of King Mountain. It grows in open places among ponderosa pine in a slowly-revegetating clearcut.

### *Potentilla gracilis* Dougl. *ex* Hook. var. *gracilis*
### GRACEFUL CINQUEFOIL

Tufted, hairy but not glandular, this perennial has palmately divided leaves with 5-7 leaflets, each oblanceolate, coarsely toothed, dark green on the upper side and white-hairy beneath. The leaflets vary in length, with the longest 3-6 cm. Sparsely-flowered, the flowering stems are 30-60 cm tall; the bright yellow petals are 8-10 mm long, notched, and much longer than the sepals.

This showy species is known only from a single Flett collection at Klickitat Meadows, northeast of the mountain.

## *Prunus* L.—CHERRY

### *Prunus emarginata* (Dougl. *ex* Hook.) D. Dietr. var. *emarginata* BITTER CHERRY

A multi-stemmed small tree or tall shrub, bitter cherry has the shiny, reddish-brown bark of the cultivated cherry and can reach about 6 m in height at Mount Adams. The leaves are often clustered on short side branchlets; they are 3-8 cm long and oval to obovate. Flat-topped clusters of 3-10 flowers are borne on lateral spurs. The 5 petals are white and 4-8 mm long; there are many stamens. The fruit is a bitter, egg-shaped, cherry-like, red drupe, accounting for the common name.

Commonly found along roadsides and other disturbed areas, this species is most likely to be encountered on the south and southwest sides of the mountain, including the edges of large meadows such as Grand Meadow. Historic collections were also made on the east side at Howard Lake and the Klickitat River.

## *Purshia* DC. *ex* Poir.—BITTERBRUSH

### *Purshia tridentata* (Pursh) DC.—ANTELOPE BITTERBRUSH

Rounded and freely branched, this shrub of dry, eastside habitats, may reach 2 m in height. The wedge-shaped leaves with a point at the base vary from 10-20 mm in length, and have 3 deeply indented teeth at the tip; they are pubescent but green on the upper surface, grayish beneath, and rolled under at the edges. Fragrant, solitary flowers are borne on lateral, leafy spurs; the yellow petals are oval to spatulate, 6-9 mm long and spreading. The sepals are nearly equal in size to the petals. The fruit is a flexible achene.

This species was collected by the authors on the southeast side at the DNR quarry, on a dry, stony slope in an open Garry oak woodland. Here at 4,100 feet the plants are depressed in height by harsh conditions: spreading to 2 m across, individual plants may be less than 30 cm high.

## *Rosa* L.—ROSE

These are thorny or prickly shrubs, with alternate, pinnate leaves on arching stems. The leaf margins may be singly or doubly toothed. The pink flowers are large and attractive, with 5 sepals, 5 petals, and numerous stamens and are followed by red fruits, called "hips." There are several woody achenes within each hip.

1 Sepals falling from the hip as the fruit matures; petals about 10 mm long .......... *R. gymnocarpa*

1 Sepals persistent on the maturing hip; petals 10-25 mm long ..... 2

2(1) Leaflets sparsely glandular; flowers generally solitary .................. ........................................................ *R. nutkana* var. *hispida*

2 Leaflets glandless; flowers several in a cyme ............ *R. pisocarpa*

### *Rosa gymnocarpa* Nutt.—WOOD ROSE, BALD-HIP ROSE

Slender, straight bristles on the stems of an open shrub distinguish this rose; the stems may reach 2 m in height. Elliptical leaves with 5 or 7 leaflets are hairless, although the stalks and midribs are glandular-hairy. Doubly toothed margins are tipped with glands, and the flowering stalks are also glandular. These bear 1-3 flowers; the pinkish to rose-colored petals are about 10 mm long with ovate, shorter sepals. The sepals are glandular on the back and united at their base, and fall as the fruit matures; the sepals remain attached to the hip in the other two *Rosa* species, hence "bald hip." The hip is 4-6 mm in diameter, elliptical in shape, and bright red-orange in color.

Wood rose is found in moist places in forests below about 4,500 feet on the west side of Mount Adams. Elsewhere and at higher elevations, the other two species are found.

### *Rosa nutkana* C. Presl var. *hispida* Fern.—NOOTKA ROSE

Less than 1 m tall, the stems of this openly-configured shrub bear straight, slightly flattened prickles, lacking the bristles of *R. gymnocarpa*. The leaves are composed of 5 or 7 sparsely hairy and glandular, elliptical to ovate leaflets, each varying from 1-7 cm in length. The leaflets are singly toothed, and the tips of the teeth are glandless. Large, solitary flowers on hairless stalks have 5 broadly notched, 1-2 cm long petals. The lanceolate sepals are equally long, tapered to a slender tip, and are mostly hairy on the back. The sepals persist on the 1 cm diameter fruit.

This showy rose has been collected at Swampy Meadows on the west side and at Hellroaring Creek and Snipes Mountain on the southeast. It grows in middle elevation forests in moist, rather open places up to 5,000 feet.

### *Rosa pisocarpa* A. Gray—CLUSTERED ROSE

Compact and upright, this 1-2 m tall shrub bears relatively few stout, broad-based prickles. There are typically 7 hairless leaflets that vary from 1.5-3 cm in length, and have singly toothed, nonglandular margins. Small clusters of 2-8 flowers are borne on hairless, nonglandular stalks from 1-2 cm long. The small petals are only 1.5 cm long with equal-length sepals. They are glandular-hairy on the back. A dark red, round hip is about 1 cm in diameter.

Preferring wet sites, this rose has been found on the southeast side near the DNR quarry, on north-facing slopes, often at the edges of logged areas.

## *Rubus* L.—BLACKBERRY, RASPBERRY

Ranging from trailing forest creepers to erect, thicket-forming shrubs, this is a diverse genus of vigorous plants. The trailing species are prickly or thorny, while the shrubby salmonberry and thimbleberry have softer prickles. The leaves are pinnately or palmately divided or lobed and typically have toothed margins. The flowers are borne in small clusters and have 5 sepals and 5 petals. There are numerous stamens and pistils. The fruit is the familiar blackberry or raspberry, technically an aggregate of many small 1-seeded drupelets borne upon a more or less conical structure called a receptacle.

The raspberries are distinguished by a fruit that slips easily from the receptacle and upon which the drupelets are borne. In the blackberries the drupelets and receptacle remain together when the ripe fruit is picked.

| | |
|---|---|
| 1 | Leaves lobed but not divided into leaflets .......... 2 |
| 1 | Leaves palmately divided into 3-5 leaflets .......... 3 |
| 2(1) | Upright shrub; flowers 15-30 mm long .......... *R. parviflorus* var. *parviflorus* |
| 2 | Trailing plant; flowers less than 10 mm long .......... *R. lasiococcus* |
| 3(1) | Stems strongly angled, with heavy and curved prickles; larger leaves with 5 leaflets; introduced shrubs, with arching stems .......... *R. laciniatus* |
| 3 | Stems slender and round, the prickles absent or slender; leaflets mostly 3 (5 in *R. pedatus*); native shrubs with upright or trailing stems .......... 4 |
| 4(3) | Tall, upright shrubs; flowers magenta; berries yellow or red .......... *R. spectabilis* var. *spectabilis* |
| 4 | Shrubs with trailing or weakly ascending stems; flowers white; berries red, purplish, or black .......... 5 |
| 5(4) | Leaflets 5; stems mat-forming, prickles absent .......... *R. pedatus* |
| 5 | Leaflets 3; stems weakly ascending or trailing, but not matlike; prickles present, hooked .......... 6 |
| 6(5) | Stems conspicuously glaucous .... *R. leucodermis* var. *leucodermis* |
| 6 | Stems not glaucous .......... *R. ursinus* ssp. *macropetalus* |

## Rosaceae

### *Rubus laciniatus* Willd.—CUTLEAF BLACKBERRY

Armed with strong, curved thorns, this stout plant is composed of heavy, arching stems. The semi-evergreen, tough leaves are divided into 5 leaflets, each leaflet ovate but deeply cut into sharp teeth or lobes, the largest 2-6 cm long. They appear green although are hairy beneath. The inflorescence is a glandular panicle with multiple flowers; each round petal is white or pinkish and is 7-15 mm long. The egg-shaped fruit is black and hairless.

This invasive, weedy species is known from a single collection made for this study at Morrison Creek on the south side, at 4,000 feet. This is higher than other collections reported in Washington. The equally-troublesome Himalayan blackberry (*Rubus armeniacus*) has not been found in the study area.

### *Rubus lasiococcus* A. Gray—DWARF BRAMBLE

Long stems that may reach 2 m and root at the leaf nodes create a trailing, ground-covering raspberry. There are no prickles on the stems. The rounded, compound leaves are borne on short lateral stems and are 3-5 lobed with fine teeth; somewhat wider than long, they measure 2-4 cm across. The flowers are white, with petals that are less than 8 mm long. A red berry of 2-5 druplets is edible but infrequently produced.

Common in middle elevation forests up to 5,000 feet, this plant can also behave as a disturbance species and is often found along roadsides, including Road 23 on the west side and the road up Snipes Mountain on the southeast.

### *Rubus leucodermis* Dougl. *ex* Torr. & A. Gray var. *leucodermis*<br>BLACKCAP RASPBERRY

Armed with short, hooked prickles, this is a trailing raspberry with clambering or weakly ascending stems. The bark of the branches appears pale green beneath a glaucous coating. The leaves of the fruiting branches are divided into 3 leaflets, while the first-year stems have larger leaves composed of 5 leaflets. The leaflets are sharply toothed, ovate, green above and white-hairy beneath; the largest varying between 2-6 cm in length. The white petals are oblanceolate and 4-5 mm long; the sepals are long. The flowers are arranged in small clusters; the fruits are purplish black, rounded, and about 1 cm broad. Covered with thin, velvety hairs, the fruits are quite tasty and sometimes produced in good numbers.

Relatively common at middle elevations in forest openings and at roadsides, this species is easily seen on Stagman Ridge Trail on the west or along the Pineway Trail on the southeast.

### *Rubus parviflorus* Nutt. var. *parviflorus*—THIMBLEBERRY

Thornless, this upright, 1-2 m tall raspberry is most readily recognized by its reddish-brown, shredded bark and the large leaves. The leaves are ovate and palmately divided into 3-5 broad, shallow lobes with sharp teeth. They are softly hairy, pale green, and vary between 5 and 15 cm in length. Flat clusters of 3-7 flowers are borne on densely glandular stalks. The oval, 1.5-3 cm long white petals are attractively textured, appearing crinkled. The red fruit is 1.5-2 cm broad and shaped as a flattened hemisphere; it has a good flavor and the fruits are usually plentiful.

Thimbleberry is most typically found in the lower elevations, reaching just above 4,000 feet, where it can be locally common; it also occurs at higher elevations at sites such as the meadows along the lower reach of Hellroaring Creek.

### *Rubus pedatus* Sm.—FIVE-LEAVED BRAMBLE

Another ground covering raspberry, this species bears shiny-green leaves divided into 5 sharply toothed, obovate leaflets that are 5-15 mm long. Solitary flowers are borne on long stalks in the leaf axils; the 5 white petals are 5-7 mm long. The tart, red fruit is composed of 1-6 smooth druplets, but is rarely seen.

Growing in middle elevation forests, this species is also found at the edges of wet meadows, such as Bathtub Meadow on the north side. It is generally in moister places than the other bramble, *R. lasiococcus*.

### *Rubus spectabilis* Pursh var. *spectabilis*—SALMONBERRY

Sometimes forming dense thickets, the 1-3 m tall stems sprout from the spreading roots of this deciduous shrub. Short, straight prickles adorn the stems while the leaves are divided into 3 leaflets. These are 7-15 cm long, ovate and toothy and sometimes lobed. Solitary or paired, the showy flowers have purplish-red petals 10-15 mm long. The edible, if bland, raspberry-like fruit is egg-shaped, smooth and typically dark red, although occasionally a plant with yellow fruits is encountered.

Most common on the north side of Mount Adams at middle elevations, this shrub was newly identified for the study area. At lower elevations, it is cosmopolitan at streamsides and in damp forest openings.

### *Rubus ursinus* Cham. & Schlecht. ssp. *macropetalus* (Dougl. *ex* Hook.) Roy L. Taylor & MacBryde—PACIFIC BLACKBERRY

The individual stems of this blackberry may reach 1 m in length, but the impression is of a widely spreading shrub, particularly in disturbed areas. The stems spread as clones from rootstocks. They are armed with short, slender, curved prickles. The ovate leaflets are configured in groups of 3 (although occasionally 5), and are toothed and tapered at the tip. The large terminal leaflet may be lobed and is 3-4 cm long. The flowers are borne in clusters of 2-5 at the tops of lateral stems. Slender, white petals are up to 2 cm long; male and female flowers occur on separate plants. The fruit is an egg-shaped, black, 1.5-cm long berry. It is the tastiest of the wild blackberries at Mount Adams.

Cosmopolitan but not seen in great numbers at the mountain, this species is confined to forests and open disturbed areas in the middle elevations.

## *Sibbaldia* L.—SIBBALDIA

### *Sibbaldia procumbens* L.—CREEPING SIBBALDIA

Forming mats with its creeping, somewhat woody stems, this species was originally classified as a *Potentilla*. The basal leaves are borne on long, slender stalks and are divided into 3 leaflets of nearly equal size; these are wedge-shaped, 1-2 cm long, and have 3 teeth at a blunt apex. Dense flower clusters cupped in 1 or 2 reduced leaves are set atop 5-15 cm tall flowering stems. The yellow petals, 2-4 mm long, are much shorter than the sepals. There are 5 (or occasionally 6) stamens. The fruit is an achene.

A subalpine to alpine species, this plant has been found at High Camp on the north side, and is known from a Suksdorf collection at Hellroaring Creek and a Henderson one near glacial margins high on Muddy Creek. It can be found at elevations up to 7,000 feet and is usually seen in meadows or flats that become seasonally dry. In harsh sites, the flowering stems may be no more than 3 cm tall.

## *Sorbus* L.—MOUNTAIN-ASH

Erect, multiple-stemmed shrubs, the mountain-ashes bear large, alternate, deciduous, pinnately divided leaves. The characteristics of the leaves are an aid in distinguishing the species, although not always definitive. The white flowers are borne in broad, showy, flattish clusters and consist of 5 sepals and 5 petals, with 15-20 stamens and 2-5 styles. The ovary is inferior and develops into a small, applelike pome that is bright red at maturity; the pomes are borne in large numbers in clusters and are attractive to birds.

Suksdorf twice collected hybrids between the two species, from about 6,500 feet on the upper end of Hellroaring Valley. They combine leaf and bud characteristics of the parents.

1 Leaflets sharply pointed and finely toothed most of their length; leaflets mostly 9 or 11 .................. *S. scopulina* var. *cascadensis*
1 Leaflets blunt at the end and toothed on the upper half or three-quarters; leaflets 9 ................................. *S. sitchensis* var. *grayi*

### *Sorbus scopulina* Greene var. *cascadensis* (G. N. Jones) C. L. Hitchc.—CASCADE MOUNTAIN-ASH

A tall shrub that varies from 2-5 m, this multiple-branched plant has sticky winter buds and new twigs, both covered with white hairs. The leaves consist of 9 or 11 oblong leaflets, pointed at the tip, and toothed most of the length of the margins. Flat clusters of many flowers are 5-10 cm across, with the individual petals 5-6 mm long. The calyx is smooth on the outside, and the fruit is scarlet and 8-10 mm in diameter.

Found at subalpine elevations on open, moist slopes, this mountain ash is less common than *S. sitchensis.*

### *Sorbus sitchensis* M. Roem. var. *grayi* (Wenzig) C.L. Hitchc. SITKA MOUNTAIN-ASH

The buds and twigs of this 2 m tall shrub are covered with reddish brown hairs, but they are not sticky. Each pinnate leaf is composed of 7 or 9 oblong leaflets, rounded at the tip and marginally toothed above the midpoint; they are 3-6 cm long. A smaller and rounder flower cluster helps distinguish this shrub from *S. scopulina.* The petals are 3-4 mm long, and the calyx is short-hairy on the outside. The red fruit measures 7-10 mm in diameter.

The most common mountain-ash at Mount Adams, this is a middle elevation to subalpine species, growing in open, moist areas, sometimes as high as 5,000 feet on the southeast flank, where plants are near the terminal ends of glaciers.

### *Spiraea* L.—SPIREA

These shrubby plants bear toothed, undivided, deciduous leaves. The small flowers have 5 petals, 5 sepals, and 15-60 stamens and are borne in small, dense clusters. There are 5 pistils that develop into follicles. The pink-flowered species prefer wet or swampy ground and often form extensive thickets, prominent features of the middle elevation meadows at Mount Adams.

One hybrid is known, of frequent-enough occurrence that it is keyed below.

1 Flowers in elongated clusters .............................................. 2
1 Flowers in flat-topped clusters ............................................. 3

2(1) Inflorescence broadly conical; flowers light pink; plants of dry hillsides .................................................... *S.* x *pyramidata*
2 Inflorescence narrowly conical; flowers dark pink; plants of swamps and lake margins .............................. *S. douglasii* var. *douglasii*

3(1) Flowers white ...................................... *S. betulifolia* var. *lucida*
3 Flowers pink to rose ........................ *S. splendens* var. *splendens*

### *Spiraea betulifolia* Pall. var. *lucida* (Dougl. *ex* Greene) C.L. Hitchc.
### BIRCH-LEAF SPIREA

Small shrubs, barely 1 m tall, the leaves of this species are toothed on the margins above the midpoint, 2-6 cm long, and hairless. Small white flowers, often with a pinkish tinge, are borne in flattish clusters 5-12 cm broad; the petals are 2 mm long.

Found on the southeast side, this species is uncommon at the mountain. It was found by the authors on Snipes Mountain at 4,500 feet and in Hellroaring Canyon at 4,850 feet, just north of Bench Lake.

### *Spiraea douglasii* Hook. var. *douglasii*
### HARDHACK, DOUGLAS'S SPIREA

Erect, branched stems form a shrub 1-2 m tall. The young twigs are short-hairy and the 4-10 cm long leaves are oval to oblong, short-hairy above, wooly beneath, and toothed on the margin near the tip. Narrow, pyramidal clusters of bright rose-pink flowers stand 8-20 cm long at the branch ends and easily serve to distinguish this species from other spireas.

Common in wet meadows and other moist habitats, typically forming extensive and impenetrable thickets, this species is found at places such as Takh Takh Meadow, Council Lake, Swampy Meadows, and Grand Meadow.

### *Spiraea splendens* Baumann *ex* K. Koch var. *splendens*
### ROSY SPIREA

An upright shrub that reaches 30-100 cm in height and most easily distinguished from *S. douglasii* by the flat-topped flower clusters, this is the most common spirea at the mountain. The elliptical to ovate leaves are 1-7 cm long and toothed on the margin near a blunt tip. Rose-pink flowers are borne in dense clusters 2-4 cm broad, wider than tall.

A species of wet meadows and hillsides, rosy spirea is cosmopolitan at the mountain, growing at places as diverse as Babyshoe Meadow, a wet, sphagnum meadow, and Potato Hill, a dry, open site.

### *Spiraea* x *pyramidata* Greene—HYBRID SPIREA

The parents of this plant are *Spiraea betulifolia* and *S. douglasii*. About 1 m tall, it has a conical, and somewhat rounded inflorescence, while the flowers are light pink, at least in bud.

The hybrid was found by Suksdorf on a dry slope in Hellroaring Canton and, during the present study, on the Island Springs Trail, probably close to the Suksdorf location.

## Rubiaceae Juss.—MADDER FAMILY

Perennial herbs at Mount Adams, typically weak-stemmed, with opposite or whorled leaves, these are common plants found in diverse habitats. The corolla is regular, 4-parted or less often 3-parted; the calyx is absent or nearly obsolete. There are 4 stamens, 2 styles, with an inferior ovary that develops into a 2-parted dry fruit that is often clothed with hooked hairs.

1 Leaves opposite; corolla funnel-shaped, pink ................ *Kelloggia*
1 Leaves whorled; corolla flat or circular-shaped, greenish to white ... ........................................................................ *Galium*

### *Galium* L.—BEDSTRAW

Common and distinctive members of a number of forest communities (except for one rare weedy species), the bedstraws have leaves in whorls on 4-angled, slender and often bristly stems. The greenish to white flowers each have a short tube on widely-spreading lobes, appearing flat-faced. The fruits form pairs of nutlets.

1 Plants annual ........................................................................ 2
1 Plants perennial .................................................................... 3

2(1) Leaves in whorls of 2-4 ............................................ *G. bifolium*
2 Leaves in whorls of 5-8 ............................................ *G. aparine*

3(1) Leaves in whorls of 4 ....................................................... 4
3 Leaves in whorls of 5 or more ................................ *G. triflorum*

4(3) Leaves 3-veined, broadly ovate; nutlets with hooked hairs ........... ....................................................................... *G. oreganum*
4 Leaves 1-veined, linear to oblanceolate; nutlets smooth .............. ................................................ *G. trifidum* ssp. *columbianum*

#### *Galium aparine* L.—GOOSE-GRASS, CLEAVERS

This annual bears weak, trailing 30-150 cm long stems with small, hooked hairs. The 2-5 cm long, linear to oblanceolate leaves are borne in whorls of 5-8. The whitish flowers are borne in clusters of a few flowers in the leaf axils; they are 2-3 mm broad, and the 2-3 mm diameter nutlets are clothed with short, hooked hairs.

A middle elevation weedy species, relatively uncommon, it was collected by the authors near Trail 75 at Salt Creek. It is also found alongside roads on the west side of the mountain.

### *Galium bifolium* S. Wats.—TWINLEAF BEDSTRAW

A simple to moderately branched, slender annual, mostly erect and 5-20 cm tall, this *Galium* is of very different appearance from the other bedstraws. The 1-2 cm long elliptic leaves are more or less rounded at the tip. The lower leaves are in whorls of 4, with fewer numbers on the upper stem. The flowers are solitary and borne in the leaf axils; the tiny 3-lobed corolla is white. The fruit is covered with short, hooked hairs and is 2.5-3.5 mm long.

Uncommon at the mountain, this species is known from Suksdorf collections at Hellroaring Canyon and the cliffs above Bird Creek, and from a Flett collection on the upper Klickitat River northeast of Mount Adams.

### *Galium oreganum* Britton—OREGON BEDSTRAW

This perennial, mostly hairless bedstraw is distinguished by the numerous short, erect stems that rise from a slender, creeping rootstock. The stems range from 10-30 cm tall. The 2-4 cm long leaves are ovate to elliptical and configured in whorls of 4. They have 3 main veins and bear short hairs on the margins. The 2 mm broad greenish-white flowers are in terminal clusters. The nutlet is covered with long, hooked hairs.

The most common bedstraw of rather open forests and meadow edges, this species grows at the Stagman Ridge trailhead on the west side of the mountain. It also is found in Midway Meadows and alongside Road 115.

### *Galium trifidum* L. ssp. *columbianum* (Rydb.) Hultén<br>SMALL BEDSTRAW

This perennial is a sprawling plant, with minutely-hairy slender stems 10-70 cm long. The 5-15 mm long linear to narrowly oblanceolate leaves are in whorls of 4-6. The white, 1-2 mm broad tiny flowers are borne in small clusters on the side branches and at the ends of the stems. The 1-1.5 mm diameter nutlet is smooth.

Preferring wet ground at the edges of meadows, this species is found on the north side of the mountain alongside Road 115 and at Spring Creek. It grows also at Takhlakh Lake on the northwest side.

### *Galium triflorum* Michx.—FRAGRANT BEDSTRAW

Similar to *G. aparine* in having 6 leaves in the whorl, this spreading native perennial with leaves up to 50 cm long tends to form loose mats. The 1-5 cm long leaves are ovate or obovate, and when bruised smell strongly of coumarin, an aroma more commonly associated with "new mown hay." The tiny cream-colored or greenish-white flowers are borne in clusters of 3 on long stalks in the leaf axils. The nutlets have hooked hairs.

Common in middle elevation, moist woods, this species has been noted by the authors at upper Swampy Meadows, and on Road 070, east of Bunnell Butte.

### *Kelloggia* Torr. *ex* Benth. & Hook.—KELLOGGIA

#### *Kelloggia galioides* Torr.—MILK KELLOGGIA

This perennial develops from robust, creeping rootstocks, with the 1-6 dm tall stems clustered. The 1.5-5 cm long lanceolate to linear, toothless leaves are opposite and sessile. The pink to white, stiffly hairy corolla is 4-8 mm long, with ascending narrow lobes nearly as long as the tube. The 3-4 mm fruit is oblong.

In habitats varying from open slopes to stream banks, this middle elevation to subalpine plant is found at Crooked Creek, the Pineway trailhead, and at Island Springs, all on the southeast side of the mountain. It also grows along Road 8040 to the South Climb trailhead.

## Salicaceae Mirb.—WILLOW FAMILY

Most typically plants of wetlands, streamsides, and other damp places, the willow family is represented by two genera and twelve species at Mount Adams. Since the study area begins at 4,000 feet, the common black cottonwood (genus *Populus*) of lower elevations is relatively rare at the mountain. The willows (genus *Salix*) are present throughout to elevations in excess of 6,500 feet.

All the willow family members bear alternate, deciduous leaves with more or less prominent stipules, although the latter may be shed early. The male and female flowers are borne in dense, spikelike racemes (commonly called catkins) on separate plants; this feature may render some of the willows difficult to identify if plants of both sexes are not present.

A small, scalelike bract is set at the base of each flower; there are no sepals or petals. The stamens number 1 to many and there is 1 pistil in the female flower. The superior ovary has a short style and 2-4 stigma lobes. The fruit is a capsule, and each seed bears a tuft of hairs, a characteristic that enables the willows to employ the wind for dispersal. Root suckering and sprouting from old trunks are other common means of regeneration.

## Salicaceae

1 Catkins pendulous, each with a bract cut into slender segments; tall trees with broadly ovate leaves .................................... *Populus*
1 Catkins ascending to erect, the bracts not divided; trees or shrubs, with narrower leaves ..................................................... *Salix*

### *Populus* L.—COTTONWOOD

Two members of this genus are known at the mountain. Quaking aspen, *P. tremuloides,* is found in small clonal groups, most typically on the east and south sides to elevations of 5,000 feet or so. Black cottonwood, *P. balsamifera,* is more common on the north and west sides at lower elevations.

The catkins are drooping and appear before the leaves; the capsules, therefore, mature before full leaf development. The bracts are divided into slender segments. The leaves are heart-shaped to triangular; glossy in the case of *P. balsamifera* and glaucous for *P. tremuloides*. Both species are trees, typically of wet environments, but occasionally on drier sites as well.

1 Smooth, greenish-white bark; bud scales not resinous; flattened leaf stalk; rounded leaves with sharp tip, to 9 cm long .................................................................................... *P. tremuloides*
1 Rough, dark gray bark; bud scales resinous; leaf stalk not flattened; heart-shaped to elongated leaves, to 15 cm long ............................................................... *P. balsamifera* ssp. *trichocarpa*

### *Populus balsamifera* L. ssp. *trichocarpa* (Torr. & A. Gray *ex* Hook.) Brayshaw—BLACK COTTONWOOD

The tallest of the non-coniferous trees at Mount Adams, the trees range from 20-50 m in height. Mature trees have deeply fissured gray bark, and a broad crown of arched branches. New buds are covered with a sticky resin; as the buds expand they become fragrant. The leaves are easily recognized by the combination of a pointed tip and a broadly ovate to triangular shape. They are 2-5 cm long, broadly toothed, dark green above and reddish-brown beneath and long stalked. Both male and female catkins appear before the leaves, with the long male catkins (3.5-6 cm) composed of multiple flowers, each with 30-60 stamens, and the female catkins from 5-10 cm long, each flower with 3 stigmas. The round capsule contains seeds enveloped by long, white, cottony hairs, from which the common name of the species is derived.

A middle elevation species of stream banks and wet meadows, black cottonwood is most common on the west and north sides. Stout trees grow near Roads 034 and 070 at the 4,000 foot elevation.

### *Populus tremuloides* Michx.—QUAKING ASPEN

Distinguished by smooth, greenish-gray bark and triangular, fluttering leaves, this species may spread by cloning, forming small groups of trees. Up to 15 m tall, the bark on old trunks may blacken; the bud scales are shiny but not resinous. The leaves are borne on a slender, laterally flattened stalk (which causes the leaf to "quake" in a breeze); they are 2.5-9 cm long and rounded to heart-shaped with a small tip. The margins of the leaves are finely toothed or wavy, with small white hairs. The male catkins are racemelike, 2 to 3 cm, with 6-14 stamens in each flower, while the female catkins range from 4-10 cm in length. The 4-6 mm fruits are borne on short stalks.

Local in small groups, this species grows at Snipes Mountain, alongside the Pineway Trail, near Road 071, and at 4,000 feet near Road 82, all on the southeast side. It is found near Morrison Creek on the south and at the lava flow alongside the Pacific Crest Trail south of Potato Hill, on the north.

### *Salix* L.—WILLOW

Most of the willows at the mountain are shrubby and some grow as dense thickets. *Salix scouleriana,* an uncommon species, can appear tree-like, and a genuine tree, *S. lucida* ssp. *lasiandra,* is present only at a few places at 4,000 feet on the west side of the mountain. In the middle to lower subalpine habitats willows often grow in thickets. Curiously, the prostrate species of alpine elevations, found farther north, as at Mount Rainier, are absent, perhaps owing to the generally drier conditions at Mount Adams.

The winter buds are covered by a single scale, the color being important in keying some of the species. Likewise, whether the catkins appear before, with, or after the unfolding of the leaves should be observed. The leaves vary from obovate to long and narrow and are borne on short stalks; it is worth noting that leaf shape may vary considerably on a single plant. Male and female flowers are borne on separate plants; identification often requires the presence of both sexes at the correct flowering stage. The catkins may be pendulous or erect. There is 1 style (occasionally so short as to appear absent) with 2 stigmas each of which is more or less 2-lobed, and 1-9 stamens. The capsule may be smooth or hairy and is usually pear-shaped.

1 Tree or "tree-sized," greater than 6 m .................................... 2
1 Shrub, less than 4 m ........................................................... 3

2(1) Stamens 3-8; glands present at base of leaf blade ........................ ........................ *S. lucida* ssp. *lasiandra*
2 Stamens 2; glands absent at base of leaf blade ....... *S. scouleriana*

3(1) Ovary and capsule short- or long-hairy ........................ 4
3 Ovary and capsule smooth ........................ 9

4(3) Leaves glaucous and often with short, reddish hairs on the underside ........................ *S. scouleriana*
4 Leaves not glaucous below; hairs, if present, not reddish ............ 5

5(4) One stamen; leaves obovate ........................ *S. sitchensis*
5 Stamens two; leaves lanceolate ........................ 6

6(5) Stigma elongated, 0.5-1 mm long ........................ 7
6 Stigma shorter, 0.2-0.5 mm long ........................ 8

7(6) Young twigs hairless; leaves hairless at maturity; catkins developing before of along with the leaves ................ *S. planifolia*
7 Young twigs with long, loose hairs; leaves with hairs at maturity, especially beneath; catkins developing after the leaves ............... ........................ *S. sessilifolia*
8(6) Male catkins 2-3 cm long; female catkins 2-6 cm long ................. ........................ *S. drummondiana*
8 Male catkins 0.5-1.5 cm long; female catkins 1-2.5 cm long .......... ........................ *S. geyeriana*

9(3) Low shrub, less than 1 m; growing in sphagnum bogs ................. ........................ *S. pedicillaris*
9 Shrub, greater than 1 m; not confined to bogs . ........................10

10(9) Subalpine shrub; young twigs dark ........................ *S. barclayi*
10 Middle elevation shrubs; young twigs light ...................... *S. piperi*

### *Salix barclayi* Anderss.—BARCLAY'S WILLOW

This shrub is composed of many spreading 1-3 m long branches. The 2-5 cm long leaves are oval to obovate in shape, silky-hairy when first opened but becoming smooth with age, glaucous beneath, with fine gland-tipped teeth on the margins. The 2-3 cm long catkins appear after the leaves have begun to open. There are 2 stamens and the style is 1-1.5 mm long. The 6-8 cm long capsule is smooth.

A subalpine willow of stream banks and open places, a large community was found by the authors along the Round-the-Mountain trail on the southwest side of the mountain at 6,200 feet, in wet places on the Avalanche Glacier debris fall. It is also known from Suksdorf collections at Hellroaring Canyon and on the northwest side.

### *Salix drummondiana* Baratt *ex* Hook.—DRUMMOND'S WILLOW

A shrub to 3 m tall, the new twigs of this willow become glaucous the first year and gradually fade. The leaf stalks are 4-10 mm long and the leaves are simple with rolled back margins, densely hairy beneath and with short, matted hairs. The leaves are broadly elliptic to lanceolate in shape, range from 4-9 cm in length, and are wider than long. The racemes are stalkless, lack bracts at the base, and the scales are blackish and long-hairy. The male catkins are about 2-3 cm long, with 2 stamens, and the female catkins are 2-6 cm long. The 3-6 mm long capsules are densely short-hairy, on short stalks.

Found along stream banks and moist meadows, this species is rare at the mountain. It was collected by Flett on the upper Klickitat River.

### *Salix geyeriana* Anderss.—GEYER'S WILLOW

Smooth, glaucous twigs and narrowly oblanceolate leaves distinguish this 3 m tall subalpine species. The 5-10 cm long leaves are toothless, tapered at the tip, dark green above and glaucous beneath, with silky white hairs. The stipules are small and obscure. The 1 cm long rounded catkins appear with the leaves. There are 2 stamens and the style is only about 0.2 mm long. The 5-6 mm long capsule is short-hairy.

Rare at the mountain, this species is known from a Suksdorf collection on the Klickitat River, east of Mount Adams.

### *Salix lucida* Muhl. ssp. *lasiandra* (Benth.) E. Murr.<br>PACIFIC WILLOW

Treelike, this willow may reach 10 m or more in height and has a slender crown and fissured, yellowish-brown bark. The young twigs are yellowish. The lanceolate leaves have a long, slender tip and are green and shiny above, glaucous beneath. They are finely toothed on the margins, while the leaf stalks are characterized by prominent glands. The 2-9 cm long catkins appear with the leaves. There are 5-9 stamens and the short style is about 0.1 mm long. The 5-7 mm long capsule is smooth.

A middle elevation streamside willow, large thickets can be found along the west shore of Council Lake on the west side of Mount Adams. The rest of the study area is probably too high to permit the occurrence of this species.

### *Salix pedicellaris* Pursh—BOG WILLOW

A slender, small, and thinly branched willow from 4-12 dm tall, this species bears hairless, dark twigs, and lacks stipules. The leaf blades are silky at first but then become smooth; they are short-stalked, pale, and glaucous beneath, elliptic to obovate and 1-6 cm long, and broadest above the middle. The catkins are borne on lateral branches with small leaves. The scales are yellowish and hairy near the tip. The 1-2 cm long male catkins are slender and the female catkins are 1-3 cm long at maturity. The style is very short and stout.

Found in bogs and boggy meadows where sphagnum is present, this is a relatively common middle elevation to lower subalpine species at the mountain. It grows at Foggy Flat at 6,100 feet, but is typically more common at lower elevations. Sites include Babyshoe, Grand, and Muddy Meadows, King Mountain, and Crofton Butte, with elevations ranging from 4,250 to 4,800 feet at these sites.

### *Salix piperi* Bebb—PIPER'S WILLOW

This 3-6 m tall, middle elevation willow forms thickets along streams and rivers. The 6-12 cm long leaves are oblanceolate to obovate, green and shiny above while glaucous beneath, and coarsely toothed. The leaves appear after the catkins. The male catkins are 3-5 mm long, with 2 stamens per flower. The female catkins range from 4-10 cm long, with the style only about 1 mm long. The 6-7 mm long capsule is smooth or only sparsely hairy.

The PLANTS Database of the U.S. Department of Agriculture synonymizes *P. piperi* with *P. hookeriana*. However, a review of plants at the University of Washington herbarium shows that plants first determined to be *S. piperi* appear to differ consistently from those first determined to be *S. hookeriana*, so the distinction cited in Hitchcock's treatment of *Salix* is used here. Nelsa Buckingham, in her *Flora of the Olympic Peninsula* (1995) reached the same conclusion and maintained the two species.

Rare at the mountain, this species was collected by the authors at King Mountain at 4,200 feet.

### *Salix planifolia* Pursh—TEA-LEAVED WILLOW

A small shrub less than 1 m in height, this willow bears erect branches. The twigs are smooth and the 3-6 cm long leaves elliptical to narrowly obovate, toothless, silky when young and dark green above at maturity while glaucous beneath. The stipules are very small or sometimes absent. The catkins are 3 cm long, appearing before the leaves. There are 2 stamens and the style is 1-1.5 mm long; the capsule is silvery in appearance from dense, short hairs.

Growing on rocky subalpine slopes, this rare species is known from Suksdorf collections, one taken at the "cliffs in Bird Creek Canyon."

### *Salix scouleriana* Barratt *ex* Hook.—SCOULER'S WILLOW

Typically a shrub although sometimes reaching the size and stature of a small tree, this willow ranges from 4-10 m in height, and is characterized by gray bark and hairy twigs. The leaves vary widely in shape, ranging from elliptical to oblanceolate, rounded or pointed at the tip, toothless or sometimes with irregular teeth on the margin, and 3-8 cm long. The upper surface of the leaves is smooth and dark green and the lower surface is short-hairy and glaucous. The 2-5 cm long catkins appear before the leaves. There are 2 stamens and the style is less than 0.5 mm long. The 7-9 mm long capsule is covered with silky hairs.

A wetland species, this is an uncommon willow at the mountain. It is known from a modern collection made by Paul Slichter on the southeast side of Mount Adams, near the DNR quarry at about 4,100 feet.

### *Salix sessilifolia* Nutt.—NORTHWEST SANDBAR WILLOW

A tall and vigorous shrub, this willow forms thickets alongside ditches and small streams at about 4,000 feet. It has multiple ascending stems that are up to 10 cm in diameter; the new twigs are dark but overlain by short, flat, silvery hairs that wear away later in the season. The stipules are very small. The leaves are notably long and narrow, from nearly linear to linear-lanceolate, and 10-15 cm long. Also notable are the catkins: the female catkins are slender, pendulous, and up to 10 cm long, appearing after the leaves have begun to unfurl. Male plants of this species were not found in the study area.

In Hitchcock and Cronquist (1973), these plants key out as *Salix fluviatilis*, but recent studies suggest that the latter species is of hybrid origin and that the name *S. sessilifolia* is to be preferred (see Brunsfeld et al, 1991, and Dorn, 1998).

This willow forms thickets that line roadside ditches and small streams on the west side of Mount Adams, especially along Road 8810 on the way to Grand Meadow.

### *Salix sitchensis* Sanson *ex* Bong.—SITKA WILLOW

This 2-5 m tall shrubby willow bears smooth and glaucous twigs. The leaves are hairy when young and become dark green and smooth on the upper surface while remaining densely silvery-hairy on the lower. They are 5-10 cm long, obovate to more or less spoon-shaped, and typically finely toothed. The 2-8 cm long catkins appear at the same time as the leaves; there is 1 stamen and the style is less than 0.5 mm long. The 4-6 mm long capsule is silky.

The most common willow at Mount Adams, Sitka willow is found along streams and wet meadow borders, typically at middle elevations although sometimes higher. It grows near Takhlakh Lake in inundated meadows, near Ollalie Lake, at Midway Meadows, and alongside Roads 034 and 23. It is also known from a Suksdorf collection at Hellroaring Canyon.

## Saxifragaceae

### Saxifragaceae Juss.—SAXIFRAGE FAMILY

A diverse family at Mount Adams, as elsewhere in the Cascades, these are all perennial herbs and conspicuous members of forest, meadow, and alpine communities. Often they have a basal rosette of leaves while the flowering stem is leafless or has leaves or bracts of reduced size. The parts of the flower are arranged on a structure called a hypanthium: the 5 sepals are partly fused into a cup which partially encloses the ovary. The 5 petals and 5-10 stamens are attached to the hypanthium, encircling the 2 styles (3 in *Lithophragma*). The fruit is a capsule or a set of paired follicles.

| | |
|---|---|
| 1 | One flower per stem; stamens 5 .............................. *Parnassia* |
| 1 | Several to many flowers per stem; stamens 5 or 10 .................. 2 |
| 2(1) | Stamens 5 .......................................................................... 3 |
| 2 | Stamens 10 ........................................................................ 6 |
| 3(2) | Leaves kidney-shaped, deeply divided into rounded segments; stems leafy, the leaves of the stem only a little smaller than the basal leaves ...................................................... *Suksdorfia* |
| 3 | Stems leafless or with 1 or 2 much-reduced leaves or a few bracts . ......................................................................................... 4 |
| 4(3) | Petals not toothed, longer than the sepals ................... *Heuchera* |
| 4 | Petals toothed, relative length various .................................. 5 |
| 5(4) | Petals as long as sepals ............................................ *Elmera* |
| 5 | Petals longer than the sepals ....................................... *Mitella* |
| 6(2) | Styles 3 ....................................................... *Lithophragma* |
| 6 | Styles 2 .............................................................................. 7 |
| 7(6) | Leaves evergreen, leathery, thick, and hairless .......... *Leptarrhena* |
| 7 | Leaves deciduous or persistent but not leathery, thin to thickish, usually with hairs ............................................................ 8 |
| 8(7) | Mature fruit with 2 valves of very unequal in size; petals very slender, obscure ....................................................... *Tiarella* |
| 8 | Valves of mature fruit of equal size; petals relatively wide and conspicuous ...................................................... *Saxifraga* |

#### *Elmera* Rydb.—ELMERA

#### *Elmera racemosa* (S. Wats.) Rydb. var. *racemosa*
#### YELLOW CORALBELLS

Long-stalked basal leaves borne on a creeping rootstock define this compact plant. Rounded to kidney-shaped, the glandular-hairy leaf blades are 3-6 cm broad, and have shallow, rounded teeth. The flowers are borne in racemes on slender glandular-hairy stems 10-25 cm tall with 1-2 leaves. The fused sepals create a barrel-shaped calyx, yellowish green in color; the 3-4 mm long petals are white, with 3-7 teeth at the tip and about as long as the free calyx lobes.

Known from two Suksdorf collections at Hellroaring Canyon, this is a species of open, stony slopes and rocky crevices but can also be seen in the upper portion of Bird Creek Meadows.

### *Heuchera* L.—ALUMROOT

Mostly coarse plants, with a tuft of basal leaves rising from a thickened, vertical rootstock, the heucheras are characteristic plants of rocky, exposed places in forests and in the subalpine. The leaves are rounded to ovate, shallowly toothed, and more or less lobed. Small flowers are arranged in panicles on leafless stems. The petals are white, slender, and untoothed – a useful way to distinguish them from the otherwise similar *Elmera racemosa.*

| | |
|---|---|
| 1 | Stamens shorter than calyx; flowers in tight panicles .......................................................................... *H. cylindrica* var. *alpina* |
| 1 | Stamens protruding; flowers in loose panicles .......................... 2 |
| 2(1) | Flowering stem hairless at the base; leaf stalks hairless .............................................................................................. *H. glabra* |
| 2 | Flowering stem and leaf stalks hairy throughout ................................................................................ *H. micrantha* var. *diversifolia* |

### *Heuchera cylindrica* Dougl. *ex* Hook. var. *alpina* Sw. ALPINE ALUMROOT

A robust perennial with a branching crown atop short and thick creeping rootstocks, the leaf blades are 1-2.5 cm broad, ovate and somewhat longer than wide. The flowering stems range widely in height, from 15-90 cm; both stems and leaves are glandular-pubescent. The cream-colored to greenish-yellow, tubular flowers are carried on an open panicle 3-12 cm long.

Growing in the subalpine to alpine environment, this plant has been found at Hellroaring Creek and on the summit of Little Mount Adams; there is Suksdorf collection made at 7,000 feet in 1881 on the south side of the mountain, probably on his first trip to so high an elevation at Mount Adams.

### *Heuchera glabra* Willd. ex Roem. & Schult.—SMOOTH ALUMROOT

A basal set of leaves create a tufted plant with several 15-60 cm tall flowering stems; both stems and leaves are hairless. The heart-shaped leaves are about 10 cm broad and feature palmate and shallow, sharply toothed lobes. The flowers are clustered toward the tips of the spreading branches. White and 2.5-3 mm long, the petals are 2-4 times as long as the sepals and are not toothed.

Found on the west side of Mount Adams along the Lewis River and on roadcuts alongside Road 23, this is a moisture loving plant with a potentially wide elevational range.

### *Heuchera micrantha* Dougl. ex Lindl. var. *diversifolia* (Rydb.) Rosend. Butters & Lakela—CREVICE ALUMROOT

Growing from a heavy rootstock, this species has densely long-hairy leaf stalks and stems. The numerous flowering stems are 15-60 cm tall; open, plumelike panicles of small flowers with white petals only 2-2.5 mm long are similar to those of *H. glabra.* The branches of the inflorescence are glandular.

Collected by the authors alongside Road 23 at 4,000 feet as well as known from a poorly-documented Flett collection, this is an uncommon *Heuchera* at the mountain.

## *Leptarrhena* R. Br.—FALSE SAXIFRAGE

### *Leptarrhena pyrolifolia* (D. Don) R. Br. *ex* Ser. in DC. LEATHERLEAF SAXIFRAGE

Rosettes of deep green, nearly stalkless evergreen leaves distinguish this saxifrage. The oblong leaves are 2-10 cm long, glossy on top, with rounded teeth on the margin. The reddish stems have 1 or 2 small leaves and are 20-40 cm tall; they are topped with a small cluster of white flowers. A reddish calyx of partially fused sepals extends more than ½ the length of the petals. The fruit is a pair of highly visible purplish-red follicles.

This species is encountered most frequently in middle elevation wetlands on the north and northwest sides of Mount Adams, including Takhlakh Lake, Babyshoe Meadow, and Muddy Meadows. It also colonizes wet places at roadsides.

## *Lithophragma* (Nutt.) Torr. & A. Gray—WOODLAND-STAR

### *Lithophragma parviflorum* (Hook.) Nutt. *ex* Torr. & A. Gray var. *parviflorum*—SMALL WOODLAND-STAR

Basal leaves on 2-6 cm long stalks with blades 1-3 cm long, divided into 5 segments that are two or three-times cleft and lobed, distinguish this species. The stems are 10-30 cm tall, glandular and pubescent and purplish in color. The racemes may reach 15 cm in length and consist of 5 to 11 flowers with erect pedicels; the calyx is cone-shaped. The 5-10 mm long flowers are white to pinkish, the blade 3-cleft and narrowing to a slender claw.

This delicate and appealing, but uncommon, species was found at the DNR quarry on the southeast side, growing among grasses in a grove of *Quercus garryana*. It is typically a species of open sagebrush desert and lower forests that become very dry by early summer.

### *Mitella* L. – MITREWORT

These delicate plants grow from rootstocks. The leaves are basal, long-stalked, and heart-shaped where the blade joins the stalk. The stems are leafless, and the flowers are in a raceme. The broad, shallow calyx has 5 widely spreading lobes and the 5 stamens are borne on very short filaments on a disk surrounding the ovary, set within the bowl-like calyx. The greenish petals of two of the species are threadlike and pinnately divided, resembling the teeth of a comb. The fruit is a capsule.

| | | |
|---|---|---|
| 1 | Petals white, with 3 teeth at the tip ................. | *M. trifida* var. *trifida* |
| 1 | Petals greenish, pinnately divided into 5-9 threadlike segments ... | 2 |
| 2(1) | Stamens alternate with the sepals and opposite the petals; calyx lobes broadly pointed in outline ............................ | *M. pentandra* |
| 2 | Stamens opposite the sepals and alternate with the petals; calyx lobes rounded in outline ...................................................... | 3 |
| 3(2) | Leaves round in outline .......................................... | *M. breweri* |
| 3 | Leaves egg-shaped in outline .................................... | *M. ovalis* |

#### *Mitella breweri* A. Gray—BREWER'S MITREWORT

The round-to-kidney shaped leaves are 3-8 cm across on this mitrewort, scalloped on the margins and wrinkled. The flowering stem is 10-20 cm tall and glandular. Greenish petals are divided into 3-6 segments turned upwards and are 1.5-2 mm long.

Cosmopolitan but not particularly common in middle to subalpine locations where it favors meadow edges and moist openings in forests, this species grows at Midway Meadows on the north and fringes wet meadows and ponds along the Pacific Crest Trail on the west.

#### *Mitella ovalis* Greene—COASTAL MITREWORT

Similar to the common *Mitella pentandra* in overall appearance, this species has markedly hairy leaves and stems. The hairs on the flowering stems and stalks of the leaves point downwards; the leaf blade is up to 3 cm long and seems to be less sharply toothed than *M. pentandra*. The major difference in the species is seen in the flowers: in *M. ovalis*, each stamen is placed upon a lobe of the calyx and, therefore, in between the adjacent petals. The petals are threadlike, 1.5 mm long, greenish, and divided into 3-5 segments. The calyx lobes are broadly rounded.

The only collection known of this species at Mount Adams was made by Henderson, at an unspecified location, but on a day when he was on the north and northeast sides. In the herbarium at the University of Washington, this specimen was annotated by an unknown person as *M. ovalis* and is on a sheet with *M. pentandra*. The top of the flowering stem was broken and lost at some time in the past (it was present when the sheet was treated, decades ago, with mercuric chloride). It was possible to dissect the single flower bud on a rudimentary stem at the base of the plant to see the key features of *M. ovalis*.

This species is usually found in moist coastal forests and wooded bottomlands. Its occurrence at Mount Adams is unusual.

### *Mitella pentandra* Hook.—ALPINE MITREWORT

As much as 8 cm in length, the leaves of this mitrewort are broadly ovate, longer than broad, shallowly toothed, and obscurely lobed. The leafless flowering stems are 10-30 cm tall, with a raceme of greenish flowers whose petals are divided into 7 or 9 segments, rather comb-like.

Collected along Road 23 on the west side, this common species was also collected by Suksdorf at Hellroaring Canyon. It grows in moist places in closed to open forests and at streamsides, reaching about 5,000 feet. Despite the common name, it does not reach above the subalpine at Mount Adams.

### *Mitella trifida* Graham var. *trifida*—PACIFIC MITREWORT

Smaller than the other *Mitella* species, this plant bears leaves 2-4 cm long and equally wide, bluntly toothed, and with obscure and rounded lobes. A stem 15-30 cm tall bears white flowers. The petals and sepals are about equal in length, reaching 2 mm, and are divided into 3 blunt teeth at their tips.

This plant was observed by the authors on the south and southeast sides of the mountain alongside the road to King Mountain, and on the South Climb route. It is also found at 4,000 feet alongside Road 782. It prefers more or less open, rocky places in forests.

## *Parnassia* L.—GRASS-OF-PARNASSUS

### *Parnassia fimbriata* Koenig var. *fimbriata*<br>FRINGED GRASS-OF-PARNASSUS

Distinguished by both leaves and flowers, this hairless plant has a short rootstock. The 2-6 cm broad, untoothed, kidney-shaped leaves are borne on slender stalks. A small leaf at the middle of the 20-40 cm tall flowering stem is also distinctive; on top a single flower 8-12 mm long has 5 rounded petals, each with a clawlike base. The claw of the petal is heavily fringed on the margin. There are 5 fertile stamens and 5 sterile staminodia, the latter short and fleshy, with 5-9 blunt teeth. The overall appearance is highly exotic, creating the appearance of a fringe on the surface of each petal.

This species grows above 4,500 feet in wet meadows and on streambanks, in sunny to partly shaded places. It was collected by Suksdorf on the southeast side of the mountain. It was also observed near the east fork of Adams Creek alongside Road 2329 on the north.

At Mount Hood, the very similar variety *hoodiana* is found. It differs in having staminodia with slender lobes, each with a ball-like tip. Despite the proximity, it has never been found at Mount Adams.

## *Saxifraga* L.—SAXIFRAGE

A genus with many species and well-represented at the mountain, all are perennial herbs. The leaves are primarily basal, although the flowering stems may bear a few small alternate leaves or leaflike bracts. The flowers are typically solitary and borne in cymes or panicles; in some species (*S. ferruginea*) they are slightly irregular. There are 5 prominent petals and the ovary is superior to slightly inferior, composed of 2 nearly distinct chambers. There are 10 stamens, sometimes showy with expanded filaments. The fruit is a capsule or follicle.

1 Leaves rounded in outline, coarsely toothed and on slender stalks ........ 2

1 Leaves longer than broad, stalked or not, even to shallowly toothed ........ 4

2(1) Teeth of the leaves doubly (or irregularly) toothed; leaf stalks hairy; some of the flowers usually replaced by plantlets .... *S. mertensiana*

2 Teeth of the leaves simple (once-toothed); leaf stalks hairless; no flowers replaced by plantlets ........ 3

3(2) Petals nearly round; inflorescence glandular-hairy ........ *S. odontoloma*

3 Petals elliptical; inflorescence with long hairs, not glandular ........ *S. nelsoniana* ssp. *cascadensis*

4(1) Leaves evergreen, not toothed, to 10 mm long ........ 5

4 Leaves deciduous, toothed (sometimes untoothed in *S. nidifica*), mostly more than 20 mm long ........ 7

5(4) Leaves hairless or with a few hairs on the margin toward the base; petals white ........ *S. tolmiei*

5 Leaves with hairs along the margins; petals white with purplish to orangish spots ........ 6

6(5) Leaves lanceolate, pointed; hairs on the leaf margin coarse, relatively few .......................... *S. bronchialis* ssp. *austromontana*

6 Leaves spoon-shaped, rounded at the tip; marginal hairs slender, many ........................................ *S. bronchialis* ssp. *vespertina*

7 F flowers often replaced by plantlets; petals, when present, with a lanceolate blade tapered to a slender claw ............................... ................................................... *S. ferruginea* var. *vreelandii*

7(4) Flowers not replaced by plantlets; petals blade often rounded, with an indistinct claw .............................................................. 8

8(7) Leaves serrate; plants to 25 cm tall ...................... *S. occidentalis*

8 Leaves entire or with small teeth; plants more than 30 cm tall ...... 9

9(8) Flowering stems 30-120 cm tall, inflorescence elongated, to 10 cm long .............................................................. *S. oregana*

9 Flowering stems less than 30 cm tall; inflorescence compact, less than 10 cm long ............................................................ 10

10(9) Leaves hairy along the edges and usually on the surfaces; leaf stalk poorly-defined and tapering to the crown .......... *S. integrifolia*

10 Leaves hairless, or with a few marginal hairs; leaf stalk well defined .................................................... *S. nidifica* var. *claytoniifolia*

**_Saxifraga bronchialis_ L. ssp. _austromontana_ (Wiegand) Piper**
**YELLOW-DOT SAXIFRAGE**

This is a tufted plant with evergreen leaves densely packed on short spreading stems. Dead, brown leaves remain on the lower stems. The lanceolate, 1-1.5 cm long leaves are more than 4 times as long as broad; they are tapered to a sharp tip, untoothed, and fringed with coarse hairs less than .3 mm long. The 10-20 cm tall flowering stems have several narrow leaves along their length and spread widely into several branches. The white petals are 5-6 mm long and have yellow or orange spots.

A subalpine species of rocky sites, this subspecies is found on the south and east sides of the mountain, including Hellroaring Creek and between Klickitat and Rusk Glaciers, growing in crevices and other protected places among rocks.

**_Saxifraga bronchialis_ L. ssp. _vespertina_ (Small) Piper**
**YELLOW-DOT SAXIFRAGE**

This subspecies differs from *austromontana* in having leaves less than 1 cm in length that are broadest at the tip. They are fringed with hairs that range from 0.3-0.5 mm in length. The petals are 4-5 mm long.

This uncommon subspecies is known from a single 1892 Henderson collection on the west side, probably high up on Killen Creek.

### *Saxifraga ferruginea* Graham var. *vreelandii* (Small) Engl. & Irmsch RUSTY SAXIFRAGE

The basal leaves of this saxifrage are wedge-to-spoon shaped, tapering gradually to the stalk, and 3-6 cm long; they have a few broad teeth above the middle. The glandular-hairy flowering stems range from 10-30 cm in length. The flowers are somewhat irregular, with 3 larger upper petals 4-6 mm long, more truncate at the base than the 2 elliptic lower petals. There are 2 yellow spots at the base of the upper petals. The flowers may be replaced by small, bulblike plantlets.

Also known as S. *ferruginea* var. *macounii*, this is a middle elevation to subalpine subspecies with a wet habitat preference, although it is also found in places that become quite dry by late summer. It is cosmopolitan at the mountain with collections from Hellroaring Creek, Bird Creek Meadows, and alongside Road 2329 at a lava flow.

### *Saxifraga integrifolia* Hook.—WHOLE-LEAF SAXIFRAGE

Rising from rhizomes or cormlike propagules, the single stems of this small saxifrage are 10-30 cm tall, and glandular-hairy in the upper half. The 2-4 cm leaves are 1-2 cm broad, hairy below, and usually untoothed; they often have bulblets in their axils. The calyx is conical with 1-2 mm long oblong-lanceolate lobes. The petals are greenish-white or yellowish, and oval to rounded in shape; they are usually 2-3 mm long (although sometimes smaller), and narrow abruptly to a clawed base. The 3.5-5 mm long follicles are reddish or purplish.

A subalpine species, this saxifrage is known from Suksdorf collections at Bird Creek Meadows and Hellroaring Canyon, growing in sunny, wet places above 5,000 feet.

### *Saxifraga mertensiana* Bong.—MERTENS'S SAXIFRAGE

This is a low-growing plant with rounded leaves that are kidney-shaped at their base. They are 3-10 cm broad, thick, and sparsely hairy, and divided into shallow, blunt lobes. The lobes have small teeth; the leaf stalks are hairy. Arranged in a loose panicle, the white flowers, with 3-4 mm long petals, are borne on slender, glandular branches. Often a few are replaced by tiny plantlets.

This uncommon species is known from a single Suksdorf collection at Hellroaring Canyon on the southeast side. It is easily confused with *S. nelsoniana*.

## Saxifragaceae

### *Saxifraga nelsoniana* D. Don ssp. *cascadensis* (Calder & Savile) Hultén—CASCADE SAXIFRAGE

Resembling *S. mertensiana,* the leaves of this saxifrage are singly-toothed on the margin and 3-7 cm broad; they are borne on hairless leaf stalks. The branches of the inflorescence are long-hairy, and the flowers are not replaced by plantlets. The oval, white, spotless petals are 3-4 mm long.

This species was collected by the authors alongside Road 23 in a wet culvert at 4,000 feet and also at Hellroaring Canyon at an unrecorded elevation. Elsewhere in the Cascades, it is very common along subalpine streams, to 6,000 feet.

### *Saxifraga nidifica* Greene var. *claytoniifolia* (Canby *ex* Small) Elvander PEAK SAXIFRAGE

Similar to *S. integrifolia,* and once considered a variety of that species, this saxifrage has distinctive leaves: they are up to 6 cm long, with a well-marked blade and sharply contracted leaf stalk. The leaves are also hairless, or, at most, have short hairs along the margin. The petals are 1-2 mm long, about equal in length to the sepals.

A species of the east and southeast sides of Mount Adams, it was collected made by Flett at Klickitat Meadows.

### *Saxifraga occidentalis* S. Wats.—WESTERN SAXIFRAGE

Twice as long as broad, the 4-8 cm long, oval to ovate leaves distinguish this saxifrage. The leaves are shallowly toothed and taper gradually to a broad stalk; young leaves are reddish-hairy on the underside. Glandular-hairy, the flowering stems vary from 5-20 cm in height. The inflorescence may by small and rounded or expanded to a pyramid-like shape. White, oval petals are 3-4 mm long, and the filaments of the stamens are slightly expanded.

This uncommon saxifrage is known from a single Suksdorf collection at Hellroaring Canyon, made at an unrecorded elevation.

### *Saxifraga odontoloma* Piper—BROOK SAXIFRAGE

This saxifrage is similar to both *S. mertensiana* and *S. nelsoniana;* like that latter, it is once-toothed, but has broader leaves (up to 8 cm). The branches of the inflorescence are minutely glandular. The round petals are 2-3 mm long, borne on a short stalk, and have 2 yellow spots at their bases.

This species is known from a single Suksdorf collection at Hellroaring Canyon.

### *Saxifraga oregana* T.J. Howell—OREGON SAXIFRAGE

The largest of the *Saxifraga* genus at Mount Adams, the 30-120 cm tall flowering stems of this erect perennial are glandular and hairy on the upper part. The oblanceolate to elliptic leaves are 10-20 cm long and contracted to a winged 3-6 cm petiole. A long, glandular-hairy, rather open inflorescence may reach 20-40 cm when in fruit; the petals of the flowers are white to greenish-white, 2-4 mm long, and half as broad. They are rounded, with awl-shaped filaments.

A common middle elevation to subalpine species, this saxifrage has been located at Hellroaring Canyon, Midway Meadows, near Bench Lake, and east of Little Mount Adams in the upper reach of Island Springs Creek. It grows in open meadows that remain wet through most or all of the summer but is absent from sphagnum meadows.

#### ***Saxifraga tolmiei*** **Torr. & A. Gray—TOLMIE'S SAXIFRAGE**

Short branches crowded with deep green leaves create a mat-forming plant of the subalpine and alpine regions. The 2-10 mm long leaves are alternate on the stems, cigar to spoon-shaped, thick, inrolled, and typically hairless, although there may be a few long hairs near their bases. Flowering stems 2-8 cm tall are usually leafless and bear 1-3 flowers on each. The white, oblanceolate petals are 5-6 mm long. Expanded filaments of the stamens appear nearly petal-like, giving an impression that this saxifrage has 10 petals. The plants are fragile, and broken pieces easily take root, allowing the species to colonize disturbed environments.

High elevation rocky sites are a favorite place for this little plant, which tends to grow in crevices and may be quite extensive. It is relatively common on the South Climb trail, found at elevations greater than 7,500 feet.

### ***Suksdorfia*** **A. Gray—SUKSDORFIA**

#### ***Suksdorfia ranunculifolia*** **(Hook.) Engl.—BUTTERCUP SUKSDORFIA**

The genus differs from the similar saxifrages by having 5 stamens. Bulblets may occasionally form in the axils of the leaves or along the rootstock. Fan-shaped leaves on long stalks are divided into 3 major lobes, each with 3 or 4 teeth. A flat-topped panicle tops a leafy, 10-30 cm tall stem. The petals are white or purplish-tinged at the base and 6-7 cm long; the triangular sepals are very glandular.

Known from a Suksdorf and a Flett collection, made on the east and southeast sides of Mount Adams, where it reaches 7,000 feet, this is a middle elevation to subalpine species of damp habitats, including those that dry out in summer.

### *Tiarella* L.—FOAMFLOWER

#### *Tiarella trifoliata* L. var. *unifoliata* (Hook.) Kurtz. FOAMFLOWER, COOLWORT

Forest plants of middle elevations, a few basal leaves and leafy stems rise from creeping rootstocks; both stems and leaves are short-hairy. The palmately lobed leaves are toothed, shallowly divided, and 3-8 cm broad. Stems 15-40 cm tall bear 1-3 smaller leaves. The flowers are configured in a narrow, loose panicle. The white petals are 2-3 mm long, and the sepals are nearly white also. There are 10 stamens; the capsule is divided into 2, unequally sized segments.

Unambiguous specimens of *T. trifoliata* var. *trifoliata,* with each leaf fully divided into three lobes, are not known at Mount Adams, although some plants of var. *unifoliata* exhibit deeply lobed leaves.

Cosmopolitan, this middle elevation to subalpine woodland species is also found at the edges of Muddy Meadows and Swampy Meadows.

## Scrophulariaceae Juss.—FIGWORT FAMILY

Some of the most conspicuous wildflowers at Mount Adams are members of the figwort family, including louseworts, monkeyflowers, paintbrushes, and penstemons. A few weedy annuals or biennials are present, but most species are perennial herbs, at most slightly woody at the base in some penstemons. The flowers are in racemes or solitary in the leaf axils and most are irregular to bilabiate, with an upper lip of two fused petals and the lower lip of three. In two genera, *Castilleja* and *Pedicularis,* the upper two lobes of the corolla are fused into a unique structure called a galea that covers and enfolds the stamens; the lower three lobes form a shorter lip. Fertile stamens typically number 2 or 4. In some genera, a fifth sterile filament or scale, called a staminode, is present. The fruit is a capsule containing numerous, small, seeds.

1 Stamens with anthers 5; corolla nearly regular ............ *Verbascum*
1 Stamens with anthers 2 or 4 (a 5th sterile filament may be present); corolla somewhat to strongly 2-lipped .................................... 2

2(1) Leaves alternate ............................................................ 3
2 Leaves opposite ............................................................ 5

3(2) Corolla spurred at the base, galea absent; uncommon weed ......... ............................................................ *Linaria*
3 Corolla not spurred; the upper lip (galea) enclosing the anthers; common native plants ........................................................ 4

4(3) Calyx lobes 5 (except in *P. racemosa* which has a down-curved galea); lower lip of the corolla evident ........................ *Pedicularis*
4 Calyx lobes 2 or 4; lower lip of corolla very reduced in size, greenish ............................................................... *Castilleja*

5(2) Stamens 2; the 2 lobes of the upper lip fused to form a single wide, flat lobe (the corolla thus appearing to be 4-lobed) .......... *Veronica*
5 Stamens 4 (a fifth may be present as a sterile filament or scale); upper lip of the corolla with 2 lobes which may be free or more or less fused, but not appearing to be a single, flat lobe ................ 6

6(5) Stems square in cross-section; sterile stamen represented by a scale ............................................................... *Scrophularia*
6 Stems round in cross-section; sterile stamen a slender filament, or absent .................................................................................. 7

7(6) Lobes of the calyx free or united only at the base; fifth stamen present as a sterile filament ................................................ 8
7 Lobes of the calyx united to form a tube (rather short in *Collinsia*); sterile stamen absent ........................................................ 9

8(7) Filaments of the stamens short hairy at their bases; plants at least 30 cm tall, leaves toothed and anthers wooly .......... *Nothochelone*
8 Filaments hairless at their bases; other features not as combined above ................................................................ *Penstemon*

9(7) Corolla bright yellow or rose-pink; calyx tube strongly angled ......... ......................................................................... *Mimulus*
9 Upper lip of corolla whitish, the lower blue or whitish; calyx tube at most weakly angled ....................................................... 10

10(9) Lower corolla lobe whitish, marked with purple lines; leaves toothed ..................................................................... *Euphrasia*
10 Lower corolla lobe blue; leaves not toothed ................... *Collinsia*

## *Castilleja* Mutis *ex* L. f.—PAINTBRUSH

The brightly colored bracts of paintbrushes add a warm color to subalpine meadows throughout the summer season. The showy, reddish *C. suksdorfii,* in particular, and the magenta *C. parviflora,* are quite common at the mountain. The yellow-tinged *C. thompsonii* is less noticeable. The plants are typically unbranched, although there may be several stems arising from a woody rootstock. The leaves are alternate, undivided or lobed, and stalkless. The flowers are borne in racemes or spikes, with the colorful bracts more conspicuous than the true flowers. The calyx, also brightly colored, is 4-lobed, forming a tube that mostly includes the corolla. The corolla itself is essentially green and 2-lipped.

## Scrophulariaceae

The upper lip (the galea) is beaklike, with its 2 lobes uniting to form a hood over the stamens; the lower lip is usually shorter and obscurely petal-like or 3-toothed. There are 4 stamens.

Paintbrushes are known as "hemiparasites," a term that refers to plants with specialized roots that enable them to obtain part of their nutrient requirements from the roots of other plants.

| | |
|---|---|
| 1 | Corolla whitish to yellowish, tube less than 2 cm; galea short, scarcely exceeding the lower lip .......................................... 2 |
| 1 | Corolla orange to red to rose-purple; galea long, slender ........... 3 |
| 2(1) | Inflorescence glandular, with long, unmatted hairs; calyx divided half-way into 4 lobes ................................. *C. pilosa* var. *pilosa* |
| 2 | Inflorescence not glandular, hairs otherwise; calyx divided less than half-way ........................................................ *C. thompsonii* |
| 3(1) | Leaves not divided; bracts not divided or with 2 short lateral teeth at the apex ............................................ *C. miniata* ssp. *miniata* |
| 3 | Leaves and bracts deeply divided into 2-6 spreading lobes ......... 4 |
| 4(3) | Plants with rough, stiff hairs ...................... *C. hispida* ssp. *hispida* |
| 4 | Plants with long, soft, tangled hairs ........................................ 5 |
| 5(4) | Stems numerous, arising from a woody base; corolla and bracts rose-purple ...................................... *C. parviflora* var. *oreopola* |
| 5 | Stems single, from a slender, creeping rootstock ....... *C. suksdorfii* |

### ***Castilleja hispida*** **Benth. ssp.** ***hispida*****—HARSH PAINTBRUSH**

An eye-catching paintbrush, this species is distinguished by roughly hairy stems 30-50 cm tall. The broadly lanceolate leaves are 2.5-5 cm long, mostly 3-5 lobed and covered with long, soft, more or less straight hairs. The 3-5 lobed calyx is scarlet, but occasionally yellow or orange, particularly at drier sites. The corolla is 25-30 mm long and the galea 10-15 mm.

Found in low to middle elevations along roadsides, and in generally dry habitats, this is a relatively uncommon paintbrush at Mount Adams. It was found by Suksdorf in lower Bird Creek meadows and in Hellroaring Canyon.

### ***Castilleja miniata*** **Dougl.** ***ex*** **Hook. ssp.** ***miniata*** **SCARLET PAINTBRUSH**

With tufted stems 20-40 cm tall, this common species is the only paintbrush at the mountain with undivided leaves. They are lanceolate with silky hairs and 30-60 mm long. The scarlet bracts are ovate, with a pair of small, sharp teeth near their tips. The corolla is approximately 30 mm long, and the galea is nearly 15 mm long.

Primarily a subalpine species of meadows and forest openings, this paintbrush is the most common at Mount Adams. It is known from a Suksdorf collection at Hellroaring Canyon and is also found on the Island Springs Trail and alongside Road 60 on the southeast side. It grows alongside Road 2329 near lower Midway Meadows on the north, as well as at the junction of the Killen Creek and Pacific Crest trails.(elevation 6,000 ft). It also grows alongside the Round-the-Mountain Trail at 6,300 feet.

### *Castilleja parviflora* Bong. var. *oreopola* (Greenm.) Ownbey
### MAGENTA PAINTBRUSH

Low growing, the 15-30 cm tall stems of this paintbrush are sparsely hairy on the upper stems and the leaves. The 2-4 cm long leaves have 1 or 2 pairs of slender lobes. Varying from rose-purple to magenta, the bracts are 2-lobed. The corolla is 20-30 mm long and the galea approximately half that length.

In open, subalpine meadows, this common species is distinguished by the color. It is found at Mirror Lake, Bird Creek Meadows, and Hellroaring Canyon on the southeast side. On the north, it was collected at 6,900 feet in High Camp meadows.

### *Castilleja pilosa* (S. Wats.) Rydb. var. *pilosa*
### PARROTHEAD PAINTBRUSH

The clustered stems of this species are curved and unbranched, ranging from 5-10 cm tall, and purplish; they bear long hairs and are somewhat glutinous. The lower leaves are linear and undivided, while the upper ones have 1 or 2 pairs of lateral lobes and are hairy. The bracts are broader than the leaves and red-purple, with 1 or 2 pairs of linear lobes. The inflorescence is dense, and the corolla is 12-15 mm long, glandular, hairy, and exserted. The galea is short while the lower lip is prominent; overall, the flower is red-purple in color.

A northeast Oregon species of the Wallowa Mountains region, this is a rare paintbrush at Mount Adams. It was found in 1892 by Henderson on "alpine bluffs," presumably on the south side of the mountain.

### *Castilleja suksdorfii* A. Gray—SUKSDORF'S PAINTBRUSH

This erect paintbrush rises as a single 30-50 cm tall stem from a slender, creeping base. The stems and leaves vary from hairless to finely hairy; the upper ones have 1-2 pairs of lateral lobes much narrower than the mid-blade, while the lower leaves are sometimes unlobed. The red bracts and calyx have a yellow band at the base of the red portion. The bracts are sparsely long-hairy, divided into 5 parts, and shorter than the flowers. The calyx is 20-30 mm long, the corolla 30-50 mm long with a short-hairy galea the length of the tube.

A frequently seen paintbrush of middle elevation to subalpine meadows at the mountain this species is found at Foggy Flat and Midway Meadows on the north side. It also grows at lower elevations in Bathtub Meadow, Babyshoe Meadow, and Killen Creek Meadow on the northwest, and at Grand Meadow on the southwest. It is found near Bench Lake in the lower Hellroaring Creek meadows. The type specimen for this species was collected by Suksdorf at Mount Adams in 1885 and named by Asa Gray at Harvard University, to whom Suksdorf sent much material.

#### ***Castilleja thompsonii*** **Pennell—THOMPSON'S PAINTBRUSH**

The clustered, 1-4 dm tall, erect or ascending stems of this perennial paintbrush are often branched above. They are hairy and occasionally purplish in color. The upper leaves have 1-2 pairs of linear lobes and the lower leaves are entire; the leaves are hairy and occasionally glandular. The yellowish bracts are divided 3-5 times; the calyx may be purplish and is 12-25 mm long. The galea has a prominent lower lip and is hidden within the calyx.

A subalpine species of dry places, this paintbrush is found at High Camp on the north side, below the Mazama Glacier on the southeast, and at the headwaters of Adams Creek on the northwest. It also was collected by Flett on the Klickitat River just east of Mount Adams and has been found alongside the trail above Hellroaring Overlook at 6,650 feet. Hitchcock considered the Mount Adams plants distinctive enough to perhaps deserve varietal status, owing to their smaller stature and the presence of longer hairs on the stems.

### ***Collinsia*** **Nutt.—BLUE-EYED MARY**

#### ***Collinsia parviflora*** **Lindl.—SMALL-FLOWERED BLUE-EYED MARY**

A small plant with tiny flowers, this annual is often obscured by the grasses and herbs of its meadow habitat. The slender stems may reach 20 cm tall. The 1-2 cm leaves are opposite, the lower ones stalked and rounded, and the upper linear and stalkless. The blue flowers are borne in the axils of the upper leaves on long, slender stalks. The 6-7 mm long corolla is strongly 2-lipped and cocked at an angle from the stem. There are 4 fertile stamens.

Common in the drier portions of meadows, along roadsides, and in other open, dry habitats below 4,500 feet, this species was found by the authors at Muddy Meadows, and alongside roads K6900, 782, 071, and 8040 (South Climb road).

## *Euphrasia* L.—EYEBRIGHT

### *Euphrasia nemorosa* (Pers.) Wallr.—COMMON EYEBRIGHT

An annual that resembles a *Veronica* at first glance, this plant has slender, solitary, unbranched stems up to 10 cm tall. The leaves are opposite, toothed, and about 1 cm long. Each flower in the short raceme is paired with a leaf-like bract and is 10-15 mm long, strongly two-lipped, and white, with purple lines on the lower lip. There are 4 stamens, covered by the hoodlike upper lip.

Introduced, this species was found once at Mount Adams by the authors in Midway Meadows close to Road 115, on ground that becomes dry by midsummer.

## *Linaria* Mill.—TOADFLAX

### *Linaria vulgaris* Mill.—BUTTER-AND-EGGS

Forming small patches from spreading rootstocks, this perennial weed bears upright, slender stems 60-80 cm tall. The plant is hairless, and the alternate, stalkless, linear leaves are somewhat glaucous and 2-5 cm long. The 2-3 cm long, bright yellow flowers are 2-lipped and borne in a tall spike.

Uncommon and found only in highly disturbed places, this species is known from the intersection of Road 23 and Road 521 on the northwest side of Mount Adams.

## *Mimulus* L.—MONKEYFLOWER

The bright yellow or pink flowers of this genus may be found in a variety of wet habitats, ranging from moist draws that dry by midsummer to meadows to streamsides, where the plants may be nearly inundated. They are annual or perennial herbs with opposite leaves. The flowers are weakly to strongly 2-lipped and borne on long stalks in the axils of the upper leaves. The calyx is 5-angled with prominent midveins on the lobes.

1 Corolla pink to rose .......................................................... 2
1 Corolla yellow, sometime marked with red .............................. 3

2(1) Perennial with multiple stems at least 30 cm tall; corolla 3.5-5 cm long .......................................................................... *M. lewisii*
2 Annual with a single (rarely branched) stem, less than 10 cm tall; corolla less than 1 cm long ........................................ *M. breweri*

3(1) Slender annuals, the stems less than 15 cm tall; corolla less than 1 cm long .................................................................... 4
3 Perennials with tall stems or spreading as mats; corollas more than 1 cm long .................................................................... 6

4(3) Corollas strongly 2-lipped; stems usually unbranched ................. ........................................................................ *M. alsinoides*
4 Corollas nearly regular; stems branched ............................... 5

5(4) Lower leaves short-stalked; lobes of the corolla rounded at the tip .. ...................................................................... *M. breviflorus*
5 Lower leaves stalkless; lobes of the corolla notched at the tip ........ ...................................................................... *M. suksdorfii*

6(3) Plant matlike, spreading by slender stolons; flowers on long, slender pedicels that appear to rise from the center of a tuft of leaves ........................................................ *M. primuloides*
6 Plants with erect or ascending stems; flowers on short or long stems from the axils of the upper leaves ................................ 7

7(6) Calyx teeth more or less equal in size; leaves pinnately veined, slimy-sticky ................................ *M. moschatus* var. *moschatus*
7 Upper calyx tooth larger than the others; leaves hairy or not, but neither sticky nor slimy ...................................................... 8
8(7) Plants typically more than 25 cm tall; flowers numerous, in a leafy-bracted raceme .................................................. *M. guttatus*
8 Plants less than 20 cm tall; flowers solitary in the axils of the upper leaves ........................................... *M. tilingii var. caespitosus*

### *Mimulus alsinoides* Dougl. *ex* Benth.
### CHICKWEED MONKEYFLOWER

Averaging 10-15 cm in height, this annual may reach 25 cm on favorable sites. The 5-15 mm long leaves are ovate to rounded, toothed, and borne on short stalks. The 8-14 mm flowers are moderately 2-lipped, marked by a large red spot or several small red ones on the lower lip.

A subalpine species of drier meadows, this species is known from Stagman Ridge and also from a Suksdorf collection designated as "6-7,000 feet," probably on the southeast side.

### *Mimulus breviflorus* Piper—SHORT-FLOWERED MONKEYFLOWER

A 5-20 cm tall annual, with many slender, glandular-hairy branches, this small species bears many 5-20 mm long leaves. They are sometimes toothed, and elliptic in shape, and most taper to a small petiole. The 4-7 mm long yellow corolla is 2-lipped and faintly spotted with red. The throat is short-hairy and less than 2 mm wide.

Preferring moist, open habitats, this species is known from a Flett collection at Klickitat Meadows on the east side of the mountain at 4,000 feet.

### *Mimulus breweri (*Greene) Coville—BREWER'S MONKEYFLOWER

From 3-10 cm tall, this small annual is distinguished by its single, slender, glandular-hairy stem. The narrowly lanceolate leaves are 1-2 cm long, stalkless, and not toothed. The 5-10 mm long light rose flowers are weakly 2-lipped.

This tiny monkeyflower is a species of drier habitats than most members of the genus and is found at the DNR quarry, on the Klickitat River (a Flett collection), and is also known from a Suksdorf collection of unspecified location. It grows in open places on sunny slopes where the soil dries quickly in the spring.

### *Mimulus guttatus* DC.—YELLOW MONKEYFLOWER

The most common of the monkeyflowers at the mountain, this perennial spreads by runners and rootstocks, and has mostly hairless stems 20-60 cm tall. The 1-5 cm long rounded to ovate leaves are toothed and palmately veined. The lower leaves are on short stalks and the upper ones are stalkless. The yellow flowers are 2-4 cm long and strongly 2-lipped, with the lower lip bearing red spots.

A middle elevation species of wet habitat, this species was observed by the authors alongside Roads K6000 and K6900 on the southeast side. On the north, it grows along Killen Creek at 6,000 feet, at Midway Meadows, and near Road 115. Flett also collected it near the Klickitat River. Occasionally, it provides a colorful companion to the pink Lewis's monkeyflower.

### *Mimulus lewisii* Pursh
### LEWIS'S MONKEYFLOWER, PURPLE MONKEYFLOWER

Clumps of stems 30-60 cm tall with bright to pale pink flowers distinguish this monkeyflower as amongst the most beautiful of wet meadow species. The stems and leaves are sticky and the 3-5 cm long leaves are lanceolate to ovate, toothed, and stalkless. The bright flowers are strongly 2-lipped with spreading lobes and yellow marks in the throat. Occasional white-flowered individuals may be encountered.

Found at Bird Creek Caves by Suksdorf and common along the upper Killen Creek Trail at 6,000 feet of elevation, this species may be encountered along stream banks and other wet, sunny to partly shaded sites in the subalpine region.

### *Mimulus moschatus* Douglas *ex* Lindl. var. *moschatus*
### MUSK MONKEYFLOWER

A middle elevation wet habitat species, often in sphagnum meadows, this perennial is spread by rootstocks. The plants are densely hairy, sticky, and slimy. The sprawling stems are 10-30 cm long. Lanceolate to ovate, the 2-5 cm long leaves are toothed, with the lower leaves short-stalked. The 2-3 cm long bright yellow flowers are weakly 2-lipped.

Relatively common at the mountain, this species was collected by the authors at Bathtub Meadows on the northwest side. It is found at Midway Meadows on the north, and was also collected by Suksdorf at Bird Creek and the Big Muddy River.

### *Mimulus primuloides* Benth.—PRIMROSE MONKEYFLOWER

A perennial with long, slender rhizomes, this species forms dense mats. The 7-25 mm long leaves are borne mostly near the ground although sometimes on the stems. They are long-hairy on 1 or both sides, oblanceolate, stalkless, and sometimes shallowly toothed. The 1-2 cm corolla is often dotted with maroon spots and is shallowly 2-lipped. Each is set atop a tall (3-4 cm) leafless stalk. The corolla lobes are notched and spreading.

A little plant with a spectacular flower, this species is common in wet subalpine habitats. It forms large mats in a sphagnum environment at Foggy Flat and is found alongside Hellroaring Creek close to Bench Lake. It also grows in Bird Creek Meadows.

### *Mimulus suksdorfii* A. Gray—SUKSDORF'S MONKEYFLOWER

A slender annual 3-10 cm tall, with many branches that are glandular and sparsely hairy, this subalpine species may grow in habitats ranging from moist to rather dry. The 2 cm long leaves are numerous, linear on the upper part of the stem and oblanceolate below. The flowers are borne on short stems, the corolla yellow and faintly spotted and only 4-8 mm long. It is shallowly 2-lipped, the lobes notched, and the narrow throat short-hairy.

An eastern Cascade species, this monkeyflower is found in drier areas adjacent to meadows in lower Hellroaring Canyon. The species was discovered at Mount Adams by Suksdorf in 1885 and named by Asa Gray in his honor.

### *Mimulus tilingii* Regel var. *caespitosus* (Greene) A.L. Grant<br>LARGE MOUNTAIN MONKEYFLOWER

Low and tufted or matted, this hairless perennial spreads by rootstocks and runners. The 5-20 cm tall branched stems bear 2-10 mm ovate, stalkless leaves. The yellow flowers are 2-3 cm long, strongly 2-lipped, and spotted with red at the throat.

This very showy monkeyflower is cosmopolitan, with specimens collected at Bird Creek, Big Muddy Creek, and Hellroaring Meadow. This is a stunning little plant, with the largest flowers of the genus at Mount Adams, a feature emphasized by its low stature and small leaves.

## *Nothochelone* Straw—TURTLEHEAD

### *Nothochelone nemorosa* (Dougl. *ex* Lindl.) Straw WOODLAND-PENSTEMON

A tall plant with erect or leaning stems that reach 30-60 cm in length, this plant resembles a large *Penstemon* and was formerly included in that genus. The difference is in the flower. In *Nothochelone* there is a specialized disk of nectar-producing glands at the base of the ovary. In addition, the filaments of the stamens are hairy at the base. In *Penstemon* the disk is absent; instead, nectar is produced at the bases of hairless filaments. The 5-10 cm, lanceolate leaves of this species are sharply toothed and borne opposite. The inflorescence is a panicle with glandular-hairy stems, and the 2.5-3 cm long corolla is purplish, tubular, slightly curved, and 2-lipped. Its wooly anthers recall those of some of the low or mounded *Penstemon* species.

Most commonly a middle elevation open forest dweller, this species also grows in the lower subalpine and in disturbed sites, reaching 6,100 feet. It is cosmopolitan at the mountain, making appearances here and there, and has been located by the authors alongside Road 23, on the Pacific Crest Trail, and on the road to King Mountain at the Tract D boundary. Historic collections include a Flett specimen at the Klickitat River and at a "moraine" on the south side, collected by Henderson.

## *Pedicularis* L.—LOUSEWORT

Perennial herbs, *Pedicularis* differs from *Castilleja* in the shape of the hoodlike upper lip of the corolla (galea) which is both colored and often curved into unique, beaklike shapes. The lower lip of the corolla takes a variety of shapes as well, in some species reduced to small lobes while in others flattened to make a "platform" for pollinating insects. Ranging in color from white to pink or purplish, rarely yellowish, the corollas tend to be larger, but the white or greenish bracts are less showy and much smaller than in *Castilleja*. The stems are more or less leafy, and there are basal leaves as well; they are toothed or lobed, and often appear fernlike. The flowers are borne in racemes or spikes. There are 4 stamens.

1 Leaves toothed but not divided .......... *P. racemosa* ssp. *racemosa*
1 Leaves pinnately divided, the lobes toothed or again divided ....... 2

2(1) Upper lip of the corolla a beak that curves upward and outward, resembling an elephant's trunk .......................... *P. groenlandica*
2 Upper lip of the corolla hoodlike, the beak short ....................... 3

3(2) Inflorescence more or less hairy; flowers purplish ........................................................................ *P. bracteosa* var. *latifolia*
3 Inflorescence hairless; flowers yellowish ................................ 4

4(3) Tips of the lateral sepals glandular, elongated, and very slender ..... ................................................ *P. bracteosa* var. *bracteosa*
4 Tips of the lateral sepals not glandular, lanceolate to triangular and relatively short .................................. *P. bracteosa* var. *flavida*

**_Pedicularis bracteosa_ Benth. var. _bracteosa_—BRACTED LOUSEWORT**

A perennial that may reach 1 m in height, with leafy stems, three subspecies of this pedicularis are found at the mountain. The leaves are pinnately divided, the linear-oblong to lanceolate leaflets are 1-7 cm long, incised and finely toothed. The uppermost leaflets are reduced. The 13-21 mm corolla is yellowish in plants seen near Bench Lake but more often are purple; the free tips of the lateral sepals are very slender and elongate, a distinguishing feature of this subspecies.

According to Hitchcock this subspecies is "isolated" on Mount Adams; other locations for this variety are found to the north and northeast, in British Columbia, Alberta, northern Idaho, northwest Montana, and the northeast corner of Washington. It was found by the authors at the meadow along Hellroaring Creek close to Bench Lake. There is also a historic Henderson collection with no specific information.

**_Pedicularis bracteosa_ Benth. var. _flavida_ (Pennell) Cronq.**
**BRACTED LOUSEWORT**

This subspecies is similar to var. *bracteosa* in the flower color, typically yellowish; it may be distinguished by the wider tips of the glandless sepals. The inflorescence is glabrous.

Common in middle elevations, often in forest openings or edges, but also found in wet meadows, this plant also is encountered in the subalpine habitats, such as alongside the trail above Hellroaring Overlook at 6,500 feet of elevation. It grows near Road 82 along a small stream west of Bird Creek, and is found at Babyshoe Meadow on the northwest side of the mountain; it also is found alongside the trail between Muddy Meadows and the Pacific Crest Trail.

**_Pedicularis bracteosa_ Benth. var. _latifolia_ (Pennell) Cronq.**
**BRACTED LOUSEWORT**

This subspecies has lateral sepals that are shorter and wider than those of var. *flavida*. The sepals also lack glands, and the hairs of the inflorescence are denser. The corolla is purplish.

This plant is known from two Suksdorf collections, one at Hellroaring Canyon and the other at an unspecified location.

### *Pedicularis groenlandica* Retz.—ELEPHANT'S HEAD

This very showy lousewort ranges from 20-60 cm tall, and bears hairless stems and leaves. The numerous, 5-20 cm long basal leaves are lanceolate, sometimes reddish in color, and pinnately divided into slender, toothed lobes. The leaves on the upper stem are reduced in size. The 10 mm long corolla is pinkish to reddish-purple, and has a 10-15 mm long and narrow beak that curves downward and outward—hence the reference to an "elephant's trunk" in the common name. The flower of this species is an unmistakable field mark.

A middle elevation to subalpine *Pedicularis* of open, wet meadows, this species is quite common in such habitats at the mountain. On the southeast side it grows at Bird Creek, Mirror Lake, and on the trail above Hellroaring overlook. On the northwest, it is found at Babyshoe Meadow and on the north in a wet meadow alongside the trail from Muddy Meadows to the Pacific Crest Trail.

### *Pedicularis racemosa* Douglas ex Benth. ssp. *racemosa* SICKLE-TOP LOUSEWORT, RAM'S-HORN LOUSEWORT

This lousewort is most easily separated from other genus members by the leaves, which are evenly toothed but not divided into separate lobes. They are 3-8 cm long, long-lanceolate, and are borne on short stalks. Young plants are reddish-purple. The 1-1.5 cm corolla is pink to purplish and the upper lip is curved sufficiently to touch the twisted, broad lower lip with its tip.

Fairly common in middle elevation forest edges and occasionally meadows, this species is cosmopolitan at the mountain. It grows at Bathtub Meadows, along Road 82 west of Bird Creek, and between Horseshoe and Green Mountain Lakes on the northwest side. It is also found alongside the Crofton Ridge trail

### *Penstemon* Schmidel—PENSTEMON

One of the brightest, showiest flowers at the mountain is the red-pink cliff penstemon, *P. rupicola.* This genus includes several species with light purple to nearly blue flowers; on the southeast side fields of *P. euglaucus,* a bluish-colored penstemon, may be encountered in open, sometimes disturbed sites. The genus also includes less colorful species, such as *P. confertus,* a rare species that typically bears creamy white flowers. Among the dicots, following the epilobiums, *Penstemon* is the most diverse genus in terms of numbers of species.

Most common on the south and east sides of the mountain, penstemons show a variety of growth forms, from spreading mats, to slender or robust erect stems. All have opposite, often toothed leaves; the lower leaves are typically short-stalked. The tubular flowers are borne in racemes, panicles, or in whorled clusters and are strongly 2-lipped and open at the throat. There are 4 stamens as well as a 5th sterile filament. Whether or not the anthers are wooly is a critical feature in separating the species. A very similar plant in overall appearance is *Nothochelone* - so similar that it is "keyed out" here as well as in the key to the Scrophulariaceae.

1 Anthers densely wooly .................................................... 2
1 Anthers hairless or with, at most, a few straight hairs ................ 7

2(1) Erect plants, 30-60 cm tall; leaves 5-10 cm long .................................................................. See *Nothochelone*, above
2 Plants with prostrate or short erect stems, never more than 30 cm tall; leaves to 6 cm long ....................................................3

3(1) Stems erect, not matlike, to 30 cm tall; leaves lanceolate, 3-6 cm long ....................................................................................4
3 Stems prostrate, forming mats, the flowering stems less than 15 cm tall; leaves rounded to obovate, less than 2 cm long ................. 5

4(3) Flowers purple to blue-violet; leaves rounded at tip ...... *P. cardwellii*
4 Flowers light purple; leaves sharp-tipped .......................................................................... *P. fruticosus* var. *fruticosus*

5(3) Leaves blue-green and glaucous; corolla bright pink to rose-red ...... ........................................................................ *P. rupicola*
5 Leaves green, not glaucous; corolla blue-purple to violet ............. 6

6(5) Leaves not toothed, rounded at the tip; corolla 1.5-2.5 cm long ....... ........................................................ *P. davidsonii* var. *davidsonii*
6 Leaves toothed, sharp at the tip; corolla 2.5-3.5 cm long.................. ........................................................ *P. davidsonii* var. *menziesii*

7(1) Anther horseshoe-shaped at maturity, the two anther sacs opening only at the top ........................................................ *P. serrulatus*
7 Anther sacs opening along their lengths and spreading apart at maturity, thus the anther not horseshoe-shaped .......................... 8

8(7) Flowers yellow ........................................................ *P. confertus*
8 Flowers blue to purplish, rarely white ........................................... 9

9(8) Stems and leaves markedly glaucous ....................... *P. euglaucus*
9 Stems and leaves not glaucous ................................................. 10

10(9) Flowers not glandular, small, to 11 mm, with a slender tube ....... 11
10 Flowers glandular or not, longer than 12 mm, with a more open tube; if small, then flowers glandular externally .......................... 12

| | | |
|---|---|---|
| 11(10) | Basal leaves few | *P. procerus* var. *procerus* |
| 11 | Basal rosette well developed | *P. procerus* var. *tolmiei* |
| 12(10) | Leaves toothed, sometimes inconspicuously so | 13 |
| 12 | Leaves not toothed | 14 |
| 13(12) | Leaves short-hairy, evidently toothed | *P. humilis* ssp. *humilis* |
| 13 | Leaves smooth, obscurely toothed | *P. subserratus* |
| 14 | Inflorescence glandular | *P. attenuatus* var. *attenuatus* |
| 14 | Inflorescence not glandular | *P. rydbergii* var. *oreocharis* |

### *Penstemon attenuatus* Dougl. *ex* Lindl. var. *attenuatus* SLENDER PENSTEMON

This *Penstemon* is a tufted plant that varies in height from 3 to 9 dm, with long petioles on deep green basal leaves that may reach 17 cm in length and 4 cm in width. The stem leaves are sessile and much reduced in size upwards. The glabrous stems support a glandular-hairy inflorescence; the flowers on short stalks are arranged in axillary pairs from the stem leaves. Corolla colors vary from blue to white, with the corolla tube ranging between 14 and 20 mm, and the calyx 4 to 7 mm. long.

Found in dry middle elevation openings, this species also thrives in disturbed ground along roadsides and trail borders. It is most commonly encountered on the southeast side of the mountain, particularly near Snipes Mountain.

### *Penstemon cardwellii* T.J. Howell—CARDWELL'S BEARDTONGUE

The stems of this 1-3 dm tall shrub ascend rather than stand erect, and occasionally root. New shoots are sparsely and finely hairy. The 1.5-3.5 cm long elliptic leaves are rounded at the tip, finely and sharply toothed, hairless, and crowded near the base. The inflorescence is somewhat glandular-hairy, with a few, crowded flowers. The corolla is bright purple to deep blue-violet, 30-38 mm long and approximately 1 cm wide at the mouth. It is keeled on the back, with long white hairs near the base of the lower lip.

This species is known from two Suksdorf collections, one at the headwaters of the White Salmon River on the southwest side and the other from Hellroaring Canyon.

### *Penstemon confertus* Dougl. *ex* Lindl.—YELLOW PENSTEMON

This is a matted, hairless *Penstemon* with a few, 20-50 cm tall, flowering stems. The 3-15 cm long leaves are lanceolate to oblanceolate and not toothed. The flowers are born in narrow whorls that are widely spaced at the tops of the stems. Creamy white to yellowish and 8-12 mm long, the corollas usually nod downwards. The tube is slender, and the throat of the flower is typically spotted with purple or streaked. The anthers spread widely.

This species is rare at the mountain, known from a collection made by the authors on the Round-the-Mountain Trail above Stagman Ridge at an elevation of 6,140 feet.

### *Penstemon davidsonii* Greene var. *davidsonii* DAVIDSON'S PENSTEMON

Dense mats from creeping woody stems characterize this low perennial that may form patches up to 50 cm broad. The 5-20 mm long, hairless leaves are oval to obovate, short-stalked, and not toothed. There are a few flowers in a compact raceme on a stem 10-15 cm tall. The flower appears disproportionately large for such a low plant: measuring 1-2.5 cm in length and a vivid shade of lavender to purple, they command attention. The anthers are enveloped in wooly hairs.

More common than subspecies *menziesii*, this is a subalpine to alpine species, cosmopolitan at the mountain and growing on talus slopes and stony flats. It grows at the summit of Little Mount Adams, alongside the South Climb trail to 7,500 feet, and alongside the trail above Hellroaring Overlook. It is found at 6,880 feet at High Camp Meadows on the north side.

### *Penstemon davidsonii* Green var. *menziesii* (D.D. Keck) Cronq. MENZIES'S PENSTEMON

Similar to variety *davidsonii*, this variety differs in the longer leaves (8-20 mm) that are toothed on the edges and have sharp tips. The flowers average somewhat larger, being 2.5-3.5 cm long.

Rare at Mount Adams, this subspecies is known from a collection at Devil's Garden at over 7,800 feet of elevation.

### *Penstemon euglaucus* English—GLAUCOUS PENSTEMON

Most common of all the penstemons at the mountain, this tufted perennial may reach 70 cm in height. With slender stems, the plants are glabrous and markedly glaucous. The leaves are entire, lanceolate in shape, with the basal leaves borne on pedicels. The 3.5 to 5 mm calyx is thinly margined with irregular teeth and a sharply pointed tip. The flowers are axillary and spread at right angles to the stem. The corolla is blue-purple and reaches 15 mm in length, with the limb spreading and the lower lip of the corolla bearded.

Found on the south side of the mountain at middle to subalpine elevations, this species prefers open flats with deep, dry soil and sometimes forms large colonies on disturbed sites. Such is the case at the trailhead to Hellroaring Creek in the Bird Creek Meadows area. It is also conspicuous on the lower portion of the South Climb trail, growing in forest openings

### *Penstemon fruticosus* (Pursh) Greene var. *fruticosus*
### SHRUBBY PENSTEMON

Reaching approximately 30 cm tall and densely branched, this rounded shrub bears lanceolate to elliptical leaves, typically toothed although occasionally toothless, pointed, and 2-4 cm long. The 3-10, blue-violet flowers are configured in a simple raceme, while the corolla tube is relatively wide and straight and distinguished by 2 prominent ridges on the lower lip. The wooly anther sacs spread widely.

Predominantly an eastern Cascades species, this penstemon is found from middle to subalpine elevations on the south and east aspects of the mountain. It has been located on the summit of Little Mount Adams, alongside the road to King Mountain, at Hellroaring Canyon, at the Klickitat River, and alongside the Round-the-Mountain trail on the southwest side.

### *Penstemon humilis* Nutt. *ex* A. Gray ssp. *humilis*
### LOW PENSTEMON

Grayish, tufted plants up to 6 dm tall, the basal leaves may reach 12 cm in length with a 2 cm width. These elliptic to ovate leaves are typically much longer than the stalkless stem leaves. The inflorescence is glandular-hairy and the blue to blue-purple flowers reach only 17 mm in length and 6 mm in width.

Rare at the mountain, and a species typically found in open, dry and rocky places east of the Cascades species, this *Penstemon* is known from one collection made by Flett near the Klickitat River northeast of Mount Adams.

### *Penstemon procerus* Dougl. *ex* Graham var. *procerus*
### SMALL-FLOWERED PENSTEMON

The basal rosette of this tufted plant is poorly developed, with only a few basal leaves. The plants are 2-4 dm tall, with pairs of cymes forming a whorl-like inflorescence from the leaf axils. The corolla is blue, 6-11 mm long, with a narrow tube barely 2-3 mm wide at the mouth; the limb is spreading and weakly 2-lipped, with the tip of the sterile filament hairy. The widely spreading anther sacs are hairless.

Found on the south and west sides of the mountain, this penstemon may behave as a disturbance species along roadsides and trails. It is not as common in these situations as the other small blue-flowered species, *Penstemon euglaucus*.

## Scrophulariaceae

### *Penstemon procerus* Dougl. *ex* Graham var. *tolmiei* (Hook.) Cronq. TOLMIE'S PENSTEMON

Multiple stems form a tufted plant characterized by lanceolate to elliptical, toothless, hairless, unstalked leaves. The plants range from .5 to 1.5 dm in height, although occasionally taller, and the basal rosette is well developed. Whorled clusters of blue to blue-violet flowers (occasionally cream-colored) are composed of 8-12 mm long corollas, each with a narrow tube and whitish throat. The widely-spread anther sacs are hairless.

Most easily recognized by the bright, small flowers, this penstemon differs from variety *procerus* in having a more developed rosette of shorter and broader leaves. It also tends to grow at higher elevations. It was found by the authors in upper Bird Creek Meadows at an elevation of 7,000 feet and is also known from a Gage and Rodman collection at High Camp on the north side of the mountain. It is most common on the south and southeast slopes of the mountain.

### *Penstemon rupicola* (Piper) Howell—CLIFF PENSTEMON

The striking deep pink to rose-red flowers set off this low, matted plant, which might otherwise go unnoticed. The flowering stems are 5-10 cm tall and the oval to ovate leaves are thick and only 5-7 mm long; they are toothed, hairy, glaucous and gray-green. Borne in a raceme on each stem, the 3-4 cm long flowers are somewhat curved and have 2 sharp ridges on the lower lip. The densely wooly anther sacs spread widely, and often protrude from the throat of the flower.

Growing on rocky sites, often tucked in crevices in cliffs or steep slopes, this species was collected by Suksdorf at Hellroaring Canyon. It grows alongside Road 23 at the gravel pit, along a cliff north of the Stagman Ridge - Pacific Crest Trail junction, and at Bird Creek Meadows.

### *Penstemon rydbergii* A. Nels. var. *oreocharis* (Greene) N. Holmgren RYDBERG'S PENSTEMON

Tufted plants that range from 2-7 dm tall rise from a surface, woody rhizome. They are slender-stemmed and mostly hairless. The 15 cm long oblanceolate to narrowly elliptic basal leaves often form rosettes on petioles, while the 10 cm stem leaves are sessile. The sometimes sparsely hairy inflorescence consists of "false" whorls of blue-purple flowers. The corolla is strongly 2-lipped, 11-15 mm long and 3-5 mm wide; the lower lip is bearded.

Resembling *Penstemon procerus* but with the corolla tube more expanded, this is a rare species at the mountain. It was collected by the authors on the north side of the mountain at Muddy Meadows, where it grew on wet ground among tall grasses and sedges.

### *Penstemon serrulatus* Menzies *ex* Rees—CASCADE PENSTEMON

Distinguished by unbranched stems 15-60 cm tall, this species bears 2-10 cm long leaves that are lanceolate to ovate, sharply and irregularly toothed, and bright green; they are short-stalked on the lower stem and stalkless above. Borne in a single, headlike cluster, the flowers are bright blue, with the relatively broad corolla 1.5-2.5 cm long. The anthers are horseshoe-shaped with a few short hairs at the top; the anthers are distinctive from the other penstemons at Mount Adams in opening only across their apices.

Found in middle elevations on dry to wet sites, this species grows near Stagman Ridge, at the DNR quarry, alongside Road 23 at 4,000 feet on a large roadcut, and at Hellroaring Canyon.

### *Penstemon subserratus* Pennell—FINETOOTH PENSTEMON

This 30-80 cm tall *Penstemon* consists of mostly hairless stems rising from a woody, branched root crown. The elliptic to ovate leaves bear small, irregularly distributed teeth and are up to 15 cm long; the basal leaves are clustered on petioles while the stem leaves clasp the stem. The inflorescence consists of open whorls of numerous bright blue, 26-35 mm long blossoms, each approximately 1 cm wide at the mouth.

A dry habitat *Penstemon* of open forests and dry flats at low to middle elevations, this species is known from a modern collection from the DNR quarry on the southeast side of the mountain. Henderson collected it in 1892 on the "subalpine slopes of Mount Adams." The elevation of Henderson's collection is not recorded. In 2006, the authors also found it along Trail 73 crossing Crofton Ridge.

## *Scrophularia* L.—FIGWORT

### *Scrophularia lanceolata* Pursh—LANCE-LEAVED FIGWORT

Rising from thickened roots, this stout 5-15 dm tall plant has 4-angled stems and leaves that diminish only slightly in size from top to bottom. The 5-15 cm leaves are triangular-ovate with a sharp tip, and rounded at the base. They are sharply toothed and sometimes irregularly "cut." The 1-5 dm long inflorescence consists of opposite branches bearing yellowish-green flowers that have a maroon tone. The corolla is 2-lobed and stout, 9-14 mm long.

Found in open and disturbed middle elevation habitats to about 4,500 feet, and preferring moist sites, this relatively rare plant at the mountain is easily distinguished by the long inflorescence and color of the flowers. It is found alongside Road K6000, near Road 8040 (South Climb route), and near the road up Snipes Mountain.

## Scrophulariaceae

### *Verbascum* L.—MULLEIN

#### *Verbascum thapsus* L.—COMMON MULLEIN

With tall stems up to 2 m in length, size alone makes this weed apparent along roadsides and other disturbed areas. The feltlike, large, pale green leaves also set the plants apart; they are thick, oblong to ovate, toothless, and 10-40 cm long. The flowers borne in a dense, long spike add to the "weed" effect. They are yellow, with a nearly-regular corolla consisting of a short tube and 16-20 mm broad, spreading lobes. There are 5 stamens.

Fortunately uncommon at the mountain, this weed has been noted at the DNR quarry, on the road to King Mountain, and alongside Road 23 at the overlook south of the Pacific Crest Trail crossing.

### *Veronica* L.—VERONICA, SPEEDWELL

Two weedy members of the genus, *Veronica officinalis* and *V. serpyllifolia* var. *serpyllifolia*, are found at Mount Adams, along with seven native species, some of which are showy wildflowers. All are perennials, with mostly opposite leaves, although leaves on the upper stems may be alternate. The stems are upright, or may sprawl if longer. There are two patterns for the inflorescence: the flowers may be arranged in a bracted raceme that terminates the stem, or they may be in racemes that arise from the axils of the upper leaves. The flowers are small and nearly regular, with four lobes; color ranges from white to pinkish to blue, often penciled with darker lines. There are 2 stamens and the capsule is 2-lobed, flattened, and often heart-shaped.

1 Flowers in racemes that arise from the axils of the leaves on the upper stem ........ 2
1 Flowers in racemes at the ends of the stems ........ 6

2(1) Plant short-hairy ........ *V. officinalis* var. *officinalis*
2 Plant hairless ........ 3

3(2) Leaves short-stalked ........ *V. americana*
3 Leaves not stalked ........ 4

4(3) Capsule flattened, notched ........ *V. scutellata*
4 Capsule inflated; scarcely notched ........ 5

5(4) Leaves toothed; flowers blue to violet; fruits upturned ........ *V. anagallis-aquatica*
5 Leaves not toothed; flowers white to pink; fruits spreading ........ *V. catenata*

6(1) Style 6-9 mm long, as long as or longer than the capsule; leaves hairless, neither toothed nor stalked ................................ *V. cusickii*

6 Style less than 3 mm long, shorter than the capsule; leaves various ........................................................................................................ 7

7(6) Subalpine perennial; leaves all opposite .................. *V. wormskjoldii*

7 Low-to mid-elevation perennials with creeping stems; upper leaves and bracts alternate ....................................................................... 8

8(7) Flowers deep blue; flower stalks with at least a few glandular hairs . ......................................................... *V. serpyllifolia* ssp. *humifusa*

8 Flowers white or pale blue; flower stalks merely short-hairy ............ ......................................................... *V. serpyllifolia* ssp. *serpyllifolia*

**_Veronica americana_ Schwein. _ex_ Benth.—AMERICAN BROOKLIME**

This is a sprawling perennial distinguished by 30-60 cm long, branched and hairless stems. The 2-8 cm long elliptical to ovate leaves are broadly toothed and short-stalked. The flowers are borne in loose racemes in the axils of the upper leaves. The 4-5 mm broad blue corolla is marked with darker veins on the lobes.

Found on Big Muddy Creek, on the Klickitat River on the east, and alongside Trail 75 on the southwest side, this is an uncommon species of swampy areas and streamsides at the mountain.

**_Veronica anagallis-aquatica_ L.—WATER SPEEDWELL**

An erect, 2-10 dm tall, fibrous-rooted biennial, except for the glandular-hairy inflorescence, this species is predominantly hairless. The sharply-toothed, 2-10 cm long leaves are elliptic to elliptic-oblong, stalkless and clasping. Flowers are numerous, arranged in axillary racemes; the 5 mm wide corolla is blue. The capsule is 2.5-4 mm high and barely notched.

Preferring wet habitats, including banks of streams and ditches, this species was found by the authors alongside Road 23 near a wetland site on the west side, alongside Road K6900 southeast of Bird Creek Meadows, at Spring Creek Meadow on the northwest, and at Midway Meadows on the north.

**_Veronica catenata_ Pennell—CHAIN SPEEDWELL**

Similar to *V. anagallis-aquatica,* this species bears leaves 3-5 times as long as wide and the flowers are white to pinkish rather than blue. The leaves, too, are toothless, and the racemes have fewer flowers.

Some authorities treat *V. catenata* as synonymous with *V. anagallis-aquatica*. However, at Mount Adams, the two are easily separated by consistent characteristics, with no intermediate forms found.

An uncommon species of wet places, this veronica grows on the north side at Horseshoe Lake on the shore in the campground and along Road 115 along the stream through Midway Meadows.

## Scrophulariaceae

### *Veronica cusickii* A. Gray—CUSICK'S SPEEDWELL

Finely hairy to hairless, this perennial forms loose mats from slender rootstocks. The 1-3 cm long dark green leaves are toothless. The flowers are borne in an elongated terminal raceme with small bracts, and the 10-12 mm broad corolla is dark blue. This species can be separated from the very similar *V. wormskjoldii* by its short style: in *V. cusickii* the style is very long, as long as or longer than the mature capsule. The stamens extend beyond the corolla.

Known from a single Henderson collection, this *Veronica* grows in subalpine meadows and along streams. This is the reverse of the pattern at Mount Rainier, where *V. cusickii* is far more common than *V. wormskjoldii.*

### *Veronica officinalis* L. var. *officinalis*—COMMON SPEEDWELL

Short-lived and finely hairy, this perennial bears 1-3 cm long, short-stalked, oval to obovate, finely toothed leaves. The flowers are borne in fairly dense, slender racemes in the leaf axils. The light blue corolla is 4-8 mm broad.

This weed was collected by the authors once alongside Road 23 at Twin Falls Creek.

### *Veronica scutellata* L.—MARSH SPEEDWELL

Rising from a rootstock, the hairless, lax stems of this perennial may reach 50 cm in length. The 2-4 cm long, untoothed leaves are narrowly lanceolate and stalkless. The flowers are borne in delicate racemes in the leaf axils, and the white to blue corolla is 5-7 mm broad.

Rare at the mountain, this native species was collected by the authors at Muddy Meadows.

### *Veronica serpyllifolia* L. ssp. *humifusa* (Dickson) Syme THYME-LEAF SPEEDWELL

This sprawling, native perennial is distinguished by a slender rootstock and stems up to 30 cm long. The elliptical to broadly ovate leaves are blunt at the tip and toothed. The flowers are borne in a slender, terminal raceme; there are a few glandular hairs on the flowering stems.

An uncommon native, this species prefers open, moist sites, and has been found at Muddy Meadows.

### *Veronica serpyllifolia* L. ssp. *serpyllifolia* THYME-LEAF SPEEDWELL

This variety differs from ssp. *humifusa* in the flower color—white to pale blue in this case. The plant is less hairy, too, and the upper stem lacks glands.

A weed, this variety is a middle elevation species fairly common on the north side of Mount Adams in disturbed areas. It has been found south of Road 56 near the Yakama Nation border on the north side, and in the campgrounds at Olallie and Horseshoe Lakes.

#### *Veronica wormskjoldii* Roem. & Schult.
#### AMERICAN ALPINE SPEEDWELL

Rising from a creeping rootstock, this perennial is similar to *V. cusickii.* The 5-30 cm long stems are erect, with long, wavy hairs. The 1-3 cm long leaves are broadly toothed or occasionally toothless, oval to ovate, and hairy. The flowers are borne in a terminal raceme on a glandular-hairy stem. The blue corolla measures 6-10 mm broad. The style is shorter than the mature capsule, and the stamens are hidden within the corolla.

The most common *Veronica* at the mountain, this middle to subalpine elevation species typically prefers moist meadows, stream banks, and other wet, open habitats. It is found at Babyshoe Meadow, Midway Meadows, Muddy Meadows, and Hellroaring Meadows. It is also known from historic collections at Big Muddy Creek and at the head of Hellroaring River.

## Urticaceae Juss.—NETTLE FAMILY

### *Urtica* L.—NETTLE

#### *Urtica dioica* L. ssp. *gracilis* (Ait.) Selander—STINGING NETTLE

Forming patches from spreading rootstocks, this perennial is characterized by the unbranched, 4-angled stems and the stinging hairs that cover stems and leaves—these render the plant unforgettable. The 5-15 cm long, opposite leaves are ovate, coarsely toothed, and somewhat pointed. The male and female flowers are borne in separate clusters in the axils of the leaves and resemble catkins. There are no petals; rather the flower consists of 4 or 5 sepals and stamens. The fruit is a small achene.

A lowland species of moist, often shaded places, it is unusual at Mount Adams, where it was collected by Suksdorf at Hellroaring Canyon.

## Valerianaceae Batsch—VALERIAN FAMILY

### *Valeriana* L.—VALERIAN

#### *Valeriana sitchensis* Bong.—SITKA VALERIAN

Reaching 60-120 cm tall, this species has hairless leaves and square stems. The 3-8 cm long leaflets are lanceolate to ovate or roundish and coarsely toothed. The basal leaves are very long-stalked. The white flowers are fragrant and borne in dense, flat, or rounded clusters. The 6-8 mm corolla has a long tube and fairly short lobes as well as a small but evident basal spur. The inferior ovary develops into an achene that is about 4 mm long.

This cosmopolitan, common subalpine species has been located at Midway Meadows, at the intersection of Roads 852 and 85, in Bird Creek Meadows and the valley of Hellroaring Creek, and on the Round the Mountain Trail near the Yakama Nation boundary.

## Violaceae Batsch—VIOLET FAMILY

### *Viola* L.—VIOLET

Violets are low growing perennial herbs, often spreading by runners and covering small patches of ground. Those at Mount Adams have alternate, toothed leaves, varying from egg- to heart-shaped. The irregular flowers are similar to those of the familiar garden plant: the lower petal is broad and more or less spurred, forming a lip, with 2 lateral petals forming wings on the sides and 2 upper petals. The petals may be bearded as well as marked by finely-penciled lines. There are 5 stamens arranged so that the anthers crowd around the style and a superior ovary, which becomes a capsule.

1 Annual; stipules large, leaflike, nearly as large as main leaf blade . ........ *V. arvensis*
1 Perennial; stipules small and not leaflike ........ 2

2(1) Flowers blue or white ........ 3
2 Flowers yellow ........ 5

3(2) Flowers white (petals sometimes tinged bluish on the back) ........ *V. macloskeyi* ssp. *macloskeyi*
3 Flowers blue or blue-violet ........ 4

4(3) Leaves arising from rhizomes on stems to 15 cm; flowering stems leafless; leaves heart-shaped with blunt tip, toothed; flowers pale violet ........ *V. palustris*
4 Leaves on flowering stems, ovate, heart-shaped at base, flowers with slender spur ........ *V. adunca*

5(2) Flowers on tips of stems only; leaves heart-shaped ........ *V. glabella*
5 Flowers along stem; leaves heart-shaped or not ........ 6

6(5) Leaves rounded to kidney-shaped, as broad as long ... *V. orbiculata*
6 Leaves not heart-shaped or kidney-shaped, longer than broad ..... 7

7(6) Leaves coarsely veined, less than 4 cm long, with few teeth; upper petals purple on back .............................. *V. purpurea* ssp. *venosa*
7 Leaves not coarsely veined, more than 4 cm long, toothed; petals not purple on back .......................................................... *V. bakeri*

### *Viola adunca* Sm.—BLUE VIOLET, WESTERN DOG VIOLET

Forming small clumps that collectively can give the impression of a large mat, this variable violet grows from thin, branched rootstocks. Both the leaves and stems are short-hairy; leaves are both basal and on the flowering stems. They are ovate, broadly toothed, occasionally heart-shaped at the base, 1-3 cm long and blunted at the tip. The 10-15 mm dark violet flowers are long-stalked and have a white spot at the throat. The slender spur is 4-7 mm long.

In middle to subalpine meadows this is often the most common violet, and typically grows close to lakes and ponds. It was found by the authors at Muddy Meadows, Midway Meadows, at Stagman Ridge, and alongside the Round-the-Mountain trail near upper Bird Creek Meadows.

### *Viola arvensis* Murr.—EUROPEAN FIELD PANSY

Introduced from Europe, this is a widely cultivated annual with a tendency to escape. It is branched, 1-3 dm tall, with short-hairy, lanceolate to ovate leaves. These are 1-3 cm long, and have rounded teeth; the petioles are of equal length and the stipules are divided into 5-9 segments. The flowers are borne singly on long stems. They are whitish to yellow with a blue tinge; the sepals are nearly as long as the petals, and the spur is short.

This weed is known from a single collection made by the authors at the viewpoint of Mount Adams alongside Road 23.

### *Viola bakeri* Greene—BAKER'S VIOLET

This violet is composed of short, erect rootstocks with stems primarily below the ground, the parts above reaching 15 cm in length. The petioles are 3-15 cm long, and the leaf blades are variable, elliptic to lanceolate, rounded to wedge-shaped at the base, and 2-5 cm long. The 5-15 mm long flowers are bright yellow with the lower petals bearing brownish-purple lines; the spur is short. The capsule is smooth, a feature distinguishing this species from *V. purpurea.*

Found in middle elevations on the south side of the mountain, this species grows near Morrison Creek, alongside the road to Aiken Lava Flow, on the flats surrounding Bunnell Butte, and near Crofton Ridge. This violet grows best in open, dry meadows, where it flowers early in the spring.

## Violaceae

### *Viola glabella* Nutt.—STREAM VIOLET, PIONEER VIOLET

This violet grows from a thick, horizontal rootstock and is deciduous, with mostly hairless basal and stem leaves. The 3-8 cm wide basal leaves are borne on long, slender stalks; they are heart-shaped, wider than long, broadly toothed, and tapered to a short, sharp tip. Below the flowers is a pair of stem leaves; the plant can reach 10 cm tall. There are 1-3 yellow flowers per stem. These are 9-13 mm long, and the lower 3 petals have purple veins.

Found near Morrison Camp, Swampy Meadows, and Crofton Ridge as well as along roadsides, this is a fairly common violet at the mountain, generally growing in shady places close to streams.

### *Viola macloskeyi* Lloyd ssp. *macloskeyi*—SMALL WHITE VIOLET

A small violet found in wetlands, this hairless plant spreads by runners and is typically less than 10 cm tall. The leaves are all basal, rounded but kidney-shaped at the base and shallowly toothed. The blades are less than 2.5 cm wide. White flowers on tall, slender stems are 5-8 mm long; dark veins line the lower peals, while the lateral petals are not bearded.

Striking with its white flowers, this tiny violet is found on the north and west sides of Mount Adams. It grows at Babyshoe Meadow and in a meadow at the junction of Road 23 and 2329 (Bathtub Meadow). This is the scarcest of the violets at Mount Adams and has a preference for sphagnum meadows.

### *Viola orbiculata* Geyer *ex* Holz.—ROUND-LEAF VIOLET

Distinguished by a more or less vertical rootstock, this violet bears both basal leaves and leaves on the stems. The 1-4 cm wide, thin leaves do not persist through the winter. They are rounded in outline, medium green, kidney-shaped at the base and blunt at the tip, and have broad, shallow teeth. The smaller stem leaves are distributed along the 4-8 cm tall stems. There are a few yellow flowers on the stem, each marked with dark veins, and about 12 mm in length.

Most common in dryish open forest in middle elevations, this cosmopolitan species grows near the Pacific Crest Trail crossing of Potato Hill Road on the north side. It was collected by the authors at the intersection of Roads 23 and 8810 on the west side of the mountain. It also grows near Road 405.

### *Viola palustris* L.—MARSH VIOLET

From both runners and a horizontal rootstock, this slender violet has basal leaves only, on stalks up to 15 cm tall. The leaf blade is 2-4 cm broad and heart-shaped with a blunt tip; it is broadly and shallowly toothed. The flowers are violet, 8-12 mm long, with dark veins on the lower petals; the upper petals are pale violet on the back.

Common at the mountain, this middle elevation violet is easily distinguished from the other purplish-colored *V. adunca* by the more pale color of the flowers and the singular stem configuration. It is found at Babyshoe, Midway, and Swampy Meadows, Bird Creek Meadows, Crofton Butte, and Takhlakh Lake, among many other locations.

#### *Viola purpurea* Kellogg ssp. *venosa* (S. Wats.) M.S. Baker & J.C. Clausen—GOOSEFOOT VIOLET

Barely 10 cm in height and configured as small tufts from a short, ascending rootstock, this small violet is short-hairy on the stems and leaves. The triangular-shaped leaves are 1-2.5 cm long, blunt or tapered at the base, deeply toothed, and purplish beneath—this is the goosefoot resemblance. Short, leafy stems bear 1 or 2 flowers, 8-12 mm long and deep yellow with brown or purplish backsides on the upper petals; the lower petals have dark brown veins on the lower petals. The capsule is short-hairy.

An eastern Cascades species, this violet is known from Flett and Suksdorf collections at the Klickitat River and Hellroaring Creek, on the east and southeast sides of Mount Adams.

## Viscaceae Batsch—MISTLETOE FAMILY

### *Arceuthobium* Bieb.—DWARF MISTLETOE

Perennial parasitic plants of conifers, the stems of the species at Mount Adams range from less than 2 cm in *A. douglasii* to nearly 20 cm in *A. americanum*. The stems may be branched or unbranched. They vary from yellow to green while the leaves are scale-like and inconspicuous. The inflorescence is a many-flowered spike on a short stock. The plants are dioecious; the male flowers with 3-4 parts, and the female flowers with only 2 parts. The fruits are berry-like, the sticky seeds explosively dispersed. The point on the host where the parasite attaches often becomes swollen.

The mistletoe species are often conifer-specific, but too few have been collected at Mount Adams to place great reliance upon this. Two species that might be expected in the study area, *A. tsugense*, parasitic on hemlocks (*Tsuga* species), and *A. laricis*, parasitic on western larch (*Larix occidentalis*) were not seen during this study.

1 Plant unbranched or few-branched; the stem no more than 2 cm long ........................ *A. douglasii*

1 Plant many-branched; the stem exceeding 2 cm in length ............ 2

2(1) Branches arranged in whorls; chiefly parasitic on *Pinus contorta* ..... ........................................................................ A. *americanum*
2 Branches in fan-like patterns, not whorled .................................... 3

3(2) Plants likely to form "witch's brooms" (conspicuously distorted tangles of branches on the host tree); parasitic on *Pinus* ................ ........................................................................ *A. campylopdum*
3 Plants not disfiguring the host; parasitic on *Abies* ........ *A. abietinum*

### *Arceuthobium abietinum* Engelm. *ex* Munz
### FIR DWARF MISTLETOE

Parasitic on true firs, this mistletoe is characterized by 6-15 cm, yellow to yellow-green stems. The leaves are scale-like, and the inflorescence is a many-flowered spike. The branches are not whorled, distinguishing it from *A. americanum.*

This species is known from a Suksdorf collection at Bird Creek Island. The identity of the host cannot be determined.

### *Arceuthobium americanum* Nutt. *ex* Engelm.
### AMERICAN DWARF MISTLETOE

The yellow-green stems of this mistletoe are 2-6 cm long, tufted, with the segments 1-2 mm thick and 7-15 times as long. The branches are whorled. The male flowers are 2 mm broad and panicle-like on short stems, 2 to several per node. The female flowers are whorled in groups of 2 or more, on short stalks. The fruit is approximately 3 mm long.

According to Hitchcock, this species is found on *Pinus* only. It was collected by Henderson at the Big Klickitat River and by Suksdorf at Bird Creek Meadows.

### *Arceuthobium campylopodum* Engelm.
### WESTERN DWARF MISTLETOE

Tufted, with 2-15 cm long orange-yellow to olive-green or brownish stems, this mistletoe bears branches that are fanlike. The male flowers are paired and 2.5-3 mm long, and vary from yellow to orange to green in color. The female flowers are borne 1 or 2 per node, and may have short stalks. The fruit is 3-5 mm long.

Henderson collected this mistletoe from *Pinus contorta* on the northeast side of the mountain. Elsewhere, it is known chiefly as a parasite of *Pinus ponderosa,* something not seen at Mount Adams.

### *Arceuthobium douglasii* Engelm.
### DOUGLAS-FIR DWARF MISTLETOE

The tufted stems of this mistletoe are greenish or bluish-green, only 0.5-3 cm long, with segments only 1 mm thick. The branches are fanlike (that is, the accessory branches are in the same plane as the primary branches.) The male flowers are greenish to yellow, and paired at the nodes on short joints. The female flowers are paired at the nodes. The fruits are about 3 mm long.

A species that parasitzes *Pseudotsuga menziesii*, it has been collected at Morrison Creek on the south side of Mount Adams.

# Angiosperms - Monocots

## Angiosperms – Flowering Plants
## Monocotyledonous Plants (Monocots)

The monocots are a large group of seed plants (angiosperms) that are prominent in the meadows, pools, lakes, and streams at Mount Adams, although the grasses are also widespread in open, dry places. All are herbaceous and most are perennials.

1 Plants aquatic, the plant wholly floating or the stems rooted on the bottom and the leaves submerged or floating, the flowering stems only reaching above the surface (late in the summer, some plants may be stranded in dried pools) .................................................. 2

1 Plants terrestrial, not aquatic; if growing in water, then the stems and leaves primarily above the surface .......................................... 5

2(1) Plant a small, oval, floating thallus with a single, threadlike root in the water ......................................................................... Lemnaceae

2 Plant with normal stems and leaves; leaves rooted in mud or soil .... ..................................................................................................... 3

3(2) Stems typically unbranched, with 3 short, more or less linear leaves per node; plant rarely flowering ........................... Hydrocharitaceae

3 Stems often branched, the leaves configured differently; plant flowering each year ..................................................................... 4

4(3) Male and female flowers in separate, rounded clusters on the same stem ......................................................................... Sparganiaceae

4 Each flower with male and female parts; flowers whorled in spikes .. ........................................................................ Potamogetonaceae

5(1) Perianth segments present, conspicuous, petal-like, white or colored (greenish in some orchids) .............................................. 6

5 Perianth segments inconspicuous, often reduced to scales or bristles, or absent, greenish to brown or black ............................... 8

6(5) Ovary superior ............................................................... Liliaceae

6 Ovary inferior .................................................................................. 7

7(6) Flowers regular .............................................................. Iridaceae

7 Flowers irregular ..................................................... Orchidaceae

8(5) Perianth segments 6, greenish-white, small; flowers in a raceme, each with a well-developed bract ........................ Scheuchzeriaceae

8 Perianth segments scalelike, not greenish-white; flowers not in a conspicuously bracted raceme ....................................................... 9

9(8) Inflorescence a thick spike surrounded by a cloaklike yellow spathe ........................................................................................ Araceae
9 Inflorescence a never greatly thickened spike with a spathe ....... 10

10(9) Fruit a capsule of fused chambers with numerous seeds; perianth segments 6, scalelike, regular, and arranged in 2 series ................. ........................................................................................ Juncaceae
10 Fruit a single achene, grain, or nutlet ......................................... 11

11(10) Stems typically triangular in cross-section, solid or stuffed with pith; flowers spirally arranged in the axis of each spikelet; each flower subtended by 1 bract (sedges, bulrushes, spikerushes) ................. ........................................................................................ Cyperaceae
11 Stems typically round, hollow; flowers arranged in 2 ranks on the axis of the spikelet (but not infrequently just 1 flower per spikelet); each flower subtended by 2 bracts (grasses) .................. Poaceae

## Araceae Juss.—ARUM FAMILY

### *Lysichiton* Schott—SKUNK-CABBAGE

#### *Lysichiton americanus* Hultén & St. John—SKUNK-CABBAGE

Blooming early in spring in swampy ground, the tall, bright yellow spathe distinguishes this species. The glossy green leaves are distinctive also—as much as 150 cm long, erect, and elliptical to oblanceolate in shape. They are borne on short stalks, embedded in the muck. The spathe is 10-30 cm long and surrounds a thick spadix, the columnar structure upon which the flowers are borne. The flowers are small and greenish yellow and have a disagreeable odor.

Found in inundated land or seasonally dry sites, this is a middle elevation species at the mountain, generally found in forest openings. It grows alongside Road 23 at milepost 39, at Babyshoe and Midway Meadows, and along the shore of Olallie Lake. It also is found on the south side of Mount Adams where Trail 73 crosses Crofton Creek.

## Cyperaceae Juss.—SEDGE FAMILY

Resembling grasses, the plants of this family are most common in wet meadows and alongside streams, where they often dominate. The leaves are 3-ranked on triangular or rounded stems. The small flowers are greenish or brown; they can be bisexual (or "perfect") -- that is, each flower has both stamens and a pistil -- or unisexual, with flowers bearing stamens or a pistil but not both. There are typically 3 stamens that are exserted when the flowers are mature. The pistil bears a style which has 2 or 3 stigmas. The flowers are borne in spikelets that are arranged in heads, spikes, or umbels. In the very large genus *Carex*, each female flower is enclosed within a structure called a perigynium, which is a modified scale, the edges of which are fused to form a sack, leaving a small opening through which the style protrudes. In some genera, the petals and sepals are reduced to mere bristles ("perianth bristles") that rise from beneath the ovary. The fruit is an achene.

Attractive with their deep green foliage and spikelet flowers, some members of the family such as the cotton-grasses (*Eriophorum*) are particularly showy when in fruit. Sedges are particularly common in wet, middle elevation meadows, although some species of *Carex* thrive in dry places and some can grow at over 6,500 feet of elevation. There are 5 genera and 58 species altogether in the Cyperaceae; the *Carex* genus alone is represented by 50 species.

1 Female flower enfolded within a perigynium (a modified scale, the edges of which are fused to form a sack); flowers unisexual, male or female .......... *Carex*
1 Female flower in the axil of a flat scale; flowers bisexual, with both stamens and a pistil .......... 2

2(1) Perianth bristles very long and conspicuous, the spike appearing white and cottony .......... *Eriophorum*
2 Perianth bristles short and inconspicuous, not much longer than the flower .......... 3

3(2) Spikelet solitary, lacking any subtending bract .......... *Eleocharis*
3 Spikelet solitary or spikelets numerous, in either case set above 1 or more leaflike bracts .......... 4

4(3) Inflorescence a single spike; bracts of the involucre very short, erect, and not leaflike .......... *Trichophorum*
4 Inflorescence of numerous spikelets on spreading branches; bracts of the involucre long, spreading and leaflike .......... *Scirpus*

## Carex L.—SEDGE

The wetlands and meadows of the mountain apparently provide excellent habitat for the sedges, as the genus is represented by 50 species. While most are to be found in meadows at middle elevations, they are by no means restricted to such habitats: some grow in forests and others on rocky slopes in the alpine zone. And while the plants range in size from small to huge, the only way to make clear identifications is to carefully examine details of the anatomy of the flowering parts, with a handlens certainly and preferably with a microscope. And, as if this were not enough of a challenge, a successful identification often depends upon having plants that are mature enough that the shape and size of the perigynium can be determined with accuracy.

The stems of *Carex* are triangular, often with sharp, raspy corners (hence, the old expression, "sedges have edges"). The leaves are thus in three ranks along the stems. The lowest leaf blades are often reduced to sheaths, while the upper blades may be flat, folded, or inrolled. Measurements of leaf width are made on the lower regular stem leaves.

*Carex* flowers are unisexual: each is male or female. The flowers of each sex may be in separate spikes, or they may form mixed spikes with one sex above the other. They are arranged in one to several spikes per stem. The words "androgynous" and "gynaecandrous" are used to indicate the relative position of the male and female flowers.

The former means "male above," and the latter "female above." These configurations are seen in *Carex* species at Mount Adams:

1. If there is a single spike per stem, the male flowers are always at the top (androgynous).

2. Where there are two or more spikes per stem, the terminal spike may be all male (androgynous) or all female (gynaecandrous). Some species have two or more terminal male spikes. In either case, the lower spikes are usually all female.

3. Where there are two or more spikes per stem, and the terminal spike is mixed, the species is androgynous if male flowers are at the top of the mixed spike and gynaecandrous if the top flowers are female. As in case 2, the lower spikes are usually all female.

Finally, in mixed spikes, there are almost always many more female than male flowers.

The male flowers typically have 3 stamens (although occasionally 2). The male spike, or portion of it, is usually more slender than the female portion; this feature alone helps to distinguish the two sexes. Even after flowering, remnant wispy anthers can often be found on at least a few flowers.

As noted above, each female flower is borne in a perigynium (plural, perigynia) formed of a modified bract. The details of the perigynium are very important in the *Carex* key—features such as shape, dimensions, color, and surface features of mature flowers must be ascertained under magnification. The perigynium may be blunt at the tip, but is more often extended to form a beak; the surface is sometimes hairy and may have distinctive veins or a winged margin. Within the perigynium is the ovary, which develops into an achene. The stigmas, numbering 2 or 3, protrude from a tiny opening at the top of the perigynium; here they are positioned to capture the wind-borne pollen. At the base of the perigynium is a scale, which more or less covers the perigynium. The color of this scale largely determines the overall hue of the spike.

| | |
|---|---|
| 1 | Solitary spike on each flowering stem; stigmas 3 (rarely 2 in *C. nardina*) .......... 2 |
| 1 | 2 or more spikes per stem; stigmas 2 or 3 .......... 7 |
| 2(1) | Plants tufted, lacking a spreading rootstock .......... 3 |
| 2 | Plants with spreading rootstocks .......... 4 |
| 3(2) | Mature perigynia spreading at maturity .......... *C. pyrenaica* ssp. *pyrenaica* |
| 3 | Mature perigynia upright or merely ascending .......... *C. nardina* var. *hepburnii* |
| 4(2) | Perigynia 1 to 3 per stem .......... *C. geyeri* |
| 4 | Perigynia more numerous .......... 5 |
| 5(4) | Leaves flat, most more than 1.5 mm wide .......... *C. nigricans* |
| 5 | Leaf margins inrolled, seldom more than 1.5 mm wide .......... 6 |
| 6(5) | Male portion of the spike inconspicuous, less than 2 mm long .......... *C. engelmannii* |
| 6 | Male portion of the spike about 5 mm long .......... *C. breweri* |
| 7(1) | Spikes gynaecandrous or at least the terminal spike female .......... 8 |
| 7 | Spikes androgynous or the terminal spike male .......... 27 |
| 8(7) | Stigmas 3 .......... 9 |
| 8 | Stigmas 2 .......... 10 |
| 9(8) | Longest spike about 2.5 cm, on a short, upright stalk .......... *C. epapillosa* |
| 9 | Longest spike 2-4 cm long, on a slender, nodding stalk .......... *C. mertensii* |
| 10(8) | Perigynia fewer than 10 in most spikes .......... 11 |
| 10 | Perigynia more numerous .......... 12 |
| 11(10) | Spikes well-spaced, the axis of the stem visible .......... *C. echinata* ssp. *echinata* |
| 11 | Spikes crowded into a head, the axis not visible .......... *C. illota* |
| 12(10) | Ligule elongated, more than 3 mm long .......... *C. fracta* |
| 12 | Ligule less than 3 mm long .......... 13 |

13(12) Spikes crowded into a head, the axis not visible or mostly obscured ........................................................................................ 14
13 Spikes more loosely arranged, the axis visible ........................... 22

14(13) Plants from open forests and meadows at middle elevations ...... 15
14 Plants growing at or above timberline .......................................... 20

15(14) Bract of the lowest 1 or 2 spikes prolonged, equaling or exceeding the length of the head ........................................... *C. athrostachya*
15 Bracts of the lowest spike less than half the length of the head ........ ........................................................................................ 16

16(15) Perigynia with 10 or more distinct nerves ................ *C. multicostata*
16 Perigynia with fewer nerves, or the nerves less evident ............. 17

17(16) Perigynia less than 3 mm long, greenish to straw-colored ............... ................................... ............................................. *C. subfusca*
17 Perigynia more than 3 mm long, some shade of brown .............. 18

18(17) Perigynia flattened, about 1 mm wide ......................... *C. microptera*
18 Perigynia rounded in one side, 1.5-3 mm wide ............................ 19

19(18) Scales smaller and more pale than the perigynia, the spikes therefore with a bicolored appearance ................. *C. pachystachya*
19 Scales more or less equal to the perigynia, concealing them, the spikes not bicolored .......................................................... *C. preslii*

20(14) Female spikes about 1 cm long ............................ *C. straminiformis*
20 Female spikes more than 1.5 cm long ....................................... 21

21(20) Perigynia 4-5.5 mm long ..................................... *C. phaeocephala*
21 Perigynia about 7 mm long ................................... *C. constanceana*

22(13) Spikes more than 10 per stem ............................................ *C. arcta*
22 Spikes fewer than 10, often 5 or fewer ....................................... 23

23(22) Perigynia winged (with a band of thin, flat tissue at the lateral margins); stems 10-30 cm tall .................................... *C. leporinella*
23 Perigynia not winged; stems 20-60 cm tall ................................. 24

24(23) Beaks of the perigynia well-developed, 0.5 mm long or more ...... 25
24 Beaks short or nearly absent ...................................................... 26

25(24) Leaves 2.5-5 mm wide; perigynia 3.5-4.5 mm long and about 1 mm wide .................................................... *C. deweyana* var. *deweyana*
25 Leaves less than 2 mm wide; perigynia 2-4 mm long and 1-1.5 mm wide ......................................................................... *C. laeviculmis*

26(24) Perigynia mostly fewer than 12 per spike ........................................ ........................................................ *C. canescens* ssp. *canescens*
26 Perigynia 15-30 per spike .......... *C. brunnescens* ssp. *brunnescens*

27(7) Stigmas 3 ........................................................................ 28
27 Stigmas 2 ........................................................................ 40

28(27) Perigynia short-hairy ................................................ 29
28 Perigynia smooth (at most with tiny hair-like teeth towards the tip of the beak) ........................................................................ 33

29(28) Perigynia with a few short, stiff hairs across the upper faces ........... ...................................................... *C. luzulina* var. *ablata*
29 Perigynia densely hairy ........................................................ 30

30(29) Spikes less than 1.5 cm long ............................ *C. inops* ssp. *inops*
30 Spikes more than 1.5 cm long .................................................. 31

31(30) Plants of moist meadows ........................................... *C. lasiocarpa*
31 Plants of dry slopes and forest openings .................................... 32

32(31) Perigynia few per spike, each spike less than 1 cm long .... *C. rossii*
32 Perigynia many per spike, each spike more than 1.5 cm long .......... ..................................................................................... *C. halliana*

33(28) Spikes stalkless ......................................................... *C. vesicaria*
33 Spikes on short to long stalks ...................................................... 34

34(33) Plants tufted, lacking a creeping rootstock; perigynia with a few short, stiff hairs across the upper faces ......... *C. luzulina* var. *ablata*
34 Plants with creeping rootstocks; perigynia smooth ...................... 35

35(34) Leaves 1-2 mm wide, channeled ..................................... *C. limosa*
35 Leaves wider than 2 mm, flat ...................................................... 36

36(35) Perigynia with a long, tapered 2-toothed beak, spreading from the axis at maturity ........................................................... *C. utriculata*
36 Perigynia beak not as above, erect or ascending at maturity ....... 37

37(36) Female spikes cylindrical, 10-20 cm long; leaves 1-2 cm wide ......... ..................................................................................... *C. amplifolia*
37 Female spikes variously shaped but shorter than 5 cm; leaves narrower ........................................................................... 38

38(37) Lowest leaves with well-developed blades .................. *C. raynoldsii*
38 Lowest leaves scale-like ............................................................ 39

39(38) Lowermost spikes with well-developed basal sheaths; female spikes slender, 2-5 cm long ........................................ *C. californica*
39 Lowermost spikes sheathless; female spikes 1-3 cm long ............... ........................................................................... *C. spectabilis*

40(27) Plants tufted, lacking extensive creeping rootstocks .................... 41
40 Stems arising from creeping rootstocks ....................................... 43

41(40) Spikes stalked ..................................... *C. lenticularis* var. *lipocarpa*
41 Spikes stalkless ........................................................................... 42

42(41) Leaf sheath prominent, cross-wrinkled on the side opposite the leaf blade ......................................................................... *C. neurophora*
42 Leaf sheath obscure, smooth ........................................... *C. hoodii*

43(40) Spikes few-flowered, each with 2-8 perigynia .............................. 44
43 Spikes many-flowered, with more than 10 perigynia each ........... 45

44(43) Spikes crowded into a compact head ............................... *C. jonesii*
44 Spikes well-spaced on a slender stem .......................... *C. disperma*

45(43) Spikes stalkless or the lowest spike with a stalk less than 2 mm ...... ........................................................................................... 46
45 Spikes stalked.............................................................................. 48

46(45) Spikes cylindrical, 2-5 cm long, well-spaced in the stem ................. ..................................................................... *C. aquatilis* var. *aquatilis*
46 Spikes egg-shaped, crowded into a loose to compact head ........ 47

47(46) Spikes closely crowded, distinguished with difficulty ... *C. vernacula*
47 Spikes more loosely grouped, the axis of the stem visible between the lower spikes ...................................................... *C. praegracilis*

48(45) Spikes cylindrical, 2-5 cm long, well-spaced in the stem ................. ........................................................................ *C. aquatilis* var. *dives*
48 Spikes egg-shaped, less than 2 cm long .................................... 49

49(48) Bract of the lowest spike with a well-developed sheath 3-12 mm long; perigynia golden-colored at maturity .......................... *C. aurea*
49 Sheath of the lowest bract absent or rudimentary; perigynia colored otherwise ..........................................................................50

50(49) Perigynia small, less than 2 mm long ......................... *C. angustata*
50 Perigynia larger, 2-3.5 mm long ........ *C. scopulorum* var. *bracteosa*

### *Carex amplifolia* Boott—BIGLEAF SEDGE

With leaves 1-2 cm wide and vigorous growth from heavy, spreading rootstocks, this sedge is easily distinguished from others that grow in swampy places. The flowering stems reach 1 m tall and are leafy on the upper portion. This is an androgynous species, with a slender male spike and 4-6 female spikes, each up to 10 cm long on slender, erect stalks. The female flower has 3 stigmas and the mature perigynia is about 3 mm long, egg-shaped with a slender beak; they tend to spread from the axis of the spike at maturity.

This *Carex* is found below 5,000 feet, in sunny, swampy areas, usually growing in shallow water, but often on ground that is dry by the end of the summer. It was found by the authors at Grand Meadow and lower Hellroaring Meadows. It is also known from historic Suksdorf and Henderson collections.

### *Carex angustata* Boott—WIDEFRUIT SEDGE

Forming wide patches that rise from a heavy, branching rootstock, this sedge can reach 50-70 cm in height, with flat leaves that are 3-5 cm wide. The terminal spike is male and about 4 cm long. The lowest of the 3 or 4 female spikes can be up to 8 cm long and is borne on a short stem; it is noteworthy for the fact that the lowest perigynia are separated from each other (accounting for a former name, *Carex interrupta*). The perigynia are obovate to nearly round and less than 2 mm long. There are 2 stigmas.

At the northern limit of its distribution at the mountain, this sedge is known for Washington only through a collection made by Flett in 1899 at Klickitat Meadows, a place apparently at about 4,000 feet on the northeast side of Mount Adams. Further southward along the west side of the Oregon Cascades, it grows on river banks and in the beds of seasonal streams.

### *Carex aquatilis* Wahlenb. var. *aquatilis*—WATER SEDGE

Stout rootstocks of this *Carex* send up many slender stems, reaching 1-1.5 m in height, with flat leaves about 7 mm wide clustered near the base of the plant. The female spikes are rather stout and 2-5 cm long; the terminal male spike is more slender and usually longer. In the variety *aquatilis*, the spikes are not stalked. The female flower has 2 stigmas and the mature perigynia are 2-3 mm long and widest above the middle.

This tall, slender plant is one of the most frequently seen sedges at the shores of ponds and lakes, occurring below 4,500 feet, chiefly on the west side of Mount Adams, as at Grand Meadow and Council Lake. This common species ranges east of the Cascade Mountains and is not known from Mount Rainier.

### *Carex aquatilis* Wahlenb. var. *dives* (Holm) Kükenth.—SITKA SEDGE

Very similar to *Carex aquatilis* var. *aquatilis*, this variety is most easily identified by the slender, nodding stalks of the lower female spikes. The latter are also more slender and longer, to 10 cm, than those of variety *aquatilis*. The plant is taller, from 1.5-2 m in height, with leaves about 1 cm wide.

The name "Sitka sedge" reflects the fact that this plant was once known as *Carex sitchensis*.

As common and abundant at Mount Adams as *aquatilis,* this variety is apt to form more dense stands, as at the campground at Takhlakh Lake. Besides lake shores, it is also found in very wet meadows, such as Grand Meadow.

### *Carex arcta* Boott—NORTHERN CLUSTER SEDGE

A tufted sedge, with flat leaves on the lower part of the stem, reaching 30-40 cm tall, *C. arcta* is easily distinguished from other high elevation sedges by an inflorescence composed, typically, of 10 or so stalkless spikes arranged in a long headlike cluster. The plants are gynaecandrous, with relatively few male flowers in each of the lower spikes. There are 2 stigmas and the perigynia are less than 2 mm long and egg-shaped with a long beak.

Northern cluster sedge has a wide range at Mount Adams, both in habitat type and elevation. On the southeast side, Peter Zika found this species at 5,360 feet in Hellroaring Meadows while J.W. Thompson found it on "rocky moraines" at 7,000 feet. On the northwest, Sarah Gage and Sharon Rodman, following Henderson's historic collecting trip, found it at Muddy Meadows at 4,380 feet. There is also a Suksdorf collection made at timberline, presumably on the southeast side of Mount Adams. The authors found it at Foggy Flat at over 6,000 feet of elevation.

### *Carex athrostachya* Olney—SLENDER-BEAK SEDGE

Slender-beak sedge grows in dense tufts of stems that reach almost 1 m tall. The 3 to 5 stalkless, gynaecandrous spikes are closely crowded into a head. It can be distinguished from similar species by the very long bracts at the bases of the lowest spikes that can reach 3 cm in length. The perigynia are 3-5 mm long, spindle-shaped with a very long, slender beak that is toothed on its upper margins.

Seldom found at Mount Adams and known from a collection made by Flett at about 4,000 feet on the upper reach of the Klickitat River. It was also found by Peter Zika at 5,412 feet in a seasonally dry meadow along Hellroaring Creek.

### *Carex aurea* Nutt.—GOLDEN SEDGE

This is a striking plant in late summer when the perigynia take on a golden color. Golden sedge sends up 1 or 2 stems from a slender rootstock. The 2 or 3 female spikes are borne on slender, upright stalks, with a few-flowered male spike at the top of the stem. The female spikes are each subtended by a very long, leaf-like bract that envelops the stem as a distinct sheath. Golden sedge has 2 stigmas and the perigynia are 2-3 mm long, oval to elliptical, and spread somewhat at maturity.

Known from a collection made by Suksdorf in a meadow at about 4,000 feet on the upper reach of the Klickitat River and from a Flett collection at Klickitat Meadows, this species grows at lower elevations throughout much of western Washington and western Oregon.

### *Carex breweri* Boott—BREWER'S SEDGE

Occurring singly or as a few stems together from an extensive, stout rootstock, this sedge may reach 20-30 cm in height although it is often only 10 cm. The leaves are stiff and only about 1 mm wide. The spike is solitary, with the male flowers at the top and easily distinguished from the wider female portion of the spike. In *C. breweri*, the male portion is about 5 mm long. There are 3 stigmas; the perigynia are almost round in outline and 4-7 mm long.

This species is very similar to *C. engelmannii*, which was once called *C. breweri* var. *paddoensis*. Hitchcock states that Brewer's sedge reaches its northern limit of distribution at Mount Adams, while Engelmann's sedge grows from Mount Adams northwards in the Cascade Mountains.

A species of talus or open rocky slopes at and above timberline, it was collected by Suksdorf on the west and east sides of the mountain.

### *Carex brunnescens* (Pers.) Poir. ssp. *brunnescens*—BROWN SEDGE

Lacking spreading rootstocks, brown sedge is tufted, with stems 20-50 cm tall and slender leaves less than 2 mm wide. The 4-8 spikes are short and loosely grouped at the top of the stem. This sedge is gynaecandrous, with 2 stigmas. The perigynia are oval, with a short, toothed beak and about 2 mm long.

Uncommon at Mount Adams, this sedge is typically found below 4,500 feet in wet meadows on well-developed soils with such plants as *Lupinus polyphyllus*. It is quite similar to *Carex canescens*, but the more numerous perigynia of *C. brunnescens*, as described in the key, will usually distinguish the two. It was collected by the authors at Spring Creek Meadow and is also known from a Flett collection.

### *Carex californica* Bailey—CALIFORNIA SEDGE

Unlikely to be seen even by serious *Carex* collectors, California sedge most closely resembles the very common C. *spectabilis*. (The latter occurs in similar wet meadow habitats but at elevations higher than 4,000 feet.)

In addition to characters in the key, it is distinguished by the reddish-brown to purple colored leaf-sheaths at the base of the stem.

The perigynia are 3.5-5 mm long, with a surface that is covered with fine, minute bumps.

This species is known only from an 1895 Suksdorf collection for which label information states only that it came from "mountains" on the west side. Elsewhere in western Washington it grows at lower elevations between the coast and the Cascades.

#### *Carex canescens* L. ssp. *canescens*—GRAY SEDGE

A tufted sedge that sometimes also has short rootstocks, this species has stems that reach 50-60 cm tall. The leaves are flat and 2-4 mm wide. The 4-8 spikes are stalkless and well-spaced on the stem. Gray sedge is gynaecandrous, with 2 stigmas. The perigynia are egg-shaped with a short beak and less than 1.5 mm long.

Also called silvery sedge for the overall color of the spikes, this species is common in wet meadows between 3,500 feet (along Cascade Creek in the southwest corner of the Wilderness Area) and 5,000 feet, as in Hellroaring Meadows. It can also be found in wet, open places in middle elevation forests.

#### *Carex constanceana* Stacey—CONSTANCE'S SEDGE

This rare, and possibly now extinct, species grows in tufts, with stems up to 90 cm tall. Leaves are borne along the stem and are flat and 2-4 mm wide. The gynaecandrous spikes, between 3 and 7, are closely arranged in an egg-shaped head. The female scales have a blunt tip and are shorter than (or rarely equal to) the perigynia in length, not covering the latter. The reddish-brown male and female scales have a thin (up to about 0.2 mm) wide margin, less than that of *C. petasata*. The perigynium is egg-shaped, with a long and slender beak, altogether 6.8-7.5 mm long and mostly straw-colored, giving the spike a bicolored appearance.

Hitchcock's opinion was that the Mount Adams plants, here called Constance's sedge, were encompassed within the range of variation of *Carex petasata*, a common species of western North America. However, Joy Mastrogiuseppe and others, in their treatment of *Carex* for the *Flora of North America*, recognize the species and distinguish it from *C. petasata*.

The plant has not been seen since it was originally collected by Suksdorf on August 16, 1909, despite the efforts of a number of botanists, including Joy Mastrogiuseppe and Peter Zika. Dr. Mastrogiuseppe has studied Suksdorf's journals and notes that the collections were made at the start of a day's work, suggesting that they were found close to his usual camp at today's Hellroaring Overlook. That suggestion points to a location at the top of Hellroaring Valley, where talus slopes plunge down from the terminus of Mazama Glacier, at 6,864 feet, according to the collector's label. The possibility certainly exists that the species is extinct, perhaps due to the severe impact of heavy grazing by sheep in the 1920s and 1930s.

### *Carex deweyana* Schwein. var. *deweyana*—DEWEY'S SEDGE

Growing in clumps and lacking a creeping rootstock, this sedge bears stems that range from 50-100 cm tall. The flat leaves are light green and 2-5 mm wide. The 4-8 gynaecandrous spikes are grouped in a loose head. There are 2 stigmas. The light green perigynia are 3.5-4.5 mm long, egg-shaped, with a long and slender beak.

Dewey's sedge is common along streams and in moist forest openings below about 4,000 feet in the Pacific Northwest. At Mount Adams its occurrence is limited to the lower reach of Cascade Creek, in the southwest corner of the Mount Adams Wilderness Area, where it reaches 3,400 feet and grows about the edges of small ponds in the shade of red alder (*Alnus rubra*).

### *Carex disperma* Dewey—SOFTLEAF SEDGE

Exceptionally slender and graceful, with one or two stems rising at short intervals from a creeping rootstock, this sedge has flat leaves that are up to 2 mm wide. The stems are up to 50 cm tall, with 4-6 androgynous spikes, each with only 2-4 flowers: typically one male and the rest female. There are two stigmas and the elliptical perigynia are 2-3 mm long.

This *Carex* was found twice by the authors at Mount Adams, on Morrison Creek at the Shorthorn trailhead, where the plants grew as a fringe around a boulder in the creek, and nearby where Trail 73 crosses Crofton Creek. No historical collections are known.

### *Carex echinata* Murr. ssp. *echinata*—STAR SEDGE, BRISTLY SEDGE

Easily separated from the other sedges at Mount Adams by the distinctive spikes that, at maturity, resemble spiny burs, this tufted plant has stems that can reach 50 cm but are often less, with leaves up to 2 mm wide. The short, stalkless spikes are gynaecandrous, with 2 stigmas. The perigynia are 3.5-4 mm long, egg-shaped with a very long, sturdy beak. At maturity, the perigynia spread away from the axis of the spike, becoming "starlike."

This species is very common in wet meadows surrounding Mount Adams, between 4,000 and 6,500 feet, often in sphagnum bogs.

### *Carex engelmannii* Bailey—ENGELMANN'S SEDGE

This high-elevation species is very similar to *C. breweri* and was once considered a variety of that species: *C. breweri* var. *paddoensis*. In Engelmann's sedge, the male portion of the single terminal spike is often difficult to discern; at most, it is 1 or 2 mm long. Another good feature is the nature of the veins on the female scales - in *C. engelmannii* there is a solitary vein compared to 3 in *C. breweri*.

Apparently less common at Mount Adams than *C. breweri*, this sedge is most often seen above timberline on the south side, as along the South Climb trail between 6,000 and 8,000 feet. It is abundant at Mount Rainier, where it reaches 9,500 feet.

### *Carex epapillosa* Mackenzie—SMOOTH-NERVE SEDGE

Similar to and sometimes mistaken for *Carex mertensii*, *C. epapillosa* is a tufted species, lacking a creeping rhizome. It is about 60 cm tall, with 3-5 spikes per stem. The lower spikes are on short stalks and are not more than 2.5 cm long. The perigynia are 3-4 mm long, with a short beak, and are widest towards the tip.

A common enough species in the Pacific Northwest, at Mount Adams it is only known from a collection made by Suksdorf at 6,500 feet in the valley of Hellroaring Creek and from a Henderson collection along Big Muddy River.

### *Carex fracta* Mackenzie—FRAGILE-SHEATH SEDGE

This is a coarse plant, with sturdy stems that are 50-100 cm tall. The flat leaves are 3-6 mm wide. The leaf sheath is distinctive: it is whitish and elongated up to 10 mm on the side opposite the leaf blade; it is easily torn. The numerous, stalkless, gynaecandrous spikes are closely grouped into an elongated head. The perigynia are greenish to straw-colored, from 2.5-5 mm long, egg-shaped with a long beak.

Uncommon and typically seen in dry, disturbed places, as along roads, this sedge is known from alongside Road 23 close to the Pacific Crest Trail crossing at Potato Hill. Suksdorf found it at a "shaded spring" at 4,200 feet in the valley of Muddy Creek.

### *Carex geyeri* Boott—GEYER'S SEDGE

This sedge is a small plant, usually less than 40 cm tall, with a few stems arising at intervals from a heavy rootstock. The leaves are flat and 2-4 mm wide. The spike is solitary, androgynous, and few-flowered - rarely more than 3 or 4 flowers are present. The perigynia are straw-colored, 5-7 mm long, and much wider at the top than at the narrow base.

Uncommon at Mount Adams, only two collections are known, both made by Suksdorf on the southeast side of the mountain, probably in dry meadows along Hellroaring Creek.

### *Carex halliana* Bailey—HALL'S SEDGE

A low sedge with stems that reach about 30 cm, this species grows in tufts from a heavy rootstock. The leaves are flat or folded and 2-5 mm wide. The spikes are long relative to the height of the stem, up to 5 cm long; the top 1 or 2 are staminate, with 3 or 4 pistillate spikes below. The bracts of the lower spikes are long and leaf-like. There are 3 stigmas and the perigynia are 3.5-5 mm long, elliptical, and densely covered with short hairs.

The most common of the dry-land sedges at Mount Adams, this species grows around the mountain between 4,000 and 5,000 feet, in forest openings, at the edges of dry meadows, and on disturbed ground at roadsides. Hall's sedge reaches its northern limit of range at Mount Adams.

### *Carex hoodii* Boott—HOOD'S SEDGE

Hood's sedge is a tufted plant, lacking a creeping rhizome, with stems 40-80 cm tall. The leaves are only about 3 mm wide and arranged on the lower part of the stem. The 5-10 spikes are androgynous and closely clustered into a dense head, obscuring the central axis. There are 2 stigmas, and the 3.5-5 mm long perigynia are copper-brown, with green edges, widest at the middle and with a long, tapered, beak that is serrate towards the tip.

This is an uncommon sedge found in a variety of habitats between 5,000 and 6,000 feet around the mountain: from dry meadows along the valley of Hellroaring Creek to dryish places about the Morrison Creek trailhead to forest openings on the Pineway trail.

### *Carex illota* Bailey—SHEEP SEDGE

Growing typically in dense patches, sometimes from a very short rootstock, the stems of sheep sedge reach up to 30 cm tall but frequently are just 10 cm in height. The spikes are gynaecandrous and crowded either into a dense head, or with the lowest spike somewhat remote. There are 2 stigmas and the perigynia are narrowly egg-shaped, 2.5-3 mm long, and dark brown to nearly black.

Very common and a major component of meadows that become dry by summer's end, this sedge is most often seen between 5,000 and nearly 7,000 feet. It is also found on rocky slopes where summer moisture is available. Babyshoe Meadow is a good place to find it.

### *Carex inops* Bailey ssp. *inops*—LONG-STOLON SEDGE

Forming tufts from extensive creeping rootstocks (not, properly speaking, "stolons"), this sedge has stems up to 40 or 50 cm tall, with relatively short leaves grouped near the bases. The species is androgynous, with a solitary, slender terminal male spike. There are usually 2 short female spikes, each with a leaf-like bract. There are 3 stigmas and the perigynia are 3-4.5 mm long, rounded over the top but with a prominent beak; the surface is densely short-hairy.

Known from several historical collections from the south and southeast sides of the mountain, *C. inops* was also observed once by the authors on Road 23 south of Babyshoe Meadow.

**_Carex jonesii_ Bailey—JONES'S SEDGE**

A small sedge with stems at short intervals on a heavy rootstock, this species has flat leaves 1-3 mm wide. The species is androgynous, with the 1-2 cm heads crowded into a dense oblong cluster. The perigynia are 3-4 mm long, widest at the base and tapered to a slender beak; there are 2 stigmas.

Jones's sedge is known from several poorly documented collections made by Suksdorf in the valley of Hellroaring Creek, between 6,000 and 6,500 feet, as well as a modern collection by the authors at Foggy Flat, on the north flank of Mount Adams. The species grows in deep soil in meadows that become dry by mid-summer.

**_Carex laeviculmis_ Meinsh.—SMOOTH-STEM SEDGE**

Densely tufted, with stems from 30-60 cm tall, this sedge also spreads by rootstocks. The flat leaves are 1-2 mm wide. The species is gynaecandrous, with 6-8 small, egg-shaped heads; the lower are well-separated while the upper are close together. The greenish to brown perigynia are 2-4 mm long, widest at the base and tapered to a slender beak; there are 2 stigmas.

Collected by Suksdorf in the valley of Hellroaring Creek, this species was also collected by the authors in an open forest along Road 23, near the Pacific Crest Trail crossing.

**_Carex lasiocarpa_ Ehrh.—WOOLY-FRUITED SEDGE**

With stems scattered on an elongated rootstock and reaching 1 m tall, *C. lasiocarpa* has leaves just 1.5 mm wide, a result of being strongly folded along the midrib, but very long. The species is androgynous, with 1 or 2 slender male spikes and usually 2 female spikes. The perigynia are 3-4.5 mm long, elliptical with a prominent beak, and velvety; there are 3 stigmas.

Known only from collections made by the authors at Swampy Meadows, where it grows on muddy ground along with *Deschampsia cespitosa* and *Vaccinium uliginosum*, this species apparently reaches its southern limit of distribution at Mount Adams. It is more common at Mount Rainier and northwards.

### *Carex lenticularis* Michx. var. *lipocarpa* (Holm) L.A. Standley
### LAKESHORE SEDGE

A tufted sedge, with a very short rootstock or rootstock absent, the stems are 15-40 cm tall. The longest leaves generally equal or exceed the flowering stem and are 1-3.5 mm wide. The male spike is uppermost, long and slender; the 3-5 female spikes are nearly cylindrical and arranged in a loose cluster. The perigynia are about 2.5 mm long, widest at the middle, and greenish. The scales are black and smaller than the perigynia, giving the spikes a two-toned appearance. There are 2 stigmas.

Very common around Mount Adams, this species is often abundant at lakeshores and in wet meadows, up to about 6,000 feet. Babyshoe Meadow is a good place to see it.

### *Carex leporinella* Mackenzie—LITTLE HARE SEDGE

Little hare sedge is named for its stature, just 10-30 cm tall, rising from a dense tuft of leaves. The leaves are more or less flat, 1-2 mm wide, and 10-20 cm long. The 3-6 stalkless, gynaecandrous spikes are in a rather loose, elliptical to egg-shaped head. The perigynia are brownish, 2-4 mm long, widest at the middle and tapered to the poorly-defined beak; the upper margins are minutely toothed.

This species was found just once by the authors, close to the Yakama Nation boundary on the north side of Mount Adams at 4,800 feet in a lodgepole pine woods, where it grows with several other *Carex* species in small meadows that are only seasonally wet.

### *Carex limosa* L.—MUD SEDGE

A slender plant, reaching about 50 cm from a widely-spreading, slender rootstock, this species has a special distinction: the major roots are covered with a yellow, felty layer of hairs. The leaves are 1-2 mm wide and folded along the midvein. The terminal male spike is uppermost, 1-3 cm long and slender, and about twice the length of the nodding, elliptical female spikes. There are 3 stigmas and the perigynia are elliptical and 2.5-4 mm long, widest at the middle.

Found just once in the Mount Adams region by the authors, at Swampy Meadows, where it is common on muddy ground at the north end of the meadow; this species should be looked for in other sphagnum meadows.

### *Carex luzulina* Olney var. *ablata* (Bailey) F.J. Herm.
### WOODRUSH SEDGE

A tufted plant, lacking a rootstock, with stems 30-90 mm tall., this species has leaves that are crowded at the base of the stem and comparatively wide, to nearly 1 cm (the common name notes their resemblance to leaves of *Luzula* species). The species is androgynous, with 3-7 elliptical, closely-grouped female spikes. There are 3 stigmas. The perigynia are light green to purplish, 3.5-4 mm long, with a long, tapered beak; it is also sparsely short-hairy, but sometimes only so toward the beak.

Seldom found at Mount Adams, where it grows in wet meadows and in wet places in open forests, to 5,500 feet, this sedge was collected by the authors on Stagman Ridge. It is more common in the Cascade Mountains to the north.

#### *Carex mertensii* Prescott *ex* Bong.—MERTENS'S SEDGE

This is a tall and robust sedge, growing in large clumps with stems reaching 120 cm. The flat leaves are 3-7 mm wide. The 5-8 gynaecandrous spikes nod on long stalks; each is elliptical, to 2 cm long and 1 cm broad; there are 3 stigmas. The perigynia are about 5 mm long, tapered towards each end with a very short beak. The perigynia are green while the much shorter scales are dark brown, giving the spikes a patterned, two-toned appearance.

A striking and attractive species, it is most often seen on wet ground along permanent streams between 4,000 and 6,000 feet, sometimes in open woods. It is a dominant plant on the deep soils of Spring Creek Meadow on the north side of Mount Adams.

#### *Carex microptera* Mackenzie—SMALL-WING SEDGE

An inconspicuous sedge, this species grows in dense clumps with stems reaching 60 cm in height. The flat leaves are 2-6 mm wide. Four to 7 gynaecandrous spikes are crowded into a tight head. The spikes appear bicolored: the perigynia are egg-shaped with a long and tapered beak and about 3-5 mm long and brown while the scales are smaller and greenish to tan. The name *microptera* refers to the narrow wing on the margin of the perigynium. There are 2 stigmas.

This sedge is known from two collections at Mount Adams: one made by Suksdorf in 1893 at an unspecified location and one by the authors alongside Road 115, a small track just east of Midway Meadows on the north side of the mountain, in a small, seasonally moist meadow at 4,500 feet. Mount Adams is close to the northern limit of the distribution of this species.

#### *Carex multicostata* Mackenzie—MANYRIB SEDGE

Much like *Carex microptera* in appearance, this clump-forming species also grows to 60 cm. The flat leaves are narrower, to about 3.5 mm wide. Four to 7 gynaecandrous spikes are crowded into a tight head, but not as closely as in *C. microptera*. There are 2 stigmas. The perigynia are 4.5-6 mm long, wing-margined, with a tapered beak that is serrate along the edges. "Multicostata" refers to the multiple fine ribs of the perigynium.

This sedge is known from just two collections at Mount Adams, one made by Henderson in 1883 at an unspecified location and one by the authors along the Pacific Crest Trail on the north side of the mountain, in a seasonally wet meadow with other sedge species. Elsewhere in the Cascades, it is found at lakeshores and on stream banks as well as in meadows.

### *Carex nardina* Fries var. *hepburnii* (Boott) Kükenth. SPIKENARD SEDGE

A little sedge found in harsh environments, the stems of this densely tufted plant are shorter than 15 cm. It has needle-like leaves that are longer than the flowering stems. A single androgynous spike tops each stem and bears about 10 female flowers. The perigynia are about 4 mm long, widest towards the top, and with a short beak. There are 3 stigmas, but rarely only 2.

Not a common sedge at Mount Adams, this species grows on rocky ridges above timberline, generally above 6,000 feet and reaching 8,000 feet. Historical collections by Suksdorf and Henderson are known from the east and southeast sides of the mountain. Mount Adams represents its southern limit of distribution in the Cascade Mountains.

### *Carex neurophora* Mackenzie—ALPINE NERVED SEDGE

Tufted, sometimes forming large clumps, with stems up to 50 cm, the leaves of this sedge are flat, 1.5-3 mm wide, and well-distributed along the stem. The leaf sheaths are distinctive: they are thin-textured, light in color, and cross-wrinkled (that is, they appear to be corrugated across the surface opposite the side where the leaf blade attaches). The 7-10 androgynous spikes are short, less than 1 cm long, and are crowded into an oblong head. The perigynia are 3-4 mm long, widest at the base and tapered to a slender tip and bear prominent veins (or "nerves"). The species has 2 stigmas.

An uncommon species at Mount Adams, it has been found between 5,300 to 6,500 feet, growing in wet meadows that may or may not become seasonally dry. The authors collected it along the Stagman Ridge trail and two Suksdorf collections are known from Hellroaring Valley.

### *Carex nigricans* C.A. Mey.—BLACK ALPINE SEDGE

This tough species is a mat-forming plant, spreading by thick rootstocks, with stems 5-20 cm tall. The leaves are flat and 1.5-3 mm wide. There is only 1 androgynous spike per stem, with perigynia that are brown to nearly black. They are 4 mm long, widest at the middle, and tapered to a slender tip; at maturity, they spread outwards and downwards before falling.

Common and often the dominant plant at timberline and above on flats where the snow is late to melt, this is sometimes the only plant growing in such places. It is also a major component of subalpine meadows and is frequently seen along the shores of small ponds, sometimes partly submerged at the start of the season. It is found at 8,100 feet on the South Climb trail and to 8,000 on the moraine at Mazama Glacier.

### *Carex pachystachya* Cham. *ex* Steud.—THICK-HEADED SEDGE

This is a small, tufted sedge, just 15-30 cm high, with slender stems and flat leaves 2-4 mm wide. Two to 7 short gynaecandrous spikes are crowded into a head that is 1-1.5 mm across. The perigynia are egg-shaped, 3-5 mm long with a tapered beak and a broad, finely-toothed marginal wing. The perigynia differ from those of the similar *C. microptera* in being rounded on the back side and wider, up to 2 mm. The scales are shorter and lighter-colored than the perigynia, giving the spike a bi-colored appearance. There are 2 stigmas.

Fairly common in perennially wet meadows and on stream banks, this species is most frequently encountered on the east and southeast sides of Mount Adams below 6,000 feet.

### *Carex phaeocephala* Piper—DUNHEAD SEDGE

A tufted plant, extending by offsets to form patches, dunhead sedge can reach 30 cm tall but is often less in harsh surroundings. The leaves are 1-2 mm wide, typically folded, and clustered at the base of the stems. Three to 5 short gynaecandrous spikes are crowded into a small head. The scales and perigynia are dark brown, giving the species its common name. The perigynia are 4-5 mm long, slender and widest at the middle, with a marginal wing and a prominent, flattened "base." There are 2 stigmas.

Very common on dry slopes and flats above timberline on all sides of Mount Adams, dunhead sedge is abundant at Killen High Camp. It is also seen on the flanks and summit of Little Mount Adams and reaches 8,500 feet between the White Salmon and Avalanche Glaciers.

### *Carex praegracilis* W. Boott—CLUSTERED FIELD SEDGE

In this species, single stems rise from a spreading rootstock and reach about 50 cm tall. The leaves are flat or folded, 1.5-3 mm wide, and arranged along the stem. Five to 10 oval, short, androgynous spikes are fairly crowded, although the lowest 1 or 2 may be separated lower on the stem. There are 2 stigmas and the 3-4 mm long perigynia are egg-shaped, with a prominent beak.

Interesting for occurring at higher elevations at Mount Adams than is typical for the species elsewhere in Washington, this sedge is known from a collection made by Suksdorf in Hellroaring Valley and by the authors along the South Climb Trail, in both cases at about 6,500 feet, among rocks on open slopes.

### *Carex preslii* Steud.—PRESL'S SEDGE

Very similar to *Carex pachystachya*, this was synonymized with that species by Hitchcock. Presl's sedge grows as more dense tufts of taller stems, ranging from 30-60 cm in height. The spikes are grouped into a looser head, with the lower 1 or 2 separate from the others. Another difference is seen in the spikes, which appear not bicolored but instead a uniform reddish brown. There are 2 stigmas.

Probably uncommon at Mount Adams, Presl's sedge is known from several collections made by Suksdorf on the south and southeast sides of the mountain. It is a plant of wet meadows and streamsides, as well as meadows that become seasonally dry. Peter Zika relocated the plant in Hellroaring Valley at 6,133 feet on a north-facing slope.

### *Carex pyrenaica* Wahlenb. ssp *pyrenaica*—PYRENAEAN SEDGE

Densely tufted and lacking spreading rootstocks, this species otherwise resembles *Carex nigricans*, a true mat-former found in similar places. The stems are typically less than 20 cm tall, with inrolled leaves about 1 mm wide. There is a single androgynous spike per stem, dark brown and 1-2 cm long. The perigynia are 3-4 mm long, brown, and lance-shaped. There are 3 stigmas.

Probably uncommon at Mount Adams, this species is known from a collection made by the authors in a dryish meadow at 5,300 feet on the Stagman Ridge trail and from an historical collection made by Suksdorf at nearly 8,500 feet at "Mount Adams." Elsewhere in the Cascades, it is a common species at and above timberline.

### *Carex raynoldsii* Dewey—RAYNOLDS'S SEDGE

Tufted and also spreading by rootstocks, Raynolds's sedge can reach 70 cm in height. The flat leaves are 3-8 cm broad and arranged along the stem. The lowest leaves have well-developed blades, a good point of contrast with the very common *Carex spectabilis*. There is a terminal male spike about 1.5 cm long and 2-5 female spikes grouped fairly closely below and about the same size; the lowest spike is often on a short, erect stalk. The perigynia are 3.5-4.5 mm long and widest at the top, with a very short beak. There are 3 stigmas.

This sedge is known from only one collection made by Henderson in 1892, at 6,000 feet at "Mount Adams," on a day when he was on the north side of the mountain. The species is widespread across the west, occurring in a wide variety of habitats. At Mount Rainier, it is known from upper Paradise Park.

### *Carex rossii* Boott—ROSS'S SEDGE

Growing tufts of stems from a thick rootstock, this species reaches about 30 cm tall. The leaves are flat and 1-3 mm wide. The terminal male spike is about 1 cm long while the 2 or 3 female spikes are a bit shorter. Usually there are 1 or 2 female spikes on short stems among the leaves at the base of the plant. The perigynia are few in number, egg-shaped and abruptly contracted to a pronounced beak and long base, and variable in size, overall up to 5 mm in length. There are 3 stigmas.

Infrequent at Mount Adams, Ross's sedge grows on dry slopes and in seasonally dry meadows below 5,500 feet. *Carex halliana,* with longer spikes, is much more common in this sort of habitat, reversing the situation at Mount Rainier, where *C. halliana* is absent.

### *Carex scopulorum* Holm var. *bracteosa* (Bailey) F.J. Herm. MOUNTAIN SEDGE

Growing in dense tufts loosely arranged on a stout rootstock, this sedge ranges to about 40 cm in height. The leaves are flat and 2-5 mm wide. The species is androgynous with fairly large, cylindrical heads, well-spaced, on very short stalks at the top of the stem. There are two stigmas and the purplish perigynia are elliptical and 2-4 mm long, with a very short beak.

A high elevation sedge, this species is found in open, moist places above timberline, reaching 8,000 on the south and southeast sides of the mountain. It has, however, also been collected at Council Pass, where R.W. Becking found it in 1953, growing at the edge of a sphagnum bog.

### *Carex spectabilis* Dewey—SHOWY SEDGE

A clump-forming plant that spreads by short rootstocks, the slender stems of this sedge are 25-70 cm tall. The flat leaves are 2.5-5 mm wide and well-spaced on the stem. Those at the bases of the stems are much reduced in size (a useful contrast with the otherwise similar *C. raynoldsii*). The inflorescence is androgynous, with a terminal male spike about 1-3 cm long (an arresting pale yellow color when in full bloom) and 3 or 4 female spikes of about the same size; the lowermost nod on short stalks. The perigynia are oval and 3-5 mm long, with a short beak; light green in color, they contrast with the darker scales. There are 3 stigmas.

The most attractive of the sedges at Mount Adams and very frequently seen, occurring in most wet meadows between 4,000 and 7,000 feet, showy sedge can be found on all sides of the mountain. It is especially easy to see at Babyshoe and Takh Takh Meadow. Sometimes it is also present in small flats that are only seasonally damp, as along the South Climb trail. On the northwest side, Peter Zika found it at the base of Adams Glacier at 6,500 feet and Sarah Gage and Sharon Rodman collected it nearby at Killen High Camp. Perhaps the loveliest plants are those that line the fast-flowing streamlets in Spring Creek Meadow.

### *Carex straminiformis* Bailey—SHASTA SEDGE

A tufted plant, lacking spreading rootstocks, the stout stems of this sedge may reach 40 cm in height, but are frequently just 10 cm tall. The flat or somewhat folded leaves are 2-4 mm wide and crowded at the base of the stem. The inflorescence is compact and head-like, of 3-8 short, gynaecandrous spikes. The perigynia are 4-5 mm long, almost round in outline with a broad marginal wing and tapered beak. There are 2 stigmas.

Shasta sedge, as suggested by the common name, is chiefly a species of California and Nevada where it grows on open slopes above timberline. It reaches its northern limit of distribution at Mount Adams and was known only from a collection made by Howell in 1882, at an undescribed location, until 2003 when Peter Zika collected it at 6,400 feet in a dry meadow on the east side of the Aiken Lava Bed.

### *Carex subfusca* W. Boott—BROWN-HEADED SEDGE

Very similar to *Carex pachystachya* densely tufted and 20-100 cm tall, brown-headed sedge has perigynia that are shorter, reaching 3 mm with a tapered, serrate beak. The perigynia and scales are both brown; the spikes in *C. pachystachya* appear bicolored due to the lighter perigynia. There are 2 stigmas.

Brown-headed sedge reaches its northern limit of distribution at Mount Adams, being more common at middle elevations in the mountains of California and Oregon. It must be considered rare at the mountain and is known only from a collection housed at Oregon State University, made in 1965 at Mirror Lake by Knut Faegri.

### *Carex utriculata* Boott—BLADDER SEDGE

Wide-spreading rootstocks and a sod-forming habit produce large clumps of this big sedge, whose stems can reach 120 cm in length. The leaves are 3-10 mm wide, with internal crosswalls that may be felt by running a blade between the fingertips. Androgynous, with 2-4 slender male spikes and typically an equal number of stalkless female spikes that may be 10 cm long, the inflorescence is long and loose. There are 3 stigmas. The perigynia are prominently veined and 4-6 mm long, tapered to a slender, 2-toothed beak. As the achene matures, the style remains attached and becomes hardened, a characteristic that can be seen with careful dissection of the perigynium.

Bladder sedge, named for the inflated perigynia that act as little rafts for the achenes, is a common species of middle elevation meadows and bogs on the east and southeast sides of Mount Adams, reaching about 4,500 feet.

### *Carex vernacula* Bailey—DRUMSTICK SEDGE

Spreading by short, branching rootstocks, this is a low-growing plant, reaching 20 cm. The stiff leaves are 2-4 mm wide and grouped at the base of the stem. The species is androgynous, with numerous small spikes grouped into a tight, brown cluster about 15 mm across. There are 2 stigmas. The perigynia are 3.5-5 mm long, with an extended base and broad marginal wing, tapered to a slender, 2-toothed beak.

This species does not appear to have a *bona fide* common name. The National Plants Database styles *Carex vernacula* "Native Sedge," an unhelpful name if ever there was one! "Drumstick" nicely describes the cluster of spikes atop the slender stem.

The species ranges widely across the West, reaching its northern limit of distribution in the Sierra/Cascades at Mount Adams, where it is rare, known only from two Suksdorf collections made at about 7,000 feet, probably on the southeast side of the mountain. Elsewhere, it is a species of moist places near and above timberline.

### *Carex vesicaria* Boott—BLISTER SEDGE

A clump-forming plant with stems that can reach 100 cm tall, this species has folded leaves from 2-6 mm wide. The terminal spikes are male, 1-3 in number, and very slender. The female spikes are cylindrical and about 2 cm long. The perigynia are held upright as they mature, a feature that separates this species from *C. utriculata*; they are greenish to straw-colored, prominently veined, 4-7.5 mm long and ovate with a tapered beak about 1/5 mm long. The style remains attached to the achene and there are 3 stigmas.

Found between 4,500 and 6,500 feet surrounding Mount Adams, this species is frequently seen in meadows that become rather dry by late summer; it can form extensive patches. It was collected by the authors on the north side of the mountain, near Midway Meadows and on the northwest at Bathtub Meadow.

## *Eleocharis* R. Br.—SPIKERUSH

Sedgelike, these plants bear solitary and bractless spikelets. The scales are membranous and spirally arranged; the flowers are borne singly in the axils of the scales. The bristles on the achene are typically short and not visible in the mature spike. The achene is topped by a tubercule, the remains of a thickened portion of the style; this may be distinctly caplike or undifferentiated from the achene.

| | | |
|---|---|---|
| 1 | Tiny, fragile plant, the stems less than 10 cm tall ......... | *E. acicularis* |
| 1 | Taller plants, at least 10 cm tall and usually 30 cm or more .......... | 2 |
| 2(1) | Stems greater than 50 cm tall; stigmas 2; achene capped with a distinct tubercule ........................................................ | *E. palustris* |
| 2 | Stems 10-30 cm tall; stigmas 3; achene merely pointed ................ | 3 |
| 3(2) | Plant with a hard, woody base, 1-2 mm thick; flowers 8-12 .............................................................................................. | *E. suksdorfiana* |
| 3 | Plant with a non-woody base, no more than 0.5 mm thick; flowers 3-7.......................................................................... | *E. quinqueflora* |

### *Eleocharis acicularis* (L.) Roemer & J.A. Schultes
### NEEDLE SPIKERUSH

"Needle" spikerush is named for its tufted, almost thread-like stems that are up to 10 cm tall. The plant is a perennial, spreading by slender rootstocks. The stem bears one purple-brown spikelet 3-6 mm long, with about 10 flowers. There are 3 stigmas and the achene bears at its top a distinct flat, cap-like tubercule.

This spikerush is found in the meadow fringing Mirror Lake, on the southeast side of Mount Adams at 5,450 feet, where it spreads across a flat of sandy mud at the inlet stream and where it has no competing vegetation. Suksdorf made a collection in Hellroaring Valley.

### *Eleocharis palustris* (L.) Roemer & J.A. Schultes
### COMMON SPIKERUSH

A vigorous plant that forms extensive colonies, common spike rush stems rise up to 1 m in height above heavy rootstocks. The spikelet is brown and 1-2.5 cm long with 20-30 flowers. There are 2 stigmas and the achene is capped with a pointed tubercule.

Common spikerush is known from an observation made by the authors on the north shore of Bench Lake at 4,850 feet, where it is common, growing in deep mud in water to about 1 m deep.

### *Eleocharis quinqueflora* (F.X. Hartmann) Schwarz
### FEW-FLOWERED SPIKERUSH

Few-flowered spikerush grows as tufts of stems from spreading rootstocks. Typically on a stem 10-30 cm tall, the spikelet itself is less than 8 mm long and holds just 3-7 flowers. There are 3 stigmas; the achene is beaked but lacks a distinct tubercule.

This is the most frequently seen spikerush in wet meadows between 4,000 and 5,500 feet, on all sides of the mountain, especially around Takhlakh Lake and nearby meadows. It can dominate small patches of ground, but more frequently blends in with other vegetation.

#### *Eleocharis suksdorfiana* Beauverd—SUKSDORF'S SPIKERUSH

Differing from *E. quinqueflora* most visibly in its hardened woody base that is 1-2 mm thick, this was recently recognized as a distinct species. The spikelets are a little longer, ranging between 5 and 10 mm, and there are 8-12 flowers. The beak is distinctly pointed but not tubercule-like.

This species is known from one collection, made by Suksdorf in Hellroaring Valley at about 6,500 feet. It was formerly labeled *E. quinqueflora,* but recently annotated by Galen Smith.

### *Eriophorum* L.—COTTON-GRASS

These sedgelike species are distinguished by the lengthened, soft, white, perianth bristles; these give the maturing spike the appearance of a cotton boll. There are 2 species at mount Adams, but *Eriophorum gracile* is very rare.

1 Inflorescence with a single, short, leaf-like bract that is much shorter than the inflorescence .......................................... *E. gracile*
1 Inflorescence with 2 or 3 bracts that may exceed the length of the inflorescence ............................ *E. angustifolium* ssp. *angustifolium*

#### *Eriophorum angustifolium* Honckeny ssp. *angustifolium*<br>TALL COTTONGRASS

Typically just one but sometimes several stems rise together from a slender, spreading rootstock, reaching 30-60 cm in height in this cotton grass. The stems are leafy (unlike *Eleocharis* species); leaves are 3-8 mm wide and folded lengthwise into a V. The 2 or 3 spikelets on short, nodding stalks are loosely grouped at the top of the stem and subtended by 2 or 3 leaflike bracts; at least one bract typically is longer than the inflorescence. The bristles are white.

Frequent in meadows all around Mount Adams, from 4,000 to 6,000 feet, this species is not abundant, but nevertheless easy to see thanks to the cottony, plume-like bristles. Babyshoe and Swampy Meadows are excellent places to find it, while Lookingglass Lake and upper Killen Creek require more hiking. It is also scattered along the length of Hellroaring Valley. Huge numbers may be seen in Takh Takh Meadow.

#### *Eriophorum gracile* W.D.J. Koch—SLENDER COTTONGRASS

A slender plant, with solitary stems that rise from a thin, spreading rootstock, slender cotton grass ranges from 20-60 cm in height. The stems are leafy from the base, the leaves only about 2 mm wide and deeply V-shaped. The 2 to 4 spikelets are on short, nodding stalks in a cluster, subtended by just 1 short, leaflike bract. The bristles are white.

Evidently rare at Mount Adams, this species is known only from a poorly documented Henderson collection made in 1892.

### *Scirpus* L.—BULRUSH

#### *Scirpus microcarpus* J. & K. Presl—SMALL-FRUITED BULRUSH

A vigorous species, with stems that reach 1-1.5 m tall, small-fruited bulrush typically forms colonies from long, heavy rootstocks. The stems are leafy and the blades broad, to 2 cm wide and channeled lengthwise. The individual spikelets are small, just 3-5 mm long, but numerous and grouped into small heads on the branches of an umbel-like inflorescence. The bracts of the inflorescence are long and leaflike.

Common below 4,500 feet, small-fruited bulrush is a prominent element of wet meadow communities on the north and west sides of Mount Adams; it also fringes ponds and lakes, growing out into shallow water. It may be seen at Muddy Meadows and at Spring Creek Meadow and was collected by the authors alongside Road 23 at milepost 41.

### *Trichophorum* Pers.—BULRUSH

#### *Trichophorum caespitosum* (L.) Hartman—TUFTED BULRUSH

Very similar in appearance to, as well as growing with, the common and abundant *Eleocharis quinqueflora*, tufted bulrush is separated by the presence of 1 or 2 small bracts beneath the spikelet; in *Eleocharis*, such bracts are absent. The plant grows in tufts and has round stems, unlike sedges. The leaves are reduced to sheaths at the bases of the stems, which may be up to 40 cm tall but are usually less. The spikelet is 3-6 mm long and contains 2 or 3 flowers.

This little bulrush, formerly known as *Scirpus caespitosus* was found by the authors at Babyshoe Meadow, a small, wet sphagnum meadow on the northwest side of Mount Adams at 4,200 feet.

## Hydrocharitaceae Juss.—FROG'S-BIT FAMILY

### *Elodea* Michx.—WATER-WEED

#### *Elodea nuttallii* (Planch.) St. John—WESTERN WATER-WEED

A forked, slender-stemmed perennial, the leaves are typically configured in groups of 3 and are 6-13 mm long, linear to linear-lanceolate, and sharply tipped, with fine teeth. The single flower is stalkless and floats on the surface. The sepals are about 2 mm long, and the petals are often lacking or very reduced in size; there are 9 stamens. The female inflorescence is enclosed in a pair of 9-15 mm long bracts, and the hypanthium is 10 cm long. The capsule is 5-7 mm in length.

This aquatic plant grows in Bench Lake, rooted in mud at a depth of about 1 m at the southwest corner of the lake. Flowering stems were not observed.

## Iridaceae Juss.—IRIS FAMILY

There are two Iris family genera at the mountain, each with a single species. Both have purplish flowers that are borne in small umbels and are composed of 6 similar perianth segments. There are 3 stamens that are tubelike for part of their length and borne opposite the outer whorl of perianth segments. The ovary is inferior and the style 3-branched. The fruit is a capsule.

Both are uncommon: one of the species is known from a meadow on the north side and the other in drier habitats on the southeast and eastern aspects.

1 Leaves flat; filaments of the anthers united nearly their whole length ........................................ *Sisyrinchium*

1 Leaves somewhat rounded; filaments united only about ½ their length........................................ *Olsynium*

### *Olsynium douglasii* (A. Dietrich) E. P. Bicknell var. *douglasii*
### GRASS WIDOW

Grass widow is a slender perennial that grows in tufts, similar in many respects to blue-eyed grass (*Sisyrinchium*). Its 15-30 cm stems are rounded rather than flattened. There are 1-5 deep reddish-purple flowers and the tepals are 15-22 mm long. The outer 3 tepals are about 18 mm long, the inner slightly shorter. The rounded capsule is 5-9 mm long.

The is a plant of dry places on the east side of the Cascade Mountains; it was collected by Flett on the upper Klickitat River.

## *Sisyrinchium* L.—SISYRINCHIUM

### *Sisyrinchium idahoense* E.P. Bicknell var. *idahoense*
### BLUE-EYED GRASS

Blue-eyed grass is a slender perennial that grows in tufts scattered through other meadow vegetation. The light green stems are flattened and "winged," 2-2.5 mm wide, and range from 20 to 40 cm tall; the leaves are flattened as well. Occasionally the stems are branched. There are 2-5 bright blue to blue-violet flowers in the inflorescence; the base of each of the tepals is yellow. The outer 3 tepals are about 18 mm long, the inner slightly shorter. The capsules are globular, 4-5 mm long, and lumpy from the seeds within.

At Mount Adams, this pretty flower grows in Midway Meadows on the north at about 4,500 feet.

## Juncaceae Juss.—RUSH FAMILY

Grasslike plants, all but one of the 20 rush family members at the mountain are perennials. The two genera include *Juncus,* the true rushes, and *Luzula,* the wood-rushes. Anatomically, the flowers resemble some lilies, although in outward appearance they are quite different from the showy flowers of that family. The perianth segments (three sepals and three petals) are alike and thus sometimes are referred to as "tepals." The small flowers are greenish, brown, or purple-brown. The inflorescence is variable: the flowers may be arranged singly along the branches of an open and spreading inflorescence or may be clustered into small heads or even into a spike.

There are 13 *Juncus* and 7 *Luzula* species at the mountain. *Scheuchzeria palustris,* a rare plant in Swampy Meadow, looks much like a rush but has three distinct pistils; in *Juncus,* the single pistil is made up of three fused carpels or chambers.

1 Leaves stiff, not hairy on the margins; capsule 3-celled, with many seeds ........ *Juncus*

1 Leaves flat, lax and grasslike, hairy on the margins; capsule 1-celled, with 3 seeds ........ *Luzula*

### *Juncus* L.—RUSH

With the exception of one annual, *J. bufonius,* the *Juncus* species at the mountain are all perennials. They are tufted, with hairless, rounded or flat leaves. The 13 species fall naturally into two groups based upon the nature of the lowest bract of the inflorescence. In some, it is rigid and upright, appearing to be a vertical extension of the stem and so the inflorescence, although in fact terminal, appears to be borne along the side of the stem. In other species, the bract is markedly different from the stem and so the inflorescence is clearly terminal. Typically there are 6 stamens, although two species, *J. effusus* and *J. ensifolius* var. *ensifolius* have just 3. The length of the anther relative to the filament is an important feature.

Rushes may be found in a variety of habitats at Mount Adams: wet meadows as well as seasonally dry meadows, open places in middle elevation forests, in ponds, on dry flats with lodgepole pine, and in disturbed places, as along roadsides.

| | |
|---|---|
| 1 | Annual, mostly shorter than 20 cm tall and much-branched; flowers arranged singly along the branches ................................ *J. bufonius* |
| 1 | Perennial, mostly taller than 15 cm; flowers in small to large headlike clusters ........................................................................ 2 |
| 2(1) | Lowest bract of the inflorescence stemlike, appearing to be an extension of the stem, the inflorescence therefore appearing to be lateral ......................................................................................... 3 |
| 2 | Lowest bract of the inflorescence not resembling an extension of the stem, the inflorescence clearly terminal ................................ 7 |
| 3(2) | Flowers 1-4 per stem; plants typically of dry places ...................... 4 |
| 3 | Flowers usually more than 8 per stem; plants typically of wet places ........................................................................................ 5 |
| 4(3) | Uppermost of the basal sheaths with well-developed leaf blades; capsule pointed ................................................................ *J. parryi* |
| 4 | Blades of the uppermost basal sheaths reduced and bristlelike; capsule blunt .................................. *J. drummondii* var. *subtriflorus* |
| 5(3) | Anthers at least 2 times longer than the filaments; inflorescence open ................................................................ *J. balticus* ssp. *ater* |
| 5 | Anthers about equal to the filaments; inflorescence congested ........ ........................................................................................ 6 |
| 6(5) | Stamens 3 .................................................... *J. effusus* var. *gracilis* |
| 6 | Stamens 6 ................................................................ *J. filiformis* |
| 7(2) | Leaf blades flattened and turned so that an edge faces the stem; leaves 3-6 mm broad ............................ *J. ensifolius* var. *ensifolius* |
| 7 | Leaf blades flattened with the flat side facing the stem, or rounded; leaves less than 3 mm broad ...................................................... 8 |
| 8(7) | Leaves without internal crosswalls, flattened ................................ 9 |
| 8 | Leaves with internal crosswalls, rounded .................................... 10 |
| 9(8) | Plant 10-25 cm tall; tepals 2-3.5 mm long ........................................ ................................................................ *J. covillei* var. *obtusatus* |
| 9 | Plant 10-40 cm tall; tepals 4-5 mm long ............................. *J. regelii* |
| 10(8) | Aquatic plant, often with floating leaves; capsule 0.5-1.5 mm longer than tepals, rounded at the tip ................................. *J. supiniformis* |
| 10 | Terrestrial; capsule no longer than perianth ................................ 11 |
| 11(10) | Heads 1, or rarely 2, per stem ............................... *J. mertensianus* |
| 11 | Heads more than 1 per stem ..................................................... 12 |

12(11) Heads 2-5; anthers slightly longer than the filaments ........................................................................................ *J. nevadensis* var. *badius*
12 Heads more than 5; anthers much longer than filaments ........................................................................ *J. nevadensis* var. *nevadensis*

### *Juncus balticus* Willd. ssp. *ater* (Rydb.) Snogerup—ARCTIC RUSH

This rush has wide-ranging rootstocks from which rise stems that may reach 60 cm in height. The leaves are reduced to long, brown scales at the base of the flowering stem. The numerous flowers are arranged as an open panicle that appears to be placed on the side of the stem, due to the upright and stemlike bract. The 3-4 mm long tepals are purplish brown. The anthers are 3-5 times longer than the filaments.

Typically a species of lower elevations in meadows, at Mount Adams this species grows between 4,000 and 4,500 feet at Spring Creek and Grand Meadow. It was also collected by Suksdorf at Hellroaring Canyon at an unspecified elevation.

### Juncus bufonius L.—TOAD RUSH

Although the stems of this annual weed may reach 20 cm in height, they are often much less and also tend to sprawl on the ground. The leaves are less than 1 mm wide and typically inrolled. The 4-7 mm long flowers are arranged singly on the multi-branched inflorescence. The anthers are shorter than the filaments.

A low to middle elevation species, the study area at Mount Adams is above the typical range of this species and thus occurrences are uncommon. A collection was made on the north side, just south of Road 56 near the Yakama Nation border, at 4,800 feet at the edge of a road through a dry meadow.

### *Juncus covillei* Piper var. *obtusatus* C.L. Hitchc.—COVILLE'S RUSH

Ranging from 20-25 cm in height, the stems of this rush form small tufts, with slender leaves only about 2 mm wide. There are 2-4 branches in the inflorescence, each with several small clusters of dark brown flowers. The tepals are approximately 3 mm long, and the anthers are slightly longer than the filaments.

A middle elevation species of river banks and lake shores, particularly on sandy soils, this is a rare plant at the mountain, known from a single Flett collection, made on a day when he was on the east side of Mount Adams on the upper Klickitat River.

### *Juncus drummondii* E. Mey. var. *subtriflorus* (E. Mey.) C.L. Hitchc. DRUMMOND'S RUSH

Matlike tufts of stems up to 35 cm tall characterize this rush. The leaves are reduced to brown bracts at the base of the stem. The lower bract of the inflorescence is 1-3 cm long, but has the appearance of being a continuation of the stem. The inflorescence consists of 1-3 flowers, and the perianth segments are brown and 5-7 mm long.

This is a relatively common *Juncus* at the mountain with a range that varies from middle elevation forest edges to near timberline. It grows at Keene's Horse Camp on the north side (elevation 4,400 feet), and along the South Climb trail near 6,800 feet. Suksdorf collected it at the Lewis River, Hellroaring Canyon, and Cowslip Springs.

### ***Juncus effusus* L. var. *gracilis* Hook.—COMMON RUSH**

Up to 100 cm in height, the leaves of this tall rush are reduced to brown sheaths at the bases of the flowering stems. Typically compact, the inflorescence appears to be horizontal on the stem, with many flowers on short branches. The tepals are 2-3 mm long, and the anthers of the 3 stamens are shorter than the filaments.

Uncommon, this species prefers wet habitats, including meadows, stream banks, and lakeshores. It is known from a single collection taken by the authors along Road 115.

### ***Juncus ensifolius* Wikstr. var. *ensifolius*—DAGGERLEAF RUSH**

A perennial with rootstocks that ranges from 20-60 cm in height, there are 1-3 leaves per stem, with 3-6 mm broad blades that are "equitant," set so that an edge of the leaf faces the stem. The common name refers to these distinctive leaves. The inflorescence is terminal and exceeds the involucral bract. There are 2-5 purplish-brown heads and the anthers are 0.5-0.7 mm long and shorter than the filaments. There are 3 stamens in this variety; variety *montanus*, with 6 stamens and present at Mount Rainier, has not been found at Mount Adams.

A species of moist areas but not of standing water, daggerleaf rush is found at Babyshoe Meadow, alongside the east fork of Adams Creek, and near ponds on Trail 75 along Cascade Creek. Suksdorf collected it at Hellroaring Canyon.

### ***Juncus filiformis* L.—THREAD RUSH**

The leaves of the slender, tufted, 20-60 cm tall stems of this rush are reduced to brownish sheaths. The long lower bract of the involucre is at least half the length of the flowering stem. The inflorescence appears to be horizontal, and is rather loose, and composed of numerous flowers. The perianth segments are 2.5-3.5 mm long, and the anthers are about equal in length to the filaments.

Uncommon at Mount Adams, this species of wet meadows and stream sides was found by the authors alongside Trail 64 on the northwest side. It was also collected by Suksdorf at Hellroaring Canyon.

### *Juncus mertensianus* Bong.—MERTENS'S RUSH

This 15-45 cm tall rush grows as closely-spaced stems along a stout rootstock, with inrolled leaves just 1-2 mm wide. The slender stems bear 1 or 2 leaves and a single, dense head of dark brown flowers. (Plants with 2 heads have been found at Adams Creek.) The tepals are 4 mm long, and the anthers are approximately the same length as the filaments.

The most common *Juncus* at the mountain, this species grows from middle elevations to the subalpine in wet sites, such as meadows and stream banks. It is also found alongside trails, such as the South Climb route, as well as in forest settings where there is moisture at least through midsummer. It grows alongside the east fork of Adams Creek (on Road 2329), at Babyshoe Meadow, and at the Yakama Nation boundary on the north side. Cotton and Suksdorf collected it at Hellroaring Canyon; there are also Suksdorf collections from Cowslip Springs and from a "butte" on the northeast side of the mountain.

### *Juncus nevadensis* S. Wats. var. *badius* (Suksdorf) C.L Hitchc. SIERRA RUSH

A slender perennial from a thin rootstock, this species ranges from 10-70 cm in height. The 2-8 cm long inflorescence is terminal, and composed of 2-5 heads that are held well above the leaves. The flower is about 3 mm long and dark brown; the tepals are lanceolate, tapering gradually to a sharp tip. The 1-2 mm long anthers are slightly longer than the filaments.

Typically an eastern Cascades variety, this rush is rare at the mountain. A collection was made by the authors alongside Forest Service Road 115 on the north side, in Midway Meadows, a place that becomes quite dry late in the summer. Suksdorf originally named this species "*Juncus badius*" from a collection made in southern Klickitat County.

### *Juncus nevadensis* S. Wats. var. *nevadensis*—SIERRA RUSH

This variety is distinguished from variety *badius* by the more numerous heads (more than 5) and a flower that is 3-5.5 mm long. The anthers are usually much longer than the filaments.

Found in wet places, particularly along streams and lakes, this is most often a lower elevation species. Suksdorf collected it at the mountain but did not give a specific location. Elsewhere, it grows from east of the Cascades south to California.

### *Juncus parryi* Engelm.—PARRY'S RUSH

This species resembles *J. drummondii,* but is separated by the pointed capsule and the leaves—those of *J. parryi* are threadlike and 3-7 cm long.

A middle elevation species typically found on open, rocky slopes, it was collected by Suksdorf at Hellroaring Canyon and is also known from collections made by the authors at Midway Meadows alongside Road 115 and under lodgepole pine at Keene's Horse Camp.

### *Juncus regelii* Buch.—REGEL'S RUSH

Typically tufted, this rush is distinguished by slender stems, 10-40 cm tall, with well-developed, 1-3 mm wide leaves. Each stem bears 1-3 dense, many-flowered heads. The brown tepals are 4-5 mm long and the filaments are about equal in length to the anthers.

A middle to subalpine species, Regel's rush is known from Suksdorf collections made at the Lewis River, Hellroaring Canyon, and a "red crater" near that canyon (that is, Little Mount Adams). This species is tolerant of places that become quite dry late in the summer

### *Juncus supiniformis* Engelm.—FLOATING RUSH

This perennial is distinguished by floating leaves and stems where the plant grows in water; it roots at the leaf nodes in shallow water and on muddy flats. The tufted stems are 10-30 cm tall and rise from slender rhizomes. There are 2-6 flower heads on each stalk, each with 3- to 10-flowers. The 3-4 mm long tepals are light to dark brown with narrowly lanceolate, sharply-tipped segments. The anthers are shorter than the filaments.

Found in wet habitats, including marshes, ponds, and streams, and often submerged early in the season, this is a rare species at the mountain. It is known from a collection made by the authors at Swampy Meadows on the southwest side of the mountain; there it grew in a shallow pool and sprawled across the mud where the pool had dried.

## *Luzula* L.—WOOD-RUSH

The flat, grasslike leaves, hairy along the lower margins, distinguish this genus from *Juncus*. The inflorescence may be configured in headlike clusters or as open, branched panicles. The tepals are greenish or brownish. As with *Juncus* (the "true rushes"), examination under magnification of tepal length and anthers and their filaments is often crucial to separating the species. The seed capsule consists of a single chamber that holds just 3 seeds.

Wood-rushes are more likely to grow on drier ground than the true rushes. At Mount Adams, they are found in open habitats from middle elevations to over 7,000 feet. Two of the species are very uncommon at the mountain.

| | | |
|---|---|---|
| 1 | Flowers on rudimentary stalks crowded into headlike clusters ...... | 2 |
| 1 | Flowers mostly solitary on slender stalks in open panicles ............ | 5 |
| 2(1) | Clusters of flowers on very short stalks and crowded into a single spikelike panicle; inflorescence nodding on the stem ....... | *L. spicata* |
| 2 | Clusters stalked, not crowed together, nodding or erect ............... | 3 |
| 3(2) | Stalk of the inflorescence very slender and nodding, 2-6 per stem; tepals about 2 mm long .................... | *L. arcuata* ssp. *unalashcensis* |
| 3 | Stalk of the inflorescence erect, generally 5 or more per stem; tepals 2.5 mm or longer .............................................................. | 4 |
| 4(3) | Heads 1-3 cm long; tepals 3-4.5 mm long; anthers twice as long as filaments .......................................................................... | *L. comosa* |
| 4 | Heads 0.5-1 cm long; tepals 2.5-3 mm long; anthers about equal to the filaments .......................................... | *L. multiflora* ssp. *multiflora* |
| 5(1) | Leaves 8-12 mm wide; anthers much longer than the filaments ....... ................................................................ | *L. glabrata* var. *hitchcockii* |
| 5 | Leaves 6-8 mm wide; anthers shorter than or about equal to the filaments .............................................................................. | 6 |
| 6(5) | Leaves of the stem 5-8 mm broad; tepals usually greenish; middle elevation forests ......................................................... | *L. parviflora* |
| 6 | Leaves of the stem 2-3 mm broad; tepals purplish-brown; subalpine to alpine open slopes and ridges ......................................... | *L. piperi* |

### *Luzula arcuata* (Wahlenb.) Sw. ssp. *unalashcensis* (Buch.) Hultén ALPINE WOOD-RUSH, CURVED WOOD-RUSH

Only 10-15 cm in height, this small wood-rush bears slender tufted stems. The 1-3 mm wide leaves are often folded. The inflorescence consists of 2-6 heads composed of several flowers on slender, curved and drooping stalks.

Known from a single collection by C. T. Shick, from a steep, rocky slope above the "Killen Creek Snowfield" at 7,080 feet, this is a rare species at Mount Adams.

### *Luzula comosa* E. Mey.—FIELD WOOD-RUSH

Distinguished by the hairy (at least when young) leaves that are 3-6 mm wide, this 10-40 cm tall wood-rush bears clusters of flowers in a dense oblong-cylindrical head, up to 30 mm in length. The light brown perianth segments are 3-4.5 mm long.

Uncommon in middle elevation wet meadows, this species was collected by the authors at Grand Meadow on the southwest side.

### ***Luzula glabrata*** **(Hoppe ex Rostk.) Desv. var. *hitchcockii* (Hämet-Ahti) Dorn—HITCHCOCK'S WOOD-RUSH**

This loosely tufted species may reach 60 cm in height. It bears broad, 8-12 mm wide leaves, although plants near timberline may be shorter. The flowers are borne at the tips of a widely branched, predominantly erect panicle. The branches sometimes droop, resembling *L. arcuata* when they do so. However, the flowers of *L. glabrata* are solitary rather than in small clusters and, at 3-3.5 mm, the dark brown tepals are longer.

Fairly common alongside trails and in meadows and sometimes forming extensive patches, this species grows alongside the Round-the-Mountain trail near upper Bird Creek Meadows at 6,300 feet. It is found near Trail 183 at nearly 5,900 feet, and also grows near the Killen Creek trail. Suksdorf collected it at Little Mount Adams and along Hellroaring Creek. Henderson also made a collection on the south side.

### ***Luzula multiflora*** **(Ehrh.) Lef. ssp. *multiflora* MANY-FLOWERED WOOD-RUSH**

The tufted stems of this wood-rush reach 50 cm in height and bear narrow leaves, 2-4 mm wide. Long white hairs fringe the joint between leaves and stem. The inflorescence is less than 1 cm long, occasionally much less. The small flowers are dark brown and the tepals are 2.5-3.5 mm in length.

Found on moist slopes and drier open habitats from middle elevations to subalpine meadows, this is a fairly common species at the mountain. It grows at Midway Meadows on the north side, as well as alongside the trail from Muddy Meadows to the Pacific Crest Trail (elevation 4,560 feet). It is found at milepost 34 alongside Road 23 on the northwest; it also grows near Road 034, and Road 82. Suksdorf collected it at Hellroaring Canyon.

### ***Luzula parviflora*** **(Ehrh.) Desv.—SMALL-FLOWERED WOOD-RUSH**

Although it may reach 60 cm in height, this wood-rush bears small flowers, 2-2.5 mm long. The numerous leaves are thin, with the stem leaves ranging from 5-8 mm in width. The long branches of the open panicle are nodding, and the flowers are typically solitary, although they may occur in groups of two.

A species of middle elevations at the mountain, found between 4,000 and 4,800 feet; wet meadows, roadsides, and trail borders are common habitats, where it often grows in abundance. It grows in the culvert south of the gravel pit on Road 23 (southwest aspect), near Bathtub Meadow on the northwest, and was collected by Suksdorf at Hellroaring Canyon, Cowslip Spring, and on the "south side."

### *Luzula piperi* (Coville) M.E. Jones—PIPER'S WOOD-RUSH

This attractive, densely tufted wood-rush varies between 10-40 cm in height, depending on the harshness and degree of exposure. The leaves are thickish and relatively few, with those of the stem measuring 2-3 mm in width. The inflorescence consists of a graceful, open panicle with nodding branches and the 1.5-2 mm long tepals are purple-brown.

Found on open slopes in stony or sandy soils at and above timberline, this is an uncommon species at Mount Adams. It grows alongside the trail above Hellroaring overlook at over 6,600 feet and near the Pacific Crest Trail north of Trail 64 (Riley Creek) at 5,900 feet.

### *Luzula spicata* (L.) DC.—SPIKED WOOD-RUSH

This densely tufted species may reach 40 cm in height, although it is typically much less, just 10 cm or so. The 1-3 mm wide leaves are narrow and usually folded. The spikelike inflorescence is congested; the flowers are stalkless or on rudimentary stalks and the separate heads are not easily discernable. The 2-2.5 mm long tepals are brown.

Found on rocky alpine slopes above timberline, this species was collected by Henderson, Flett, and Suksdorf, the last at Hellroaring Canyon. For the others, there is little collection information.

## Lemnaceae Gray—DUCKWEED FAMILY

### *Lemna* L.—DUCKWEED

### *Lemna minor* L.—SMALL DUCKWEED

The sole duckweed and the smallest flowering plant at Mount Adams, this would be an easy plant to overlook but for the fact that it grows in such large numbers. An individual plant consists of a single "thallus," a flat, oval body about 1-2 mm long, with a shiny, green surface. The plants multiply by budding, so pairs or triads of thalli are often seen. From the underside dangles a single, unbranched root that may be up 1 cm long. Flowers are rarely seen in any of the *Lemna* species.

Small duckweed has been found in the ponds alongside Trail 75, at about 3,500 feet in the valley of Cascade Creek. It grows in sunny to partly shaded, still water and is capable of forming dense mats.

## Liliaceae Juss.—LILY FAMILY

The lilies vary widely in form and appearance and are among the showiest flowers at Mount Adams. All have six "tepals," or perianth segments. With the exception of camas and trillium, these tepals are so similar in size and color that it makes sense to call them collectively, petals, as we do here for familiarity and convenience.

The flowers may be quite small, although collectively showy, as in the case of false-hellebore or amongst the largest and most easily noticed of the mountain's flowers, as with trillium. Colors and form range widely, too, from the orange flower with turned-back petals of the Columbia lily to the small rose hanging flowers of the rosy twistedstalk. There are six stamens and one or three styles. The leaves are simple and vary from narrow and linear to straplike and wide.

There are 21 species and 16 genera, the latter number matched by the Brassicaceae and exceeded only by the Asteraceae.

| | | |
|---|---|---|
| 1 | Petals 3, colored, larger than the 3 sepals that are green or only weakly colored | 2 |
| 1 | Petals and sepals essentially alike in color and size | 3 |
| 2(1) | Leaves 3, ovate, in a whorl at the top of the stem | *Trillium* |
| 2 | Major leaf basal, long and flat (sometimes a smaller stem leaf is present) | *Calochortus* |
| 3(1) | Flowers in an umbel on a leafless stem; leaves basal, grasslike | *Allium* |
| 3 | Flowers single, or in racemes, panicles or heads; leaves various but the plant never with basal leaves and a leafless stem | 4 |
| 4(3) | Leaves tough, firm, basal and persisting more than one season | *Xerophyllum* |
| 4 | Leaves, if basal, not tough and firm, dying back in winter | 5 |
| 5(4) | Flowers single (or 2 or 3) on recurved stalks | 6 |
| 5 | Flowers numerous, in racemes, panicles, or heads; if single, then not on a recurved stalk | 8 |
| 6(5) | Leaves basal | *Erythronium* |
| 6 | Leaves on short to tall stems | 7 |
| 7(6) | Flowers yellow, usually single; plant to about 20 cm tall | *Fritillaria* |
| 7 | Flowers orange, 3 or more on a plant over 50 cm tall | *Lilium* |
| 8(5) | Flowers single; leaves basal | *Clintonia* |
| 8 | Flowers more than 1 per plant, on more or less leafy stems | 9 |
| 9(8) | Flowers solitary in the axils of the leaves | *Streptopus* |
| 9 | Flowers in racemes or panicles, or in 2s or 3s at the ends of leafy branches | 10 |

10(9) Flowers in 2s or 3s at the ends of leafy branches ............ *Prosartes*
10 Flowers in racemes, panicles, or heads ...................................... 11

11(10) Flowers congested, in head-like clusters ............................ *Triantha*
11 Flowers in a raceme or panicle .................................................. 12

12(11) Leaves arranged along the stem, never basal, lanceolate to ovate .. .................................................................................................. 13
12 Leaves chiefly basal, narrow to linear; any stem leaves much reduced in size ...................................................................... 14

13(12) Flowers green, on erect stems 1.5 m tall or more ............ *Veratrum*
13 Flowers white, on ascending stems less than 1 m tall ...................... ........................................................................ *Maianthemum*

14(12) Style 1; flowers blue ..................................................... *Camassia*
14 Styles 3; flowers some other color ............................................. 15

15(14) Flowers cream-colored, with a prominent yellow-green gland at the base of each petal ......................................................... *Zigadenus*
15 Flowers purple-brown, gland absent ........................... *Stenanthium*

## ***Allium* L.—ONION**

### ***Allium acuminatum* Hook.—TAPERTIP ONION**

The bulbs of this onion are brownish on the outside and whitish beneath with prominent ridges visible in the skins. Plants tend to be clustered. Two or 3 grasslike leaves, scented like onion, rise from near the soil level; they are 1-3 mm broad, and tend to wither at flowering time. The flowering stem is 10-40 cm tall, well above the height of the leaves. There are 2-3 ovate bracts with short, sharp tips beneath the umbel. The flowers are borne on leafless stalks 10-20 mm long, are pink to whitish and configured in an umbel on a leafless stem. The 10-12 mm long petals are lanceolate in shape and tend to become papery with age. The fruit is a capsule marked with 3 small crests.

Rare, this dry habitat species was collected by the authors at the DNR quarry on the southeast side of Mount Adams at an elevation of 4,125 feet.

## ***Calochortus* Pursh—MARIPOSA LILY**

### ***Calochortus subalpinus* Piper—SUBALPINE MARIPOSA LILY**

The usually leafless stem of this species ranges between 5 and 30 cm in height, sometimes nodding, but more often erect. A single, pale green, flat basal leaf, 10-30 cm long, tapers at both ends and is usually longer than the stem. The 1-5 cm long, lanceolate to linear bracts are sharply tipped. The flowers are yellowish-white, often spotted with a purple crescent above the gland on each petal, and also bear a purple spot near the base of the sepal. The inner face of the petals has bumpy projections and is fringed with hairs. The sepals are shorter than the petals and are hairy on the inner face.

Most commonly found in open, dry subalpine habitats, this lily enjoys an extended blooming period. The South Climb Trail boasts a large number; it is also found on the Round-the-Mountain trail, alongside Road 82, at the junction of Road 782 and Road 8040, and at Hellroaring Canyon.

### *Camassia* Lindl.—CAMAS

#### *Camassia quamash* (Pursh) Green ssp. *breviflora* Gould<br>COMMON CAMAS

Each plant consists of an ovoid bulb 2-4 cm long, 3 or more basal leaves, and a leafless flowering stem, with the flowers borne in a raceme. The basal leaves are linear, deep green, 8-20 mm broad, and up to 50 cm long. The flowers are numerous, with deep blue-violet petals 15-25 mm long and yellow anthers. The petals twist together over the immature capsule after flowering; eventually, the expanding capsule ruptures the "knot." The fruit is an ovoid capsule 10-20 mm long.

Ephemerally blooming in large numbers in Muddy Meadows, this subspecies is otherwise rare at the mountain.

### *Clintonia* Raf.—BEADLILY

#### *Clintonia uniflora* (Menzies *ex* J.A. & J.H. Schultes) Kunth<br>QUEEN'S CUP, BRIDE'S BONNET

A lily found in closed forests, the plants bear 2 or 3 oval, glossy green leaves up to 20 cm long. The single, 5-10 cm tall stem bears a single flower, with showy white petals that spread widely. They mature to a single, dark blue, beadlike fruit approximately 1 cm in diameter; another name for this plant is beadlily.

Lovely in flower and unique when in fruit, this middle to subalpine forest dweller is also found at meadow edges. It has been located near King Mountain, alongside Road 23 on the south and southwest sides, on the south shore of Bench Lake, and in the meadows of Hellroaring valley, where it grows at nearly 5,000 feet.

### *Erythronium* L.—FAWN-LILY

Typically the earliest flowers in subalpine meadows, often pushing their leaves upward through the melting snow, the fawn-lilies are heralds of spring. The plants grow from deeply-buried bulbs. The basal leaves surround a naked stem that bears one to several nodding flowers. The petals curve backward to display the downward-hanging stamens. The fruit is a fleshy, elongated capsule.

These lilies are common and often abundant in Cascade mountain meadows, particularly at Mount Rainier where they may dominate the early blooming scene. With the exception of the southeast side, Mount Adams lacks the extensive subalpine wet meadows; thus these species are locally common but typically do not cover large areas.

1 Flowers white; leaves narrowed to a slender stalk ..... *E. montanum*
1 Flowers yellow; leaves not clearly stalklike at the base .................... ................................................... *E. grandiflorum* ssp. *grandiflorum*

### ***Erythronium grandiflorum*** **Pursh ssp.** ***grandiflorum*****—GLACIER LILY**

Typically bearing just 1 yellow flower per stem, the stems of this species reach about 30 cm in height. The petals measure 2-3 cm long and are wider than those of *E. montanum*. The flowers have a light, sweet scent.

Glacier lily grows on wet, open sites between 4,000 and 6,000 feet, nowhere in great numbers, but nevertheless encountered on the west and southeast sides of the mountain.

### ***Erythronium montanum*** **S. Wats.—AVALANCHE LILY**

Typically bearing 2 or 3 white flowers on 15-40 cm tall stems, the white petals measure 2-3 cm long and are fairly narrow on this early season lily. Often, single leaves are seen, as the plants require many years to mature sufficiently for blooming.

A subalpine species of wet, open sites between 4,500 and 6,000 feet, large colonies grow near the lava flow on Road 2329. This species is less common on the south side of the mountain.

## ***Fritillaria*** **L.—FRITILLARY**

### ***Fritillaria pudica*** **(Pursh) Spreng.—YELLOW BELLS**

Bearing 2 opposite leaves, or sometimes more in a semi-whorled configuration, the flowers of this uncommon lily are solitary on 10-30 cm tall stems. The leaves are 3-16 cm long, and linear to linear-oblanceolate. The pendant, bell-shaped flowers are yellow with purplish to brownish streaks near the base and are 12-26 mm long. The capsule is 18-30 mm long and contains numerous flattened, winged seeds.

This species is known only from the DNR quarry on the southeast side of Mount Adams, at 4,100 feet, where it grows on a stony, south-facing talus slope as well as nearby in a Garry oak woodland.

## *Lilium* L.—LILY

### *Lilium columbianum* Hanson—COLUMBIA LILY

Bright red-orange flowers on stems that may reach 200 cm, although typically are much shorter, characterize this unmistakable lily. The narrow leaves, borne in whorls on the lower stem and spread on the upper, may reach 20 cm in length. The flowers hang downward from long, slender, and curved stalks. The 3-4 cm long petals curve backwards. They are spotted with purple. The 2.5 cm high capsule is 6-sided, and the seeds are flattened. This lily is also known as "tiger-lily" in acknowledgement of its resemblance to the tiger-lilies of eastern North America.

Although common in many Northwest forests, this species is relatively uncommon at Mount Adams, typically being found in small numbers. It is known at Hellroaring Canyon and Muddy Canyon. It is also found alongside Road 23 on the west side of the mountain and near the small stream west of Bird Creek on Road 82 on the southeast.

## *Maianthemum* G.H. Weber *ex* Wiggers—SOLOMON'S SEAL

Formerly included in *Smilacina*, these species bear small, white flowers in racemes or panicles at the ends of leafy stems. The stems are not branched. The leaves are alternate, heart-shaped to ovate, and not much reduced in size toward the top of the stem.

At Mount Adams, both species are found in subalpine meadow habitats above 5,000 feet; they also are local in lower elevation moist forested or roadside locations.

1 Stems 30-50 cm tall; flowers few, in an open raceme ........................................................................................ *M. stellatum*

1 Stems 50-100 cm tall; flowers many, in a dense panicle ................................................................... *M. racemosum* ssp. *amplexicaule*

### *Maianthemum racemosum* (L.) Link ssp. *amplexicaule* (Nutt.) LaFrankie—LARGE FALSE SOLOMON'S-SEAL

The tall stems of this vigorous plant may reach 100 cm. The 6-12 cm long leaves are ovate to lanceolate and clasp the stem at their bases. The flowers are configured in plumelike panicles. Individual flowers are 1-2 mm long and the stamens are exserted. The red berries are 5-7 mm in diameter.

A middle elevation forest species, this large lily is cosmopolitan at the mountain. It achieves its greatest size in open thickets on moist slopes and is found at elevations up to 4,000 feet.

### *Maianthemum stellatum* (L.) Link
### STAR-FLOWERED FALSE SOLOMON'S-SEAL

Smaller than *M. racemosum*, this species bears small numbers of white, starlike flowers in a zig-zag raceme at the end of the 20-50 cm tall stems. The 5-12 cm long leaves do not clasp the stem. The 4-6 mm long flowers exceed the length of the stamens and the 7-10 mm diameter berries are purplish.

More common than *M. racemosum*, this species grows alongside Road 23, near the South Climb road (Road 8040), and at Hellroaring Canyon. It is cosmopolitan at the mountain and grows both in forests and at meadow edges, to 4,800 feet.

## *Prosartes* D. Don—FAIRY BELLS

### *Prosartes hookeri* Torr.—HOOKER'S FAIRY BELLS

The sparingly branched stems of this plant are 30-80 cm tall and bear leaves that are ovate, 5-12 cm long, with pointed tips and margins fringed with short hairs. The flowers are paired and hang at the branch tips. The petals spread outward from the midpoint, making the stamens visible. This species was formerly named *Disporum hookeri*.

A lower elevation species of moist sites through the rest of the Cascade Mountains in Washington, at Mount Adams this lily is uncommon. It is usually seen in rather dry locations on the southeast side of the mountain, often in regrowing clearcuts, as on King Mountain. It grows in an open Pacific silver fir forest alongside the Pineway Trail at 4,600 feet, and at Bunnell Butte on Forest Road 071 at 4,100 feet.

## *Stenanthium* (A. Gray) Kunth—STENANTHIUM

### *Stenanthium occidentale* A. Gray
### BRONZE BELLS, MOUNTAIN BELLS

The 2 or 3 grasslike leaves of this attractive species rise from the base of the flowering stem and are 10-20 cm long. The purple-brown, bell-shaped flowers have a sharply-sweet scent. Approximately 1.5 cm long, they are arranged in an open raceme or panicle on 15-40 cm tall stems. The fruit is an oblong capsule.

Rare at Mount Adams, this is a species of moist slopes. It is known from a poorly-documented Suksdorf collection taken at the "base of the mountain."

## *Streptopus* Michx.—TWISTED STALK

The common name of these lilies is taken from the manner in which the stalk of each flower, borne singly in the leaf axil, is twisted so that the flower is held beneath and hidden by the leaf. The plants spread by rootstocks and look somewhat like the false Solomon's-seals, but can be separated by the unique arrangement of the flowers. At Mount Adams the two species occur from middle elevation wet meadows and disturbed sites to subalpine open meadows.

1 Flowers greenish-white; leaves glaucous on the underside .................................................................................. *S. amplexifolius* var. *amplexifolius*

1 Flowers rose-colored; leaves not glaucous on the underside ..................................................................................................... *S. lanceolatus*

### *Streptopus amplexifolius* (L.) DC. var. *amplexifolius* CLASPING-LEAF TWISTED STALK

The species name refers to the configuration of the leaves, which clasp and surround the stem at their bases. They are ovate, 5-10 cm long, glaucous below, with teeth on the margins. The leafy stems range from 50-100 cm in height and the bell-shaped flowers are 9-15 mm long with the tips of the petals spread or curved backward. The berry is 10-15 mm in diameter.

Found in middle elevation forests and wet meadow edges, this species grows alongside the Island Springs trail at an elevation of 4,850 feet. It is also known from Hellroaring Canyon, at the intersection on Road 8040 and Road 781, near Crofton Creek at Trail 73, and alongside the Cascades Creek Trail at lower elevation on the southwest side of the mountain.

### *Streptopus lanceolatus* (Ait.) Reveal—ROSY TWISTED STALK

Beautiful pinkish flowers distinguish this species. The stems may reach 30 cm in height. The 3-8 cm long leaves are stalkless; they do not clasp the stem and are not glaucous on the underside. The 10-12 mm long flowers are bell-shaped and the petals do not spread at the tip. The berry is 7-10 mm in diameter. The species was formerly known as *S. roseus* var. *curvipes*.

Locally common in moist middle elevation sites, including meadow edges and forests, this species sometimes forms colonies. It has been located on the west shore of Council Lake on the west side of Mount Adams. It grows at the Chain of Lakes on the northwest and is also known on the east and southeast from Suksdorf collections. A large group grows near the Muddy Meadows trailhead; similar large numbers are found near Crofton Creek alongside Trail 73.

## Liliaceae

### *Triantha* (Nutt.) Baker—TRIANTHA

#### *Triantha occidentalis* (S. Wats.) Gates ssp. *brevistyla* (C.L. Hitchc.) Packer—STICKY TOFIELDIA

Previously known as *Tofieldia glutinosa* ssp. *brevistyla,* that species name referred to the many sticky glands on the upper part of the 30-40 cm tall stems of this small-flowered lily. The whitish or greenish-white flowers are only about 4 mm long and are crowded in a compact raceme at the top of the stem. The 3-5 mm broad grasslike leaves are shorter than the flowering stem. Bright reddish-purple seed capsules follow flowering.

A species of wet middle elevation to subalpine meadows, often growing in inundated habitats, plants are found in most of the big meadows, including Muddy Meadows, Spring Creek Meadow, Takh Takh Meadow, and Babyshoe Meadow.

### *Trillium* L.—TRILLIUM

#### *Trillium ovatum* Pursh ssp. *ovatum*—WESTERN TRILLIUM

The species name is in reference to the three-parted nature of this beautiful lily. There are 3 leaves at the top of the stem, where the single flower is composed of 3 sepals and 3 petals. The leaves vary from 5-20 cm in length and are broadly ovate. The flowers are fragrant and set atop a 3-5 cm long stalk. The 1-3 cm long sepals are greenish while the pure white petals are 2-5 cm long; they fade to pink and purple as they age. The stigma is 3-lobed, and the fruit is a fleshy, 3-faced capsule.

A middle elevation forest species or sometimes found at the edges of meadows, and preferring moist ground, this is often one of the earliest spring-flowering species. Cosmopolitan at the mountain and reaching 6,400 feet, trillium has been recorded at Cold Springs on the south side, alongside Road 82 to Bird Creek Meadows, on Crofton Ridge, and at Hellroaring Canyon.

### *Veratrum* L.—FALSE HELLEBORE

#### *Veratrum viride* Ait. var. *eschscholtzii* (A. Gray) Breitung GREEN FALSE HELLEBORE

Tall, with large leaves, this species is also commonly known as "corn lily" for its slight resemblance to cultivated corn: reaching 2 m in height, the leafy stems and flowers borne in panicles to some degree resemble corn tassels. The 15-30 cm long leaves are stalkless and heavily ridged along the lengthwise veins. The many flowers cause the branches of the large, open panicle to droop. The greenish flowers have green veins and a dark green center. The petals are 8-10 mm long.

This species prefers middle elevation to lower subalpine meadow openings and trailside habitats on moist ground. It is found at Hellroaring Canyon, Spring Creek and Swampy Meadows, and alongside Road 405 at 4,550 feet.

### *Xerophyllum* Michaux—BEARGRASS

#### *Xerophyllum tenax* (Pursh) Nutt.—BEARGRASS

The tough basal leaves of this plant were used by Native Americans for many articles, including mats, baskets, and capes. The grasslike leaves may reach 1 m in length. Short, stiff leaves also line the stout 1.5 m length stems. Dense rounded racemes of white, starry flowers form a bulbous top to stems. Each flower is borne on a 2-5 cm long stalk. The widely spreading oblong petals are approximately 1 cm long. The 5 mm long fruit is a dry, 3-lobed capsule.

Not necessarily flowering every year, in "good" years fields of the showy flowers may be found in select locations. Such is the case at Olallie Lake on the north side of the mountain. Commonly considered a subalpine meadow plant, forest colonies are as typical at Mount Adams. Cosmopolitan at the mountain, this species grows from 4,000 to nearly 6,000 feet.

### *Zigadenus* Michx.—DEATH-CAMAS

The common name refers to the poisonous bulb. With their grasslike basal leaves and dense cluster of flowers at the top of the stem, the plants resemble *Tofieldia*. The flowers vary from white to yellowish-green. The petals are ovate to lanceolate, and slightly unequal in length. There are 6 stamens and 3 styles.

Typically found in dry, and apparently restricted to the east and southeast sides, these species are uncommon at Mount Adams.

1 Inflorescence a panicle; outer petals pointed, claw absent; stamens exserted .................................................................. *Z. paniculatus*

1 Inflorescence a raceme, sometimes branched; outer petals rounded, with a claw; stamens not exserted .................................... ........................................................ *Z. venenosus* var. *venenosus*

#### *Zigadenus paniculatus* (Nutt.) S. Wats.—FOOTHILL DEATH-CAMAS

Flowers borne in panicles distinguish this death-camas. The stems range from 30-50 cm, and the 15-30 cm long leaves are primarily basal. The tepals lack claws and are ovate-triangular and 3-4.5 mm long. The panicle ranges from 10-30 cm in length.

An eastern Cascade mountain species in habitats that range from sagebrush desert to ponderosa pine forest, *Z. paniculatus* is known from a Suksdorf collection at Muddy River Canyon at 4,600 feet and a Flett collection on the upper Klickitat River.

### *Zigadenus venenosus* S. Wats. var. *venenosus*
### MEADOW DEATH-CAMAS

Distinguished from the previous species by the racemose configuration of the flowers, the outer petals of this death-camas typically have a 0.3-1 mm long claw and are 4.5-5 mm long.

A species of both sides of the Cascades, it is most common on the east side of the mountain, including the dry, stony site at the DNR quarry.

## Orchidaceae Juss.—ORCHID FAMILY

Many of the 15 orchid species at Mount Adams are middle elevation wetland specialists, including one Washington state sensitive species, western ladies' tresses (*Spiranthes porrifolia*). Other species, such as the calypso orchid (*Calypso bulbosa*) are quite uncommon at the mountain, being found in select forest habitats on the southeast side. The forest dwelling *Corallorhiza* species are also local, occasionally found in groups, but more often as individuals; none of the three species are really common. Most orchids prefer organically rich soils and are found at middle elevation sites. In general, the orchids most likely to be encountered at Mount Adams grow in the extensive wet meadows on the north and west sides, where *Platanthera* species, in particular, are common.

Although most of the orchids at Mount Adams have small flowers, even the smallest demonstrate features in common with the florist's hothouse orchid. The flowers are bilaterally symmetrical and more or less irregular. The 3 sepals resemble petals; the upper sepal may be erect or ascending and the lateral sepals spreading. There are 3 petals, two of which resemble one another, with the third broadened into a "lip." The lip is typically distinct in shape, color, and pattern of markings; in some genera, it bears a prolonged, backward-pointing spur. Where other monocots have 3 stamens, in the orchids the number is reduced, with the result that the anthers form a structure called a pollinium that is fused with the style to form what is called the column. The ovary is inferior and twists through a 180 degree turn as the flower bud develops. Such a flower is said to be "resupinate," and what was initially the upper petal becomes the characteristic lip of the flower. The fruit is an oblong capsule and within are nearly countless tiny seeds.

Well-represented at Mount Adams, there are seven genera and 15 species of orchids present in the flora.

| | | |
|---|---|---|
| 1 | Green leaves absent | *Corallorhiza* |
| 1 | Plants with green leaves, at least up until flowering time | 2 |
| 2(1) | Lip with a spur | 3 |
| 2 | Lip lacking a spur | 4 |
| 3(2) | Leaves basal only, withering by flowering time; plants of dryish places | *Piperia* |
| 3 | Leaves basal and on the stem, green at flowering time; plants of wet meadows | *Platanthera* |
| 4(2) | Plant with 1 leaf and 1 flower; petals 1.5 cm or longer | *Calypso* |
| 4 | Plants with more than 1 leaf; flowers several to many; petals less than 1 cm long | 5 |
| 5(4) | Leaves 2, opposite, at the top of a short stem | *Listera* |
| 5 | Leaves several, basal or arranged along the stem | 6 |
| 6(5) | Leaves in a basal rosette, stem leaves absent | *Goodyera* |
| 6 | Basal rosette absent, stem leafy | *Spiranthes* |

### *Calypso* Salisb.—FAIRY-SLIPPER, CALYPSO

#### *Calypso bulbosa* (L.) Oakes var. *occidentalis* (Holz.) Boivin CALYPSO

This small plant with an oversized flower has a single 2-5 cm long, dark green, ovate leaf arising from a bulblike corm. A single flower is borne on the top of a 10-15 cm tall stem. The flower has a spicy fragrance and is bright pink, a classic orchid form, with flaring pink petals. The lip is slipper-shaped, white to pinkish, mottled with purple-brown spots and streaks, and fringed with yellow hairs on the center of the lip. The 1.5-2.5 cm long sepals and petals are lanceolate in shape.

Rare at the mountain and first observed in this study, calypso orchid grows on the southeast side of Mount Adams, on the east side of Bunnell Butte at 4,000 feet, where a small, clonal group grows in a pocket of deep, rich soil on the side of a small lava flow, under Pacific silver fir and ponderosa pine.

### *Corallorhiza* Gagnebin—CORALROOT

Members of the genus *Corallorhiza* lack chlorophyll and thus must acquire their nutrients by other means: they are "mycotrophic," doing so through a symbiotic relationship with soil fungi. The scientific and common names refer to the heavily-branched root system of this orchid, resembling coral. The stems of two of the species are reddish in color (although yellowish color variants are known) and the third is a pale yellow-green. That third species, *C. trifida*, apparently retains enough chlorophyll to color the plant and to produce some carbohydrates through ordinary photosynthesis. The leaves are present merely as sheathing scales on the lower stem. The flowers are borne in tall, slender racemes. None of these orchids is common at Mount Adams, perhaps because of the dryness or the starting elevation of the study area.

1 Plants pale yellow or greenish-yellow; lip white and unmarked ........ ........................................................................................ *C. trifida*

1 Plants typically magenta, reddish, or reddish-brown (rarely yellowish); lip whitish to pinkish, as well as spotted or lightly veined ........................................................................................ 2

2(1) Lip spotted; spur absent or represented by a small bump ............... ........................................................ *C. maculata* var. *occidentalis*

2 Lip lightly veined; short spur present ...................... *C. mertensiana*

**_Corallorhiza maculata_ (Raf.) Raf. var. _occidentalis_ (Lindl.) Ames**
**SPOTTED CORALROOT**

Most easily recognized by the white lip spotted with magenta, this orchid tends to favor dry ground. The plants are reddish-brown in color with shades varying from light to dark. The stems are 20-30 cm tall. The narrow sepals and petals are 5-10 mm long, with a short, broad lip that is bluntly toothed at the apex. There are 2 very short lobes on the sides at the base of the lip, and the spur is a mere bump less than .5 mm long, or may be absent entirely.

The expanded middle lobe of the lip of variety *occidentalis* distinguishes it from the variety *maculata,* in which the end of the middle lobe is scarcely expanded; they also differ in details of the bracts of the flowers. Both varieties occur in the Pacific Northwest, although only one is known at Mount Adams.

For reasons not clearly understood, *Corallorhiza* genus members are surprisingly rare at Mount Adams. This species is less common than *C. mertensiana* and is apt to be found in open, dryish forests and is known from Island Springs trail at 5,050 feet, and along Rusk Creek, the latter a Suksdorf collection.

**_Corallorhiza mertensiana_ Bong.—WESTERN CORALROOT**

The most common coralroot at the mountain, the 20-40 cm tall stems are occasionally found in large groups. The 7-10 mm long sepals are narrowly oblong. A shorter and broader lip has 3 dark reddish veins and 2 small teeth at either side of its base; the veins may be partially broken up into spots or dashes. The spur measures 0.5-2.5 mm long. Typically, the entire flower is reddish-purple, although sometimes the color may be pink or yellow.

A colony with several hundred stems grows near Road 80 at an elevation of 4,150 feet in a young Pacific silver fir woods; it includes stems ranging from yellow to reddish to purplish. Western coralroot also grows alongside the Island Springs trail northeast of Bench Lake, alongside Road 8040 near Gotchen Creek, on the east side of the Aiken Lava Flow, and near the Snipes Mountain Trail at an elevation of 4,950 feet.

#### *Corallorhiza trifida* Chatelain—EARLY CORALROOT

Shorter stems distinguish this coralroot from the other two at the mountain. The stems are 20-25 cm tall, and the few flowers are a yellowish or pale yellowish-green in color. The lateral sepals vary from 4-6 mm in length and the pure white lip is approximately 5 mm long. Another distinguishing feature is the curve of the upper petals of the flower, touching their tips above the column.

This species is known from the end of Trail 75, at about 3,500 feet along Cascade Creek and in the forest on the east side of Swampy Meadows at 4,000 feet. It was collected by Suksdorf at Hellroaring Valley and near "an island in Bird Creek." It appears to require a forest habitat that is both moister and older than that required by the other two coralroot species.

### *Goodyera* R. Br.—RATTLESNAKE-PLANTAIN

#### *Goodyera oblongifolia* Raf.—RATTLESNAKE-PLANTAIN

The flattened rosettes of this orchid occasionally form colonies from spreading rootstocks in the middle elevation forest. Variable, the attractive 3-6 cm long lanceolate to elliptical leaves are typically dark green and streaked with white, netlike markings, although on occasion entirely green leaves are found. The individual, greenish-white flowers are 6-8 mm long, and are configured in dense racemes on 20-30 cm tall stems. The upper petals and sepal are fused, forming a hoodlike structure over the column while the lip is concave, almost pouchlike. The backs of the sepals are short-hairy.

Locally common and occurring both as individual plants and small colonies, this orchid is an understory plant in dense forests. It is cosmopolitan at the mountain, reaching about 4,500 feet of elevation, with plants noted by the authors at Swampy Meadows, at the intersections of Roads 8040 and 781, and at the end of Road 050.

### *Listera* R. Br.—TWAYBLADE

The common name is derived from the two opposite leaves at the middle of each stem. The 2-5 cm long, stalkless leaves vary from ovate to rounded. The small plants rarely are more than 20 cm tall. Each slender stem bears a raceme of a few widely-spaced green (sometimes reddish-brown), flowers. The flowers have wide-spreading sepals and petals that range from 2-4 mm in length; a spur is absent.

Uncommon at Mount Adams, the twayblades are most typically found in lower elevation moist forests on the west side.

1 Lip deeply forked with pointed lobes; leaves heart-shaped at the base ........................................................................ *L. cordata*

1 Lip blunt, or shallowly notched with blunt lobes; leaves rounded at the base ........................................................................ 2

2(1) Lip shallowly notched at the tip; ovary glandular .. *L. convallarioides*

2 Lip blunt or rounded at the tip; ovary smooth.................... *L. caurina*

### *Listera caurina* Piper—WESTERN TWAYBLADE

Two short, flaring, hornlike structures at the base of the lip help distinguish this plant from *L. convallarioides.* The lip declines at an angle of approximately 45° from the ovary (observe this in side view) and the column is approximately 2 mm long. The plants reach 10-30 cm in height and have leaves 3-6 cm long.

The most frequently seen twayblade at Mount Adams, this species is nevertheless uncommon, growing on rich soil in moist forests, chiefly on the west side of the mountain. It has been found at the Pacific Crest Trail crossing on Road 23 and in forests along Hellroaring Creek.

### *Listera convallarioides* (Sw.) Nutt. *ex* Ell. BROAD-LIPPED TWAYBLADE

Taller and with longer leaves than *L. caurina,* the column of this twayblade is about 3 mm long, and, rather than angled, the lip is more or less in a straight line with the ovary.

A low to middle elevation species of rich, damp soils in old forests, this orchid was found by the authors at the end of Trail 75 alongside Cascade Creek at 3,500 feet on the southwest. It is also known from a Suksdorf collection at Rusk Creek on the east side.

### *Listera cordata* (L.) R. Br.—HEART-LEAF TWAYBLADE

Heart-shaped leaves up to 4 cm long and a long-forked lip distinguish this plant. The flowers are typically greenish in color; elsewhere in the Cascades, plants with reddish or reddish-brown flowers may be seen but this has not been noted at Mount Adams.

Rare at the mountain, this species is known from a Suksdorf collection on the White Salmon River, for which other details are not given, and a modern collection by Paul Slichter, from a meadow at 4,400 feet on Dairy Creek, on the southeast.

### *Piperia* Rydb.—REIN-ORCHID

This genus was formerly placed in *Habenaria* and is thus described in Hitchcock. (Presently only four species of *Habenaria* are recognized in North America, all limited to the Gulf Coast and Florida.) The leaves of the two *Piperia* species at Mount Adams tend to be basal and to have withered by flowering time; the stems are leafless or bear leaf-like bracts. The white to green flowers are spurred, and the size and shape of the spur helps distinguish the species. The sepals have one prominent vein.

A dry habitat, lower elevation species, *P. unalascensis* is much less common at the mountain than *P. elegans*, which grows in meadows and open sites at middle to subalpine elevations.

1 Spur 2-3 mm long; flowers 5-6 mm across at the mouth .................. *P. unalascensis*

1 Spur about 10 mm long; flowers 10-12 mm across .................. *P. elegans* ssp. *elegans*

### *Piperia elegans* (Lindl.) Rydb. ssp. *elegans*
### ELEGANT REIN-ORCHID

The whitish flowers of this lovely orchid are borne in dense, slender spikes on 30-50 cm tall stems. The 2-4 oblanceolate leaves are 5-25 cm long. The upper petals are slightly narrower than the sepals, but they and the lower lip differ little. They are widely spread, while the long flower spurs are approximately 10 mm in length, slender, and curved downward.

Preferring dry, lower elevation forests, this uncommon species is found at the DNR quarry on the southeast side of the mountain, at an elevation of 4,100 feet where it grows in a Garry oak woodland.

### *Piperia unalascensis* (Spreng.) Rydb.—ALASKAN REIN-ORCHID

The flowers of this species are relatively few in number and widely spaced on the stems, which are typically less than 40 cm tall. The oblanceolate, 7-15 cm long basal leaves number 2 or 3. The lower sepals are wider than the upper sepal and the petals; they do not spread as widely as those of *P. elegans*. The slightly curved spur is 2-3 mm long.

More commonly found than *P. elegans*, this species is known from the trailhead at Trail 75 in the Cascade Creek drainage on the southwest side of Mount Adams. It was collected by Suksdorf on the east side at Rusk Creek, Hellroaring Valley, and on Little Mount Adams (that collection label is not specific, but the most likely location is in the forest on the lower slope close to Hellroaring Creek).

### *Platanthera* L.C. Rich.—BOG ORCHID

Once included in *Habenaria,* these are orchids of moist to wet, open habitats, often in perennially inundated meadows (although on more elevated ground than the wettest parts). Unlike *Piperia,* the leaves are retained throughout the flowering period. A small, leaflike bract is set below each flower. The flowers of *Platanthera* have a hooded appearance formed by the partially-fused upper sepal and 2 petals. The lateral sepals are widely spread and there is a spur.

*P. dilatata* var. *leucostachys* and *P. stricta* are common in the middle elevation wet meadows at the mountain. *P. dilatata* var. *dilatata,* found along Hellroaring Creek on the southeast side, is more restricted in range. A hybrid of *P. stricta* and var. *dilatata* is known from Mount Rainier but has not been observed at Mount Adams.

1 Spur about 3 mm long, sackline; flowers greenish ........... *P. stricta*
1 Spur 6-10 mm long, slender and not sacklike ............................... 2

2(1) Spur about equal to lower lip, nearly straight and somewhat stout ... ....................................................................... *P. dilatata* var. *dilatata*
2 Spur half again as long as lip, very slender, curved ......................... ............................................................ *P. dilatata* var. *leucostachys*

### *Platanthera dilatata* (Pursh) Lindl. *ex* Beck var. *dilatata* DILATED BOG ORCHID

This species resembles *P. dilatata* var. *leucostachys* in most respects, differing primarily in the spur, which is approximately as long as the lip, more or less straight, and not particularly slender.

Uncommon, this species is known from the meadow along Hellroaring Creek (close to Bench Lake) at 4,800 feet and from a Suksdorf collection made somewhere in Hellroaring Valley.

### *Platanthera dilatata* (Pursh) Lindl. var. *leucostachys* (Lindl.) Luer WHITE BOG ORCHID

The 20-80 cm tall stems of this variable orchid are very leafy, with the larger leaves lanceolate in shape and up to 20 cm long. The inflorescence is a dense spike. The sepals and upper petals are 4 mm long, and the longer lip measures 6-8 mm in length. It is wide at the upper part and narrow towards the tip. The 10 mm long, slender spur is curved downward from the ovary. The flowers are scented like cloves.

Nicknamed "bog candles," this is a relatively common and easily-seen orchid in middle elevation wet meadows where it may occur in dense colonies. It is found at Babyshoe Meadow on the northwest side of the mountain, and at Spring Creek and Grand Meadow on the southwest. On the north side it grows in Midway Meadows and on the southwest at Hellroaring Valley and the slopes above the valley.

#### *Platanthera stricta* Lindl.—SLENDER BOG ORCHID

The greenish stems and flowers blend well with the grasses and sedges common to the preferred habitat of this orchid. The stems measure 20-60 cm tall and the lanceolate leaves may reach 15 cm in length. The flowers are borne in a loose to dense spike; the sepals vary from 3-6 mm in length, and the slender lip is 5-7 mm long. The sacklike spur is approximately 3 mm long, and is rather difficult to see, as it tucks behind the lip.

Common and often found with *P. dilatata* var. *leucostachys*, this orchid grows at Babyshoe, Muddy, and Midway Meadows. It is also found in the meadow at the intersection of Road 23 and Road 2329 (Bathtub Meadow) at 4,100 feet. This orchid also colonizes roadside ditches and grows along streams, reaching 4,500 feet.

### *Spiranthes* L.C. Rich.—LADIES' TRESSES

One common species and one listed "sensitive" species comprise the members of this genus of lovely, meadow-dwelling orchids. The species differ in the characteristics of the lower lip, which is more expanded at the tip in *S. porrifolia.* The fragrant flowers are set in 3 ranks that twist in spirals along the stem. The leaves are primarily basal; any stem leaves are reduced in size. The flowers are whitish to creamy-yellow in color.

1 Lip narrow at the tip, short-hairy on the upper surface, with a protuberance (callosity) at each side of the base ........... *S. porrifolia*

1 Lip expanded and nearly triangular at the tip, lacking hairs and protuberances ........................................................ *S. romanzoffiana*

#### *Spiranthes porrifolia* Lindl.—CREAMY LADIES' TRESSES

The flowers of this lovely orchid are set in 3 ranks that twist in spirals along the 30-40 cm tall stems. The 7-15 cm long leaves are primarily basal, while the stem leaves are much shorter. The 1 cm long cream-colored flowers are narrow. The lip is slightly tapered to a narrower tip, with a small protuberance at each side of the base and short hairs near the apex. The other petals and sepals spread a bit at their tips, giving the flower a more tubular appearance. There is no spur.

On the Washington State Department of Natural Resources list as a "sensitive" species, and known in the state from a small number of locations, in southern Washington this species was previously known only along the Columbia River. It is much more abundant southwards into California.

This uncommon orchid was found by the authors at Muddy Meadows on the southwest side of the mountain, and at Midway Meadows and Foggy Flat (elevation 6,050 feet) on the north. Nowhere at Mount Adams has it been found growing with *S. romanzoffiana*.

### *Spiranthes romanzoffiana* Cham.—HOODED LADIES' TRESSES

Similar to *S. porrifolia*, this species differs in the shape of the lip, which is constricted below the expanded tip (a condition called "pandurate"); it also lacks protuberances and hairiness. The lip is also recurved to a greater degree and the upper sepals and petals curve together, giving the flower a shorter, "hooded" appearance.

Found in middle elevation to subalpine meadows, this common species grows at an elevation of 6,500 feet alongside the trail above Hellroaring Overlook on the southeast side. It is also found in Killen Creek Meadow on the northwest, at Snipes Mountain, and in Hellroaring Valley.

## Poaceae (R. Brown) Barnhart—GRASS FAMILY

Grasses can be found everywhere at Mount Adams, from the swampy pools of Cascade Creek at 3,200 feet on the southwest side to stony slopes far above timberline. With 96 separate taxa, including species with more than one subspecies or variety, in 32 genera, the grasses pose a challenge to the student of the mountain's flora. Add to the sheer number of species the fact that grass anatomy is complex and calls for a specialized vocabulary, the task of identifying a particular specimen may seem daunting. Success with grasses is really just a matter of learning the terminology and becoming aware of features of the plants that require careful observation, aided by a handlens and sometimes by a dissecting microscope. (It should be noted that the remarks that follow apply to the grasses at Mount Adams, and not necessarily to all members of the grass family worldwide.)

The leaves of grasses may be primarily basal, or the stem may be leafy. In either case, each leaf attaches to a **node**, a solid junction in the stem. The lower portion of the leaf wraps around the stem, forming a **sheath**; the lengthwise edges of the sheath may be open and more or less overlapping or may be fused together, or some condition in between. The upper part of the leaf, free of the stem, is the **blade**.

A tongue-like structure called the **ligule** is present at the base of the free portion of the leaf; it represents an extension of the sheath. In a few grasses, it is reduced to a mere fringe of hairs, but more commonly it is membranous, whitish or translucent, and of variable length and shape.

The stem, at the top of which the inflorescence is borne, is round in cross-section, unlike the triangular sedges and often flattened rushes. The inflorescence is arranged in spikes, racemes, or panicles.

Individual flowers, called **florets** in the grasses, are grouped into **spikelets** and it is the nature of the parts of the spikelet that is most frequently referred to in the key. At the base of each spikelet is a pair of **glumes**. Since spikelets are unitary, never compound, locating the glumes is sufficient to isolate a spikelet.

Glumes are empty bracts; that is, they themselves contain no florets; that is, the florets are placed on the rachilla *above* the glumes. Typically membranous, they may be short, long, sharp-tipped or blunt. In a few genera, the spikelet separates (**disarticulates**) from the stem at a point below the glumes, falling as a unit and, in a breeze, rolling across the ground like a miniature tumbleweed. However, in most of the grasses at Mount Adams, the spikelet disarticulates above the glumes, so that the inflorescence, once the seeds have been shed, consists of an arrangement of empty glumes.

Within each pair of glumes are one or more **florets**. The number of florets per spikelet is important: one only in common genera such as *Agrostis*, seven to ten or more in *Bromus*. The floret itself is comprised of another pair of bracts, the **lemma** and the **palea**. The lemma enfolds the palea, which is often smaller than the lemma or, in some genera, rudimentary or absent. The lemma should be observed closely: it may be smooth or hairy, green or colored, veined or not, and may be blunt or pointed. A lemma is said to be **awned** if it bears a short to long needle-like point; this represents a continuation of the major vein of the lemma. Furthermore, the point at which the awn is attached is significant: at the tip, part-way down the back, or near the base.

The glumes, lemmas, and paleas are attached to an axis that runs the length of the spikelet, called a **rachilla**; the florets, if there are more than one, are two-ranked, alternating on the axis. The rachilla may be prolonged a short ways beyond the last floret.

The reproductive portions of the floret – the stamens and pistil – are seldom referred to in the key or the descriptions. There is one pistil per floret, with two feathery stigmas (an adaptation to wind pollination) and usually three stamens, but sometimes two. Florets may be perfect, with a pistil and stamens, or may be pistillate or staminate only. Some grasses have a combination of fertile and sterile florets within a spikelet. The fruit, or grain, develops from a one-celled ovary and remains enveloped by the lemma and palea when it is mature and shed.

1 Ligule a fringe of hairs ........ *Danthonia*
1 Ligule membranous, although sometimes ragged or cut along the upper margin ........ 2

2(1) Florets all replaced with small bulblets; stamens and pistils absent ........ *Poa bulbosa*
2 Normal florets present ........ 3

3(2) Floret 1 per spikelet ........ 4
3 Florets 2 or more per spikelet ........ 12

4(3) Inflorescence spikelike ........ 5
4 Inflorescence branched, sometimes obscurely so ........ 6

5(4) Lemma with a bent awn ........ *Alopecurus*
5 Lemma awnless ........ *Phleum*

6(4) Base of the lemma bearded with straight hairs half or more as long as the lemma ........ *Calamagrostis*
6 Base of the lemma not bearded, or with much shorter hairs ........ 7

7(6) Awn of lemma 15-40 mm long ........ 8
7 Awn, if present, less than 3 mm long ........ 9

8(7) Awn more than 15 mm long; ligule 3-6 mm long ........ *Hesperostipa*
8 Awn about 15 mm long; ligule less than 1 mm long ........ *Achnatherum*

9(7) Leaf blades more than 7 mm wide ........ *Cinna*
9 Leaf blades up to 5 mm wide ........ 10

10(9) Annual, with loosely spreading, decumbent stems less than 10 cm tall ........ *Muhlenbergia*
10 Perennial, tufted, with upright stems, usually more than 10 cm tall ........ 11

11(10) Palea long, 2/3 to 3/4 the length of the lemma ........ *Podagrostis*
11 Palea less than 1/4 the length of the lemma ........ *Agrostis*

12(3) Inflorescence unbranched, spikelike ........ 13
12 Inflorescence branched, sometimes obscurely so ........ 19

13(12) Inflorescence of unlike, paired fertile and sterile spikelets, appearing "brush-like" due to closely-set, erect, long-awned glumes and lemmas; rare weed ........ *Cynosurus*
13 Spikelets alike; if lemmas awned, then inflorescence not brush-like ........ 14

14(13) Spikelets arranged equally around the axis of the inflorescence ...... ........................................................................................ *Trisetum*

14 Spikelets in two rows on opposite sides of the axis of the inflorescence ........................................................................ 15

15(14) Spikelets 1 per node ................................................................. 16
15 Spikelets 2 or 3 per node ........................................................... 17

16(15) Lemma awned .................................................... *Pseudoroegneria*
16 Lemma not awned ......................................................... *Thinopyrum*

17(15) Lemma fringed with short teeth below the awn ..................... *Secale*
17 Lemma smooth-edged below the awn ........................................ 18

18(17) Spikelets mostly 2 per node, with 2 fertile florets per spikelet .......... ........................................................................................ *Elymus*
18 Spikelets mostly 3 per node, with 1 fertile floret and 2 sterile florets per spikelet ...................................................................... *Hordeum*

19(12) One or both glumes longer than the first lemma .......................... 20
19 Both glumes shorter than the first lemma .................................... 27

20(19) Lemma not awned ........................................................................ 21
20 Lemma awned ............................................................................. 22

21(20) Branches of the panicle erect, densely-flowered; plant more than 1 m tall ........................................................................................ *Phalaris*
21 Branches spreading, few-flowered; plant less than 1 m tall ............. ........................................................................... *Anthoxanthum*

22(20) Glumes at least 20 mm long ............................................... *Avena*
22 Glumes no more than 10 mm long ............................................. 23

23(22) Leaves sweet-scented; upper floret fertile, lower 2 florets sterile ...... ........................................................................... *Anthoxanthum*
23 Leaves not sweet-scented; all florets fertile ................................. 24

24(23) Nodes along the stem short-hairy; uncommon weed ............ *Holcus*
24 Nodes smooth; native plants ...................................................... 25

25(24) Axis of the spikelet hairy; lemma pointed at the tip ............ *Trisetum*
25 Axis smooth; lemma blunt at the tip ........................................... 26

26(25) Leaf blades 1-3 mm wide; lemma awned from below the middle of the back ........................................................................ *Deschampsia*
26 Leaf blades 4-6 mm wide; lemma awned from the middle of the back ........................................................................................ *Vahlodea*

27(19) Lemma awned; if unawned then the base of the flowering stem bulbous .................................................................... 28
27 Lemma not awned ............................................................ 33

28(27) Inflorescence a 1-sided raceme; spikelet 1 per branch .................... ............................................................ *Pleuropogon*
28 Inflorescence a panicle, rarely 1-sided; spikelets typically more than 1 per branch ............................................................ 29

29(28) Leaf sheath closed one-quarter of its length or more .................. 30
29 Leaf sheath closed less than one-quarter its length or nearly entirely open ............................................................ 32

30(29) Glumes papery, translucent; base of stems often bulbous .... *Melica*
30 Glumes membranous, green; stems never bulbous .................... 31

31(30) Rare introduced grass; inflorescence asymmetrical, 1-sided ............ ............................................................ *Dactylis*
31 Common native as well as weedy grasses; inflorescence symmetrical with branches surrounding the axis ................ *Bromus*

32(29) Annuals; 1 stamen ............................................................ *Vulpia*
32 Perennials; 3 stamens ...................................................... *Festuca*

33(27) Lemma keeled on the back, often purplish at the tip, the veins converging at tip ............................................................ *Poa*
33 Lemma rounded on the back, greenish throughout, the veins parallel and not converging ................................................... 34

34(33) Second (upper) glume with 1 major vein; leaf sheath closed to near top ............................................................ *Glyceria*
34 Second glume with 3 major veins; leaf sheath open......................... ............................................................ *Torreyochloa*

## Achnatherum Beauv.—NEEDLEGRASS

These are tufted, native perennials with 1-flowered spikelets that are bent above the glumes. The inflorescence is panicle-like, narrow, and most often ascending. The lemma is awned from the tip and may be roughened at the base or hairy. The plants vary considerably, from 20-180 cm.

Needlegrass species are fairly uncommon at the mountain. They are found at sites ranging from dry, open hillsides to alpine habitats. They were formerly included in the genus *Stipa.*

1 Basal segment of awn rough .......................... *A. nelsonii* ssp. *dorei*
1 Basal segment of awn hairy, some more than 1 mm long ............ 2

2(1) Awn completely hairy ..................... *A. occidentale* ssp. *occidentale*
2 Tip of awn smooth or slightly rough .................................................
........................................................ *A. occidentale* ssp. *pubescens*

### *Achnatherum nelsonii* (Scribn.) Barkworth ssp. *dorei* (Barkworth & Maze) Barkworth DORE'S NEEDLEGRASS

This species differs from *A. occidentale* in the characteristics of the lower part of the awn. It is roughened and somewhat short-hairy (with a few longish hairs at the top of the lemma), but not feathery with long-hairs, as is the case with *A. occidentale.*

Named *Stipa occidentalis* var. *nelsonii* in Hitchcock, this species is known from a Suksdorf collection made at "6-7,000" feet at the mountain, probably on the southeast side, on open talus slopes.

### *Achnatherum occidentale* (Thurb. *ex* S. Wats.) Barkworth ssp. *occidentale*—WESTERN NEEDLEGRASS

This tufted grass may reach 50 cm in height and bears narrow branches in an ascending panicle. The awns are nearly 4 cm long, hairy its entire length, and twice bent. The hairs of the lemma are about as long as the hairs of the awn.

A middle elevation species of dry sites, including rocky slopes, it was collected at Bunnell Butte and at Rush Creek.

### *Achnatherum occidentale* (Thurb. *ex* S. Wats.) Barkworth ssp. *pubescens* (Vasey) Barkworth—HAIRY NEEDLEGRASS

This subspecies is distinguished from ssp. *occidentale* in having lemma tip hairs that are longer than the hairs of the awn. Furthermore, the uppermost portion of the awn (above the second bend) is not hairy.

Occurring at higher elevations than ssp. *occidentale,* this plant was collected above 6,000 feet on the southeast side of Mount Adams by both Suksdorf and Thompson.

## *Agrostis* L.—BENTGRASS

The spikelets of this genus are 1-flowered and borne in open to compact, relatively small panicles, overall with a characteristic light and airy appearance. The common name refers to the awns of some species, which are bent at midlength. There are 3 stamens. The ligules are membranous and softly short-hairy.

One perennial weedy species is included among the 6 more common native species. Bentgrasses are typically found in middle elevation meadows and forest openings; two species are known from subalpine elevations. Check the very similar genus *Podagrostis* for "agrostis-like" plants that do not key well here.

1 Plants tufted, less than 20 cm tall .............................. *A. variabilis*
1 Plants 20-120 cm tall, tufted or with creeping rootstocks and spreading .......................................................................... 2

2(1) Plants with well-developed runners or rootstocks .......................... 3
2 Runners and rootstocks absent .................................................... 4

3(2) Plants more than 50 cm tall (reaching 120 cm); panicle open .......... ........................................................................... *A. capillaris*
3 Plants 15-30 cm tall; panicle various ........................... *A. pallens*

4(42 Lemmas awned ............................................................. *A. exarata*
4 Lemmas not awned ...................................................................... 5

5(4) Panicle very diffuse, the branches spreading-ascending and reaching 15 cm long ...................................................... *A. scabra*
5 Panicle contracted to open, the longest branches less than 6 cm long ........................................................................................ 6

6(5) Panicle less than 15 cm long; lower leaf blades to 5 cm long and 2 mm wide ................................................................... *A. idahoensis*
6 Panicle 15-30 cm long; lower leaf blades 10-30 cm long and 2-4 mm wide ................................................................ *A. oregonensis*

### *Agrostis capillaris* L.—COLONIAL BENTGRASS

This bentgrass is a strongly-spreading species, with flowering stems that reach about 80 cm tall. The 3 mm wide leaves are mostly flat and up to 15 cm long. The inflorescence is an open panicle with widely-spreading branches. The spikelets are purplish; the 1.5-2 mm long lemmas are usually awnless. The palea is about half as long as the lemma.

This is the one non-native species of bentgrass at Mount Adams, probably because of the overall high elevation of the study area. It was collected on the southeast side of the mountain alongside Road 170 in a logged stand of ponderosa pine on the west side of King Mountain.

### *Agrostis exarata* Trin.—SPIKE BENTGRASS

This tufted species ranges from 30-90 cm in height, with flat leaf blades that are 7-8 mm wide. The common name is in reference to the congested panicle, although it is not technically a spike: the panicle is dense and narrow compared to other *Agrostis* species. The branches are short and erect and bear spikelets nearly to the base. The lemma is 1.5-2 mm long and unawned; the palea is minute.

Fairly common in middle elevation wet sites, this species is found in the upper part of Swampy Meadows, at Rush Creek, and Hellroaring Canyon.

### *Agrostis idahoensis* Nash—IDAHO BENTGRASS

Characterized by a loose, branched panicle up to 10 cm long, this is a small grass, tufted and less than 30 cm in height. The 2 mm wide leaf blades are flat. The branches spread widely but are not quite horizontal, bearing only a few spikelets towards the end of each very slender branch. The lemma is about 1.5 mm long and unawned; the palea is minute or absent.

A middle elevation species of moist or at least seasonally wet places, it was collected by the authors near the lava flow along the Pacific Crest Trail on the north side of the mountain. It was also collected at Hellroaring Canyon by Suksdorf.

### *Agrostis oregonensis* Vasey—OREGON BENTGRASS

Similar to Idaho bentgrass, this species is both taller, to 90 cm in height, and has a widely-branched panicle that is about 30 cm high. The flat leaves are 2-4 mm wide. The lemmas are longer than in *A. idahoensis*, averaging about 2 mm in length; it is unawned and the palea is minute.

A lower elevation species elsewhere in the Cascades, it is uncommon at Mount Adams, and was collected by Suksdorf at Hellroaring Canyon and along Hellroaring Creek by Cotton. It grows in wet meadows.

### *Agrostis pallens* Trin.—SEASHORE BENTGRASS

This is the tallest of the bentgrasses at Mount Adams, reaching 120 cm in height and spreading from a stout rootstock. The ligules are 1-4 mm long and the leaf blades are flat and up to 3 mm broad and 15 cm long. The panicle is narrowly open, with ascending branches; spikelets are borne nearly to the bases of the branches. The lemma is 2-2.3 mm long, awned or awnless, and the palea is absent.

This species is uncommon at Mount Adams, known from old collections made by Flett along the upper Klickitat River and by Suksdorf along the upper Lewis River. In these places, it presumably grew in moist forest openings and on open streamside slopes.

The common name reflects a change in the concept of the species. At one time, plants of the coastal strand from Washington to California were called *A. pallens*, seashore bentgrass, while similar plants inland were named *A. diegoensis*. Current thinking treats the coastal plants as no more than an ecotype so, since the epithet "pallens" has priority, the Mount Adams plants inherit the name "seashore bentgrass."

### *Agrostis scabra* Willd.—ROUGH BENTGRASS, TICKLEGRASS

This tufted perennial grass may reach 60 cm in height. The very diffuse panicle can equal half the height of the plant. The flat leaf blades are 2-3 mm wide and the panicle has very long, ascending branches with purplish spikelets borne near the branch tips. The lemma may be awnless or bear a short awn and is about 1.5 mm long; the palea is very short.

Relatively common in moist to wet places in meadows and open woods as well as along roadsides, this species grows at Muddy Meadows on the north side and is also found at Bird Creek, Hellroaring Canyon, and at the Pineway trailhead on the southeast.

### *Agrostis variabilis* Rydb.—MOUNTAIN BENTGRASS

This tufted grass reaches about 30 cm in height; the inflorescence is a contracted panicle. The inrolled leaf blades are less than 7 cm long and 1 mm wide. The lemmas are typically not awned, although on occasion a short (less than 2 mm) straight awn is present. The absence of a palea distinguishes this species from the similar *Podagrostis humilis.*

Showing a preference for dry meadows and rocky ridges, typically in the subalpine regime, although sometimes lower, this species is locally common. It grows at a low elevation near the confluence of Cascade Creek and Salt Creek and is also found as high as the Highline Trail, west of Foggy Flat (approximately 6,100 feet of elevation). Suksdorf collected it in Hellroaring Canyon.

## *Alopecurus* L.—FOXTAIL

### *Alopecurus pratensis* L.—MEADOW FOXTAIL

This stout perennial weed ranges from 30-90 cm in height. The ligules of the lower leaves are 1.5-2 mm long, while those of the upper stem leaves may be 6 mm long and are irregularly toothed. The 3-10 mm broad leaf blades are roughened by very short hairs. The panicle appears spike-like and is 3-10 cm high. The glumes are 5 mm long; they are long-hairy on the keel. The lemmas are slightly shorter than the glumes, with awns that are bent and exserted above the tips of the glumes. A palea is absent.

Introduced from northern Eurasia, this weed is found at Muddy Meadows, growing amidst dense stands of native grasses and sedges, along with *Camassia quamash* ssp. *breviflora.*

## *Anthoxanthum* L.—VERNALGRASS

The native northern sweetgrass was formerly included in a separate genus, *Hierochloe;* that genus has recently been combined with *Anthoxanthum,* based upon the unusual nature of the spikelet: each spikelet is three-flowered, only the uppermost of which is perfect, this is, containing both stamens and a pistil. More easily noticed is the strong, sweet fragrance of the plants, especially at the roots and when dried.

1 Lower two flowers consisting of empty lemmas only; lemmas awned; fairly common weed of disturbed places ........ *A. odoratum*

1 Lower two flowers staminate; lemmas awnless; rare native in wet meadows .............................................................. *A. hirtum*

**_Anthoxanthum hirtum_ (Schrank) Y. Schouten & Veldkamp**
**NORTHERN SWEETGRASS**

A purplish-tinged perennial that ranges from 30-50 cm tall, this showy grass spreads from rootstocks to form loose patches. The ligules are 3-5 mm long and wavy on the edges, with small hairs. The leaf blades, clustered at the base of the stem, are 3-5 mm broad and as much as 25 cm in length, while the stem leaves are only 1-2 cm long. The 5-10 cm-long panicle is pyramidal, and the spikelets are 5-6 mm long, almost round in outline. The lemmas, not quite 2 mm long, are covered by short hairs.

This is a species of moist sites in middle elevation to subalpine meadows and slopes. At the mountain, it grows in Muddy Meadows at 4,400 feet. The species is of very limited occurrence in Washington and is on the "review" list of the Washington Natural Heritage Program.

**_Anthoxanthum odoratum_ L.—SWEET VERNALGRASS**

This tufted, weedy perennial grass is about 60 cm tall. The inflorescence is a congested, spikelike panicle, yellow-brown in color. It has a "spiky" appearance, from the awns of the 2 sterile lemmas in each spikelet; the third floret is fertile and unawned. The common name refers to the strong, sweet scent of the roots.

A middle elevation, non-native species at the mountain, of open forests and wet sites, sweet vernalgrass is found alongside Road 23 near the summit overlook, at Keene's Horse Camp, and at Olallie campground.

## *Avena* L.—OATS

**_Avena fatua_ L.—WILD OATS**

The tall, dry, straw-colored stems of the mature plants distinguish this weedy, annual grass. Reaching close to 1 m in height, there is typically just one stem per plant, with an openly-branched inflorescence. Configured in a loose panicle, the 3-flowered spikelets, each about 2 cm long, nod at the ends of slender branches. The bent awns of the lemmas are about 30-40 mm in length. The palea is shorter than the lemma and the seed is densely clothed with straight hairs.

Found in middle elevation disturbance areas, this species grows at the Morrison Creek trailhead and near Road 23 at the Riley Creek trailhead, both places where horse trailers regularly park.

### *Bromus* L.—BROME-GRASS

Three weedy species, fortunately quite rare, are included in this genus of annual and perennial grasses. The native species are locally common in meadows as well as in open, disturbed sites; they are also seen in dry forests. The bromes tend to be tall and vigorous, with broad, flat leaf blades that are variously roughened or hairy. The ligules are relatively short, and auricles are present in some species. The spikelets have several to many florets in flattened spikelets that are borne in open to contracted panicles.

1 Annual plants .......... 2
1 Perennial plants .......... 3

2(1) Nerves of lemma prominent; inflorescence congested and erect; spikelets longer than pedicels ........ *B. hordeaceus* ssp. *hordeaceus*
2 Nerves of lemma barely elevated; inflorescence open, spikelets shorter than pedicels .......... *B. commutatus*

3(1) Plants with rhizomes; lemmas unawned or with small tip .......... 4
3 Plants without rhizomes; lemmas with awn at least 4 mm long .... 5

4(3) Glumes broadest at the midsection; stem nodes short-hairy .......... *B. pumpellianus*
4 Glumes broadest at the base; stem nodes hairless .......... *B. inermis*

5(3) Narrow, contracted panicle, branches erect .......... 6
5 Panicle open, branches spreading, longer than spikelets .......... 7

6(5) Sheaths and blades glabrous; panicle branches erect; awn less than 4 mm long .......... *B. suksdorfii*
6 Sheaths long-hairy; panicle branches stiffly spreading; awn 5-7 mm long .......... *B. orcuttianus*

7(5) Ligules about 1 mm long; awn 2-4 mm long .......... *B. ciliatus*
7 Ligules 2-8 mm long; awn more than 5 mm long .......... 8

8(7) Panicle large, up to 35 cm tall .......... *B. sitchensis*
8 Panicle small, 15 cm high or less .......... *B. vulgaris*

### ***Bromus ciliatus* L.—FRINGED BROME**

The stems of this tufted perennial are 50-100 cm tall. The sheaths vary from glabrous to thickly long-hairy and the ligules average about 1 mm long and are minutely toothed and hairy. The blades are flat and 5-10 mm broad and may be hairy beneath. The 7-13 cm long panicle is loose with slender, drooping branches, and the spikelets are 15-23 mm long and composed of 7 to 9 flowers. The first glume is narrow and 5-7 mm long, while the second varies from 6-8 mm, is 3-nerved and rounded to abrupt. The lemmas are 8-11 mm long, hairy, with a straight 3-4 mm long awn.

Elsewhere in Washington, fringed brome is typically found along riverbanks, lake shores, and wet to dry slopes; relatively rare at the mountain, this species was collected by Suksdorf at Hellroaring Canyon.

### ***Bromus commutatus* Schrad.—MEADOW BROME**

This annual grass may reach 60 cm in height and is distinguished by the moderate length ascending to spreading panicle branches. The sheaths and the lower portion of the leaf blades are softly long-hairy.

A rare roadside weed, meadow brome was collected by the authors alongside Road 23, at the Mile 34 post, in a sunny place on disturbed soil.

### ***Bromus hordeaceus* L. ssp. *hordeaceus*—SOFT BROME**

A weedy, annual grass that reaches about 60 cm in height (but often less on poor ground), this brome is characterized by its soft-hairy leaf blades and sheaths. The spikelets are arranged in a contracted, upright panicle, helping to distinguish the species from the similar *B. commutatus*. The veins of the short-awned lemma are noticeably raised, forming ridges with intervening shallow troughs.

Formerly called *Bromus mollis*, this species was found by the authors on trampled soil partly shaded by lodgepole pine at the Keene's Horse Camp on the north side of the mountain.

### ***Bromus inermis* Leyss.—SMOOTH BROME**

Rising 20-120 cm from strong rhizomes, this species is primarily hairless. The stem leaves number 4-6 and the minutely hairy and toothed ligules are less than 1 mm in length. The glumes are broadest at their bases. The flat blades are 3-10 mm broad and glabrous to hairy. The panicle is 7-20 cm long, narrow, with the branches ascending to erect. The narrow spikelets are 1.5-3 cm long and purplish to greenish-tinged. The lemmas are unawned or sometimes have a small, sharp tip, while the glumes are broadest at their bases.

A weed of disturbed areas, meadows and streambanks with a wide elevational range, it is found at Keene's Horse Camp. It also has the potential to invade intact habitats, as is seen in the lower Paradise Meadow at Mount Rainier.

### *Bromus orcuttianus* Vasey—ORCUTT'S BROME

The leaves of this 45-100 cm tall brome are densely hairy at and below the nodes. The plants lack rhizomes. The sheaths overlap and are long-hairy to smooth; auricles are lacking. The minutely toothed ligules are 1-1.5 mm long, and the leaf blades are flat and 5-10 mm broad. The panicle branches are short and stiffly spreading, with 18-32 mm long spikelets at the tips. The lemma is 11-14 mm long and finely short-hairy and short-awned.

Most typically a dry habitat, open forest species, it was collected on the north slope of Hellroaring Canyon by Suksdorf. It also grows alongside Road 115 on the north side of the mountain. Suksdorf also found it on "slopes."

### *Bromus pumpellianus* Scribn. ssp. *pumpellianus*—ARCTIC BROME

This *Bromus* is distinguished most readily in the field by the reddish-purple color of the spikelets. More reliable characteristics that separate it from the weedy species *inermis* are the presence of small auricles on the leaves and leaf nodes that are short-hairy; the ligules are 1-2 mm long. The glumes are broadest at their midsections.

This native species, once considered a variety of *B. inermis*, was collected by the authors at the upper edge of Muddy Meadows, on ground that becomes dry by midsummer. Historical collections were made by Suksdorf and Eyerdam in the area of Hellroaring Valley. The color of the spikelets is eye-catching.

### *Bromus sitchensis* Trin.—ALASKA BROME

This common perennial brome forms clumps on dry soil in open forests. Its numerous flowering stems reach about 1.5 m in height, with 6 or 7 stem leaves that are 8-15 mm broad and lack auricles; the leaves are usually hairy on the lower surface. The ligules are 5-6 mm long. The branches of the large panicle spread widely, each bearing 1-2 spikelets. Each spikelet has 5-8 florets. The lemmas are short-hairy and 10-15 mm long, each with a straight awn 5-7 mm long.

The authors collected this grass alongside the Pineway Trail, west of the road to Bird Creek Meadows, in an open forest of *Pinus contorta* and *Abies grandis*. Suksdorf collected it on the upper Klickitat River.

### *Bromus suksdorfii* Vasey—SUKSDORF'S BROME

A perennial without rhizomes, this species varies from 50-100 cm in height and is hairless. The ligules are very small and minutely toothed and hairy. The blades are flat, 6-10 mm broad, and the narrow, almost spikelike, panicle is erect, with the branches shorter than the spikelets; these are 2.5-3.5 cm long and broadest above the midlength. The 13 mm long lemmas bear flattened, short hairs, while the awn is les than 4 mm long.

Found in open meadows and slopes from middle to subalpine levels, this is a southern Cascades species that reaches the Sierra Nevada in California. It is the most common native brome at Mount Adams and grows at the confluence of Cascade Creek and Salt Creek. It is also found near Road 23 on a cliff, and was collected by Suksdorf at Muddy River Canyon and Hellroaring Canyon.

### *Bromus vulgaris* (Hook.) Shear—COLUMBIAN BROME

This vigorous perennial grass may reach 120 cm in length. The flat leaf blades are 5-10 mm broad, auricles are absent and the ligule is 3-5 mm long. The lower stem and sheaths are soft-hairy. The panicle is relatively small, about 15 cm in height, with long, drooping branches. The large spikelets are 25 mm long. The lower portion of the lemma is finely hairy and there is a short awn.

Primarily a low elevation species, Columbian brome is a prominent member of the camas meadow community at Muddy Meadows and was collected by Suksdorf at Hellroaring Canyon.

### *Calamagrostis* Adans.—REED-GRASS

These are attractive, graceful, usually tall, perennial grasses, rising from spreading rootstocks and often found in meadows and alongside streams. The spikelets bear just 1 floret; they are arranged in dense to open panicles. The base of each floret bears short to long straight hairs; the lemmas are awned, although the awn may be inconspicuous.

1 Awn bent, exserted beyond the glume tips by 1.5-10 mm ............. 2
1 Awn straight, sometimes bent, exserted 1 mm or less beyond the glumes ............................................................................................ 3

2(1) Awn strongly bent, exserted less than 1.5 mm ........... *C. rubescens*
2 Awn not strongly bent, exserted at least 1.5 mm ............................................................................................................. *C. purpurascens*

3(1) Inflorescence dense, lower branches appressed to ascending ......................................................................................... *C. stricta* ssp. *stricta*
3 Inflorescence open, lower branches spreading to ascending ........................................................ *C. canadensis* var. *canadensis*

### *Calamagrostis canadensis* (Michx.) Beauv. var. *canadensis* BLUEJOINT

Upwards of 120 cm in height, with smooth stems, and flat, 5-10 mm wide leaf blades, this perennial has stout rootstocks. The panicle is relatively short for the height of the plant and has straight, spreading branches. The greenish to purplish glumes range from 3-3.8 mm long and taper to a sharp tip; they are longer than the blunt lemma. The awn is attached below the terminal 1/3 of the lemma.

Included here is the variety *imberbis*, formerly recognized based upon its longer glumes (at least 3.8 mm) that are narrow and tapered to a long tip. The glumes are purplish but edged with a brown color. It occurs widely at Mount Adams.

The common species is primarily a meadow dweller at the mountain. It grows in the upper part of Swampy Meadows, at Grand Meadow, at Takh Takh Meadow, alongside Hellroaring River, and in Hellroaring Canyon, where Suksdorf collected it. He also collected this variety at Bird Creek.

### *Calamagrostis purpurascens* R. Brown—PURPLE REED-GRASS

With short rootstocks, and more or less tufted, this species ranges in height from 30-60 cm. Softly-hairy on the upper surface, the leaf blades are up to 5 mm wide. The slender panicle is purplish and the hairs at the base of the lemma are short. The awn is exserted a short distance from the glumes, helping distinguish this species from *C. stricta*.

Although typically considered to be a species of open places on dryish, rocky slopes, particularly in ponderosa pine forests, at Mount Adams this uncommon plant is found at Babyshoe Meadow, a seasonally dry site.

### *Calamagrostis rubescens* Buckl.—PINEGRASS

The stems are smooth on this 50-110 cm tall stout perennial. The sheaths are mostly smooth although they may have stiff hairs on the front of some of the collars. The flat blades are 2-4 mm broad, roughened, and short and stiffly-hairy on the margins. The 1-5 mm long ligules are truncated and membranous and pale greenish-white to purplish. The 4-5 mm long glumes are sharply tipped and the lemma is slightly shorter, with 4 teeth. The awn is twisted and attached above the base, and extends beyond the glumes.

A species of openings in dry to moist forests, pinegrass is primarily an eastern Cascades plant. It is found at the DNR quarry and was collected by Suksdorf at Rush Creek, Muddy River Canyon, and Hellroaring Canyon. It was also collected by the authors on the north side of the mountain.

### *Calamagrostis stricta* (Timm) Koel. ssp. *stricta* SLIMSTEM REED-GRASS

Loosely tufted, this grass may range from 20-90 cm in height. The ligule is 1-3.5 mm long and the leaf is generally inrolled, with the upper surface smooth to somewhat roughened. The inflorescence is dense, 5-12 cm in length, while the branches ascending to flatly pressed against the axis. The glumes are 2-4.5 mm and thin, while the lemma is 2-4 mm in length. The awn is slender and straight, almost as long as the glumes.

A subspecies of coniferous forest, meadows, and slopes from middle elevations to the subalpine, it was collected by the authors at Muddy Meadows. Suksdorf collected it at Hellroaring Canyon, and Howell also made a collection at the "base" of the mountain.

## *Cinna* L.—WOODREED

### *Cinna latifolia* (Trev. *ex* Goepp.) Griseb.—SLENDER WOODREED

Growing from a thin spreading rootstock, this tall, slender grass, which at a distance resembles a *Calamagrostis*, may reach 120 cm in height. The flat, lax leaf blades droop from the stem. The panicle is open, about 30 cm high, with spreading to drooping branches. The spikelet is 1-flowered and the lemmas may have a rudimentary awn at the tip.

Rare at Mount Adams, this is an open woods or wetland plant, typically found at middle elevation sites. Suksdorf collected it at the Lewis River on the northwest side and at Hellroaring Canyon and Rusk Creek on the southeast.

## *Cynosurus* L.—DOGTAIL

### *Cynosurus cristatus* L.—CRESTED DOGTAIL

This tufted perennial reaches 60 cm in height and is distinguished by the dense, spikelike panicles that curve toward the top. The fertile spikelets are paired with sterile ones; the latter have flattened glumes that are toothed at the top, and the lemmas are empty. "Crested" refers to the distinctive appearance of the spikelets. The leaves are narrow, up to 2.5 mm wide, mostly at the base of the plant.

Found along roadsides and other open areas, this southern European native grows on the south aspects of the mountain. It was found by the authors at the junction of Road 8040 and 781, and also grows along the road up Snipes Mountain.

### *Dactylis* L.—ORCHARD GRASS

#### *Dactylis glomerata* L.—ORCHARD GRASS

This weedy perennial is a vigorous, strongly-spreading grass that may reach 150 cm in height. The panicle appears rather disjointed, with the spikelets arranged in 1-sided small clusters—the "glomerules" of the name. These are on short, ascending branches. The backs of the glumes and the edges of the lemmas bear short, stiff hairs. The bristly appearance of the spikelet is enhanced by the short awns of the lemmas.

A weed of open sites that extends its range to the subalpine, plants have been found by the authors at 6,100 feet at Foggy Flat on the north side of the mountain and at Bathtub Meadow on the northwest.

### *Danthonia* Lam. & DC.—OATGRASS

#### *Danthonia intermedia* Vasey—TIMBER OATGRASS

This tufted perennial reaches 60 cm in height and is characterized by slender stems and narrow, purplish, spikelike panicles. The inflorescence has only about 6-10 spikelets. These, however, are relatively large, making the individual parts of the floret easy to study. The glumes are about 15 mm long and the lemmas 10 mm. The 10 mm awns are both bent and twisted.

Common in moist meadows at middle to lower subalpine elevations, reaching 6,600 feet, this species grows at Spring Creek Meadow and just south of Road 56 on the north side of the mountain. It is also found alongside the Riley Creek trail on the west and at Grand Meadow on the southwest, as well as at Hellroaring Canyon and Muddy River Canyon.

### *Deschampsia* P. Beauv.—HAIRGRASS

The three hairgrass species present at Mount Adams are quite dissimilar in appearance at first glance. Two are perennials that are taller than the single annual, and all have narrow, folded or inrolled, mostly basal leaves. There are 2 florets per spikelet and the rachilla is both hairy and prolonged beyond the upper floret. The glumes and lemmas are shiny, adding a unique appearance to the spikelet. The lemma is toothed at the tip and an awn, which may be bent, is present.

*Vahlodea atropurpurea*, with flat leaf blades, was formerly included in *Deschampsia*.

1 Plants annual; stems 15-40 cm tall ........................ *D. danthonioides*
1 Plants perennial; stems 30-90 cm tall ............................................. 2

2(1) Inflorescence contracted and spikelike; lower leaf blades about 1 mm wide ........................................................................ *D. elongata*

2 Inflorescence open, the branches spreading; lower leaves 1.5-3 mm wide ........................................................................ *D. cespitosa*

### *Deschampsia cespitosa* (L.) Beauv.—TUFTED HAIRGRASS

This hairgrass may reach 120 cm in favored locations, although it is often much reduced in stature at high elevations. The leaf blades are up to 3 mm wide, folded along the midvein, and rather stiff. The loosely-configured panicle may reach 30 cm in height, and the branches are horizontally whorled.

Fairly common at the mountain, this species is found primarily in middle elevation wet meadows. It grows at the north end of Swampy Meadows and Grand Meadow (including the roadside there). Suksdorf collected this hairgrass at Hellroaring Canyon, where it reaches 6,560 feet, and near Bird Creek.

### *Deschampsia danthonioides* (Trin.) Munro—ANNUAL HAIRGRASS

This annual grass bears 2 or 3 flowering stems to about 50 cm tall. The inrolled leaf blades are few and 1-2 mm wide. The spikelets are also few in number, set at the ends of ascending branches. The awn is bent and about twice the length of the lemma.

A species of dry sites east of the mountain, it grows at the DNR quarry and was collected at Klickitat Meadows by Flett.

### *Deschampsia elongata* (Hook.) Munro—SLENDER HAIRGRASS

Resembling *Deschampsia cespitosa* in its dense tuft of basal leaves, the spikelets of this hairgrass distinguish it from that species: they are borne on very short, erect stalks; thus the panicle has a spikelike appearance, more dense than that of *D. danthonioides*. The lemmas are 2.5 mm long, with a straight awn.

Found in middle elevation wet sites, this species is relatively rare at the mountain. It grows at the confluence of Cascade Creek and Salt Creek on the southwest side, and was collected by Suksdorf at Hellroaring Canyon.

### *Elymus* L.—WILD-RYE

These are not the true ryegrasses (genus *Lolium*) of agriculture or horticulture, which have markedly flattened spikelets set so that an edge of the spikelet faces the axis of the stem. In *Elymus*, the spikelets are somewhat more cylindrical, with a flattened side that faces the stem axis. The plants vary from short to tall due to environmental influences. The leaf blade is flat and auricles are present. The inflorescence is spikelike, with closely-crowded, 2-flowered spikelets (3-flowered in one variety of *E. elymoides*). The glumes may be awned and the lemmas are awned as well.

At Mount Adams, *Elymus* are native species of middle elevations to subalpine meadows, although they also colonize disturbed areas. In these grasses, the spikelets disarticulate at a point just below the glumes; in the squirrel-tail grasses this allows the spikelet to be blown about by the wind, scattering the seeds.

The genus *Sitanion*, squirrel-tail grass, is now included with *Elymus*. Hybridization among *Elymus* species adds to the challenges posed by this group of grasses. *Hordeum*, foxtail grass, is superficially similar, but more distantly related.

1 Glumes pointed to short-awned; lemmas not awned or, more often, short-awned, the awn rarely more than 20 mm long .................................................................................. *E. glaucus* ssp. *glaucus*
1 Glumes awnlike, more than 30 mm long, sometimes divided; lemmas very long, 20-90 mm, and widely divergent ...................... 2

2(1) Inflorescence 8-18 cm long; glumes not divided; awns of the lemmas erect ........................................................... *E. x hansenii*
2 Inflorescence 2-8 cm long; glumes divided, with 2 awns; awns of the lemmas spreading ..................................................................... 3

3(2) Spikelets 2 per node .......................... *E. elymoides* ssp. *elymoides*
3 Spikelets 3 per node .......................... *E. elymoides* ssp. *hordeoides*

### ***Elymus elymoides*** **(Raf.) Swezey ssp.** ***elymoides*** **SQUIRREL-TAIL GRASS**

The reddish-tawny, bushy "squirrel-tail" panicle of this species is due to the long, sharply spreading awns of the glumes and lemmas; these may reach 4-7 cm in length. The plants range from 30-60 cm in height. There are 2 spikelets per node, at least in the lower half of the spike in this subspecies, and the spikes themselves range from 2-8 cm in length.

Fairly common in open Pacific silver fir woods and at meadow edges, this is a middle elevation to alpine species, reaching 7,500 feet and found primarily on the south and southeast sides of the mountain. Sarah Gage and Sharon Rodman collected it at High Camp on the north.

### ***Elymus elymoides*** **(Raf.) Swezey ssp.** ***hordeoides*** **(Suksdorf) Barkworth—SQUIRREL-TAIL GRASS**

This subspecies typically bears 3 spikelets per node, with the lateral ones reduced, or sometimes represented solely by 3 or more glumes. The plants are shorter, reaching only 20 cm in height.

A plant of dry habitats, this subspecies is often found in ponderosa pine forests and reportedly growing east and south of the Cascades. However, at Mount Adams it was found by the authors alongside Road 115 on the north side.

### *Elymus glaucus* Buckl. ssp. *glaucus*—BLUE WILD-RYE

The common name is in reference to the glaucous, blue-green leaf blades. This grass may reach 100 cm in height. The 10 mm wide leaf blades are flat, and the awns of the lemmas are about 25 mm in length, giving the inflorescence a much different appearance than that of *E. elymoides*.

Found on dry ground near roads and trails, as well as in open woods, this species grows alongside Forest Service Road 115 on the north side of the mountain. Suksdorf collected it at "Clover Vale," which is a small valley near Bird Creek Meadows.

### *Elymus* x *hansenii* Scribn.—HYBRID WILD-RYE

This grass is said to be a sterile hybrid of *Elymus elymoides* ssp. *californicus* (formerly *Sitanion hystrix* var. *californicum*) and *E. glaucus*. Like the latter, it is a tall plant, reaching about 80 cm. The panicle is also tall, up to 18 cm, and purplish in hue. The awns are very long, reaching 8 cm and oriented upwards.

This hybrid, not uncommon in western North America, is known from Mount Adams from a collection made by Suksdorf on a "steep north slope" in the valley of Hellroaring Creek.

## *Festuca* L.—FESCUE

These are perennial bunchgrass species, with mostly smooth stems and leaf blades. All species at the mountain are natives. The leaf blades are flat or inrolled and the panicle varies from loose and open to fairly compact. The glumes are shorter than the lowest floret and of unequal size. The lemmas of most species are awned (sometimes the awn is absent in *F. viridula*).

Annual species of fescue are now in their own genus, *Vulpia*.

1 Blades lax and flat; and panicle branches dropping ....... *F. subulata*
1 Blades stiff and folded or inrolled, or panicle branches stiff and erect ........ 2

2(1) Blades rolled inward; lemmas without awns ............... *F. campestris*
2 Blades flat; lemmas awned ........ 3

3(2) Panicle open, more than 15 cm long; some awns longer than lemmas ........ *F. occidentalis*
3 Panicle narrow to congested, less than 15 cm long; awns shorter than or as long as lemmas ........ 4

4(3) Panicle congested, less than 10 cm. long; blades threadlike ......... 5
4 Panicle open or over 10 cm long; blades over 10 cm long or not threadlike ........ 7

5(4) Flowering stems 5-20 cm tall ...... *F. brachyphylla* ssp. *brachyphylla*
5 Flowering stems greater than 20 cm tall ........ 6

6(5) Spikelets colored green or reddish; leaf sheath fused to ¼ its length ........ *F. saximontana* var. *saximontana*
6 Spikelets green mottled with purple; leaf sheath fused to 1/3 to ½ its length ........ *F. saximontana* var. *purpusiana*

7(4) Blades flat, 1.5-2.5 mm broad; lemmas awnless or with small awn 0.3 mm long ........ *F. viridula*
7 Blades folded or rolled, less than 1.5 mm broad; awn greater than 1 mm long ........ 8

8(7) Plants tufted, without rhizomes; sheaths firm and greenish, not shredding into fibers ........ *F. idahoensis*
8 Plants curved and rising from ground level; sheaths reddish to brown, thin, shredding into thin fibers ........ *F. rubra*

### ***Festuca brachyphylla*** **Schult. & Schult. f. ssp.** ***brachyphylla*** **ALPINE FESCUE**

Less than 20 cm tall, this grass grows in dense tufts among rocks at high elevations. The needlelike leaf blades are tightly folded and up to 5 cm long, with ligules to 0.5 mm long. The 4 mm long spikelets, of 5 to 7 flowers each, are arranged in a more or less contracted, spikelike panicle.

This species is also known as sheep fescue, from an earlier name *Festuca ovina*; it is common on open slopes, typically above timberline. It was collected by Suksdorf at Mazama Glacier and Hellroaring Canyon; Henderson collected it at Muddy River Canyon.

### ***Festuca campestris*** **Rydb.—ROUGH FESCUE**

A densely-tufted perennial with thick mats of persistent stems, this species ranges from 60-100 cm in height. The ligules are less than 0.5 mm long and are hairy on the margins. The stems are inrolled near the base and flattened above; they are 2.5-4 mm broad and erect. The panicle is 10-15 cm long, and the spikelets typically number 5. The lemmas are sometimes minutely awn-tipped and 7-8 mm long.

Found in dry habitats, particularly in grasslands or on open slopes, this species was collected by Suksdorf at "Springs". This location was on the west side of Mount Adams, to judge by the collection date, although this would be considered west of the typical range. It was also found on the Ridge of Wonders on the southeast side. In Hitchcock, the synonym is *Festuca scabrella*.

### *Festuca idahoensis* Elmer—IDAHO FESCUE

Heavily tufted, and typically glabrous or slightly roughened, the stems of this species are 40-100 cm tall. The leaves are mostly basal, rolled to the outside or folded, and up to 10 cm long. The narrow panicle has ascending to erect branches 7-15 cm long, and the spikelets are 5- to 7-flowered. The lemmas are rounded, 4.5-7.5 mm long, and there is a stout awn 2-5 mm long.

Most common in grasslands and sagebrush, but ranging upwards in elevation along mountain slopes, this species grows along the south and southeast sides of the mountain. It was found by the authors at the Island Springs Creek crossing on the Hellroaring Creek trail, and alongside Trail 71. Suksdorf collected it at Hellroaring Canyon, and Flett collected it near the Klickitat River. It is also found in openings on Crofton Ridge.

### *Festuca occidentalis* Hook.—WESTERN FESCUE

The stems may reach nearly 100 cm in this vigorous, loosely clumped plant. The 10-25 cm long leaf blades are inrolled. The lower branches of the open, loosely structured panicle usually droop. The spikelet is 7-8 mm long and may be purplish. The awns of the lemmas are 5-6 mm in length.

A middle elevation species of open forests and open slopes, it was collected by Suksdorf at Rusk Creek on the east side of the mountain and by the authors on the west side of King Mountain.

### *Festuca rubra* L. ssp. *rubra*—RED FESCUE

Reaching 100 cm in height, although typically much less at higher elevations, this is a loosely tufted grass. The stems are reddish at the base and the sheaths of the basal leaf blades tend to shred with maturity. The leaf blades are smooth, inrolled, and lack auricles. The spikelets typically are reddish-purple and the awns of the lemmas are only about 3 mm long.

Finding a variety of habitats suitable, this species grows in middle elevation wet and dry sites at the mountain. It was found by the authors at the Road 23 overlook, and at upper Swampy Meadows.

### *Festuca saximontana* Rydb. var. *purpusiana* (St.-Yves) Frederiksen & Pavlick—ROCKY MOUNTAIN FESCUE

This subspecies is very similar to *F. saximontana* ssp. *saximontana* and is most readily distinguished by the color of the spikelets: they are green mottled with purple in *purpusiana*.

Rare at the mountain, Suksdorf and Flett both collected this subspecies on Little Mount Adams at about 6,800 feet, in the crater area.

### *Festuca saximontana* Rydb. var. *saximontana* ROCKY MOUNTAIN FESCUE

This perennial is distinguished by dense tufts of basal leaves. It is a small plant, from 20-35 cm in height; sometimes less on harsh sites. The ligules are barely 0.4 mm long, with minute hairs on the margins. The leaves are primarily basal and are folded to inrolled, very narrow, and less than 10 cm long; they are smooth to roughened. The panicle is strongly compressed, 3-7 cm long and the spikelets are 3- to 4- flowered. The lemmas are 3-5.5 mm long, with an awn 1-3 mm in length; occasionally the awn is absent.

Rare at the mountain, Suksdorf located it on the northeast side near an unspecified glacier. Elsewhere, it is a species of rocky alpine slopes. This species is named *F. ovina* in Hitchcock.

### *Festuca subulata* Trin.—BEARDED FESCUE

This grass is distinguished by the stems, which are leafy for most of their length, up to the panicle. The stems range from 50-120 cm tall. The leaf blades are flat, the lower ones about 1 cm wide; there are no auricles. The panicles are open, while the branches, borne in 2s or 3s along the axis, tend to droop. The awn of the lemma is quite variable, ranging from 5-20 mm in length.

Found in middle elevation open forests, this species was collected by Suksdorf near the Lewis River, probably close to the present Road 23 bridge.

### *Festuca viridula* Vasey GREEN FESCUE, MOUNTAIN BUNCHGRASS

This species is typically 60 cm tall, although it may reach 100 cm on favorable sites and form broad clumps. It has flat to slightly inrolled leaf blades. The panicle is somewhat open, while the branches are generally in pairs and typically erect. The lemma is usually not awned, although occasionally it has a very short awnlike tip.

Emerald-green, this lovely grass is locally common in middle to subalpine elevation meadows that are not inundated. It was collected by Suksdorf at Hellroaring Canyon and Bird Creek Meadows and by

Cotton along Hellroaring Creek. The authors found it along the South Climb trail.

### *Glyceria* R. Br.—MANNAGRASS

Species of wet places, these perennial grasses spread by rootstocks. They may sometimes be found in standing water, as well as in moist meadows, alongside streams, and the margins of ponds. The leaves are bright green, folded, and have prominent ligules; the sheaths are closed. The panicles of the species at Mount Adams are open, with spreading branches. The spikelets are flattened, less than 1 cm long, and less than 3 times as long as broad; unawned, they resemble the spikelets of *Poa*.

These are middle elevation to subalpine species at the mountain; *G. striata* is typically at higher elevations than *G. elata*.

1 Plants 3-8 dm tall; ligules closed in front, the lower ones 1.5-3 mm. long; glumes ovate, rounded at the tip ................................ *G. striata*
1 Plants 10-15 dm tall; ligules open in front, the lower ones 3-6 mm long; glumes lanceolate-ovate, pointed at the tip ................ *G. elata*

#### *Glyceria elata* (Nash *ex* Rydb.) M.E. Jones—TALL MANNAGRASS

Distinguished by its height of 10-15 dm, greater than any other of the mannagrasses, the panicle of this species is widely spreading; the branches may droop, creating quite a graceful plant. The spikelets are small and ovate, and the lemmas are 2 mm long. The species spreads by heavy rootstocks and may form patches.

A middle elevation species of stream and river banks, this species is uncommon at Mount Adams. It was found by the authors at Horseshoe Lake and collected at Swampy Meadow Creek on the southwest side and in a small meadow off Trail 73 at Crofton Creek.

#### *Glyceria striata* (Lam.) A.S. Hitchc.—FOWL MANNAGRASS

Shorter than *G. elata*, this species ranges from 30-80 cm in height. The plants are strongly tufted. The blades are only 2-5 mm broad, and the ligules are usually closed at the front of the throat (an unusual feature even in grasses with closed sheaths). The panicle is more narrowly pyramidal.

A wet meadow to boggy habitat species, this plant ranges from middle to subalpine elevations. It is more common than *G. elata* at the mountain. Suksdorf collected it at Bird Creek Island, Rush Creek, and Hellroaring Canyon, reaching at least 5,800 feet. It also grows on the west side at lower elevations, as at the outlet stream of Swampy Meadows.

### *Hesperostipa* (Elias) Barkworth—NEEDLEGRASS

#### *Hesperostipa comata* (Trin. & Rupr.) Barkworth ssp. *comata* NEEDLE-AND-THREAD

This tufted perennial may reach up to 70 cm in height, with foliage that may be smooth or short-hairy. The ligules are 3-5 mm long and finely short-hairy. The leaf blades are 1-2 mm broad and inrolled, while the contracted but loose panicle ranges from 7-20 cm in length. The lemma (the "needle" of the common name) is 8-12 mm long and sparsely hairy while the awn (the "thread") may reach 15 cm in length and is twisted and bent 2 or 3 times, the terminal segment being more than 5.5. cm long.

Formerly named *Stipa comata* var. *comata,* this species was collected by Cotton on Snipes Mountain, probably at its upper elevational limit at Mount Adams.

### *Holcus* L.—VELVET GRASS

#### *Holcus lanatus* L.—VELVET GRASS

The stems of this introduced perennial grass may reach 100 cm in height, but are often shorter on poor soil. The leaf blades are 3-10 mm broad, flat, both basal and well-distributed along the stem. The panicle is congested, with short, erect branches. The glumes are 3-4 mm long, about twice the length of the lemmas. There are 2 florets per spikelet and the lemma of the upper floret awn is distinctively hooked, about the length of the glume. The entire plant is densely covered with short, soft hairs, hence "velvet" grass.

The only representative of its genus at Mount Adams, this weedy grass is known from Keene's Horse Camp, at 4,350 feet, growing on packed ground in the parking area. It seems surprising that it is not more frequently seen.

### *Hordeum* L.—BARLEY

Tall native grasses with a rather weedy appearance and the ability to colonize disturbed habitats, both *Hordeum* species at Mount Adams bear spikes that are dense and cylindrical. There are 3 spikelets per node on the axis; these consist of 2 sterile spikelets placed immediately below a central fertile one. Each lemma, as well as the glumes, bears an awn, imparting a brushy appearance to the plants, especially in the case of *H. jubatum.*

1 Awns of the lemmas 20-60 mm long, widely divergent .................... ................................................................ *H. jubatum* ssp. *jubatum*
1 Awns of the lemmas 4-6 mm long, erect ........................................ ........................................ *H. brachyantherum* ssp. *brachyantherum*

### *Hordeum brachyantherum* Nevski ssp. *brachyantherum* MEADOW BARLEY

This slender, tufted barley ranges from 30-90 cm tall. The leaves are 2-5 mm broad; auricles are absent and the ligule is very short. The spike is 5-10 cm long and narrow, with a brownish color overall. The awns are only 1 cm in length, giving a compact appearance to the plants.

A species of moist middle elevation meadows, and rare at Mount Adams, plants were found by the authors alongside Road 115 at 4,450 feet in upper Midway Meadows, a location that becomes quite dry late in the summer.

### *Hordeum jubatum* L. ssp. *jubatum*—FOXTAIL BARLEY

The stems of this perennial may reach 50 cm in height, and the leaves appear gray-green, from short, soft hairs. Sometimes flowering in its first year, the spikes are brushy-looking, owing to the long, spreading awns of the glumes and lemmas; these are 20-60 mm in length. The spike is typically reddish-purple in color, although occasionally pale green.

Uncommon, this is a species of open woods and disturbed areas, including roadsides. It is found at the DNR quarry on the southeast side of the mountain and on the north alongside Road 115 through upper Midway Meadows.

## *Melica* L.—MELIC GRASS, ONIONGRASS

The stems of two of the melicas at Mount Adams have enlarged, onionlike bases. These are perennial grasses, with closed leaf sheaths, membranous ligules, and no auricles. The upper florets are sterile, consisting of lemmas only, the lowermost enfolding the uppermost. The lemmas may be awned or not. There are 3 stamens.

1 Lemmas awned; stem not bulbous .................................. *M. aristata*
1 Lemmas unawned; stem bulbous .................................................... 2

2(1) Lemmas narrow and sharply tipped; panicle open, lower branches spreading ................................................ *M. subulata* var. *subulata*
2 Lemmas not sharply tipped; panicle narrow, erect, with short branches ..................................................................... *M. spectabilis*

### *Melica aristata* Thurb. *ex* Boland.—BEARDED MELIC

The stems of this tufted perennial are erect and roughened. The sheaths are short-hairy to roughened and closed to near the top. The ligules are 3-5 mm long and are finely hairy; the blades 2.5-5 mm broad and very rough. The panicle is 10-20 cm in length and narrow, with paired, erect branches and spikelets to near the base. The spikelets are about 15 mm long and 3- to 5- flowered; they are purplish in color. The awns are 8 mm long, with short teeth.

Found in dry forests and, according to Hitchcock, ranging from the southwest Cascades of Washington to California, this species was collected alongside the Lewis River by Suksdorf, apparently the only collection of this melic made in Washington.

### *Melica spectabilis* Scribn.—PURPLE ONIONGRASS

The stems of this perennial range from 30-80 cm in height; they are widely spaced on a spreading rootstock. The sheaths are roughened and opened only a short distance at the top. The ligules are collar-like, 2-4 mm broad, and are stiffly-hairy to smooth. The narrow panicle is 7-15 cm long, with slender, erect branches. The purplish spikelets are 9-15 mm long and somewhat compressed. The glumes are short, the second as much as 7 mm long; the lemmas are about the same length.

Found in habitats ranging from wet to dry meadows and open forests up to the subalpine region, this species is rare at the mountain. Flett collected it along the upper Klickitat River.

### *Melica subulata* (Griseb.) Scribn. var. *subulata*<br>ALASKA ONIONGRASS

The stem bases in this species are broadly expanded and thickened. The tufted stems range from 60-120 cm tall. Additional onionlike bulbs are borne on short, thick rootstocks, allowing the plant to reproduce vegetatively from the bulbs. The narrow leaf blades are 5 mm broad, flat and shiny. The narrow panicle is erect, and the glumes are papery and translucent. The lemmas are 9-12 mm long and not awned.

A species of stream banks, meadows and open slopes, this is the only common species of *Melica* at Mount Adams, growing on the southeast side of the mountain. Suksdorf collected it at Hellroaring Canyon. Plants have also been located alongside Road 071 at approximately 4,100 feet, near Bunnell Butte.

## *Muhlenbergia* Schreb.—MUHLY GRASS

### *Muhlenbergia filiformis* (Thurb. *ex* S. Wats.) Rydb. PULL-UP MUHLY

This small, annual grass is tufted and up to 10 cm tall; the stems are often decumbent, lying along the ground at their bases. The leaves are quite narrow, to 2.5 mm wide; with ligules 1-3 mm long. The leafy stems bear a very narrow panicle. The spikelets are 1-flowered, and the lemma, about 2 mm long, bears an awn-like tip that is less than 1 mm long.

Uncommon at the mountain, this is a species of moist meadows and stream banks from middle to subalpine elevations. It was collected by Suksdorf at Hellroaring Canyon. It was also found by Gage and Rodman at Muddy Meadows and by the authors near the DNR quarry and alongside Trail 73 near Crofton Creek.

## *Phalaris* L.—CANARY-GRASS

### *Phalaris arundinacea* L.—REED CANARY-GRASS

A highly invasive perennial, and weedy in wet meadows, the plants spread by rootstocks and the stems may reach 150 cm in height. The flat leaf blades are 1-2 cm wide and the sheaths are open. The inflorescence is a tall, open panicle; the branches tend to become erect as the seed matures. An unusual feature is that the spikelets often fall as a unit, leaving behind the glumes. Each spikelet typically has 3 florets, the lower one merely an empty lemma. The lemma of the fertile florets is 3-4.5 mm long.

Uncommon, this noxious species has been found at the Horseshoe Lake campground on the northwest side of the mountain, and also occurs scattered alongside the side of Road 23 close to the Lewis River bridge.

## *Phleum* L.—TIMOTHY

One weed and one native species are separated by the shape of the inflorescence and the height of the plants. Both have 1-flowered spikelets in which both the glumes and lemmas are short-awned, giving the compact spike a bristly appearance. The leaf blades are flat and the sheaths open; both species often have small auricles. The weedy timothy, *P. pretense*, grows only at lower elevations.

1 Inflorescence 5-10 cm long ...................... *P. pretense* ssp. *pratense*
1 Inflorescence 2-3 cm long .......................... *P. alpinum* ssp. *alpinum*

## Poaceae

### *Phleum alpinum* L. ssp. *alpinum*—ALPINE TIMOTHY

Borne on a 20-60 cm tall stem, the inflorescence of this species is densely congested, elliptical to egg-shaped in outline, and more than 1 cm thick. The awn of the lemma is 2-3 mm long.

Common in middle elevation to subalpine meadows and rocky slopes, this species grows at Muddy Meadows, alongside Road 115, and near the trail above Hellroaring Overlook at 6,500 feet of elevation. Suksdorf collected it on lava beds on the south side of the mountain (a location he named "Trummerthal" - possibly the Aiken Lava Beds) and at Hellroaring Canyon.

### *Phleum pratense* L. ssp. *pratense*—COMMON TIMOTHY

A weed, this robust timothy reaches 100 cm in height. It bears a long (10 cm or more), cylindrical, and tightly congested inflorescence less than 1 cm thick. The base of the stem is often somewhat enlarged and bulblike.

Uncommon at Mount Adams, this species is found alongside roadsides. It grows south of the overlook near Road 23. Suksdorf also collected it at Hellroaring Canyon.

### *Pleuropogon* R. Br.—SEMAPHORE-GRASS

### *Pleuropogon refractus* (A. Gray) Benth. *ex* Vasey NODDING SEMAPHORE-GRASS

This distinctive grass bears narrow spikelets, widely-spaced in a 1-sided raceme. There are 7 to 11 florets per spikelet and perhaps 5 to 9 spikelets per stem. The stems are 100-150 cm tall and loosely tufted, with flat leaf blades from 5-7 mm wide; the sheaths are closed up to half their length. The awn of the lemma is 5-10 mm long.

A middle elevation to subalpine species of moist areas in open forests, this semaphore-grass is cosmopolitan at the mountain. Henderson located it on the west side, and Suksdorf collected it on the northwest and at Bird Creek Island and Muddy River Canyon on the east. The authors also collected this species alongside Road 115 on the north side.

### *Poa* L.—BLUEGRASS

Three weeds and nine native species make this the largest genus of grasses at Mount Adams. Suksdorf collected two of the weedy species, *P. pratensis* and *P. annua* over a hundred years ago in the Hellroaring Canyon and Bird Creek areas. Modern collections of weedy *Poa* species are from campground areas and near lakes, roadsides, and trailheads. These grasses range from middle to alpine elevations, including one, *P.*

*lettermanii* at the "Lunchcounter" on the South Climb route. Bluegrasses are both cosmopolitan and well-adapted to a range of conditions.

The plants bear characteristic leaves: at their tips, the edges curve together in a way that resembles the prow of a canoe. The sheaths are partly open and auricles are absent; the ligules are membranous and vary in size. Four to 7 florets per spikelet are typical. Most species have lemmas with a purplish band across the back near the tip. Cobwebby hairs at the base of the lemmas distinguish some of the species; hairs along the margins and veins of the lemmas may be diagnostic as well. The panicle is highly variable in size and configuration.

1 Plants annual ........................................ *P. annua*
1 Plants perennial ........................................ 2

2(1) Most of the florets replaced by plantlets; base of the stems bulbous ........................................ *P. bulbosa* ssp. *vivipara*
2 Florets all normal; stems not bulbous ........................................ 3

3(2) Lemmas cobwebby at base ........................................ 4
3 Lemmas not cobwebby at base ........................................ 6

4(3) Plants with spreading rootstocks ........... *P. pratensis* ssp. *pratensis*
4 Plants tufted, not spreading ........................................ 5

5(4) Lower branches of panicle reflexed, 1-3 per node ........... *P. reflexa*
5 Lower branches of panicle not reflexed, in pairs ...... *P. paucispicula*

6(3) Spikelets slightly compressed, over twice as long as broad .......... 7
6 Spikelets compressed, usually less than twice as long as broad ... 8

7(6) Lemmas hairless; ligules less than 2 mm long ........................................ *P. secunda* ssp. *juncifolia*
7 Lemmas short-hairy; ligules more than 2 mm long ........................................ *P. secunda* ssp. *secunda*

8(7) Lemmas short-hairy on keel and nerves .......... *P. alpina* ssp. *alpina*
8 Lemmas smooth above base, or with very short hairs .................. 9

9(8) Plants less than 1 dm tall ........................................ *P. lettermanii*
9 Plants more than 1 dm tall ........................................ 10

10(9) Panicles open; sheaths of stem leaves softly hairy and reddish-purple ........................................ *P. wheeleri*
10 Panicles congested; sheaths of stem leaves rarely softly hairy or reddish-purple ........................................ 11

11(10) Panicle narrow, less than 1 cm thick, purplish, shorter than basal leaves at flowering time ............................................ *P. suksdorfii*
11 Panicle broader, more than 1 cm thick, tawny or greenish, longer than basal leaves at flowering time ............................................ 12

12(11) Lemmas hairless above base; stem leaves folded, less than 2.5 mm broad ............................................ *P. cusickii* ssp. *epilis*
12 Lemmas long-hairy on keel; stem leaves flat, 2-3.5 mm broad ............................................ *P. cusickii* ssp. *purpurascens*

### *Poa alpina* L. ssp. *alpina*—ALPINE BLUEGRASS

Densely tufted with mats of basal leaves, this 10-30 cm tall smooth perennial has nearly open sheaths, and 1.5-3 mm long ligules that encircle the stem. The 2-4 mm broad blades are flat; there is typically just 1 short leaf at the midpoint of the stem. The 2-6 cm long panicle is compact and pyramidal in shape, with spreading branches. The purplish spikelets are 3- to 6-flowered, 4-6 mm long and flattened in outline. The 3.5-4 mm long lemmas are not cobwebby at the base but do have soft, long hairs on the keel and veins.

A species of subalpine to alpine meadows, ridges and talus slopes, it is known from a single Suksdorf collection for which no data other than "Mount Adams" is given. The occurrence of this species at Mount Adams is surprising - other locations in Washington include the North Cascades and Okanogan County.

### *Poa annua* L.—ANNUAL BLUEGRASS

The stems of this annual are only about 10 cm tall and tend to bend over and root at the nodes, creating small mats. The plants appear yellow-green in color, while the spikelets, borne in an open panicle, are pale green, although the lemmas are often banded with light purple. The lemmas, 3-4 mm long, are hairy on the lower veins, but do not have a tangle of hairs at their bases.

Low growing and capable of spreading rapidly, this introduced species was found by the authors at Ollalie Lake and Horseshoe Lake, and was also collected at Hellroaring Canyon by Suksdorf.

### *Poa bulbosa* L. ssp. *vivipara*—BULBOUS BLUEGRASS

This weedy, highly invasive species can reach 30 or 40 cm in height, but is often less. The leaves are flat and up to 2.5 mm wide. Most of the florets of this unusual grass are replaced by small, purplish plantlets that resemble small bulbs. The panicle is cylindrical, and the bulblets are borne on short ascending branches, being rather crowded. The stem bases are also somewhat bulbous, similar to *Melica subulata*, although in that species the florets are normally formed.

A weed, this species grows at Keene's Horse Camp and at the Stagman Ridge trailhead. It is not seen, at least at Mount Adams, off of heavily disturbed soils.

### *Poa cusickii* Vasey ssp. *epilis* (Scribn.) W.A. Weber
### CUSICK'S BLUEGRASS

Smooth to roughened, this strongly tufted perennial is 20-40 cm tall, with sheaths closed less than half their length. The panicle is compact, egg-shaped, and 2-6 cm long, greenish to purple, and with spikelets of 3-5 florets. The ligules are 1-3 mm long, sharply-tipped, and typically hairless. The leaf blades are flat, at least 1-2.5 mm broad and less than 10 cm long. The lemmas are 4.5-6 mm long, smooth to roughened, and not hairy.

Found in sagebrush flats to alpine meadows and ridges, this subspecies grows at High Camp Meadows on the north side. It was also found by Suksdorf on the "northeast side."

### *Poa cusickii* Vasey ssp. *purpurascens* (Vasey) Soreng
### CUSICK'S BLUEGRASS

Differing from ssp. *epilis* in several details, the lemmas of this subspecies are 5.5-7 mm long and are long and softly hairy on the keel, with a slight basal mat of hairs. The stem blades are flat and 2-3.5 mm broad.

Found in subalpine to alpine habitats, this subspecies was collected by both Suksdorf and Morton Peck, the latter collection from the "south slope."

### *Poa lettermanii* Vasey—LETTERMAN'S BLUEGRASS

Dwarfed and delicate in appearance, this species is densely tufted, and may reach as much as 10 cm in height, although often it is much shorter. The leaf blades are up to 1.5 mm wide, and the narrow panicle is up to 3 cm tall. The lemmas are 2.5-3 mm long and hairless.

Found on high ridges and ledges, this species was collected in 2005 by Paul Dixon at the "Lunchcounter" on the South Climb route at an elevation of over 9,200 feet. Suksdorf also collected it "near the Mazama Glacier."

### *Poa paucispicula* Scribn. & Merr.—BOG BLUEGRASS

The flattened leaf blades of this 10-30 cm tall grass are only about 2 mm wide. The open panicle is composed of spreading branches. The lemmas are pointed at the tip, and hairy with a sparse web of tangled hairs on the lower half of the veins. High elevation plants are much reduced in size.

Rare at the mountain, and formerly called *P. leptocoma* var. *paucispicula* by Hitchcock, this species is known from a single Suksdorf collection at Hellroaring Canyon, made at 6,500 feet.

**_Poa pratensis_ L. ssp. _pratensis_—KENTUCKY BLUEGRASS**

This lawn and pasture grass forms dense mats from extensive rootstocks. The flowering stems may reach 120 cm in height, although they are often shorter. The leaves are flat and 2-4 mm wide. The panicle is loose, open, and has spreading branches arranged in whorls. The nerves of the 3.5 mm lemma are prominent and long-hairy; the lemma is cobwebby at the base.

Introduced, this species grows alongside Road 23. It was also collected at an "island" in Bird Creek and at Hellroaring Canyon by Suksdorf.

**_Poa reflexa_ Vasey & Scribn. _ex_ Vasey—NODDING BLUEGRASS**

A hairless, tufted perennial, the smooth stems of this species range from 20-50 cm in height. The sheaths are closed for approximately half their length, and the jagged ligules (or sometimes sharply tipped) may reach 2.5 mm in length, although are often much shorter. The leaf blades are flat and 1-4 mm broad. The 5-15 cm long panicle is open, sometimes nodding, with the lower branches numbering 1-3 per node. The spikelets are 3- to 5- flowered, about 5 mm long, and the lemmas are keeled, cobwebby at the base, and about 3 mm long.

Found in subalpine to alpine meadows, stream banks, and slopes, this is a rare species at the mountain. Suksdorf collected a specimen at Hellroaring Canyon.

**_Poa secunda_ J. Presl ssp. _juncifolia_ (Scribn.) Soreng**
**SANDBERG'S BLUEGRASS**

Favoring moister habitats than the subspecies *secunda*, this was collected by Suksdorf in Hellroaring Canyon. It is distinguished by lemmas that are hairless and leaves that tend to stay green through the growing season. The ligules are less than 2 mm long.

**_Poa secunda_ J. Presl ssp. _secunda_—SANDBERG'S BLUEGRASS**

This densely tufted perennial ranges from 15-100 cm in height; the ligule is 0.5-10 mm and occasionally roughened. The 0.5-3 mm wide leaf blade varies from flat to folded or inrolled and tend to wither as the growing season progresses; the ligule more than 2 mm long. The 2-25 cm long inflorescence is densely packed, sometimes 1-sided, with appressed to ascending branches. The spikelet is cylindrical. The 3.5-5 mm lemma is only weakly keeled or sometimes rounded and sparsely to densely short-hairy.

This is a variable species, to which many names have been applied. The *Flora of North America* recognizes just these two subspecies. One of these other names, *Poa nevadensis*, has been applied to plants with both long ligules and hairless lemmas; such plants are occasionally seen at Mount Adams and may represent hybrids between subspecies *juncifolia* and *secunda*.

Common in middle elevation dry and open habitats, this species also is occasionally found above timberline. This versatility is reflected in a presence at High Camp at 7,050 feet, as well as at the DNR quarry on stony ground at 4,125 feet. It is found on the lower slope on the north side of Little Mount Adams as well as at the Road 23 overlook. It also grows at Spring Creek and was collected by Suksdorf "near a glacier."

#### ***Poa suksdorfii*** **(Beal) Vasey *ex* Piper—WESTERN BLUEGRASS**

This tufted bluegrass is 20 cm in height at the most, and has narrow, inrolled leaf blades to 5 cm long. The narrow panicle is about 5 cm high, and is characterized by branches held close to the axis and an overall purplish color. The lemmas, 4.5 mm long, are most often smoothed although occasionally roughened by minute, stiff hairs.

An alpine species of rocky or sandy slopes, this species was collected "near the glacier" above Hellroaring Canyon by Suksdorf. He also collected it on the northeast side of the mountain and at Muddy River Canyon.

#### ***Poa wheeleri*** **Vasey—HOOKER'S BLUEGRASS**

This 30-60 cm tall native perennial spreads by rootstocks. The 10 cm high panicle is loose, and composed of relatively few spikelets. The florets are large and almost entirely female, as florets with rudimentary anthers are rare. There are prominent veins on the lemma and short hairs across the back but no web of hairs at the base; the lemma is about 5 mm long.

A middle elevation species that also makes it to the subalpine region on the southeast side of the mountain, plants have been found in the summit crater of Little Mount Adams at 6,800 feet, at Horseshoe Meadow, and at Bathtub Meadow. Suksdorf also collected it at an unspecified location "on damp ground."

### ***Podagrostis*** **(Griseb.) Scribn. & Merr.—BENTGRASS**

#### ***Podagrostis humilis*** **(Vasey) Bjőrkman—ALPINE BENTGRASS**

As presently treated in the *Flora of North America*, this is a species that is variable in appearance, depending upon the elevation at which it grows. At the highest limits of plant growth at Mount Adams, it grows just 10 cm in height, with tightly folded leaf blades just 1 mm wide and 3 cm long; here, it has a slender, constricted panicle. At lower elevations, the plant is both taller, to about 30 cm, with flat leaves about 3 mm wide and 5 cm long.; the panicle is narrow, with ascending branches. The panicle is colored purplish by the glumes of the small spikelets. The lemmas are about 2 mm long and unawned and the paleas about 1.5 mm.

The presence of a palea distinguishes this species from dwarfed, alpine specimens of *Agrostis variabilis*.

Formerly treated as two separate species in the genus *Agrostis*, the two forms of alpine bentgrass are common at Mount Adams. The larger is most common in middle elevation meadows and near ponds and is not seen above 5,000 feet. It was found by the authors at Babyshoe Meadow on the northwest side, in the meadows south of Potato Hill near the Yakama Nation boundary on the north, in the meadow along Hellroaring Creek close to Bench Lake, and near the ponds alongside Trail 75 at Cascade Creek. The more dwarf form, although known from as low as Hellroaring Canyon, is an alpine plant of open talus slopes on the south and southeast sides of the mountain, reaching at least 7,000 feet in places that are moist through midsummer.

### *Pseudoroegneria* (Nevski) Á. Löve—WHEATGRASS

#### *Pseudoroegneria spicata* (Pursh) Á. Löve forma *inermis* (Scribn. & J.G. Sm.) Barkworth—BEARDLESS WHEATGRASS

A tufted perennial from 60-100 cm tall, the slender leaf blades are 1-4 mm wide and flat to loosely rolled; the uppermost blade is typically spreading. The 8-16 cm tall inflorescence is narrow and spikelike; there are 6-8 florets in each spikelet. The 9-14 mm lemmas are almost always awnless.

Found in habitats ranging from sagebrush steppe to open woodlands, this species was collected by Beth Skaggs Ryan at Bunnell Butte on the south side. Suksdorf collected it on the northeast side of the mountain. The authors found it near Pineway Trail on the southeast side.

### *Secale* L.—RYE

#### *Secale cereale* L.—RYE

This genus is characterized by spikelets borne 1 per node in a terminal spike. These are bent above the glumes and are 2-flowered; the awns are long. The plants are annual, those of *S. cereale* ranging from 60-150 cm in height. The leaf blades are 4-10 mm broad. The spikes are 8-15 cm long and the awns 4-7 cm in length. The ligules are finely toothed, membranous, and only 1 mm long.

Introduced, this is a widely cultivated plant. It is known from a single collection made by Beth Skaggs Ryan on the south side of the mountain, alongside Road 712 near Lower Butte at 4,000 feet.

### *Thinopyrum* Á. Löve—WHEATGRASS

#### *Thinopyrum intermedium* (Host) Barkworth & D.R. Dewey ssp. *intermedium*—INTERMEDIATE WHEATGRASS

This perennial, which grows from heavy, spreading rootstocks, has stiff, inrolled 2-5 mm broad leaf blades that are smooth or roughened. The sheaths are long-hairy on the margins, and the tiny ligules are only .5 mm long. The stems may reach 100 cm in height, and the spike is slender, stiff, and 10-20 cm long. The lemmas lack awns and are blunt, with a shallow notch in the tip. Overall, the plant has a pronounced bluish color, from the glaucous leaves and stems.

This is an introduced species, formerly placed in the *Agropyron* genus. It grows alongside Road 170 on the southeast side of the mountain, near King Mountain.

### Torreyochloa Church—FALSE MANNAGRASS

#### *Torreyochloa pallida* (Torr.) Church var. *pauciflora* (J. Presl) J.I. Davis—WEAK MANNAGRASS

Open the full length along the stem, the leaf sheaths distinguish this genus from *Glyceria*. The stems may reach 100 cm in height and the leaf blades are up to 15 mm wide. The panicle is loose, with slender, spreading branches, and purplish, oblong spikelets. The lemma is prominently veined, minutely roughened, and about 2.5 mm long.

Formerly named *Puccinellia pauciflora,* this plant has very much the appearance of a *Glyceria* or *Poa.*

A middle to subalpine elevation meadow species at the mountain, it was collected by Suksdorf at Hellroaring Canyon and upper Bird Creek. Cotton also collected it at Hellroaring River. The authors located it at Horseshoe Lake.

### *Trisetum* Pers.—TRISETUM

Trisetums are tufted perennials, with open sheaths, membranous ligules, and flat to somewhat inrolled blades; auricles are absent. The panicle of these species varies from open and spreading to upright and spikelike. The spikelets are 2-flowered, and the lemmas lack awns in one species and are awned in the other three. There are 3 stamens and the rachilla is hairy.

Trisetum means "three bristles" in reference to the unique nature of the lemmas of many of the species: these have 2 slender teeth at the tip as well as a much longer, often bent awn that arises from the back of the lemma.

There is one uncommon species, and one found only at high elevations; the other two are common and range from middle to subalpine elevations.

| | | |
|---|---|---|
| 1 | Lemmas awnless, or if present, the awn rarely exceeding the lemma ........................................ | *T. wolfii* |
| 1 | Lemmas awned, the awn curved ........................................ | 2 |
| 2(1) | Panicle strongly contracted and spikelike; stems 10-50 cm tall ........................................ | *T. spicatum* |
| 2 | Panicle open to congested but not spikelike; stems 50-100 cm tall ........................................ | 3 |
| 3(2) | Panicle open, the lower branches spreading or drooping ........................................ | *T. cernuum* |
| 3 | Panicle congested, the lower branches erect ............ | *T. canescens* |

### ***Trisetum canescens*** **Buckl.—TALL TRISETUM**

A tufted perennial that ranges from 50-100 cm in height, the sheaths are typically long hairy although sometimes roughened only. The 1.5-4 mm ligules are small toothed and irregularly fringed and are smooth. The flat leaf blades are 4-10 mm broad, roughened to long hairy, with long hairs on the ligule. The 10-20 cm long panicle is narrow, with short, upright branches. The spikelets are typically 3- flowered. The lemmas are 5-7 mm long, with two 2 mm long teeth at the tip as well as a longer, 10-14 mm awn that arises from the back of the lemma and is sharply bent.

Found along streambanks as well as dry sites in lower elevations, and often growing in ponderosa pine forests, but not restricted to the eastern Cascades, this species is relatively common at the mountain. It grows alongside Trail 73 close to Crofton Butte on the southwest side, and at Babyshoe Meadow on the northwest side. Cotton collected it at Soda Springs, and Suksdorf at Hellroaring Canyon, Cowslip Spring, and Lewis River.

### ***Trisetum cernuum*** **Trin.—NODDING TRISETUM**

A tall, perennial grass, this species is very similar to *T. canescens* and both were once considered separate varieties of *T. cernuum*. "Cernuum" refers to the nodding or drooping habit of the long, widely-spreading branches of the inflorescence. Another difference is that the second glume is shorter, up to 4 mm in length, compared to that of *T. canescens* at 4-7 mm.

Occupying similar habitats at Mount Adams, nodding trisetum is much less frequently seen than tall trisetum: it is known from Suksdorf collections made alongside the Lewis River at about 4,000 feet, and from Cowslip Spring on the southeast side.

### *Trisetum spicatum* (L.) Richter—SPIKE TRISETUM

The stems of this densely tufted perennial reach 50 cm in height. The 2-3 mm wide leaf blades are stiff, typically folded, and more or less hairy. The purplish panicle is 10-15 cm long, densely flowered, and spikelike. The lemmas are 4-5 mm long and the awn is strongly bent and about 5 mm long.

Found on open slopes and rocky ridges, often above timberline, it grows at Killen High Camp at 6,800 feet and was also collected by Suksdorf at Hellroaring Canyon.

### *Trisetum wolfii* Vasey—AWNLESS TRISETUM

Loosely tufted and varying from 40-80 cm tall, the sheaths of this perennial are roughened to long and softly hairy. The ligules are 2.5-4 mm long, and are abrupt and irregularly toothed. The leaf blades are flat and 2-4 mm broad; the 8-15 cm long panicle is narrow, with erect or ascending branches. The purplish spikelets are 2- to 3- flowered, and the glumes are longer than the first or second floret. The blunt lemmas are 4.5-5.5 mm long.

Growing in wet meadows east of the Cascades, this species is known from a single Suksdorf collection at Hellroaring Canyon.

## *Vahlodea* Fries—ARCTIC HAIRGRASS

### *Vahlodea atropurpurea* (Wahlenb.) Fries *ex* Hartman MOUNTAIN HAIRGRASS

This species is loosely tufted and may reach 100 cm in height. The open panicle is composed of wide-spreading or sometimes drooping branches. The purplish spikelets are about 5 mm long and the lemmas are about 2.5 mm long, with a bent awn about as long as the lemma.

Although this genus was once grouped with *Deschampsia*, the difference is in the wider, generally flat leaf blades and in the lemmas--these are awned at the middle of the back.

Typically an alpine species of open slopes and rocky ridges, Suksdorf collected it on Lynx Creek in the Muddy River Canyon, and in Hellroaring Canyon. It was collected by the authors along the Riley Creek trail and by Gage and Rodman at High Camp Meadows.

## Poaceae

### *Vulpia* C. C. Gmelin—SIX-WEEKS GRASS

One weed and two varieties of a native species constitute this genus, once included in *Festuca*. The species resemble fescues, with awned lemmas and glumes. The flowers have 1 stamen rather than the 3 of *Festuca*. All three are annuals.

1 Plants hairless (or short-hairy on the undersides of the leaves only); spikelets 3-6 flowered .......................................... *F. bromoides*
1 Plants hairy on the sheathes and leaves; spikelets 1-3 flowered ... 2

2(1) Panicle branches erect; lemmas smooth .................................................................................. *V. microstachys* var. *pauciflora*
2 Panicle branches spreading; lemmas hairy ............................................................................. *V. microstachys* var. *microstachys*

### *Vulpia bromoides* (L.) S.F. Gray—BROME FESCUE

Except for the roughened to short hairy underside of the leaf blades, this is a hairless annual, 10-50 cm tall. The ligules are .2-.6 mm long with tiny teeth. The leaf blades are at most 1.5 mm broad, and are folded and rolled inward toward the upper side. The 3-10 cm long, narrow panicle has short, erect branches and the spikelets are 3- to 6- flowered. The lemmas are 5.5-7.5 mm in length and roughened to glabrous, and the awn is 5.5-13 mm long.

Introduced from Europe and formerly named *Festuca bromoides,* this is a rare weedy species at the mountain with a single collection known from along the trail between Horseshoe and Green Mountain Lakes.

### *Vulpia microstachys* (Nutt.) Munro var. *microstachys* SMALL FESCUE

A tufted annual that reaches about 50 cm in height although it may reach maturity and flower at a much lower height, this native grass resembles a true fescue: inspection of the crown of the plant may be necessary to determine the presence or absence of perennial structures in taller plants. The leaves are slender and inrolled, to about 0.5 mm wide. The panicle branches are spreading and the number of florets per spikelet ranges between 1 and 3. The lemmas are hairy and about 6 mm long.

Behaving as a weed, although a native, this species is found at Keene's Horse Camp on the north side. It was also collected by Suksdorf at an unspecified location.

#### *Vulpia microstachys* (Nutt.) Munro var. *pauciflora* (Scribn. *ex* Beal) Lonard & Gould—SMALL FESCUE

This variety may be distinguished from var. *microstachys* by the upright orientation of the panicle branches and the smooth lemmas. Typically, there are no more than 2 florets per spikelet.

A rare annual, it is known from a single Suksdorf collection, made at an unspecified location at and elevation of "6,000-7,000" feet, probably high up in Hellroaring Canyon based upon the collection date.

## Potamogetonaceae Dumort.—PONDWEED FAMILY

### *Potamogeton* L.—PONDWEED

The extensive wetlands at the mountain provide excellent habitat for these aptly named species. Two are quite rare and none have been found above 4,500 feet. All are submerged plants, with floating leaves, a characteristic not always found in other members of this genus. They are most readily distinguished by the size of the leaves and the degree of similarity between the submerged and floating leaves. *P. natans* bears the largest leaves. The flowers are held above the surface of the water in spikes; quite small and non-descript, they have 4 tepals, 4 pistils, and 4 stamens that are fused to the bases of the tepals. The fruit is an achene.

1 Submersed leaves narrowly linear, less than 2 mm broad and more than 10 cm long; floating leaves rounded to heart-shaped at base ... ........ *P. natans*

1 Submersed leaves not both more than 2 mm broad and less than 10 cm long; floating leaves tapered at base ........ 2

2(1) Plant reddish tinged; floating leaves similar to submersed leaves .... ........ *P. alpinus*

2 Plant greenish; floating leaves different than submersed leaves ... 3

3(2) Submersed leaves linear, limp, 10-20 cm long, with a broad median stripe ........ *P. epihydrus*

3 Submersed leaves less than 10 cm long, without a broad median stripe ........ *P. gramineus*

#### *Potamogeton alpinus* Balbis—ALPINE PONDWEED

The round stems of this species are up to 100 cm long, simple or sparingly branched, and often reddish. The floating leaves are also reddish. The 7-12 cm long submersed leaves are stalkless, thin and linear-lanceolate to linear-oblong in shape. The 4-6 cm-long floating leaves are similar, with a short petiole. The flower stalks are 7-15 cm long, and the whorls of flowers are crowded into a spike only 1.5-3 cm in length. The achenes are 4 mm long, including the curved beak.

Rare at Mount Adams, this species is known from Swampy Meadows, where it was found by the authors in one shallow pool.

### *Potamogeton epihydrus* Raf.—RIBBONLEAF PONDWEED

The somewhat flattened, 50-150 cm long stems of this pondweed are simple or sparingly branched. The submersed leaves are linear, stalkless, and 10-20 cm long; the midvein has several rows of air chambers, giving the appearance from beneath of a stripe running down the leaf. The floating leaves are elliptic to oblong-elliptic, 4-8 cm long, and borne on flattened petioles that are shorter than the blade. The spikes are densely flowered, 2-4 cm long in fruit, and the achenes are 3-4 mm long with a short beak, and sharply keeled on the back.

Typically found in shallow to deep ponds, this is the rarest *Potamogeton* at the mountain. It grows in a single deep pool at Bathtub Meadow on the northwest side of the mountain.

### *Potamogeton gramineus* L.—VARIABLE-LEAF WATERWEED

The nearly round stems of this pondweed are branched and 30-60 cm long. The submersed leaves vary between 3 and 9 cm in length and are linear or lanceolate to oblanceolate, sessile, and narrowed at the base. The floating leaves are 2-5 cm in length with long petioles and narrow to broadly elliptic or oblong-elliptic in shape. The spikes are 1.5-2.5 cm long, with 6-10 whorls of densely packed flowers. The achenes are 2-2.8 mm long, including a short beak.

This species grows in both standing and running water. It is found at Muddy Meadows, Grand Meadow (the east end), and in a small pond near the bridge on Trail 114, east of Muddy Meadows.

### *Potamogeton natans* L.—FLOATING PONDWEED

The slender stems of this pondweed vary widely from 15-150 cm in length. The submerged leaves are linear and persist for only a short time, to be followed by oval, floating leaves 3-10 cm long and reddish in color. The inconspicuous flowers are borne in dense whorls on spikes that rise 2-5 cm above the water surface. The achene is 3-5 mm long.

The most common *Potamogeton* at the mountain, this plant grows in shallow ponds at the east end of Grand Meadow, in Swampy Meadow, at Horseshoe Lake, and in Cascade Creek near Trail 75.

## Scheuchzeriaceae F. Rudolphi—SCHEUCHZERIA FAMILY

### *Scheuchzeria* L.—RANNOCH-RUSH

#### *Scheuchzeria palustris* L.—RANNOCH-RUSH

The 10-30 cm basal leaves of the stems of this 20-40 cm tall rush-like plant tend to wither early; the stem leaves are much smaller. The flowers are borne in 3-to-12-flowered racemes with pedicels up to 25 mm long when fruiting. The greenish-white flowers are 6-parted into oblong segments approximately 3 mm in length. The 5-8 mm-long follicle is light greenish-brown, cone-shaped at the base, with a 0.5-1 mm long beak (remnant of the style).

Named for Johan Jakob Scheuchzer (1672-1733), a Swiss botanist, this is the only species in the family. The plants are found in Swampy Meadows on the southwest side of the mountain, growing close to a shallow pool, in deep, mucky soil, along with *Drosera anglica, Platanthera dilatata, Deschampsia* species, and *Menyanthes trifoliata.*

## Sparganiaceae F. Rudolphi—BUR-REED FAMILY

### *Sparganium* L.—BUR-REED

Aquatic plants, the *Sparganium* species are characterized by floating leaves and by their showy round heads of inconspicuous flowers. The leaves may be immersed or, in the case of two species, floating on the surface. The female flowers mature to heads of burlike fruits.

The bur-reeds are found in swamps, shallow ponds, and at lakeshores and are at their most obvious in mid-summer when the flowering stem projects above the water level. The nomenclature here follows that in the *Flora of North America,* where the Sparganiaceae and Typhaceae (cattails) are treated as separate families. No cattails are known from the study area at Mount Adams.

1 Male flowers in 1 head; female heads 5-12 mm broad at maturity .... ........ *S. natans*

1 Male flowers in 2 to several heads; female heads 10-20 mm broad at maturity ........ 2

2(1) Some leaves rising above the water; leaves 7-15 mm wide ............ ........ *S. emersum* ssp. *emersum*

2 Leaves floating on the surface; leaves 2-4 mm wide ...................... ........ *S. angustifolium*

## Sparganiaceae

### *Sparganium angustifolium* Michx.—NARROW-LEAF BUR-REED

This species has slender stems and long, narrow leaves that float on the water's surface. The 2-5 brownish male flowering heads set on top of a stem that rises above the water. Below the male heads are 2-4 green female heads, each 10-20 mm broad.

Common in ponds and lakes at middle elevations, this species is found at Mirror Lake, along the Riley Creek trail, near Trail 64, and at Hellroaring Canyon.

### *Sparganium emersum* Rehmann ssp. *emersum* EMERGENT BUR-REED

The leaves of this bur-reed are most typically above the water. The 20-50 cm stems are stiff and erect and the 20-60 cm leaves are keeled or triangular below the middle; the submersed leaves are approximately half as long. There are 3-4 female flower heads, 12-20 mm in diameter; the inflorescence may be branched. The male flower heads are well separated and number 4-7. The fruit is 3.5-5.5 mm wide and spindle-shaped—it is brown and shiny.

Found in middle elevation ponds and streams, this species was collected by the authors at the Horseshoe Lake campground, where it forms extensive patches at 4,140 feet.

### *Sparganium natans* L.—SMALL BUR-REED

This aquatic plant is distinguished by slender stems that vary from 10-40 cm in height and by the long, slender grasslike leaves that float on the water. There is a single, somewhat oblong male head at the top of the stem and 2 or 3 female heads that are about 10 mm broad at maturity.

Found in middle elevation ponds, this species grows at Swampy Meadows and Bathtub Meadow. It also occurs in small pools in Takh Takh Meadow.

## Glossary

Discussions of terminology specific to certain groups of plants - chiefly the grasses, sedges, and sunflowers - are found in the introductions to those families.

**achene**—A dry, one seeded fruit, not at all fleshy.
**acute**—Tapered to a point with straight sides.
**alpine**—An elevational zone above timberline.
**alternate**—Describing leaves borne singly on a stem.
**androgynous**—Plants with both male and female flowers, with the male flowers above the female, in reference to some *Carex* inflorescences.
**annual**—A plant species that completes its life cycle within one growing season, typically with a taproot or fibrous roots, lacking a rootstock that survives more than one season.
**anther**—A sack in which pollen is produced.
**apex**—A tip, farthest from the point of attachment.
**appressed**—Pressed against.
**aril**—A fleshy, thickened seed coat, referring to *Taxus.*
**ascending**—Growing upward, usually curving, from a base or point of attachment.
**awn**—A needlelike or bristlelike tip of a leaf or flower part.
**axil**—The space in the angle where a leaf attaches to a stem.
**banner**—The upper petal of pea (*Fabaceae*) flowers.
**basal**—positioned at the base; usually describing a cluster of leaves at the base of a stem.
**beak**—A (usually) short tip at the top of the seed (or at the end of the galea in some flowers).
**biennial**—A plant species that completes its life cycle within two growing seasons.
**bilaterally symmetrical**—Symmetric with respect to only one axis; typically an irregular flower.
**blade**—The expanded portion of a leaf, typically attached to a leaf stalk. In grasses, the portion of the leaf that is free from the stem. Also used for the wider part of a petal that has a narrower, stalklike claw.
**bloom**—A white powdery or waxy coating on a surface.
**bract**—A small leaflike or scalelike structure that is placed beneath a flower, flower stalk, or branch.
**bulblet**—an aboveground small bulb, usually borne in a leaf axil.
**calyx**—The sepals of a flower, taken together, whether they are fused or not; usually green.
**capsule**—A dry, often thin-walled fruit, composed of more than one carpel, and containing (usually) numerous seeds.

## Glossary

**catkin**—A (usually) downward-hanging spike; the flowers are unisexual and inconspicuous, lacking petals.
**claw**—The narrowed, stalklike part of a petal that has a wider blade.
**cordate**—heart-shaped.
**corm**—A thickened, underground, bulblike stem.
**corymb**—A flat-topped inflorescence, with the lower flower stalks longer than the upper.
**corolla**—The petals of a flower, taken together, whether fused or not; usually colored.
**cotyledon**—Seed leaf; in the angiosperms, this is a modified leaf found within the seed.
**crown**—The top part of a tree or the persistent base of a herbaceous perennial.
**cyme**—A branched inflorescence in which the flower bud at the end of a branch opens first.
**deciduous**—A tree or shrub that loses all of its leaves at the end of the growing season and produces new leaves the following season.
**decumbent**—Lying on the ground with the stem pointing upward.
**deltate, deltoid**—Shaped like an equilateral triangle, although usually with rounded corners.
**dioecious**—Male and female flowers borne on different plants.
**dimorphic**—Taking on two distinctive forms or shapes, as in some ferns where the fertile and sterile fronds are very different in appearance.
**disk flower**—In the sunflowers, an individual flower that lacks a ligule; usually making up the inner portion of the head. See ray flower.
**dissected**—Very deeply and irregularly divided, usually describing leaves.
**divided**—Describing a leaf that is deeply lobed or cut to the midvein.
**drupe**—A fruit like a cherry, with a stonelike seed at the center, surrounded by a pulpy flesh.
**ecotype**—Plants of a species adapted to a specific environment.
**elliptical**—Shaped like an ellipse; a flattened and stretched circle.
**fibrous**—Referring to a highly branched, spreading root system, each branch of about equal thickness. Contrast with taproot.
**filament**—The stalk of an anther.
**follicle**—A dry, thin-walled fruit, usually elongated and slender, with numerous seeds, opening along one side.
**frond**—The leaf of a fern.
**galea**—The hood-like upper lip of a two-lipped corolla, especially in the Scrophulariaceae.
**glaucous**—Having a whitish or silvery-gray waxy sheen, typically on leaves and stems.
**globose**—Nearly spherical, usually describing a fruit.
**glomerule**—A dense cluster, or head-like cyme.

**gynaecandrous**—In the *Carex*, with the female flowers borne above the male flowers.
**herbaceous**—Not woody; a general term for plants that may be annual or perennial, in contrast to trees or shrubs.
**hypanthium**—A cup-like organ surrounding or enclosing the pistils, as in Rosaceae and Saxifragaceae.
**indusium**—A flap or veil of tissue that covers a sorus in some ferns.
**inferior**—Referring to an ovary that is placed below the petals and stamens.
**inflorescence**—The general term for an entire cluster of flowers, including the blossoms and stems.
**involucre**—The set of bracts beneath the flower head in the sunflowers. To be distinguished from a calyx.
**irregular**—A flower that is not radially symmetrical (that is, which does not follow the general petals-around-the-center model).
**keel**—A lengthwise ridge in some leaves or flower parts, usually seen on the lower surface. In pea flowers, a keel is formed by the two lowermost fused petals.
**krummholz**—German for "crooked wood." These are trees growing at timberline that are shrublike even when many decades old, with twisted branches and no leading trunk.
**lanceolate**—Shaped like the blade of a spear: widest at the base, elongated, and tapered to the tip.
**lemma**—In grasses, the lower of a pair of bracts at the base of the flower.
**lenticel**—In young trees, a raised, lens-shaped area on the surface of the trunk or branch.
**ligule**—In some grasses, an extension of thin tissue partly or wholly surrounding the stem at the point where the sheath of a leaf joins the blade. In the sunflowers, the petal-like blade of flowers (in disk flowers, a ligule is absent).
**linear**—Narrow and elongated, with straight or nearly straight sides.
**node**—On the stem the place where leaves or branches originate.
**nutlet**—A small, dry, fruit in which the single seed is surrounded by a hard shell or covering.
**obcordate**—A shape the opposite of cordate, with the attachment at the narrow end.
**oblanceolate**—A shape the opposite of lanceolate, with the widest part of the leaf above the middle.
**obovate**—A shape the opposite of ovate, with the widest part of the leaf above the middle.
**opposite**—Placed directly across from one another, usually describing a pair of leaves on a stem.
**ovary**—The ovule-producing part of the female organ of a flower. See pistil.
**ovate**—Egg-shaped, usually describing leaves that are widest below the middle.

**ovule** — An immature seed, prior to fertilization.
**palea** — The uppermost of the bracts at the base of a grass floret.
**palmate** — Like the palm of a hand, with the parts radiating from a common point; used to describe a leaf shape or a pattern of veins.
**panicle** — A branched inflorescence in which the lowest flower on a branch opens first. A branched raceme.
**pappus** — In the sunflowers, a crown of awns, bristles, or scales at the top of the seed.
**pectinate** — Comb-like.
**pedicel** — The stalk of a single flower or a grass spikelet.
**perennial** — A plant species that lives for two years or more, typically with a heavy rootstock that survives more than one season. The stems may or may not survive the winter.
**perianth** — A collective term for the calyx and corolla; often used when the parts are difficult to distinguish.
**petal** — An individual part of the corolla, usually flattened and colored or white.
**phyllary** — A single bract in the involucre of a flower head in the sunflowers.
**pinnate** — Describing a compound leaf, in which the individual leaflets are placed on opposite sides of the midrib of the leaf. "Twice-pinnate" is used to describe the situation where the individual leaflets are again pinnately divided.
**pistil** — The female organ of a flower, comprising an ovary, (usually) a style, and a stigma.
**pistillate** — A flower lacking stamens.
**pome** — A fruit like an apple, in which the seeds are at the core of a fleshy body.
**pubescent** — Covered with soft, short hairs.
**raceme** — An unbranched inflorescence in which the flowers are stalked.
**rachilla** — The axis of a grass or sedge spikelet.
**ray** — An individual flower stalk in an umbel.
**ray flower** — In the sunflowers, an individual flower that has a ligule, usually former an outer circle in the head.
**receptacle** — An enlargement of the tip of a flower stalk to which the petals of the flower are attached. In the sunflowers, the broad disk to which the individual flowers are attached.
**reflexed** — Bent or turned downward or backward.
**rootstock** — An underground, sometimes thickened, stem by which a plant may spread in a creeping fashion. Contrast with a runner.
**rosette** — A cluster of leaves, often flattened, at the base of a plant, arising directly from the crown of the roots of the plant.
**runner** — An above-ground, horizontal stem that roots as it creeps and from which new plants arise. Contrast with rootstock.
**samara** — A dry, winged fruit that does not open along the seam.

**schizocarp**—A dry fruit which splits into one-seeded segments.
**scree**—An accumulation of rocks, similar to a talus, but the fragments relatively small, and not always located at the foot of a cliff.
**sepal**—An individual part of the calyx, usually greenish and seldom colored.
**serrate**—Sharply and rather coarsely toothed.
**sheath**—Describing a thin tissue at the base of a leaf that encircles ("sheathes") the stem below the point at which the leaf is attached to the stem. Seen in many Poaceae and some Polygonaceae.
**silicle**—A two-valved, dry fruit that opens along the seam and is less than twice as long as wide, referring to the Brassicaceae.
**silique**—A two-valved, dry fruit that opens along the seam and is more than twice as long as wide, referring to the Brassicaceae.
**simple**—Unbranched; not compound; not lobed.
**sorus**—In ferns, a cluster of sporangia, found on the underside of the frond. Plural: sori.
**spathe**—A large bract or bracts beneath and enclosing an inflorescence.
**spike**—An unbranched inflorescence in which the flowers are not stalked.
**spikelet**—The smallest unitary structure of grass and sedge flowers.
**sporangium**—In ferns, a tiny structure in which the spores develop. Plural: sporangia.
**spore**—The reproductive unit in ferns, grapeferns, horsetails, quillworts, and clubmosses.
**stamen**—The male organ of a flower, with a stalklike filament and a pollen-producing anther; usually several stamens are present in a flower.
**staminate**—A flower with male parts only.
**stigma**—The expanded tip of a pistil, which receives the pollen; often on a short stalk called a style.
**stipule**—A leaf-like appendage at the base of the leaf stalk.
**stomate**—Pore or opening on a leaf surface, for gas exchange. Plural: stomata.
**strigose**—With straight, stiff, sharp, flattened hairs.
**style**—The slender stalk that elevates the stigma above the ovary in the pistil of a flower.
**subalpine**—An elevational zone just below timberline but above the reach of more or less continuous tree or shrub cover.
**succulent**—Thick and fleshy stems or leaves.
**superior**—Referring to an ovary that is placed above the petals and stamens.
**talus**—An accumulation of rock fragments on a slope at the foot of a cliff.
**taproot**—A main root of a plant, one that grows straight down.
**tendril**—An extension of the midvein of a leaf, which twines and helps support a stem.
**terminal**—Occurring at the end of a stem or branch.
**trifoliate**—Three leaves or leaflets.
**tubercule**—A small projection on a seed or fruit.

**tufted**—In a dense cluster.
**umbel**—An inflorescence in which the multiple flower stalks radiate from a common point, often flat-topped.
**unisexual**—Describing a flower that has either fertile stamens or pistils but not both.
**whorl**—Arranged in a ring, as in a stem where three or more leaves join the stem at the same level.

## Bibliography


Andalkar, A. 2006. Cascade snowfall and snowdepth. Internet URL: <http://skimountaineer.com/CascadeSki/CascadeSnow.html> [accessed 4 September 2006].

Biek, D.E. 2000. *Flora of Mount Rainier National Park*. Corvallis, OR: Oregon State University Press.

Bilderback, D.E. 1987. *Mount St. Helens, 1980: Botanical consequences of the explosive eruptions*. Berkeley: University of California Press.

Brackenridge, W.D. 1931. *The Brackenridge journal for the Oregon Country*. Edited by O.B. Sperling and reprinted from The Washington Historical Quarterly, 1930-1931. Seattle: University of Washington Press.

Brunsfeld, S.J. et al. 1991. Patterns of genetic variation in Salix section Longifoliae (Salicaceae). *American Journal of Botany* 78(6): 855-869.

Buckingham, N.M. et al. 1995. *Flora of the Olympic Peninsula*. Seattle, WA: Northwest Interpretive Association.

Burnett, R.E. 1985. Flowering plants of the Mt. Hood area. *Mazama* 47: 45-56.

Cascades Volcano Observatory. 2006. *Mount Adams, Washington*. Internet URL: <http://vulcan.wr.usgs.gov/Volcanoes/Adams/summary_mount_adams.html> [accessed 4 September 2006].

Chambers, K.L. and S. Sundberg. 2001. Oregon Vascular Plant Checklist – Asteraceae. Corvallis, OR: Oregon Flora Project. Internet URL: <http://www.oregonflora.org/asterlist/Asteraceae.html> [accessed 4 September 2006].

Del Moral, R. and D.M. Wood. 1988. The high elevation flora of Mount St. Helens, Washington. Madroño 35: 309-319.

Douglas, W.O. 1960. *My wilderness, the Pacific west*. Garden City, NY: Doubleday.

Douglas, W.O. 1950. *Of men and mountains*. New York: Harper & Row.

Ferguson, C. J. and R. K. Jansen. 2002. A chloroplast DNA phylogeny of eastern Phlox (Polemoniaceae): implications of congruence and incongruence with the ITS phylogeny. Am. J. Bot. 89:1324-1335.

Flora of North America Editorial Committee. *Flora of North America*. Internet URL: <http://www.efloras.org/flora_page.aspx?flora_id=1> [published volumes used include 1, 2, 3, 4, 5, 19, 20, 21, 22, 23, 24, 25, 26] [accessed 4 September 2006].

Franklin, J.F., and C.T. Dyrness. 1988. *Natural vegetation of Oregon and Washington*. Corvallis, OR: Oregon State University Press.

Harris, J.G. and M.W. Harris. 2001. *Plant identification terminology: an illustrated glossary*. Spring Lake, UT: Spring Lake Publishing.

## Bibliography


Hickman, J.C., editor. 1993. *The Jepson manual: higher plants of California*. Berkeley, CA: University of California Press.

Hildreth, W. and J. Fierstein. 1995. *Geologic map of the Mount Adams volcanic field, Cascade Range of Washington*. Reston, VA: U.S. Geological Survey. [map, data sheet, + text].

Hitchcock, C.L. and A. Cronquist. 1976. *Flora of the Pacific Northwest*. Seattle, WA: University of Washington Press.

Hitchcock, C.L. et al. 1959-1967. *Vascular plants of the Pacific Northwest*. Seattle, WA: University of Washington Press.

Hopkins, K.D. 1976. *Geology of the south and east slopes of Mount Adams volcano, Cascade Range, Washington*. Thesis (Ph. D.) University of Washington.

Hummel, S.S, et al. 2001. Ecological and financial assessment of late-successional reserve management [Gotchen LSR]. Portland, OR: Pacific Northwest Research Station. [Research Note 531]

*International Plant Names Index*. 2004. Internet URL: <http://www.ipni.org> [accessed 4 September 2006].

Jolley, R. 1988. *Wildflowers of the Columbia Gorge*. Portland, OR: Oregon Historical Society Press.

Kendall, K.C. *Whitebark pine*. West Glacier, MT.: Glacier Field Station Science Center. Internet URL: <http://biology.usgs.gov/s+t/SNT/noframe/wm147.htm> [accessed 4 September 2006].

Korosec, M.A. 1987. *Geologic map of the Mount Adams quadrangle, Washington*. Olympia, WA: Washington Division of Geology and Earth Resources. [map + text]

Kozloff, E.N. 2005. *Plants of western Oregon, Washington, & British Columbia*. Portland, OR: Timber Press.

Kruckeberg, A.R. and R. Ornduff. [n.d.] "Thomas Jefferson Howell (1842-1912): the untutored, impoverished botanist." [excerpted] Internet URL: <http://www.oregonflora.org/ofn/v9n2/howell.html> [accessed 4 September 2006].

Lawrence, D.B. Continuing research on the flora of Mt. St. Helens, a progress report. *Mazama*: 21(12): 49-54.

Lawrence, D.B. 1938. Trees on the march: notes on the recent volcanic and vegetational history of Mount St. Helens. *Mazama* 20(12): 49-53.

Love, R.M. 2001. Louis F. Henderson (1853-1942): the grand old man of Northwest botany. Eugene, OR: Native Plant Society of Oregon. [NPSO Occasional Paper no. 2]

McDougall, S.C. 2001. *The Trees of Mt. Rainier*. [s.l.]: Xlibris Corp.

McDougall, S.C. 2006. *Wildflowers of Mount Adams, Washington*. Tacoma, WA: Sound Books.

Moerman, D. 1998. Native American ethnobotany. Portland, OR: Timber Press.

National Atlas of the United States. Mount Adams [Nationalatlas.gov dynamic map] Internet URL: <http://nationalatlas.gov/dynamic/dyn_vol-adam.html#> [accessed 4 September 2006].

National Climate Data Center, 2004 and 2006. *Climatological data.* Internet URL: <http://www.ncdc.noaa.gov/oa/ncdc.html> [accessed 4 September 2006].

National Resources Conservation Service. [n.d.] *PLANTS Database.* Internet URL: <http://plants.usda.gov/> [accessed 4 September 2006].

Pavlick, L.E., and J. Looman. 1984. Taxonomy and nomenclature of rough fescues, Festuca altaica, F. campestris (F. scabrella var. major) and F. hallii in Canada and the adjacent part of United States. *Canadian Journal of Botany* 62(8): 1739-1749.

Peck, M.E. 1941. *A manual of the higher plants of Oregon*. Portland, OR: Binfords & Mort.

Piper, C.V. 1906. *Flora of the State of Washington*. Washington, D.C.: Government Printing Office.

Plamondon, M. 2004. *Lewis and Clark trail maps, a cartographic reconstruction, Volume III, Columbia River to the Pacific Ocean ... Outbound, 1805, return 1806*. Pullman, WA: Washington State University Press.

Rusk, C.E. 1919. *Mount Adams: towering sentinel of the lower Columbia basin. Reasons for its preservation and maintenance as a national park.* Yakima, WA: Yakima Commercial Club.

Scott, W.E. 1995. *Volcano hazards in the Mount Adams region, Washington*. Reston, VA: U.S. Geological Survey.

Stacey, J.W. 1938. Notes on Carex [C. constanceana]. *Leaflets of Western Botany* 2:121-124.

Strickler, D. 1997. *Northwest penstemons: 80 species of Penstemon native to the Pacific Northwest*. Columbia Falls, MT: Flower Press.

Suksdorf, W.N. 1867-1935. *Papers*. Pullman, WA: Washington State University, Manuscripts, Archives, and Special Collections.

Valliance, J.W. 1999. *Postglacial lahars and potential hazards in the White River system on the southwest flank of Mount Adams, Washington*. Reston, VA: U.S. Geological Survey.

Van Pelt, R. 1996. *Champion trees of Washington State*. Seattle: University of Washington Press.

Washington Natural Heritage Program. 2006. *List of Plants Tracked by the Washington Natural Heritage Program.* Olympia, WA: Washington State Department of Natural Resources. Internet URL: <http://www.dnr.wa.gov/nhp/refdesk/lists/plantrnk.html> [accessed 4 September 2006].

## Bibliography

Washington State Noxious Weed Control Board. 2006. *Washington State noxious weed list*. Internet URL: < http://www.nwcb.wa.gov/weed_list/weed_list.htm> [accessed 4 September 2006].

Watershed Professionals Network. 2005. *Klickitat Basin (WRIA 30) watershed management plan*. Appendix A, Chapter 2: Hydrologic framework. [s.l.]

Weber, W.A. 1944. The botanical collections of Wilhelm N. Suksdorf, 1850-1932. *Research Studies of the State College of Washington* 12: 51-119.

William, G.D. and W.A. Babcock. 1983. *The Yakima Indian Nation forest heritage: a history of forest management on the Yakima Indian Reservation, Washington, for the 1983-1992 forest management plan*. Missoula, MT: Heritage Research Center.

Wood, C.A. and J. Kienle. 1990. *Volcanoes of North America*. Boston: Cambridge University Press.

# Index

The Index covers names, both scientific and common, of families, genera, and species. A few cross references are given in parentheses; this is done where a plant is better or more widely known by a name other than the name we have adopted.

# Index

# Index

# Index

# Index

# Index

# Index

www.ingramcontent.com/pod-product-compliance
Lightning Source LLC
Chambersburg PA
CBHW071948270326
41928CB00009B/1385
*9780977628513*